MW01092501

About Island Press

Island Press, a nonprofit organization, publishes, markets, and distributes the most advanced thinking on the conservation of our natural resources—books about soil, land, water, forests, wildlife, and hazardous and toxic wastes. These books are practical tools used by public officials, business and industry leaders, natural resource managers, and concerned citizens working to solve both local and global resource problems.

Founded in 1978, Island Press reorganized in 1984 to meet the increasing demand for substantive books on all resource-related issues. Island Press publishes and distributes under its own imprint and offers these services to other nonprofit organizations.

Support for Island Press is provided by The Geraldine R. Dodge Foundation, The Energy Foundation, The Charles Engelhard Foundation, The Ford Foundation, Glen Eagles Foundation, The George Gund Foundation, William and Flora Hewlett Foundation, The James Irvine Foundation, The John D. and Catherine T. MacArthur Foundation, The Andrew W. Mellon Foundation, The Joyce Mertz-Gilmore Foundation, The New-Land Foundation, The Pew Charitable Trusts, The Rockefeller Brothers Fund, The Tides Foundation, and individual donors.

Renewable
Resource
Policy

Renewable Resource Policy

The Legal-Institutional Foundations

David A. Adams

ISLAND PRESS

Washington, D.C. • Covelo, California

The author gratefully acknowledges permission to use the following photographs:

Figures 5.1, 5.4, and 6.2 by permission of the Forest History Society, Durham, North Carolina; Figure 7.1 is from the Harry Walsh Collection, Chesapeake Bay Maritime Museum, St. Michaels, Maryland.

Library of Congress Cataloging-in-Publication Data

Adams, David A. (David Arthur), 1931-
    Renewable Resource Policy : the legal-institutional foundations/
David A. Adams.
        p. cm.
    Includes bibliographical references and index.
    ISBN 1-55963-225-9 (c).
    1. Renewable natural resources—Law and legislation—United States.
    2. Conservation of natural resources—Law and legislation—United
States. 3. Environmental Law—United States. 4. Conservation of nat-
ural resources—United States. 5. Environmental Protection—United
States. I. Title.
    KF5505.A93 1993
    344.73'046—dc20   936543
    [347.30446]   CIP

Printed on recycled, acid-free paper

Manufactured in the United States of America
10 9 8 7 6 5 4 3 2

Contents

Preface   xi

Acknowledgments   xvii

CHAPTER 1.   ANCIENT FOUNDATIONS   3
             The Bible   3
             Roman Law   5
             Magna Carta   13

CHAPTER 2.   OUR CONSTITUTIONAL GOVERNMENT   27
             Background   27
             The Constitution   28
             The Bill of Rights   43
             Common Law and Other Legal Principles   48

CHAPTER 3.   THE PUBLIC DOMAIN   55
             Early Land Tenure Systems   55
             The New Republic   57
             Federal Landownership   58

CHAPTER 4.   GRAZING LANDS   90
             Free Land, Competition, and Conflict   90
             The Coming of Regulation   91
             Implementing the System   94
             A Word about Powell   95
             Closing the Frontier: The Taylor Grazing Act   104
             Grazing Fees on Public Land   107
             The National Grasslands   109

CHAPTER 5.   FORESTLANDS AND NATIONAL FORESTS   114
             Reserves   114
             Preserves or Managed Forests?   118
             A Word about Pinchot   122
             A Permanent Home   125

	Forests in the East	127
	Forests for Everyone	135
	Forest Management Outside the National Forests	155
	Persistent Problems	169
CHAPTER 6.	OUTDOOR RECREATION AND THE NATIONAL PARKS	178
	Yosemite: The Beginnings?	179
	A Word about Olmsted	179
	Yellowstone, the First "National Park"	181
	Toward a National Park System	184
	A Word about Mather and Albright	187
	The Eastern National Parks	191
	The CCC Days	194
	Mission 66	197
	The Modern National Park System	202
	Outdoor Recreation	204
CHAPTER 7.	THE NATION'S WILDLIFE AND THE NATIONAL WILDLIFE REFUGE SYSTEM	223
	A National Perspective	223
	A Word about Leopold	234
	Wildlife on Federal Land	229
	Enforcing Federal Law	234
	Animal Control	243
	Research and Management	248
	Rare, Threatened, and Endangered Species	250
	The National Wildlife Refuge System	272
CHAPTER 8.	WILDERNESS	285
	Early Rumblings	285
	A Word about Marshall	288
	Toward a National Wilderness System	291
	The Act and the System	295
	Toward a Bigger and Better System	296
	RARE II—and Beyond	298
	Wilderness in Other Agencies	302
CHAPTER 9.	SOIL CONSERVATION	306
	Bennett's Crusade	306
	Internecine Warfare	309
	The Districts: Governments within Governments	310
	The Other Part of the Story	312
	Accommodation	314
	National Land Use Planning: You Can't Win 'Em All	315
	Achievements	317

CHAPTER 10.	WATER LAW	324
	Tidelands, Streambeds, and Shores	324
	The Waters Within	328
	Littoral and Maritime Considerations	332
CHAPTER 11.	FEDERAL WATER RESOURCE DEVELOPMENT	351
	The U.S. Army Corps of Engineers	351
	The Bureau of Reclamation (BuRec)	359
	The Tennessee Valley Authority (TVA)	359
	The Soil Conservation Service (SCS)	362
	The River Basin Concept	364
	Benefits and Costs	366
	What of Tomorrow?	368
CHAPTER 12.	WATER RESOURCE PROTECTION	375
	Navigation	375
	Water and Wetlands	384
CHAPTER 13.	FISHERIES	412
	Institutional Matters	412
	Federal Aid to the States	416
	Regulatory Functions	419
CHAPTER 14.	THE COASTAL ZONE	428
	Legislative Precursors	429
	Within the Executive Branch	433
	The Coastal Zone Management Act of 1972 (CZMA)	435
	Amendments to the Act	446
	The National Program	453
CHAPTER 15.	A NATIONAL ENVIRONMENTAL POLICY	472
	The Environmental Setting	472
	Legislative History	477
	Organizing the Bureaucracy	490
	The Other Branch: Assistance from the Judiciary	492
	NEPA and the EIS: Guts or Facade?	496
	Environmentalism and Reaganism	498
APPENDIX A	FEDERAL GOVERNMENT ORGANIZATION	508
APPENDIX B	TREATIES AND FEDERAL STATUTES CITED	526
APPENDIX C	CASES CITED	540
	Index	542

Preface

This is a book about the foundations of renewable natural resource management in the United States. It is primarily a story of laws, agencies, and issues rather than of people, though the people are also important. It deals with the "mays," the "musts," and some of the "hows" of the business. The "cans" and most of the "hows" compose the technological basis and are treated elsewhere.

The book is intended to serve two functions—a text for students in advanced-level policy courses and a reference for the serious practitioner. It emphasizes the common origins and similarities among the classic natural resource fields. As approaches to natural resource management become more holistic, these similarities are becoming more evident. Only in the more detailed levels of policy development—when one intends to produce trees or turkeys rather than to influence the future condition of a piece of the earth—do agency and/or resource differences become obvious and overriding. Yet texts emphasizing this common heritage are rare if not nonexistent, while the individual resources—trees, water, range, wildlife, and so forth—are amply covered. Thus it is easier for universities to offer, and for instructors to teach, courses in the classic fields than to attempt to integrate bits and pieces into a more unified approach. Compounding the problem is much of our traditional academic approach to educating (training?) natural resource managers. Since the days of Pinchot and Leopold, we have emphasized the technocratic, science-oriented approach and neglected the legal, administrative, bureaucratic, and interpersonal skills, which are equally important. Thus advanced-level college students come to a policy course with a poor background in these matters and a deep and well-nurtured bias against the "political" aspects of their profession. The instructor is indeed challenged to awaken and maintain their attention in a subject that so many students feel is irrelevant.

Unfortunately, awakening frequently does come with graduation and employment, when the novice resource manager discovers the maze of agencies and laws within which he or she must work. Those employed in the private sector do not escape, for government is increasingly involved in their activities through taxes, incentives and subsidies, regulations, and interactions in the marketplace. An understanding of these relationships is essential. A fair analogy may be drawn between the resource manager and an athlete—both must understand the rules of the game, the teams, and the players before they can effectively compete.

Those who are already involved in the resource management game—whether in government or industry; as teachers, activists, or landowners; or simply as interested spectators—frequently have cause to refresh their memory on some aspect. I hope that this book will be of value to them as well. I have attempted to cover the spectrum of information that might be desired, and I have made a concerted effort to document all sources. Those seeking superficial coverage should find it here; those wishing additional information should find the citations helpful. In addition the book contains appendices listing all federal treaties, laws, and cases cited, with complete references to the source documents.

Organizing this mass of material posed a formidable challenge. Three interwoven themes appear. The first is chronological; the book traces the history of renewable natural resource policy and management in the United States. Within this matrix are secondary themes developed along resource lines—water, forests, recreation, and the like—presenting the evolution of the major resource areas and current policies for administering each of them. I have attempted to make the third theme, emphasizing individual agencies, subordinate to the first two. However, in many instances a single agency is paramount, and discussion of resource and agency become inseparable. Of course, there are always some elements, such as coastal zone management and environmental policy, that do not fit the mold very well.

The book first traces our heritage of laws and legal customs from early civilizations to the U.S. Constitution. This is the primary foundation—our inheritance of ethics, mores, and principles,.which we continually amend and apply to changing conditions but which we rarely violate outright. The discussion goes far beyond natural resource issues, and it provides a linkage between natural resources and the other elements of our society.

Having made this beginning, the book discusses our heritage of public land. It describes our westward expansion, our attitude toward the public lands, and the evolution of public land policy. Most of the federal resource management agencies can trace their history to some aspect of this story. It is, to a large degree, the common origin that produced the national parks, forests, recreation areas, wildlife refuges, and water resource developments and their cognizant agencies.

The book then develops each of these natural arenas in greater detail. I have chosen to organize the discussion generally around the types of resources and the products they provide, reserving a special place for the coastal zone. In doing so I have accepted a certain amount of historical and legal redundancy and some dispersal of agency programs but have attempted to emphasize the primacy of the resources being managed. In each resource area, the discussion includes basic underlying legal principles, proprietary and custodial government activities, and nonfederal considerations.

The final chapter describes the national environmental policy, which provides an umbrella over all federal activities and has been precedent for much state and local policy development. It exemplifies the degree of integration and holism that characterizes current natural resource policy development and that promises to be the way of the future.

Following the body of the text are three appendices. Appendix A is a litany of federal agencies—the lineup. Dull as it may be to the reader, a knowledge of the agencies and their missions is essential to an understanding of natural resource policy. Bureaucrats are proud of their agencies and sensitive to misstatements about duties and responsibilities. Professionals know the agencies and what they do—it's as simple as that! Appendix B provides a list of treaties and federal laws cited. It obviates the need for complete in-text citations and provides ready access to the sources. It addition, citations to the *United States Code* enable a reader to find the current relevant laws (in most cases), even if changes have occurred since this writing. Appendix C lists all cases cited, providing the same function as appendix B.

In presenting the material this way and attempting to serve two functions, I have accepted a number of calculated risks. Attempting to cover the entire renewable natural resource area in one treatise rather than concentrating on forests, wildlife, range, or other, more classic, organization may be overly ambitious; but I am convinced that these resources share a common heritage and an interwoven management network—it is only in its ultimate considerations that each discipline becomes unique. My early emphasis on historical precedent may alienate some readers; yet chronology provides a simple, easy-to-follow basis for organization, and members of the legal profession place great weight on precedents. The review of legislative process and executive rule making may bore those with a good background in government; but I notice that many university upperclassmen have forgotten much of their high school and freshman civics and government courses. Discussions of administrative principles and political process may appear out of place in such a text; yet I am continually amazed at the lack of understanding of these essential ingredients exhibited by college students. The numerous in-text citations interrupt the reader's train of thought and detract from a smooth flow of material; but such documentation is essential to avoid plagiarism, to establish legitimacy, and to assist those who want more. On balance, I feel that my choices increase the quality and utility of the presentation. Should any of these elements offend the reader, they can easily be passed over.

On the other hand, I have given short shrift to "pollution" and have avoided the topic of nonrenewable resources. These were deliberate omissions. Pollution is emphasized in treatments of environmental science and environmental law and properly belongs there. Public pollution control policy is more narrowly focused and more user- and process-oriented than that affecting renewable resources in general. Pollution concerns the injection of a class of products into an ecosystem rather than the production of an array of products from one. It overlaps with, but is somewhat apart from, the central thrust of renewable resource management. Omission of nonrenewable natural resources may be more difficult to defend, for the same lands and agencies produce both. Yet the philosophy and policy are different, and the concept of "conservation" is much different, when dealing with such depletable resources as petroleum and hard minerals. I simply elected to omit them—though I brought in mineral development on the continental shelf in discussing maritime law and coastal zone management.

I have sprinkled a goodly amount of my personal observations and opinions throughout the text, not in excess, I hope. Perhaps I should have supplied more interpretation, but I hesitate to subject equally qualified instructors and professionals to too much of my personal bias. The substance, I believe, is here. Each reader can apply some of his or her own thought to the analysis and interpretation, perhaps learning even more in the process. My contributions should be evident by their lack of documentation and can be taken with a grain of salt.

The book contains many, and long, quotes from earlier sources. These may detract from the continuity and in many cases could have been paraphrased. They are included for three reasons: (1) they provide the reader with original wording, undistorted by any prejudice I might have; (2) they illustrate the composition and rhetoric of their times, which itself is of aesthetic and historical significance; and (3) the original writers probably expressed their ideas better than I could. Those who are bothered by these inclusions will probably skip over them, losing much of the flavor in the process.

The same could be said regarding the minibiographies that appear throughout the book. I intended to base the treatise on the laws and institutions rather than on the people, but it is impossible to separate them. People made the laws, governed the agencies, received the benefits, and bore the costs. Furthermore, so few persons produced so much of our heritage, and so many similarities exist among these personalities and their careers. Their stories need telling.

I have deliberately underemphasized two essential elements—case studies and current events. The former provide the depth necessary to understand detailed interrelationships; the latter provide connections to present-day happenings. Both are essential to a good course offering. But case studies should be relevant to the geographic area and interests of the class, and current events should be current. I hope that readers and instructors will provide their own supplements in these areas.

Preparation of this volume has consumed a great deal of time over a number of years. I have profited immensely from the undertaking, and I hope that the reader will also derive some benefit from it.

Acknowledgments

I am indebted to my family and to the friends, students, professors, colleagues, and associates who taught me what I know about natural resource policy and management; to the lawmakers, bureaucrats, and entrepreneurs who made and implemented the policy that I now try to relate; to the authors who have preceded me, particularly those who wrote the classics in each natural resource area and upon whom I have so heavily relied; to the following persons, who graciously consented to review the chapters indicated and have given me many valuable comments and suggestions and much constructive criticism:

Alvin L. Alm (11, 14), J. David Almand (3, 4), Richard N. L. Andrews (15), Randall T. Bell (1), Franklin E. Boteler (1, 2, 3, 5, 6, 8), Peter T. Bromley (7), William A. Campbell (1, 3), Anita Clark (6), Walter F. Clark (10, 13, 14), Marion Clawson (3, 4), William B. Davis (6, 8), William L. Evans (4), John J. Garrett (9), Neil S. Grigg (10, 11, 12), Douglas Helms (9), Larry D. Henson (2, 5), F. Eugene Hester (6, 8), Lawrence W. Hill (2, 5), M. Casey Jarman (12), David E. Ketcham (15), Robert W. Knecht (13, 14), Dennis C. Le Master (4, 5), Richard MacComber (10, 11, 12), Larry A. Nielsen (13), George A. Olson (5, 8), R. Max Peterson (2, 5), Edward R. Smith (7, 9), Robert B. Smythe (8, 9), Robert P. Spivey (8), Kit J. Valentine (10, 11, 12), J. D. Wellman (6, 8), and Edward Wenk, Jr. (14); and to my God, who loaned me these resources during my lifetime.

Renewable
Resource
Policy

CHAPTER I

Ancient Foundations

As precedent for natural resource actions we often cite recent court cases, legislation of the environmental decade of the 1970s, or the awareness of profligacy that arose in the mid- to late 1800s. But all these are merely the last stages in an evolution that dates to the dawn of history. The ethics that govern our use of natural resources are as much a part of our heritage as those that govern work, charity toward the unfortunate, and tolerance of those of different race or religious persuasion. These roots are not buried in the past; they form the foundation of modern legislation and frequently are referenced in contemporary legal decisions.

This chapter discusses three sources of our legal heritage: the Judeo-Christian background of most Americans, the Roman *Code of Justinian*, and the Magna Carta of King John. Each has contributed differently; combined, they provide the foundation of our modern legal system.

THE BIBLE

Those who have searched the Bible for a strong conservation or natural resource stewardship ethic have come away largely empty-handed; those seeking reasons for Western civilization's consumptive attitude toward these resources (White 1967) have had somewhat more success. Authors of the Old Testament were more concerned with chronicling Jewish history and prescribing rules of conduct for the Jewish people, while those of the New Testament concentrated on salvation through Jesus Christ. Abundant natural resources were frequently considered gifts of the Almighty to deserving mankind, whereas scarcity, drought, and plague were attributed to mankind's transgressions.

God's intention that mankind was to be separate from and superior to other creatures and the ecosystems that support them is supported by the classic quotation from Genesis:

Then God said "Let us make man—someone like ourselves, to be master of all life upon the earth and in the skies and in the seas."

And God blessed them and told them, "Multiply and fill the earth and subdue it; you are masters of the fish and birds and all the animals." (Living Bible 1971, Gen. 1:26, 28)

Clearly, God was apart from and superior to the creatures he created. Mankind, created in his image, must be likewise and was directed to exercise dominion over the environment that surrounded him.

Much of the Old Testament emphasizes that natural resources were gifts of God placed on earth for the enjoyment of mankind:

"I have given you the seedbearing plants throughout the earth, and all the fruit trees for your food." (Living Bible 1971, Gen. 1:29)

...[T]he Lord God has given us this land. Go and possess it as he told us to. Don't be afraid! Don't even doubt! (Deut. 1:21)

And he will love you and bless you and make you into a great nation. He will make you fertile and give fertility to your ground and your animals, so that you will have large crops of grain, grapes, and olives, and great flocks of cattle, sheep, and goats. (Deut. 7:13)

For the Lord your God is bringing you into a good land of brooks, pools, gushing springs, valleys, and hills; it is a land where...nothing is lacking; it is a land where iron is as common as stone, and copper is abundant in the hills. (Deut. 8:7-9)

And if you will carefully obey all of his commandments that I am going to give you today, and if you will love the Lord your God with all your hearts and souls, and will worship him, then he will continue to send both the early and late rains that will produce wonderful crops of grain, grapes for your wine, and olive oil. He will give you lush pastureland for your cattle to graze in, and you yourselves shall have plenty to eat and be fully content.

But beware that your hearts do not turn from God to worship other Gods. For if you do, the anger of the Lord will be hot against you, and he will shut the heavens—there will be no rain and no harvest, and you will quickly perish from the good land the Lord has given you. (Deut. 11:13-17)

Only one passage prescribes limits for man's exploitive activities:

If a bird's nest is lying on the ground, or if you spy one in a tree, and there are young ones or eggs in it with the mother in the nest, don't take the mother with the young. Let her go, and take only the young. The Lord will bless you for it. (Deut. 22:6-7)

Thus the principle of removing the harvestable surplus while maintaining the breeding stock was a part of the Jewish tradition, but no other direct guidance is provided in the Bible. Those who argue that stewardship of natural resources is inherently part of the Judeo-Christian ethic (Berry 1979) do so from the standpoint that to be otherwise would violate other doctrines (e.g., that man must revere God, nature is from God and of God, and any desecration of nature would be an abomination). The argument is persuasive, but documentation is sketchy.

ROMAN LAW

Much of our law regarding wild animals, use of riverbanks and the edge of the sea (riparian and littoral law), admiralty, and the public trust can be traced directly to Roman law. Even today, courts may cite these ancient documents as precedent and basis for their findings.

Justinian's Codification

The Roman legal system consisted of customs and traditions that were part of Latin culture, laws enacted by popular assemblies, rulings of the courts, and imperial proclamations. From time to time, as origins became hazy and intentions became vague, efforts were made to clarify and codify the body of Roman law (Buckland 1963, 1-12). The most famous of these were a series of codifications issued under the emperor Justinian, who ruled the eastern Roman empire from Byzantium during the early sixth century A.D. (Severy 1983).

The *First Code* appeared in A.D. 529 and consolidated and updated existing laws. Within a year, work began on a second compilation, and the *Digest of Justinian* (*Pandectae*) was issued in A.D. 533. This work collected earlier juristic writings and laws in a systematic arrangement and contained many transcription errors and deliberate changes from the older laws. Two other compilations, the *Institutes of Justinian* and the *Quinquaginta Decisiones*, were issued at about the same time. The *Institutes* was organized into four books covering the law of persons, things (property), obligations, and actions. *Quinquaginta Decisiones* contained Justinian's imperial enactments. In A.D. 534, the *Codex Repetitae*

Praelectiones was issued, containing legislation adopted since publication of the *First Code* and making that document obsolete. The final codification, the *Novellae Constitutiones*, issued in A.D. 546, contained enactments subsequent to the *Codex* (Buckland 1963, 39-47). Many inconsistencies exist between and within the documents, as might be expected from manual transcription from diverse sources (and perhaps intentional modification). Thus, one may find citations that both confirm and refute a position, just as one can with contemporary court decisions.

The Law of Things (Property)

Of the foregoing documents, the *Digest* and the *Institutes* contain provisions most relevant to natural resource issues. In particular, the law of things (*res*) provides the foundation for much of the natural resource and environmental law we practice today. The Romans recognized two basic classes of things, *res in patrimonio*, things that belonged to someone and were therefore private property, and *res extra patrimonium*, things that were outside private ownership but some kinds of which could be acquired by individuals under certain circumstances (*J. Inst.* 2.2.1). (Note: Unless otherwise indicated, citations to Justinian's codification come from Scott's [1973] translation.)

Res extra patrimonium included public property such as highways, rivers, harbors, and other transportation facilities (*res publicae*) and theaters, stadia, and universities owned by society in general (*res institutiones*). They also included common property resources (*res communes*)—the air, water, and seashore, which were owned by and open to everyone—and those that were owned by no one (*res nullius*)—either because they were incapable of private ownership, they had not yet been acquired by private interests, or they had been abandoned. This last category contained emergent but unclaimed land, wild animals, and churches, tombs, and cemeteries. The *Institutes* further distinguished between *res extra patrimonium* that were held by the central government as a private right (*jus privatum*) and could be treated as private property (e.g., highways and public buildings) and those that were held in public trust (*jus publicum*) and could not be conveyed (e.g., seashores and navigable waters) (*J. Inst.* 2.2.1).

Two methods were provided for private acquisition of *res extra patrimonium*. Wild animals, unclaimed islands, and other *res nullius* could be obtained by taking (*occupatio*) (*J. Inst.* 2.2.1[12]). Riparian owners could acquire accreted lands by incorporating them into existing ownerships (*accessio*) (*J. Inst.* 2.2.1[20]).

Animals

Animals were classified as wild (*ferae naturae*, literally "of a wild nature") or domestic (*domitae naturae*, "of a tame nature"). The latter were *res in patrimonio* whether or not they were under the owner's control. Should ducks, geese, or other domestic fowl escape and damage adjacent property, ownership was unchanged and their owner could be held responsible for the damage. Conversely, if escaped fowl were confined by the neighbor, he would have committed a theft (*Dig.* 41.1.5.6). Animals *ferae naturae* were owned by no one (*res nullius*) unless captured, killed, or otherwise prevented from returning to the wild (Buckland 1963, 182, 204-206). Bees and pigeons, animals *ferae naturae*, were *res in patrimonio* only so long as they returned to the hive or dovecote (*animus revertendi*); should they cease doing so they became *res nullius* and could be acquired by new owners through *occupatio* (*Dig.* 41.1.5.5). Prior owners of animals *ferae naturae* that were lost through escape were not liable for damages caused by the animals, however, for ownership—and thus liability— ceased when the animals escaped (*Dig.* 41.1.3.2).

Animals *ferae naturae* were granted the same status on private and public land, but a private landowner could deny access (*Dig.* 41.1.3.1). Ownership of a wild animal occurred only when it was physically possessed—mortal wounding or temporary restraint apparently did not suffice (Buckland 1963, 204-206). An anecdote from the *Digest* illustrates many of these provisions:

> A wild boar was caught in a trap which you set...and after being caught, I released him, and carried him away....[Have I] taken away your wild boar? [And if I released him] and let him go into the woods, would he still remain your property? What action would be entitled against me?
>
> The answer was...we should first take into consideration [whether the trap were set]...on public or private land; and if on private land, whether or not I did so upon my own or that of another, and if I set it upon that of another, whether I did so with the permission of the owner.
>
> Moreover...was [the boar] caught in such a way that he could not release himself? (*Dig.* 41.1.55)

If the boar were securely held within a trap, lawfully set on public land, the trapper's land, or land on which he had permission to trap, and the animal clearly was unable to escape without assistance, the trapper probably would acquire ownership though *occupatio*. In such a case, unauthorized release would be actionable. If, on the other hand, the trap were set on private land without the landowner's permission, the acquisition itself would be unlawful; the trapper would never acquire ownership; and no action could ensue. If the boar could have freed himself without assistance, it would never have become the possession of the trapper.

Although many present-day hunting customs award the game to the hunter who has drawn "first blood," our law is, as it was in the days of Justinian, that wild animals must be reduced to possession to become private property. In the early 1920s, Dapson and Daly were hunting deer in the same area in Massachusetts. Dapson wounded a deer, but before he could claim it, the deer ran by Daly, who killed it and carried it away. Dapson sued, alleging that he was entitled to the animal, but the state supreme court disagreed:

> The controlling principle of the common law is that the huntsman acquires no title to a wild animal by pursuit alone, even though there is wounding, unless the animal is followed up and reduced to occupation, that is to actual possession. (*Dapson v. Daly*)

(Note: Appendix C contains a complete listing of cases referred to in the text.)

Land

Land could be *res in patrimonio* or *res extra patrimonium*. Land above the influence of flooding was generally in private ownership unless dedicated to a public purpose (e.g., highways, which were *res publicae*). Open navigable waters were clearly outside private ownership, were held in trust as *res communes* as a public right (*jus publicum*), and could not become private property (Buckland 1963, 182, 183). The boundary between land and water, the shore or beach, presented a complicated interweaving of private and public interests, as it does today. In this area, our courts lean heavily on precedent and custom inherited from the Romans.

The shore (*littus*) extended shoreward to the point reached by the "highest wave of the sea" or the "highest winter floods." Such areas were *res communes*, generally open to all and incapable of private ownership. Structures could be built on the shore, however, provided they were found to be in the "public interest" and were duly permitted (Buckland 1963, 183):

> Although whatever we construct on the public shore or in the sea will belong to us, still, a decree of the Praetor [magistrate] must be obtained to

permit this to be done; and, indeed, if anyone should do something of this kind which inconveniences others, he can be prevented by force; for I have no doubt that he who puts up a building will have no right of civil action. (*Dig.* 41.1.50)

Prior to the *Novellae Constitutiones*, adjacent landowners could be fined for denying access to the shore, but beach access appears to have been a controversial subject during Justinian's time, as it is now, and later Roman courts found that

> [T]he law which abolishes the common ownership of maritime lands...those situated on the shores of the sea, and compels the owner of such lands to pay damages for forbidding persons to fish thereon, does not seem to us to be just....We hereby decree that everyone shall be the actual owner of his land on the seashore, and that no one shall be permitted to enjoy the advantages thereof without his permission. (*Nov. Const.* LVI)

Riparian lands (those bordering on rivers) and littoral lands (bordering on tidal shores) changed from privately owned *res in patrimonio* to publicly owned *res communes* and vice versa through gradual hydrogeologic processes. A littoral or riparian owner could gain land through accretion (the gradual and imperceptible accumulation of land through natural causes), from dereliction (the recession of the sea or river to expose new ground), or from alluvion (the washing in of sand or soil so as to form new ground). He could lose land through erosion (the gradual and imperceptible loss of land through natural causes [Black 1979, 486]). The precise process might be difficult to define; the essential ingredient was that of a shifting *littus* due to gradual and natural processes. As the *littus* moved landward or seaward, so did ownership of the land:

> If, however, [the river changes its channel by degrees]...and carries the soil elsewhere, this is acquired under the right of alluvion by the person to whose land it is added.
> Moreover, anything which a river adds to our land as alluvium is acquired by us under the Law of Nations...[provided it is] added little by little, so that we cannot perceive the amount which is added at each moment of time. (*Dig.* 41.1.7.1)

Islands and stream meanders presented special situations. Generally, when a channel broke through the neck of an oxbow, creating an island, ownership of the island remained with the former owner, but the newly created channel reverted to *res communes*. If an island appeared in the middle of a channel, ownership was apportioned among adjacent riparian owners, but if it were obviously closer to one bank, it became the property of the nearest riparian owner. Islands forming in the ocean were *res nullius* and became the property of the first claimant.

> If a river overflows on one side, and begins to run in a new channel, and afterwards the new channel turns back to the old one, the field which is included between the two channels and forms an island will remain the property of him to whom it formerly belonged. (*Dig.* 41.1.7.4)

> If, however, the stream, having abandoned its natural bed, begins to flow elsewhere, the former bed will belong to those who have land along the bank, in proportion to the extent of the land situated there, and the new bed will come under the same law as the river itself. (*Dig.* 41.1.7.5)

> Where an island is formed in the sea (which rarely happens) it becomes the property of the first occupant for it is considered to belong to no one. Where an island is formed in a river (which takes place very frequently), and it occupies the middle of the stream, it becomes the common property of those who have land near the banks on both sides of the stream in proportion to the extent of the land of each person along the banks. If the island is nearer to one side than the other, it will belong to him alone who has land along that side of the stream. (*Dig.* 41.1.7.3)

> When an island is formed in a stream, it becomes the common property of those who own property along the bank, not undivided, but separated by distinct boundaries; for each one of them will have a right to that portion of it which is opposite to his land on the bank of the stream, just as if a straight line were drawn through the island. (*Dig.* 41.1.29)

A riparian landowner might lose all his holding due to erosion and cease to exercise any property interest. Subsequently, stream meander or accretion resulting from other causes might restore upland within his prior boundaries. Ownership under such circumstances became extremely difficult to establish. If his upland boundary were itself a natural feature or its location were difficult to reestablish, he probably would be unable to establish any interest in the newly created riparian land. If, on the other hand, his upland boundary were a fixed and well-established landmark, it would also be the seaward boundary of the next landward owner. Under such circumstances, the landward owner could acquire riparian or littoral rights only as far seaward as this fixed boundary, and any additional accretion became the property of him whose holding had previously been eliminated by erosion.

> Where the new bed occupies all the land, even though the river may have returned to its former channel, he to whom the land belonged cannot, strictly speaking, assert any right to the bed of the stream, because the land which formerly belonged to him has ceased to be his; having lost its original form; and since he has no adjoining land, he cannot, by reason of neighborhood, be entitled to any part of the abandoned bed. To rigidly observe this rule, however, would be a hardship. (*Dig.* 41.1.7.5)

> Attius had a property adjoining a public road; beyond the road lay a river and the holding of Lucius Titius. The river gradually flowed over and ate away the land lying between the road and the river and made away with the road and then gradually receded and, by alluvion, returned to its former bed. The opinion was that the river having destroyed the land and the public road, the land so destroyed became the property of the man who held the land beyond the river [that is, Lucius Titius]; but later, when the river slowly receded, it took the restored land away from the man who had acquired it and added it to that of the owner beyond the road [that is, Attius], since his land was nearest to the river; but what had been public became no one's property. And he said further that the road did not prevent the land again exposed, with the recession of the river, on the other side of the road from becoming the property of Attius, since the road itself was part of his land. (*Dig.* 41.1.38, translated by Mommsen, Krueger, and Watson 1985, 496, 497)

> Alluvium restores a field to the state in which it was before the force of a stream entirely removed it. Therefore, if a field which is situated between a public highway and a river is covered with water by the overflow of the stream, whether it is inundated little by little, or not, and it is restored by the same force through the receding of the river, it will belong to its former owner. (*Dig.* 41.1.30.3)

> It is established that alluvium does not exist with reference to land having boundaries. (*Dig.* 41.1.16)

These citations were among those used by a South Carolina court of appeals in deciding ownership of a tract of littoral land on the border between North Carolina and South Carolina. At one time, the state line was in Little River Inlet, west of Bird Island, which was owned by a North Carolinian. During the early 1900s, the inlet migrated toward South Carolina, extending Bird Island westward across the state line, where the South Carolina portion was granted to a resident of Horry County, South Carolina. Subsequently, the inlet again migrated eastward, eroding away all of Bird Island in South Carolina. By the 1980s, however, the inlet had returned to its approximate 1903 location, reestablishing about 20 acres of land in South Carolina. At this time, the U.S. Army Corps of Engineers proposed to acquire the property as part of an inlet jetty project. The owner of the North Carolina portion of the island claimed the new land in South Carolina under the general principles of accretion, alleging that any prior rights were extinguished by past erosion. Successors to the South Carolina grantee also claimed the land, arguing that they owned the part of Bird Island that extended across the state line, as shown in the original grant, and that the North Carolinian's land was always bounded on the west by the state line. The appeals court found for the South Carolinian (*Woodward v. Price*).

Navigation

A number of Roman laws addressed the issue of transportation over public waterways (*res publicae*). Many of these originated as edicts or interdicts ("an order of a magistrate giving rise to further proceedings if disregarded" [Buckland 1963, 729]—similar to our court order), which became codified in the *Digest*. In sum, they protected the public right of navigation and described the navigational servitude attached to riparian property:

> Nothing shall be thrown into a public river or deposited on its banks by means of which the landing of merchandise, traffic, or the movement of shipping may be interfered with. (*Dig.* 43.12.1)

> The Praetor does not absolutely prohibit any work being done in a public river, or on the bank of same, but only whatever may interfere with the landing of goods, or navigation. Therefore, this interdict only applies to public rivers which are navigable, and not to any others. (*Dig.* 43.12.12)

> The anchorage and the course of navigation are also considered to be interfered with where the use of the same is interrupted, or rendered more difficult, or diminished, or made less frequent, or entirely destroyed...if anything is done to inconvenience navigation, make it more difficult, or entirely prevent it; there will be cause for the interdict. (*Dig.* 43.12.15)

> I forbid anything to be built in a public river or upon its banks, or anything to be placed in such a river or on its banks, by means of which the water may be caused to flow in a different direction. (*Dig.* 43.13.1)

One cannot help but be struck with the similarity of these laws and sections 9, 10, and 13 of the River and Harbor Act of 1899 (see chapter 12), which for more than seventy years constituted the federal authority for regulating land use in the coastal zone. (Note: Appendix B contains complete references for all federal statutes cited.)

While Justinian's *Corpus Juris Civilis* provided much of the legal foundation for Europe and much of the Western world, it served Romans more as a chronicle of past events than as a model for the future. Rome and the western empire fell prior to publication of the *First Code*, and the eastern empire became Greek in speech soon after Justinian's time (Severy 1983).

The Romans provided much of our legal background for management of natural resources—particularly in the areas of public trust and admiralty law. But most of our basis for criminal law and civil rights came from another source—our Anglo-Saxon heritage.

MAGNA CARTA

Events preceding creation of the Magna Carta and its companion document, the Carta de Foresta, illustrate relationships between natural resource management and civil rights in medieval England. Conditions in the Royal Forests precipitated, at least in part, issuance of both documents, whose greatest value to succeeding generations was in defining and protecting individual rights.

Prelude

For six centuries following the decline of the Roman Empire, barbarians periodically overran England. Feudal systems came and went; life was tenuous, peace and security fleeting (Swindler 1965, 9). Real property and wildlife were possessions of the ruler, and use was a privilege bestowed on but a few. The right to hunt was precious, and royalty treated transgressions as serious crimes. The Danish king Canute (A.D. 1018) declared:

> I will and grant that each one shall be worthy of such venery [hunting places] as he by hunting can take either in the plains or in the woods within his fee or dominion, but each man shall abstain from my venerie in every place, where I will that my beasts shall have firm peace and quiet-

ness, upon pain to forfeit as much as a man may forfeit. (Manwood [1615]
1976, 30)

Thus did Canute confirm a landowner's right to hunt on his own land,
deny all men the right to hunt on the king's land, and declare wildlife on
such lands to be "my beasts." No longer were wild animals *res nullius*, the
property of no one until possessed. They were now the property of the
landowner, who received land through grant from the sovereign. Hunting
(particularly big game hunting and falconry) became the coveted, protected property of the few, and one must wonder just how far Canute may
have gone in requiring a man "to forfeit as much as a man may forfeit."

The Royal Forests

The concept of forests as preserves was neither new nor unique to feudal
England. The word "forest" is derived from *ferae*, "wild," and *statio*, "to
remain." Forests were therefore areas that were to remain wild and had
little to do with the production of trees. Although the concept dates at
least to Philip of Macedonia, who maintained forests for hunting and
other recreation, it gained its greatest notoriety in England during the
Middle Ages.

The defeat of Harold (a Saxon) by William the Conqueror (a Norman)
at the Battle of Hastings in A.D. 1066 marked the beginning of the
Anglo-Saxon state and societal structure. William decreed a national levy,
declared all freeholds forfeit (although some few surviving lords were permitted to redeem their lands), and distributed the formerly Saxon land to
Normans. Thus all landholders became "tenants," holding their estates at
the pleasure of the king, vowing to "bear...faith against all men," and to
supply men and provisions to the king. In return, the tenant received
protection for himself and his landholdings (Swindler 1965, 10, 11).

Land brought wealth and power, but fewer than 10 percent of the
English people were landed. These composed the nobility, extending
from crown tenants (barons) through mesne (intermediate) lords to
knights and minor nobles. Peasants, churls, villeins, and other nonlanded
people composed the remainder of England's 1.5 million people (during
William's reign). This group held no real property, had few rights, and
lived under domination of the nobility.

Prior to the Norman Conquest, Saxon kings had hunting preserves
scattered throughout England, but the concept of Royal Forests with
their unique judicial system was a distinctly Norman invention (Young

1979, 2). The Royal Forests were a special class of land. Originally (under William) they consisted of unoccupied wastelands scattered irregularly throughout England (McKechnie 1958, 416), and covered about one-third of the country. They were a legal, rather than a biophysical, entity and could include moors (open, rolling, infertile land), bogs, heaths (level, uncultivated, poorly drained land), downs (treeless hills), plowed lands, fields, and even villages and "owned" lands:

> [A] Forest is a Certain Territory of wooded grounds and fruitful pastures, privileged for wild beasts and fowls of the Forest, Chase, and Warren, to rest and abide in, in the safe protection of the king, for his princely delight and pleasure...and therefore a Forest doth chiefly consist of four things...of vert, venison, particular laws and privileges, and of certain meet [suitable] officers appointed for that purpose. (Manwood [1615] 1976, 18)

Royal Forests were the highest class of "game preserve." They were the exclusive hunting territory of royalty and were designed to protect the royal game—red deer (hart and hind), fallow deer (buck and doe), roe deer (roe), boar, and wolf (Manwood [1615] 1976, 19). Other preserves were maintained by lesser nobles. Chases were unenclosed former Royal Forests granted to individuals, who maintained exclusive hunting rights. Parks were enclosed areas containing animals, and warrens were privately "owned" game lands (sometimes royal lands) on which royal game and lesser wildlife were protected (McKechnie 1958, 422, 423). Characteristic animals of the chase were the buck, doe, fox, martin, and roe; those of the warren were the hare, coney, pheasant, and partridge (Manwood [1615] 1976, 20). All such lands were protected by common-law remedies against trespass and theft, but only the Royal Forests were governed by the Forest laws (McKechnie 1958, 422, 423).

The "vert," then, was the woody vegetation and food (i.e., the habitat) required to maintain game populations. The "venison" was the animals of the forest, chase, or warren; the "particular laws and privileges" were the Forest laws; and the "meet officers appointed" were the Forest officers.

The Forest Laws and Forest Officers

The Forest laws constituted a special legal system, distinct from and more restrictive than English common law. Transgressors were tried in special Forest courts, which all persons living within two leagues of the Forest were required to attend (Young 1979, 22). At their highest level (eyres), the courts were held infrequently. Sometimes as many as twenty-five years passed between eyres; juries were not utilized; and trials consisted of little more than presentation of the charges and assessment of penalties (Young 1979, 89). Although much has been made of the harsh penalties for crimes against the venison, the number of cases tried in each eyre was usually very small—either unlawful deer hunting was rare (which seems unlikely) or the foresters and verderers (and the entire forest judicial system) were inefficient (Young 1979, 99). Crimes against the vert were much more common, with unlawful clearing for agriculture (assarts), construction of houses and other structures (purprestures), and cutting of wood being the most common (Young 1979, 108, 109). Fines were assessed more on the ability to pay than on the nature of the offense, with larger amounts assessed barons, clergy, and Jews—but those of lower social rank tended to appear in court more often (Young 1979, 104, 108).

The Forests were managed by a hierarchy of paid and unpaid officers. Each Forest was in charge of a justiciar (chief forester), under whom worked professional wardens (supervisors) and foresters (gamekeepers). A separate system of magistrates consisted of verderers (who reported conditions in the Forests to the king), regarders (twelve knights who inspected conditions every three years), and agistors (who enforced grazing regulations). Forest officers frequently paid for the right to hold office (Young 1979, 14); each officer was dependent upon his superiors (and ultimately to the king) for job security (Young 1979, 51); many unpaid foresters "lived upon the country"; and graft and bribery were rampant (McKechnie 1958, 418).

A few examples illustrate the severity of the Forest laws:

• "[T]he Killing of any wild beast within the forest was punishable by the King at his will and pleasure...: and therefore the King might have punished a man for killing a Hare, or a Fox, or a Martin, or any other beast of the Forest, before the granting of the great charter of the Forest, even with the loss of life, or the loss of an arm" (Manwood [1615] 1976, 47, 48).

• Lands could be added to the Royal Forests by royal proclamation (McKechnie 1958, 424); few were given back.

• In some cases, barons could kill one or two royal game while passing through a Forest if they did so in sight of a forester or after blowing a horn (McKechnie 1958, 425).

- "[B]y the Laws of the Forest, no man may cut down his woods, nor destroy any coverts, within the Forest, without the view of a Forester and license of the Lord chief justice in Eyre of the Forest" (Manwood [1615] 1976, 60).

- "In one instance, hedges were ordered burned and ditches leveled, so that animals [boar] could feed on crops" (McKechnie 1958, 416).

- Freeholders within a Forest could not clear their lands, nor plough wastelands, nor root out trees, nor build a pond or mill, nor enclose a space with a hedge (for Forests were "unenclosed"), nor cut a tree or lop off limbs without permission (and payment) (McKechnie 1958, 425).

- When a hare was found dead, twenty men of four townships were assembled and determined that it died of disease, but the townships were fined because no culprit was identified. When a hart was found dead, the whole town was seized by the king (McKechnie 1958, 428). No one living near a Forest could keep bows and arrows, nor could one own large dogs (mastiffs or greyhounds) near a Forest unless the dogs were "lawed"—had their knees cut or toenails removed to impair their running ability (McKechnie 1958, 427).

- "[N]o man may hawk or hunt in the Forest, even on his own land, except Earls, Barons, and Noblemen of the Realm, being therefore licensed or authorized by the King or his Justiciar in Eyre" (Manwood [1615] 1976, 124).

- During fence month (thirty-one days beginning fifteen days before midsummer), all livestock in the Forest were required to be confined; swine, sheep, or goats found in the Forest were confiscated and became the king's property; persons could not go "wandering up and down in the Forest" nor drive cattle through the Forest "for fear of troubling or disquieting of the wild beasts in the time of their fawning" (Manwood [1516] 1976, 92).

- "[T]he Assize of Woodstock had provided for physical punishment (probably the death penalty) only for the third offense...[whereas] Richard's Assize of 1198 set the penalty for killing deer as mutilation by removal of the offender's eyes and testicles" (Young 1979, 30).

The Forest laws were intended to protect both the vert and the venison, and special provisions governed excessive timbering and reforestation:

> But if woods are so severely cut that a man, standing on the half-buried stump of an oak or other tree, can see five other trees cut down round

about him, that is regarded as "waste," which is short for "wasted." Such
an offence, even in a man's own woods, is considered so serious, that he can
in no way be quit of it by his session at the Exchequer, but must all the
more suffer a money penalty proportionate to his means. (*Dialogus de
Scaccario*, 61, cited in Young 1979, 35)

Fines collected at the infrequent Forest eyres were important sources of
royal income, but the amounts collected from defendants were frequently
far less than anticipated "because some are dead, some are fugitives, and
some have nothing" (Young 1979, 39).

Enactment

During the 150 years between the Battle of Hastings and the creation of
the Magna Carta, increasing conflict developed between the kings' desire
to protect their hunting rights and freeholders' efforts to make their lands
more profitable. Originally, the Royal Forests consisted largely of vacant
wastelands, but as development pressures intensified and habitat for big
game diminished in quality and quantity, successive monarchs found it
necessary (or desirable) to designate more and more land as Royal Forests.
In addition to nonarable lands, these permanent additions included fields,
pastures, and even entire villages. In such areas, freeholds continued to
exist in theory, but use was vastly restricted through imposition of the
Forest laws.

Kings used another ploy to reserve lowlands along rivers. These areas
supported waterfowl and other game of interest to nobility and were particularly valuable for falconry. They, and access across the rivers, were also
important from the standpoint of defense. Such lands often were placed *in
defensum*. Access was limited or prohibited, and nearby residents were
required to build and maintain bridges. This practice also proliferated
until much English bottomland was *in defensum* and became additional
royal game lands (but not Royal Forests) (Swindler 1965, 296).

The Royal Forests were more than mere game preserves; they were also
important sources of income. The king could grant a right of chase
(which established a private forest), of warren (control over the hunting of
animals other than beasts of the Forest), or of common (pasturage of
domestic animals); the right to develop assarts (cleared and cultivated
areas) (Young 1979, 46, 47); and other privileges. He could collect rent
from the cutting and sale of wood, range for pigs (pannage), operation of
cattle farms (vaccaries), and the production of iron, hides, grain, salt, and
peat (Young 1979, 55-58). There were also fees for carts and wagons

using roads though the Forests (cheminage), and for use of windfallen timber, hay, nuts, and firewood (Young 1979, 115)—and for almost everything else that could be produced in the Forest. During the reigns of Richard and John, sale of privileges within the Forests and of the Forests themselves became particularly profitable, and large areas of Royal Forest were disafforested (Young 1979, 20).

By the early thirteenth century, expansion of the Forests and curtailment of individual rights had become critical issues throughout England. Diversion of resources to support the Crusades and other foreign wars, coupled with a high rate of inflation, had depressed the economy; adultery and bastardy were considered only "incidents of the age," and graft and bribery were commonplace. On August 25, 1214, Archbishop Stephen Langton told a gathering of nobles at St. Paul's Church that "a charter of Henry the first of England [successor to William the Conqueror] has just now been found by which you may, if you wish it, recall your lost rights and former condition." Armed rebellion followed and raged for almost a year. In early June 1215, King John sent word to the barons that he was ready to come to terms, and a meeting was arranged. On June 15, 1215, the king and the barons met on the south bank of the Thames River, in a meadow called Runnymede (Swindler 1965, 71-79).

Considerable confusion surrounds what happened that day and during the ten years prior to issuance of the Great Charter of 1225. Articles were agreed upon during the first day of the meeting, and an agreement was sealed by both parties four days later (June 19). Objections from the pope caused rejection of the agreement sixty-six days after its enactment, and it was reissued in 1216 with changes to overcome the papal objections. In 1217, two documents emerged: the Carta de Foresta contained revisions to the Forest law, and the more comprehensive Magna Carta de Libertatibus guaranteed civil rights of the subjects. It was not until 1225 that the definitive Great Charter was issued. Any or all of the foregoing documents have become known as the Magna Carta, despite differences in the various versions and omission of most amendments to the Forest law from both the Magna Carta de Libertatibus and the Great Charter of 1225.

Provisions of the Great Charter of 1225

The Great Charter's most significant contribution to the body of law affecting natural resources was its declaration of the civil rights to which all freemen were entitled. At the time of its enactment, these rights pertained only to "freemen"—the less than 10 percent of the population that held land. In time, application broadened to apply to all English subjects, including those who settled in the New World. These are the precedents for determining the limits of government and the liberties of the individual (which we still debate today).

While most provisions pertaining to forests and other natural resources appear in the Carta de Foresta, a few provisions of the Great Charter do affect navigation and land use.

Liberties of the Subject (Article 1)

First, we have granted to God, and by this our present Charter we have confirmed, for us and our heirs forever, that the English Church shall be free, and shall have all her rights entire and her liberties inviolate; we have also granted to all freemen of our kingdom, for us and ours forever, all the liberties underwritten, to be had and held by them and their heirs, of us and our heirs, for ever. (Swindler 1965, 250)

For clerics, this article ensured the right to trial by clerical, rather than laic, court and preservation of church property following death of the clergyman in charge. For freemen, it preserved the "liberties of the subject." This principle states that a subject is free to speak or act as he chooses, providing that he violates no law nor transgresses the rights of others; public authorities, including the Crown, however, may do only what is authorized by some rule of common law or statute.

Just Punishment (Article 14)

A freeman shall not be amerced for a small offence, except in proportion to the measure of the offence; and for a great offence he shall be fined in proportion to the magnitude of the offence, saving his countenance; and none of the above fines shall be imposed except by the oaths of honest and lawful men of the neighborhood. Earls and barons shall be amerced only by their peers, and only in proportion to their offence. (Swindler 1965, 291)

Prior to enactment of this provision, freemen could lose all their property to satisfy a small debt or crime. Subsequently, "cruel and unusual punishments" were forbidden, and trials were conducted and penalties assessed by local courts. Still, rights were class privileges, and only freemen were entitled to this protection. Only gradually did they come to apply to the vast unlanded majority of Englishmen.

Due Process (Article 29)

No freeman shall be taken or imprisoned or disseised of any freehold or liberties, or free customs, or outlawed or banished, or in any other way destroyed, nor will we go upon him, nor send upon him, except by the legal judgment of his peers or by the law of the land. To no one will we sell, to no one will we deny, or delay right or justice. (Swindler 1965, 316, 317)

This, the most famous provision of the Magna Carta, ensured for freemen the rights of due process and equal protection. The former grew to encompass the rights of notice, opportunity to be heard, and defense in an orderly proceeding and the ability to present evidence and rebut opposing witnesses in open court that we enjoy today (Black 1979, 449). The latter prohibited prejudicial treatment resulting from social or economic status or political leanings.

Riverbanks *In Defensum* (Articles 15 and 16)

No town nor freeman shall be distrained to make bridges at riverbanks, except those who were obliged to do so of old and by right. (Swindler 1965, 295)

No riverbanks shall be defended henceforth, except those which were in defense in the time of King Henry our grandfather, by the same places and in the same bounds as they were wont to be in his time. (Swindler 1965, 295, 296)

Correcting some of the injustice perpetrated in the name of national security and implementing provisions discovered by Archbishop Langton, these articles reduced the size of the kings' hunting preserves outside the Royal Forests. They returned all lands placed *in defensum* during the approximately 100-year period since the reign of King Henry I and lifted the requirement that citizens build and maintain bridges in such areas.

Hazards to Navigation (Article 23)

All the fishweirs in the Thames and the Medway, and throughout all England, shall be removed forthwith, except those along the coast. (Swindler 1965, 307)

As the land became more densely settled and river commerce became more important, use conflicts occurred between fishermen and vessels.

Weirs—fixed fishing devices consisting of walls (leads) and traps (hearts or pounds) of stones, brush, or netting—in navigable waters encroached upon channels and created hazards to navigation. This provision recognized the conflict and resolved it in favor of the paramount navigational servitude.

Provisions of the Magna Carta and Carta de Foresta Relating to the Forests

Provisions of the Magna Carta and Carta de Foresta addressed injustices contained within the special set of Forest laws and those committed by Forest officers. Few of them are reflected in modern law; they do, however, illustrate the depth of concern over administration of the Royal Forests and the seriousness with which medieval England treated violations of hunting laws.

Attendance at Forest Court (Magna Carta, Article 44)

Men who dwell outside the forest shall not henceforth come before our Justiciars of the forest [chief foresters], on general summons, unless they are impleaded or are sureties for any person or persons who are attached on account of the forest. (Swindler 1965, 327, 328)

Previously, persons living in and around the Royal Forests were required to attend periodic Forest courts whether they were parties to the proceedings or not. This requirement imposed a severe hardship upon the citizenry, forcing them from work and family obligations with no compensation. This article brought relief, limiting required attendance to those who were essential.

Forest Officers and Practices (Magna Carta, Articles 45 and 48)

We will not make Justiciars, constables, sheriffs, or bailiffs except as such know the law of the realm and are well inclined to observe it...and all the bad customs concerning the forests and warrens [privately or royally owned game lands which were not governed by Forest laws] and concerning foresters and warrenors, sheriffs and their servants, riverbanks and their guardians shall be inquired into immediately in each county by twelve sworn knights of the same county,...and within forty days after the inquisition has been made, they shall be entirely destroyed by them. (Swindler 1965, 329-332)

These were among the most controversial of the charter's provisions. In an attempt to rid the Royal Forests and other game lands of graft and corruption, groups of knights, called inquisitors, were established to investigate the "bad customs" and to take remedial action. In many cases, inquisitors were agents of the rebels who had fought against King John and who were dedicated to destroying the Forest administration. The archbishops recognized the extent to which reform might be carried under such conditions and protested, resulting in Pope Innocent's intervention. The pope's objections to these and other sections of the original charter (of June 19, 1215) led to revisions, which were issued in 1216. Subsequently, the foregoing articles resurfaced in later versions of the charter (Swindler 1965, 101).

Disafforestation (Magna Carta, Article 47)

All forests which have been afforested in our time shall be disafforested immediately, and so it shall be concerning river banks which in our time have been in defense. (Swindler 1965, 331)

This was an attempt to reduce the area of Royal Forests and lowlands *in defensum* and to return the lands to private management. Difficulties arose, however, in defining "our time." Through the years, it grew to apply to all lands taken since the reign of Richard I, then to Henry II. The matter was controversial for years and was not finally resolved until 1327. (A somewhat similar but unsuccessful attempt was made to "disafforest" much of the U.S. National Forest System during the first Reagan administration.)

Forest Game Laws (Carta de Foresta, Cap. 11 and 13)

Whatsoever Archbishop, Bishop, Earl, or Baron, coming to us at our commandment, passeth by our Forest, it shall be lawful for him to take and kill one or two of our deer, by view of the forester if he be present, or else he shall cause one to blow a horn for him, that he seem not to steal our deer. And likewise they shall do returning home from us....Every freeman shall have within his own woods, ayries of hawks, sparrow hawks, falcons, eagles, and herons, and shall also have the honey that is found within their woods. (Manwood [1615] 1976, 7)

These provisions somewhat relaxed hunting restrictions within and around the Royal Forests. Previously, deer were protected royal game, and only noblemen were permitted to use falcons on their own land within the Forest. Subsequently, noblemen on royal missions were permitted a few deer (provided that they gave "notice" by being accompa-

nied by a Forest officer or by blowing a horn), and landholders were permitted to own and use falcons on their own lands within Royal Forests
(but probably not elsewhere within the Forests).

Punishment for Poaching (Carta de Foresta, Cap. 10)

No man from henceforth shall loose neither life nor member for killing
our deer, but if any man be taken therewith, and convicted for taking our
venison, he shall make a grevious fine, and if he have nothing to loose [sic]
he shall be imprisoned for a year and a day, and after the year and a day
expired (if he can find sufficient sureties) he shall be delivered. And if not,
he shall abjure the realm. (Manwood [1615] 1976, 7)

While death and dismemberment were no longer appropriate penalties
for killing royal game, poaching was still a very serious crime. Those
unable to pay the fine could be imprisoned, and if unable to make bond
upon being released, they could be exiled. Moreover, law enforcement
officers were empowered to employ what today would easily be deemed
"excessive force" in bringing violators to justice:

If any forester, parker, or warrenor, do find any trespasser wandering within his liberty, intending to do damage therein, and after hue and cry made
to him to stand unto the peace, will not yield himself, but doth continue
and execute his malice, and disobeying the king's peace doth flee or defend
himself with force and arms, although such foresters, parkers, and warrenors...do kill such offendor or offendors...they shall not be arraigned
before the king and his justices...or suffer any other punishment. (Statute
of Trespassers in Parks, from Manwood [1615] 1976, 11)

So game law violations were still very serious matters.

The civil rights guaranteed by the Magna Carta were originally accorded
only to freemen. The vast majority of the people continued to have few
individual rights, living oppressed, dependent upon the landed few. In
time, however, these provisions came to be applied to all English citizens
and provided the foundation for many of our state constitutions and the
United States Constitution and Bill of Rights.

The charter's impact upon natural resource management was far less
salutary. Lands that once were protected under the oppressive Forest laws
became open to timber and wildlife poaching to the detriment of both
resources (Cross 1928, 11, 12). During the fourteenth and fifteenth cen-

turies, massive sales of timber occurred, and large areas of the Royal Forests were cleared for agriculture. Income from the Forests shifted from that produced by fines and privileges to that derived from farming (Young 1979, 122, 123). So depleted were England's timber resources that trees for masts, spars, and other naval requirements were among the most valuable imports from the American colonies, and foresters were commissioned to locate and mark superior specimens as Crown property to be used by the Royal Navy (Dana and Fairfax 1980, 5, 6). A letter written in 1770 recommended seeding oak, beech, hazel, ash, and other hardwoods in fenced enclosures; coppice management; thinning; and selective cutting (favoring oak) in the remaining Royal Forests to ensure a supply of timber for the navy (Cross 1928, 128). Between 1787 and 1793, a royal commission reported on the condition of the Forests, finding that "endless unlicensed enclosures had been effected; timber was stolen, mines neglected, plantations mismanaged;...[and] only twenty forests which could supply timber to the navy [existed]..." (Cross 1928, 11). Unfortunately, the 1770 recommendations were not implemented in the Royal Forests (though they were to some degree on privately managed land), and conditions continued to decline. How many times has this scenario been repeated in well-intentioned "land reform" schemes?

REFERENCES

Berry, Wendell. 1979. "The Gift of Good Land." *Sierra* 64:20-26.
Black, Henry C. 1979. *Black's Law Dictionary.* 5th ed. St. Paul, MN: West Publishing Company.
Buckland, W. W. 1963. *Textbook of Roman Law from Augustus to Justinian.* Cambridge, England: Cambridge University Press.
Cross, A. L. 1928. *Eighteenth Century Documents Relating to the Royal Forests the Sheriffs and Smuggling.* Selected from the Shelborne Manuscripts in the William L. Clements Library. New York: Macmillan Company.
Dana, Samuel T., and Sally K. Fairfax. 1980. *Forest and Range Policy: Its Development in the United States.* New York: McGraw-Hill Book Company.
Living Bible. 1971. Wheaton, IL: Tyndale House Publishers.
McKechnie, W. S. 1958. *Magna Carta: A Commmentary on the Great Charter of King John.* New York: Burt Franklin & Company.
Manwood, John. [1615] 1976. *Treatise of the Lawes of the Forest.* Published in fascimile. Norwood, NJ: W. J. Johnson.
Mommsen, Theodor, and Paul Krueger, eds. 1970. *Corpus Juris Civilis: Volumen Primum.* 21st ed. Dublin, Ireland: Weidmann.
Mommsen, Theodor, Paul Krueger, and Alan Watson, eds. 1985. *The Digest of Justinian.* Philadelphia: University of Pennsylvania Press.

Scott, Samuel P., ed. 1973. *The Civil Law, Including the Twelve Tables, the Institutes of Gaius, the Rules of Ulpian, the Opinions of Paulus, the Enactments of Justinian, and the Constitutions of Leo.* 17 vols. New York: AMS Press.

Severy, Merle. 1983. "The Byzantine Empire." *National Geographic* 164 (6): 709-737, 746-767.

Swindler, William F. 1965. *Magna Carta: Legend and Legacy.* Indianapolis: Bobbs-Merrill Company.

White, Lynn, Jr. 1967. "The Historical Roots of Our Ecological Crisis." *Science* 55:1203-1207.

Young, Charles R. 1979. *The Royal Forests of Medieval England.* Philadelphia: University of Pennsylvania Press.

CHAPTER II

Our Constitutional Government

BACKGROUND

At the conclusion of our Revolutionary War, this country consisted of thirteen independent colonies and a vast amount of unsettled (by Europeans) and unorganized western territory. While the colonies recognized the need to continue the alliances forged during the conflict, they were also reticent to relinquish any of their newly won power to a central government. The first attempt at unification, under the Articles of Confederation, was a failure—the central government possessed insufficient power to govern. The convention that drafted the second attempt—our Constitution—was likewise determined to retain maximum power in the states. Thus the document that resulted transferred to the central government only those powers that are enumerated, reserving all else to the states or the citizens (Grant and Nixon 1968, 34). The Constitution does not mention natural resources, nor does it say much about "responsibility"; it is, however, the basis for all federal government intervention into natural resource and environmental matters—*the federal government can take no action or engage in any activity unless authorized by the Constitution.*

The charters or constitutions of nine of the thirteen original states were based on the Magna Carta, and many of these provisions were carried over to the U.S. Constitution. Among the most important were the following concepts:

- Due process ("no free man shall be taken...except by...the law of the land" [Magna Carta, article 29]). This right guarantees an accused notice and an opportunity to be heard in a competent court; prescribes a course of legal procedure according to accepted rules and proceedings; and entitles the accused to be present at trial, to confront accusers, and to controvert evidence brought against him or her (Black 1979, 449). It is incorporated into the Fifth, Sixth, and Thirteenth Amendments of the U.S. Constitution.

• Equal protection ("To no one will we sell,...deny, or delay...justice" [Magna Carta, article 29]). All must be treated alike before the law. Courts are open to all under the same conditions, and equal protection is given to all under like circumstances (Black 1979, 481, 482). In practice, "all" may apply to a group or class (e.g., all hunters sixteen years of age or older, all nonresident fishermen, or citizens of states bordering the oceans or Great Lakes), but the class so identified must be relatively homogeneous, be different from other classes, and be treated uniformly. Equal protection is guaranteed by the Fourteenth Amendment.

• Local trial ("none of the above fines shall be imposed except by...men of the neighborhood" [Magna Carta, article 14]). Unless there are over-riding circumstances (excessive adverse publicity, safety considerations, etc.) an accused must be tried in the jurisdiction in which the alleged crime occurred. Violations of federal waterfowl laws will be tried in the appropriate state; violations of state game laws will be tried in the appro-priate county. The Sixth Amendment contains these provisions.

• Excessive bail or cruel and unusual punishment ("A freeman...shall be fined in proportion to the offence, saving his countenance" [Magna Carta, article 14]). The punishment must fit the crime. A timber poacher may be fined more than the stumpage value as a deterrent to others, but his or her equipment probably will not be confiscated. An oysterman who risks the health and lives of others by taking and selling shellfish from pollut-ed waters may lose his or her boat. This prohibition is embodied in the Eighth Amendment.

THE CONSTITUTION

When one reflects on the group of citizens assembled in Philadelphia more than 200 years ago to commence a great new experiment in govern-ment, one cannot help but be struck by their success in creating the resilient and functional document we call the Constitution. Its strength lies in its breadth and flexibility, for although interpretations vary from time to time as our societal values change, we have found it necessary to amend it only sixteen times (not counting the first ten amendments, which were added soon after ratification).

In understanding the legal basis for government action (or inaction), bureaucrats are wont to cite regulations promulgated by their executive branch agencies, yet such regulations are invalid if not authorized by a statute, and no statute is valid unless it is consistent with the Constitution. We frequently forget this relationship and the importance of constitutional law to natural resource management.

Article VI

This Constitution, and the Laws of the United States which shall be made in Pursuance thereof; and all Treaties made, or which shall be made, under the Authority of the United States, shall be the supreme Law of the Land; and the Judges in every State shall be bound thereby, any Thing in the constitution or Laws of any State to the Contrary notwithstanding.

Amendment 10

The powers not delegated to the United States by the Constitution, nor prohibited by it to the States, are reserved to the States respectively, or to the people.

Treaties (e.g., the Migratory Bird Treaty of 1916) and federal laws empowered by the Constitution (e.g., the Clean Water Act of 1977) thus take precedence over state law, and conflicts are resolved in favor of the federal law. Exceptions occur when the federal statutes themselves are found to be invalid (unconstitutional) because they go beyond the powers granted in the Constitution, violate personal liberties granted by that document, or infringe upon the "reserved rights of the States" or "liberties of the Subject." While civil rights appear to have strengthened in recent decades, states' rights have experienced extreme erosion. About the only natural resource area that so far has survived federal intervention has been the management and intrastate use of resident wildlife occurring on nonfederal land. Application of one or more constitutional provisions has enabled the federal government to subjugate state expression in every other field.

Three branches of government—legislative, executive, and judiciary—implement the Constitution, each with complementary, but sometimes overlapping, powers.

Article I: The Legislative Branch

Section 1. All legislative Powers herein granted shall be vested in a Congress of the United States, which shall consist of a Senate and House of Representatives.

Section 2. The House of Representatives shall be composed of Members chosen every second Year.

Representatives...shall be apportioned among the several States which may be included within this Union, according to their respective Numbers.

Section 3. The Senate of the United States shall be composed of two Senators from each State...[elected for terms of] six Years.

Section 5.....Each House may determine the Rules of its Proceedings.

Each House shall keep a Journal of its Proceedings, and from time to time publish the same.

Section 7.....Every Bill which shall have passed the House of Representatives and the Senate, shall, before it become a Law, be presented to the President of the United States; If he approve he shall sign it, but if not he shall return it, with his Objections to that House in which it shall have originated, who shall enter the Objections at large on their Journal, and proceed to reconsider it. If after such Reconsideration two thirds of that House shall agree to pass the Bill, it shall be sent, together with the Objections, to the other House, by which it shall likewise be reconsidered, and if approved by two thirds of that House, it shall become a Law....If any Bill shall not be returned by the President within ten Days (Sundays excepted) after it shall have been presented to him, the Same shall be a Law, in like manner as if he had signed it, unless the Congress by their Adjournment prevent its Return, in which case it shall not be a Law.

Every Order, Resolution, or Vote to which the Concurrence of the Senate and House of Representatives may be necessary...shall be presented to the President of the United States; and before the Same shall take Effect, shall be approved by him, or being disapproved by him, shall be repassed by two thirds of the Senate and House of Representatives.

Congress passes many types of laws. Enabling legislation confers new powers upon persons, corporations, or agencies, authorizing them to do what before they could not. Criminal statutes define crimes and may prescribe punishment; punitive statutes describe penalties or impose punishment. General statutes (or public statutes) relate to persons generally and have broad application, whereas private statutes (or special statutes) relate to individuals or particular circumstances and have narrow application (Black 1979, 1265). Of special interest to natural resource practitioners is the organic legislation, which describes the organization and functions of the agencies with which we work.

The Legislative Process

Natural resource legislation begins with citizens' perception of a problem, issue, or opportunity. The laws originate in the Congress, but we initiate the process. We bring matters to the attention of our elected officials and demand that they take action, and their form of action is to enact laws that may bring us relief. In the process, original motivations may become clouded and distorted by political expediency, and organized interest groups and their professional spokespersons (lobbyists) may become the dominant actors. The legislation that results often resolves the original problem, but it also may (1) expand the federal bureaucracy, (2) constrain our freedom, or (3) require additional taxes—or all three. All events that transpire during the legislative process (figure 2.1) are governed by the Constitution and by the intricate set of rules adopted by each house under the powers of the Constitution.

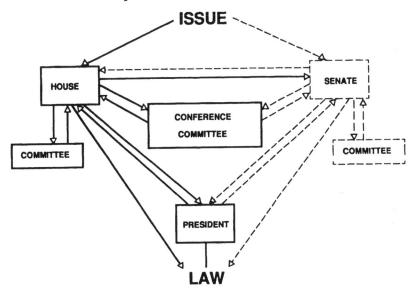

FIGURE 2.1. The Legislative Process

If we are successful in obtaining the interest of our congressional representative or senator, he or she will introduce a bill addressing our concern. A bill, then, is a proposed law. Each bill has a prefix denoting the house ("S." for Senate, "H.R." for House of Representatives) and a sequential number (the first bill introduced in the Senate during a given session of Congress would be "S. 1," etc.). Each bill also has a title, and the title remains unchanged regardless of what subsequently may happen to the content. Completely irrelevant amendments may be added (that is how the amortization provisions of the federal Forestry Incentives Program came to be part of the Recreational Boating Safety and Facilities Improvement Act of 1980), or the entire text may be deleted and replaced with text on a different subject.

TABLE 2.1

Major Congressional Committees Considering Natural Resource Issues

Subject	House Committee	Senate Committee
Air pollution	Energy and Commerce	Environment and Public Works
Endangered species	Merchant Marine and Fisheries	Energy and Natural Resources
Coastal zone management	Merchant Marine and Fisheries	Commerce, Science, and Transportation
Environment	Merchant Marine and Fisheries Works	Environment and Public
Energy	Energy and Commerce Resources	Energy and Natural
Fisheries	Merchant Marine and Fisheries and Transportation	Commerce, Science,
Forestry	Agriculture; Interior and Insular Affairs	Agriculture, Nutrition, and Forestry
Parks	Interior and Insular Affairs Resources	Energy and Natural
Public works	Public Works and Transportation	Environment and Public Works
Soil conservation	Agriculture	Agriculture, Nutrition, and Forestry
Water pollution	Public Works and Transportation	Environment and Public Works
Wilderness	Interior and Insular Affairs; Agriculture	Environment and Public Works; Agriculture, Nutrition, and Forestry
Wildlife	Merchant Marine and Fisheries	Environment and Public Works

Source: Charles B. Brownson, ed., *1987 Congressional Staff Directory* (Mount Vernon, VA: Congressional Staff Directory, 1987), pp. 217-235, 411-457.

Much of the work of Congress is performed by standing committees and their subcommittees (General Services Administration 1986, 25), and each bill is referred to one or more committees for consideration before action by the full House or Senate. Committee membership is chosen by a vote of each house, chairpersons are appointed by the majority party leadership of each house, and the majority party also comprises the majority of each committee. Committee chairs (who usually reach their positions through seniority) are extremely influential; the fate of a bill is frequently determined by the chair of the committee to which it is referred. Major committees for consideration of natural resource legislation are listed in table 2.1.

Committees and subcommittees usually hold hearings on proposed legislation. Any person wishing to provide testimony may do so (part of a citizen's "right to be heard"), and witnesses are subject to examination by committee members. Witnesses usually show a certain amount of deference toward members of the Congress, but committee members may be relentless in their interrogation of witnesses. Such interchanges may be efforts to obtain a complete and accurate record; they may also reflect committee members' attempts to appeal to their various constituencies. All testimony is recorded and appears later in a "committee report on hearings" (witnesses and committee members may have an opportunity to edit their remarks prior to publication, however, so the written record may not be completely accurate). Based on the record of hearings and whatever the committee and its staff may discover, a committee may report a bill out in its original form (favorably or unfavorably), or it may propose amendments. A bill may also die in committee without action (the positions of the chairperson and influential members may be extremely important here).

If a bill is considered favorably, it is presented for consideration to the full House (or Senate), as originally introduced or with suggested amendments. Accompanying the bill is a committee report, which documents the committee's deliberations and the basis for its recommendations. On the floor of the House (Senate), the bill is subject to debate and amendment and may be passed as referred by committee, passed with amendment, referred to a second committee, or defeated. If passed, it is sent to the Senate (House) and referred to a Senate (House) committee, and the process begins anew. Eventually, the bill may pass both houses, but usually not in an identical form. In this case, both houses appoint members to a conference committee, which attempts to work out differences and to report identical, agreed-upon versions back to their respective houses. Deliberations on the floor are reported daily in the *Congressional Record*; the day-to-day progress of legislation is recorded in the *Calendar of the U.S. House of Representatives and History of Legislation* (one publication); and results of conference committee deliberations are published in conference committee reports.

Eventually, a bill may emerge in identical form from both houses of Congress, but it is not yet a law. It must now be signed by the Speaker (or Speaker *pro tempore*) of the House and the vice president (or president *pro tempore* or acting president *pro tempore* of the Senate) and be presented to the president (General Services Administration 1986, 27). If the president favors the legislation and wishes to be identified with it, he may sign it, and it becomes law. If he favors the legislation but does not wish to be identified with it, or if he opposes it but does not have the support to sustain a veto, he may do nothing, and the bill will become law in ten days (Sundays excepted) if Congress is still in session (if Congress adjourns within the ten-day period, the bill does not become law—it has sustained a "pocket veto"). If the president opposes the bill and feels that he can sustain a veto (or simply has strong negative feelings about it), he may veto the bill and return it to Congress with a message explaining his objections. In the event of a presidential veto, each house must repass the bill by a two-thirds majority, or it dies. Presidential action is recorded in the *Congressional Record,* the House *Calendar,* and the *Weekly Compilation of Presidential Documents.*

Once a bill becomes law ("law," "act," and "statute" are synonymous), it is first published as a "slip law"—a pamphlet containing the text, the *Statutes at Large* page numbers that will be assigned, marginal notes and comments (including *United States Code* citations to current legislation), and a guide to legislative history (General Services Administration 1980, 8). As a slip law, the act is assigned a public law (Pub. L. or P.L.) prefix, a number denoting the Congress, and a second number reflecting its place in the sequence of passed legislation. While this designation is soon superseded, it frequently becomes the title by which a statute is known (e.g., the Commercial Fisheries Research and Development Act of 1964 frequently is called P.L. 88-309). All laws and resolutions enacted during a session of Congress are compiled into a volume of the *Statutes at Large,* which is published annually. The full text of each law is printed, arranged chronologically by approval date, along with finding aids and notes on legislative history (General Services Administration 1980, 8). The law now receives a new designation—the volume of the *Statutes at Large* in which it appears, "Stat.," and the page on which it first appears. P.L. 88-309 has become 78 Stat. 197.

If a statute does not affect the general public (is a "private law") or is of a temporary nature (as are appropriations, civil works authorizations, and general policy statements), the publication process may end with the *Statutes at Large.* Acts or portions of acts that are generally applicable and reasonably permanent become codified in the *United States Code*. In this process, the legislation is classified by subject and inserted into the existing body of federal law (General Services Administration 1980, 8). The code is published annually as cumulative supplements, with complete editions appearing every six years. Parts of a public law may appear in several places in the federal code, depending on the subject addressed. Each part receives a number designating the title within the code, "U.S.C.", and the number of its section. The codified parts of 78 Stat. 197 are in 16 U.S.C. 779-779f. Annotated versions of the federal code are also published (e.g., the *United States Code Service*), which contain cross-references among the statutes, case law notations, and statutory history.

Congressional Powers

Article I
Section 8. The Congress shall have Power To...provide for the common Defence and general Welfare of the United States.

To regulate Commerce with foreign Nations, and among the several States, and with the Indian Tribes.

To make all Laws which shall be necessary and proper for carrying into Execution the foregoing Powers, and all other Powers vested by this Constitution in the Government of the United States.

Section 10. No State shall, without the Consent of Congress,...enter into any Agreement or Compact with another State, or with a foreign Power.

Article IV
Section 3. The Congress shall have Power to dispose of and make all needful Rules and Regulations respecting the Territory or other Property belonging to the United States.

These sections, together with the treaty powers discussed later, compose the package of constitutional powers that authorize federal involvement in natural resource issues. They illustrate the beautiful flexibility of the document. Our founding fathers could never have foreseen the array of future situations requiring federal action, yet their words have generally sufficed.

The Commerce Clause (Article I, Section 8)
The commerce clause has been extended to include virtually every kind of traffic, trade, or transportation, whether for strictly commercial purposes or not, and to apply toward social objectives, whether or not economic considerations exist. In one classic application, it was applied to prevent

filling of a mangrove swamp in Tampa Bay, Florida, because of the damage that would result to estuarine fisheries and thus to interstate commerce:

> [D]redge and fill projects are activities which may tend to destroy the ecological balance and thereby affect commerce substantially. Because of these potential effects Congress has the power to regulate such projects. (*Zabel v. Tabb*)

Application of the commerce clause may conflict with reserved rights of the states, particularly when the states' use of police powers affects interstate commerce. When the impact is not severe or exclusionary (as in the case of higher fees for nonresident hunting and fishing licenses), courts have generally upheld the state laws (*Baldwin v. Montana Fish and Game Commission*). When fees are clearly and excessively discriminatory or nonresidents are excluded, however, courts have frequently found the state laws to infringe upon interstate commerce and thus to be unconstitutional and invalid (*Foster-Fountain Packing Co. v. Haydel, Douglas v. Seacoast Products*).

The Federal Property Clause (Article IV, Section 3)

The congressional right to control federal property extends far beyond acquisition and disposition of material goods and real estate. Congress *manages* federal property, and federal property includes all that is contained on or in the land (as well as material goods). Thus it falls to Congress to designate wilderness areas (a right reinforced by statute), to dispose of the National Forest System (the Reagan administration could not do it within the executive branch), and to manage resident wildlife on federal lands:

> [The] power of the United States to thus protect its lands and property does not admit of doubt...the game laws or any other statute of the state notwithstanding. (*Hunt v. United States*)

> [T]he furthest reaches of...the Property Clause have not yet been... resolved...[but it] includes the power to regulate and protect the wildlife living there. (*Kleppe v. New Mexico*)

In most instances, Congress exercises its property authority by delegating specific duties to the executive branch. Thus the secretary of the Department of Agriculture was given authority to manage the National Forest System, and the secretary of the Department of the Interior has similar authority over the National Park System. But Congress reserves the right to create and abolish national forests and parks.

Other Legislative Provisions

The specific powers discussed here are reinforced by the broader and more general directives to the legislative branch (article 1, section 8) to "provide for the common Defence," the general welfare provision, and the exclusive authority "[t]o make all Laws which shall be necessary...for carrying into Execution the foregoing Powers." The first authorizes acquisition of vast areas of land and the natural resources they contain in the interests of "defense" (remember how lands were placed *in defensum* in medieval England). The general welfare provision underlies park and recreation, pollution control, and general environmental legislation. However, the exclusive legislative authority is not as exclusive as one might think, for, as we shall see later, regulations of the executive branch have the effect of law, and the judicial branch makes "new law" as it interprets the old.

Article II: The Executive Branch

Section 1. The executive Power shall be vested in a President of the United States of America.

Section 2. He shall have Power, by and with the Advice and Consent of the Senate, to make Treaties, provided two thirds of the Senators present concur; and he shall nominate, and by and with the Advice and Consent of the Senate, shall appoint Ambassadors,...Judges of the Supreme Court, and all other Officers of the United States, whose Appointments are not herein otherwise provided for...but the Congress may by Law vest the Appointment of such inferior Officers, as they think proper, in the President alone, in the Courts of Law, or in the Heads of Departments....

Section 3. [H]e shall take Care that the Laws be faithfully executed....

Section 4. The President,...and all civil Officers of the United States, shall be removed from Office on Impeachment for...High Crimes and Misdemeanors.

The executive branch carries out the laws. To most citizens, it characterizes the day-by-day workings of government and constitutes the target of most complaints about the bureaucracy. Some such complaints result from ineptitude (or worse) within the executive branch. Many, however, have their foundations in the laws passed by Congress. Because most people cannot differentiate between the two sources, public servants of the executive branch receive much criticism that they do not deserve.

Treaty Powers

Many natural resource and environmental issues transcend national boundaries. Article I, section 10 reserves foreign affairs to the federal government ("No State shall...enter into any Agreement...with a foreign Power"), and the power to appoint ambassadors and to make treaties establishes the president, and thus the executive branch, as the primary instrument for international affairs. Initiative and precedent obtained through these powers frequently carry over into domestic legislation. Thus the Migratory Bird Treaty with Great Britain provided the foundation for the Migratory Bird Treaty Act of 1918, and the Convention on Trade in Endangered Species and Wild Fauna and Flora underlies our Endangered Species Act of 1973. Treaties are not binding upon the United States unless approved by a two-thirds vote of the Senate (article II, section 2), but even draft treaties and those to which the United States is not a party can influence legislation. Sometimes legislation is even passed in anticipation of, or to expedite passage of, a pending treaty. The United States was one of the prime movers in developing a Law of the Sea Treaty through the United Nations, yet the Senate refused to endorse the resulting convention. Nevertheless, Congress passed the Deep Seabed Hard Mineral Resources Act, one purpose of which was "to encourage the successful conclusion of a comprehensive Law of the Sea Treaty" (94 Stat. 553).

Personnel Matters

While Congress permits executive discretion in most personnel actions within that branch, it reserves the right to approve appointment of senior officials. Cabinet officers, agency heads, ambassadors, and others in high policy-level positions are subject to Senate confirmation. The exposure afforded by this process provides protection from flagrant political favoritism at the expense of the public interest and gives Congress an opportunity to put nominees "on notice" concerning congressional interests and reservations. James Watt, President Reagan's first secretary of the interior, was ultimately confirmed but was subjected to extensive interrogation and berating in the process; William Ruckelshaus, Reagan's second administrator of the Environmental Protection Agency (EPA) and a proponent of sound environmental policy, received only token examination.

Two other classes of federal executive branch employees deserve mention. Middle- to upper-class policy-level positions (staff to agency heads, personnel of the Executive Office of the President) are frequently occupied by personnel who come and go as administrations change. These positions are exempt from Senate confirmation and from civil service protection. They attract administration supporters, businessmen, and academicians who wish to serve a particular administration or who seek a short term of duty and are not bothered by the fact that they can be dismissed at the whim of their supervisor. The majority of federal employees, the public servants who make the system work, are career professionals committed to a life of service within government. They are protected by civil service legislation, must be hired and promoted on the basis of merit, and may be dismissed only for cause.

Rules and Regulations

One means by which the executive branch "take[s] Care that the Laws be faithfully executed" is by promulgating documents that interpret and amplify statutes passed by the legislative branch. These regulations have the effect of law if they are authorized by statute, and they constitute the framework for bureaucratic action. An EPA employee may not be familiar with details of the Clean Water Act, but he or she can quote the titles and sections of the "regs" that guide his or her everyday activities. Executive rule making has many similarities to the legislative process. Just as statutes must be authorized by a higher authority (the Constitution), executive regulations must be authorized by statute. An executive agency cannot enact regulations having the "force and effect of law" unless so authorized; violations of such regulations are not crimes unless specified by statute; and penalties cannot be assessed unless authorized by statute (Arbuckle et al. 1983, 47).

Federal rule making frequently begins with publication of an "advance notice of proposed rule making" in the *Federal Register*—the executive branch's counterpart of the *Congressional Record*. The *Federal Register* provides notice to the citizenry and is published daily; entries are cited by volume, "Fed. Reg." or "FR" page, and date—for example, 45 Fed. Reg. 49,953 (July 28, 1980). Publication of a "proposed rule" follows the advance notice. This publication briefly summarizes the statutory basis for the regulation, gives the proposed text, solicits comments, indicates a deadline for submission of comments, and may announce one or more public hearings at which testimony will be taken. Usually at least thirty days are provided for submission of comments. Eventually, a "final rule" is published in the *Federal Register*. In addition to providing the text of the regulation, this notice will repeat the statutory authority, summarize events along the path toward the final rule, and enumerate and respond to comments received in response to the proposed rule. Within a year of enactment, the text of final regulations is codified in the *Code of Federal Regulations* (analogous to the *United States Code* for statutes); entries are cited by title, "C.F.R.," and part (e.g., 33 C.F.R. 320).

A second type of regulation is issued by the executive branch to govern internal operations. These "executive orders" are issued by the president to consolidate and clarify statutes affecting more than one department or to espouse some particular policy. Executive orders affect only government agencies and are not enforceable in criminal or civil proceedings, but agencies avoid being exposed as "violating their own regulations." Thus publicity is frequently sufficient to persuade a bureaucrat to mend his or her ways. Executive orders are published as they are issued, appearing in the *Weekly Compilation of Presidential Documents*. Many federal agencies also have their own sets of internal regulations—engineer policies (EPs) and engineer regulations (ERs) for the U.S. Army Corps of Engineers, directives in the *Forest Service Manual*, and so forth. These are usually published in limited quantities for internal distribution, contain detailed descriptions of how agency business is to be conducted, and are frequently difficult for the general public to obtain.

The Budgetary Process

Promulgation of regulations gives the executive branch an opportunity to develop and enunciate policy, but development and defense of a budget may play an equally important role. Organic legislation and enabling legislation authorize programs and funds to support them but do not by themselves provide the funds. The budget is developed jointly by the executive and the legislative branches and reflects their consolidated concept of current national priorities. Initially a budget is prepared for the president by the Office of Management and Budget (see appendix A) and is presented to Congress and the nation in the president's annual State of the Union address. Once presented, the budget follows the path of all legislation, being considered by committees, supported and attacked in testimony, and subjected to much compromise before emerging as a law. From proposals developed in the individual executive agencies to final enactment by Congress, preparation of an annual budget may encompass more than two years. Rarely does the federal government begin a fiscal year with a completed budget for that year.

The budget is not codified in the *United States Code*, however; it is of a temporary and narrow interest. Nevertheless, an administration's performance in developing, presenting, and supporting the annual budget signals, probably more than anything else, its program priorities. The Reagan administration had difficulty convincing the nation that it was really "environmentally oriented" after it proposed reducing the budgets of most environmental agencies.

Article III: The Judicial Branch

Section 1. The judicial Power of the United States, shall be vested in one supreme Court, and such inferior Courts as the Congress may from time to time ordain and establish....

Section 2. The judicial Power shall extend to all Cases, in Law and Equity, arising under this Constitution, the Laws of the United States, and Treaties made...under their Authority;...—to all Cases of admiralty and maritime Jurisdiction; —to Controversies to which the United States shall be a Party; —to Controversies between two or more States; between a State and Citizens of another State; —between Citizens of different States....

In all Cases...in which a State shall be Party, the supreme Court shall have original Jurisdiction. In all the other Cases..., the supreme Court shall have appellate Jurisdiction, both as to Law and Fact...

The federal court system is organized in three levels—ninety-four district courts, eleven courts of appeals, and one Supreme Court (Arbuckle et al. 1983, 3). Cases start in the district court that serves the location in which the alleged offense occurred. An adverse opinion may be appealed up through the system, eventually reaching the United States Supreme Court, which can either agree or refuse (*"certiorari denied"*) to hear the appeal. In instances in which one state sues another, however, litigation begins (and ends) in the Supreme Court.

Case Law

By interpreting statutory and common law in their decisions, courts create another form of law, "case law." Case law is accepted throughout the geographic area of a court's jurisdiction and may serve as legal precedent elsewhere. Few cases of any significance end at the district court level; decisions of a court of appeals become case law throughout that circuit; decisions of the Supreme Court are case law throughout the country. If the Supreme Court denies *certiorari*, it has in effect confirmed the circuit court's decision. *Zabel v. Tabb*, the landmark dredge and fill case, was decided by the U.S. Court of Appeals for the Fifth Circuit, which overturned the district court's decision. Upon appeal to the Supreme Court, *certiorari* was denied, so the circuit court's decision is universally accepted as case law.

Prosecution of Natural Resource Cases

The first notice of a violation of natural resource law frequently comes through a private citizen, who reports it to a federal agent, or from an agent who personally observes it. In most cases, the federal employee represents the U.S. Fish and Wildlife Service, the National Marine Fisheries Service, the Environmental Protection Agency (EPA), the U.S. Army Corps of Engineers, or some other department of the executive branch. He or she will attempt to obtain evidence sufficient to prosecute the case and if successful will turn the matter over to the district office of the Executive Office for United States Attorneys (in the Department of Justice) that has jurisdiction over the location in which the alleged violation occurred. In a large district office, the case may be referred directly to a lawyer in the Land and Natural Resources Division; in smaller offices, it may be handled by a representative of the Civil Division or the Criminal Division, with notice given to Land and Natural Resources at the next higher office level. Many environmental and natural resource statutes provide both civil and criminal penalties, and the government may elect either route of prosecution.

If the evidence warrants prosecution, the U.S. attorney will bring the case before the relevant U.S. district court—the trial court. (Note: One must not confuse the Department of Justice, an agency of the executive branch, personnel of which represent the government in litigation, and the courts, agencies of the judicial branch, which try the cases.) If the district court's opinion goes against the government, the U.S. attorney may, with the concurrence of the solicitor general, appeal to the court of appeals for the circuit in which the district court is located. The circuit court may confirm or overturn the lower court's opinion or, if errors in the trial are found, may remand the case to the district level for retrial. A second level of appeal lies in the U.S. Supreme Court. The losing party at the appellate level (sometimes both sides may lose) may petition the Supreme Court for a writ of *certiorari* (literally ordering the circuit court to forward its records for review). If the petition is granted the Supreme Court agrees to review the case, and it may confirm or overturn the circuit court's decision or remand the case for retrial. If the Supreme Court denies the petition, thereby refusing to hear the case, the circuit court's opinion stands and no further appeal is possible. Whatever the outcome at the Supreme Court level, no appeal is possible.

The level of the final judicial determination is extremely important, for it determines the geographic area over which the court's opinion sets legal precedent and becomes case law. Few important decisions are left at the district level. Final determinations of a circuit court are accepted over its area of jurisdiction. If *certiorari* is denied by the Supreme Court, a circuit court's decision becomes case law throughout the United States, as are all determinations of the Supreme Court. The importance of case law goes far beyond simple determinations of innocence and guilt. The courts' written opinions contain discussion, analysis, and interpretation of fine details hidden within the Constitution, statutes, and regulations. They investigate the legislative intent: What did Congress mean to accomplish by the legislation? What did it mean to say? How did it intend portions of the law to be interpreted? They relate regulations to enabling legislation: Did the executive branch go beyond the rule-making power authorized by the legislative branch? Was the delegated authority too broad or too vague? They determine the constitutional authority for statutes: Were reserved rights infringed upon? Were other constitutional guarantees violated? Case law is the law of the lawyer. The bureaucrat will quote statutes and regulations; the lawyer will quote cases.

THE BILL OF RIGHTS

The Constitution was ratified on September 17, 1787, twelve years after the end of the Revolutionary War. Four years later, on December 15, 1791, the first ten amendments were added in response to beliefs that the original document did not adequately protect the rights of individuals. Most of the provisions in this Bill of Rights came directly from similar provisions of the Magna Carta; they were guaranteed to free Englishmen in colonial times and were properly a part of Americans' inheritance.

Amendment II

A well regulated Militia, being necessary to the security of a free State, the right of the people to keep and bear Arms, shall not be infringed.

Originally justified on the basis of national defense, this amendment

has produced a controversy between those who wish to limit the possession of firearms in the interest of crime prevention and those who encourage their sporting use. To outsiders, many of the arguments may seem
illogical and trite (making an act a crime has rarely deterred criminals;
shotguns and sporting rifles are poorly adapted to a warfare based on
guided missiles), but proponents on both sides are sincere and dedicated.
As a result, any congressional effort in this area immediately becomes
embroiled in controversy and leads nowhere.

Amendment IV

The right of the people to be secure in their persons, houses, papers, and
effects, against unreasonable searches and seizures, shall not be violated,
and no Warrants shall issue, but upon probable cause, supported by Oath
or affirmation, and particularly describing the place to be searched, and
the persons or things to be seized.

Law enforcement officers in all natural resource areas are confronted
with situations addressed by this amendment. They must enforce the
laws; to do so they must obtain evidence of violations; and to obtain evidence they must invade the privacy of persons and the sanctity of their
possessions. Specific federal (and state) statutes, such as the Occupational
Safety and Health Act (OSHA) and the Resource Conservation and
Recovery Act (RCRA) may authorize warrantless searches, but the
Supreme Court found the search provisions of OSHA unconstitutional
(*Marshall v. Barlow's*), and RCRA has not yet been tested (Arbuckle et al.
1983, 25, 26).
    The most common incidents in natural resource cases occur when
wildlife agents apprehend suspected violators and the evidence is con-
cealed inside a car; when fisheries agents must board a vessel and search
below decks; when water quality enforcement agents must enter the
property of a potential polluter; or when drugs or other contraband are
discovered during a warranted search for other evidence. If permission to
search is granted, no problem results; if it is denied, the agents must proceed carefully.

Amendment V

No person shall be...deprived of life, liberty, or property, without due
process of law; nor shall private property be taken for public use, without
just compensation.

Due process requires that a person be given notice and an opportunity to be heard and that proceedings be conducted in an orderly manner adapted to the nature of the case (Black 1979). All proceedings must conform to accepted legal principles and cannot be unreasonable, arbitrary, or capricious. A defendant must be served process detailing the nature of the complaint, must be entitled to be present and to confront his or her accusers before a competent court, and must have the right to be heard and to controvert, by proof, evidence brought against him or her. Laws that are unreasonable or are applied arbitrarily violate these provisions and are unconstitutional and void. Due process is reflected in the disclosure requirements of the National Environmental Policy Act, the rulemaking procedures of all agencies, and agencies' administrative appeals processes.

The central government has the ability to acquire private property for public use through the power of eminent domain. In doing so, it is exercising its right to reassert its dominion, to *resume* possession of the property whenever the public interest requires it (Black 1979). The concept that we hold private property as a privilege bestowed by central authority rather than by an inherent right emanates from feudal law, under which all rights to real property were granted by the Crown. It runs counter to current American attitudes regarding use of private property, but it provides the underlying rationale for acquisition of land for highways, parks, harbors, airports, and other public purposes. Two elements must accompany the valid exercise of eminent domain: (1) the acquiring agency must have statutory authority for the use to which the acquisition will be put, and (2) the owner must be paid fair market value or an otherwise acceptable sum for the property. If either element is missing, the act is an unconstitutional taking of private property and is invalid. Taking need not apply only to ownership of the land or other property. If government action results in denying an individual all beneficial use of the property, and no compensation is paid, a taking may have occurred.

The taking issue is somewhat different when viewed from the state perspective. One of the reserved rights of the states is the exercise of police power. If the valid exercise of this power, in the interest of "the maintenance or advancement of the public safety, health, welfare, and morals" (Grant and Nixon 1968, 96) results in the loss of beneficial use, no unconstitutional taking may have occurred and the owner may not be entitled to compensation.

Amendment VI

In all criminal prosecutions, the accused shall enjoy the right to a speedy and public trial, by an impartial jury of the State and district wherein the crime shall have been committed,...and to be informed of the nature and cause of the accusation; to be confronted with the witnesses against him; to have compulsory process for obtaining witnesses in his favor, and to have the Assistance of Counsel for his defence.

The Sixth Amendment further defines and guarantees the right of a citizen to the due process of law. Criminal trials are to be conducted in the area in which the alleged offense occurred, where jurors will be knowledgeable of local conditions, and the trial itself is to be open to the public. Visibility is one of the most effective means of keeping government honest. Justice is best served when prosecutions are conducted openly in the public arena, with legal counsel and open examination of conflicting testimony. At the same time, one may wonder if the public interest is always best protected when market hunters may be tried before a jury composed (at least in part) of market hunters.

Amendment VIII

Excessive bail shall not be required, nor excessive fines imposed, nor cruel and unusual punishments inflicted.

Taken directly from the Magna Carta ("A freeman shall not be amerced for a small offence, except in proportion to the measure of the offence" [article 14]), this provision ensures that "the penalty must fit the crime." Until recently, however, violations of environmental and natural resource laws were treated rather lightly. Fish and game law violators were frequently assessed only the costs of court; polluters were fined token amounts; commercial fishermen working in closed waters could recover the costs of their penalties with only a few more hours of illegal activities.

The decade of the 1970s saw a shift from this rather light-handed treatment of environmental law violators. Public awareness of environmental values was reflected in statutory authorization of higher penalties, and government prosecutors asked the courts to award greater damages for environmental degradation. The far-reaching and long-lasting effects of waste disposal practices were also becoming apparent, adding to acceptance of the notion that violations of environmental laws were serious matters and should be treated accordingly. The Federal Water Pollution Control Act Amendments of 1972 (33 U.S.C. 1319[c][1]) authorize criminal penalties of "not less than $2,500 nor more than $25,000 per day of violation, or imprisonment for not more than one year, or both" for an initial offense and "a fine of not more than $50,000 per day of violation, or...imprisonment of not more than two years, or...both" for subsequent violations. Failure to notify the government of a hazardous waste spill or operation of an unauthorized hazardous waste disposal facility may result in a fine of up to $10,000 per day (42 U.S.C. 9603). Violators of the Endangered Species Act (as amended) are subject to a civil penalty of not more than $25,000 for each violation, which may be assessed by the secretary of the interior, and upon conviction of a criminal violation may be fined $50,000 or imprisoned for not more than one year, or both (16 U.S.C. 1540).

Amendment X

The powers not delegated to the United States by the Constitution, nor prohibited by it to the States, are reserved to the States respectively, or to the people.

The federal government was a creature of the states, created by them and possessing only those powers with which the states wished to endow it. At the time (1787), the states were very distrustful of a powerful central government (after all, we had just fought an expensive eleven-year war against one) and wished to limit its authority as much as possible. In natural resource matters, the federal government received exclusive rights over foreign relations, foreign and interstate commerce, and maritime law. As successors to the Crown, the states retained jurisdiction over common property resources, including fish and game, and rights to the exclusive exercise of police power.

This last authority, the power of a state legislature to make and enforce laws that protect the "peace, good order, morals, and health of the community" (Black 1979, 1041), is the basis for zoning and other land use legislation at the state level. In the proper exercise of police power, the states (and local governments, which are a part of the states) may deny all beneficial use of a person's property under extreme or unusual circumstances, without payment to the owner. Such an action by the federal government would be an unconstitutional taking without compensation in violation of the Fifth Amendment. The limits of the states' police power are never well defined, and they constantly change with changing societal values.

Recent decades have seen an erosion of states' rights in favor of more powerful central authority. As we shall see in later discussions, combinations of the commerce and federal property clauses and the treaty and general welfare provisions of the U.S. Constitution have enabled the federal government to become involved throughout natural resource and environmental matters and have left very little to the exclusive domain of the states.

COMMON LAW AND OTHER LEGAL PRINCIPLES

Interwoven with the Constitution are a number of other legal principles that guide natural resource managers. Litigation is conducted according to a series of fixed principles, and not everyone may bring suit in all situations. These elements involve the concepts of due process and standing.

Complementing legislative law is another body of law that we have inherited through time by custom and accepted use. This "common law" contains principles "derived from the application of natural reason, an innate sense of justice, and the dictates of conscience" (Arbuckle 1983, 7). It is simply "not right" to annoy another beyond reason; we call such an offense a "nuisance." Nor is it accepted conduct to enter upon and damage the property of another; and we call that a "trespass." The body of common law evolves as courts decide each new case in the social, economic, environmental, and political context in which it occurs.

Due Process

The concept of due process has both procedural and substantive aspects (Bockrath 1977, 73). Procedurally, it encompasses the sequence of events designed to afford a defendant just and adequate opportunity to defend himself or herself. Substantively, it addresses whether a government act is a "reasonable" exercise of police power and thus constitutional and valid or an "unreasonable, arbitrary, or capricious" act and thus unconstitutional. Due process is guaranteed, but not defined, in the Fifth and Fourteenth Amendments. The Fifth Amendment applies to the federal government ("No person shall...be deprived of life, liberty, or property, without due process of law"), while the Fourteenth Amendment addresses the states ("nor shall any State deprive any person of life, liberty, or property without due process of law").

The essential procedural elements include the following:

1. Notice and an opportunity to be heard and to defend oneself in an orderly proceeding adapted to the nature of the case.
2. Right to a hearing before a court under the general law.
3. Assurance that proceedings will progress according to established and accepted rules.
4. Hearing before a competent tribunal.
5. Right to be heard, to confront adversaries, and to controvert by proof every material fact brought against one. (Black 1979, 449)

The substantive context is more difficult to define. If a law is unreasonable or is exercised arbitrarily or capriciously, it is a taking without due process. Environmental legislation may violate due process where standards have no factual basis, where substances or activities to be regulated have no demonstrable environmental effects, or where the type of land affected cannot be logically and reproducibly defined and delineated. Similar legislation, when based on some reasonable premise, may be found valid. Thus the Court upheld (Arbuckle 1983, 28) a city ordinance that sought to preserve a small town's character with open space and low population density by limiting issuance of new building permits (*Constr. Indus. Ass'n. v. City of Petaluma*).

Equal Protection

The concept of fair and impartial treatment was incorporated into the Magna Carta ("To no one will we sell, to no one will we deny, or delay right or justice" [article 29]). A similar provision was added to our Constitution after the Civil War. The Fourteenth Amendment prevents any state from denying "to any person within its jurisdiction the equal protection of the laws." When read with section 2 of article IV ("The Citizens of each State shall be entitled to all Privileges and Immunities of Citizens in the several States"), these provisions appear to guarantee that all persons will be treated "alike" before the law. The full range of the privileges and immunities clause is open to debate, but it has been used to protect the rights of residents from one state who wished to pursue a trade or other activity in another (Marine Law Institute 1982), and it was the basis, at least in part, for requiring the state of Virginia to permit nonresidents to harvest crabs in the Virginia portion of Chesapeake Bay (*Tangier Sound Waterman's Ass'n v. Douglas*). In practice, it is illogical and impossible to treat all equally, for groups of citizens have innately different characteristics (you would not want a five-year-old to be licensed to hunt), and different geographic and ecological areas have different potentials (waters supporting trout may require more stringent quality standards than those containing carp). Thus "equal protection" has come to mean that all individuals under like circumstances be treated equally (Black 1979, 481). Applied in this way, it is possible to define a "coastal zone," which is different from inland areas and is subject to a different land management strategy (provided, of course, that all areas within the defined coastal zone are treated similarly).

Torts

Torts are wrongful acts for which civil actions can be brought by the injured party (Arbuckle et al. 1983, 23). Tort actions are most frequently employed to alleviate nuisances and trespasses and traditionally have rarely been applied in natural resource and environmental matters (in most instances, we wait for Big Brother to wield his statutory power). A small but growing element of society has recently begun espousing the creation of private property rights in such resources, many of which have traditionally been considered "common property." If such occurred, environmental violations would become torts and would be addressed by civil action among the private parties concerned rather than by government regulatory intervention (Dennis 1982).

Standing

You may strongly object to an environmentally degrading action being committed by an individual or public agency and wish to sue, but you cannot do so unless you have standing. Standing concerns an individual's right to a judicial determination in a controversy (Bockrath 1977, 8) and protects society against unjustified litigation while protecting the right of due process. A person has standing in the following circumstances:

1. He has been instructed by government to do something,
2. He belongs to a group or class addressed by the statute concerned,
3. The challenged action has caused him economic or other injury,
4. Standing is granted as a matter of law. (Bockrath 1977, 8)

In all cases, however, the plaintiff (the party who brings suit) must establish that he or she has standing. In the 1972 Mineral King case (*Sierra Club v. Morton*), which attacked the legality of a proposed ski resort in the Sierra Nevada, the Sierra Club did not assert that its activities or those of its members would be directly affected, relying instead upon its general interest in protecting natural areas (Council on Environmental Quality 1972, 250). The Supreme Court found that only users and representatives of users directly affected by the injury to aesthetic and recreational values that would result from the project had a right to bring suit and that the Sierra Club had not asserted a sufficient basis for suit. In its opinion, the Court outlined bases for a proper showing of standing— advice that has been heeded in subsequent Sierra Club litigation.

The next year, the Supreme Court accepted its first National Environmental Policy Act (NEPA) case, *Students Challenging Regulatory Agency Procedures v. United States,* which challenged an Interstate Commerce Commission's action. Students Challenging Regulatory Agency Procedures (SCRAP), a group of Washington University law students, claimed that a proposed 2.5 percent surcharge would discourage the movement of recyclable goods and was an environmentally significant action requiring an environmental impact statement (Council on Environmental Quality 1973, 239-241). While failing to resolve the NEPA issue, the Court concluded that the plaintiff's allegations were sufficient to support standing because the proposed action could harm "all persons who utilize the scenic resources of the country, and indeed all who breathe its air" (5 E.R.C. 1455).

The Clean Air Act and the Federal Water Pollution Control Act Amendments grant standing as a matter of statute to any person commencing a civil action against violators or against the administrator of the Environmental Protection Agency for failure to enforce the act. In such situations, standing is a matter of law and need not be established by the plaintiff.

Nuisance

While a person generally may use property as he or she sees fit, such use must be reasonable and must not cause material injury or annoyance to the property owner's neighbor (Arbuckle et al. 1983, 9). Such action, even if otherwise lawful, constitutes a nuisance and is subject to a tort action. Abatement is within the police power of the state and may be effected without compensation, even though considerable economic harm to the defendant may result.

Almost anything may constitute a nuisance; the court must decide the degree to which a nuisance may be offensive or indecent or may cause hurt, inconvenience, or damage, and the court must also determine the appropriate remedy. In natural resource situations, fish houses, boat-launching ramps and marinas, rock quarries, pulp mills, campgrounds, and bathing beaches frequented by nudists may be found to constitute nuisances. Air pollutants constitute nuisances only if they alter the normal air quality to the extent that they cause harm to ordinary people to an unreasonable extent (Arbuckle et al. 1983, 12). In a New York case (*McCarty v. Natural Carbonic Gas Co.*) the court held that smoke from the defendant's manufacturing plant caused the plaintiffs discomfort, annoyance, and injury and that they were entitled to relief (Arbuckle et al. 1983, 12). In a somewhat similar case (*Chicago v. Commonwealth Edison*) the court found that the public had a right to clean air but that the definition of cleanliness must be consistent with the character of the locality and attending circumstances; as the plaintiff failed to show substantial harm, no actionable nuisance existed (Arbuckle et al. 1983, 13).

Trespass

Trespass results from an act that causes injury to another's person or property (Black 1979, 1347, 1348). It may be attended by violence, as in an assault, or not, as in peaceable but unlawful entry upon another's land. Trespass does not require personal entry upon the property of another but may result from discharge of material that subsequently enters or passes over such property (but not from sound or light, which are usually treated as nuisances).

Generally, there must be some physical invasion of property to constitute a trespass (Arbuckle et al. 1983, 16, 17). Natural resource situations involving trespass include timber poaching; damage to property by hunters, campers, and hikers; and sedimentation from upslope land development activities.

Common Property Resources and the Public Trust

Deeply ingrained within the philosophy of natural resource management is the concept of common resources, resources held in trust for the people. The Romans identified such as *res communes, res nullius,* and *res extra patrimonium,* those things that either were incapable of private ownership or were not privately possessed at the time in question (Buckland 1963,

182). Under English law, the Crown held land as an individual and as the sovereign. In the former case, such lands were freely alienable—the king could sell them or give them away just as we do with our private property; he held them as a private right, *jus privatum*. In the latter case, however, lands were held for the benefit of all the people in common and could not be conveyed to private individuals; they were held as a public right, *jus publicum* (Rice 1968, 4-8). Many early discussions of the public trust revolved around this principle—whether real property, held in trust by government, could be conveyed to a private interest (Sax 1970). More recently, concern has shifted and expanded to focus on the degree to which government can restrict private activities in protecting the public trust.

In the United States, many renewable natural resources are considered common property resources and are protected by the public trust (or in the public interest). A recent codification of this interest appears in regulations concerning processing of U.S. Army Corps of Engineers' permits:

> The decision whether to issue a permit will be based on an evaluation of the probable impact...of the proposed activity on the public interest....[—]conservation, economics, aesthetics, general environmental concerns, wetlands, historic properties, fish and wildlife values, flood hazards, floodplain values, land use, navigation, shoreline erosion and accretion, recreation, water supply and conservation, water quality, energy needs, safety, food and fiber production, mineral needs, considerations of property ownership and, in general, the needs and welfare of the people. (33 C.F.R. 325.3(c)(1) (July 1, 1989))

The concept of public trust and public interest changes as social objectives change. During the environmental decade of the 1970s, the public trust doctrine appeared to have potential as the guardian of many natural resources (Sax 1970, 474). During the 1980s, some argued that common ownership of natural resources *was* the environmental problem; the solution lay in conveying as many resources as possible into the private sector, where they could be protected under the laws governing torts, nuisance, and trespass (Stroup and Baden 1983). With the reawakening of environmentalism in the 1990s, the pendulum again appears to be swinging toward an expanded public trust.

REFERENCES

Arbuckle, J. Gordon, G. William Frick, Ridgway M. Hall, Jr., Marshall Lee Miller, Thomas F. P. Sullivan, and Timothy A. Vanderver, Jr., eds. 1983. *Environmental Law Handbook.* 7th ed. Rockville, MD: Government Institutes.

Black, Henry C. 1979. *Black's Law Dictionary.* 5th ed. St. Paul, MN: West Publishing Company.

Bockrath, Joseph T. 1977. *Environmental Law for Engineers, Scientists, and Managers.* New York: McGraw-Hill Book Company.

Brownson, Charles B., ed. 1987. *1987 Congressional Staff Directory.* Mount Vernon, VA: Congressional Staff Directory.

Buckland, William W. 1963. *Textbook of Roman Law from Augustus to Justinian.* Cambridge, England: Cambridge University Press.

Council on Environmental Quality. 1972. *Environmental Quality—1972.* Washington, DC: Government Printing Office.

———. 1973. *Environmental Quality—1973.* Washington, DC: Government Printing Office.

Dennis, William C. 1982. "Environmental Protection and Individual Liberty." *Environmental Professional* 4:233-239.

General Services Administration. 1980. *How to Find U.S. Statutes and U.S. Code Citations.* 4th rev. ed. Washington, DC: Government Printing Office.

———. 1986. *The United States Government Manual 1986/87.* Washington, DC: Government Printing Office.

Grant, Daniel R., and H. C. Nixon. 1968. *State and Local Government in America.* Needham Heights, MA: Allyn & Bacon.

Marine Law Institute. 1982. "*Tangier Sound Waterman's Association v. Douglas:* Chesapeake Bay Residency Restrictions Held Unconstitutional." *Territorial Sea* 2 (2): 2-5, 10-11.

Rice, David A. 1968. *Estuarine Lands of North Carolina: Legal Aspects of Ownership, Use and Control.* Chapel Hill, NC: University of North Carolina, Institute of Government.

Sax, Joseph L. 1970. "The Public Trust Doctrine." *Michigan Law Review* 68:471-566.

Stroup, Richard L., and J. A. Baden. 1983. *Natural Resources, Bureaucratic Myths and Environmental Management.* Cambridge, MA: Ballinger Publishing Company.

Swindler, William F. 1965. *Magna Carta: Legend and Legacy.* Indianapolis: Bobbs-Merrill Company.

United States Code Service: Lawyers Edition. 1980-. Rochester, NY: Lawyers Co-operative Publishing Company.

CHAPTER III

The Public Domain

EARLY LAND TENURE SYSTEMS

When European settlers first reached the coast of North America, they found a society with little sense of landownership. The land was as free as its inhabitants, and resources were shared in common by all (Clawson, Held, and Stoddard 1968, 41). While Indian families enjoyed exclusive use of the land on which their dwellings rested and the fields they cultivated, their society was mobile, and land rights changed as communities migrated (Cronon 1983, 62). Their concept of ownership of the broader resources was more of a usufruct—a right to use—than ownership of the land itself (Cronon 1983, 65). Commerce in land was alien to the native American (Udall 1963, 6). Upon this communal system the colonists imposed their Old World concepts of land tenure, of proprietorship that conveyed not only wealth but also social rank, eminence, and privileges.

Settlers of Jamestown and Plymouth brought with them a system of land tenure based on a combination of the feudal relationships embodied in the English manorial system and the concept of village organization. English land tenures were composed of many variations of two basic types—free tenures (freeholds) maintained in the king's courts through various forms of service (military and religious obligations, and personal and administrative services) and unfree tenures (villein tenures) usually issued by the lord of a manor in return for tribute in money or kind and service obligations and subject to the lord's arbitrary will. Freeholders were also bound to the lord through oaths of loyalty (fealty); financial obligations associated with marriage of the lord's eldest child, ransom, and right to inherit; and other social and financial relationships (Johnson and Barlowe [1954] 1979, 15-19).

Rights associated with the various forms of tenure lay somewhere between what we now attribute to a landowner and those of a lessee, but they were closer to the latter. Remember that land "ownership" was a class privilege extending ultimately from the sovereign. No one could simply buy or sell land just because he wished to and was financially able to; freeholds could revert upon death of the freeholder; and villein tenures frequently existed only for the life of the holder.

Villages were organized as largely self-sufficient, primarily agrarian systems. Dwellings were typically clustered fairly closely together. Each family had custody of a small "in-lot" containing the dwelling, a garden, and livestock pens and shared in the enclosed common agricultural lands of the village. Woodlands and other nonarable lands were held in common and used for pasture and the production of firewood (Johnson and Barlowe [1954] 1979, 16).

During precolonial and colonial times, the rigid structure of English land tenure was eroding. Land was beginning to be bought and sold in commerce. The right of ownership was being expanded, and freehold tenure was moving toward ownership as we know it today.

Land in the New World was of little value to England unless it was settled and developed, however, and the Crown employed several variations on a theme to encourage emigration to the New World. Property rights were conveyed to individual proprietors or corporations by royal charter, upon condition that the lands be settled. Subgrants were then issued to colonists (before or after emigration) upon payment of a fee or fulfillment of other conditions. The village system of land organization was most characteristic of New England settlements, and it persists today in the town commons and township political power characteristic of that region. Farther south development patterns were more diffuse, leading to large individual rural landholdings and a plantation system (Johnson and Barlowe [1954] 1979, 22).

Because of the abundance of land and the desire to establish Englishmen and English rule upon it, methods of conveying subgrants were frequently somewhat slipshod. In the early years of the Virginia Colony, a person desiring to acquire land could obtain a warrant for a given area without specifying its location. He could then select any unclaimed tract meeting his requirements, present the land office with a warrant of survey and a description of boundaries, and be granted a patent conveying title to the property. Although expeditious under the frontier conditions of early Virginia, the system contained serious flaws. Land was cheap and surveying methods crude; many conveyances described much more land than was specified in the original warrants. The process necessitated two trips to the land office—one for the warrant and one for the patent; because travel was expensive and time-consuming, persons often simply "squatted" on lands without obtaining formal title. With all the error inherent in the system, opportunities existed for "claim jumping"—obtaining a patent for land already occupied by another or duplicate claims to the same parcel or tampering with boundary marks. In later years, and in other colonies, many of these deficiencies were corrected by requiring a survey prior to issuance of a warrant and by auctioning identified parcels subject to minimum prices (Johnson and Barlowe [1954] 1979, 23, 24).

A "headright" policy, under which an emigrant could obtain 50 acres of land upon settling himself at his own expense or paying the expense of another settler, also encouraged colonization. Under this policy (employed throughout the colonies), one could acquire considerable holdings by transporting indentured servants to the colonies and acquiring the lands to which they were entitled by headright or by buying the headrights of others. Headrights were sometimes awarded in the names of slaves and fictitious persons, and these practices were condoned because they resulted in more land being developed and more quitrent (traditional payment to the lord of the manor) accruing to the proprietor (Johnson and Barlowe [1954] 1979, 24).

THE NEW REPUBLIC

At the close of the Revolutionary War, the newly created states became successors to the Crown, and all vacant and unappropriated lands within the original colonies succeeded to state ownership (*People v. Livingston, State v. Pinckney,* cited in Winter [1932] 1979, 69). Most of the colonies had asserted claims to vast areas of "western lands"—Virginia claimed much of what is now Kentucky; North Carolina claimed Tennessee; Georgia's claims extended to the Mississippi River. Many claims were poorly defined and/or overlapped, and states granted large areas of the western lands to individuals. To correct this potential source of conflict and to quiet dissension from the six states that claimed no western lands (New Hampshire, Rhode Island, Delaware, New Jersey, Maryland, and Pennsylvania), the Continental Congress proposed in 1777 that all such lands be placed at its disposal. As a result of this cession, the western boundaries of the original states became defined and the central government obtained a vast source of wealth (Johnson and Barlowe [1954] 1979, 27).

A New Land Ethic

Concurrent with the political evolution, an evolution in ideology, land ethics, and property rights was also occurring. During the eighteenth century, the practice of buying and selling land as a commodity became more prevalent throughout the colonies. Landownership became more complete, less a leasehold and more as we view it today; and quitrents were becoming taxes. The writings of the philosopher John Locke were influencing political thought. According to Locke, property rights in land arose from the relationship of man to nature, not from the relationship of man to man; they accrued to individuals because of their labors and were not dependent upon the consent of others; and property was a natural right, not derived from the state. Adam Smith and other contemporary economists added their doctrines of the self-interest of individuals, free competition, and the labor theory of values—that the individual is best able to maximize his welfare, that government restrictions simply thwart the individual, that the role of government should be minimal and be restricted to maintaining order and protecting citizens from external violence, and that maximal social well-being would be achieved through noninterference. These philosophies were shared by Thomas Jefferson, who believed in a wide diffusion of property interests in land and felt that government should encourage numerous freeholds. Thus our nation came through the Revolution with a strong sense of the value of land as property and with the desire to convert the public domain to private property, unrestricted by government, as expeditiously as possible (Johnson and Barlowe [1954] 1979, 29). We were utilitarians, believing that "natural resources were inexhaustible and...should be used to raise individual and collective standards of living" (Culhane 1981, 3).

FEDERAL LANDOWNERSHIP

In 1957 Clawson and Held ([1957] 1966, 16) identified five major, overlapping eras of federal landownership: acquisition, disposal, reservation, custodial management, and intensive management. Later Clawson (1983, 39) added a sixth era, consultation and conflict, which began in the 1960s and continues today. During the first period, the United States added all lands westward to the Pacific Ocean to the original states and their ceded western lands. During the second it attempted to get these lands into productive private ownership (without too much regard for process, equity, or results). Excesses in disposal led to the reservation of large areas of the public domain for public purposes and ushered in the custodial caretaking period. A decade of intensive management began in the 1950s, during which production was emphasized and gross receipts from the federal lands exceeded the costs of management. The current period began during the early 1960s and is exemplified by a plethora of environmental legislation, new public attitudes and greater citizen involvement in public land management, and a new role for the courts (Clawson 1983, 43). Culhane (1981, 41) recognized the same first five periods as Clawson but titled the last "extensive preservation." The periods obviously overlap, and elements of all exist throughout our nation's history. They are useful, however, in illustrating the sequence of dominant themes in the evolution of public land policy.

Acquisition

As the Revolution ended, almost all land of the present United States east of the Mississippi River (except Florida) was in the possession of the states. Lands west of the current boundaries of the thirteen original states were ceded to the federal government between 1781 (New York) and 1802 (Georgia) and became the nucleus of the public domain (Clawson and Held [1957] 1966, 18). The differences between these two classes of land are profound. The original states were successors to the Crown; vacant and unappropriated lands became state property; and any proprietary or custodial sovereign rights fell to them. States carved from the public domain had no such heritage. Although such states were admitted on an "equal footing" (*Coyle v. Smith*), except for Texas they were never sovereign. The unallocated land within them is federal property, and the federal government has much more influence upon their state and private activities.

The first major addition to our fledgling nation came in 1803 with purchase of the Louisiana Territory from France for $15 million. This single acquisition of almost 530 million acres (Mahoney 1950, cited in Johnson and Barlowe [1954] 1979, 31) almost doubled the area of the United States and opened up the heartland of the continent and its agricultural and other resources via the Mississippi River (Clawson and Held [1957] 1966, 18). In 1819 Spain ceded its claims to Florida for about $6 million, adding another 46 million acres (Mahoney 1950, cited in Johnson and Barlowe [1954] 1979, 31) and removing the remaining foreign influence in the eastern half of the country. The next acquisitions were more turbulent. Texas was annexed in 1845, following its war for independence from Mexico and nine years of independent rule (it entered the Union as a sovereign entity, as did the original thirteen states, and was never a part of the public domain). Following prolonged and bitter negotiations with Great Britain, United States territory was extended to the Pacific Ocean by the Oregon Compromise of 1846 (Clawson and Held [1957] 1966, 19, 20), which added another 183 million acres. Continuing boundary disputes with Mexico led to a peace treaty under which the United States gained an additional 339 million acres (Mahoney 1950, cited in Johnson and Barlowe [1954] 1979, 31).

The final acquisitions were more peaceful. Texas ceded 79 million acres of disputed territory in 1850. The Gadsden Purchase of 1853 added 19 million acres along the southern boundary of Arizona, and the purchase of Alaska in 1867 completed the continental United States by contributing 375 million acres (Clawson and Held [1957] 1966, 20, 21). In only sixty-four years, the United States grew from about 500 million acres along the eastern seaboard to a transcontinental nation of more than 2.3 billion acres (table 3.1), most of which was unoccupied (by white men) and lay open to exploitation.

TABLE 3.1
Summary of Land Acquisitions, 1776-1867 (in Millions of Acres)

Source	Date	Acquisition	Total
Original states	1776	305	305
Cessions by original states	1781-1882	237	542
Red River Basin	1782-1817	30	572
Louisiana Purchase	1803	530	1,102
Florida Purchase	1819	46	1,148
Annexation of Texas	1845	170	1,318
Oregon Compromise	1846	183	1,501
Mexican Treaty	1848	339	1,840
Purchase from Texas	1850	79	1,919
Gadsden Purchase	1853	19	1,938
Alaskan Purchase	1867	375	2,313

Source: Marion Clawson and Burnell Held, *The Federal Lands: Their Use and Management* (Baltimore: Johns Hopkins University Press, [1957] 1966), p. 21; U.S. Department of the Interior, Bureau of Land Management, *Manual for the Survey of the Public Lands of the United States* (Washington, DC: Government Printing Office, 1973), table 1.

Although the purchase of Alaska in 1867 marked the end of the era of acquisition, the federal government subsequently has acquired additional lands for defense, transportation, forests and parks, and other public purposes. While these lands may be termed "public lands," they are not properly part of the "public domain" (Dana and Fairfax 1980, 8). Only lands acquired from other nations and those received in exchange for such lands should be included in the concept of "public domain" or "original public domain" (Clawson and Held [1957] 1966, 22). The distinction is important, for (with some few exceptions) the dispositional policies and laws discussed in the following section apply only to the public domain—those "unentered, unreserved unoccupied lands of the original public domain which were or are in public ownership and were subject to disposition under the general land laws until 1976 and are managed by the Bureau of Land Management" (Dana and Fairfax 1980, 8).

Disposal

From cession of the western lands onward, the prevailing policy governing the public domain was generally one of federal trusteeship (Winter [1932] 1979, 63, 64). Disposition to states, corporations, and individuals was generally favored in the absence of some demonstrable national need or value, but the motives, methods, and conditions governing disposal were varied and complex. Superimposed upon this public policy was the changing concept of private ownership. In colonial days land "ownership" as we know it today did not exist. Freeholds were "held" upon continuing conditions of allegiance, quitrents, and other constraints, and rights of inheritance (demise), lease, and sale were uncertain—a socage tenure (Johnson and Barlowe [1954] 1979, 22). Toward the time of the Revolution, the difficulty in collecting quitrents, their small value, and the general inability to protect vacant lands from trespass (abetted by the teachings of Locke, Smith, and others) caused a transition from the concept of socage tenure toward that of alodial tenure in fee simple. Under this system the grantor retains no residual control over land conveyed and the grantee may sell, devise, or bequeath (and generally use) his real property without restraint. The transition to fee simple ownership as the accepted norm was completed in the Ordinance of 1787, which provided that estates in the Northwest Territories could be bequeathed by wills and conveyed by lease, bargain, and sale and that elected representatives must own at least 200 acres within their district in fee simple (Johnson and Barlowe [1954] 1979, 32).

Motivation

The purposes to be served by disposal of the public domain and the motives behind various forms of disposition were legion. Representatives of newly formed states argued that such lands should be ceded to the states. Easterners generally believed that the public domain should be conveyed to individuals. Some believed the greatest value of the lands was as a source of revenue for the federal treasury. Daniel Webster and others felt that "the national domain [should never be] regarded as any great source of revenue" and that the primary objective should be to get the lands settled. Still others pushed payment of war debts, enticement to military service, financing of education, and other public purposes (Winter [1932] 1979, 58-60).

In sum the forces behind divestiture were overwhelming, and until about 1891 the predominant national policy governing the public domain was to pass it into nonfederal ownership as expeditiously as possible. Although this period and the policies governing disposal of the public domain are often criticized, they were, at the time, perfectly understandable. Land and natural resources were cheap—there was no need to conserve (Dana and Fairfax 1980, 12). The new nation needed revenues—disposition of large and unused land resources appeared to be a ready source (Johnson and Barlowe [1954] 1979, 34). Émigrés from the Old World desired to escape the burdensome land tenure policies there and to acquire land in their own right—the public domain provided the solution (Clawson and Held [1957] 1966, 22). And ineptitude, greed, and corruption are almost inevitable fellow travelers in any program of such size, value, and complexity.

TABLE 3.2
Receipts from Sale of the Public Domain, 1800-1860

Period	Average Annual Sales (Acres)[a]	Average Price Per Acre Actual Price When Sold[a]	1990 Value Discounted at 4 Percent Per Year
1800-1809	330,219	$2.08	$2,946
1810-1819	1,432,319	$2.68	$2,564
1820-1829	866,991	$1.41	$911
1830-1839	6,231,612	$1.27	$555
1840-1849	1,773,695	$1.17	$345
1850-1860	8,238,538	$0.91	$181

[a]From Benjamin H. Hibbard, *A History of the Public Land Policies* (New York: Macmillan Company, 1924), cited in V. Webster Johnson and Raleigh Barlowe, *Land Problems and Policies* (New York: Arno Press, [1954] 1979), p. 36.

Much has been made of the low prices commanded by public domain lands, and in truth many tracts were sold for less than $1 per acre. Yet if one looks at average receipts per acre over reasonable bases of time and area, the picture is not quite so bleak (table 3.2). Discounted at 4 percent per year, prices received prior to 1820 were actually extremely high by present-day standards. Those received between 1820 and 1850 were reasonable for unimproved remote land. Only in the decade between 1850 and 1860 is a "giveaway" obvious.

Public Land Surveys

One of the first (and most long-lasting) accomplishments of the disposal era was adoption of a national system of public land surveys (Dana and Fairfax 1980, 13). Land surveys in the original colonies were based on "metes and bounds" descriptions, generally following topographic features, which were often tied to movable or short-lived landmarks and were frequently difficult to recover. As established by the Continental Congress in the General Ordinance of 1785, subsequent surveys of public lands (and, by inference, of lands conveyed from the public domain) were to conform to a rectilinear system based on true meridians (lines of longitude). Beginning at an initial point in each state or region to be surveyed, a principal meridian was established, a baseline conforming to a true parallel of latitude was constructed through the initial point, and standard parallels of latitude extended east and west of the principal meridian at 24-mile intervals (figure 3.1). North-south guide meridians were then established intersecting the standard parallels at 24-mile intervals. Each of the 24-by-24-mile squares so created contained sixteen 36-square-mile townships. Each township was further divided into thirty-six sections, each of which contained 640 acres (1 square mile). Townships were designated incrementally north or south of the baseline and east or west of the principal meridian, and sections within each township were numbered 1 through 36, beginning in the northeastern corner of the township (U.S. Department of the Interior, Bureau of Land Management 1973, 62). Thus the extreme northwestern section in the township immediately southwest of the initial point would be designated section 6 in township 1 south, range 1 west.

While metes and bounds descriptions were troublesome to surveyors and the neat, linear township and section system was much more suited to their needs, attributes are reversed in their effects on land use, planning, and management. The older system tended to follow watershed divides, streams, and other natural features, many of which had ecological significance. Roads also tended to follow these natural features, and acquisition and management of watersheds and other natural land units were facilitated. The linear system of public land survey recognizes no such natural boundaries—lines run straight regardless of terrain, drainage, or anything else. Boundary line roads run indiscriminately up and down slopes and back and forth across streams and contain numerous right-angle curves. Farmers plowing parallel to their property lines likewise ignore the topography, intensifying erosion, and efforts to acquire natural units as watersheds are thwarted by the straight lines of the public land survey (Dana and Fairfax 1980, 13).

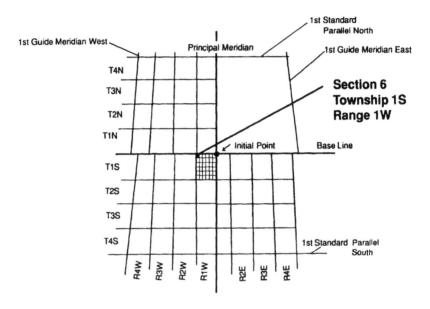

FIGURE 3.1. System of Public Land Surveys. *Source*: U.S. Department of the Interior, Bureau of Land Management. *Manual for the Survey of the Public Lands of the United States* (Washington, DC: Government Printing Office, 1973), figure 2, p. 9; figure 15, p. 62.

Public Land Sales

The disposal era itself can be divided into three phases of differing dominant policy. Until 1830 emphasis was upon sale; 1830 to 1862 saw increased recognition of squatters' rights and movement toward homesteading; from 1862 onward homesteading was the primary means of acquiring portions of the public domain. Under various ordinances and acts, public lands were sold at auction. Although a minimum per-acre price was usually specified by law (ranging from $1.25 to $2.00), the practice permitted numerous means of avoiding full payment. Payment sometimes was made in depreciated Confederation obligations; allowances were made for poor-quality lands; and payments could be deferred (Johnson and Barlowe [1954] 1979, 35). The maximum purchasable area was usually specified by law, but schemes to circumvent these restrictions were easily conceived. Large tracts were sold to speculators, and credit was freely extended (Dana and Fairfax 1980, 14). Occupation of unsurveyed lands was technically illegal but was widely supported by local opinion (Johnson and Barlowe [1954] 1979, 37). Toward the end of the sales phase, many landowners were in arrears of payment and squatting was prevalent throughout the public domain (Dana and Fairfax 1980, 14, 15).

Preemption and Squatters' Rights

Squatters' rights were exercised through the principle of preemption— "the preferential right of a settler on public lands to buy his claim at a moderate price" (Gates 1968, 219). While this right had been generally conceded, particularly along the frontier, adoption of a revenue policy emphasizing sales through public auction (in 1785 and 1796) required that squatting be curtailed. During the early 1800s, a number of acts were passed prohibiting squatting on the public domain and permitting ejection by military force, fines, and imprisonment. But the squatters had become too strong a political force (Gates 1968, 19-21). They were the pioneers who had braved the dangers of the wilderness, who had wrested their land from nature and defended it against Indian attack and other trespassers, and who for the most part had the sympathy of the general public. They had also organized into formal "claim associations" that settled disputes among members and defended themselves from outside interests. They appeared at land auctions and intimidated prospective purchasers and confirmed their claims through rigged bids (Johnson and Barlowe [1954] 1979, 38; Dana and Fairfax 1980, 15).

Between 1800 and 1830, a number of acts were passed authorizing preemption in specified areas of the public domain (e.g., parts of the Mississippi Territory, the Illinois Territory, Indiana, and Missouri), and in 1830 Congress passed the first general, but temporary, preemption act. The most significant of a number of subsequent preemption laws was the "Log Cabin Bill" of 1841 (Dana and Fairfax 1980, 16). This law, the Act of September 4, 1841, permitted any head of a household, widow, or single man over twenty-one years of age, who was a citizen, to acquire up to 160 acres of surveyed, unoccupied, unreserved public land by settling upon it and paying $1.25 per acre, provided the preemptor did not already own more than 320 acres within the United States.

> This new policy in general recognized four important principles: first, it was evident that Congress at last regarded the settlement of the public domain as more desirable than the revenue that might be obtained from it; second, that Congress intended that the domain should not fall into the hands of those who already had enough land; third, that the domain should be settled in small farms so as to extend the blessing of cheap land to the largest number; and fourth, that settlers should be protected from all intrusion and allowed a reasonable time to earn or gather together a sufficient sum to buy the land. It was at last intended that the actual settler be placed on an equal basis with the speculator in competition for land. (Robbins 1942, cited in Johnson and Barlowe [1954] 1979, 39)

Homesteading

Conversion of a sales policy to one of preemption through occupancy and use became essentially complete with passage of the Homestead Act of 1862—though numerous exceptions occurred in practice. New settlers and westerners had always favored a policy of free land but were opposed by easterners and southerners who feared out-migration and competition with southern plantations. Ultimately resistance was overcome by a combination of social and economic arguments, political activism (including formation of a Free Soil party), and appeals to a new dogma of natural rights that included the right to own sufficient land for the support of one's family (Johnson and Barlowe [1954] 1979, 43). On May 20, 1862, in the absence of most southern members, Congress passed the Homestead Act. Initially the act provided that any family head over twenty-one years of age who was a citizen or had declared the intention of becoming one could obtain a patent to up to 160 acres for cultivation upon payment of certain fees and proof that he had resided upon and cultivated the land for at least five years (Dana and Fairfax 1980, 21, 22). While on the surface this was a reasonable approach, Dana and Fairfax (1980, 22) point out, "Thus began one of the most durable and destructive myths in American folklore." Two primary factors contributed to its downfall: (1) most of the remaining public domain available for homesteading was unsuited for traditional agriculture and incapable of supporting a family on 160 acres, and (2) inherent weaknesses in the legislation and efforts to correct the first factor created numerous opportunities for graft and corruption.

Congress attempted to remedy the first defect by passing a series of acts addressing particular ecological and economic situations. Subsequent legislation expanded general homestead size to 320 acres, then to 640 acres; changed residency requirements to three years; then permitted entrymen to purchase their claim for $1.25 per acre after only six months' (later fourteen months') residence (Dana and Fairfax 1980, 24). The Timber Culture Act of 1873 granted 160 acres to persons who would plant trees, 12 feet apart, on 40 acres and cultivate the tract for ten years; and later amendments reduced the period of cultivation to eight years and the requisite area to 10 acres. The Desert Land Act of 1877 granted 640 acres to each settler who would irrigate the land within three years of filing and pay a fee of $1.25 per acre. The Timber and Stone Act of 1878 permitted a citizen to purchase 160 acres of nonmineral land, valuable primarily for timber and stone resources, for no less than $2.50 per acre. The Carey Act of 1894 shifted administrative responsibility to the states by authorizing grants of 1 million acres to each state provided that the state would cause the lands to be occupied, irrigated, and cultivated. The Forest Homestead Act of June 11, 1906, authorized homesteading within the national forests provided a homesteader could locate agricultural land and describe its location by metes and bounds and that the tract claimed did not extend more than a mile (Johnson and Barlowe [1954] 1979, 46-51).

Other Forms of Disposal

In addition to disposal of the public domain to individuals through various forms of sales and homesteading, vast areas were conveyed for public purposes. Section 16 (and later section 36) of each township was granted to the states to support education, and still later two additional sections per township were added. After 1841 each new state was granted 500,000 acres, which could be sold for not less than $1.25 per acre and the proceeds used for public purposes. Swamplands were granted to states, with proceeds from sales to be used for construction of levees and drains—determination of which areas were "swamplands" was left to the states, and extremely liberal definitions resulted. Other lands passed to the states for schools, highways, canals, the "land grant colleges," and other purposes (Dana and Fairfax 1980, 17-19), and more than 131 million acres were acquired by railroads (94 million directly and 37 million through the states) to expedite transportation to the West (Gates 1968, 384, 385).

Table 3.3 summarizes disposals of public domain lands as of 1987. In retrospect one can easily criticize the process. It was profligate—about half of the area acquired (including Alaska), almost three-fourths of the coterminous area, and almost all of the agriculturally productive land was subsequently granted. It was poor economics—particularly in the latter half of the nineteenth century, the price received was far below true value. It illustrated poor natural resource management—lands were conveyed for normal, dryland, and wetland agriculture; timber production; and mineral exploitation with no effort to determine their inherent productivity, their suitability for the purpose intended, or the adverse environmental impacts that might result from development. It was plagued by poor administration—the system was a bonanza for speculators, thieves, and grafters; and reformation efforts were halfhearted and ineffective. Yet when one considers how our generation has handled very large, very popular, and very intensive programs in the military-industrial area, aerospace activities, pollution abatement, the savings and loan industry, and even research administration and environmental impact analysis—would we have done any better?

TABLE 3.3
Disposal of the Public Domain, 1781-1987

Method	Area (Million of Acres)	Percentage of Total
Public, private, and preemption sales; miscellaneous grants	304	27
Homestead grants and sales	287	25
Grants to states	328	29
Grants to railroads	94	8
Grants to veterans	61	5
Confirmed private claims	34	3
Miscellaneous grants and sales	36	3
Total	1,144	100

Source: U.S. Department of the Interior, Bureau of Land Management, *Public Land Statistics 1987* (Washington, DC: Government Printing Office, 1988), table 2, p. 4.

Reservation and Custodial Management

A shift in public land policy began to occur around the middle of the nineteenth century, based primarily on concerns over timber and wildlife depletion (The Nature Conservancy 1977, 10). In addition to the large grants of land to timber companies, timber on the public lands and other unprotected areas was considered public property (more *res nullius* than *res communes*), subject to appropriation by the first settler, steamboat crew, or timberman to come along (Gates 1968, 534). Wildlife populations also suffered. Big game and fur animals were extirpated throughout much of their range. Bison went from 50-100 million animals to about 500; passenger pigeons, from about 5 billion birds to extinction (The Nature Conservancy 1977, 10-12). George Perkins Marsh, a Vermont lawyer, congressman, ambassador, and writer and a leader in the movement toward public awareness, wrote as follows:

> The earth is fast becoming an unfit home for its noblest inhabitant, and another era of equal human crime and human improvidence...would reduce it to such a condition of impoverished productiveness, of shattered surface, of climatic excess, as to threaten the depravation, barbarism, and even the extinction of the species. (Marsh 1864, cited in The Nature Conservancy 1977, 13)

A century later another author summarized:

> In the space of 40 years, between 1860 and 1900, the face of the continent—or at least that portion within the United States—was altered irretrievably. Wildlife was decimated, whole species becoming extinct, or nearly so. The sea of grass which covered the prairies was plowed under. And the trees came down like match sticks, fated to build homes and factories, provide ties for railroads, timbers for mines, charcoal for furnaces, potash for soap. Giant rafts of logs choked river after river as the timber was floated to mill and market. As the loggers exhausted one source of supply they moved on to the next; from Bangor to Burlington to Albany to Williamsport to Saginaw to Cloquet to Gray's Harbor. So went the timberman's boom and bust.
>
> Farmers and homesteaders contributed equally to the toll, only to discover—too late—that the same land that supported trees might not support crops. By the time this revelation dawned on a family, however, it all too often was bankrupt—and so was the soil.
>
> So the land was raped and left to die. Fires raced across immense reaches of denuded forest country blanking out the sun hundreds, even thousands, of miles away. (Widner 1968, xvi)

This thinking culminated in a growing uneasiness over the supply of natural resources for the future. Would we have "enough"? Enough unoccupied land? Enough timber? Enough wildlife? Enough water? Or should we begin to retain some of those resources that were becoming scarce? The utilitarian philosophy of the pioneers was yielding to the "progressive conservation" of the late 1800s (Culhane 1981, 3-6).

Reservation provided the easiest means for retaining natural resources that were still publicly owned. In this context reservation means "a withdrawal of a specified portion of the public domain from the administration of the Land Office and from disposal under the land laws and the appropriation thereof for the time being to some particular use or purpose of the General Government" (*Territory v. Burgess*, cited in Winter [1932] 1979, 70). The act of reservation is basically a bookkeeping entry; a given area of land simply is moved from one side of the ledger (where it could be disposed of through sale, grant, preemption, or other process) to the other (where it is committed to a specific public use). Congress may reserve lands within the public domain—"the Congress shall have Power to dispose of and make all needful Rules and Regulations respecting the Territory or other Property belonging to the United States" (U.S. Constitution, art. IV, sec. 3). Presidential power to reserve portions of the public domain seems less clear (absent specific congressional authorization), but presidents did so "from an early period in the history of the Government") (Winter [1932] 1979, 70). Although this right was subsequently substantiated by the U.S. Supreme Court (in a split decision), Congress found it desirable to clarify the situation through legislative action (Winter [1932] 1979, 72).

The Beginnings

The first major reservation took place in 1872, when Yellowstone National Park was set aside by an act of Congress (Clawson and Held [1957] 1966, 27). The policy gained impetus with passage of the Forest Reserve Act of 1891, also known as the Creative Act of 1891, which stated:

> Sec. 24 That the President of the United States may, from time to time, set apart and reserve, in any State or Territory having public lands wholly or in part covered with timber or undergrowth, whether of commercial value or not, as public reservations. (26 Stat. 1103)

Discounting the facts that section 24 was drafted by a conference committee, was never subjected to extensive debate and deliberation, was passed only four days before congressional adjournment, and received little publicity or interest at the time, it marked a milestone in declaration of public land policy (Dana and Fairfax 1980, 56, 57). Less than a month after the Forest Reserve Act passed, President Benjamin Harrison employed it to enlarge Yellowstone National Park by designating the Yellowstone Park Forest Reservation (Dana and Fairfax 1980, 58). Passage of the Antiquities Act of 1906 rounded out congressional delegation of general reservation authority to the president. This act authorized the president to designate historic landmarks, historic or prehistoric structures, and other objects of historic or scientific interest on public lands as national landmarks. It was used extensively by Presidents Theodore Roosevelt, William Taft, and Woodrow Wilson, and by 1916 it had been employed to create twenty national monuments (seven historic and thirteen scientific), including Grand Canyon, Petrified Forest, Dinosaur, and Katmai (The Nature Conservancy 1977, 28).

Impacts of Reservation

The ease with which withdrawals and reservations could be effected was attractive to both the executive and the legislative branches, and by 1932 more than 375 million acres had been withdrawn from the public domain (table 3.4) (Winter [1932] 1979, 88).

TABLE 3.4
Withdrawals from the Public Domain as of 1932

Purpose	Acres
National forests (net)	135,971,883
Indian lands	70,993,326
Mineral rights	125,558,576
Power, reservoir sites, and water rights	8,335,804
Reclamation	19,034,330
National parks and monuments	8,066,511
Miscellaneous	7,668,627
Total	375,629,057

Source: Summarized from Charles E. Winter, *Four Hundred Million Acres* (New York: Arno Press, [1932]), pp. 87, 88.

While reservation is regarded by easterners as a practical and efficient means of protecting the nation's common property resources, many westerners view the system as an unwarranted denial of the "equality" with which they were to have entered the Union. After all, the older states shared, through the federal government, in receipts from all sales of public lands, whereas the younger states shared less so. The original states, upon their independence, fell heir to all vacant and unappropriated lands within their boundaries; new states received only those that the federal government saw fit to give them. Almost all of the land in the original states was privately owned and tax generating, whereas about 30 percent of the eleven western states was forever beyond their control (Winter [1932] 1979, 89). Moreover, the highest-quality remaining public lands were reserved—the most unusual scenic areas, the most valuable watershed and grazing areas, and virtually all of the commercial forestlands (Clawson and Held [1957] 1966, 29). Smoldering resentment over these perceived injustices led to the creation and attitude of the Public Land Law Review Commission in 1964, organization of the "Sagebrush Rebellion" of the 1970s, and many of the Reagan administration's natural resource policies of the 1980s.

Custodial Management

With the advent of reservation, the concept of the public domain as marketable real estate over which the federal government was broker began to erode. If land were to be permanently "reserved," then the government must begin to act as a landowner and not as only a temporary steward. Agencies and infrastructure must be provided and operating policies developed. The Bureau of Reclamation, the National Park Service, and the U.S. Fish and Wildlife Service in the Department of the Interior and the Forest Service in the Department of Agriculture (or their predecessors) were created to fill this need. Each agency began as a recipient of lands withdrawn from the public domain for a specific purpose or purposes, received organic legislation defining its authority and responsibility, and eventually was authorized to purchase lands (through exercise of eminent domain if necessary) in furtherance of its mission. At the end of the custodial management period, the final extent of public lands was reasonably well defined and the lands were allocated among these agencies (and the Department of Defense). Agency missions were narrowly defined, however, and little program planning was practiced. With the exception of the Bureau of Reclamation, little actual resource management (in the sense of deliberate manipulation) was practiced. Multiresource considerations, intensive management, and broad environmental awareness awaited the following period—that of intensive management.

The Forest Management Act of 1897 established policy for managing the forest reserves (Gates 1968, 569, 570) and became the main statutory basis for activities of the Forest Service (Dana and Fairfax 1980, 62). The Transfer Act of 1905 created the Forest Service in the Department of Agriculture and transferred jurisdiction of the forest reserves from the General Land Office in the Department of the Interior to the new agency (Gates 1968, 579, 580); two years later the name "forest reserves" was changed to "national forests" (Clawson and Held [1957] 1966, 30).

The Newlands Act of 1902 provided that all receipts from sales of arid or semiarid public lands were to be deposited into a reclamation fund, from which irrigation projects benefiting both private and public lands were to be financed (Gates 1968, 654, 655). The Reclamation Service was created in the Geological Survey by action of the secretary of the interior to provide this service, was separated from the Geological Survey in 1907, and became the Bureau of Reclamation in 1923 (General Services Administration 1984, 322). Lands withdrawn for reclamation were transferred to the new agency; the secretary was authorized to withdraw lands from the public domain or to purchase private lands for reclamation purposes; and water users were to pay fees "sufficient to repay the cost of construction" (Gates 1968, 655). Initially all reclamation projects were financed from the reclamation fund (Winter [1932] 1979, 251), but eventually general fund appropriations were added, and by the late 1960s reclamation activities were funded about equally from the two sources (Gates 1968, 691). By 1930 twenty-nine reclamation projects had been constructed, serving more than 2.5 million acres of irrigable land (Winter [1932] 1979, 251). Perhaps even more significant was the impact upon land settlement and entry. The total number of homestead entries in the eleven arid states of the Far West more than tripled (from 17,806 to 63,931) between 1900 and 1910 in anticipation of irrigation (Gates 1968, 668).

Prior to 1916 national parks and monuments were administered by three federal departments—Interior, Agriculture, and War (construction activities in the parks were conducted by the U.S. Army Corps of Engineers, and army troops were often used to manage and patrol parklands) (Mogren 1980, 52, 161). The National Park Service was created in 1916 and received custody of the fourteen national parks and twenty-one national monuments previously withdrawn from the public domain (Everhart 1983, 18). The first federal wildlife refuge was established by presidential proclamation on Afognak Island, Alaska, in 1892 and was soon followed by Pelican Island, Florida, in 1903 (Bean 1983, 22). The National Bison Range in Montana and areas within the Wichita Forest Reserve (National Forest) and Grand Canyon Forest Reserve (National Forest) followed soon thereafter (Bean 1983, 120). Numerous waterfowl refuges were added in the years following passage of the Migratory Bird Conservation Act of 1929, but the federal refuge system was not unified under a single agency with clear organic legislation until the National Wildlife Refuge System Administration Act was passed in 1966 (Bean 1983, 125).

The Taylor Grazing Act of 1934 provided a land classification system for public domain lands and authorized the secretary of the interior to withdraw and place in designated grazing districts lands best suited for that purpose. Although the act did not eliminate homesteading where otherwise authorized, it did greatly curtail it (total homestead entries fell from almost 3 million acres per year in 1933 and 1934 to less than 100,000 acres per year in 1938 and thereafter (Gates 1968, 613). Unfortunately the phrase "pending its [the public land's] final disposal" (Gates 1968, 611) in the act's preamble served to continue debate over the ultimate fate of the public domain (Clawson and Held [1957] 1966, 34).

The process just described methodically removed from under the General Land Office (GLO) virtually all lands reserved for their renewable resource, historic, cultural, and aesthetic values, leaving the GLO with mineral lands and the remaining public domain. The GLO was established in the Department of the Treasury in 1812 to deal with lands recently acquired through the Louisiana Purchase (Mogren 1980, 19). In 1849 the office was transferred into the newly created Department of the Interior (Mogren 1980, 26, 27). By tradition the GLO was staffed by political appointees, many of whom participated in land speculation (Clawson 1951, 84). Fraud, bribery, and theft existed on a large scale (Clawson [1962] 1968, 450). Gifford Pinchot developed an early and negative impression of GLO management, characterizing it in 1899 as being "lax, stupid, and wrongheaded" (Pinchot [1947] 1972, 161) and later (p. 264) comparing "the blundering of political Land Office appointees" with "the skilled and honest judgment and action of trained foresters and experienced Western men."

On July 16, 1946, President Harry Truman joined the GLO and the Grazing Service to form the Bureau of Land Management (BLM) (Reorganization Plan no. 3 of 1946, sec. 403). In so doing he consolidated administration of the withdrawn grazing district lands with those remaining in the public domain, coupled the highly centralized organization of the GLO with the highly decentralized system of the Grazing Service (Clawson [1962] 1968, 454), and linked one of the oldest units of government (the GLO, established in 1812) with one of the youngest (the Grazing Service, established as the Division of Grazing in 1934) (General Services Administration 1985, 326).

Understandably grazing district users wished to place a sympathetic person in charge of the new bureau and, through the National Advisory Board Council and Senator Patrick McCarran, lobbied hard for their man. They overplayed their hand, however, in recommending a grazing district licensee for the post over the temporary director (Fred W. Johnson, commissioner of the GLO 1933-1946 [Carstensen 1968, 509]), and lost on both counts (Peffer 1951, 306-308). In 1948 Marion Clawson (Ph.D. in economics from Harvard University; economist, Bureau of Agricultural Economics [USDA]; regional director, BLM, California-Nevada region) was appointed director, and he held the post until 1953 (Carstensen 1968, 509).

Clawson summarizes accomplishments during the early days of the bureau in words that both bureaucrat and layperson can understand:

> In 1948 the Bureau of Land Management had an appropriation of $5,000,000 and collected in revenues the then unheard-of sum of $15,000,000; its budget request for fiscal 1958 is over $29,000,000, and it anticipates revenues in that year of $237,000,000. Impressive as this growth in size is, the growth in competence and quality of work has been even greater—admitting that it is most difficult to define competence and quality, to say nothing of measuring it. The humble origin is often part of the American success story. (Clawson [1962] 1968, 458, 459)

Intensive Management

During the short period of intensive management, from about 1950 to about 1960, the public lands produced a profit for the federal Treasury. The volume of timber cut from the national forests increased from less than 4 billion board feet in 1950 to more than 9 billion by 1960, yielding a profit of more than $20 million. Oil and gas leases increased from fewer than 30,000 to almost 140,000, and the area affected increased from fewer than 25 million acres to over 100 million. Total receipts from grazing, oil and gas, recreation, minerals, and coal (excluding those from outer continental shelf leases) increased nearly fourfold. As originally envisioned by Clawson and Held ([1957] 1966), this period was to continue indefinitely. In reality it was but a short interlude, soon replaced by the complexities and confrontations of the 1960s (Clawson 1983, 37-39).

Consultation and Confrontation

By the end of World War II, the total area of federal lands (exclusive of the outer continental shelf) was generally fixed (Clawson and Held [1957] 1966, 35). Relatively few acquisitions have been made since then, and those were generally small, for specific projects, and/or to eliminate inholdings or to round out boundaries. After the war the American public found itself with greater disposable income and more leisure time and turned increasingly to outdoor recreation on public lands. More diverse and more intense use led to conflict and competition for resources, necessitating a more complex and holistic management system. The "romantic preservation" philosophy of Thoreau and Muir (Culhane 1981, 6) experienced a reawakening and was joined by a new ethos, "environmentalism..., committed to maintaining the integrity of the biosphere" (Culhane 1981, 7, 9). Culhane (1981, 41) termed the period one of "extensive preservation." Clawson (1983, 39) called it "consultation and confrontation." It could as well be titled "conflict, complexity, and confusion."

Clarifying the Federal Role

Congressionally mandated study commissions containing private citizens—the Outdoor Recreation Resources Review Commission (ORRRC), the Public Land Law Review Commission (PLLRC), the Commission on Marine Science, Engineering, and Resources (COMSER), and the National Water Commission (NWC)—reviewed almost every area of federal natural resource management. In almost all cases, they recommended more planning, a more integrated approach to management, and more efficient resource production.

New organic legislation was enacted, or existing legislation amended, defining the authorities and responsibilities of all federal natural resource agencies. The Multiple-Use Sustained Yield Act of 1960, the Forest and Rangeland Renewable Resources Planning Act of 1974, and the National Forest Management Act of 1976 defined the role of the Forest Service. The Fish and Wildlife Act of 1956 created the United States Fish and Wildlife Service (FWS) in the Department of the Interior and described its duties. Federal civilian marine activities were largely consolidated in the National Oceanic and Atmospheric Administration following recommendations in the COMSER report.

During the 1960s and early 1970s, events also proceeded toward long-delayed enactment of a BLM organic act. In 1963 Charles H. Stoddard became director, adding a touch of enlightened leadership at a time of rapidly changing attitudes toward use of public land. During his tenure Stoddard was a staunch supporter of the Classification and Multiple Use Act of 1964 and of legislation establishing the Public Land Law Review Commission (Voigt 1976, 303, 304)—both of which were precursors to organic legislation.

The Classification and Multiple Use Act bore the same general relationship to the BLM as the Multiple-Use Sustained Yield Act of 1960 did to the Forest Service, but it was a temporary statute "pending implementation of recommendations to be made by the Public Land Law Review Commission." It directed the secretary of the interior to develop criteria by which to classify public lands in the contiguous states and Alaska as to their desirability for disposal or retention "at least during this period" in federal ownership and management. Lands were to be disposed of if they were "required" for community growth and development, "chiefly valuable for residential, commercial, agricultural..., industrial, or public uses or development." If retained they were to be managed for "(1) domestic livestock grazing, (2) fish and wildlife development and utilization, (3) industrial development, (4) mineral production, (5) occupancy, (6) outdoor recreation, (7) timber production, (8) watershed protection, (9) wilderness preservation, or (10) preservation of public values that would be lost if the land passed from Federal ownership" (78 Stat. 986). Having developed the criteria, the secretary "as soon as possible" was to classify the public lands and publish notice of the proposed classifications. Once notice was published, no classified lands could be otherwise disposed of unless final action was not taken within two years. Noteworthy as the provision of the Classification and Multiple Use Act might have been, it was only a temporary measure, awaiting the definitive action of the commission.

A second precursor, the Public Land Law Review Commission, was formed:

Sec. 2. Because the public land laws of the United States have developed over a long period of years through a series of Acts of Congress which are not fully correlated with each other and because those laws, or some of them, may be inadequate to meet the current and future needs of the American people and because administration of the public lands and the laws relating thereto has been divided among several agencies. (78 Stat. 982)

The commission was given a broad mission: to "study the statutes and regulations governing the retention, management, and disposition of the public lands;...review the policies and practices of the Federal agencies charged with administrative jurisdiction over such lands...[; and] to recommend such modifications as will...carry out the policy set forth..." (78 Stat. 982, sec. 4). It looked at the public domain, reserved and withdrawn lands, national forests, and national wildlife refuges and ranges. It looked at mineral resources; timber; intensive agriculture; water; fish and wildlife; outdoor recreation; and residential, commercial, and industrial development (Public Land Law Review Commission 1970, ix-xi)—and it looked at grazing on BLM and Forest Service lands (105-118).

Although the commission never recommended, per se, that a BLM organic act be passed, its oblique and peripheral recommendations accomplished the same effect. It noted that the Classification and Multiple Use Act, though commendable, was *temporary* legislation and recommended "that BLM be provided permanent multiple use management authority" (Public Land Law Review Commission 1970, 51). It commented that as of April 1, 1970, BLM had classified 154.4 million acres of public land for retention and only 4.5 million acres for disposal under the act, commending the agency for moving swiftly under its congressional mandate to act "as soon as possible" but expressing concern that the decisions "were made in a hurried manner on the basis of inadequate information." As a result the commission recommended that Congress review all BLM retention and disposal classifications (pp. 52, 53). It recommended that "statutory goals and objectives should be established as guidelines for land-use planning under the general principle that within a specific unit, consideration should be given to all possible uses and the maximum number of uses permitted" (p. 3). And finally it observed that the Forest Service was the only "major public land agency" outside the Department of the Interior and stated that "*the Forest Service should be merged with the Department of the Interior into a new department of natural resources*" [emphasis added] (p. 282).

Perhaps the crowning glory was the continued degradation of rangelands administered by the BLM and the growing public awareness of that situation. When the Taylor Grazing Act was passed in 1934 to "stabilize the livestock industry, increase grazing capacity, and protect the range," 90 percent of the public domain rangeland was deteriorating. In 1975, 83 percent of the BLM grazing lands were in fair, poor, or bad condition and 50 million acres (an area the size of Utah) were in poor or bad condition. Ten percent of the national resource lands were subject to critical or severe erosion and another 35 percent to moderate erosion (Council on Environmental Quality 1975, 212-214).

Given the climate of the times, something had to happen; yet it was only in the final days of the Ninety-fourth Congress that the BLM was finally given its legislative mandate, the Federal Land Policy and Management Act of 1976 (FLPMA) (Council on Environmental Quality 1977, 75, 76). Widely different bills were passed by the two houses, and compromises were forced in conference "in a dramatic race against the clock." As frequently happens agreement was reached relatively easily on most important national issues, but major controversies arose over efforts to protect special interests (Dana and Fairfax 1980, 338, 339).

Prior to FLPMA, BLM officers had no law enforcement authority on the public lands and had to rely on local authorities—an inefficient and unpopular remedy (Dana and Fairfax 1980, 338). Although the bureau did not get strong congressional endorsement, it did receive authority to "authorize Federal personnel or appropriate local officials to carry out...law enforcement responsibilities with respect to the public lands and their resources" (90 Stat. 2764).

A second controversy revolved around inclusion of the Forest Service, which already had ample organic legislation, within FLPMA. The issue here was primarily an intercommittee struggle between the House Interior and Insular Affairs and Agriculture committees. Although almost all interests other than the Committee on Interior and Insular Affairs opposed involving the Forest Service, it remains affected by sections of the act concerning coordination of land use planning (sec. 202), land acquisitions (sec. 205) and exchanges (sec. 206), establishment of "national forest townships" (sec. 213), grazing fees (sec. 401), grazing advisory boards (sec. 403), and rights-of-way (title V). In many cases these provisions of FLPMA duplicate or conflict with similar provisions of the Forest and Rangeland Renewable Resources Planning Act (RPA) passed two years earlier and the National Forest Management Act (NFMA) passed by the same session of Congress—adding more complexity and confusion to the Forest Service's planning process.

A third debate concerned authority to withdraw lands from mineral entry and pitted the legislative branch (which wanted more control over withdrawals) against the executive branch and the conservation lobby (Dana and Fairfax 1980, 339). The conflict was resolved through a complicated process by which the secretary of the interior is to report to Congress a description of conditions under which areas of more than 5,000 acres are proposed for withdrawal, and the Congress may by concurrent resolution veto the proposal (sec. 204).

Grazing fees constituted the fourth major (and eternal) controversy (Dana and Fairfax 1980, 339). Differences between Forest Service and BLM rates, between grazing fees for public and private land, and between the viewpoints of graziers and other users of the public lands will probably never be reconciled, but the act at least addressed the issue. It directed the secretaries of agriculture and the interior to "jointly cause to be conducted a study to determine the value of grazing on the lands under their jurisdiction in the eleven Western States with a view to establishing a [grazing] fee...which is equitable to the United States and to the holders of grazing permits and leases" (sec. 401(a)), and froze grazing fees until the study could be completed. In recognition of the deteriorated condition of the public rangelands, FLPMA also directed that 50 percent of the grazing fees received be placed in a special fund for "range rehabilitation, protection, and improvements" (sec. 401(b)(1)).

But above all FLPMA gave the BLM official recognition from the legislative branch, legitimizing its position in the bureaucracy and providing it with a statutory basis and legal framework for doing business. It declared the government's intention to retain most of the public lands and to manage them for the long-term benefit of all citizens (Council on Environmental Quality 1977, 77) and outlined the administrative organization and planning and management procedures by which the BLM is to operate:

> In the end, careful planning and sensitivity to the trade-offs and impacts of management activities still will not make it possible to meet all the demands of forest and rangelands. At best, we have a process for assessing conflict and making decisions. Nothing can prevent the conflict or keep it from growing as public demands proliferate and compete. To succeed, land management professionals must recognize that they are part of a confusing policy arena, increasingly controversial, increasingly politicized, and increasingly uncertain. The objective must not be to seek certainty, but to learn to live with complexity. (Dana and Fairfax 1980, 346)

The Federal Land Policy and Management Act of 1976 also clarified the secretary of the interior's authority to withdraw lands from the public domain, provided a comprehensive framework for activities of the Bureau of Land Management, and repealed a number of acts affecting withdrawals, administration of public lands, and rights-of-way.

Efforts were made to coordinate activities better among agencies with similar (and sometimes antagonistic) missions. The Fish and Wildlife Coordination Act of 1934 was amended in 1958 to strengthen the ability of the U.S. Fish and Wildlife Service and state fish and game agencies to obtain mitigation for habitat losses resulting from water development projects, and a Water Resources Council (WRC) was created at the secretary's level to develop unified planning procedures and oversee the conservation and development of "water and related land resources." In the marine area, the National Council on Marine Resources and Engineering Development in the Executive Office of the President performed similar coordinative functions between 1966 and 1969.

Particular classes of natural resources were emphasized, regardless of agency jurisdiction. Provisions for preserving lands "where the earth and its community of life are untrammeled by man, where man himself is a visitor who does not remain" were included in the Wilderness Act of 1964 and the Eastern Wilderness Act of 1974. Protection for threatened and endangered species of fish, wildlife, and plants was provided by the Marine Mammal Protection Act of 1972, the Endangered Species Act of 1973, and several international treaties. The Coastal Zone Management Act of 1972 identified the continental margin as a unique class of land and developed a special federal-state mechanism to "preserve, protect, develop, and where possible to restore" it. Presidential executive orders were issued to minimize the adverse impacts of federal activities upon floodplains (Exec. Order No. 11,988, May 24, 1977) and wetlands (Exec. Order No. 11,990, May 24, 1977).

Several measures were enacted to provide sustained funding for programs that were most sensitive to the ups and downs of the annual budget cycle. The Migratory Bird Hunting Stamp Act of 1934 requires every person sixteen years of age and older hunting migratory waterfowl to purchase a "duck stamp," the proceeds from which are deposited in a special migratory bird conservation fund for acquiring and managing lands as migratory bird refuges. The most comprehensive natural resource special fund was established by the Land and Water Conservation Fund Act of 1965. As provided in this act, proceeds from entrance, admission, and other recreation user fees charged by federal agencies; proceeds from sale of federal surplus property; and federal motorboat fuel taxes are deposited in a separate fund, the Land and Water Conservation Fund. If subsequently appropriated by Congress, monies from the fund may be used by federal, state, and local park, recreation, and wildlife agencies. As modified by later amendments, revenues from outer continental shelf leases are now deposited in the fund, and up to $900 million per year may be made available from it.

And serving as an umbrella over "the policies, regulations, and public laws of the United States...[and] all agencies of the Federal Government" is the National Environmental Policy Act of 1969 (NEPA). This ambitious, far-reaching, and controversial law has the following purposes:

To declare a national policy which will encourage productive and enjoyable harmony between man and his environment; to promote efforts which will prevent or eliminate damage to the environment and biosphere and stimulate the health and welfare of man; to enrich the understanding of the ecological systems and natural resources important to the Nation; and to establish a Council on Environmental Quality. (83 Stat. 852)

The act directs all federal agencies to "use all practicable measures" to further its objectives and requires detailed statements of environmental impacts to accompany all "proposals for legislation and other major Federal actions significantly affecting the quality of the human environment" (42 U.S.C. 4332 [1982]). Environmental impact statements (EISs) require full disclosure of the government's intentions and elicit public input.

By the 1980s virtually all of the public domain outside of Alaska had been reserved for some special or dominant use. The authority and responsibility of administering agencies had been well defined by comprehensive organic legislation; activities were guided by program and project planning to which the public had ready access; and almost all were engaged in multiple-use, multiresource management emphasizing some optimal mix of products. Only the National Park Service retained its original narrow mission—protection and preservation of unique natural, historic, and cultural areas and objects—and even it is required to balance this objective with the opportunity for public use and enjoyment.

Public Participation

While "the public" has always been involved to a degree in agency decision making, citizen involvement prior to the 1960s was generally limited in the spectrum of its interests and geographic representation. Direct resource users, be they miners, graziers, loggers, or to a lesser extent recreationists, developed relationships with the land managers, the nature of which is still subject to debate. Nonparticipants and remote residents were generally not part of the process.

Culhane (1981, 322) denoted the extremes of these agency-clientele relationships as "capture" and "conformity." In the former, agency personnel are so closely allied to the interests of a user group that they and their policies are "captured" by the group—the agency is "in bed with the special interests." In the case of conformity, a strong agency organization and doctrine successfully sway public opinion toward its position, using the constituency primarily as a source of approval and political support. In the minds of many observers, the Bureau of Land Management was captured by the grazing interests, whereas the Forest Service exemplified conformity (Clawson 1983, 249; Culhane 1981, 322,

323). Whatever the validity of the capture-conformity argument, the situation changed swiftly and drastically during the 1960s and early 1970s.

Citing Truman (1951), Culhane argues that groups are effective in influencing government policy in direct relation to their interests, power, and access. "Interests" are defined narrowly as positions on specific issues. "Power" is the influence exerted, by whatever means. "Access" is the ability to inject the group's interests into an agency's policy-making or decision-making process (Culhane 1981, 23, 24). It takes little imagination to conclude that all three factors expanded during the past two decades. As a result agencies often "can play their more extreme constituents off against each other to reinforce the agencies' preferred middle course" (Culhane 1981, 336). Culhane's discussion was limited to the Forest Service and the Bureau of Land Management, but the principle is applicable much more widely. The balancing game is neither easy nor free of political pitfalls, however, and many agencies had difficulty in accepting as allies interests that had previously been considered enemies.

The Voice of the Courts

Clawson describes the increased role of the judiciary as the result of four factors:

> First, some of the new legislation has provided openings for litigation. Particularly, as it has worked out, the National Environmental Policy Act of 1969, with its requirements for Environmental Impact Statements, opened the door to many suits....
>
> Second, the courts generally have taken more generous attitudes toward letting interest groups and even individuals sue in the name of larger groups....
>
> Third, the judiciary...is far more activist today than it was many years ago....
>
> Fourth, but perhaps the more important[,] factor has been the changing attitudes of the public, or at least large sectors of it. With the new laws on the books, conservation groups hire lawyers and devote considerable sums to legal action. Law has become a key area of expertise for environmentalists, on a par with their expertise in natural sciences....(Clawson 1983, 55, 56)

One might add that your reading this book is also a manifestation of the fourth factor. No longer does a scientific-technical-administrative background suffice for a natural resource manager. He or she must also have legal-political expertise.

The Federal Land Managers

Table 3.5 summarizes the distribution of land within the United States among federal agencies. Following admission of Alaska and Hawaii as states in 1959, the area of public lands "within the United States" rose to almost 770 million acres. Alaska itself added 378 million acres—more than doubling the area (U.S. Department of the Interior, Bureau of Land Management 1987, table 1). Since that time the area of public lands has diminished—slowly through about 1976, by 15 million acres during the Carter administration, and by an additional 15 million acres during the first year of the Reagan administration. Lands administered by the Bureau of Land Management (BLM) decreased by 128 million acres (27 percent) between 1973-1976 and 1981-1983, reflecting the impact of the Federal Land Policy and Management Act of 1976 and the Reagan administration's intent to privatize as much as possible of the nation's natural resource base. The area of land administered by the U.S. Army Corps of Engineers grew by 3.6 million acres (75 percent) between 1957-1960 and 1981-1983, indicating the Corps' small but growing role as a natural resource manager. Holdings of the U.S. Fish and Wildlife Service (FWS) increased by 71.5 million acres (almost sixfold) and those of the National Park Service (NPS) increased by 58.1 million acres (threefold) during the same period, primarily as a result of acquisitions provided through the Land and Water Conservation Fund Act. The Forest Service (FS), the FWS, and the NPS all benefited from settlement of the Alaska lands controversy in 1981 (but the BLM lost).

About 60 percent of the public lands is used predominantly for forests and wildlife (table 3.6). The Department of the Interior (BLM and FWS) provides about 60 percent of these lands, with the remainder in the Department of Agriculture (FS). The total area of federal forestlands and wildlife lands diminished by 70 million acres (14 percent) between 1973-1976 and 1981-1983. Grazing lands comprise about 22 percent of the federal lands, with the Department of the Interior (BLM) providing almost 90 percent and the Department of Agriculture (FS) providing the remainder. The total amount of grazing lands has been relatively constant (a little more than 160 million acres) since 1961-1964, despite the efforts of the Sagebrush Rebellion to place more of these resources in private hands. The greatest increase in public lands during the past twenty-five years has been for parks and historic sites, almost entirely within the Department of the Interior (NPS). These holdings almost tripled between 1957-1960 and 1977-1980 and almost doubled between 1977-

1980 and 1981-1983. The Alaska oil and gas reserves entered the inventory in 1959 and were removed upon disposition of the Alaska lands. In 1981-1983 military lands decreased by about 30 percent from average holdings during the twenty-year period of 1957-1960 to 1977-1980.

TABLE 3.5

United States Land Administered by Major Federal Land Management Agencies
(Four-Year Averages, in Millions of Acres)

	Area						
Agency	1957-1960	1961-1964	1965-1968	1969-1972	1973-1976	1977-1980	1981-1983[a]
Forest Service	76.4	186.2	186.6	186.7	187.8	186.9	192.2
Bureau of Land Management	338.7	487.9	477.0	474.5	471.0	419.4	342.3
U.S. Fish and Wildlife Service	12.1	27.2	26.8	27.9	30.1	46.7	83.6
National Park Service	18.1	22.4	23.1	24.4	25.1	47.4	76.2
Bureau of Reclamation	9.4	9.1	8.9	8.2	7.3	6.3	4.3
U.S. Army Corps of Engineers	4.8	5.8	6.8	7.3	7.8	8.2	8.4
Department of Defense	23.1	22.8	23.6	23.2	22.9	23.0	16.4
Other	5.9	8.4	8.8	9.0	9.0	7.2	7.5
Total	588.5	769.8	761.6	761.2	76.1	745.1	730.9

Source: General Services Administration, "Summary Report on Real Property Owned by the United States Throughout the World" (Washington, DC: Government Printing Office, 1958-1985), table 7.
[a] Data for 1984 and succeeding years are not available.

Flood control and navigation (primarily by the U.S. Army Corps of Engineers) is a small but growing component, increasing by 3.2 million acres (62 percent) over the period 1957-1960 to 1981-1983; and reclamation and irrigation are diminishing in importance, declining by 28 percent between 1957-1960 and 1977-1980 and by an additional 34 percent in 1981-1983.

TABLE 3.6

United States Land Administered by Major Federal Land Management Agencies
(Four-Year Averages, in Millions of Acres)

Use	Area						
	1957-1960	1961-1964	1965-1968	1969-1972	1973-1976	1977-1980	1981-1983[a]
Forests and wildlife							
Dept. of the Interior	181.9	347.2	337.0	336.1	335.4	299.6	260.8
Dept. of Agriculture	156.8	166.8	167.3	167.4	168.1	166.6	172.3
Other	—	—	—	.01	—	0.1	0.2
Subtotal	338.7	514.0	504.3	503.6	503.5	466.3	433.3
Grazing							
Dept. of the Interior	158.4	146.4	145.4	144.8	144.2	143.4	142.2
Dept. of Agriculture	19.3	19.1	19.0	19.0	19.4	19.7	19.7
Subtotal	177.7	165.5	164.4	163.8	163.6	163.1	161.9
Parks and Historic Sites							
Dept. of the Interior	18.7	22.4	23.1	24.5	25.2	53.2	99.3
Other	—	—	—	0.1	0.1	0.4	0.4
Subtotal	18.7	22.4	23.1	24.5	25.2	53.6	99.5
Alaska oil and gas							
Dept. of the Interior	11.5	23.0	23.0	23.0	23.0	17.2	—
Military (e.g., airfields)	8.8	16.6	15.8	16.6	17.6	18.9	12.7
Flood control and navigation							
U.S. Army Corps of Engineers	4.3	5.2	6.1	6.6	7.0	7.3	7.5
TVA	0.7	0.7	0.7	0.7	0.7	0.7	0.7
Other	0.2	0.2	0.2	0.2	0.2	0.2	0.2
Subtotal	5.2	6.1	7.0	7.5	7.9	8.2	8.4
Reclamation and irrigation							
Dept. of the Interior	8.0	8.0	7.7	7.2	6.7	5.8	3.8
Other uses	10.6	14.2	16.3	14.9	13.4	12.0	11.3
Total	589.2	769.8	761.6	761.2	761.0	745.1	730.9

Source: General Services Administration, "Summary Report on Real Property Owned by the United States Throughout the World" (Washington, DC: Government Printing Office, 1958-1985), section 15 (1957-1960), section 10 (1961-1981), section 11 (1982, 1983).

[a]Data for 1984 and succeeding years are not available.

The constitutional authority for the federal government to hold and manage land is derived primarily from the commerce clause (U.S. Constitution, art. I, sec. 8), treaty provisions (art. II, sec. 2), and the power to "provide for the common Defence and general Welfare of the United States" (art. I, sec. 8). Public lands may be residual areas of the public domain or may be acquired through gift, purchase, or condemnation for a public purpose related to one of the constitutional powers cited above. Once an area becomes part of the federal public lands,

> the Congress shall have Power to dispose of and make all needful Rules and Regulations respecting the Territory or other Property belonging to the United States....(U.S. Constitution, art. IV, sec. 3)

Although it may delegate some regulatory authority over federal property to the executive branch, Congress's power to control the use of the public lands is supreme "the...Laws of any State to the Contrary notwithstanding" (U.S. Constitution, art. VI; *Kleppe v. New Mexico*). In practice, however, Congress and federal land managers attempt to avoid conflicts with relevant state land management policies wherever possible (the law and the politics are sometimes different).

Grazing lands, forests, parks and recreational areas, wildlife refuges, and wilderness preserves constitute the major kinds of public lands from the perspective of renewable natural resources. All had a common origin in the public domain and have evolved along generally parallel paths—reservation, organic legislation, acquisition, and multiple use.

REFERENCES

Bean, Michael J. 1983. *The Evolution of National Wildlife Law.* New York: Praeger Publishers.

Carstensen, Vernon, ed. 1968. *The Public Lands.* Madison: University of Wisconsin Press.

Clawson, Marion. 1951. *Uncle Sam's Acres.* New York: Mead & Company.

———. [1962] 1968. "Reminiscences of the Bureau of Land Management." In *The Public Lands,* edited by Vernon Carstensen, 449-459. Madison: University of Wisconsin Press.

———. 1983. *The Federal Lands Revisited.* Baltimore: Johns Hopkins University Press.

Clawson, Marion, and Burnell Held. [1957] 1966. *The Federal Lands: Their Use and Management.* Baltimore: Johns Hopkins University Press.

Clawson, Marion, R. Burnell Held, and Charles H. Stoddard. [1960] 1968. *Land for the Future.* Baltimore: Johns Hopkins University Press.

Council on Environmental Quality. 1975. *Environmental Quality—1975.* Washington, DC: Government Printing Office.

———. 1977. *Environmental Quality—1977.* Washington, DC: Government Printing Office.

Cronon, Edmund D. 1983. *Changes in the Land: Indians, Colonists, and the Ecology of New England.* New York: Hill & Wang.

Culhane, Paul J. 1981. *Public Lands Policy: Interest Group Influence on the Forest Service and the Bureau of Land Management.* Baltimore: Johns Hopkins University Press.

Dana, Samuel T., and Sally K. Fairfax. 1980. *Forest and Range Policy: Its Development in the United States.* New York: McGraw-Hill Book Company.

Everhart, William C. 1983. *The National Park Service.* Boulder, CO: Westview Press.

Gates, Paul W. 1968. "History of Land Law Development." Public Land Law Review Commission study report. Washington, DC: Government Printing Office.

General Services Administration. 1958-1985. "Summary Report on Real Property Owned by the United States Throughout the World." (Published annually.) Washington, DC: Government Printing Office.

————. 1984. *The United States Government Manual 1984/85.* Washington, DC: Government Printing Office.

————. 1985. *The United States Government Manual 1985/86.* Washington, DC: Government Printing Office.

Hibbard, Benjamin H. 1924. *A History of the Public Land Policies.* New York: Macmillan Company.

Johnson, V. Webster, and Raleigh Barlowe. [1954] 1979. *Land Problems and Policies.* New York: Arno Press.

Mahoney, J. R. 1950. "Natural Resources Activity of the Federal Government." Public Affairs Bulletin no. 76. Washington, DC: Library of Congress.

Marsh, George P. 1864. *Man and Nature.* New York: Charles Scribner.

Mogren, Paul A. 1980. "The Development of a Philosophy of Land Reservation on General Land Office, United States Forest Service, and National Park Service Lands: 1787 to 1947." Ph.D. diss., University of Utah. (Available from University Microfilms, Ann Arbor, MI.)

The Nature Conservancy. 1977. *Preserving Our Natural Heritage.* Prepared for U.S. Department of the Interior, National Park Service, Office of the Chief Scientist. Washington, DC: Government Printing Office.

Peffer, E. Louise. 1951. *The Closing of the Public Domain.* Stanford, CA: Stanford University Press.

Pinchot, Gifford. [1947] 1972. *Breaking New Ground.* Seattle: University of Washington Press.

Public Land Law Review Commission. 1970. *One Third of the Nation's Land.* Washington, DC: Government Printing Office.

Robbins, Roy M. 1942. *Our Landed Heritage: The Public Domain, 1776-1936.* Princeton, NJ: Princeton University Press.

Truman, David B. 1951. *The Governmental Process.* New York: Alfred A. Knopf.

Udall, Stewart L. 1963. *The Quiet Crisis.* New York: Holt, Rinehart and Winston.

U.S. Department of the Interior, Bureau of Land Management. 1973. *Manual for the Survey of the Public Lands of the United States.* Washington, DC: Government Printing Office.

———. 1988. *Public Land Statistics 1987.* Washington, DC: Government Printing Office.

Voigt, William, Jr. 1976. *Public Grazing Lands.* New Brunswick, NJ: Rutgers University Press.

Widner, Ralph R., ed. 1968. *Forests and Forestry in the American States.* Washington, DC: National Association of State Foresters.

Winter, Charles E. [1932] 1979. *Four Hundred Million Acres.* New York: Arno Press.

CHAPTER IV

Grazing Lands

Of all the private uses of public land, grazing has the longest history and still affects the greatest area. About 373 million acres—thirty-one percent of the nation's rangeland—are on the public lands. Two federal agencies—the Forest Service and the Bureau of Land Management—provide the vast majority (about 268 million acres) of the public grazing land (Council on Environmental Quality 1975, 212). Together they administer over 30,000 grazing allotments on approximately 318 million acres of federally owned rangelands throughout the western states (U.S. Department of Agriculture, Forest Service 1984, 15). The Forest Service and the Bureau of Land Management are converging toward a common goal, but their evolution has been by different routes and varying land use philosophies.

FREE LAND, COMPETITION, AND CONFLICT

In the early days of western land settlement, grazing on public land was limited to a narrow strip around settlements, "for Indians were as fond of beef as of the meat of any wild animal" (Clawson 1951, 112). Technically all such use of the public domain was a trespass, but land was plentiful, and much of it had little use other than for grazing. Gradually a philosophy of ranching developed, based upon permanent use of the public lands (Clawson 1951, 113).

The western cattle industry was based on these large expanses of free range and transportation corridors to eastern markets. As early as 1846, cattle were being driven from Texas to as far east as Ohio (Wellman 1939, cited in Stoddart, Smith, and Box 1975, 83), and by the mid-1880s, cattle trails extended from grazing lands to railheads throughout the West. With expansion of the railroads came the sheep industry, which required the rails for wool shipment, and the rivalry and range wars between sheepherders and cattlemen began (Stoddart, Smith, and Box 1975, 84, 85).

Cattle were left to graze freely over the range, but sheep were maintained in closely controlled bands, always under the close supervision of a herder who lived with the band. Sheep required little water and were better able to survive harsh winters. Sheep thus were able to outcompete cattle for the range resources. Sheep also produced two products, whereas cattle produced only one; and the market for mutton and wool was more stable than that for beef (Stoddart, Smith, and Box 1975, 16-18). As the nineteenth century came to a close, western cattlemen found themselves facing increasing pressure from this efficient competitor, more conflict among themselves, blockage of cattle trails by homesteaders' fences, and continual range degradation from overstocking (the classic "tragedy of the commons" [Hardin 1968]).

Yet the western cattle industry boomed during the two decades following the Civil War, and the great cattle drives from Texas grazing lands to eastern markets (often lasting more than a year) became etched in American history (Stoddart, Smith, and Box 1975, 83). In only a few years, the seemingly infinite grass resources of the West Texas ranges were consumed, their roots destroyed and trampled into the dust. Reckoning came with the severe winters of the mid-1880s. Many herds were almost entirely wiped out by cold, hunger, and thirst; fortunes were lost; and the limitations of free and unlimited use of the public rangelands were becoming apparent. From this disaster came two developments that changed the ranching industry forever—the science of range management and regulation of grazing on the public domain (Stoddart, Smith, and Box 1975, 88-89).

THE COMING OF REGULATION

Passage of the Creative Act in 1891 provided the first legislative step toward protecting grazing lands on the public domain. During the first two years of the act's existence, almost 40 million acres were reserved—ostensibly protected from timbering, mining, farming, and grazing. The reserves were created to protect *timber* resources, but the principal commercial product was livestock, the primary use was grazing, and the stock owner's power was too strong to withstand. By 1899 the forest reserves were officially open to grazing and the General Land Office had instituted a grazing permit program (Rowley 1985, 4, 5).

Regulation came neither swiftly nor painlessly. During the 1890s troops were employed to eject sheepherders, and to a lesser degree cattlemen, from Yosemite National Park. Beginning in 1892 Congress began deliberating utilization of the forest reserves, but no legislation emerged until 1897 (Rowley 1985, 23, 24). In 1894 the first regulations were passed prohibiting "'driving, feeding, grazing, pasturing, or herding of cattle, sheep, or other livestock'" on all forest reserves (Coville 1898, 10, cited in Rowley 1985, 24). In the same year, Secretary of the Interior Hoke Smith requested troops to protect the reserves from fires set by sheepherders. Smith's request was denied—absent specific congressional authorization, the secretary of war believed that he lacked constitutional authority to intervene (Ise 1920, 121). Thus passage of regulations had little impact; stockmen simply continued their traditional practices (Rowley 1985, 24).

During 1896 and early 1897 events were proceeding toward a climax. Despite lengthy debate over several years, Congress was unable to produce any meaningful legislation. The National Academy of Sciences Committee's report (National Academy of Sciences 1897) attacked grazing and other western interests (Rowley 1985, 28). President Grover Cleveland added 21 million acres to the forest reserves and vetoed appropriations legislation shortly before the end of his administration. Incoming president William McKinley was the victim of Cleveland's monumental squeeze play. Faced with near rebellion in the West and no funds to run the government, McKinley obtained the funding and passage of the Organic Act during a special session of Congress on June 4, 1897.

Shortly thereafter the secretary of the interior issued the following clarification of the department's position concerning grazing on the reserves:

> The pasturing of livestock on public lands in forest reserves will not be interfered with, so long as it appears that injury is not being done to the forest growth, and the rights of others are not thereby jeopardized. The pasturing of sheep is, however, prohibited in all forest reserves except those in the states of Oregon and Washington, for the reason that sheep grazing has been found injurious to the forest cover....(Rowley 1985, 32)

That same summer, in 1897, Fredrick V. Coville, a botanist with the Department of Agriculture, surveyed the Washington-Oregon sheep region and returned to the nation's capital with a more objective appraisal of sheep grazing in the reserves and a plan for its control. Under Coville's proposal each sheep owner would be "granted a permit to graze a specified number of sheep in a designated forage area which the area could support without damage." Sheepherders agreed to abide by the limitations and to refrain from setting fires; the government granted them exclusive grazing rights within their permit areas. The cost of the program was to have been borne by the permittees. In accord with Coville's recommendations (and those of a 1900 Pinchot-Coville investigation), sheep grazing was permitted in eight reserves by 1901—but no fees were charged (Rowley 1985, 32-40). Regulation had come to grazing on the public land but only on the *forest reserves, for sheep, and without charge.* A 1902 General Land Office report "allowed the forest supervisor to issue cattle and horse grazing permits to reserve residents who owned not more than one hundred head of cattle and horses combined," but in practice cattle and horses trespassed on the reserves with impunity (Rowley 1985, 46, 48).

With the transfer of the forest reserves to the Department of Agriculture in 1905, authority over grazing on public lands became divided between Gifford Pinchot's new Forest Service, with its doctrine of scientific management, and the unreserved public domain under the administration of the General Land Office in the Department of the Interior, with its laissez-faire attitude toward natural resource management.

Pinchot lost little time in initiating permit fees, and he used an artful ploy to obtain administrative sanction for his move. The authority to charge fees is usually granted by statute. The Forest Service had no such authority, and the livestock interests would have blocked the congressional route. In May 1905 Secretary of Agriculture James Wilson asked the attorney general three questions prepared, of course, in the Forest Service (Pinchot [1947] 1972, 270)—concerning "an application for the use of forest reserve land in Alaska for a fish saltery, oil, and fertilizer plant." Could such a permit be issued? Could the permit be for longer than one year? Could he "require reasonable compensation or rental for such permit?" When all three answers came back in the affirmative, Pinchot had his authority. If fees could be charged for fish saltery permits, they could be charged for grazing permits! But the fight was not yet over, and when fees were assessed beginning January 1, 1906, the stock owners sued. After protracted litigation the Supreme Court in 1911 overturned lower court precedent and confirmed Pinchot's position (*Grimaud v. United States, United States v. Light*):

First, the Court found that congressional authority over the public lands is plenary and that the 1891 [Forest Reserve] and 1897 [Forest Management] acts passed by the Congress providing for reservation and administration of the national forests were constitutional. Second, the

[C]ourt held that the authority given the Secretary to regulate use of the forest reserves was not, as the stockmen had argued, an unconstitutional delegation of legislative power. Third, the Court concluded that the authority to charge for a grazing permit is implied both in the 1897 act and in other acts disposing of revenues from the national forests. Finally, the Court held that any previous implied license to graze stock on public lands did not confer any vested right on the users, nor did it deprive the United States [of] the power of recalling such licenses. (Dana and Fairfax 1980, 88, 89)

From that day forward, the Forest Service had a firm legal basis for managing grazing within the reserves, but the fee issue would never disappear.

IMPLEMENTING THE SYSTEM

Four years before the Transfer Act, Pinchot had employed Albert F. Potter to administer the grazing branch within the (then) Bureau of Forestry. Potter was a sheepman, secretary of the eastern division of the Arizona Wool Growers Association, defender of sheepherder's rights, and instigator (at least in part) of the Coville-Pinchot investigation of 1900. His performance as a rational advocate of the grazing interests had greatly impressed Pinchot, so—"if you can't lick 'em, join 'em." Until the reserves were transferred to Agriculture, Potter and Pinchot offered advice to Secretary of the Interior Wilson; after the transfer, Potter was prepared to follow his own advice (Rowley 1985, 38, 39).

Potter translated the findings of scientific studies into workable policies and programs. He served the Forest Service until his retirement in 1920, becoming assistant forester and chief of the grazing branch in 1907, associate chief forester in 1910, and acting chief forester during World War II.

Potter's soft, unemphatic, knowledgeable speech, his thorough mastery of his business, his quiet, persistent steadiness, his complete fearlessness and fairness, gave him a standing and an influence that were remarkable....As head of the Branch of Grazing,...[he] was more than able to meet any sheepmen or cattlemen on their own ground. He was the cornerstone upon which we built the whole structure of grazing control. (Pinchot [1947] 1972, 181, 182)

In 1902, still prior to the transfer, the Interior Department issued a policy statement stipulating the order of preference to be followed in awarding grazing permits:

...stock "of all kinds" would receive preference in the following order:

1. Stock of residents within the reserve.
2. Stock of persons who own permanent stock ranches within the reserve, but who reside outside the reserve.
3. Stock of persons living in the immediate vicinity of the reserve, called neighboring stock.
4. Stock of outsiders who have some equitable claim. (Rowley 1985, 47)

This policy, which undoubtedly had Pinchot's and Potter's blessing, became one of the cornerstones of the Forest Service grazing program for decades to come (Rowley 1985, 47). By emphasizing the desirability of a secure and permanent nearby base, it virtually eliminated the nomadic graziers from the reserves—forcing these more controversial users (usually sheepherders) onto the already overgrazed adjacent public domain (Voigt 1976, 46). It also recognized one of the principles in John Wesley Powell's *Report on the Lands of the Arid Region of the United States* (Powell 1962, 32)—that users of public pasturage require a lowland base of irrigable land.

A second cornerstone of the Forest Service grazing policy was an analysis of the land's capability to support stock. In 1908 Potter provided instructions to local forest officials, based "upon a close physical observation of the land, water resources, type of forage, climatic conditions, the manner of handling, and a 'consideration of the interests involved'...[—] the economic and political impact...upon the local stock industry" (Rowley 1985, 69). Preference and capability met in an annual working plan, prepared by each forest supervisor, which also discussed enforcement activities, game protection, activities of livestock associations, and other topics (Rowley 1985, 74-76).

The basic planning policy related to grazing on the forest reserves and their successors, the national forests, has changed little since this early development. Through the years the same issues arise over and over again—fee schedules, bias toward small or large producers, permitted numbers of livestock, and competitive uses.

A WORD ABOUT POWELL

In these days of extreme specialization and high technology, we have difficulty envisioning, much less appreciating, the breadth of inquiry pursued and the magnitude of operations executed by natural resource pioneers of the late nineteenth century. John Wesley Powell was one of these. A teacher, scientist (geologist, anthropologist, ethnologist, conchologist, and hydrologist, among others), army officer, bureaucrat, politician, writer, and philosopher, he grasped and conveyed an understanding of arid land behavior that was to form the foundation of land and water management in the West. Unfortunately he also suffered the lot of many who get too far in front of the troops—many of his ideas were ignored or opposed for decades, and some have only lately become appreciated.

Born on March 24, 1834, in Mount Morris, New York, Powell was the son of a Methodist minister. Preaching being what it was (and is), the reverend's profession took him successively through New York, Ohio, Wisconsin, and Illinois, and he spent much time away from his family. John (Wes) was left to run the farm, which furnished the family's primary source of financial support (Gilbert 1903, 633). As the son of an avowed abolitionist, he did not get along well with his schoolmates, fought regularly, and was eventually withdrawn from public school and placed in a small private school run by a Calvinist neighbor, George Crookham. There he was introduced to scientific inquiry through field trips and experimentation—novel forms of education in that day (Goetzmann 1966, 532).

At the age of eighteen, Powell began his teaching career—short of a college education and in a one-room country school. He was determined to go to college, however, and spent the next seven years teaching, attending college (Illinois College, Illinois Institute, and Oberlin College), and traveling (U.S. Department of the Interior, Geological Survey 1969, 4). He traversed much of Wisconsin, Illinois, Iowa, and Missouri on foot, collecting all manner of plant, shell, mineral, and fossil specimens and expanding his largely independent education (Gilbert 1903, 633). His reputation as an explorer and collector grew, and he was elected secretary of the Illinois Natural History Society (Goetzmann 1966, 532).

By 1860 he had become superintendent of the Hennepin, Illinois, schools, but war interrupted his career, and in 1861 he enlisted as a private in the Twentieth Illinois Infantry. Soon thereafter the unit was moved to Camp Girardeau, near St. Louis, and Powell was given the responsibility to fortify the camp and town and to recruit and train a company to man the siege guns. During the battle of Shiloh, on April 6, 1862, Powell raised his arm to signal the battery to fire and was struck in the wrist by a Minnieball—an injury that cost him his right arm (U.S.

Department of the Interior, Geological Survey 1969, 5, 6). The wound caused him much pain and inconvenience through his later life but, as one author put it, may have been a mixed blessing:

> On the one hand, the wounded arm caused him at various periods much pain, and thus weakened an exceptionally strong constitution. On the other, he was led in early manhood to employ an amanuensis [secretary] and the resulting freedom from the mechanical factor in writing was a distinct advantage to his literary work. (Gilbert 1903, 633)

Returning to duty Powell became commanding officer of the Seventh Army Corps artillery brigade and rose to the rank of brevet lieutenant colonel (though he preferred the title "Major") before leaving the military in January 1865 (U.S. Department of the Interior, Geological Survey 1969, 6, 7).

He became a professor of geology at Illinois Wesleyan University, where he taught botany, zoology, comparative anatomy, entomology, natural philosophy, and logic of natural science in addition to geology—employing the techniques learned from Crookham (Goetzmann 1966, 534), but he moved to Illinois State Normal University in 1866 (Powell 1962, xxvi). There he "organized the first important geological excursion of American students, taking a party of sixteen to the mountain region of Colorado...before the building of the transcontinental railways, and the journey across the plains was long" (Gilbert 1903, 634). Funding for the expedition illustrates Powell's ability to "put together a package." The Illinois Museum of Natural History allocated $500; the Illinois Industrial University provided $500; the Chicago Academy of Sciences furnished $100; and the Smithsonian Institution loaned the scientific equipment—all the foregoing in return for specimens and data. He obtained rations from army posts at government rates, rode the railroads free, and contributed his own salary to ease the financial burden (U.S. Department of the Interior, Geological Survey 1969, 8, 9). Following this prolonged "field trip," Powell's students returned home, while he remained in the West to begin his next career (Gilbert 1903, 634).

Of Powell's western adventures, the most famous were his boat trips on the Colorado River. In 1869 Powell completed the first successful transit of the Grand Canyon and laid the political and financial foundation for much of his later career:

> The undertaking was...of phenomenal boldness and its successful accomplishment a dramatic triumph. It produced a strong impression on the public mind and gave Powell a national reputation which was afterwards

of great service, although based on an adventurous episode by no means essential to his career as an investigator. (Gilbert 1903, 634)

The second expedition, in 1871, was to last one and one-half years. Provisions were cached along the route, and much of 1870 was spent determining supply routes and establishing friendly relations with the Indians (three men of the first expedition had been killed by Indians who refused to believe that they had traveled down the river) (U.S. Department of the Interior, Geological Survey 1969, 15). During these reconnaissances Powell developed an understanding of Indian culture and a deep interest in Indian ethnology—a subject that came to mean far more to him than did geology (Goetzmann 1966, 554, 555).

With the exception of Almon H. Thompson, a surveyor and Powell's brother-in-law, and E. O. Beaman, an experienced photographer, most of the expedition's members were inexperienced, nonprofessional friends and relatives (U.S. Department of the Interior, Geological Survey 1969, 15). Comments of expedition artist Frederick S. Dellenbaugh illustrate the simplicity of life and attention to detail that characterized the endeavor:

...our supplies were flour, beans, bacon, dried apples, and dried peaches, tea, and coffee, with, of course, plenty of sugar. Canned goods at the time were not common, and besides, would have been too heavy. Bread must be baked three times a day in the Dutch oven....It was Andy's first experience as a cook....

The white boats [figure 4.1] were thoroughly gone over with caulking iron and paint. Upon the decks of the cabins, canvas, painted green, was stretched in such a way that it could be unbuttoned at the edges on three sides and thrown back when we wanted to take off the hatches. When in place this canvas kept the water, perfectly, out of the hatch joints. Each boat had three compartments, the middle one being about four feet long, about one-fifth the length of the boat, which was twenty-two feet over the top. Two places were left for the rowers, before and abaft the middle compartment, while the steersman with his long oar thrust behind was to sit on the deck of the after-cabin.... [W]hen the hatches were firmly in place and the canvases drawn taut over the decks, even if a boat turned over, as was expected might be the case, the contents of these cabins would remain intact and dry.... [E]verything was carefully put in rubber sacks, each having a soft mouth inside a double lip with a row of eyelets in each lip through which ran a strong cord. When the soft mouth was rolled up and the bag squeezed, the air was forced out, and the lips could be drawn to a bunch by means of the cord. When in this condition the bag could be soaked a long time in water without wetting the contents. Each rubber bag was encased in a heavy cotton one to protect it; in short, we spared no effort to render our provisions proof against the destroying elements. (Dellenbaugh 1908, 4-6)

FIGURE 4.1. Powell's 1871 Colorado River Expedition. The expedition leaving Green River Station, Wyoming. Major Powell is standing on the deck of the center boat. (Photo courtesy of the National Archives)

The second expedition completed much of the surveying begun in 1869, returning with much information, photographs (some stereoscopic), and notes (U.S. Department of the Interior, Geological Survey 1969, 16, 17). Powell frequently left the river expedition, delegating much of the work to Thompson while he ranged across the uplands and even returned to Washington to obtain additional funding and to purchase a house (Goetzmann 1966, 555, 556). The journey was concluded at the mouth of Kanab Creek, short of the Virgin River, reached by the earlier voyage, and Powell began the next facet of his life (U.S. Department of the Interior, Geological Survey 1969, 17). While the scientific data and information gathered on the expedition were monumental, of far greater import was Powell's realization that land use institutions and techniques developed in the humid East could not be successfully transplanted to the arid West. The rest of his life was devoted to espousing this doctrine (Goetzmann 1966, 562, 563).

During the 1870s four major surveys were being conducted in the West—Ferdinand Vandeveer Hayden's Geological and Geographical Survey of the Territories (Interior Department), Lieutenant George Montague Wheeler's Geographical Surveys West of the Hundredth Meridian (War Department), Clarence King's Geological Survey of the Fortieth Parallel (also War Department) (Powell 1962, vii), and Powell's (sponsored by the Smithsonian Institution [Goetzmann 1966, 556]). Intense rivalry developed among the expeditions, especially between civilian and military interests. Congress was unable to resolve the matter and in June 1878 called on the National Academy of Sciences for assistance (Powell 1962, xvii).

In making its recommendations the academy had access to Powell's *Report on the Lands of the Arid Region of the United States,* which contained not only a physiographic description but also Powell's personal philosophy of western land use, his criticism of the existing system of land allocation and land management, and even draft legislation to implement his ideas. (Note: Powell's original report was published in 1878 as H.R. Exec. Doc. 73, 45th Cong., 2d sess. It was reprinted in March 1879 with minor revisions and corrections. This latter version was reprinted in 1962, with annotations and an editor's introduction, by the Belknap Press of the Harvard University Press [Powell 1962] and is the basis of the discussion that follows.)

Powell divided the arid region of the West into three classes of lands—irrigable, timber, and pasturage—each with its distinctive characteristics and land use policy. He discussed the advantages of irrigation, the desirability of cooperative ventures to manage irrigation projects, and the need to construct large reservoirs (Powell 1962, 20-23). In describing timberlands Powell seemed obsessed with losses due to wildfire and failed to perceive demands of the coming century:

> [T]he timber regions are fully adequate to the growth of all the forests which the industrial interests of the country will require if they can be protected from desolation by fire. No limitation to the use of the forests need be made. The amount which the citizens of the country will require will bear but a small proportion to the amount which the fires will destroy; and if the fires are prevented, the renewal by annual growth will more than replace that taken by man. The protection of the forests of the entire Arid Region of the United States is reduced to one single problem—Can these forests be saved from fire? (Powell 1962, 27)

In his scheme of landownership and use based on land capability, societal interests were distributed geographically based on these resources:

The pasturage lands that in a general way intervene between the irrigable and timber lands have a scanty supply of dwarfed forests, as already described, and the people in occupying these lands will not resort, to any great extent, to the mountains for timber; hence timber and agricultural enterprises will be more or less differentiated; lumbermen and woodmen will furnish to the people below their supply of building and fencing material and fuel. In some cases it will be practicable for the farmers to own their timber lands, but in general the timber will be too remote, and from necessity such a division of labor will ensue. (Powell 1962, 29)

To the third class, pasturage lands, Powell devoted his greatest attention:

[T]here yet remain vast areas of valuable pasturage land bearing nutritious but scanty grass. The lands along the creeks and rivers have been relegated to that class which has been described as irrigable, hence the lands under consideration are away from the permanent streams. No rivers sweep over them and no creeks meander among their hills. (Powell 1962, 31)

To accommodate the needs of those using such lands, Powell suggested a complex social system. Each farm unit was to have a base of irrigable land "for gardens and fields where agricultural products can be raised... and where a store of grain and hay may be raised for their herds when pressed by the severe storms by which the country is sometimes visited" (1962, 32). As a source of pasturage, he recommended units that "must be of at least 2,560 acres, and in many districts they must be much larger" (p. 32)—far larger than the 160 acres authorized under the Timber Culture Act of 1873 and the Timber and Stone Act of 1878 or the 640 acres provided in the Desert Land Act of 1877 and amendments to the Homestead Act of 1862.

He correctly recognized that graziers without adequate hay lands and a protected lowland base were too susceptible to the vagaries of weather (as happened during the winters of the mid-1880s) and that extensive holdings were required to support a viable economic unit. To facilitate "local social organizations of civilization—as schools, churches, etc., and the benefits of cooperation in the construction of roads, bridges, and other local improvements," Powell proposed that the farm residences be grouped along the streams "to give the greatest possible number of water fronts" (Powell 1962, 34). Powell (p. 34) notes that the *métis* system of settlement, which evinced similar concepts and "divided the land into long narrow strips reaching back from a river frontage and merging with a large common pasture," was implemented in the arid lands of Saskatchewan and Manitoba and proved superior to the American rectangular grid system. Powell went further in attacking the public land survey, noting that its artificiality could circumscribe all water in several townships within one section, the owner of which would control the others. "[D]ivisional surveys should conform to the topography, and be so made as to give the greatest number of water fronts" (p. 33).

Although it is not clearly evident from the language, Powell's report had the effect of providing for "the reform of the notoriously corrupt General Land Office, the transfer of the cadastral surveys to the Coast and Geodetic Survey, the elimination of all contract surveying, and the consolidation of the geological and geographical surveys of the West into one bureau under the Department of the Interior" (Powell 1962, ix).

The first edition of the *Arid Lands* report was available to the National Academy of Sciences Committee, composed largely of Powell's friends, which in November 1878 recommended (not surprisingly) "consolidation of the four western surveys under Interior; elimination of the Office of Surveyor-General and of the practice of contracting land surveys; transfer of the land-parcelling surveys to the Coast and Geodetic Survey, and transfer of that Survey from Treasury to Interior" (Powell 1962, xvii). Bills implementing the academy's recommendations were drafted and introduced, but with one exception—consolidation of the western surveys into the United States Geological Survey—they failed. The western bloc in Congress saw Powell's proposals as favoring the big cattle rancher over the small rancher and an imposition of federal authority over local matters, and it defeated all other provisions. Thus only one, bureaucratic, recommendation emerged immediately from the *Arid Lands* report. Germs of ideas must also incubate, however, and traditional ways are hard to change. The thinking that Powell catalyzed developed (and was accepted by society) slowly, but it became the basis for much of western public land policy well into the twentieth century (Smith 1966, 60, 61).

Despite his active involvement in its creation, Powell did not become the first director of the Geological Survey—his past competitor and more recent ally Clarence King was awarded that position (U.S. Department of the Interior, Geological Survey 1969, 18; Goetzmann 1966, 588, 589). Instead Powell, *of his own choosing,* moved on to pursue his interests in Indian ethnology, becoming director of "his" Bureau of Ethnology in the Smithsonian Institution (Powell 1962, xvii). In 1881 King resigned from the Geological Survey, and Powell was immediately named his successor—retaining directorship of the Bureau of Ethnology for life and administering both agencies until 1894 (Gilbert 1903, 635).

Powell's greatest power came as director of the Geological Survey during the late 1880s. Cold winters of the mid-1880s had destroyed many of the western cattle herds, and a severe drought during the summer of 1887 caused many farmers to consider irrigation—situations that Powell had correctly foreseen. The Irrigation Service, part of the Geological Survey, had the task of locating water sites, which local communities would then develop (Goetzmann 1966, 596). There followed a classic sequence of *intense public issue leading to congressional action creating an opportunity for large private profits limited by bureaucratic control.* Following "gusts of Populist oratory and clamors for government help," Congress passed the Joint Resolution of March 20, 1888, which directed the secretary of the interior through the Geological Survey to examine

> that portion of the arid regions of the United States where agriculture is carried on by means of irrigation, as to the natural advantages for the storage of water for irrigation purposes with the practicability of constructing reservoirs, together with the capacity of streams and the cost of construction and the capacity of reservoirs, and such other facts as bear on the question. (25 Stat. 619)

Powell now had the opportunity to implement his concept of western water development; he also could make owners of the lands benefited enormously wealthy. Rather than continuing the piecemeal approach practiced in the past, Powell embarked upon a "general topographical survey of the whole region and its interrelated watersheds[,]...the work of a decade at least" (Goetzmann 1966, 596, 597). Faced with immediate problems, westerners and their congressional representatives objected to such delays, but the full force of Powell's power dawned only belatedly. Hidden in the joint resolution were two amendments. The first, to forestall land speculation, "temporarily withdrew from settlement 'all lands made susceptible of irrigation' by the reservoirs and canals which the survey would designate"; the second, to provide a loophole, authorized the president to restore any of the withdrawn lands for entry under the Homestead Act. Together they closed 850 million acres of the public domain unless restored by the president, and he would not do so unless certified by Powell (Powell 1962, xxi). Powell had become czar of the public domain.

Such power was not to last, however, and western society was ready to accept neither the scientific logic of Powell's scheme nor his inordinate delay. Senator William Stewart of Nevada, once a staunch supporter, turned against him and set about dismantling his empire. Through the Sundry Civil Expenses Appropriation Bill of 1890, the $720,000 requested for the Irrigation Survey was reduced to $162,500—forcing abandonment of Powell's grand plan and a return to the previous practice of merely locating water development sites (Powell 1962, xxiii). Congress also eliminated the power to reserve irrigable land, reopening the public domain (U.S. Department of the Interior, Geological Survey 1969, 21). Then Stewart and his cronies turned on the Geological Survey itself, cutting $90,000 from its 1891 budget and further reducing appropriations in 1892. Powell saw the writing on the wall and resigned as director on May 4, 1894 (Goetzmann 1966, 597, 599).

During his waning years, he turned even from his love of Indian ethnology (though he remained director of the Bureau of Ethnology until his death), devoting his last eight years to psychology and natural philosophy and publishing two books on the subjects (Gilbert 1903, 639). After a number of years of poor health, he died at his summer home in Haven, Maine, on September 23, 1902, at the age of sixty-nine (U.S. Department of the Interior, Geological Survey 1969, 21). Grove Karl Gilbert, veteran of the Wheeler and Powell surveys (Goetzmann 1966, 566) and chief geologist of the Geological Survey (1889-1892) provides a fitting epitaph:

> To the nation he is known as an intrepid explorer, to a wide public as a conspicuous and cogent advocate of reform in the laws affecting the development of the arid West, to geologists as a pioneer in a new province of interpretation and the chief organizer of a great engine of research, to anthropologists as a leader in philosophic thought and the founder, in America, of the new regime. (Gilbert 1903, 640)

CLOSING THE FRONTIER:
THE TAYLOR GRAZING ACT

By the 1930s fees and a land use policy had been well established and accepted on Forest Service lands. Permits for specific numbers of animal units per month (AUMs) were let to landowners who had sufficient "base property" to support their herds, and grazing was limited to prevent damage to the range. But grazing on the public domain, under the jurisdiction of the Department of the Interior, continued largely uncontrolled (Public Land Law Review Commission 1970, 105, 106). Two factors combined to change the nation's policy toward homesteading and pasturage on the public domain. During the 1920s drought conditions forced abandonment of much of the arid land under homesteading—just as Powell had predicted—demonstrating the incapability of these areas to support traditional agriculture (Peffer 1951, 168). Between 1931 and 1933, livestock prices fell by 50 percent, forcing cattle ranchers to produce more stock for the same return, further overstocking the public domain and compounding the degradation of the range (Gates 1968, 607).

The solution fell to Congressman Edward T. Taylor of Colorado, a staunch advocate of conveying public lands to the states, an opponent of withdrawals for any conservationist objective, and an adversary of all those who advocated leasing the public domain. But by 1934 even Congressman Taylor had become convinced that individual citizens and the states were incapable of dealing with the situation and that "'conservation of the public domain under Federal leadership'" was required. Early in the first session of the Seventy-third Congress, Taylor introduced the bill that he later called "'the magna carta of American conservation'" (Peffer 1951, 216, 217, 220).

Western congressional representatives were torn between their opposition to expanding federalism and grazing fees and their support of homesteading on one hand and on the other, their recognition that the arid lands of the West were being destroyed by a combination of nature and mismanagement (Gates 1968, 611, 612). In the end reason prevailed, and the Taylor Grazing Act passed the House on April 11 and the Senate on June 12, 1934. Midway between these dates

> occurred what was later considered the most devastating of conceivable condemnations of past land policy. The dust storms of May 11 carried sands from the Western deserts to the sidewalks of New York and sifted them down around the dome of the Capitol in Washington. They provided what Senator Gore of Oklahoma later called 'the most tragic, the most impressive lobbyist, that [has] ever come to this Capital.' [But at the time,]...the dust storms received little mention in the Senate debates on the grazing bill. Their significance appears not to have been realized in this connection. (Peffer 1951, 220)

The act authorized the secretary of the interior to create grazing districts in suitable areas, to grant grazing permits for up to ten years, to lease disconnected tracts of grazing land to adjacent landowners, to cooperate with local associations of stock owners, and to enact regulations necessary for the law's implementation (Peffer 1951, 221). Lands proposed for inclusion in grazing districts were withdrawn from all forms of entry, but areas subsequently found to be more valuable for agricultural crops could be sold in 320-acre tracts. Isolated tracts of up to 760 acres and small mountainous or rough tracts of not over 160 acres could also be sold (Gates 1968, 611).

As enacted the withdrawal provisions applied to 80 million of the approximately 166 million acres then in the public domain, a little more than half of the area for which grazing licenses were subsequently requested. A 1936 amendment (49 Stat. 1976) increased the withdrawal area to 142 million acres, but by November 1935 President Franklin D. Roosevelt had withdrawn the remaining public lands in the coterminous United States, effectively ending large-scale entry of public lands there (Peffer 1951, 222-224). Homesteading in the lower forty-eight continued on a reduced scale, however. No stock-raising entries were filed after 1955, but 6,159 original homestead entries totaling 776,216 acres were filed between 1955 and 1966, more than 90 percent of which were in Alaska (Gates 1968, 613).

The Taylor Act provided that 25 percent of the grazing fees collected were to go to range improvements (if subsequently appropriated by the Congress), 25 percent were to go to the federal Treasury, and 50 percent were to be distributed to the states in which the lands were located. In contrast only 25 percent of the receipts from grazing and stumpage in the national forests went to the states (Gates 1968, 611)—but a 1947 amendment reduced the state share of Taylor Grazing Act fees to 12.5 percent, reversing the local political advantage.

While the land classification and leasing provisions of the Taylor Grazing Act brought administration of grazing on the public domain closer to the policies prescribed for Forest Service land—and to Powell's recommendations—there were sharp philosophical and political differences between the two programs. Forest Service personnel were largely technically trained, and proud of it. As a result they sometimes were ridiculed "for being mere college boys" (Rowley 1985, 152), but they adhered to Pinchot's theme of scientific resource management with a minimum of (outside) political meddling. The Interior Department's Division of Grazing, however, "was to stand out among new Federal agencies in that its appointees were not drawn from the major universities and law schools. Its chief officers[, by statute,] were selected from men who had been residents of public land states at least a year before receiving their appointments" (Gates 1968, 614).

Both the Forest Service and the Division of Grazing emphasized consultation with local grazing interests. The Division of Grazing relied on local advisory boards, elected by the stock owners themselves. The boards provided a source of local knowledge and experience (Penny and Clawson

[1962] 1968, 465) and, perhaps more important, a means of settling disputes and making decisions at the local level. As a result of their success, the boards were given statutory recognition in 1939 (53 Stat. 1002) and were organized into a National Advisory Board Council in 1940 to "'consider and make recommendations on grazing administration and problems of a national scope'" (Foss 1960, p. 61). Although they were only advisory, the boards "assured local users a large and determining part in the administration of the grazing districts" and ensured their cooperation in and support of the program (Peffer 1951, 231).

The Forest Service and its predecessor agencies in the Department of Agriculture had a comparable system. As early as 1902, grazing allotment permit recommendations from local wool growers' associations received official endorsement from the Forest Service (although forest supervisors retained the final decision-making authority), and the local associations assisted in enforcing rules and regulations on national forest land (Rowley 1985, 47). By 1910 the local boards were recognized in the Forest Service's manual *Use of the National Forest Reserves* (or simply the Use Book)—they were

> to receive notice of proposed action[s] and have an opportunity to be heard by the local Forest officer in reference to increase or decrease in the number of stock to be allowed for any year, the division of the range between different classes of stock or their owners, or the adoption of special rules to meet local conditions. (Rowley 1985, 80)

While the effectiveness of the advisory boards utilized by the Forest Service has varied with time, geography, and local conditions, their existence and consultation are now guaranteed by federal regulation (36 C.F.R. 222.2 (1992)) and by the current social, political, and legal realities of public natural resource management.

GRAZING FEES ON PUBLIC LAND

At least as early as 1925, the Forest Service was on record that forage resources in the forests should be treated as any other commodity, "sold at their commercial value[,]...worth just as much as private land" (Voigt 1976, 60). In contrast the Division of Grazing determined "[f]rom the outset...not to base fees for the use of public range within the [grazing] districts on their economic value" (Gates 1968, 614), basing fees instead on their administrative cost (Rowley 1985, 152). As a result Forest Service lease fees invariably were higher than Division of Grazing fees for comparable land. In 1963 the BLM charged $.19 per AUM, the Forest Service charged $.60, the Indian Bureau charged $1.25, and some private owners charged $3.00 (Gates 1968, 632). Under these conditions graziers understandably felt "closer" to the Department of the Interior than to Agriculture. Conversely the conservation lobby has felt closer to Agriculture, *at least regarding grazing on the public lands.*

In 1969 a program was begun to raise grazing fees to fair market value by 1980. By 1976 rates were as follows: BLM $1.51, Forest Service $1.60, private land (1975) $5.75 per AUM (Council on Environmental Quality 1976, 86, 87). The program did not achieve its objective in reference to private land, but during the decade of the 1970s BLM fee rates reached and surpassed those charged by the Forest Service (table 4.1).

Congress addressed the grazing fees issue in the Public Rangelands Improvement Act of 1978 (PRIA) (92 Stat. 1803), which established a statutory formula for setting grazing fees on public rangelands administered by the BLM and the Forest Service. For the grazing years 1979 through 1985, PRIA set a base rate of $1.23 per AUM

> multiplied by the result of the Forage Value Index (computed annually from data supplied by the Economic Research Service) added to the Combined Index (Beef Cattle Price Index minus the Price Paid Index) and divided by 100: Provided, That the annual increase or decrease in such fee for any given year shall be limited to not more than 25 per centum of the previous year's fee. (92 Stat. 1806)

The PRIA formula (1) created a uniform fee system for both agencies, (2) linked the fee to both range and market conditions, and (3) prevented large year-to-year fee fluctuations. It also increased grazing fees to $1.81 per AUM by 1990 and $1.97 in 1991 (Jamison 1991, 174).

TABLE 4.1

Grazing Fees Charged by the Forest Service and the Bureau of Land Management, 1960-1978 (Five-Year Averages)

Years	Forest Service	BLM
1960-1964	$ .42	$ .23
1965-1969	$ .43	$ .33
1970-1974	$ .64	$ .67
1975-1978[a]	$1.09	$1.31

Source: Marion Clawson, *The Federal Lands Revisited* (Washington, DC: Resources for the Future, 1983), pp. 281, 282.

[a]Forest Service data for 1979 are not included in the original table.

PRIA expired on December 31, 1985, but its grazing fee formula has been continued under Executive Order No. 12548 (22 WEEKLY COMP. PRES. DOC. 222 (Feb. 14, 1986), 51 Fed. Reg. 5985).

PRIA quieted criticism of agency bias, but it did not settle the controversy between those who wished to increase fees and those who wished to maintain or reduce existing levels. The former argued that "present fee levels either are (1) unfair to nonpermittees, or (2) result in a Federal subsidy to a small and economically insignificant number of permittees" (Obermiller 1991, 220). The latter maintained that the difference in fees charged for grazing on public and private land was offset by the quality of the land, the nature of improvements, and the general efficiency of use; that no real subsidy existed; and that raising fees would put many ranchers out of business (U.S. Congress, House 1991, 56, 69, 102).

Congress again addressed the grazing fee issue in 1987 and 1989 but failed to pass a bill (Obermiller 1991, 220). Four related bills were introduced in the Hundred and Second Congress (H.R. 481, H.R. 944, H.R. 1096, and H.R. 1292). The first two would have increased fees; H.R. 1292 would have retained the existing structure; and H.R. 1096 did not address the fee issue. H.R. 481 and H.R. 944 were uniformly opposed by ranchers and by the Bush administration (Jamison 1991, 175-177; U.S. Congress, House 1991, 178). A March 1991 hearing amassed 654 pages of testimony, most of which reiterated long-standing and well-known positions (U.S. Congress, House 1991). H.R. 1096 was the bill that emerged from committee. During more than three hours of floor debate, an attempt was made to insert provisions increasing grazing fees, but the final effect was merely to increase the allowable annual fluctuation from 25 percent (as per PRIA) to 33.3 percent (137 CONG. REC. H5692 (July 23, 1991)). H.R. 1096, as amended, passed the House on July 23, 1991, by a vote of 254 to 165 (14 not voting) (137 CONG. REC. H5703 (July 23, 1991)), and was sent to the Senate, and referred to the Committee on Energy and Natural Resources (137 CONG. REC. S10,768 (July 24, 1991)). Although reported out of committee during the last days of the Hundred and Second Congress no vote was taken, and the grazing issue awaits the Clinton administration and the Hundred and Third Congress.

THE NATIONAL GRASSLANDS

In 1954 the Forest Service received almost 4 million acres of rangeland acquired for the federal government during the 1930s by the Resettlement Administration. These marginal to submarginal farmlands were purchased as part of the New Deal programs of President Roosevelt in an effort to take people off farms that could not support them. Between 1938 and 1954, the Resettlement lands were administered by the Soil Conservation Service (SCS), which initiated soil and water conservation practices and extended grazing privileges to interested ranchers (Rowley 1985, 224, 225).

SCS grazing policies differed from those of the Forest Service. Whereas the Forest Service dealt directly with individual lessees and its policies concerned only federal land, the SCS worked through local grazing associations and incorporated private land conditions into its policy. Many Forest Service range management specialists found the SCS land use philosophy difficult to accept—fifty years of precedent was hard to overcome. Eventually, with the assistance of a number of former SCS employees who joined the Forest Service and some cooperative and forward-thinking range chiefs within the service, appropriate SCS policies and practices were adopted and inappropriate ones discarded. The resulting blend became management policy for the national grasslands. In 1975 the Forest Service and the Bureau of Land Management agreed to develop coordinated resource management plans for large areas of adjacent lands owned by the BLM, the Forest Service, and private citizens, extending the policy merger one additional step (Rowley 1985, 226-229). The BLM, within the Department of the Interior, had a different lineage and its own land use philosophy.

In the early days of the Forest Service and the BLM and their predecessors, a considerable gap existed between agencies of the Department of the Interior and those of the Department of Agriculture. Each had different resource management and personnel policies. Forest Service personnel had little contact with members of the Division of Grazing (Rowley 1985, 152, 153). Each took swipes at the other whenever convenient, and numerous attempts at jurisdictional piracy erupted in Congress over the years. Most of these problems have since been corrected, and currently some personnel of both agencies have "aptly compared this interagency sniping to a college football rivalry" (Culhane 1981, 105).

Similar progress has been made in the condition of rangelands managed by the Forest Service and the BLM, particularly since the 1975 evaluation (Council on Environmental Quality 1975, 212-214). Part of the improvement in range conditions on the public lands may be attributable to reduced grazing intensity. Between 1945 and 1985, the number of AUMs grazed in national forests declined by 35 to 40 percent (but rose by about 10 percent in 1985), and those provided by BLM lands decreased by 37 percent. However, credit also must be given to improved management, concerns for environmental quality, and increased emphasis on multiple use—particularly on BLM lands (Council on Environmental Quality 1985, 107).

While considerable progress in managing the public rangelands has been achieved, controversy remains and will always remain. Ranchers continue to resist efforts to reduce stocking levels and to increase multiple-use considerations, while conservation and environmental interests strive for the contrary (Council on Environmental Quality 1985, 108).

REFERENCES

Clawson, Marion. 1951. *Uncle Sam's Acres.* New York: Mead & Company.

———. 1983. *The Federal Lands Revisited.* Washington, DC: Resources for the Future.

Council on Environmental Quality. 1975. *Environmental Quality—1975.* Washington, DC: Government Printing Office.

———. 1976. *Environmental Quality—1976.* Washington, DC: Government Printing Office.

———. 1982. *Environmental Quality—1982.* Washington, DC: Government Printing Office.

———. 1985. *Environmental Quality—1985.* Washington, DC: Government Printing Office.

Coville, Fredrick V. 1898. *Forest Growth and Sheep Raising in the Cascade Mountains of Oregon.* Washington, DC: Government Printing Office.

Culhane, Paul J. 1981. *Public Lands Politics.* Washington, DC: Resources for the Future.

Dana, Samuel T., and Sally K. Fairfax. 1980. *Forest and Range Policy: Its Development in the United States.* New York: McGraw-Hill Book Company.

Dellenbaugh, Frederick S. 1908. *A Canyon Voyage: The Narrative of the Second Powell Expedition down the Green-Colorado River from Wyoming, and the Explorations on the Land, in the Years 1871 and 1872.* New York: Putnam.

Foss, Phillip O. 1960. *Politics and Grass.* Seattle: University of Washington Press.

Gates, Paul W. 1968. "History of Land Law Development." Public Land Law Review Commission study report. Washington, DC: Government Printing Office.

Gilbert, G. K. 1903. "John Wesley Powell." In "Annual Report of the Board of Regents of the Smithsonian Institution for the Year Ending June 30, 1902," 633-640. Washington, DC: Government Printing Office.

Goetzmann, William H. 1966. *Exploration and Empire.* New York: Alfred A. Knopf.

Hardin, Garrett. 1968. "The Tragedy of the Commons." *Science* 163:1243.

Ise, John. 1920. *The United States Forest Policy.* New Haven, CT: Yale University Press.

Jamison, Cy. 1991. "Statement of Cy Jamison, Bureau of Land Management, United States Department of the Interior, before the Subcommittee on National Parks and Public Lands, Committee on Interior and Insular Affairs, United States House of Representatives, on H.R. 481 and H.R. 944, Bills to Establish Grazing Fees for Domestic Livestock on the Public Rangelands." U.S. Congress, House, Committee on Interior and Insular Affairs, Subcommittee on National Parks and Public Lands, "BLM Reauthorization and Grazing Fees," 169-177. 102d Cong., 1st sess., March 12, 1991. Serial 102-2. Washington, DC: Government Printing Office.

National Academy of Sciences. 1897. "Senate Report of the National Academy of Sciences upon the Inauguration of a Forest Policy for the Forested Lands of the United States." 55th Cong., 1st sess. S. Doc. 105. Washington, DC: Government Printing Office.

Obermiller, Frederick W. 1991. "1991 Federal Grazing Fee Policy Debate." U.S. Congress, House, Committee on Interior and Insular Affairs, Subcommittee on National Parks and Public Lands, "BLM Reauthorization and Grazing Fees," 218-227. 102d Cong., 1st sess., March 12, 1991. Serial 102-2. Washington, DC: Government Printing Office.

Peffer, E. Louise. 1951. *The Closing of the Public Domain.* Stanford, CA: Stanford University Press.

Penny, J. Russell, and Marion Clawson. [1962] 1968. "Administration of Grazing Districts." In Carstenson, Vernon, ed., *The Public Lands,* 461-477. Madison: University of Wisconsin Press.

Pinchot, Gifford. [1947] 1972. *Breaking New Ground.* Seattle: University of Washington Press.

Powell, John W. 1962. *U.S. Geographical and Geological Survey of the Rocky Mountain Region: Report on the Lands of the Arid Region of the United States.* Cambridge, MA: Harvard University Press, Belknap Press.

Public Land Law Review Commission. 1970. *One Third of the Nation's Land.* Washington, DC: Government Printing Office.

Rowley, William D. 1985. *U.S. Forest Service Grazing and Rangelands.* College Station: Texas A&M University Press.

Smith, Frank E. 1966. *The Politics of Conservation.* New York: Pantheon Books.

Stoddart, Laurence A., A. D. Smith, and Thadis W. Box. 1975. *Range Management.* 3d ed. New York: McGraw-Hill Book Company.

U.S. Congress. House. Committee on Interior and Insular Affairs. Subcommittee on National Parks and Public Lands. 1991. "BLM Reauthorization and Grazing Fees." 102d Cong., 1st sess., March 12, 1991. Serial 102-2. Washington, DC: Government Printing Office.

U.S. Department of Agriculture. Forest Service. 1984. "Appraisal Report Estimating Fair Market Value of Grazing on Public Lands." 2 vols. Washington, DC: Government Printing Office.

U.S. Department of the Interior. Geological Survey. 1969. *John Wesley Powell: Soldier, Explorer, Scientist.* Washington, DC: Government Printing Office.

Voigt, William, Jr. 1976. *Public Grazing Lands.* New Brunswick, NJ: Rutgers University Press.

Wellman, P. I. 1939. *The Trampling Herd.* New York: Carrick and Evans.

CHAPTER V

Forestlands and National Forests

National forest policy began with the concept of "reservation"—that these renewable resources could be withdrawn and protected from private exploitation, to be used at some time in the future for public purposes. Initially the forests (actually the trees) were treated as nonrenewable resources, their supply conserved and stretched over as much time as possible, with little regard for their dynamic nature. During the last decade of the nineteenth century and the first decade of the twentieth century there followed a period of intense debate over the purpose and management policy governing the forests. During this time "forest management," the intentional manipulation of the forest ecosystem, and "scientific forestry," efforts to increase the quantity and improve the quality of forest products, entered the picture. The current phase began after World War II, with increased utilization of national forest land by an increasingly diverse population of users and with efforts to diversify production accordingly.

RESERVES

Early efforts toward reservation of timberlands were motivated by national defense needs. In time the concept of reservation broadened to encompass much more, and timber production became entwined with land ethics.

Early Naval Reserves

From before the Revolution to the coming of the ironclads, efforts were taken to reserve to the central government sufficient timber resources to sustain a viable navy of wooden-hulled ships. The British government was painfully aware that the security of England lay in its navy and merchant marine. The quality timber had long since been removed from the forests of the British Isles, and efforts toward reforestation and stand improvement in the Royal Forests had been unsuccessful. Timber for masts was in particularly short supply, and the vast forests of the New World appeared to contain the solution. Even in America, however, trees of sufficient quality for masts were uncommon—not surprisingly, high-quality timber was also in demand for domestic shipbuilding and construction timbers (Dana and Fairfax 1980, 5). In order to protect what remained of this resource and to ensure a continuing supply for the Royal Navy, a provision was inserted into the 1691 Charter of Massachusetts Bay:

> *And lastly* for the better provideing and furnishing of Masts for Our Royall Navy Wee doe hereby reserve to Vs Our Heires and Successors all Trees of the Diameter of Twenty Four Inches and vpwards of Twelve Inches from the ground growing vpon any soyle or Tract of Land within Our said Province or Territory not heretofore granted to any private persons And Wee doe restraine and forbid all persons whatsoever from felling cutting or destroying any such Trees without the Royall Lycence of Vs Our Heires and Successors first had and obteyned vpon penalty of Forfeiting One Hundred Pounds sterling vnto Ous Our Heires and Successors for every Tree soe felled cutt or destroyed without such Lyence. (Swindler 1975, 5: 87)

The same charter joined the Maine Territory, Plymouth Colony, and Massachusetts Bay Colony to form the province of Massachusetts; New Hampshire had become a separate royal province in 1679 (*Encyclopedia Americana* 1978, 18:411a, 20:179). Such trees were marked with three blazes forming a broad arrow, the symbol of the British navy. In 1711 the "Broad Arrow Policy" was extended to include all of New England, New Jersey, and New York (Dana and Fairfax 1980, 5). Even with the heavy penalties prescribed for unauthorized cutting, the Broad Arrow Policy was a failure. It simply ran counter to accepted concepts of freedom in the colonies. Trespass was common, enforcement lax, and public opinion hostile (Gates 1968, 532).

Despite this precedent the United States was to adopt a similar policy within two decades of its creation—with similar results. In 1799 Congress appropriated $200,000 for the purchase of timber or timber-lands as a reserve for the navy (Dana [1956] 1968, 74). Live oak was of particular interest, for the spreading form of this species produced natural ribs and knees, and the species was remarkably resistant to rot. In 1799 the supply available to the United States Navy was deemed adequate, but by 1815 the stocks in Virginia, the Carolinas, and Georgia were seriously depleted (Hutchins 1941, 88, 89, 91). Two islands off the coast of Georgia containing "fair amounts of live oak" were therefore purchased and became the first "forest reserves" of the new nation (Dana [1956] 1968, 74). Subsequently the practice was extended to Alabama, where the Louisiana Purchase provided extensive resources of live oak and red cedar, and to Florida, which contained vast stands of live oak. In Alabama 19,000 acres were withdrawn from the public domain; in Florida acquisition was through a combination of withdrawal and purchase (Gates 1968, 533). While the naval timber reserve concept existed on paper until 1923, the program was never really successful. Timber poaching and entry were commonplace and graft and corruption rampant. By 1831 Congress had authorized fines up to triple the value of the timber cut, prison terms of one year, and payment of one-half of the fines to informers (Acts of March 19, 1828, and March 2, 1831), but to little avail. As the nineteenth century progressed, changes in naval construction, an abundance of alternate timber resources, and public opposition and lagging congressional support all contributed to the demise of the naval timber reserves (Gates 1968, 533).

In 1843 reservations in Louisiana were set aside or annulled (Gates 1968, 533). Most lands in Florida were restored to the unreserved public domain in 1879. Those in Alabama and Mississippi and the remainder of the Florida reservations were abolished in 1895, and the last 3,000 acres (in Louisiana) were relinquished in 1923 (Dana [1956] 1968, 77). Despite its ineffectiveness the naval timber reserve policy illustrated the importance of the public domain as a source of raw materials and the complete authority of Congress to exercise control over those lands in the national interest. It also showed that natural resource policies (and other public policies) cannot be successful without public support—in this case trespass on the public domain was an accepted way of life, and the resources it contained appeared inexhaustible (Dana and Fairfax 1980, 35).

The Beginnings of Forest Reserves

The concept of forest reserves, or preserves, began to develop in a more general sense during the mid-1800s. The first applications were not in the federal public domain but on state-owned lands in New York. Following more than a decade of concern over destruction of forests in the Adirondacks, the law of 1885 established a state Forest Commission and the Adirondack and Catskill Forest Preserves. These lands, decreed the legislature, "shall be forever kept as wild forest lands. They shall not be sold, nor shall they be leased or taken by any person or corporation, public or private" (Widner 1968, 7-9).

Almost immediately the newly created Forest Commission was confronted by those who wished to leave the preserve lands alone, relying upon nature to heal the wounds of lumbering and fire, and those who believed in protection from fire and trespass but felt that timber on the reserves should be harvested. The first round was won by the lumber lobbies, and in 1893 the Forest Commission was authorized to sell timber from the forest preserves. Preservation interests responded with force, however, and on January 1, 1895, the New York Act of 1885 (amended to conclude "nor shall the timber therein be sold, removed, or destroyed") became article VII, section 7, of the New York State Constitution by a vote of 122 to 0 in a state constitutional convention (Widner 1968, 10, 11). New York had decided that it would have reserves and that they would be "preserves" in which the timber resources would be protected and not harvested. The federal government and every other state were to face the same issue, with varying results.

The Forest Reserve Act of 1891

By the early 1880s, continued exploitation of the nation's timber resources and trespassing on the public domain had attracted the attention of Congress and a number of influential citizens. Charles S. Sargent, a Harvard professor, prepared a report, "Forests of America," for the census of 1880, containing alarmingly low estimates of remaining stands of white pine in the Lake states (Gates 1968, 563). In 1876 Bernhard Eduard Fernow, the first professionally trained forester to visit the United States, came to see the Philadelphia Centennial Exposition—and stayed (Widner 1968, 26). The secretary of agriculture established a Division of Forestry in 1883, and President Grover Cleveland appointed Fernow head of the division in 1885 (Gates 1968, 565)—Fernow is also credited with teaching the first forestry course in the United States, at Massachusetts Agricultural College in 1887 (Cook ca. 1961, cited in Widner 1968, 129). The American Forestry Association was formed in 1887, held a number of forestry congresses, and lobbied for better forestry legislation (Gates 1968, 563, 566). State forestry agencies were created in New York, California, Colorado, and Ohio in 1885 (Widner 1968, 8-9). After fifteen years of unsuccessful attempts to obtain meaningful forest reserve legislation (Dana and Fairfax 1980, 55), these interests persuaded Secretary of the Interior John W. Noble to suggest the addition of section 24 to the act of 1891 (Gates 1968, 565). This section was attached to the bill in violation of a rule prohibiting such action by a conference committee and passed with little debate on March 3, 1891, during the closing hours of the session (Dana and Fairfax 1980, 56, 57). It stated:

> Section 24. That the President of the United States may, from time to time, set apart and reserve, in any State or Territory having public land bearing forests, in any part of the public lands wholly or in part covered with timber or undergrowth, whether of commercial value or not, as public reservations, and the President shall, by public proclamation, declare establishment of such reservations and the limits thereof. (26 Stat. 1103)

Other parts of the act of 1891 (the Forest Reserve Act) extended provisions of the Free Timber Act and the Timber and Stone Act to all public land states—spreading opportunities for graft, corruption, and destruction of the public forests—and repealed the Timber Culture Act and the Preemption Act—constructive changes (Dana and Fairfax 1980, 57). The act is most remembered, however, as the first clear congressional authorization to establish forest reserves from the public domain.

Within a month of the Forest Reserve Act's passage, President Benjamin Harrison withdrew 1,239,040 acres of the public domain north and east of Yellowstone National Park for the Yellowstone National Park Timberland Reserve (26 Stat., Proclamation No. 17; amended by 27 Stat., Proclamation No. 6). During the remainder of his administration, Harrison designated fourteen additional forest preserves (27 Stat., Proclamation Nos. 8, 12, 15, 21, 28, 29, 37, 38, 40, 43, 44, 45, 47, 48), totaling an additional 13,053,440 acres. President Cleveland added two more areas with a combined area of 4,501,300 acres in 1893 (28 Stat., Proclamation Nos. 6, 7; General Land Office 1893, cited in Gates 1968, 567, 568) and thirteen additional areas with a gross area of 21.3 million acres during the closing days of his administration (29 Stat., Proclamation Nos. 19-31) (Dana and Fairfax 1980, 60).

PRESERVES OR MANAGED FORESTS?

By the end of the nineteenth century, actual and potential users of the forest reserves were beginning to actively debate policy and ethical considerations affecting their use—a debate which continues today.

The National Forest Commission and the Cleveland Reserves

Congress had clearly declared its intention that some of the public domain be reserved to protect its forest resources, and the executive branch was anxious to oblige. By the end of Cleveland's second administration (1897), the forest reserves contained more than 39 million acres (Hibbard 1924, cited in Johnson and Barlowe [1954] 1979, 65). Yet the guidelines for selecting potential forest reserves, the criteria for subsequent use, and the administration for management did not exist. The first professional assistance in developing policy for the forest preserves came from the National Forest Commission, established by the National Academy of Sciences in 1896 upon request of Secretary of the Interior Hoke Smith. Seven distinguished men composed the commission, including Charles S. Sargent, mentioned previously; William H. Brewer, a distinguished Yale botanist; Alexander Agassiz, mine administrator, zoologist, and patron of science (son of Jean Louis Agassiz, eminent nineteenth-century naturalist and founder of the Museum of Comparative Zoology [now the Agassiz Museum] at Harvard University [*Encyclopedia Americana* 1978, 1:329]); Oliver Wolcott Gibbs, president of the academy; and Gifford Pinchot (Gates 1968, 568). Although the commission's report was released too late to influence passage of the Forest Management Act in early 1897 (Dana and Fairfax 1980, 60), its findings were "leaked" prematurely to the president (over Pinchot's objections), precipitating hasty action to create the thirteen additional Cleveland Reserves. The commission's findings and recommendations were noteworthy, however, and must have influenced the thinking of Pinchot and others involved in developing national forest policy during this critical time. The commission's report stated that (1) the forest reserves belonged to, and should be managed for, all the people; (2) steep slopes should not be cleared; (3) grazing of sheep should be regulated; (4) lands better suited for mining or agriculture should be eliminated from the reserves; (5) mature timber should be cut and sold; and (6) settlers and miners should be allowed to cut only such timber as they needed. The commission also criticized the administration of the reserves—patronage, low pay, insecurity, poor quality of personnel—and recommended remedies (Gates 1968, 560, 568).

Cleveland's precipitous creation of the thirteen forest reserves (without local or congressional coordination and including towns, cities, developments, and millions of acres of land suitable for agriculture) caused a storm of protest in Congress. A spate of legislative maneuvering ensued to nullify Cleveland's action and to modify the manner in which reserves could be established and vacated. The end result of this skirmishing was Cleveland's pocket veto of the appropriations bill (to which the forest reserve provisions had been attached) shortly before William McKinley was inaugurated, leaving the new president with no funds to run the government and the forest issues unresolved. McKinley had no choice but to call a special session of Congress (Dana and Fairfax 1980, 60, 61). On June 4, 1897, McKinley had his funds, and the forest reserves had their first organic legislation.

The Forest Management Act of 1897 (The Organic Act)

Among the most significant provisions of the Forest Management Act (Organic Administration Act, or Organic Act) were the following:

> That to remove any doubt which may exist pertaining to the authority of the President thereunto, the President of the United States is...authorized...to revoke, modify, or suspend any and all...Executive orders...establishing any forest reserve as he shall deem best for the public interests,...and by such modification may reduce the area or change the boundary lines..., or may vacate altogether any order creating such forest reserve. (30 Stat. 34, 36)

> No public forest reservation shall be established, except to improve and protect the forest within the reservation, or for the purpose of securing favorable conditions of water flows, and to furnish a continuous supply of timber for use and necessities of the citizens of the United States; but it is not the purpose or intent of these provisions...to authorize the inclusion therein of lands more valuable for the minerals therein, or for agricultural purposes, than for forest purposes. (30 Stat. 35)

> For the purpose of preserving the living and growing timber and promoting younger growth on forest reservations, the Secretary of the Interior, under such rules and regulations as he shall prescribe, may cause to be designated and appraised so much of the dead, matured, or large growth of trees found on such forest reservations as may be compatible with utilization of the forests thereon, and he may sell the same for not less than the appraised value....Such timber, before being sold, shall be marked and designated, and shall be cut and removed under the supervision of some person appointed by the Secretary....(30 Stat. 35)

> The Secretary...may permit...the use of timber and stone found upon such reservations, free of charge, by bona fide settlers, miners, residents, and

prospectors for minerals, for firewood, fencing, buildings,...and other domestic purposes; such timber to be used within the State or Territory...where such national forest may be located. (30 Stat. 35)

All waters on such reservations may be used for domestic mining, milling, or irrigation purposes, under the laws of the State..., or under the laws of the United States and the rules...established thereunder. (30 Stat. 36)

[A]ny public lands embraced within...any such forest reservation which...shall be found better adapted for mining or for agricultural pur- poses than for forest usage, may be restored to the public domain. And any mineral lands in any forest reservation which have been shown to be such, and subject to entry under the existing mining laws of the United States..., shall continue to be subject to such location and entry, notwith- standing provisions herein contained. (30 Stat. 36)

The Organic Act clarified the role of the forest reserves—to protect the forests so that citizens may have a reliable supply of water and tim- ber. It established a system of relative values for determining whether an area should become, or be retained within, a reserve—if the area's value as a forest resource was greater than its value for mineral extraction or agriculture, it should; otherwise, it should not. The act continued the practice of permitting local residents to use the timber, stone, and water on the reserves, subject to state and federal regulation, and it declared mineral lands within the reserves subject to entry. (Note: The Organic Act speaks of "forest reserves." The designation was changed to "national forests" by the Agricultural Appropriations Act of 1907 and appears as such in the United States Code.)

Another section of the Organic Act suspended creation of Cleveland's thirteen forest reserves (except for the two in California) until March 1, 1898 (30 Stat. 34). Although this action permitted entry for another year, very little area was lost (Pinchot [1947] 1972, 117). Further, the act authorized the secretary of the interior to sell "dead, matured, or large growth of trees" in the national forests provided that they had been indi- vidually "marked and designated" (30 Stat. 35). Pinchot ([1947] 1972) noted that these provisions created "another door wide open for the forester" ([1947] 1972, 117). Future events proved Pinchot in error on this point. More than seventy years later, conservation groups were to use these restrictions on timber sales to contest the Forest Service's clear-cutting prac- tices (*West Virginia Division of the Izaak Walton League of America v. Butz, Zieske v. Butz*), "those old and unnoticed phrases in that much-praised statute came to haunt the Forest Service" (Dana and Fairfax 1980, 316).

Despite these minor difficulties, the act of 1897 settled for all time the question of whether the reserves were to be "preserves" or "managed forests" and remains the primary organic legislation governing administration of the National Forest System today (Dana and Fairfax 1980, 62).

A WORD ABOUT PINCHOT

There were no American foresters in the 1890s. The pure biological sciences—zoology, botany, and geology—were taught in this country, but the applied natural sciences—forestry, wildlife management, and range science—were slow in coming. Professional forestry was practiced in Europe, however (though under much different social, ecological, and economic conditions than existed in the New World), and the first foresters in the United States were European trained. Gifford Pinchot was one of these. A product of upstate Pennsylvania and of a father with a keen interest in forestry (Widner 1968, 26, 100), Pinchot was trained at the French Forestry School at Nancy by Sir Dietrich Brandis (Widner 1968, 82n.) and returned to this country in 1890. One of his early jobs was to prepare management plans for several tracts of forestland in New York, during which time he met and became friends with the governor, Theodore Roosevelt (Whipple 1935, cited in Widner 1968, 92). In the following year, he was offered a position as assistant to Bernhard Fernow (head of the new Division of Forestry), but he turned it down to "take to the forest instead" (Pinchot [1947] 1972, 49). He journeyed south to the Biltmore Estate, near Asheville, North Carolina,

> a little over 7,000 acres of rolling hills and bottom lands on both sides of the French Broad River...[which] had been put together from small impoverished farms, the forest on which had been burned, slashed, and overgrazed until it was little more than the shadow of its former self. In Europe I had seen nothing like it, but millions of acres east of the Mississippi were its brothers and sisters. (Pinchot [1947] 1972, 50)

The Biltmore Experience

The Biltmore Estate had been established by George W. Vanderbilt, the railroad tycoon, and designed by Frederick Law Olmsted (we shall meet him again). Olmsted, in turn, was responsible for attracting Pinchot to Biltmore in December 1891 (Widner 1968, 82, ed. note).

Despite the gloomy predictions of Fernow ("If you can 'make forestry *profitable*' under the conditions at Biltmore within the next ten years, I shall consider you the wisest forester and financier of the age") (Pinchot [1947] 1972, 50), and the inapplicability of much of his European training (Dana and Fairfax 1980, 52, 53), Pinchot's activities at Biltmore were a success.

In 1895 Pinchot hired a young German forester, (Carl) Alvin Schenck, to assist him at Biltmore. Schenck apparently never really fit in ("Schenck had very much to learn....I did my best to break him in, but never quite succeeded....[H]e had far less understanding of the mountaineers than he had of the mountains and the woods"). He lasted two years with Pinchot, and another two with Vanderbilt, before being discharged in 1899. During his short tenure, however, Schenck established the first forestry school in the United States (figure 5.1), taking his first students in 1896, opening the Biltmore Forest School in 1897, and continuing operations until 1913 (Pinchot [1947] 1972, 65).

Sometime in 1892 or 1893, Joseph A. Holmes, the state geologist of North Carolina, suggested to Pinchot that the federal government should

FIGURE 5.1. The Biltmore Forest School. Carl A. Schenck (third from left) with students in front of the nation's first forestry school near Asheville, North Carolina. (Forest History Society photo courtesy of Champion-International Corporation)

purchase timberland in the southern Appalachian Mountains and practice forestry on it (Pinchot [1947] 1972, 56). In 1916 the Pisgah Forest, a tract of some 100,000 acres "beyond the Biltmore Estate" purchased by Vanderbilt in 1895, was acquired by the United States government to form the Pisgah National Forest (Pinkett 1970, 28, 29; Frome 1984, 24)—the nucleus of the National Forest System in the Southeast and the fulfillment of Holmes's dream.

The Pinchot Philosophy

Pinchot left Biltmore in 1898 to succeed Fernow as head of the Division of Forestry (Dana and Fairfax 1980, 65). Fernow, in turn, joined the faculty of Cornell University, where he founded the first professional school of forestry in an American university (Whipple 1935, cited in Widner 1968, 93). The division was renamed the Bureau of Forestry in 1901 (Dana and Fairfax 1980, 80). During this period Pinchot became embroiled in efforts to clarify policy governing the forest reserves and to transfer the reserves to the Department of Agriculture. His basic philosophy was technical and utilitarian—forests generate products that man can use; they are wasted through death and decay if not used in a timely manner but can be destroyed through negligence and overexploitation; forests are renewable and can be regenerated indefinitely.

This philosophy was opposed by those who advocated complete protection of the forest reserves, led by (among others) Charles Sprague Sargent and John Muir. Muir, one of the founders of the Sierra Club in 1892 (Fox 1981, 107), had camped with Pinchot during the western excursion of the National Forest Commission and again in 1898 and 1899 (Fox 1981, 115). Pinchot "took to him at once" (Pinchot [1947] 1972, 100), whereas Muir "felt himself drawn to Pinchot as they went camping together for the first time" (Fox 1981, 112). But the "Pinchot forestry tradition cut down trees so humans might use them in improving on nature...[whereas the] Muir tradition protected trees for their own sake" (Fox 1981, 208). Muir and Pinchot continued sniping at each other until Muir's death in 1914. In the short run Pinchot appeared to win—he was the better politician, his positions in government placed him closer to the seat of power, and his philosophy permeated Forest Service thinking through at least the middle of the twentieth century. Muir's thinking became the foundation of the National Park Service, however, and was incorporated into the Wilderness Act of 1964 and the Eastern Wilderness Act of 1974.

A PERMANENT HOME

Separation of the national forestland base, in Interior, from the technical expertise and political clout, in Agriculture, created an inherently unstable situation. It was not to last.

Building a Power Base

The turn of the century found Pinchot entrenched as head of the Division of Forestry in the Department of Agriculture and the new national forests, with their organic legislation, under the General Land Office (GLO) in the Department of the Interior. Our nation's chief forester had no forestland to manage! However, the GLO had requested that Pinchot's Division of Forestry prepare management plans for the forest reserves (Pinchot 1902, 117). Pinchot also ingratiated himself with the timber industry by providing it with consulting services, personally examining seventeen areas in eleven states during 1901 alone (Gates 1968, 571, 572). These two activities broadened and strengthened the division's base of operations, greatly expanding its knowledge, professional competence, and political support—attributes of extreme value in Pinchot's campaign to acquire the reserves. His "noise, turmoil, excitement, and propaganda" attracted the attention of Congress, which increased appropriations to the division (the bureau, as of 1901) almost fifteenfold between 1897 and 1904. And his old acquaintance, Theodore Roosevelt, assumed the presidency in 1901, increasing Pinchot's influence within the executive branch. The GLO did not sit idly during this time, however. A new management program was instituted in 1897; a corps of investigating agents was created to prevent fire, control grazing, and collect fees for stumpage and use of power sites; and by 1901 the staff had grown to 400 persons. The GLO still lacked the personnel (in quality and quantity) and the resource management philosophy required for effective administration of the national forests, however, and continued to be racked by scandals (Gates 1968, 573-575).

The Transfer Act of 1905

After numerous trials and many setbacks, Pinchot received the forestlands he sought on February 1, 1905.

What I had been hoping for and working for, from the moment I came into the old Forestry Division seven long years before, had finally arrived. It had been a long pull, and, as it turned out, a strong pull. Now it had to be a pull all together, if we were to make good use of the chance which perseverence, common sense, T. R. [Theodore Roosevelt], and the American Forest Congress had given us. (Pinchot [1947] 1972, 256)

The Transfer Act of 1905 transferred all lands reserved under the provisions of the Forest Reserve Act of 1891 from the Department of the Interior to the Department of Agriculture. During his first administration, Roosevelt had added twenty-six new reserves and 16.3 million acres to the 46.4 million acres he had inherited from McKinley; thus the amount of forestland transferred was about 62.7 million acres (Gates 1968, 580). The act also provided that for five years after its passage, all receipts from sales of timber, water rights, grazing rights, or any other product or use of land within the forest reserves were to be placed in a separate fund for use in managing the preserves (Pinchot [1947] 1972, 257)—in essence, permitting Pinchot to control his finances independently of congressional appropriations. Additional authority was conferred by a clause in the Agricultural Appropriations Act of 1905, which empowered Forest Service employees to "make arrests for the violation of the laws and regulations relating to the forest reserves and national parks" and to participate "in the enforcement of the laws of the States and Territories in the prevention and extinguishment of forest fires and the protection of fish and game" (Pinchot [1947] 1972, 257). Two years later, in the Agricultural Appropriations Act of 1907, Congress renamed the forest reserves "national forests," removing any connotation that these areas were to be locked up as inviolate sanctuaries.

The End of an Era

Pinchot now had the complete package—land, money, and power—and he lost no time in enlarging his domain. By the end of the Roosevelt era, the National Forest System contained 194.5 million acres—148.1 million of which were added by the Pinchot-Roosevelt team (Gates 1968, 580). The Forest Service was molded into a professional, decentralized field organization with high esprit de corps (Dana and Fairfax 1980, 83). Unfortunately, success did not come without a price. The haste with which reserves were created, their large area, inclusion of lands with little forest resource significance, imposition of grazing fees where none had existed before, abuses of the Forest Lieu Lands Act (which permitted owners of lands within reserves to exchange them for equivalent areas of vacant land open to settlement [Gates 1968, 570]), and the crusading ardor and sometimes high-handed methods of Roosevelt and Pinchot created enemies as well (Gates 1968, 581-593). Congress repealed the Forest Lieu Lands Act in 1905 (Gates 1968, 591), and in 1907 eliminated Pinchot's independent funding source and forbade creation of any additional forest reserves in Washington, Oregon, Idaho, Montana, Wyoming, and Colorado except by act of Congress (Agricultural Appropriations Act of 1907) (Dana and Fairfax 1980, 91). William Howard Taft became the new president in 1909, and Gifford Pinchot was fired as chief of the Forest Service in January 1910. The "Golden Era of Roosevelt and Pinchot" had ended (Dana and Fairfax 1980, 91-95). (Note: Pinchot's public career continued until his death on October 4, 1946, at the age of eighty-one. He was an unsuccessful candidate for senator from Pennsylvania, a leading spokesman for the Progressive party, commissioner of forestry for Pennsylvania, and twice governor of Pennsylvania [1923-1927 and 1931-1935] [Pinkett 1970, 130, 136, 147, 149].)

FORESTS IN THE EAST

Through the end of Roosevelt's administration, national forests could be created only by reserving lands within the public domain—east of the 100th meridian there were only six (the Ouachita and Ozark national forests in Arkansas, the Ocala in Florida, the Huron in Michigan, and the Chippewa and Superior in Minnesota, all of which were established between 1907 and 1909 (Shands and Healy 1977, 265, 266). Yet many people in New England and the southern Appalachians were concerned over protection of watersheds and wilderness areas (Gates 1968, 595), and Holmes's suggestion to purchase reserves in the Appalachians "was never out of. . . [Pinchot's] head for long" (Pinchot [1947] 1972, 239).

Public Concern

As early as 1794, parts of New England were experiencing shortages of timber and fuelwood and concomitant price increases. Timothy Dwight, writing in 1821, noted that "in the 240-mile journey from Boston to New York a traveler passed through no more than twenty miles of wooded land, in fifty or sixty parcels," and by the middle of the nineteenth century, southern New England was as much as three-fourths deforested (Cronon 1983, 121, 156).

Most of the Appalachian forests had been cut over during the late 1800s and the land left to burn and erode (figure 5.2). On January 2, 1900, a memorial (proposal) for government purchase and protection of the Appalachian forests was presented to Congress by the Appalachian Mountain Club of New England and the Appalachian National Park Association of the South Atlantic States. Congress responded with an appropriation of $5,000 "to investigate forest conditions in the Southern Appalachian Mountain region of western North Carolina and adjacent States" ("Message from the President" 1902, 157). (Note: Pinchot [(1947) 1972, 239] states that the memorial was presented to Congress on January 2, 1901, which seems doubtful.) During fiscal year 1900-1901, the Division of Forestry, in cooperation with the U.S. Geological Survey, examined and mapped 9.6 million acres, and on January 16, 1901, President McKinley transmitted a preliminary report to Congress recommending "the purchase of land for a national forest reserve in western North Carolina, eastern Tennessee, and adjacent States" ("Message from the President" 1902, 166).

FIGURE 5.2. Cutover Forests in the Southern Appalachians. (Photo from C. F. Korstian, "Perpetuation of Spruce on Cutover and Burned Lands in the Higher Appalachians," *Ecological Monographs* 7 (1937): 125-167, courtesy of USDA Forest Service, Southeastern Forest Experiment Station)

The final report on southern Appalachian forests, transmitted to Congress on December 19, 1901, repeated the recommendation ("Message from the President" 1902, 36, 37). (Note: The report, "Forests and Forest Conditions of the Southern Appalachian Mountain Region," was written in the first person and signed by James Wilson, secretary of agriculture. Nonetheless, there seems little doubt that "I" was Gifford Pinchot.) The report outlined the function of the proposed eastern reserve in typical Pinchot terms:

> [T]he early movement for the purchase and control of a large area of forest land in the East by the Government chiefly contemplated a national park, but the idea of a national park is conservation, not use; that of a forest reserve is conservation by use, and I therefore recommend the establishment of a forest reserve instead of a park. If, however, the present proposal for the establishment of a national forest reserve is favorably acted upon by Congress, and at some future time it should prove desirable that some considerable portion of this region be set aside and opened up more especially for use as a national park, I can see in advance no objection whatever to the carrying out of such a plan....
>
> I confidently expect that the reserve now proposed in the Southern Appalachians will in the course of a few years be self-supporting, and that subsequently, as the hard-wood timber supplies in other portions of the country become more scarce, the lumbering operations will yield a considerable net return to the Government. ("Message from the President" 1902, 36, 37)

While the report recommended forest reserves and discussed the potential for practicing modern forestry on these lands, much of the underlying justification was tied to soil conservation, water supplies, and flood control. Agriculture in mountainous areas (figure 5.3) was similar to the slash-and-burn migratory agriculture practiced in many developing countries today:

> From some of the peaks one may count these mountain-side patches by the score. They have multiplied the more rapidly because their fertility is short lived, limited to two, three, or five crops at the most. They are cleared, cultivated, and abandoned in rapid succession. Out of twenty such cleared fields, perhaps two or three are in corn, planted between recently girdled trees; one or two may be in grain; two or four in grass, and the remainder—more than half of them—in various stages of abandonment and ruin, perhaps even before the deadened trees have fallen to the ground. ("Message from the President" 1902, 23, 24)

Wilson's report described forest resources by river basin as well as by mountain group ("Message from the President" 1902, 46-55, 69-93) and emphasized damages wrought by the floods of 1901 and 1902. (Note: The letter of transmittal was signed by President Roosevelt on December 19, 1901 [p. 5], yet the report cited "floods occurring during...January, February, and March 1902" [plate 36].) A close relationship between forest cover, erosion protection, dependable water supplies, and flood control was made throughout the text and was used in large part to justify the eastern reserves.

Early in 1901 the legislatures of Virginia, North Carolina, Tennessee, and South Carolina passed almost identical resolutions consenting to federal acquisition of lands for a national forest reserve (Georgia passed one consent resolution on December 18, 1900, and another on December 13, 1901) ("Message from the President" 1902, 172-179). In that same year, legislation authorizing purchase funds was introduced in Congress, but none was forthcoming then or for several succeeding Congresses (Shands and Healy 1977, 13). "One year a bill would pass the Senate, but die in the House. Then another bill would go through the House, but die in the

FIGURE 5.3. Early Appalachian Farming. (Photo courtesy of the National Archives)

Senate" (Pinchot [1947] 1972, 239). In 1908 the Forest Service determined that 23 million acres in the southern Appalachians and 2 million acres in the White Mountains should be permanently forested and recommended purchase of 5 million acres in the former and 600,000 acres in the latter (Pinchot 1908, 28). In the next year, following disastrous floods along the Monongahela River in 1907, the West Virginia legislature authorized federal purchase of lands that were to become the Monongahela National Forest (Shands and Healy 1977, 14, 15).

Theodore Roosevelt was now president, and in his message to Congress on December 3, 1907, he proposed:

> We should acquire in the Appalachian and White Mountain regions all the forest lands that it is possible to acquire for the use of the nation. These lands, because they form a national asset, are as emphatically national as the rivers which they feed, and which flow through so many States before they reach the ocean. (U.S. Congress, House 1908, 1)

Bills supporting these recommendations were introduced, directing the secretary of agriculture to acquire such lands and appropriating $5 million for that purpose. But no precedent existed for forest reserves in the East, and the Constitution was interpreted much more narrowly then than now. As a result the House passed a resolution referring both that part of the president's message just quoted and the pending bills to the House Judiciary Committee, requesting its views as to the federal government's power "to acquire for the purpose of forest reserves lands within a State wherein the Government of the United States has no public domain, and to make appropriation therefore" (U.S. Congress, House 1908, 1). In due course the report came back:

> *Resolved,* That this committee is of the opinion that the Federal Government has no power to acquire lands within a State, solely for forest reserves; but under its constitutional power over navigation the Federal Government may appropriate for the purchase of lands and forest reserves in a State, provided it is made clearly to appear that such lands and forest reserves have a direct and substantial connection with the conservation and improvement of the navigability of a river actually navigable in whole or in part; and that any appropriation made therefor is limited to that purpose....[T]he bills referred to...are not confined to such last-mentioned purpose and are therefore unconstitutional. (U.S. Congress, House 1908, 14)

The Weeks Act of 1911

On March 1, 1911, more than ten years after the southern Appalachian forest report was released and more than twenty years after Holmes's suggestion, the Weeks Act was passed with solid public and congressional support, opening the door for eastern national forests—the final Senate vote was 57 to 9 in favor (Gates 1968, 595):

> Sec. 6. That the Secretary of Agriculture is hereby authorized and directed to examine, locate, and recommend for purchase such lands as in his judgment may be necessary to the regulation and flow of navigable streams...Provided, That before any lands are purchased...said lands shall be examined by the Geological Survey and a report made...showing that the control of such lands will promote or protect the navigation of streams on whose watersheds they lie. (36 Stat. 962)

> Sec. 11. That,...the lands acquired under this Act shall be permanently reserved, held, and administered as national forest lands. (36 Stat. 963)

Pinchot ([1947] 1972, 240) noted that twenty years is "about the time it usually takes to get a new idea through Congress" and attributed success to two facts: "one, the proof that forests do affect the flow of streams; and the other, that the Federal Government, under the Constitution, has power to deal with the Conservation and improvement of navigable rivers and their tributaries."

The act provided that a National Forest Reservation Commission, composed of the secretaries of War, Interior, and Agriculture, was to approve all acquisitions, as were the Geological Survey, the attorney general, and the legislatures of the states concerned (Gates 1968, 595). Lands recommended for acquisition did not have to be forested or suitable for forest management, and appropriations were authorized only for acquisitions of "lands located on the headwaters of navigable streams or those which are being or which may be developed for navigable purposes" (36 Stat. 961). Although cumbersome in appearance, these provisions ensured that the constitutional concerns of the House Judiciary Committee were accommodated, that interests of the U.S. Army Corps of Engineers and agencies in the Department of the Interior were adequately represented in the decision-making process, that no title questions persisted, and that state-federal political issues were resolved. In addition restricting acquisitions to lands that would affect navigable waters firmly tied the program to interstate commerce, allaying the fears of some congressional representatives (Dana and Fairfax 1980, 112) and forestalling constitutionality tests that might otherwise have arisen.

Implementation was swift and dramatic. Ten years of investigations had provided a wealth of information concerning potential purchase areas. For fiscal year 1911, $2 million in acquisition funds had been appropriated, and an attempt was made to purchase as much land as possible before the end of that year. The first tract approved for purchase was about 31,000 acres in Fannin, Gilmer, Lumpkin, and Union counties, Georgia, offered by Andrew and N. W. Gennett by proposal on April 14, 1911 (U.S. Department of Agriculture, Forest Service n.d., 29). By June 30 (only four months after the act was passed), the service had received thirty sale proposals covering 1,250,641 acres, of which 832,464 were within the general area selected for purchase, and had examined 140,787 acres (U.S. Department of Agriculture 1911, 61, 62). During the same period, the National Forest Reservation Commission had approved thirteen purchase units for acquisition (U.S. Department of Agriculture, Forest Service n.d., 3). By July 30, 1912, the commission had approved for purchase 255,822 acres and service personnel had examined 840,453 acres, of which 225,352 were under purchase agreements. Unfortunately, the 31,000 acres approved for purchase during the preceding year proved not to have an acceptable title; acquisition by purchase failed, and the government initiated condemnation proceedings (U.S. Department of Agriculture 1912, 72, 73).

The thirty-five examiners (U.S. Department of Agriculture 1911, 62) assigned to the acquisition effort faced a tremendous task. The government desired tracts of "25,000 to 100,000 acres well situated for protection, administration, and use"—but in practice it accepted units of at least 15,000 to 20,000 acres. Speculators ("certain individuals who sought to precede the government and tie up the desired lands by options in the hope that they might themselves sell them to the government at a handsome profit") became involved, prompting the secretary to announce that no optioned lands would be considered. Lands were appraised by the government based on timber and soil characteristics, and negotiations were undertaken leading to a price not greater than the government estimate. All lands were surveyed prior to purchase or condemnation, with "shrinkage amounts to from 8 to 10 percent."

Lands placed under purchase contract or condemnation during the first two years were "partly cut over, partly more or less culled of their best timber, and partly virgin timberland. The average price [was] $5.95 per acre, with a range of from $1.16 to $15 per acre" (U.S. Department of Agriculture 1912, 74). In the four southern Appalachian states (Virginia, Tennessee, North Carolina, and Georgia), the lands approved for acquisition "were of high quality, 28 percent of all such lands being virgin timber" (U.S. Department of Agriculture, Forest Service n.d., 3). By the end of fiscal year 1913, over 3 million acres of land had been offered to the government and 713,415 had been approved for purchase by the National Forest Reservation Commission (U.S. Department of Agriculture 1913, 46). By the end of the next year, almost 200,000 acres had been acquired and paid for (U.S. Department of Agriculture 1914, 156).

[By] 1916, sufficient land had been acquired to establish the first eastern forest, Pisgah National Forest in North Carolina. In 1918, the Pisgah was joined by three more—the Shenandoah in Virginia (now a part of the George Washington); the Natural Bridge, also in Virginia (now a part of the Thomas Jefferson); and the White Mountain [in New Hampshire and Maine]. (The Alabama—now the William B. Bankhead—also was established from public domain land in that year.)

In 1920 five more Appalachian forests were created—the Boone, now part of the Pisgah, and the Nantahala in North Carolina, South Carolina, and Georgia; the Cherokee in Tennessee; the Unaka in North Carolina, Tennessee, and Virginia; and the Monongahela in West Virginia. The Allegheny National Forest in Pennsylvania was established in 1922. Through the remainder of the 1920's, acquisition focused on filling in the established forests. (Shands and Healy 1977, 15)

Eastern Forest Reserves

In 1924 the Clarke-McNary Act removed the requirement that forest-lands be acquired only to protect navigable streams, giving the Forest Service a clear mandate to acquire *forestlands* for the practice of *forestry* (the act did several other things, which we shall examine later).

Sec. 6. That section 6 of the Act of March 1, 1911 (thirty-sixth Statutes at Large, page 961) is hereby amended to authorize and direct the Secretary of Agriculture to examine, locate, and recommend for purchase such forested, cut-over, or denuded lands within the watersheds of navigable streams as in his judgment may be necessary for the regulation of the flow of navigable streams or *for the production of timber* [emphasis added]....(43 Stat. 654)

Little change in legislation and policy occurred for the next three decades. During the 1930s some twenty-six additional national forests were established in the East; the Civilian Conservation Corps (CCC) provided a ready source of labor for reforestation, soil conservation projects, and related work in the forests (Shands and Healy 1977, 16); and the wilderness issue gained steam (Dana and Fairfax 1980, 155). In general, however, the Forest Service was left to manage the National Forest System as Pinchot had envisioned—by professional foresters with a minimum of outside interference. But all that was to change.

FORESTS FOR EVERYONE

The United States emerged from World War II as a recognized world leader, and its citizens emerged with a new feeling of importance. They had the time, money, and inclination to use the public lands to their utmost, for all the resources the lands could produce, but especially for outdoor recreation. At the same time, timber production from the national forests first became significant during the war, and forest industries had become dependent on continued (and expanded) production from national forest lands for their survival. Emergence of the forest products industry itself as a "major political force" was a product of the war (Dana and Fairfax 1980, 199), and the industry began exerting its political power shortly thereafter. And the wilderness movement was demanding that more and more land be set aside for "nonuse," regardless of the administering agency's organic legislation. Over all was the increasing clamor of the vox populi, demanding to be heard and insisting on a greater influence over the workings of government.

As if these outside interests were not enough, the Forest Service was engaged in a continuing struggle with the Department of the Interior. Relations between the two departments had never been harmonious. After all, Agriculture had acquired the reserves from Interior; Pinchot had been fired because of his feud with Richard A. Ballinger (former commissioner of the General Land Office, then secretary of the interior) over administration of the Alaskan coal fields (Pinkett 1970, 115-125); and the National Park Service was constantly attempting to gain control of national forest land, promoting public discontent with Forest Service policies, and opposing funding for Forest Service recreation programs (Dana and Fairfax 1980, 193, 201).

The Multiple-Use Sustained Yield Act of 1960

The Forest Service turned to Congress for assistance, drafting and lobbying for the bill that was to become the Multiple-Use Sustained Yield Act of 1960 (MUSY) (Dana and Fairfax 1980, 201). The act is short but far reaching:

> Sec. 1. It is the policy of the Congress that the national forests are established and shall be administered for outdoor recreation, range, timber, watershed, and wildlife and fish purposes. The purposes of this Act are declared to be supplemental to, but not in derogation of, the purposes for which the national forests were established. (74 Stat. 215)

> Sec. 2. The Secretary of Agriculture is authorized and directed to develop and administer the renewable surface resources of the national forests for multiple use and sustained yield of the several products and services obtained therefrom. (74 Stat. 215)

The act went on to define multiple use and sustained yield:

> (a) "Multiple use" means the management of all the various renewable surface resources of the national forests so that they are utilized in the combination that will best meet the needs of the American people; making the most judicious use of the land for some or all of these resources or related services over areas large enough to provide sufficient latitude for periodic adjustments in use to conform to changing needs and conditions....

> (b) "Sustained yield of the several products and services" means the achievement and maintenance in perpetuity of a high-level annual or regular periodic output of the various resources of the national forests without the impairment of the productivity of the land. (74 Stat. 215)

MUSY provided what the Forest Service requested—legislative sanction of the multiple-use philosophy inherent in the service and protection from the "dominant use" or even "exclusive use" demands of some elements of the timber industry. But in some respects, it may have been more confusing than clarifying. Consider yourself a forest administrator. How do you determine the "needs of the American people," how best to meet them, and the "most judicious use of land"? When may the land provide "all of these resources," and when may it provide only "some"? And which "some...without the impairment of the productivity of the land"? Some ambiguities were introduced in efforts to strengthen the Forest Service's role in new areas of resource management without weakening its position with the timber and grazing interests (Dana and Fairfax 1980, 203). Others were inevitable (and sometimes desirable) consequences of broad organic and enabling legislation—agencies prefer having some maneuvering latitude within statutory limits. Despite its weaknesses, however, MUSY established that recreation, range, timber, watershed, and wildlife and fish all had legitimate interests in national forest management, and it served as a model for the BLM organic act sixteen years later. (Note: Forest Service activities related to range management and grazing are discussed in chapter 4; recreation, in chapter 6; wildlife, in chapter 7; and wilderness, in chapter 8.)

Wilderness, Environmental Quality, and Clear-cutting

While the Forest Service was trying to understand and adjust to this legislation and the public interest it awakened, the service was confronted by the Wilderness Act of 1964. This act, which is discussed in greater detail in chapter 8, "established a National Wilderness Preservation System to be composed of federally owned areas designated by Congress as 'wilderness areas'...to be administered for the use and enjoyment of the American people in such manner as will leave them unimpaired for future use and enjoyment as wilderness" (16 U.S.C. 1131). The act can apply to any federal land and particularly affected national forest land.

Coming a little more than five years after the Wilderness Act, the National Environmental Policy Act of 1969 (see chapter 15) required preparation of environmental impact statements for every major federal action "significantly affecting the quality of the human environment," and in 1975 the Eastern Wilderness Act facilitated establishment of wilderness areas in the eastern national forests. At about the same time, the Forest Service was confronted with lawsuits attacking its ability to manage timber resources in accordance with the law and with accepted modern forestry techniques (as the service saw them).

Increased timber production from the national forests after World War II and maturing stands in the eastern forests combined to foster more widespread use of clear-cutting—an entirely legitimate harvest practice under many conditions but one that can easily be abused. Clear-cut areas appear devastated during their early years of regeneration (figure 5.4), and local citizens and conservation organizations were not prepared for such sights in "their" national forests, nor did they understand the principles of silviculture involved. Organized opposition to clear-cutting first arose in the Monongahela National Forest in 1954, where the Forest

FIGURE 5.4. Clear-cutting on the Western National Forests. Clear-cuts of 40 to 60 acres in old-growth stands of Douglas fir, Gifford Pinchot National Forest, Washington. (Photo courtesy of the USDA Forest Service and the Forest History Society)

Service attempted a small experimental cut (Dana and Fairfax 1980, 226). While clear-cutting was the issue that mobilized the opposition, public concern was much broader, involving increased levels of timber harvest, alleged contravention of the sustained-yield provisions of MUSY, and silvicultural practices in the national forests in general (Le Master 1984, 17, 18).

During the early 1970s, the crescendo of opposition began to rise, fueled by the Sierra Club (Wood 1971), the Izaak Walton League of America (Pankowski 1970; "Conservationists Fight to Preserve Monongahela Forest" 1970), and other conservation organizations and sporting magazines (Frome 1971, 1972). In their view:

> Under this form of so-called "sound forest management,"...entire moun-
> tainsides are stripped of trees, thousands of acres at one whack, running as
> much as three miles in length and a mile or more in width. Such a practice
> has an enormously devastating environmental effect which includes soil
> destruction, stream siltation, and a stinging blow to the aesthetic sense.

The truth is that clearcutting is the most destructive tool ever applied to the American forest....The most severe effect of clearcutting is the disruption of age-old soil conditions in the forest, which could leave the land barren in less than 200 years.

The next worse effect of clearcutting is sedimentation caused by erosion when logging occurs on steep slopes or upon unstable soils....Sedimentation from poor logging practices chokes stream beds many miles downstream. This causes loss of natural stream vegetation and destroys fish habitat....Clearcutting also leads to greater spring runoff, increasing the danger of floods.

What does a clearcut area look like?

Imagine the mountains, ridge after ridge of them, rolling slopes of dark green conifers punctuated with aspen—an emerald empire of stately trees against the severity of granite.

But now there are no trees. They have been cut down...not a single tree remains nor a shrub nor a flower. (Wood 1971, 14, 16)

Observations such as these were not necessarily true in all respects, but they possessed sufficient factual basis to be believed by those who were so inclined. Their main purpose was to mobilize forces against clearcutting, and in that they succeeded.

A flurry of studies ensued—the Forest Service conducted its own study in the Bitterroot, Monongahela, and Wyoming (now Bridger-Teton) national forests; deans of five forestry schools investigated clearcutting practices; and a Senate subcommittee conducted its own investigation; the West Virginia legislature, not to be outdone, launched an investigation of conditions in the Monongahela, and a team of scientists from the University of Montana looked at management practices in the Bitterroot (Council on Environmental Quality 1974, 380). Congressional testimony alone covered more than a thousand pages (U.S. Congress, Senate 1971). All this concern and intervention from outside interests surprised, perplexed, and perhaps antagonized the career professionals in the Forest Service, whose attitude was later expressed by Thomas C. Nelson, then deputy chief of the service:

But, in the final analysis, it is the agency that knows the most about the status of the lands it manages and the environmental, social, and economic needs that must be met. Therefore, within the bounds of overall congressional direction, the agency is in the best position—indeed has the obligation—to set the policy for the hundreds of rule-issues that are necessary steps between broad policy direction and action on the ground. (Nelson (1977, 193)

All the rhetoric did not stop the clear-cutting (though it may have substantially modified the practice), and during the 1970s the battleground extended from the Bitterroot in Montana through the Shoshone and Teton (now Bridger-Teton) in Wyoming to the Monongahela in West Virginia (Council on Environmental Quality 1975, 224). Although the Forest Service responded in 1971 with a detailed analysis of harvesting systems, including clear-cutting (U.S. Department of Agriculture 1971), it was too late.

The Monongahela Controversy

On May 14, 1973, environmental groups filed suit on the Monongahela (*West Virginia Div. of the Izaak Walton League of America v. Butz*), alleging that three timber sales advertised in April 1973 violated conditions of the Organic Act of 1897 in that 428 acres of the 1,077 acres offered for sale would be clear-cut, generally in blocks of 5 to 20 acres, and that none of the trees in areas to be clear-cut would be individually marked. Such actions, argued the plaintiffs, were contrary to the requirements that only "the dead, matured, or large growth of trees found upon such national forests [may be sold and that]...such timber, before being sold, shall be marked and designated, and shall be cut and removed" (30 Stat. 35). The Forest Service, in its defense, argued that "the Organic Act directs that the national forests be managed scientifically, and leaves the choice of specific management practices to the discretion of the Secretary of Agriculture." The defendants contended that the purpose of the Organic Act was to "improve and protect the forest...to furnish a continuous supply of timber" and that "this language emphasizes utilization of the forest and development of the forest for future growth." In such context, they asserted, the designating and marking requirements should be read in a general context and should not apply to each individual tree (6 E.R.C. 1019).

The plaintiffs wanted to stop clear-cutting in the national forests because they felt it was detrimental to "their" mountains, they wanted to delay harvesting pending designation of possible wilderness areas in the Monongahela National Forest, or they simply wanted to end timber harvesting in the national forests (Fairfax and Achterman 1977, 485, citing interview with Helen Cohn Needham, counsel for the plaintiff, *West Virginia Div. of the Izaak Walton League of America v. Butz*).

A court case does not always assess the logic, reasonableness, or public or professional acceptability of the acts in question, however; it may merely address whether they are in accordance with law. Neither can litigation build forward—it cannot formulate prospective policy, plans, or programs. It can only judge the past. Furthermore, once litigation is initiated, the lawyers' job is to win, using whatever tools are available, admissible, and legal; and their strategy may lead far from the original issue.

The district court's decision gave little comfort to the Forest Service:

Accordingly, it appears that over a period of years, by what would be almost imperceptible gradations, compromises of expressed legislative goals happened in the public forest harvest practices. These, for the purpose of this civil action, ripened into maturity in 1964, with the embrace of clearcutting and its progeny by the Forest Service as an acceptable harvesting practice....

The attempt to lessen legislative control over the sale of timber from the public lands by policies and practices of the Forest Service, although understandable and perhaps proper in a business, industrial and even in a scientific sense, cannot be sanctioned under the law as this Court finds the same to exist.

If the reasons for the policies and practices of the Forest Service are valid and represent the appropriate state of the science of silviculture, business, forest management and administration, and are needed tools to properly develop uses of and benefits to and from the forest, then such evidence should be presented to the Congress. After studies and hearing from all of the obviously interested parties, Congress can and will make a reasoned judgment in the matter....

Efforts toward regulatory blighting of congressional controls by administrative siege cannot be permitted. Public land means public ownership. The most direct control of public forest resources in a republic rests, once asserted as in the case here, with the Congress and until expressly relinquished, that control is reserved. (6 E.R.C. 1023)

In sum, the Organic Act of 1897

...forbids U.S. Forest Service's sale of Monongahela National Forest timber that will be harvested by clearcutting, and requires the Service to sell only timber that is dead, matured, or large, to designate each such area of timber, to mark each individual tree authorized for sale, and to insure removal of all timber cut. (6 E.R.C. 1016)

The Monongahela case was appealed by the government, and before the appeal could be heard, an almost identical case was filed concerning timber sales in the Tongass National Forest in Alaska (*Zieske v. Butz*). In *Zieske*, however, the plaintiff alleged violation of the National Environmental Policy Act, the Multiple-Use Sustained Yield Act, the Federal Water Pollution Control Act, and the Refuse Act (section 13 of the River and Harbor Act of 1899) but failed to mention the Organic Act (9 E.R.C. 1062).

The United States Court of Appeals for the Fourth Circuit affirmed the Monongahela decision, citing the legislative history that "demonstrated that the concern of Congress in passing the Organic Act was the preservation of the national forests....[O]nly those trees which were dead, physiologically mature or large [could be removed], and then only when such cutting would preserve the young and growing timber which remained" (8 E.R.C. 1081). The appellate court concluded:

> We are not insensitive to the fact that our reading of the Organic Act will have serious and far-reaching consequences, and it may well be that this legislation enacted over seventy-five years ago is an anachronism which no longer serves the public interest. However, the appropriate forum to resolve this complex and controversial issue is not the courts but the Congress. (8 E.R.C. 1083)

Shortly after the court of appeals rendered its opinion, the U.S. District Court for the District of Alaska, in *Zieske v. Butz*, found that the Forest Service did not violate any of the acts cited by the plaintiffs but did violate the Organic Act. In its decision the court followed the precedent of *Izaak Walton League v. Butz*, and issued a permanent injunction "barring the cutting of trees other than those which are large, physiologically matured, or dead...[and] individually marked prior to cutting" (9 E.R.C. 1062, 1063).

The courts heard only legal arguments, not objective discussions of value preferences and differences of opinion about how to manage the national forests—nor was it their function to act as experts in technical fields (Spurr 1977, 199). None of the plaintiffs (in *Izaak Walton League*) argued the merits or legality of clear-cutting per se, nor did the court by any means settle the clear-cutting issue (Fairfax and Achterman 1977, 485).

The Monongahela and Tongass cases were neither inconsequential nor monumental. While they did not solve the problem, they did serve to (1) illustrate the power of citizens' groups and litigation in national forest management issues, (2) demonstrate the inability of litigation to solve natural resource management issues, (3) indicate deficiencies in the

Organic Act of 1897 as applied in the 1970s, (4) generate national interest and concern over forest management issues, and (5) convince many national leaders that further congressional action was necessary:

> The Monongahela controversy involved the Congress, the courts, the Forest Service, and interested groups in a discussion of priorities in public land management...[and] is merely one exchange in a continuing conversation. Policy-making in forestry is like decision-making in any other area, a series of compromises and tradeoffs in a variety of arenas. Forestry professionals must learn to recognize the process as a continuing debate if public policy is to be informed by technical expertise [and vice versa]. (Fairfax and Achterman 1977, 487)

New Legislation

During the time that the clear-cutting issue was in litigation, Congress was wrestling with additional legislative direction for the Forest Service. The service was being buffeted from one side by those who felt it was not responding adequately to the concerns of environmentalists and other private citizens and from the other side by those who felt just the opposite. Reports generated in the clear-cutting controversy showed program deficiencies, as did the report of a presidential advisory panel (President's Advisory Panel on Timber and the Environment 1973) and the service's own appraisal (U.S. Department of Agriculture 1971). It fell to the Congress to try to develop a remedy.

In response to an unprecedented rise in softwood lumber and plywood prices during the late 1960s and predicted increases in future demands, the timber industry approached Congress with a proposal to increase production from the national forests. Supported by testimony from Forest Service chief Edward P. Cliff that "'allowable cuts could—in time—be increased by about two-thirds by intensifying timber culture on the more productive portions of national forest commercial timberlands,'" (Le Master 1984, 21), officials of the National Forest Products Association proposed legislation "'to increase substantially the timber yield'" from the National Forest System (Le Master 1984, 21). Initially the proposal garnered strong bipartisan support in Congress and unclear, indefinite opposition from conservation interests. As the debate intensified, however, opposition became better organized and effective. Vocal objections came first from spokespersons for the National Wildlife Federation, the Sierra Club, and The Wilderness Society. They were later joined by the Audubon Society, the Izaak Walton League of America, the National

Rifle Association, the Wildlife Management Institute, Trout Unlimited, Friends of the Earth, and the Committee on Natural Resources—virtually the entire conservation-environmental lobby. The conservationists had two major concerns: the bill placed timber above other resources identified in MUSY, and it would open to timbering de facto wilderness areas, foreclosing their future wilderness designation. In the end the conservationists won, and the bill never cleared the House (Le Master 1984, 19-26). Its major contribution may have been to further polarize and organize constituency groups involved with the national forests and to pave the way for future legislative battles.

A number of variants of the Timber Supply Act were brought before the Ninety-third Congress, but none affecting the national forest system was successful (Le Master 1984, 26, 27). Congress turned instead to much more comprehensive legislation. The first law, the Forest and Rangeland Renewable Resources Planning Act of 1974 (RPA), prescribed a framework for forest planning nationwide. The second, the National Forest Management Act of 1976 (NFMA), added additional detail to the RPA planning procedure and prescribed standards and guidelines for development of management policy through agency regulations.

Together, RPA and NFMA provided the framework for addressing the issues faced by the Forest Service in the 1970s and 1980s, but by themselves they cannot solve the service's problem of allocating multiple resources (in increasingly short supply) among competing and conflicting users in ever-increasing numbers.

RPA contains two major provisions:

Sec. 2. Renewable Resource Assessment.—...the Secretary of Agriculture shall prepare a Renewable Resource Assessment...not later than December 31, 1975...and updated during 1979 and each tenth year thereafter,...[to] include...

(1) an analysis of present and anticipated uses, demand for, and supply of the renewable resources...

(2) an inventory...of present and potential renewable resources, and an evaluation of opportunities for improving their yield of tangible and intangible goods and services...

(3) a description of Forest Service programs and responsibilities...and the relationship of these...to public and private activities...

(4) a discussion of important policy considerations, laws, regulations ...expected to...affect...the use, ownership, and management of forest, range, and other associated lands. (88 Stat. 476)

The assessment provides a detailed description of available renewable forest and range resources nationwide, on public and private land, and an estimate of anticipated demands for these resources. As such it furnishes the basis for a program designed to meet demands within the limits of resource capabilities:

Sec. 3. Renewable Resource Program.—...[T]he Secretary...shall prepare and transmit to the President a recommended Renewable Resource Program...[which] may include alternatives, and shall provide in appropriate detail for protection, management, and development of the National Forest System....The Program shall be prepared not later than December 31, 1975...and at least each of the [next] four fiscal decades...and shall be updated no later than during the first half of the fiscal year beginning September 30, 1980, and the first half of each fifth fiscal year thereafter...[and] shall include—

(1) an inventory of specific needs and opportunities for both public and private program investments...

(2) specific identification of Program outputs, results anticipated, and benefits [expected]...in such a manner that the anticipated costs can be directly compared with the total related benefits...

(3) a discussion of priorities for accomplishment of inventoried Program opportunities...

(4) a detailed study of personnel requirements. (88 Stat. 477)

The program includes management plans for units of the National Forest System, is developed through a systematic, interdisciplinary approach, and is coordinated with planning processes of local and state governments and other federal agencies (88 Stat. 477). But RPA, as originally passed, made no provision for input from individual citizens.

Coming during a period of intense environmental emotion and polarization following the Timber Supply Act and the Monongahela controversy, RPA was remarkably noncontroversial. Less than three dozen witnesses outside of the administration testified at the hearings, and most testimony was supportive (Le Master 1984, 44, 45). Yet Senator Hubert Humphrey, who introduced S. 2296 (which was to become RPA), was initially apprehensive and at one time "told the committee staff that he could expend no further effort on the bill unless there was clear evidence of its having broad appeal" (Le Master 1984, 35). Much of the credit must go to the staff of the Senate Committee on Agriculture, Nutrition, and Forestry, which was assigned the mission of garnering support, and to William E. Towell, executive vice-president of the American Forestry Association. Following the Timber Supply Act fiasco, Towell had set up an informal voluntary ad hoc Areas of Agreement Committee, consisting of many of the participants in that controversy. This group was enlarged by James W. Giltmier, committee staff member, and because the group met in September 1973, it became known as the "September Group." Virtually all the interests were represented—forest products industries, professional and lay wildlife and fish organizations, professional foresters, the Forest Service—but not the "preservationists," who were somewhat mistrusted. Based on an interview with Giltmier, Le Master (1984, 37) describes what may have been the turning point in passage of RPA:

> One fall day, Senator Humphrey walked through the committee room on his way to another meeting. He saw the September Group and stopped when he sensed they were discussing S. 2296. Much impressed that people representing such varied interests could be negotiating the contents of a legislative proposal in a constructive way, he sat down and joined in the discussion. It was this experience, in Giltmier's opinion, that caused Humphrey to believe that something of substance could be accomplished by S. 2296. He saw the bill's basis of support, and he began enthusiastically to push the bill through the legislative process.

Passage of RPA was a major accomplishment for the Forest Service and a personal triumph for John R. McGuire, who became chief in 1972 (Clary 1986, 189). The act was generally supported by the forest products industries and by professional forestry, wildlife, and park and recreation organizations, but it was opposed by representatives of the Sierra Club and Friends of the Earth, who desired more emphasis on wilderness preservation (U.S. Congress, Senate 1973). The Nixon administration also had reservations:

> [W]e are seriously concerned with those provisions...which would restrict Presidential flexibility and discretion in formulating annual operating plans and budget requests[, requiring] the President and the Secretary of

Agriculture to request sufficient funds to meet the forestry objectives specified by Congress and to justify any requests for less than those amounts. (Testimony of Paul A. Vander Myde, deputy assistant secretary for conservation, research and education, U.S. Department of Agriculture [U.S. Congress, Senate 1973, 37, 38])

Forest Planning under RPA and NFMA

The first assessment and program were completed on December 31, 1975 (Council on Environmental Quality 1976, 101). Among their most important recommendations were the following:

1. Increase recreational use in dispersed areas from 125 million recreation visitor days (RVDs, defined as 12 visitor-hours in the aggregate) in 1975 to between 128.8 and 140.0 million RVDs in 1980 and 176.0 to 220.0 million in 2020.

2. Increase National Forest wilderness acreage to between 25 and 30 million acres by the year 2020 [about double the 1975 acreage (Council on Environmental Quality 1976, 101)].

3. Increase fish and wildlife habitat improvement from 175,000 acres in 1976 to between 957,000 and 1,040,000 acres in 1980 and between 2,195,000 and 2,744,000 acres in 2011-2020. Increase endangered species habitat from 19,000 acres in 1975 to about 60,000 acres in 1980.

4. Increase livestock grazing on National Forest land from 11.3 million animal-unit-months (AUMs) in 1975 to between 15.4 and 16.3 million AUMs in 1980 and 18.0 to 20.4 million AUMs in 2020.

5. Increase timber sale offerings from National Forest land from 2.4 billion cubic feet in 1975 to between 2.7 and 2.9 billion cubic feet in 1980 and between 3.3 and 4.0 billion cubic feet in 2020. (U.S. Department of Agriculture, Forest Service 1976, 626, 627)

The program essentially proposed that national forests produce more of everything from increased expenditures of public funds. Thus everyone wins (except, perhaps, the taxpayer who does not use the national forests). Among the more serious cited flaws in the first attempt to implement RPA were that (1) the program and assessment were developed simultaneously, yet the program was supposed to be based on the assessment; (2) in assessing management options, the service only varied investment levels, without analyzing the assumptions behind such investments; and (3) the program was not an additive combination of unit, area, and regional plans (i.e., the whole was not the sum of the parts) (Dana and Fairfax 1980, 325, 326). Despite these weaknesses, the first program was a good start—after all, the Forest Service was plowing new and rocky ground. The 1976 report received a cool reception from the OMB, a lukewarm reception from the White House and Congress, and adverse comment and criticism from Monday-morning quarterbacks—but it resulted in increased Forest Service appropriations, increased public involvement, and additional congressional action (Dana and Fairfax 1980, 326, 327).

In 1976 Congress constructed the capstone for national forest planning, the National Forest Management Act (NFMA). Congress had before it the Organic Act of 1897, the policy enunciated in the Multiple-Use Sustained Yield Act of 1960, RPA and its initial products, and the Monongahela case, which cited discrepancies between practice and law and forcefully dumped the matter in the lap of Congress. NFMA coalesced existing authorities into a more cohesive directive, providing a comprehensive and complete planning framework for the Forest Service. It did so principally by amending RPA, inserting a section of congressional findings and generally expanding the planning criteria and refining the planning procedures. Section 13 of NFMA repealed that troublesome section of the Organic Act, removing the "dead, matured, or large growth" restrictions (an unsuccessful attempt to do so had been made during consideration of RPA in 1973 [Le Master 1984, 43]). Sections 4 and 11 addressed reforestation and timber removal, respectively, and section 11 opened virtually all Forest Service activities to public scrutiny:

> In exercising his authorities under this Act and other laws applicable to the Forest Service, the Secretary, by regulation, shall establish procedures, including public hearings where appropriate, to give the Federal, State, and local governments and the public adequate notice of and an opportunity to comment upon formulation of standards, criteria, and guidelines applicable to Forest Service programs....In providing for public participation in the planning for and management of the National Forest System, the Secretary...shall establish and consult with advisory boards as he deems necessary to secure full information and advice on the execution of his responsibilities. (90 Stat. 2958)

The congressional debate on NFMA centered on two opposing legislative philosophies. Should the legislative branch (a) prescribe in detail administrative and operational elements of an executive branch agency or (b) provide broad statutory limits within which the agency may develop its own operational framework through the rule-making process? In theory the former, prescriptive, approach ensures that the people (through their proxy, Congress) maintain firm control over agency activities and that those activities adequately reflect public values; however, it frequently embroils the legislative branch in controversies over minutia and technical issues that it has neither the time, the inclination, nor the requisite scientific background to understand. In actuality Congress cannot invest sufficient resources to do this job, nor is it a proper legislative function. The latter, nonprescriptive approach, risks loss of public control over agency activities but places the majority of technical and scientific considerations with the technicians and scientists. Those who distrust the executive branch tend toward the prescriptive approach, while those who generally approve of recent agency actions will lean toward the nonprescriptive approach. In the NFMA deliberations, environmentalists were incensed over the clear-cutting issue and were generally distrustful of the Forest Service. Their mentor, Senator Jennings Randolph of West Virginia, sponsored a bill that would have prescribed, in detail, management practices that could or could not be used within the National Forest System. The timber industry would have preferred no constraints at all, and the Forest Service favored as few as possible (Dana and Fairfax 1980, 328). Senator Hubert Humphrey's nonprescriptive bill was more to their liking. In the end the nonprescriptive approach won out, but the environmental interests came back strongly during development of implementing regulations.

The planning process prescribed by RPA and NFMA is hierarchical and iterative. The initial national program was developed in 1975 and revised in 1980, based on information from each forest region. Each region, in turn, assigned its share of national production levels to individual forests through a regional guide. Standards, guidelines, and objectives in regional guides and regulations implementing NFMA (36 C.F.R. 219 (July 1, 1987)) provided the framework within which each forest plan was developed. Approved forest plans may or may not provide the RPA production levels assigned by the previous RPA program, however, and actual work on the ground may not conform to programs or plans because of budgetary constraints, timber market and other socioeconomic conditions, fires and other environmental conditions, or other factors. Forest plan implementation is reviewed through an intricate monitoring system, and monitoring reports and forest plans prepared or revised since the last RPA program become input to the next. The RPA program and regional guides are updated every five years; forest plans ordinarily are revised on a ten-year cycle or at least every fifteen years (36 C.F.R. 219.10(g) (July 1, 1987)).

The process for developing forest plans consists of ten steps:

1. *Identification of purpose and need*—identify and evaluate public issues, concerns, and opportunities and which ones to be addressed in the planning process.

2. *Planning criteria*—develop planning criteria to guide the planning effort, derived from laws and regulations; RPA goals and objectives; results of step 1; plans and programs of other agencies; and ecological, technical and economic factors. Criteria are to include those designed to maximize net public benefits.

3. *Inventory data and information collection*—the Interdisciplinary (ID) team determines what data are required to address expressed issues and concerns, utilizes existing data where possible, and obtains new data where necessary.

4. *Analysis of the Management Situation (AMS)*—determine the planning area's ability to supply goods and services in response to societal demands through a series of "benchmarks," each of which addresses a major concern and all of which conform to existing regulations but are not constrained by existing policies or budgets (except for the "current direction" benchmark). Minimal benchmarks include a) maintain current direction, b) obtain minimum management level to maintain the unit of the National Forest System, c) maximize physical and biological production of goods and services, and d) maximize present net value based on established market values or assigned values.

5. *Formulation of alternatives*—utilize information obtained during preceding steps to formulate a broad range of alternative management plans, some of which support the benchmarks (including the current level or "no action" alternative), some [of which] provide different ways to address public issues, some [of which] may require changes in existing law or policy, and at least one of which must respond to and incorporate the current RPA Program.

6. *Estimated effects of alternatives*—analyze physical, biological, economic, and social effects of each alternative as required by NEPA procedures, including costs and benefits. Both marketable and nonmarketable goods and services are to be considered, and the decrease from maximum present net value associated with various levels of resource outputs that were not assigned monetary values is to be estimated.

7. *Evaluation of alternatives*—compare the present net value, outputs of goods and services, and overall protection and enhancement of environmental resources provided by each management alternative.

8. *Preferred alternative recommendation*—after reviewing the ID team's evaluation, the Forest Supervisor selects a preferred alternative for recommendation to the Regional Forester. This alternative becomes the "proposed action" in the draft environmental impact statement.

9. *Plan approval*—after reviewing the proposed plan and the final environmental impact statement, the Regional Forester prepares a record of decision, indicating whether he approves or disapproves the plan and comparing the selected alternative with any which are more environmentally preferable or come nearer to maximizing present net value.

10. *Monitoring and evaluation*—at intervals established in the plan, implementation is evaluated through a monitoring program which a) compares outputs and services delivered with those projected in the plan, b) documents effects including any changes in land productivity, c) compares costs of effecting prescriptions with those estimated in the plan. Recommendations for plan modifications are based on these evaluations. (36 C.F.R. 219.12 (July 1, 1987))

In the years following RPA, the Forest Service has made impressive improvements in its planning process. Little time was available for preparation of the 1975 RPA assessment and program. Most of the work on the documents was done in Washington, with little interagency coordination or public input. President Ford's statement of policy was at best a cautious endorsement and reemphasized the OMB's concern that the program might dictate budgetary considerations. Even Senator Humphrey indicated to Chief McGuire that "all that was expected of the Forest Service was its best effort to meet the requirements of RPA" (Le Master 1984, 138, 139).

The 1980 assessment and program attempted to correct weaknesses in the original document, considered resource interactions, improved linkages between the assessment and the program, and strengthened the planning methodology (Davis 1981, 383). Alternatives were developed around feasible scenarios of Forest Service activities rather than attempting to attain fixed goals, as in the 1975 version. Participation by other federal and state agencies and by the public in general was much greater, and the service made much more use of quantitative analyses and computer simulations (Le Master 1984, 142). Without question RPA, NFMA, and NEPA have opened the Forest Service's planning and management to public scrutiny and provided a means for public desires and values to be reflected in the service's activities. The resource itself is extremely complex, however; public aspirations frequently conflict, and the legal-institutional-technical mechanisms to resolve conflicting and competing demands and to manage the forest environment with certain results are still quite primitive.

Discrepancies between plan and performance continue to plague the Forest Service and will do so for a long time. RPA program and forest plan implementation are contingent upon sufficient appropriations, and their development was not constrained by existing levels. During fiscal years 1978-1981 appropriations for forestland management averaged 80 percent of the 1975 recommended program level, forest research received only 76 percent, and state and private forestry received only 63 percent of the funding required to implement the plan (Le Master 1984, 152-155).

The linear program utilized to analyze benchmarks in the forest plans (FORPLAN) may accept values for outputs such as water, sediment, recreation visitor days (Johnson 1986, 13), and wildlife (U.S. Department of Agriculture, Forest Service 1984, II-16 to II-51). These outputs do not provide income to the Forest Service, but their realization is dependent upon agency expenditures. Thus full implementation of the 1975 RPA would have required a direct subsidy, through appropriations, of almost $400 million in 1977, $1 billion in 1980, and $1.5 billion by 2020, without adjustment for inflation (Walker 1977, 715). In times of budgetary constraints, such appropriations are extremely unlikely. In addition plans developed during the late 1970s and early 1980s reflect high and increasing stumpage prices and expanding markets—both of which evaporated by the mid-1980s. Forest plan alternatives reflecting the "current direction" benchmark are far different from those that "attain RPA objectives." Such divergence can quickly erode public confidence in the entire planning process, even though the limiting factors are beyond control of the planners.

NFMA also introduces or expands upon some complex and controversial management concepts. The act does the following:

> [P]ermit[s] increases in harvest levels based on intensified management practices, such as reforestation, thinning, and tree improvement if (i) such practices justify increasing the harvests in accordance with the Multiple-Use Sustained Yield Act of 1960, and (ii) such harvest levels are decreased at the end of each planning period if such practices cannot be implemented....
>
> [I]nsure[s] that, prior to harvest, stands of trees throughout the National Forest System shall generally have reached the culmination of mean annual increment of growth (calculated on the basis of cubic measurement or other methods of calculation at the discretion of the Secretary): Provided, That these practices shall not preclude the use of

sound silvicultural practices, such as thinning or other stand improvement measures....(16 U.S.C. 1604)

[L]imit[s] the sale of timber from each national forest to a quantity equal to or less than a quantity which can be removed from such forest annually in perpetuity on a sustained yield basis: Provided, That, in order to meet overall multiple-use objectives, the Secretary may establish an allowable sale quantity for any decade which departs from the projected long-term average sale quantity that would otherwise be established: *Provided further,* That any such planned departure must be consistent with the multiple-use management objectives of the land management plan. (16 U.S.C. 1611)

The first provision permits the Forest Service to use the allowable cut effect (ACE) to justify increased appropriations for forest management. It can argue that such investments will increase future timber productivity, justifying increases in the current allowable cut (which may come from old growth). Even if sufficient appropriations to support the planned management practices are not forthcoming, ambiguities in timing the harvest level adjustments may permit raising the level of old-growth cut on the assumption of increased appropriations and deferring compensatory harvest reductions to the future (Walker 1977, 717).

The second provision ensures that harvested trees are generally beyond their maximum rate of growth and that overall stand productivity is declining at time of harvest. This requirement may cause little difficulty—old-growth stands being harvested in western forests are well beyond culmination of mean annual increment, and rotations being prescribed for eastern forests are generally long enough to meet this restriction. But the discretion afforded the secretary ("rotation age for ponderosa pine on site class 120 varies from 39 to 107 years, depending on the unit of measurement employed and the utilization standards assumed" [Zivnuska 1977, cited in Dana and Fairfax 1980, 231]) and the exception for "sound silvicultural practices" create considerable latitude.

The third provision, addressing nondeclining even flow, has been the most controversial. It appears to ensure that no more will be harvested from a forest in any one year than can be harvested every year in perpetuity. It sounds good. It is extremely conservative, ensuring (to many readers) that timber production from the national forests may increase, but will not decrease, in the future. The Forest Service interpreted it as a general endorsement of the nondeclining even flow policy (Walker 1977, 717) adopted in 1973 (Dana and Fairfax 1980, 331). It provided support

from environmental groups and shelter from timber interests that favored
accelerated cut of old growth in the western forests. It prevented boom-
and-bust cycles (up during old-growth harvest, down during regeneration, up again as new growth matured), which would be disastrous to
communities dependent upon national forest timber. Yet strict adherence
would waste (from a strictly timber utilization standpoint) much of the
old growth now standing in the western forests; its effectiveness is dependent upon the relative contributions of national forest and private timber
to the local economy (Dana and Fairfax 1980, 332); and the provision
that the secretary may depart from nondeclining even flow if such depar-
tures are "planned" and "consistent with multiple-use management
objectives" permits considerable administrative discretion.

By January 1990 the Forest Service had released draft forest plans for
all but 1 (Klamath National Forest in California) of the 156 units in the
National Forest System and final plans for 98 units. Ninety-five of the
final plans have been appealed, mostly by environmental interests, and
suits have been filed against four of the plans (The Wilderness Society
1990, 5, 6). Many of the appeals are being settled by agreement between
the appellants and the chief of the Forest Service (The Wilderness Society
1989, 6).

The 1970s marked the beginning of a new era in national forest planning and management. While NFMA will "mean whatever the courts say
it means" (Walker 1977, 717, quoting Brock Evans of the Sierra Club), it
is having a profound impact upon management of the national forests.

In 1992 the Office of Technology Assessment (OTA) summarized the
status of planning within the Forest Service (U.S. Congress, Office of
Technology Assessment 1992). The OTA reviewed the statutory framework and other elements, identified four major findings, and suggested
fourteen congressional options for improving the situation. The OTA
found the following:

Finding 1: Plan development emphasizes timber and other physical outputs....

Option   1: Clarify legislative direction....
            2: Broaden the information base....
            3: Establish targets for all resources....
            4: Improve public involvement....
            5: Expand use of information technologies....

Finding 2: Monitoring of forest management activities is inadequate....

Option   6: Separate the monitoring function....
          7: Require linkage between actions and results....
          8: Require public involvement in monitoring....

Finding 3: Budget decisions overwhelm planning decisions....

Option   9: Eliminate appropriations by resource....
          10: Require realistic budgets in forest plans....
          11: Control special accounts and trust funds....
          12: Compensate counties fairly and consistently....

Finding 4: National targets can nullify local decisions....

Option   13: Specify forest plans as the baseline for RPA planning....
          14: Require RPA direction for all resources and all branches.
          (U.S. Congress, Office of Technology Assessment 1992, 10-14)

The OTA report succinctly describes the present situation and proposes a
worthy array of alternative remedies. It might serve as the outline for
public discussion and congressional action in the 1990s; it might not.

FOREST MANAGEMENT OUTSIDE
THE NATIONAL FORESTS

As early as 1898, Gifford Pinchot's Division of Forestry was furnishing
technical assistance to industrial forest owners in the East and South, and
in 1902 the division provided such assistance on 535,000 acres of timberland. Cooperative state-federal studies of forest conditions were also
carried out with Maine, New Hampshire, and California early in the
twentieth century (Gates 1968, 571, 572), but specific legislative
authority and programs did not appear until the Weeks Act of 1911 (fire
protection), which was later joined by the Clarke-McNary Act of 1924
(fire control, reforestation, education, and land acquisition) and the
McSweeney-McNary Act of 1928 (research). Relative newcomers are the
McIntire-Stennis Act of 1962 (research), the Cooperative Forestry Assistance
Act of 1978 (rural forestry assistance, forestry incentives, insect and disease
control, fire prevention and control, and other technical assistance), and the
1980 amendments to the Forestry Incentives Program (FIP).

Cooperative Research

Forest Service research dates at least to the beginning of the old Division of Forestry (Pinchot claims to have authored the "first systematic study of American trees, by foresters for foresters," in 1896—a 100-page book, *The White Pine,* by Pinchot and Henry Solon Graves) (Pinchot [1947] 1972, 306). The first forest experiment station was established in Coconino National Forest near Flagstaff, Arizona, in 1908, and two others followed in Colorado in 1909 and 1910 (Pinchot [1947] 1972, 309). Research gained additional stature in 1915, when Earle H. Clapp, head of the Branch of Research, was successful in making the branch independent of National Forest System administration (Frome 1984, 221).

The McSweeny-McNary Act of 1928 provided additional impetus. Based on a 1925-1926 study by a committee of the Society of American Foresters headed by Clapp, the bill was introduced in December 1927 and passed in less than six months (Dana and Fairfax 1980, 129).

The act authorizes and directs the secretary of agriculture to conduct investigations

> in order to determine, demonstrate, and promulgate the best methods of reforestation and of growing, managing, and utilizing timber, forage, and other forest products, of maintaining favorable conditions of water flow and the prevention of erosion, of protecting timber and other forest growth from fire, insects, disease, or other harmful agencies, of obtaining the fullest and most effective use of forest lands, and to determine and promulgate the economic conditions which should underlie the establishment of sound policies for the management of forest land and the utilization of forest products. (45 Stat. 699-700)

Thirteen regional forest experiment stations were authorized in the contiguous states, plus one each in Alaska, Hawaii, and U.S. possessions in the West Indies (not all of which were constructed). Specific appropriations were authorized for studies of tree diseases, forest insects, forest wildlife, the relationship between weather conditions and forest fires, timber management, and forest product utilization (45 Stat. 700, 701).

The McIntire-Stennis Act of 1962 (as amended by section 1441 of the Agriculture and Food Act of 1981) rounds out legislative authority for the Forest Service research program. The act

> recognize[s] that the total forestry research efforts of the several State colleges and universities and of the Federal Government are more fully effec-

tive if there is close coordination between such programs, and...that forestry schools are especially vital to the training of research workers in forestry, and...that the provisions of this Act are essential to assist in providing the research background that undergirds the Forest and Rangeland Renewable Resources Act of 1974..., the Renewable Resources Extension Act of 1978..., and the Soil and Water Resources Conservation Act of 1977. (16 U.S.C. 582a [1982])

The act authorized financial assistance to "land-grant colleges or agricultural experiment stations" and "other State-supported colleges and universities offering graduate training in...forestry and having a forestry school...for the purpose of encouraging and assisting them in carrying out programs of forestry research" (76 Stat. 806). Federal funds are limited to no more than one-half the amount appropriated for in-house Department of Agriculture forestry research (based on the year before the year in which the budget is prepared) and to no more than the amount of each institution's forestry research funded from nonfederal sources (76 Stat. 806).

In addition to creating cooperative research programs with the states, section 9 of the McSweeney-McNary Act directed the secretary of agriculture to conduct "a comprehensive survey of the present and prospective requirements for timber and other forest products in the United States." This precursor of the Forest and Rangeland Renewable Resources Planning Act of 1974 (RPA) established the forest survey (changed to "renewable resources evaluation" following passage of the Forest and Rangeland Renewable Resources Research Act of 1978) and the beginning of regular, periodic inventories of the nation's forest resources.

The McSweeney-McNary Act was repealed by the Forest and Rangeland Renewable Resources Research Act of 1978, which continued most of the programs previously authorized but partially reoriented the research program to better support RPA.

The linkage between research and operations has not been an easy one. Pinchot contrasts the early days of the service with those of later enlightenment:

In those days the research men were not on their own, but were attached to the Forest Supervisors, to help with technical problems. Their presence was often resented on the ground that they were Eastern tenderfeet..., but more commonly because of their persistent and sometimes unreasonable habit of asking embarrassing professional questions. (Pinchot [1947] 1972, 308)

Because the research man did his job well, forest executives are now eager to turn results of scientific investigation to practical use. (Pinchot [1947] 1972, 310)

But the same move that made the research arm more autonomous, removing it from under the National Forest System to answer directly to the chief forester, also broke the thread that might have made research findings more accepted by those in the line:

Although a certain degree of freedom is necessarily sacrificed through research's affiliation with an action agency, the loss need not prove unduly detrimental to science....Consolidation and divorce are not in themselves ultimate desiderata. Premature unification may stifle research; unduly prolonged separation may limit its usefulness. Only as organizational schemes are related to the programmatic objectives of both administrators and scientists do they acquire meaning. Inquiries into the nature of professionalism, and into the character of research and administrative corps, may reveal when either alternative, or its variants, is no longer justified. (Schiff 1962, 180, 181)

Perhaps it is time for reunification, for as Michael Frome noted twenty-two years later:

[H]ighly qualified researchers have turned up choice independent findings, but getting them applied in practice has proven something else again. (Frome 1984, 221)

Fire Protection

Fire! "Keep America Green!" Smokey Bear. "Remember, Only You Can Prevent Forest Fires!" Nothing in the natural resources field stirs the emotions so much as a roaring crown fire, stampeding wildlife before it, consuming everything in its path. Yet the history of forest fires, their control and management, is a somewhat tortuous path.

Fire was a part of the North American environment long before the coming of the white man and affected virtually all areas that produced sufficient fuel to support a burn. Lightning fires, once started, ran until extinguished by rain or stopped by rivers or other natural firebreaks. Indians started fires as a means of clearing land and fertilizing the soil for their maize agriculture, for hunting, for wildlife habitat management, to remove concealment of potential use to their enemies, to clear village sites, and to create and maintain grasslands. Early settlers adopted and continued the Indian fire practices (Pyne 1982, 46-51). Numerous writings confirm that the "virgin" forests encountered by pioneers were open and parklike, were easily transited by horse and rider, and contained frequent and large expanses of meadow and grassland maintained by frequent and often intense fires—they were not the dense stands that have developed during the past century or two in the relative absence of fire, which many equate with virgin forests today.

Many fires during the 1800s and early 1900s were very large and destructive:

> The Mirimichi and Maine fires of 1825, the North Carolina fire of 1898, the 1910 fires in Idaho and Montana,...exceeded 3 million acres. The Wisconsin fires of 1894, the Michigan fires of 1871, and the Washington and Oregon fires of 1910 exceeded 2 million acres. (Pyne 1982, 537 [citing several sources])

Natural or not, fires of this magnitude could not be tolerated in a nation rapidly occupying and developing "wilderness" areas and beginning to practice intensive forestry.

As early as 1631, the Massachusetts Bay Colony had passed an ordinance providing penalties for setting destructive woods fires, and it later prescribed the death penalty "for anyone convicted of willfully setting fires." In 1891 Maine created the first State Forest Commission with a fire suppression mission, with little fanfare, "more than likely a behind-the-scenes proposal of the big timber owners who needed state help to protect their lands from fire" (Widner 1968, 18, 19). Minnesota followed in 1895 with appointment of a chief fire warden "for the prevention and suppression of forest and prairie fires" (Widner 1968, 40). In the same year, Wisconsin authorized the state forestry warden to appoint a fire warden in each organized township (Widner 1968, 188). In 1910 private timber owners in Michigan and Wisconsin organized the Northern Forest Protective Organization. But state and private efforts of those days tended to wax and wane with the severity of recent fires, and it was left to the Weeks Act of 1911 to lend coherence and permanence to national forest fire control efforts (Pyne 1982, 213).

A rash of fires during the early 1900s coincided with national concern over floods and damaged watersheds, a possible timber famine, and other environmental concerns. A Governor's Conference on Conservation was held at the White House in 1908 (Pyne 1982, 61). The North American

Conservation Conference was held at the same location in 1908 (Pinchot [1947] 1972, 362). The National and Southern conservation congresses were convened in 1910, and the American Forestry Association and other conservation groups were active and effective lobbying forces. It was in this environment that the Weeks Bill was debated. Controversy surrounded the proposal to purchase eastern lands for national forests, but the provisions regarding fire protection evoked little interest (Widner 1968, 212-215).

The Weeks Act gave the consent of Congress "to each of the several states...to enter into any agreement or compact...for the purpose of conserving the forests and the water supply" and authorized the secretary of agriculture to "agree with any State or group of States to cooperate in the organization and maintenance of a system of fire protection on private or State forest lands." Federal cooperation was conditioned on the lands being "situated upon the watershed of a navigable river," on each participating state's developing a system of forest fire prevention, and on each providing at least one-half of the cost (36 Stat. 961). The sum of $200,000 was appropriated for federal participation (Ise 1920, 221).

Gifford Pinchot was preoccupied with his controversy with Secretary of the Interior Ballinger at the time, gave the Weeks Bill little attention (Widner 1968, 213), and scarcely mentions it in *Breaking New Ground* (Pinchot [1947] 1972). (Note: The Weeks Bill was initially introduced on April 24, 1907, in the Sixtieth Congress, but it failed to pass the Senate prior to adjournment. A new Weeks Bill was introduced on July 23, 1909, in the Sixty-first Congress, was passed by both houses, and became law on March 1, 1911. Pinchot was dismissed by President Taft on January 7, 1910, and was not present for the final legislative debates, but he was chief during most of the congressional deliberations [Widner 1968, 212-214].) On the other hand, William Greeley, chief forester from 1920 to 1928, cited the cooperative program provisions as

"another bit of legislation which has proved even more important than the forest purchases in steering the course of Federal policy....This was the first in a great cooperative expansion of national forestry." (Widner 1968, 216)

When the Weeks Act was passed, only eleven states could qualify for assistance, but by 1924 all but thirteen had made a start. Still, "[n]early half of all state and private woodlands were still without organized protection, and a fourth of our annual timber crop was going up in smoke....Fire was plainly recognized as forest enemy No. 1" (Greeley 1951, 24, 26).

The Clarke-McNary Act of 1924 authorized the secretary to recommend "for each forest region of the United States, systems of forest fire prevention and suppression," extended federal participation to any "timbered or forest producing lands" within the cooperating states (removing the "navigable streams" restriction of the Weeks Act), and increased the annual fire prevention funding authorization to $2.5 million (43 Stat. 653).

Following the disastrous New England fires of 1947, Congress approved the Northeastern Interstate Forest Fire Protection Compact on June 25, 1949, and three years later approved Canadian participation in the compact—but it was not until June 9, 1970, that the complete compact of seven states and two provinces (Quebec and New Brunswick) was finalized (Wilkins 1978, 82, 83). Other sections of the country were also moving toward regional arrangements: the Southeastern and South Central Interstate Forest Fire Protection compacts were approved in 1954; the Middle Atlantic Compact, in 1956; and the Pacific Northwest and California compacts, in 1978; and two larger, informal coordinative groups were established—the Northeast Forest Fire Supervisors (1973) and the Southern Forest Fire Chief's Association (1974) (Pyne 1982, 358).

Although details of the compacts vary, they contain the same major provisions (examples are from the Southeastern Compact). State foresters or comparable officers administer the program, assisted by "an advisory committee of legislators, forestry commission representatives, and forestry or forest products industries representatives." Compact administrators develop a regional forest fire plan, of which each state plan is a component (art. III). "Whenever the state forest fire control agency of a member state requests aid from...any other state in combatting, controlling or preventing forest fires,...that state [shall]...render all possible aid..." (art. IV). The requesting state assumes liability for the actions of individual participants from cooperating states (other than for negligence) and compensates the cooperating states for all expenses (art. V). Compact administrators may request the Forest Service to "act as a research and coordinating agency (art. VII). By the late 1970s, then, an administrative network of private and local, state, and federal government interests had been perfected sufficiently to handle almost any fire situation (given that there are times when no amount of resources can "handle" a fire).

As the technical, logistic, and institutional approaches to forest fire control were improving, the Forest Service was also developing an intense public education program. The Cooperative Forest Fire Prevention Campaign (CFFP) began in 1942, fed by the patriotism of the war effort, bolstered by professional advertising agencies, and assisted by the Wartime Advertising Council. In 1945 Smokey Bear first appeared. A black bear cub, "Little Smokey," was rescued from a fire in Lincoln National Forest, New Mexico, in 1950 and became the living symbol of the nation's forest fire prevention effort (Pyne 1982, 175-177).

No other natural resource information and education program has been as successful as Smokey Bear. Aimed primarily at children, it is sponsored jointly by the Forest Service, the Department of the Interior, and the National Association of State Foresters, with assistance from the Ad Council—and it convinced children of the 1950s and 1960s beyond any doubt that forest fires were bad and the Forest Service was a fire-fighting agency (and perhaps little else) (Pyne 1982, 177).

During this period—about 1935 to 1970—Forest Service fire management policy centered around the "10 A.M. policy." Simply stated, the service attempted to "control all fires during the first duty shift after fire detection; but if that was not possible, try to control all fires by 10 A.M. the next day" (U.S. Congress, Senate 1989, 37). No distinction was made between fires in wilderness and nonwilderness areas; all fires were suppressed.

But during the 1960s and early 1970s, research was showing fire to be a natural component of forest ecosystems and a silvicultural tool. Fire research was being conducted at the Florida-based Tall Timbers Research Station, and exposure was afforded by the Tall Timbers fire ecology conferences (Pyne 1982, 153, 154, 159). The service's own research and management activities were showing that fire was essential to maintenance of the pineries of the South (Schiff 1962). Suppression of wilderness fires was determined to be "undesirable in the larger perspective of wilderness management"—and extremely expensive (Pyne 1982, 179).

During the same period, Herbert L. Stoddard's classic *The Bobwhite Quail: Its Habits, Preservation, and Increase* (Stoddard 1931), which advocated fire as a bobwhite management tool, was beginning to receive its rightful recognition. All these efforts (and others) were telling the same story: Fire in the woods definitely is not all "bad," and in many cases it is "good." The problem became one of public education (or reeducation)—distinguishing between (1) low-intensity, frequent fires under controlled conditions (i.e., "prescribed fires"), which release nutrients, reduce fuel levels, increase ground cover and browse, and aid in suppressing hardwoods in pine stands, and (2) high-intensity, uncontrolled, infrequent fires (i.e., wildfires), which may destroy the forest and most of its inhabitants.

By 1971 the Forest Service had expressed concern over the buildup of fuels in wilderness areas resulting from effective fire suppression and the high cost and lack of management flexibility in its existing program, and it began relaxing the 10 A.M. policy. The modified policy allowed lightning fires in wilderness areas to burn if carefully specified conditions were met. Such fires were described as "prescribed fires of natural origin" (U.S. Congress, Senate 1989, 37).

The Cooperative Forestry Assistance Act of 1978 rewrote the fire prevention and suppression provisions of the Clarke-McNary Act, emphasizing "rural fire prevention and control" rather than forest fires and raising "prescribed use of fires" to the same status as "prevention, control, [and] suppression" (sec. 7). But the reeducation problem may be as difficult as the original education problem (Pyne 1982, 180), and we have two generations of Americans who have learned that forest fires are "bad."

By the mid 1980s, Forest Service fire management policy was described as follows:

OBJECTIVES: The objective of the Forest Service fire management policy is cost effective integration of fire protection and use in land and resource management planning and direction....

TWO CATEGORIES OF FIRES: Fires occurring on National Forest lands are designated as either wildfires or prescribed fires. A prescribed fire is any wildland fire burning under preplanned, specified conditions to accomplish specific planned objectives....A wildfire is any wildland fire not designated and managed as a prescribed fire within an approved prescription.

WILDFIRE SUPPRESSION: Forest Service suppression policy is to conduct wildfire suppression action in a timely, energetic, and thorough manner with a high regard for public and firefighter safety....

PRESCRIBED FIRE MANAGEMENT: Prescribed fire plans are prepared in advance of all prescribed fires. Personnel conducting prescribed fires must meet training and qualification requirements.

The fire management policy was sorely tested during the 1988 fire season, during which 30,000 fire fighters battled 70,000 fires over 3.7

million acres in the western United States and another 2 million acres in Alaska, expending $600 million in fire suppression efforts (Jeffery 1989, 265). The situation in and around Yellowstone National Park provides a graphic example.

Prior to the 1970s, park policy had been to extinguish all fires as soon as possible, and organic residue had been allowed to accumulate in the dry climate of Yellowstone for ninety years (Jeffery 1989, 258). Mature to overmature stands of lodgepole pine, a highly flammable and fire-dependent species, occupied much of the burned area, and in some stands more than 50 percent of the trees had previously been killed by a beetle epidemic (McCleese 1989, 4). During late summer dry cold fronts accompanied by lightning ignited numerous fires, and high winds quickly spread them beyond control (Jeffery 1989, 258).

Eventually, thirteen major fires burned within the greater Yellowstone area. Of the approximately 1.6 million acres burned, about 1 million were within the national park and about 600,000 were in the five national forests that surround it. All but approximately 200,000 acres were either within the park or in designated wilderness areas in the National Forest System (McCleese 1989, 4; U.S. Congress, Senate 1989, 35). Most of the affected land was under National Park Service (Department of the Interior) administration, but suppression efforts were coordinated principally by the Forest Service (Department of Agriculture). In the eyes of the public, and of Congress, it made little difference—forestland was going up in smoke all over the nightly television news—and wilderness and wildland fire management policy did not differ substantially between the agencies.

While the fires still raged, Congress began hearings on fire management policies. Senators from Montana (Max Baucus and John Melcher), Idaho (James A. McClure), and Wyoming (Alan K. Simpson and Malcolm Wallop) decried the "natural burn policy," the "devastation," the "economic impact of the fires . . . [upon] the tourist seasons," and blamed much of the "Leopold Report, which stated that Yellowstone should be managed in a 'natural' manner; that Yellowstone should be 'an illusion of primitive America'" (U.S. Congress, Senate 1989, 2, 3, 10).

Despite the emotion and political implications, several senators also mentioned the fire policy that had worked for fifteen of the past sixteen years, a policy that "appears reasonable on its face," that "one can find little in the stated language to disagree with" (U.S. Congress, Senate 1989, 4, 6, 8). Testimony from the Department of the Interior and the Department of Agriculture dispassionately reviewed the history of fire management and the conditions that affected the Greater Yellowstone Area fires and promised an early review by agency representatives.

By mid-December the review had been completed. A Fire Management Policy Review Team, composed of representatives of the Forest Service, the National Park Service, the Bureau of Land Management, the U.S. Fish and Wildlife Service, the Bureau of Indian Affairs, and the National Association of State Foresters and cochaired by representatives of the two departments, presented a twenty-five-page report of their findings (Fire Management Policy Review Team 1988). The report covers only "fire management in national parks and wilderness" and thus does not deal with nonwilderness portions of the National Forest System. Among the team's more important findings were the following:

> The objectives of policies governing prescribed natural fire programs in national parks and wilderness are sound, but the policies themselves need to be refined, strengthened, and reaffirmed....
>
> There are risks inherent in trying to manage fire, but they can be reduced by careful planning and preparation. Use of planned burning and other efforts to reduce hazard fuels near high value structures and to create fire breaks along boundaries help[s] to reduce risks from both prescribed natural fires and wildfires.
>
> The ecological effects of prescribed natural fire support resource objectives in parks and wilderness, but in some cases the social and economic effects may be unacceptable. (Fire Management Policy Review Team 1988, i)

And its major recommendations were that

> [p]rescribed natural fire policies in the agencies be reaffirmed and strengthened.
>
> [f]ire management plans be reviewed to assure that current policy requirements are met and expanded to include interagency planning, stronger prescriptions, and additional decision criteria....
>
> [a]gencies consider opportunities to use planned ignitions to complement prescribed natural fire programs and to reduce hazard fuels.
>
> [a]dditional research and analysis relating to weather, fire behavior, fire history, fire information integration, and other topics be carried out so that future management programs can be carried out more effectively and with less risk. (Fire Management Policy Review Team 1988, ii)

While the review team suggested a number of improvements, it endorsed and even strengthened the use of prescribed fire in wilderness areas. In fact the present policy generally has been successful, particularly in the national parks, and damage caused by wildfire and escaped prescribed fires frequently is far less than initially supposed. Between 1968 and 1987, more than 1,600 lightning-caused fires were permitted to burn more than 320,000 acres of national park land—with only one serious problem (the community of Allenspark, Colorado, was threatened by one fire). In addition, park personnel ignited more than 1,400 prescribed burns covering more than 325,000 acres (Fire Management Policy Review Team 1988, 9, 10). Within the two Forest Service regions having the most active wilderness prescribed fire programs, only 23 of 503 prescribed natural fires became wildfires, but these burned more than 500,000 acres (the remainder burned 209,000 acres) (Fire Management Policy Review Team 1988, 25). Two years later, in May 1990, the General Accounting Office (GAO) submitted an evaluation of changes made in federal fire management following the Yellowstone fires and the review team's report. The GAO found that implementation of the team's recommendations was "taking longer than anticipated, [but] both the Park Service and the Forest Service have revised their guidance and are developing the called-for plans" (Duffus 1990, 11). The GAO was concerned, however, that interagency coordination continued to be a problem and that some jurisdictions were unlikely to adopt the prescribed natural fire program because

> wildfires must receive priority, [and] prescribed fires can be allowed to burn only if there are sufficient [resources]...to keep them under control. But over the last 10 years, these resources have declined substantially. Second, the money specifically allocated to the prescribed fire program is less than what many Park Service and Forest Service managers say they need. And third, some managers still subscribe to the old philosophy of suppressing all fires. (Duffus 1990, 12)

The GAO believed that

> government may still lack the organizational structure essential to respond to national fire emergencies,...[and that] increases in funding and fire-fighting resources, as well as changes in attitudes, are necessary...[, but that for] the long term, the program offers promise of restoring wildlands to their natural state and reducing the severity of future wildfires. (Duffus 1990, 13)

The test will come with the next extreme fire season.

And what of the damage to Yellowstone? For a time the land lay gray and desolate. Yet a "significant share of those trees will survive the fire…as a mosaic…[T]he damage has not been as severe as might have been anticipated" (U.S. Congress, Senate 1989, 23, 24). Park personnel expect plant diversity to increase up to tenfold during the next twenty years and animal diversity to increase likewise. Elk and bison mortality was less than that expected from a hard winter, and burned meadows should have recovered by the following summer. In three to five years, ground vegetation should carpet the forest floor—and more people visited Yellowstone during October 1988 than during any previous October in its history (Jeffery 1989, 271, 272).

Reforestation

Pinchot was convinced that "the practice of Forestry on private lands" would not be implemented without federal intervention:

> We saw that only Federal control of cutting on private land could assure the Nation the supply of forest products it must have to prosper. We demanded that control, which has long been in effect in the most democratic and the most civilized nations, but in vain.…
>
> That the United States will eventually exercise such control is inevitable, because without it the safety of our forests and consequently the prosperity of our people cannot be assured. So far the lumber industry, by its highly organized and very expensive campaign, has succeeded in preventing what the public interest so clearly requires. (Pinchot [1947] 1972, 293, 294)

Pinchot placed his reliance on eventual control over the harvest by fiat; William B. Greeley adopted a more moderate position and shifted emphasis from harvest to reforestation:

> The conviction became strong in my mind that industry itself was the greatest latent force for reforestation if the government could give it a lift, shake off some of its shackles and get it going. (Greeley 1951, 108)

"The diversion of Gifford Pinchot's interest to a new arena in Pennsylvania politics left the supporters of forest regulation without a leader," and Greeley's cooperative philosophy was incorporated into the

Clarke-McNary Act of 1924 (Greeley 1951, 109). Section 4 of the act authorized the secretary of agriculture to provide federal cost sharing to pay up to 50 percent of state costs to supply "forest-tree seeds and plants, for the purpose of establishing windbreaks, shelter belts, and farm wood lots upon denuded or nonforested lands." Section 5 authorized similar assistance to "owners of farms in establishing, improving, and renewing wood lots, shelter belts, windbreaks, and other valuable forest growth, and in growing and renewing useful timber crops" (43 Stat. 654).

Initially described in section 1009 of the Agriculture and Consumer Protection Act of 1973 and expanded by the Cooperative Forestry Assistance Act of 1978, the Forestry Incentives Program (FIP) extended federal reforestation subsidies directly to the landowner (generally owners of no more than 1,000 acres of "private forest land"). Section 4 of the 1978 act (92 Stat. 367) authorized reimbursement of up to 75 percent of a landowner's costs for "afforestation of suitable open lands, reforestation of cutover or other unstocked or understocked forest lands, timber stand improvement practices, including thinning, prescribed burning, and other silvicultural treatments, and forest resources management and protection" in accordance with an approved forest management plan (later administrative actions have reduced the federal share to about 50 percent of costs).

Justified primarily as an adjunct to "cost-effective timber production," the first year of the 1974 program was estimated to produce 1,045 million cubic feet of wood over the first rotation (primarily softwood sawtimber) and provide an internal rate of return (IROR) of 9.4 percent based on total costs and 14.9 percent based on private costs (Mills and Cain 1979, 663, 664). A similar study of the 1979 program estimated wood production at 1,307 million cubic feet, total IROR at 8.3 percent, and private IROR at 10.9 percent (Risbrudt, Kaiser, and Ellefson 1983, 299, 300).

Title XII of the Food Security Act of 1985 has the potential to greatly expand federally subsidized reforestation. The Conservation Reserve Program (CRP) established by that act authorized the secretary of agriculture to enter into contracts with owners and operators of farms and ranches, for not less than ten nor more than fifteen years, to remove highly erodible lands from cultivation and to convert them to less intensive uses such as "pasture, permanent grass, legumes, forbs, shrubs, or trees." During the 1986-1988 crop years, not less than 25 million nor more than 45 million acres of cropland were to be placed in the CRP (99 Stat. 509, 510). "To the extent practicable, not less than one eighth [of the land placed in the CRP]...in each of the 1986 through 1990 crop years shall be devoted to trees" (99 Stat. 511). Payments are based on "bids" offered by the landowners and operators and may be paid in cash or commodities (99 Stat. 512). Through the February 1987 sign-up period, the CRP contained 19.5 million acres of erodible land, 1.1 million of which were to be planted in trees (Wildlife Management Institute 1987a, 1; 1987b, 3). By June 1988 enrollment had reached 25.5 million acres (Wildlife Management Institute 1988, 1), surpassing the minimum goal in the act. Through 1989 almost 34 million acres had been enrolled, of which nearly 2.2 million had been planted in trees (Wildlife Management Institute 1990, 3). The total enrollment goal was achieved, but reforestation fell somewhat short. Nevertheless, 2 million additional acres of forest, established on highly erodible sites over a period of three years, is a commendable accomplishment.

PERSISTENT PROBLEMS

Legislation of the 1970s provided a structure for Forest Service planning and mechanisms for citizen input throughout Forest Service activities. But serious problems remain within the service, the National Forest System, and the practice of forestry in general. No single cause or simple causes are evident, few examples of malfeasance or malice have surfaced, and all three branches of government and numerous special-interest groups have looked for solutions—yet conflicts over forest management seem to be intensifying rather than ameliorating. At least three interrelated elements are involved: concepts of multiple use and sustained yield, desires of the forest owners, and "the system."

Multiple Use and Sustained Yield

Attractive as the goals of multiple use and sustained yield appear, they become increasingly difficult to attain with decreasing temporal and spatial scales. Within infinite space and time, one can produce a great variety of goods and services; at a single point in space and time, perhaps only one. Forests exhibit a tremendous variety of scales. Stands may be only a few acres or several thousand; silvicultural rotations may be two or three decades or more than a century.

Producing a continuous flow of products through time from a tract of land poses similar scalar problems. Again, the smaller the scale the more difficult it becomes to approach "nondeclining even flow." In the extreme case, a small even-aged stand, income may be possible only at intervals of a decade or more—the intervening years produce nothing salable. As temporal and spatial scales increase, it becomes possible to even out these irregularities, producing in the aggregate something approaching a sustained yield.

Further confounding the multiple-use and sustained-yield issues is the fact that some uses are inherently conflicting, incompatible, or exclusive and that MUSY "mixes resource protection with use and output production without defining the balance among resource values" (U.S. Congress, Office of Technology Assessment 1992, 46). Lands dedicated to wilderness or perpetuation of old growth cannot produce timber; lands producing timber cannot provide the attributes of wilderness and old growth. Cutover lands lose their value as aesthetic amenities for several decades, eventually regaining it as the new timber stand matures. Logging operations are difficult or impossible to conduct in areas frequented by hikers, hunters, campers, and others attracted by woodland aesthetics.

And each of us is seeing different consumptive and nonconsumptive forest products coming from areas of different sizes over varying lengths of time and is trying to equate these observations with the concepts of multiple use and sustained yield—what the laws have promised us. Multiple-use decisions are inherently compromises, and thus no one is fully satisfied.

Desires of the Forest Owners

In the first edition of his classic text, *The Practice of Silviculture*, Ralph C. Hawley states the purpose of silviculture to be "the production and maintenance of such a forest as shall best fulfill the objectives of the owner" (Hawley 1921, 5). The eighth edition (Smith 1986, 335) contains a similar admonition:

> The objectives of ownership clearly dictate the relative amounts of attention paid to management for timber, wildlife, forage, water, recreation, scenery, or other benefits that forests may provide. On land managed for multiple use, the silviculture logically differs from that on similar land that might be owned by a lumber company for growing saw timber; this would in turn differ from a paper company's silviculture for pulpwood production. If an owner is mostly interested in wildlife or in preserving some old-growth timber purely for aesthetic purposes, the forester should

modify the silviculture accordingly. In fact, the forester's occupational bias in favor of efficient timber production can be more of a liability than an asset. (Smith 1986, 336)

But who are the forest owners, and what are their desires? In the case of the national forests, they are all citizens, ostensibly with equal representation, and with an almost infinite array of aspirations. Even on privately owned forestlands, the magnitude of common property resources affected ensures considerable influence in the public interest. The diversity of interests represented by the citizenry causes almost any action by a forestland manager to be opposed (and supported) by a substantial population.

Large clear-cuts may be desirable from a harvest economics standpoint, but they are undesirable from an aesthetic and wildlife habitat point of view. Regulated forests produce a generally reliable flow of goods and services over time but are incompatible with the desires of those favoring old growth. Short rotations favor wildlife species preferring fields and brushland; long rotations favor canopy species and cavity nesters. Large populations of grazing animals may be desired by wildlife observers and some hunters but may retard forest regeneration and compete with domestic stock. Softwood silviculture produces greater financial returns but fewer wildlife dependent on hard mast and nesting cavities. Short rotations provide greater edge and species diversity across large areas; long rotations and mature stands produce greater within-stand variation; and so on. In the interests of providing roaded recreation and habitat for successional species, and/or to achieve social objectives, timber sales may be justified that by more stringent accounting would be "below cost" and economically inviable. And "the system" provides a variety of opportunities for each interest to influence forestland management decisions.

"The System"

Our legal and political systems combine to give each interest a voice in the decision-making process, overtly or covertly, and a chance to affect the outcome of each issue. The most obvious avenues are those provided by statute and regulation—participation in the planning process, access to government documents, review of environmental impact assessments and statements, protection of endangered species, administrative appeals and judicial review of forest plans, enforcement of pollution control regulations, and so forth. The most important avenues, however, are the underlying processes, and these may not be so evident. Provisions of the Endangered Species Act may be invoked to protect the northern spotted owl, whereas the real motive is to prevent harvesting of old-growth stands. Best management practices (BMPs) may be sincere efforts to adopt environmentally sensitive forest practices or simply attempts to avoid more stringent regulation. Local politicians may favor logging in the national forests on the pretext of supporting struggling local industry but really want to increase payments to local governments in lieu of taxes. Environmentalists may oppose clear-cutting but really want to prevent all (or most) timbering in the national forests. Forest Service personnel may argue for a higher allowable cut, justified on a silvicultural and economic basis, when they really are supporting projections that have been established at higher levels in the organization.

The means by which influence is exerted (some call these "politics") can be just as varied and murky. Outright confrontation through lawsuits may work but can be expensive, and the outcome is at best uncertain and delayed. How about a "public education" program? Workshops and symposia? Television features? All of these can sway public opinion and influence decision makers. Perhaps an environmental assessment leaves some questions unanswered. Merely raising the issue may delay action, commit scarce agency resources, reduce the agency's effectiveness, and blemish its reputation. Votes can be registered in many ways. Candidates can incorporate "environmental" or "economic development" planks in their platforms; incumbents can vote for or against agency programs and budgets; congressional hearings can be painful or supportive.

All of this process descends upon a forest ranger or forest supervisor, a person educated and trained as a technocrat, steeped in the how-to elements of the profession. His or her job is to manage forests. He or she may have had one or two courses in policy and law and a little exposure to interpersonal skills, but the emphasis was on trees, not people. Furthermore, that ranger or supervisor is part of an organization that, with justifiable pride, has for more than seven decades subscribed to the utilitarian ethic of Pinchot. It should come as no surprise that Forest Service personnel have had difficulty coping with post-1970 developments.

With all its defects, however, the system is beginning to show signs of working for the public benefit. Many appeals of national forest plans have been settled through negotiation, and other, inadequate, plans have been remanded to regional offices for revision. Within the Forest Service and with the endorsement of the chief, personnel are reevaluating their roles as resource managers and recommending policy changes. Congress has addressed the special treatment afforded the Tongass National Forest and investigated the Forest Service's controversial bookkeeping system. Retention of old growth is beginning to stand on its own merits rather than being shored up by an endangered species crutch. Allowable cuts in many national forests have been reduced to more realistic levels and the area to be cut and roaded reduced concomitantly. Perhaps most important, prospective land managers and colleges and universities are taking a broader look at natural resource management, with more emphasis on policy and the social sciences (Westoby 1989, 213)—all of which bodes well for the future.

REFERENCES

Clary, David A. 1986. *Timber and the Forest Service.* Lawrence: University Press of Kansas.

"Conservationists Fight to Preserve Monongahela Forest." 1970. *Outdoor America* (May 1970): 11.

Cook, Harold O. n.d. *Fifty Years a Forester.* Boston: Massachusetts Department of Natural Resources.

Council on Environmental Quality. 1974. *Environmental Quality—1974.* Washington, DC: Government Printing Office.

———. 1975. *Environmental Quality—1975.* Washington, DC: Government Printing Office.

———. 1976. *Environmental Quality—1976.* Washington, DC: Government Printing Office.

Cronon, Edmund D. 1983. *Changes in the Land: Indians, Colonists, and the Ecology of New England.* New York: Hill & Wang.

Dana, Samuel T. [1956] 1968. "Live Oaks and Pine." In *Forests and Forestry in the American States,* edited by Ralph R. Widner, 73-78. Washington, DC: National Association of State Foresters. (Reprinted from Dana and Fairfax 1980.)

Dana, Samuel T., and Sally K. Fairfax, 1980. *Forest and Range Policy: Its Development in the United States.* New York: McGraw-Hill Book Company.

Davis, Lawrence S. 1981. "The RPA Process: 1980. Report Summary of the Task Force on RPA Implementation." *Journal of Forestry* 79:382-385.

Duffus, James, III. 1990. "Federal Fire Management: Evaluation of Changes Made After Yellowstone," Committee on Government Operations, Subcommittee on Environment, Energy, and Natural Resources, in U.S. Congress, House, "Federal Fire Management Policy: Evaluation of Changes Made After Yellowstone," 5-13. 101st Cong., 2d sess., May 24, 1990. Washington, DC: Government Printing Office.

Encyclopedia Americana. International Edition. 1978. 30 vols. Danbury, CT: Americana Corporation.

Fairfax, Sally K., and Gail L. Achterman. 1977. "The Monongahela Controversy and the Political Process." *Journal of Forestry* 75:485-487.

Fire Management Policy Review Team. 1988. "Report on Fire Management Policy." Washington, DC: U.S. Department of Agriculture; U.S. Department of the Interior.

Fox, Stephen R. 1981. *John Muir and His Legacy.* Boston: Little, Brown & Company.

Frome, Michael. 1971. "Clearcutting the National Forests." *Field and Stream* 76 (3): 32, 34.

———. 1972. "Truth in Timber." *Field and Stream* 77 (2): 38, 40, 45.

———. 1984. *The Forest Service.* Boulder, CO: Westview Press.

Gates, Paul W. 1968. "History of Land Law Development." Public Land Law Review Commission study report. Washington, DC: Government Printing Office.

General Land Office. 1893. "General Land Office Annual Report." Washington, DC: Government Printing Office.

Greeley, William B. 1951. *Forests and Men.* New York: Doubleday & Company.

Hawley, Ralph C. 1921. *The Practice of Silviculture.* New York: John Wiley & Sons.

Hibbard, Benjamin H. 1924. *A History of the Public Land Policies.* New York: Macmillan Company.

Hutchins, John G. B. 1941. *The American Maritime Industries and Public Policy: 1789-1914.* Cambridge, MA: Harvard University Press.

Ise, John. 1920. *The United States Forest Policy.* New Haven, CT: Yale University Press.

Jeffery, David. 1989. "Yellowstone: The Fires of 1988." *National Geographic* 175 (2): 255-273.

Johnson, K. Norman. 1986. *FORPLAN Version 1: An Overview.* Washington, DC: Government Printing Office.

Johnson, V. Webster, and Raleigh Barlowe. [1954] 1979. *Land Problems and Policies.* New York: Arno Press.

Korstian, C. F. 1937. "Perpetuation of Spruce on Cutover and Burned Lands in the Higher Appalachians." *Ecological Monographs* 7:125-167.

Le Master, Dennis C. 1984. *Decade of Change: The Remaking of the Forest Service Statutory Authority During the 1970s.* Westport, CT: Greenwood Press.

McCleese, William. 1989. "The Environmental Effects of Wildfire." *Fire Management Notes* 50 (2): 3-8.

McKechnie, W. S. 1958. *Magna Carta: A Commentary on the Great Charter of King John.* New York: Burt Franklin & Company.

"Message from the President of the United States Transmitting a Report of the Secretary of Agriculture in Relation to the Forests, Rivers, and Mountains of the Southern Appalachian Region." 1902. Washington, DC: Government Printing Office. (Note: This report is referenced elsewhere as U.S. Department of Agriculture 1901 and was published as S. Doc. 84 of the 57th Congress, 1st session.)

Mills, Thomas J., and Daria Cain. 1979. "Financial Efficiency of the 1974 Forestry Incentives Program." *Journal of Forestry* 77:661-666.

Nelson, Thomas C. 1977. "Problems in Implementing Federal Forestry Laws." *Journal of Forestry* 75:192-194.

Pankowski, Ted. 1970. "Walton Officials Tour Clearcut Timber Area." *Outdoor America* (February 1970): 12.

Pinchot, Gifford. 1902. "Report of the Forester for 1902," 109-136. (From U.S. Department of Agriculture's "Annual Reports.") Washington, DC: Government Printing Office.

————. 1908. "Report of the Forester for 1908." (From U.S. Department of Agriculture's "Annual Reports.") Washington, DC: Government Printing Office.

————. [1947] 1972. *Breaking New Ground.* Seattle: University of Washington Press.

Pinkett, Harold T. 1970. *Gifford Pinchot: Private and Public Forester.* Champaign: University of Illinois Press.

President's Advisory Panel on Timber and the Environment. 1973. "Report." Washington, DC: Government Printing Office.

Pyne, Stephen J. 1982. *Fire in America.* Princeton, NJ: Princeton University Press.

Risbrudt, Christopher D., H. Fred Kaiser, and Paul V. Ellefson. 1983. "Cost-Effectiveness of the 1979 Forestry Incentives Program." *Journal of Forestry* 81:298-301.

Schiff, Ashley L. 1962. *Fire and Water.* Cambridge, MA: Harvard University Press.

Shands, William E., and Robert G. Healy. 1977. *The Lands Nobody Wanted.* Washington, DC: The Conservation Foundation.

Smith, David M. 1986. *The Practice of Silviculture.* New York: John Wiley & Sons.

Spurr, Stephan H. 1977. "Use of Professional Competence by the Judiciary." *Journal of Forestry* 75:198-200.

Stoddard, Herbert L. 1931. *The Bobwhite Quail: Its Habits, Preservation, and Increase.* New York: Charles Scribner's Sons.

Swindler, William F., ed. 1975. *Sources and Documents of United States Constitutions.* 10 vols. Dobbs Ferry, NY: Oceana Publications.

U.S. Congress. House. 1908. "Power of the Federal Government to Acquire Lands for National Forest Purposes." 60th Cong., 1st sess., H. Rept. 1514. Washington, DC: Government Printing Office.

————. Committee on Government Operations. Subcommittee on

Environment, Energy, and Natural Resources. 1991. "Federal Fire Management Policy: Evaluation of Changes Made After Yellowstone." 101st Cong., 2d sess., May 24, 1990. Serial 101-2. Washington, DC: Government Printing Office.

U.S. Congress. Office of Technology Assessment. 1992. "Forest Service Planning: Accommodating Uses, Producing Outputs, and Sustaining Ecosystems." OTA-F-505. Washington, DC: Government Printing Office.

U.S. Congress. Senate. 1902. "Report of the Secretary of Agriculture in Relation to the Forests, Rivers and Mountains of the Southern Appalachian Region." 57th Cong., 1st sess., S. Doc. 84. Washington, DC: Government Printing Office.

U.S. Congress. Senate. Committee on Agriculture and Forestry. Subcommittee on Environment, Soil Conservation and Forestry. 1973. "National Forest Environmental Management Act." 93d Cong., 1st sess., November 20, 1973. Washington, DC: Government Printing Office.

U.S. Congress. Senate. Committee on Energy and Natural Resources. Subcommittee on Public Lands, National Parks and Forests. Committee on Agriculture, Nutrition, and Forestry. Subcommittee on Conservation and Forestry. 1989. "Current Fire Management Policies." 100th Cong., 2d sess., September 29, 1988. Washington, DC: Government Printing Office.

U.S. Congress. Senate. Committee on Interior and Insular Affairs. 1971. Subcommittee on Public Lands. "'Clear-cutting' Practices on the National Timberlands." 92d Cong., 1st sess., April 5-6, 1971, pts. 1-3. Washington, DC: Government Printing Office.

U.S. Department of Agriculture. 1911. "Report of the Forester for 1911." Washington, DC: Government Printing Office.

———. 1912. "Report of the Forester for 1912." Washington, DC: Government Printing Office.

———. 1913. "Report of the Forester." Washington, DC: Government Printing Office.

———. 1914. "Report of the Forester." Washington, DC: Government Printing Office.

———. 1971. "National Forests Management in a Quality Environment." Washington, DC: Government Printing Office. Included as appendix B in U.S. Congress, Senate 1971.

———. 1974. "Environmental Program for the Future." (Draft.) Washington, DC: Government Printing Office.

U.S. Department of Agriculture. Forest Service. 1976. "Final Environmental Statement & Renewable Resource Program: 1977 to 2020." Washington, DC: Government Printing Office.

———. 1984. "Draft EIS: Land and Resource Management Plan for the Nantahala and Pisgah National Forests." Atlanta, GA: U.S. Department of Agriculture, Forest Service, Southern Region.

————. n.d. "The National Forests and Purchase Units of Region Eight." Unpublished file report. Asheville, NC: U.S. Department of Agriculture, Forest Service, National Forests in North Carolina.

Walker, John L. 1977. "Economic Efficiency and the National Forest Management Act of 1976." *Journal of Forestry* 75:715-718.

Westoby, Jack C. 1989. *Introduction to World Forestry: People and Their Trees.* Cambridge, MA: Basil Blackwell.

Whipple, Gurth A. 1935. *Fifty Years of Conservation in New York State: 1885-1935.* Albany, NY: J. B. Lyon Company.

Widner, Ralph R., ed. 1968. *Forests and Forestry in the American States.* Washington, DC: National Association of State Foresters.

The Wilderness Society. 1989. "Status of the Forest Planning Process." *Forest Issues Bulletin* (October-November 1989): 5, 6.

————. 1990. "Status of the Forest Planning Process." *Forest Issues Bulletin* (December 1989-January 1990): 5, 6.

Wildlife Management Institute. 1987a. "Conservation Reserves up 10.5 Million Acres." *Outdoor News Bulletin* 41 (7): 1. (April 3).

————. 1987b. "CRP Tree Planting Reviewed." *Outdoor News Bulletin* 41 (15): 3 (July 24).

————. 1988. "CRP Climbs 3.3 Million Acres." *Outdoor News Bulletin* 42 (12): 1 (June 17).

————. 1990. "CRP Nearly 34 Million Acres." *Outdoor News Bulletin* 44 (1): 3 (January 19).

Wilkins, Austin H. 1978. *Ten Million Acres of Timber.* Woolrich, ME: TBW Books.

Wood, Nancy. 1971. "Here Comes a Grim Reaper: Today the Forests, Tomorrow the National Parks." *Sierra Club Bulletin* 56 (8): 14-19.

Zivnuska, John. 1977. "Timber Harvesting and Land Use Planning Under the National Forest Management Act of 1976." Address given to meeting of the Committee of Scientists, Denver, August 1977.

CHAPTER VI

Outdoor Recreation and the National Parks

It is desirable that some large and easily accessible region of American soil should remain, as far as possible, in its primitive condition, at once a museum for the instruction of the student, a garden for the recreation of the lover of nature, and an asylum where indigenous tree...plant...[and] beast, may dwell and perpetuate their kind. (Marsh 1874, 327)

Writings of George Perkins Marsh (above), Henry David Thoreau, Ralph Waldo Emerson, John Muir, and others during the mid-1800s awakened the nation to the severity of land modification, the consequences of wholesale divestiture of the public domain, and the need to preserve at least a part of our heritage for future generations (The Nature Conservancy 1977, 13, 14). Not only was the land being used and abused, but also the most outstanding examples of natural phenomena frequently became the target of "freak show"-type exploiters. Beginning in 1806 promoters began buying land around Niagara Falls, and by the 1860s tourists were unable to view the falls without paying an entry fee (Sax 1976). In 1854 a group of promoters removed portions of bark from several redwoods in California's Mariposa Grove of bigtrees (*Sequoiadendron giganteum*) and shipped them to London, where they were exhibited for a fee. Ironically, the incredulous Britishers derided the show as "'a Yankee invention,' a fabrication 'made from the beginning to end'"; they believed "'that it was an utter untruth that such trees grew in this country; that it could not be'" (Runte [1979] 1981, 29), and the venture was a financial failure (Sax 1976).

From this background emerged our national parks—yet few of the old writers speak of parks as we know them today, and the concept of a system of national parks was slow in coming. Even the meaning of the word "park"—originally a fenced-in private game refuge (McKechnie 1958, 422)—has changed a great deal through time.

What was the first effort toward a national park system? There are at least three candidates and no clear answer.

YOSEMITE: THE BEGINNINGS?

Although Congress in 1832 reserved four sections of the Hot Springs of Arkansas for "future disposal" (4 Stat. 505) and these lands later became part of the National Park System, the area "known as the Yo-Semite Valley" and the "Mariposa Big Tree Grove" (Gates 1968, 566) is often cited as the first national (federal) expression of a national park concept in the United States (Runte [1979] 1981, 29; Sax 1976). The mechanism of dedication was simple and straightforward enough: in 1864 Congress passed a law (13 Stat. 325) granting the Mariposa Grove of giant redwoods to the state of California for "public use, resort, and recreation" to be held "inalienable for all time" (Gates 1968, 566). No congressional debate preceded passage; no overall policy was espoused; and motivation remains obscure. The act's sponsor was Senator John Conness of California, who acted upon the request of Israel Ward Raymond, California representative of the Central American Steamship Transit Company, and other gentlemen "of fortune, of taste and of refinement" (Sax 1976). Raymond, in turn, may have been influenced by Frederick Law Olmsted, who was at that time managing the nearby Mariposa Estate (Runte [1979] 1981, 28). Conness may have exploited an opportunity to rebuke the British for their earlier comments about the redwoods (Runte [1979] 1981, 29); or maybe the act was just one of those flukes of history that happen from time to time. Whatever the motivation, the experiment was a failure. State administration of the area was unsatisfactory, and it was returned to the federal government in 1905 and became part of Yosemite National Park in 1906 (Gates 1968, 566, 567).

A WORD ABOUT OLMSTED

Immediately upon creation of Yosemite Park, Frederick Law Olmsted was appointed chairman of its board of commissioners. His role in establishment of the park and in its subsequent administration is a bit clouded, but his impact upon natural resource management—and particularly landscape architecture and outdoor recreation policy and practice—is unquestioned. Initially a historian and public administrator (he wrote on the pre-Civil War South and was executive secretary of the U.S. Sanitary Commission, predecessor of the Red Cross, during the war), Olmsted moved west in 1863 to manage the Mariposa mining estate. There he became involved in efforts to rescue the Mariposa Grove and assumed his role as commissioner. In 1865 he prepared a report that "formulated the philosophic base for the establishment of state and national parks." The document advocated government intervention to prevent the nation's scenic resources from becoming "a monopoly of the very few, very rich people"—it might have been an important historical document had it not become lost until 1952 (Sax 1976).

By 1869 Olmsted had begun a campaign to combat the desecration of Niagara Falls. He engineered a barrage of magazine articles and a petition containing, among others, the signatures of all sitting members of the Supreme Court. Largely as a result of these activities, the New York legislature passed a bill authorizing creation of a state reservation at the falls in 1883 (Sax 1976).

Olmsted moved on to design a park on the outskirts of a great city, remote from the bulk of the populace and accessible primarily to the affluent—Central Park in New York City. He had the foresight to envision this park as a future enclave within a ring of concrete, stone, and steel mountains, a rural respite from the urban environment (Sax 1976).

During the 1880s Olmsted was retained by George W. Vanderbilt, the railroad tycoon, to design the Biltmore Estate, near Asheville, North Carolina (Widner 1968, 81). His landscaping achievements at Biltmore continue to attract throngs of admiring tourists today. He also attracted Gifford Pinchot to Biltmore, establishing the first scientifically managed forest in the United States and propelling Pinchot toward his destiny as first chief of the USDA Forest Service.

In 1899 Olmsted joined with Charles S. Sargent (chairman of the original New York Forest Commission and the Commission on National Forests, director of Harvard's Arnold Arboretum, and author) and others to found the Massachusetts Forestry Association, which was instrumental in creating forest reservations in that state (Widner 1968, 127-128).

Perhaps Olmsted's greatest attribute was his ability to perceive future needs, plan for them, execute the plans, be convinced of the validity of his position—and be right. Yosemite was set aside for the masses long before many could get there. The artificial environment surrounding Niagara Falls was removed with the conviction that reduction in physical amenities would only enhance the falls' attractiveness. Central Park was constructed on the urban fringe with the certainty that one day the city and its people would surround it. And always there was the conviction that the citizenry would appreciate the value of the natural landscape and would willingly bear the additional inconvenience of access with a minimum of human-provided conveniences.

YELLOWSTONE, THE FIRST "NATIONAL PARK"

Eight years after the cession of the Mariposa Grove and the Yosemite Valley, Congress established Yellowstone National Park, the third candidate for the first permanent federal parkland reservation. Among the first Europeans to extol the virtues of the Yellowstone was the mountain man Jim Bridger, who probably visited the valley before 1830 but whose stories were so grandiose as to be largely disbelieved. In the fall of 1869, Charles W. Cook, David E. Folsom, and William Peterson journeyed to Yellowstone, confirming Bridger's stories and stirring the public's imagination with accounts of the Grand Canyon of the Yellowstone River, Yellowstone Lake, and the Lower Geyser Basin (Runte [1979] 1981, 34, 35).

During the following summer, a nineteen-man expedition led by Henry Dana Washburn, surveyor-general of Montana and former congressman from Indiana, left Fort Ellis, Montana, for a month-long adventure in the Valley of the Yellowstone. Accompanying Washburn were (among others) Nathanial Pitt Langford, "a native of New York turned politician," and Lieutenant Gustavus C. Doane, who commanded the six-man military escort. The Washburn-Langford-Doane expedition confirmed the Cook expedition's reports and discovered the Upper Geyser Basin and Old Faithful geyser (figure 6.1). Publicity resulting from this expedition did much to arouse public interest in Yellowstone and to attract congressional attention (Runte [1979] 1981, 36-39).

In 1871 Congress appropriated $40,000 to support a third expedition led by Ferdinand Vandeveer Hayden, director of the United States Geological and Geographical Survey of the Territories, and including entomologists, topographers, a zoologist, a mineralogist, a meteorologist, an artist (Thomas Moran), a photographer (William Henry Jackson), and a physician. The return of the Hayden expedition signaled the beginning of a well-instrumented campaign to secure congressional action. The works of Jackson and Moran were widely distributed—Congress purchased Moran's 7-by-12-foot painting *The Grand Canyon of the Yellowstone* for $10,000 (Runte [1979] 1981, 39-41). Hayden lobbied actively, reminding Congress that private interests were already preparing to claim the geyser basins along the Firehole River and raising the specter of another Niagara Falls (Runte [1979] 1981, 44, 45); 400 copies of Langford's article on the Yellowstone, published in the May and June 1871 issues of *Scribner's Monthly*, were distributed to senators and representatives prior to congressional debates. And the politicking paid off— President Ulysses S. Grant signed the Yellowstone Park Act on March 1, 1872 (Runte [1979] 1981, 46).

FIGURE 6.1. Old Faithful Geyser, Yellowstone National Park. The first photo of Old Faithful geyser, taken by William Henry Jackson in August 1872. (Photo courtesy of the National Archives)

The act reserved 2 million acres near the headwaters of the Yellowstone River in the Wyoming Territory "as a public park or pleasuring ground for the benefit and enjoyment of the people" (17 Stat. 32). But passing a law does not necessarily make it so, and no national policy or institutional structure existed to implement the legislation. In fact the term "national park" did not emerge for another three years, appearing in an act dedicating public lands on Mackinac Island, Michigan, as a "National public park" (18 Stat. 517).

The attraction of curios and game—one of the last herds of bison resided in Yellowstone—the absence of strong statutory prohibitions, and the light penalties attached to transgressions proved too great a temptation, however, and poaching continued to be a severe problem. Regulations published by the secretary of the interior in 1877 prohibited commercial hunting, trapping, and fishing; cutting of timber without permission; removal of natural deposits; and careless use of fire (Ise [1961] 1967, 19). Implementation and enforcement did not necessarily follow. The park superintendent, Nathaniel P. Langford (remember the Washburn-Langford-Doane expedition?), a competent and dedicated individual, served without pay and had no budget for his first five years; park boundaries were unmarked and were established without regard to the topography (Ise [1961] 1967, 20, 21); and the only penalty for poaching was ejection from the park—after which a poacher was free to return and resume unlawful activities (Ise [1961] 1967, 24).

Army troops provided the most available source of manpower for the early parks. Their use was specifically authorized in Yellowstone in 1883 and extended to Sequoia and General Grant in 1900 (31 Stat. 618):

> The Secretary of War, upon request of the Secretary of the Interior, is authorized and directed to make the necessary details of troops to prevent trespassers and intruders from entering the park for the purpose of destroying the game or objects of curiosity therein, or for any other purpose prohibited by law, and to remove such persons from the park if found within. (22 Stat. 627)

Were it not for the army's providing engineers to construct roads and mark boundaries (Ise [1961] 1967, 27, 47) and cavalry for patrol and protection, the parks would have fared even worse. Speaking of the army administration in Yosemite, John Muir said:

> "In pleasing contrast to the noisy, ever changing management, or mismanagement, of blustering, plundering, money-making vote sellers who receive their places from boss politicians as purchased goods, the soldiers do their duty so quietly that the traveler is scarcely aware of their presence." (Ise [1961] 1967, 45)

Although the troops did their best, they had little law to back them up, and Congress was reluctant to assist them for eleven years. In March

1894 a poacher was caught in the act of skinning a bison in Yellowstone National Park; four other bison lay nearby, and six heads and hides were found in his camp (in 1891 bison heads were worth $400 to $1,000 in Bozeman, Montana [Ise (1961) 1967, 25]). A writer for *Forest and Stream* magazine was in the park at the time, wrote an article describing the incident, and stirred up such a public outcry that Congress had to do something (Ise [1961] 1967, 45). The result was the Lacey Act for the Protection of Yellowstone Park, enacted May 7, 1894, which prescribed severe penalties for hunting in the park, for destruction of timber, and for removal of minerals (28 Stat. 73). Violations of any rule of the secretary were now punishable by a fine of not more than $1,000 or imprisonment of not more than two years and forfeiture of all guns, traps, horses, and other equipment. The position of federal commissioner was created and a jail constructed. Although the Lacey Act provisions were perhaps too severe for the times and were reduced in 1916 (39 Stat. 238), they at least got the attention of poachers and other trespassers (Ise [1961] 1967, 46).

During the early days of Yellowstone, protection of big game—particularly elk and bison—successfully preserved populations of these species for posterity. As they increased in later years, however, they exerted a considerable influence on park vegetation and competing animals (particularly beavers, and to a lesser degree white-tailed deer, mule deer, and bighorn sheep), embroiling the Park Service in a controversy that continues in some units of the system today (chapter 7) (Chase 1986).

TOWARD A NATIONAL PARK SYSTEM

By 1900 the national parks comprised six units and more than 4 million acres (Gates 1968, 567), but there was no national park system. Each park was reserved from the public domain by special act of Congress and placed under the charge of the secretary of the interior. Each park was a separate, independent unit, unrelated to the others. Each had its own legislation and budget, and no overall administrative unit existed to provide continuity and cohesion (Ise [1961] 1967, 185, 186). In 1906 Congress took the first step toward more comprehensive legislation, transferring more authority over federal property to the executive branch in the process. The Antiquities Act authorized the president to declare historic landmarks, historic or prehistoric structures, and other objects of historic or scientific interest to be national monuments, provided they were on federally owned or controlled lands. The act, another product of Congressman John F. Lacey of Iowa, is sometimes called The Lacey Act

(Ise [1961] 1967, 152). (Note: This title is confusing, however, for it also refers to the Lacey Act for the Protection of Yellowstone Park, the Lacey Act of 1900, and the 1981 amendments to the act of 1900.)

By 1916 the Antiquities Act had been used to create twenty national monuments (seven historic and thirteen scientific), including the Petrified Forest, Grand Canyon, Dinosaur, and Katmai (The Nature Conservancy 1977, 28). National monuments remained under the jurisdiction of the secretary otherwise administering the lands—Interior for the public domain, Agriculture for forest reserves, and War for lands controlled by the War Department (Ise [1961] 1967, 153). While this provision created some confusion in later years, as did the appellation "monument," versus "park" or "reserve," the act provided an expedient by which the executive branch could move swiftly to preserve areas that might otherwise have been lost, creating, in many instances, the nuclei of future national parks (Ise [1961] 1967, 154, 155).

And yet each unit was separate and distinct, and there was no "national park" agency. The secretary of the interior managed this loose assemblage through various officers, culminating in Robert B. Marshall, chief geographer of the Geological Survey, who was named superintendent of national parks on December 10, 1915 (Ise [1961] 1967, 187). During this time Congress considered numerous bills that would have created a national park agency—Congressman Lacey introduced the first in 1900 (Ise [1961] 1967, 188)—but none was successful until 1916. In that year, following a camping trip and promotional campaign orchestrated by Stephen T. Mather (then assistant to the secretary), Congress passed and President Wilson signed the National Park Service Organic Act. Shortly thereafter Mather became the first director of the National Park Service. Assisting him was Horace M. Albright, an attorney who joined the Department of the Interior in 1904, who was to become superintendent of Yellowstone National Park in 1919, and who was to succeed Mather as director in 1929. The Mather-Albright team created the system and developed the philosophy that continues to govern the National Park Service today (Wirth 1980, 16-19).

The organic act established the National Park Service, specified key employees and their salaries, authorized the secretary of the interior to enact regulations governing the system, authorized the sale or disposition of timber when necessary to conserve resources of the parks, permitted destruction of animals and plants when they were detrimental to the parks, and authorized the secretary to grant concessions for twenty years for tourist accommodations and leases for livestock grazing (except in

Yellowstone) when such would not be detrimental. But above all the act stated the brief yet comprehensive, firm yet flexible, policy that has governed administration of the system since its inception. The national parks are

> to conserve the scenery and the natural and historic objects and the wildlife therein and to provide for the enjoyment of the same in such manner and by such means as will leave them unimpaired for the enjoyment of future generations. (39 Stat. 535)

At first blush the policy statement appears to be an interesting bit of nice-sounding rhetoric; at second it seems to be a non sequitur, an impossible Catch-22. How can the service "conserve" yet "provide for the enjoyment," "provide for the enjoyment" yet "leave unimpaired?" In truth it has provided a framework within which the service has ably maneuvered, leaning alternatively toward "conserve" or "enjoyment" when the politics were favorable, leaning on the same mandates when necessary to thwart unfavorable, unwanted, or detrimental proposals.

The railroads were a powerful influence in obtaining enactment of the organic act and in developing policy and the early parks themselves—not because of any environmental or conservation leanings but because the park system would attract tourists and the tourists would travel by rail and use other railroad accommodations. In essence the parks meant profits to the railroads. The vice-president of the Southern Pacific Railroad was a member of Mather's famous camping trip to the Sierra Nevada. The Northern Pacific had endorsed the Yellowstone Park Act of 1872—and subsequently underwrote a string of hostelries serving the area. The Santa Fe Railroad completed the El Tovar Hotel on the south rim of the Grand Canyon in 1904. The Great Northern Railway constructed two sprawling lodges and a series of Swiss-style chalets within and immediately adjacent to Glacier National Park (Runte [1979] 1981, 91, 94). The Union Pacific provided accommodations in Zion, Bryce Canyon, and the north rim of the Grand Canyon (Ise [1961] 1967, 198). In 1915 the Santa Fe and Union Pacific railroads spent $500,000 for national park exhibits, and in the next year seventeen railroads cooperated to produce 275,000 copies of *National Parks Portfolio*, a collection of photographs by Robert Sterling Yard (Ise [1961] 1967, 196). Although one might challenge the motives of the railroads and attempt to separate preservation of scenic resources for the sake of profit from preservation for the sake of preservation, the resources of the western railroads went a long way toward securing and defending our National Park System in its infancy. The alliance between these capitalistic entities and the altruistic preservationists repeatedly won out over Gifford Pinchot and others who wanted the program handled "efficiently, economically, and satisfactorily by the Forest Service" (Runte [1979] 1981, 99).

A WORD ABOUT MATHER AND ALBRIGHT

Stephen Mather epitomizes the small group of wealthy, powerful, politically astute, and public-spirited men who formed this nation's natural resource policy during the late 1800s and early 1900s. He was an avid outdoorsman and mountain climber, was a member of the American Civic Association and the Sierra Club, and made a fortune from the mining and distribution of borax (Ise [1961] 1967, 193; Runte [1979] 1981, 101). After a trip to the Sierra during the summer of 1914, Mather expressed his anger over the poor management of Sequoia and Yosemite national parks in a letter to Secretary of the Interior Franklin K. Lane (a fellow University of California alumnus). Lane replied, "Dear Steve, If you don't like the way the national parks are being run, come on down to Washington and run them yourself." He did, and he stayed fourteen years, the first two as assistant to the secretary and the remainder as director of the National Park Service (Runte 1987, 101, 102).

Joseph Sax relates an example of Mather's political acumen and managerial style:

Perhaps Mather's most characteristic, successful, and widely known achievement occurred in 1915 as part of an effort to garner support for the upcoming congressional consideration of the bill to create a National Park Service....To set the stage for the coming legislative session, Mather decided to have a little outing with some opinion leaders, to imbue them with the mystique of the parks and persuade them to put their influence behind the bill to establish the National Park Service, all the while having a splendid time in the high country. Among Mather's guests were Fairfield Osborn, head of the American Museum of Natural History; Emerson Hough, one of the most renowned writers of the day; Fred H. Gillett, the future speaker of the House of Representatives and ranking Republican on the Appropriations Committee; Gilbert H. Grosvenor, editor of *National Geographic;* E. O. McCormick, vice president of the Southern Pacific Railway; and Burton Holmes, a travel lecturer. [Note: The party also included an additional writer, Peter Scott Macfarlane; the owner and publisher of two influential California newspapers, Ben M. Maddox; and Mather's right-hand man and successor-to-be, Horace

Albright (Albright and Cahn 1985, 25).] For nearly two weeks, the distinguished party saw the best of the Sierra. As one magazine article put it,

> Mather had spared no expense in outfitting his guests. Each man had a new sleeping bag and air mattress which combined to make a classy and perfectly comfortable wilderness bed. There were horses to carry the men and mules to carry the supplies, which included a bountiful stock of fresh fruit, fresh eggs, and other delicacies....As camp was pitched, Tie Sing, a marvelous camp cook whom Mather had borrowed from the U.S. Geological Survey for the occasion, would construct a dining table, usually out of logs, and then...a linen table cloth would show up, and real napkins for everybody. Tie Sing would put together his collapsible stoves and calmly prepare soup, lettuce salad, fried chicken, venison and gravy, potatoes, hot rolls, apple pie, cheese, tea, and coffee.

> Just as Mather had hoped, generous support and lavish publicity in favor of the parks began to roll out; the April 1916 issue of *National Geographic* was wholly devoted to the national parks. By August 25, right on schedule, President Wilson signed the bill creating the National Park Service and Mather became its first director. (Sax 1976)

Before Mather could take office, however, he suffered a nervous breakdown from overwork and internal squabbles within the agency and was unable to accomplish much for eighteen months. During this time the task of organizing the new National Park Service fell to Horace M. Albright (Ise [1961] 1967, 195, 196). Albright was a young lawyer who had been educated at the University of California, Berkeley, where he met two men who were to greatly influence his future—John Muir, who strengthened his interest in the outdoors, and Adolph C. Miller, chairman of the economics department, who was to become assistant secretary of the interior in 1913 and take Albright with him as "Confidential Clerk to the Secretary" (Kieley 1981, 3). In 1914 Albright was assigned to Mather to help manage the national parks and to assist in getting organic legislation through Congress (Wirth 1980, 16). Upon Mather's incapacitation, Albright (assistant director and, at age twenty-seven, the youngest person on the Washington Park Service staff) was appointed acting director. Albright prepared the first annual report for the service (Kieley 1981, 3), organized and conducted the legislative program that provided the first appropriations for the new service, handled the delicate personnel matters of the early years, and convinced Mather to return to active service (Albright and Cahn 1985, 53-60).

It was Albright who oversaw final passage of the organic act and who engineered presidential approval:

> There remained the matter of getting President Wilson's signature on the bill. On August 25 Albright happened to be in the office of the enrolling clerk of the House when the clerk was told by the White House that the President would like to have the Army appropriation bill sent over at once. Horace took a chance with a bold stroke and brought it off. He persuaded the enrolling clerk to slip the National Park Service bill into the envelope with the other one. Then Horace sped to the White House where he persuaded the legislative clerk to put the Park Service bill before the President. As Albright turned to leave he pressed his luck further by casually asking the clerk to reserve the pen with which the Park Service bill would be signed. He got that too, and it remains in the possession of the Service....
>
> Now, at last, was the hour of triumph. Horace fired off a telegram to Mather in California; "Park Service bill signed 9 o'clock last night, have pen used by President for you." (Kieley 1981, 6)

During the remainder of Mather's tenure, Albright served as a dependable backup, troubleshooting where needed, ready and able to step in when Mather suffered recurrent physical and emotional problems, a loyal personal friend and professional colleague (Albright and Cahn 1985).

In May 1918 Secretary Lane (with Mather's assistance) published the first National Park Service "regulations" in the form of a letter to Mather:

> First, that the national parks must be maintained in absolutely unimpaired form for the use of future generations as well as those of our own time; second, that they are set aside for the use, observation, health, and pleasure of the people; and third, that the national interest must dictate all decisions affecting public or private enterprise in the parks.
>
> In all parks but Yellowstone grazing by cattle but not by sheep might be permitted in areas not frequented by visitors.
>
> There should be no leasing for summer homes.
>
> There should be no cutting of trees except for buildings and where it would not hurt the forests or landscape.
>
> Roads must harmonize with the landscape....
>
> Private holdings should be eliminated.
>
> All outdoor sports, including winter sports, should be encouraged.
>
> Educational as well as recreational use of the parks should be encouraged.

Low-priced camps should be maintained, and high-class hotels....

In studying new park projects, the Service should seek to find "scenery of supreme and distinctive quality or some natural features so extraordinary or unique as to be of national interest and importance."

The national park system as now constituted "should not be lowered in standard, dignity, and prestige by the inclusion of areas which express in less than the highest terms the particular class or kind of exhibit which they represent." (Ise [1961] 1967, 194, 195)

During the remainder of his tenure as director, Mather attempted to carry out these principles. Several—those in the first paragraph, grazing, and cutting of trees—were directed by statute. Others—those involving sports, camps, and hotels—were means of publicizing the parks and obtaining public support for the system. Still others—elimination of inholdings and maintenance of quality standards—protected the integrity of the system he had created.

Mather was an astute politician; at times he was also quite firm. Louis W. Hill, president of the Great Northern Railway, constructed a sawmill, planing mill, and temporary kiln to provide lumber for use in building the Many Glacier Hotel in Glacier National Park. Hill was to dismantle the mills, which were on park property in full view of visitors at the hotel, upon completion of construction. He delayed too long, however, and Mather destroyed them with dynamite charges. Hill had reneged on his agreement, and Mather had every right to have them removed; "relations between the two were cool at best afterwards" (McMillon 1983, 17, 31-33).

On November 5, 1928, Stephen Mather was stricken with paralysis, and on January 22, 1930, he died. For fourteen years he had served the National Park System, for twelve years as its director. In that time he had created the physical and administrative organization and much of the policy and park philosophy that pervade the system today (Ise [1961] 1967, 321, 322). He had devoted his life, health, and personal fortune to the establishment of organic legislation, guiding principles, and an exemplary ranger tradition. He had set standards for others to follow and laid the framework for the "politics of parks," which is still relevant.

Albright, then superintendent of Yellowstone National Park, became director on January 12, 1929, and served in that capacity until August 9, 1933. He then left the service to become vice-president and general manager, and later president, of the United States Potash Company. Although no longer in the service, Albright remained active in national park affairs—lobbying for establishment of Everglades National Park, expansion of Sequoia National Park, and completion of Jackson Hole; serving on the Advisory Board on National Parks, Historic Sites, Buildings, and Monuments; and assisting in other capacities (Kieley 1981, 5). At the age of ninety-five, he finished dictating his recollections of the early days of the National Park Service to Robert Cahn (Albright and Cahn 1985, 312, 226, 331). Of Albright, Conrad L. Wirth, onetime employee and future park service director, had this to say:

> Stephen T. Mather is considered the founder of the National Park Service and its basic policy, but the records of Mather and Albright and the relationship between these two stalwarts often cause them to be called cofounders....No one can really hope to do justice in describing Horace Albright. To know him, to say nothing of working for him, is an honor....I can't remember ever hearing anything but praise and admiration for him. Everyone still looks to him on national park matters. (Wirth 1980, 15-17)

THE EASTERN NATIONAL PARKS

Interest in eastern national parks centered initially in the southern Appalachians. In 1894 the North Carolina Press Association petitioned Congress for a park in that state. In 1899 the Appalachian National Park Association (formed in Asheville, North Carolina) joined the campaign, and a number of other preservation groups became involved soon thereafter (Runte 1987, 114). In 1900 and 1901, bills were introduced in Congress to establish "national parks" or "national forests" in Tennessee and North Carolina, and the next four Congresses saw more than a score of similar bills. But the concepts and functions of "parks" and "forests" were confounded, the proposals got nowhere (Ise [1961] 1967, 249, 250), and the precedent for eastern national parks shifted to New England.

The Antiquities Act of 1906 was the expedient. Faced with continued vandalism and destruction of archaeological ruins in the West (Ise [1961] 1967, 152), Congress had passed this act prescribing a penalty for "any person who shall appropriate, exacavate, injure or destroy any historic or prehistoric ruin or monument, or any object of antiquity, situated on lands controlled by the Government of the United States" and authorizing the president to "declare by public proclamation historic landmarks, historic and prehistoric structures, and other objects of historic and scientific interest situated on...[such] lands...to be national landmarks." If the lands were privately claimed, the secretary of the interior was authorized to accept them as gifts (34 Stat. 225). This last provision provided the tool.

In 1901 a group of wealthy and influential New Englanders became concerned about the impending development of Mount Desert Island, on the coast of Maine. With financial assistance from John D. Rockefeller, they began acquiring and protecting the threatened area and by 1916 controlled about 6,000 acres. At that time they pursuaded President Woodrow Wilson to accept their land as a national monument (Runte [1979], 1981, 114)—under provisions of the Antiquities Act and a finding that

> [the] island was discovered by Samuel de Champlain and upon which he first landed when, acting upon the authority of Sieur de Monts, he explored and described the present New England coast, an exploration and discovery of great historic interest. The topographic configuration, the geology, the fauna and the flora of the island, largely embraced within the limits of the Monument, also, are of great scientific interest. (39 Stat. 1791)

Thus the dedication met the statutory requirements that a national monument must contain "objects of historic or scientific interest" (34 Stat. 225).

Mather placed this park among his highest priorities (Foresta 1984, 36), and, largely at his urging, Congress declared Sieur de Monts National Monument (now Acadia National Park) to be a national park in 1919 (40 Stat. 1178). Acadia's first superintendent was George B. Dorr, an adjacent landowner (40 Stat. 1178), one of the leaders in acquisition, and one who had "spent much of his own money buying land for the park" (Wirth 1980, 44).

National parks in the southern Appalachians came more slowly. Mather first established a study commission, the Southern Appalachian National Park Commission, chaired by Congressman H. W. Temple of Pennsylvania—five men appointed by Secretary Hubert Work in early 1924, who served without compensation. Their task was to survey the area for possible park sites, each of which contained at least 500 square miles and the following attributes:

1. Mountain scenery with inspiring perspectives and delightful details.
2. Areas sufficiently extensive and adaptable so that annually millions of visitors might enjoy the benefits of outdoor life and communion with nature without the confusion of overcrowding.
3. A substantial part to contain forests, shrubs, and flowers, and mountain streams, with picturesque cascades and waterfalls overhung with

foliage, all untouched by the hand of man.

4. Abundant springs and streams available for camps and fishing.

5. Opportunities for protecting and developing the wild life of the area, and the whole to be a natural museum, preserving outstanding features of the southern Appalachians as they appeared in the early pioneer days.

6. Accessibility by rail and road. (Southern Appalachian National Park Commission 1931, 7)

While the Temple Commission was touring the southern Appalachians and dealing with the hostility of lumber companies and the enthusiasm of state park commissions (Southern Appalachian National Park Commission 1931, 6, 7, 12-17), Congress was considering a multitude of proposals for Appalachian parks. Eventually Congress passed the Act of February 21, 1925 (43 Stat. 958), directing the secretary of the interior to determine boundaries of the areas that were to become Shenandoah, Great Smoky Mountains, and Mammoth Cave national parks and authorizing the receipt of gifts of land and money to further the acquisition. This act definitely established Congress's intent to create eastern national parks, but much work remained to be done. The next step, on May 22, 1926, was to better define the maximum and minimum areas proposed for Shenandoah (521,000 and 250,000 acres) and for the Great Smoky Mountains (704,000 and 150,000 acres) and to set guidelines for acquisition and development (44 Stat. 616, 617).

Still no Appalachian parks had been created, nor had any funds been appropriated, other than for the Temple Commission's expenses. Congress intended for acquisition funds to come from the respective states—Virginia, Tennessee, and North Carolina—but money was scarce during the late 1920s, and by 1927 it was apparent that the effort would fail. At this time John D. Rockefeller, Jr., came forward with an offer of $5 million, to be matched by other donations. Several more years of fund-raising passed, and still efforts fell short of the standards set by Congress. Finally, in 1934, Congress decided that "enough was enough" and established Great Smoky Mountains National Park (48 Stat. 964), and two years later sufficient acreage had been acquired to permit Shenandoah to be established without additional legislation (Ise [1961] 1967, 259, 263).

Establishment, however, did not ensure the completion of parks meeting the standards of the Southern Appalachian National Park Commission. The area of the Great Smokies was far smaller than intended;

numerous inholdings and residual rights existed; nonfederal funding sources had been exhausted, and no federal acquisition funds had yet been appropriated. Four years later Congress finally appropriated $743,265.29 for acquisition of the remaining lands in Great Smoky Mountains National Park (52 Stat. 29).

THE CCC DAYS

As a result of the Great Depression, direct appropriations to the National Park Service were cut by more than 50 percent in 1934—from $10.8 million to $5.1 million—just as the eastern parks were being created and demand for facilities and services throughout the system was steadily increasing (Ise [1961] 1967, 359). Yet the service (and natural resource conservation in general) was to emerge from the depression a winner, the beneficiary of programs designed to "put men back to work,...restore family incomes,...strengthen the national morale, avert panic, and at the same time create a breathing spell that would permit the mobilization of the nation's forces...[to correct] the underlying causes of the depression" (Wirth 1980, 69). As part of the New Deal, President Franklin Roosevelt asked Congress to approve a program of land improvement and unemployment relief within three weeks of his inauguration, and ten days later the Civilian Conservation Service Act of 1933 became law (Dana and Fairfax 1980, 144).

The Civilian Conservation Corps (CCC) created by the act constituted a rare exercise of interagency cooperation. Five days after the act passed, Roosevelt created an Office of Emergency Conservation Work and named Robert Fechner as its director (Ise [1961] 1967, 360). Fechner, a product of the labor movement who had risen to general vice-president of the International Association of Machinists, was assisted by an advisory council composed of representatives of the Departments of War, Agriculture, the Interior, and Labor (Wirth 1980, 78-80). Labor selected the men; War moved them into camps and managed the camps; and Agriculture (national, state, and private forests) and Interior (national and state parks, Indian reservations, and public lands) directed their activities (Ise [1961] 1967, 360; Wirth 1980, 82, 83, 107). The CCC program went far beyond supplying the bare necessities of life, and its accomplishments reflect the high ideals with which it was conceived. As described in a letter from National Park Director Horace Albright:

"While this program involves hard work placed on the shoulders of every one of us, a large responsibility and a great deal of hard work, it also permits us to play a very important role in one of the greatest schemes ever devised for the relief of our fellow citizens in this present crisis and the rehabilitation of many young men of the nation who have as yet had no opportunity for decent occupation and have been the subjects of unfortunate attitude toward their native land and conditions in general. We therefore have a wonderful opportunity to play a leading part in the development of a wholesome and patriotic mental attitude in this younger generation." (Wirth 1980, 86, 87)

Mobilization was virtually instantaneous:

"The selection and enrollment of 250,000 unmarried young men between the ages of 18 and 25 was initiated at once. On April 7, 1933, the first man was selected and enrolled for C.C.C. work. Ten days later, on April 17, the first 200-man C.C.C. camp was established at Luray, Virginia."

"On May 16, enrollment jumped 5,890 to a total of 62,450, the next day added 8,100 men, the next 10,500 men. On June 1st a peak daily enrollment of 13,843 men was reached. The average daily gain in strength for this period was 8,700 men. During part of May, 150,000 men were in reconditioning camps being organized and equipped for the field."

"Within 3 months the 250,000 young men, together with an additional 25,000 war veterans and 25,000 experienced woodsmen, had been assembled and placed in 1,468 forest and park camps extending to every section of the Union. Since July 1, 1933, the strength of the C.C.C. has averaged about 300,000. The highest strength present for any given date has been 346,000." (Letters from CCC director Bob Fechner, cited in Wirth 1980, 93, 94)

Enrollees were provided with a complete program—clothing, medical care, education (particularly reading and writing for illiterates), good food, physical conditioning, adequate lodging, recreational opportunities, and on-the-job training (Wirth 1980, 96-99)—and they were paid $30 per month for their labors (Wirth 1980, 70). During the nine years of the program, almost 17,000 camps were operated, about one-fourth of which were supervised by Interior and only 5 percent of which were in national parks. Of all the federal agencies, the Forest Service hosted the most CCC camps (table 6.1); one source stated that "more than half of the fourteen hundred CCC camps were on Forest Service lands" (Clary 1986, 95).

TABLE 6.1
Civilian Conservation Corps Camps, 1933-1942

Location	Number
Department of the Interior National Parks	841
State parks	2,507
Other bureaus	1,055
Total Interior	4,403
Department of Agriculture national forests	4,286
State and private forests	2,364
Other bureaus	5,469
Total Agriculture	4,286
Other agencies	431
TOTAL CCC	16,953

Source: Conrad L. Wirth, *Parks, Politics, and the People* (Norman: University of Oklahoma Press, 1980), p. 127.

The CCC performed many different tasks (figure 6.2)—reforestation; building of cabins and other buildings; clearing of fire trails; construction of bridges, dams, water and sewer systems, and campgrounds; reduction of fire hazards and fire fighting (Ise [1961] 1967, 360)—virtually anything and everything that could and should be done on the public lands, and some that should not. In the rush to create work, supervisors often did not question whether a road should be built, a forest cleared, or a campsite created, and their zeal sometimes resulted in overexploitation and overdevelopment of the resources with which they were working. Despite these occasional criticisms, however, the CCC was among the most popular and successful New Deal programs (Dana and Fairfax 1980, 144). Many of the lodges, museum buildings, and even cabins constructed by CCC labor are still in use today—more than fifty years later. In the national forests, the CCC's greatest employment was in fire control, but workers also engaged in timber management that otherwise could not have been accomplished, and they planted "[h]alf the trees that [were] ever planted in the United States" (Clary 1986, 95, 96). But even more important, 3.6 million young men (Wirth 1980, 146) were provided the opportunity to live in, work with, and appreciate the forests and parks of this nation, and this appreciation and understanding was expressed in later years in conservation careers, voting records, and political activities.

World War II brought an end to the Great Depression, unemployment, and the initial justification for the CCC, and on June 30, 1942, Congress voted to terminate the program (Wirth 1980, 143). Despite numerous efforts to reactivate the system and/or to establish a permanent

FIGURE 6.2. A CCC Crew at Work. Horse Creek Road project in the San Joaquin Valley, California (ca. 1940). The CCC built the fire crew station in the rear and is constructing the access road. (Photo courtesy of the Forest History Society)

conservation corps (a test program was instituted in Interior and Agriculture in 1972), none has been successful (Wirth 1980, 151-157). The CCC was an idea whose time came, went, and returned a generation later with the Jobs Corps of the Great Society and its successors.

MISSION 66

During World War II, park attendance and funding dropped as the nation turned its attention to higher priorities, and after the war the National Park System was forgotten for a time. In 1940, with 161 areas, 21.5 million acres, and almost 17 million visitors, its budget was $33.6 million (including CCC funds). In 1955, with 181 areas, 23.8 million acres, and 57 million visitors, it was $32.6 million (Wirth 1980, 238). Of 718 persons interviewed during the summer of 1955, all of whom had visited national parks within the preceding five years, 69 percent had complaints—primarily about facilities. About one-third mentioned overcrowding, and about one-half were dissatisfied with overnight accommodations. Living conditions for park personnel were substandard, with obvious effects on marital harmony and morale (Wirth 1980, 244). Conrad L. Wirth was director at the time, and his account of this period (Wirth 1980, 237-284) is a lesson in effective government administration and political astuteness. Unless otherwise noted the following discussion is based on Wirth's account (italics have been added to emphasize note-worthy administrative elements).

Wirth first analyzed the National Park Service's attempts to obtain increased funding, none of which had cleared the Bureau of the Budget (now the Office of Management and Budget), and concluded that he had asked for too little over too short a time (1980, 238). Not only were the needs of the service large and complex, but also the bureau (and Congress) seemed to look more favorably toward the larger and longer-range proposals of the Bureau of Public Roads, the Bureau of Reclamation, and the U.S. Army Corps of Engineers. Perhaps a bolder approach would be more successful. *After discussion with staff,* a committee was established representing the branches of the service (Design and Construction, Programs and Plans Control, Conservation and Protection, Natural History, History, and River Basin Studies). Members of the committee *"were relieved of all their regular duties and would devote full time to the plan until it was completed."* A second *"steering committee,"* composed of supervisors of members of the working group, was also instituted (Wirth 1980, 239) to ensure vertical continuity throughout the organization and to *provide oversight and support.*

As yet the project had no name, no identity. It needed *"a title that was short, expressive, easy to remember, and provocative."* After some thought and discussion, "Mission 66" was selected—"mission" to denote "all that we hoped to accomplish"; "66" for 1966, the fiftieth anniversary of the establishment of the service and the year by which project objectives were to have been attained (Wirth 1980, 240, 241). The next step was to involve field personnel. A preliminary questionnaire had already been sent to the superintendent of each park unit. A second memorandum was then sent, informing the superintendents of the committees' work, clarifying objectives, summarizing the more troublesome issues, *asking each superintendent to outline a course of action for his park,* and inviting suggestions and general comments (p. 243). *"{E}verybody had a responsibility to help put Mission 66 together"* (p. 244).

Next senior members of the Washington staff (the chairs of both committees) were *sent to the field to "give a thorough explanation of Mission 66 and to answer questions....* In this way, by the end of June [1955], a rather complete indoctrination of the purpose and scope of Mission 66 had been spread throughout the personnel of the Service." Eventually Mission 66 was to contain prospectuses for each unit in the system, outlining the "plan for park development and public use...the best protection of the parks' unique resources and...the most enjoyment for the people." But before this full-scale effort was undertaken, *pilot studies* were initiated on representative areas to test the planning and analysis process (Wirth 1980, 249).

To this point Mission 66 was an internal exercise, closely held within the service, and Wirth's comments reflect the proud and somewhat autocratic attitude frequently exhibited by service personnel (at least prior to today's emphasis on public involvement):

> Mission 66 was a Park Service project, we wanted it to ourselves, and we did not want higher authorities to lay down any requirements for us. We relied on our own professional ability and judgment. We did keep the department posted on our general progress, but I asked Secretary Douglas McKay and Assistant Secretary Orem Lewis to give us a free hand in this matter, and they did except toward the end. (Wirth 1980, 251, 252)

The "coming out party" for Mission 66 was the Public Services Conference at Great Smoky Mountains on September 20, 1955. Pilot studies had been completed, legislation drafted, principles to guide the study written, and a balanced program for the decade prepared (p. 250). A summary of the major purposes of Mission 66 was the first item on the agenda. The presentation was *reported in newspapers throughout the country, and "because of the constant reference to Mission 66 in the daily press, readers were rapidly becoming aware of it and of the National Park Service's plans for the future"* (p. 251). The service's constituency had been informed and was becoming mobilized, but there was still no official sanction—a supplemental budget request was submitted in late fall of 1955 to provide funds for an early start but was turned down (p. 252).

On the previous May 12, Wirth had been informed of the possibility of an opportunity to present the Mission 66 plan to the president (actually, the White House was unaware of Mission 66, but the secretary to the cabinet had read of the deplorable park conditions in a *Saturday Evening Post* editorial and thought that national parks would be a good subject for cabinet discussion). All through the summer, the cabinet appearance was postponed, affording Wirth additional *time to complete his plan and to rehearse and perfect his presentation.* In the interim the 1957 fiscal year budget was submitted, containing a request for Mission 66 funding supported by (1) a popular-style booklet for general distribution (*Our Heritage*); (2) a detailed official report containing statistics, charts, and other data in the form used for appropriation estimates; and (3) a final prospectus for each park (p. 252).

On January 5, 1956, President Dwight D. Eisenhower included a reference to the parks in his State of the Union address, pledging his administration to "submit recommendations to provide more adequate facilities to keep abreast of the increasing interest of our people in the great outdoors." Bureaucrats read the State of the Union address with great care, and any favorable mention of their programs is considered a blessing from on high. As Wirth put it, "we began to breathe a little easier" (p. 254). And still no cabinet meeting.

Finally, on January 27, the opportunity arrived. Unbeknownst to the National Park Service, the Bureau of the Budget had approved Mission 66 funding in fiscal year 1957 prior to the meeting. If the president were to ask Budget Director Roland R. Hughes's opinion of the project, he was prepared to endorse it. The skids were greased. The presentation went off without a hitch. Secretary Douglas McKay gave a short opening statement. Wirth outlined existing problems and the program to correct them, speaking for about sixteen minutes with the aid of slides, showing a three-minute film illustrating conditions in some of the larger parks, and concluding with charts summarizing the financial schedule and legislative needs. Assistant Secretary Wes D'Ewart, previously a member of Congress, ended the presentation with his prediction of a favorable congressional reaction. After about twenty minutes of discussion, the president asked Secretary McKay if he could start Mission 66 at once (p. 255), and before proceeding to the next agenda item Eisenhower remarked, "This is a good project; let's get on with it" (p. 256)—SUPPORT FROM THE TOP.

There then ensued an exchange between the legislative and the executive branches that afforded Wirth direct access to the Congress without going through the customary bureaucratic channels:

A day or two after the cabinet presentation we appeared before Representative Mike Kirwan's Subcommittee on Interior Appropriations. Mike opened the meeting by saying he had heard about Mission 66, that it sounded good to him, but that he saw nothing in the budget about it. He then asked me, "If I added $5 million to your 1956 appropriation for Mission 66, could you get started?" All I said was, "Yes, sir." A few days later we got a call from the Bureau of the Budget asking us to send them a justification to submit to Congress requesting a $10 million supplement for Mission 66. I told them that they had our request for $12 million [which had been turned down]...and that they could use all or any part of it. About two weeks later I got a call from Mike Kirwan, who wanted to know what I was trying to do to him. He called my attention to his promise to give us $5 million to get started on Mission 66 and asserted that now we were sending up a request for $12 million. I told him what had happened but that I had not seen the request before it went up and really didn't know the Bureau of the Budget had sent it until I got his call. He was very disturbed and told me that if they wanted to play poker that was all right with him. He said he would allow the $12 million they requested but was going to raise them another $5 million. I was not to say anything about it until the bill was reported out. This was certainly a bit of plain good luck, and of course I did as the chairman requested. (Wirth 1980, 262)

So Mission 66 obtained a $17 million windfall before it officially started. Over the next two years, total National Park Service funding more than doubled (from $33 million in fiscal year 1955 to 68 million in 1957), and by 1966 it had almost doubled again (to $128 million). Capital improvement funds more than quadrupled over the same period (from $14 million in 1955 to $66 million in 1966), while park attendance increased by 135 percent (from 57 million to 133 million). The total cost of Mission 66 was slightly over $1 billion (pp. 261, 262).

Almost 3,000 miles of roads were constructed or reconstructed; 575 campgrounds containing over 17,000 campsites were added; 535 water systems, 521 sewer systems, and 271 power systems were provided; 1,239 residences, dormitories, and apartments were constructed; 2 training centers and 114 visitor centers were built; and countless other physical improvements were made (pp. 262-269). Although Mission 66 did not emphasize land acquisition (The Nature Conservancy 1977, 53), almost 3 million acres were added to the National Park System during and shortly after Mission 66 (p. 260). As measured by bureaucratic yardsticks—size of program and budget, growth, and so on—Mission 66 was an outstanding success. But it was not without its detractors. Wirth's objective was "to develop the parks so that they could properly accommodate the visitors expected" (Ise [1961] 1967, 547), estimated to be 80 million visits by 1966 (p. 261). This estimate was 53 million visits lower than the actual 1966 visitation—catalyzed by greater leisure time, increased interest in the out-of-doors, and improved facilities provided by Mission 66 itself. As a result the program greatly aided the human visitor to the parks but did little to increase protection of the natural and historical resources of the parks themselves (Runte 1987, 173).

THE MODERN NATIONAL PARK SYSTEM

In recent decades the National Park System has continued to expand its scope—in natural, historical, and cultural preservation and in outdoor recreation. As it has done so, it has encountered (and will continue to encounter) increased competition and conflicts among user constituency groups and greater similarity between its land management policies as practiced and those of other public agencies.

The "great natural areas" have always been the mainstay of the National Park System and probably will continue to be so into the foreseeable future (Foresta 1984, 93), but as demand has intensified so has the polarization between groups that emphasize the "conserve" provisions of the organic act and those who stress the "provide for the enjoyment" provisions. Superimposed upon these conflicting desires has been, at least in the past two decades, a considerable amount of political interference in what was once a proud professional corps (Wirth 1980, 264-388) and not a little pork barrel politics in expansion of the system (Foresta 1984, 77-80). Despite such criticisms significant areas meeting Director George Hartzog's criteria for natural areas have been added to the system (Foresta 1984, 107). The previous requirement that lands for national parks outside the public domain be purchased by nonfederal interests was relaxed (Runte 1987, 147). Moneys appropriated from the Land and Water Conservation Fund became available, and the rising power of the environmental movement supported expansion of the system (Foresta 1984, 71).

Reinforcing these actions was part two of the 1972 National Park Service System Plan, which emphasized (among other things) preservation of outstanding representative examples of the nation's physiographic and biological features (U.S. Department of the Interior, National Park Service 1972b, 1). The result was addition of many new natural areas—the Big Cypress and Big Thicket national preserves, representing forest types not previously in the system; Theodore Roosevelt National Park, 70,000 acres of badland topography; Guadelupe Mountains National Park, the world's most extensive Permian fossil reef; Congaree Swamp National Monument, the last virgin stand of bottomland hardwoods in the Southeast; and the greatest areal addition of all time, the Alaskan national parks, which doubled the size of the system "in a single stroke" (Foresta 1984, 116, 117). This last action, authorized by the Alaska Native Claims Settlement Act, withdrew 80 million acres from the public domain "for possible recommendations to the Congress as additions to or creations of units of the National Park, Forest, Wildlife Refuge, and Wild and Scenic Rivers Systems" (37 Fed. Reg. 5579-5583 (Mar. 16, 1972)).

A number of acquisitions reflect our attraction to water. Cape Cod National Seashore (Massachusetts), established in 1961, represented the first commitment of federal funds for purchase of an entire park unit, and it was followed by eight additional seashores and four national lakeshores (along the Great Lakes). Authorization of the Ozark National Scenic Riverways (Missouri) sparked attention to the scenic and recreational values of these resources and led to passage of the Wild and Scenic Rivers Act four years later. Eight additional streams were designated wild and scenic rivers by that legislation, initiating a system of national riverways. (Note: When wild and scenic rivers were designated on lands managed by agencies other than the National Park Service, custody was generally left with those other agencies [Runte 1987, 224-228].)

In 1933 the Civil War battlefields were taken into the National Park System (Foresta 1984, 130), and in 1935 the Historic Sites Act extended the service's role in historic preservation. That act directed that a national survey of historical and archaeological resources be undertaken to determine which of them had "exceptional value as commemorating or illustrating the history of the United States" (49 Stat. 666). Under these and other authorities, the National Park System has acquired a vast and diverse assemblage of historic sites—the boyhood homes of presidents, the Vanderbilt mansion, the Salem Maritime National Historic Site, a Hopewell iron-making village (Foresta 1984, 131), and many others. Concern over the destruction of historic sites during the housing boom of the 1950s and early 1960s prompted passage of the National Historic Preservation Act of 1966, which authorized the secretary of the interior

(1) to expand and maintain a national register of districts, sites, buildings, structures, and objects significant in American history...the National Register

(2) to establish a program of matching grants-in-aid to States for...the preservation for public benefit of properties that are significant in American history....

(3) to establish a program of matching grant[s]-in-aid to the National Trust for Historic Preservation in the United States.

The provisions of this act greatly expanded national consciousness of our historical and cultural heritage and were reflected in part one of the 1972 plan (U.S. Department of the Interior, National Park Service 1972a).

In 1986 the National Park System contained more than 337 units— national parks and monuments; scenic parkways, riverways, seashores, lakeshores, recreation areas, and reservoirs; and historic sites (General Services Administration 1986, 325). The basic philosophy espoused by Mather and contained in the National Park Service Organic Act persists, but many of the parks are bursting at their seams with visitors, and current trends toward increasing accessibility show an emphasis on "provid[ing] for the enjoyment of the same." The Legacy of Parks program announced by President Richard Nixon in 1971 and implemented in part in 1974 through creation of the 23,000-acre Gateway National Recreation Area near New York City and the 24,000-acre Golden Gate National Recreation Area near San Francisco (Council on Environmental Quality 1974, 190) was a definite move in that direction. How long the service can continue to play the balancing game required by its organic legislation is anybody's guess.

OUTDOOR RECREATION

Until late in the nineteenth century, outdoor recreation was largely the province of the rural and the wealthy. The rural had hunting, fishing, and other outdoor pursuits close at hand, and the wealthy had the time and money to travel from congested cities to privately operated spas and resorts—no government intervention was needed or desired. Under such circumstances it was easy for national park policy to emphasize the "conserve" and "leave them unimpaired" provisions of the organic act over the directive "to provide for the enjoyment of the same." But proliferation of the automobile after World War I opened remote areas to the masses and inserted the federal government into the outdoor recreation business (Fitch and Shanklin 1970, 25).

False Starts

The government's first formal efforts toward providing outdoor recreation opportunities were farsighted, comprehensive, and unsuccessful. On April 14, 1924, President Calvin Coolidge stated that the federal government's efforts to promote outdoor recreation had been expressed "'in an incoherent manner'" and appointed a committee of cabinet secretaries to prepare a national outdoor recreation policy. On the committee's recommendation, a National Conference on Outdoor Recreation was held in Washington, DC, one month later (May 22-24, 1924) and was attended by representatives of 128 organizations (Fitch and Shanklin 1970, 42, 43).

After a second meeting, the conference published a report containing several recommendations "suggested as elementary in the formation of a Federal recreation policy" (National Conference on Outdoor Recreation 1928, 89) that predated similar proposals of the Outdoor Recreation Resources Review Commission (ORRRC) by almost thirty-five years. The conference recommended the following:

> Creation by law or Executive order of a continuing agency or commission to promote and develop a Federal outdoor recreation policy; to advise concerning means of coordinating the common functions of various agencies of the Government which relate to outdoor recreation and the conservation and administration of natural plant and animal life resources, including forestry, fisheries, game and bird life, the national forests, parks, monuments, and public domain; to serve as a means of bringing the agencies of the Government into active cooperation with national and other bodies in the field of outdoor recreation and conservation; and to promote specific projects of research and plans of practical application for the utilization and enjoyment of the recreational values of the Federal natural resources. (National Conference on Outdoor Recreation 1928, 89)

The conference report went far beyond a narrow definition of outdoor recreation. Among its recommendations were the following:

4. Establishment by law of the objects and standards of the national parks system in order to (a) differentiate this system clearly from other land systems, Federal and State, and (b) provide a definite basis for development of recreation in the parks in coordination with recreation in national forests and other permanent Federal reservations....

6. Elimination from the present national park system of units or areas not fully meeting standards as measured by the major parks and the transfer of these units to other administrative agencies, Federal and State.

7. A definite long term program for the acquisition of national forest lands in the Lake States, the Appalachian Range of New England and the mountain States of the South, and in the coastal plains region of the South. (Reference, McNary-Woodruff bill as enacted by the 70th Congress, Public No. 326.)

8. Formal delimitation by proclamation of the Secretary of Agriculture of wilderness areas within the national forests and suppression of the exploitation of social uses or speculative economic uses inimical to the enjoyment of simple wilderness sports. (Reference, the Leavitt bill, H.R. 10659, 70th Cong.)....

21. Classification of lands of the public domain chiefly valuable for recreation under the terms of the act of June 14, 1926, and their administration by the State or minor political units.

22. A definite long term program establishing a firm basis for forest research and the relation of wild life and recreation to forestry. (Reference, McSweeney bill as enacted by the 70th Congress, Public No. 466.) (National Conference on Outdoor Recreation 1928, 89, 90)

Impressive as these recommendations were, they failed to arouse sufficient interest in a national outdoor recreation program, and the accomplishments of the National Conference on Outdoor Recreation were overtaken by the Great Depression (Fitch and Shanklin 1970, 44, 45).

With the advent of President Roosevelt and the New Deal, natural resource planning achieved legitimacy in the federal government. Roosevelt's National Resources Board, created by executive order on June 7, 1935, was to "'prepare and present to the President a program for the development of and use of land, waters and other national resources.'" The National Park Service was commissioned to prepare a study of outdoor recreation. Its report (U.S. Department of the Interior, National Park Service 1938) was prepared in consultation with other land management agencies in Interior and Agriculture, but *they were not permitted to review the final proposals prior to publication* (Fitch and Shanklin 1970, 46, 47). Thus the report illustrates more the National Park Service's autocratic operating style and its desire to acquire whatever outdoor recreation role might develop than a coordinated consensus among federal agencies—and for this reason, among others, it failed. Among the committee report's recommendations were that the *Park Service* study and maintain an inventory of the nation's outdoor recreation resources, assist states and local governments in recreation planning, and assist other federal agencies in protecting and developing recreation resources on lands they controlled, and that lands controlled by the Forest Service and those in the public domain be studied to determine their best use—including their possible transfer to the National Park Service (Fitch and Shanklin 1970, 48).

Within a year of the board's report, Congress enacted the Park, Parkway, and Recreational Area Study Act of 1936. The act authorized the National Park Service to study public park, parkway, and recreational area programs and to aid state and local agencies in recreation planning and authorized two or more states to make agreements relative to recreation planning (with approval of the state legislatures and of Congress—

remember the Constitution). The statute prohibited the National Park Service from considering lands under the jurisdiction of the Department of Agriculture, but these provisions were largely ignored. The Park Service's report (U.S. Department of the Interior, National Park Service 1941) provided a foundation for the ORRRC report twenty-one years later but contained much of the proprietary tenor of its predecessor: "'If any existing agency is to be charged with coordination of all Federal activities in this field, the National Park Service is the logical choice for the task'" (Fitch and Shanklin 1970, 50-53).

During the same time that the Park Service was developing recommendations under the Park, Parkway, and Recreational Area Study Act, a second, broader-based and more aggressive group was traveling a parallel path. The Technical Committee on Recreation was composed of representatives of Agriculture, Interior, the Children's Bureau, the Office of Education, and four New Deal agencies—the National Youth Administration, the Civilian Conservation Corps, and the Resettlement Administration. It evaluated the national situation and need for coordination from a "recreational" rather than an "outdoor recreational" perspective. The committee recommended a new agency, and its proposals greatly resembled those of the ORRRC, which was to follow:

[A] separate bureau should

(1) Act as a coordinating instrument for all Federal agencies with recreation programs, but should not itself operate any such programs.

(2) Assist State and local governments in recreation planning and administration....

(3) Administer a grant-in-aid program to the States for the purpose of encouraging recreational experimentation....

(4) Maintain a recreation library and act as a clearing house for information....

(5) Promote recreation research on the part of other Federal agencies and, itself, initiate such research.

(6) Assist Federal, State and local governments not only by providing technical advice and assistance but by making recreation experts available on a temporary loan basis. (Fitch and Shanklin 1970, 55)

The technical committee repeated many of the recommendations of its predecessors and was the first to suggest creation of a new agency, but it too failed to stimulate any real action. A number of other studies were conducted, bills introduced, and committees formed during the 1940s and 1950s, but no program emerged—the time had not yet come.

The Outdoor Recreation Resources Review Commission (ORRRC)

With the end of World War II and an increase in leisure time and disposable income, Americans turned to the nation's parks, forests, and other public lands as sources of outdoor recreation. In 1958 Congress responded with Public Law No. 85-470, establishing the Outdoor Recreation Resources Review Commission. The commission was charged with the following objectives:

> To determine the outdoor recreation wants and needs of the American people now and... in the years 1976 and 2000.
>
> To determine the recreation resources of the Nation available to satisfy those needs now and in the years 1976 and 2000.
>
> To determine what policies and programs should be recommended to ensure that the needs of the present and future are adequately and efficiently met. (ORRRC 1962a, 2)

The act was administered by a fifteen-member commission chaired by Laurance S. Rockefeller, assisted by an advisory council composed of high-level federal officials and twenty-five citizens representing a broad array of interest groups and geographic regions and contact officers representing each state. In addition to the assistance of its staff, the ORRRC was supported by a number of contracted studies, resulting in twenty-seven published reports containing almost 5,000 pages (ORRRC 1962b-1962bb).

The ORRRC's findings were largely self-evident— "Opportunities are most urgently needed near metropolitan areas," "Money is needed," "Water is a focal point," "Outdoor recreation is a major leisure time activity" (ORRRC 1962a, 3, 4). Many of its recommendations simply repeated those of its predecessors—states should have a key role; government should assist the private sector; federal grants-in-aid should be made available to states on a matching basis; research should be expanded. But its primary recommendation was that a new agency, the Bureau of Outdoor Recreation, be created in the Department of the Interior to coordinate a national outdoor recreation program (but not to manage land or facilities itself) and to carry out the work of the ORRRC. In this effort the commission was successful. The time had come.

The Bureau of Outdoor Recreation (BOR)

On April 2, 1962, scarcely two months after release of the ORRRC report, Secretary of the Interior Stewart Udall created the Bureau of Outdoor Recreation (BOR) by Departmental Manual Release No. 497 under the general authority in Reorganization Plan No. 3 of 1950. He assigned the new agency duties previously given to the National Park Service by the Park, Parkway, and Recreational Area Study Act of 1936—to conduct resource surveys, promote coordinated research, and initiate a national outdoor recreation plan. Chiefly a planning, coordination, and funding agency, the BOR was to manage no lands or facilities of its own. Later in the same month, on April 27, President John F. Kennedy created a cabinet-level Recreation Advisory Council by Executive Order No. 11,017. These moves included measures to link activities of the Department of Agriculture and the Department of the Interior—secretaries of the two departments alternated as council chair. Edward C. Crafts, assistant chief of the Forest Service, was named first director of the BOR (The Nature Conservancy 1977, 152).

Legislative work was also under way, culminating in the Outdoor Recreation Programs Act of 1963 and the Land and Water Conservation Fund Act of 1965. The former gave statutory authority to activities already being carried out by the BOR:

> Prepare and maintain a continuing inventory and evaluation of outdoor recreation needs and resources...[, p]repare a system for classification of outdoor recreation resources...[, f]ormulate and maintain a comprehensive nationwide outdoor recreation plan...[, p]rovide technical assistance and advice to and cooperate with States, political subdivisions, and [other interests, etc.]. (77 Stat. 49)

The Outdoor Recreation Programs Act is often referred to as the "Organic Act" of the BOR (The Nature Conservancy 1977, 152), but it never mentioned the bureau. In fact, the BOR did not then, nor did it ever, have statutory legitimacy, and it paid for that deficiency. The bureau's real clout came with the authority granted the secretary, and delegated to the BOR, in the Land and Water Conservation Fund Act. The act created a substantial pot of money, the Land and Water Conservation Fund (LWCF), from which to finance (among other things) outdoor recreation activities and projects.

As described in the original act, the LWCF was to be composed of "proceeds from entrance, admission, and other recreation user fees" charged by federal agencies, proceeds from the sale of surplus federal property (78 Stat. 897, 898), and a portion of the federal tax on fuels used by motorboats (78 Stat. 904). Moneys in the fund were to be available for expenditure *only when subsequently appropriated by Congress,* and those not appropriated within two years of receipt were to be transferred to miscellaneous receipts of the Treasury (78 Stat. 899); that is, they were to become available to meet the general financial needs of the nation and would no longer be earmarked for outdoor recreation.

Appropriations from the fund generally were to be allocated 40 percent to federal agencies and 60 percent to the states and could be used by the states for planning, acquisition of lands and waters for outdoor recreational purposes, or development (78 Stat. 900). However, no state could receive funds for acquisition or development until it had an approved state comprehensive outdoor recreation plan (SCORP) (78 Stat. 901) and the proposed acquisition or development was in accordance with the SCORP (78 Stat. 902).

Although the pay-as-you-go system based on user fees may be good economic theory, imposition of such fees for activities that had generally been "free" met with considerable public opposition, and receipts fell far short of perceived needs. The original act set no limits on the LWCF but authorized that up to $60 million in "advance appropriations" could be provided from general Treasury funds (78 Stat. 900). Amendments in 1968 (82 Stat. 355) inserted a new section, which provided that revenues from outer continental shelf (OCS) mineral leases were to be deposited to the LWCF to provide a minimum of $200 million per year. The minimum was subsequently raised to $300 million per year by the amendments of 1970 and to $900 million per year by the amendments of 1976 and 1977. While these statutory "minimums" appear impressive, far less has been appropriated (table 6.2). In 1968 the provisions for recreational user fees were deleted except for a few designated areas, and the LWCF is financed today primarily from OCS revenues.

During its first six years (through 1968) the BOR was an outstanding success. It was instrumental in accomplishing the following:

• Enacting the original Land and Water Conservation Fund Act and later amendments guaranteeing $200 million per year to the fund.

• Acquiring 462,000 acres of Federal recreational lands at a cost of $131.6 million.

• Approving 3,452 grants, totaling $197.1 million, to the states.

• Conducting and/or coordinating numerous resource area studies of potential national recreation areas, trails, and wild and scenic rivers.

TABLE 6.2

Land and Water Conservation Fund Appropriations, Fiscal Years 1965-1989
(in Thousands of Dollars)

Fiscal Year	LWCF Total[a]	State Grants Portion	Federal Portion
1965	16,000	10,375	5,555
1966	125,000	82,409	39,183
1967	110,000	56,531	41,737
1968	119,191	61,557	51,416
1969	164,500	45,000	116,725
1970	131,100	62,000	65,900
1971	357,400	185,400	167,841
1972	361,500	255,000	101,669
1973	300,000	181,800	112,957
1974	76,223	66,000	5,000
1975	307,492	180,000	121,092
1976	316,986	175,840	134,953
1976TQ[b]	75,988	43,960	30,480
1977	537,799	175,516	355,597
1978	805,000	306,070	490,166
1979	737,025	369,790	359,988
1980	509,194	300,000	201,801
1981	288,593	173,745	107,282
1982	179,927	0	167,386
1983	335,093	110,619[c]	212,593
1984	295,913	72,919	213,113
1985	286,612	71,853	206,245
1986	169,202	45,993	116,883
1987	193,096	32,700	153,126
1988	170,464	16,567	144,040
1989	206,233	16,700	179,992
Total	$7,175,531	$3,098,344	$3,902,720

Source: U.S. Department of the Interior, National Park Service, "Land and Water Conservation Fund Grants-in-Aid Program, Fiscal Year 1988" (Washington, DC: Government Printing Office, 1989), p. 62.

[a]Includes some federal administration costs for federal land acquisition and state grants.

[b]Transition quarter, July 1, 1976, to September 30, 1976, because of adoption of new fiscal year calendar.

[c]Regular appropriation—$70,619,000 plus $40,000,000 in fiscal year 1983 supplemental funding (Emergency Jobs Bill).

• Passing at least twenty-five bills affecting outdoor recreation, natural areas, and environmental issues, including the Wild and Scenic Rivers Act, the National Trails System Act, the Federal Water Project Recreation Act, and those creating fifteen national parks, seashores, and recreation areas (Crafts 1969, 14, 15).

Despite its firm fiscal foundation, the BOR was an inherently weak agency from the political standpoint. Its creation had alienated many of the old-line bureaucrats in the National Park Service (and their state counterparts); it served a diffuse and poorly organized constituency; it managed no real estate or strong internal program of its own; and, perhaps most important, it was a creature of the executive branch and was never blessed by Congress, and as such it was vulnerable to the wishes of each succeeding administration. Early in the Nixon administration, on May 29, 1969, the Council on Environmental Quality replaced the President's Council on Recreation and Natural Beauty, and the Citizens' Advisory Council on Environmental Quality replaced the Citizens' Advisory Committee on Recreation and Natural Beauty (Fitch and Shanklin 1970, 190), signaling a shift of emphasis and downgrading of outdoor recreation within the Executive Office of the President—and G. Douglas Hofe, Jr., replaced Crafts.

> Since February 1969 the Bureau of Outdoor Recreation has been on the toboggan. Little good and much bad has happened to it.... Outdoor recreation no longer is the magic phrase of five years ago. No longer are people and agencies trying to climb on the recreation band wagon. Recreation has become as mundane as forestry. (Crafts 1969, 15, 60, cited in Fitch and Shanklin 1970, 198)

By the time the much-revised report "The Recreation Imperative" was transmitted to Congress in draft form in 1974 (U.S. Congress, Senate 1974), more than six years after the deadline set by the original legislation, national priorities had indeed changed. In his letter of transmittal to the president (July 17, 1970) Secretary Walter J. Hickel stated, "This plan focuses on one of today's major domestic challenges—protecting the quality of our environment" (U.S. Congress, Senate 1974, iii). Its recommendations are directed toward the following:

1. A concentrated effort to provide recreation in the major metropolitan areas where the largest inequities now exist.
2. Assisting States and local governments in their efforts to guide suburban growth.
3. Insuring that ALL Federal programs are carried out in a way that preserves outdoor recreation resources and expands recreation opportunity through improved coordination, better use of existing resources and programs, and additional land acquisition where necessary to protect those resources that are needed for continued enjoyment of the environment. (U.S. Congress, Senate 1974, iv-v)

Senator Henry M. Jackson, chairman of the Senate Committee on Interior and Insular Affairs and a member of the Outdoor Recreation Resources Review Commission, circulated copies of "The Recreation Imperative" and a subsequent draft, "Outdoor Recreation: A Legacy for America," to state outdoor recreation officials for their review and comment, although neither report "ever received final approval of either the Johnson or the Nixon Administrations" (U.S. Congress, Senate 1974, 7). Other responses were generally cool to lukewarm; three times as many state administrators favored "The Recreation Imperative" over the later version (U.S. Congress, Senate 1975, 4).

Nixon was not the last president to tinker with the BOR. President Jimmy Carter changed the bureau's name to the Heritage Conservation and Recreation Service in 1978 (Council on Environmental Quality 1978, 244), and President Ronald Reagan abolished the agency, returning its functions to the National Park Service, from whence they came. Reagan also appointed a President's Commission on Americans Outdoors, which examined existing outdoor recreation lands and resources and the roles of federal, state, and local government and the private sector in providing outdoor recreation opportunities. The commission's report, *Americans Outdoors: The Legacy, the Challenge*, recommended, among other things, that

[c]ommunities establish Greenways, corridors of private and public recreational lands and waters, to provide people with access to open spaces close to where they live, and to link together the rural and urban spaces in the American landscape.

[c]ongressionally-authorized land acquisitions be expedited, making full use of alternative land protection techniques, and exchange procedures be streamlined.

[t]he Land and Water Conservation Fund be succeeded by a dedicated trust—providing a minimum of $1 billion a year—to help pay for federal, state, and local land acquisition, and state and local facility development and rehabilitation. Congress should consider creating an endowed trust which, over time, would be self-sustaining. (President's Commission on Americans Outdoors 1987, 142, 168, 254)

If implemented, this last recommendation would be by far the most significant. How it will fare in times of budgetary constraints and changing priorities is open to question, however. At least a hint is afforded by the fact that Congresswoman Barbara Vucanovich of Nevada and Senator

Malcolm Wallop of Wyoming, two of the four congressional members of the commission, failed to support the recommendation, feeling instead that funding should be justified in the annual budgetary process (President's Commission on Americans Outdoors 1987, 254).

The commission also addressed the subject of executive branch organization, finding that

> there is a clear need for a central organization whose purpose would be to elevate the importance of recreation and the outdoors....
>
> The purpose of the institution would be to stimulate leadership, encourage innovation, and reward excellence in recreation delivery across the nation....
>
> The institution would encourage leadership, innovation and excellence primarily through two means: awarding grants and sharing information....
>
> The institution would have a critical role in promoting an outdoor recreation ethic. (President's Commission on Americans Outdoors 1987, 248, 249)

The foregoing is a fair description of the functions of the Bureau of Outdoor Recreation, dissolved by the same president who appointed the commission.

Despite its rather stormy history, the Department of the Interior's outdoor recreation program and the funds provided though the LWCF have been a boon to public outdoor recreation. Through fiscal year 1984, the LWCF provided almost $3 billion in state grants and slightly more for use by federal agencies—more than $6 billion in total (table 6.2). It supported 31,777 state and local projects; 389 were for the preparation of SCORPs, 7,903 of which acquired over 2,786,172 acres of parkland, and the remaining 23,485 provided for the development of outdoor recreational facilities (U.S. Department of the Interior, National Park Service 1985, 2).

The Forest Service and Outdoor Recreation

Recreation in the national forests has come a long way since Pinchot noted, "'Quite incidentally, also the National Forests serve a good purpose as playgrounds for the people...and their value in this respect is well worth considering'" (Robinson 1975, 120). In the early days of the National Forest System, few persons utilized, or even appreciated, the national forests' recreational potential. After World War II, however, the national forests were caught up in the general increase in public outdoor recreation, and (as in the case of the national parks) by the mid-1950s their facilities were sorely taxed. While the National Park Service was conducting Mission 66, the Forest Service was engaged in Operation Outdoors, a five-year planning program begun in 1956 and targeted to meet the demands of 1962. In 1959 the Forest Service followed Operation Outdoors with the National Forest Recreation Survey, designed to provide quantitative resource data that could be used to plan to the year 2000 (at the same time the ORRRC was developing its report) (Robinson 1975, 121). Despite these efforts toward recreation planning and the mandate of the Multiple-Use Sustained Yield Act, management of national forest lands has been dominated by the desire to produce timber. Recreation was produced as a by-product of timber production (Clary 1986, 170-173).

Yet the kind of recreational opportunity provided by the national forests and desired by forest users requires little development or intensive management. With the exception of ski resorts and some other facilities developed by private interests through licenses, leases, and other arrangements, Forest Service recreation accommodations tend to be more modest, and their publicity less intense, than those available through the National Park Service or private enterprise. Of the 188 million visitor-days experienced in the national forests in 1973, fewer than 40 percent were on developed sites—most were dispersed along trails through undeveloped forest areas (Robinson 1975, 122). During the same year, 218 ski areas located in whole or in part within national forests accommodated 8.5 million visitor-days of use (Robinson 1975, 126). By 1980 the National Forest System had recorded 223 million recreation visitor-days, compared with only 87 million within the national parks—and the national forests "are said to furnish more outdoor recreation use than any other system, public or private" (Frome 1984, 140).

Recreational use of the National Forest System is projected to rise considerably faster than the nation's population as a whole (Robinson 1975, 130), and users' desires are shifting toward more elaborate accommodations—a move that may lead to greater use of user fees within the system (Robinson 1975, 130, 138-143). Countering this trend is the power of the environmental movement, which desires less development and more wilderness (Clary 1986, 171).

In response to the rising public interest in recreational opportunities on national forest land and a perception of the need for "innovative and creative ways for the National Forests to meet America's growing need for open space and outdoor recreation," Forest Service Chief F. Dale Robertson appointed six commissions from within the agency, each of which was to investigate one facet of the issue and recommend corrective actions. The result, presented at a national recreation strategy symposium (U.S. Department of Agriculture, Forest Service 1987), emphasized the following, among other objectives:

• Providing services and facilities to satisfy more customer preferences for national forest recreation.

• Developing a better national forest recreational transportation system.

• Strengthening application of multiple use to reflect better the importance people attach to the scenery, wildlife, and special places.

• Improving career and training opportunities for recreation and related professions.

Implementation, of course, depends upon adequate appropriations in a time of budget tightening. Yet public recreational use of the national forests will continue to increase, with increasing conflicts among competitive uses, regardless of the amount of funding available.

Recreation on Other Federal Lands

Virtually all types of federal lands, even parts of military reservations, support some kind of public outdoor recreation. Outdoor recreation in the 90.4-million-acre National Wildlife Refuge System is authorized by the Refuge Recreation Act of 1962, provided that it does not interfere with the major purpose of the refuge.

The U.S. Army Corps of Engineers has no explicit recreation mandate, but recreational facilities on Corps projects are authorized by the Flood Control Act of 1944, and in many cases the recreational benefits outweigh those accruing to navigation, flood control, or other project purposes.

The Bureau of Reclamation administers 6 million acres of western lands, much of which is open to public recreation.

The Tennessee Valley Authority (TVA) administers 1 million acres of lands and waters, including the 170,000-acre Land Between the Lakes National Recreation Demonstration Area in Kentucky and Tennessee (President's Commission on Americans Outdoors 1987, 170).

The Need for Management (and Money)

As competition for outdoor recreation opportunities and open space in general continues to intensify, greater emphasis will be placed on managing recreational resources. The 1980s marked the end of major park and wilderness allocation; the 1990s must bring structure to the use of these lands for outdoor recreation and other purposes (Wellman 1987, 235-237).

Problems to be faced extend far beyond typical users' conflicts of interest, however. Events outside public land boundaries threaten the continued existence of the natural systems that support quality outdoor recreation. Air pollution over vast areas, water withdrawals and energy developments (Wellman 1987, 237-242), and climatic changes—all affect the future of outdoor recreation. These are "mega-issues"; their solutions will profoundly affect outdoor recreation, but they lie at a much higher level.

Of more immediate and local concern, and more easily addressed, are issues developing on the recreation lands themselves. Recreational use of federal parkland and forestland increased by about 10 percent per year between 1910 and 1960. In many areas vegetation damage, soil erosion, and wildlife disturbance are already serious problems. The mere presence of other people degrades the wilderness recreational experience for many; and outright conflicts develop between canoeists (or tubers) and fishermen, hikers and pack trains, skiers and snowmobilers, trail bikers and hikers (Wellman 1987, 243-247).

Better management is an obvious approach to increased competition and conflict among users and damage to the supporting resource base. The concept of management implies guidance toward a desired objective. In the case of outdoor recreation, the objective might be to accommodate the greatest volume and diversity of the highest quality of outdoor recreation with a minimum of conflicts among users while not degrading the resource base. Conflict resolution itself is difficult enough, but keeping use below the "carrying capacity" from both quality and quantity standpoints becomes virtually impossible.

A greater degree of management must come, however, and with it increased costs. Whether the public at large is willing to pay through general taxes and congressional appropriations remains to be seen. Bills implementing the President's Commission on Americans Outdoors' recommendation for a trust fund that would produce $1 billion per year were introduced in both houses of the Hundred and First Congress (proposed American Heritage Trust Act), but none passed. The same economists who argue that pollution costs should be "internalized" also argue that outdoor recreation costs should be borne by the users. With more demand for management in the face of declining general funds, new and increased user fees are probably a certainty (Wellman 1987, 251-258).

REFERENCES

Albright, Horace M., and Robert Cahn. 1985. *The Birth of the National Park Service: The Founding Years, 1913-33.* Salt Lake City, UT: Howe Brothers.

Bean, Michael J. 1983. *The Evolution of National Wildlife Law.* New York: Praeger Publishers.

Chase, Alston. 1986. *Playing God in Yellowstone.* New York: Atlantic Monthly Press.

Clary, David A. 1986. *Timber and the Forest Service.* Lawrence: University Press of Kansas.

The Conservation Foundation. 1987. "Commission Gives Recreation a Shot in the Arm." *Conservation Foundation Letter* 1987, No. 2.

Council on Environmental Quality. 1974. *Environmental Quality—1974.* Washington, DC: Government Printing Office.

———. 1978. *Environmental Quality—1978.* Washington, DC: Government Printing Office.

Crafts, Edward C. 1969. "High Noon for the Bureau of Outdoor Recreation." *American Forests* 75:12-15, 58-60.

Dana, Samuel T., and Sally K. Fairfax. 1980. *Forest and Range Policy: Its Development in the United States.* New York: McGraw-Hill Book Company.

Fitch, Edwin M., and John F. Shanklin. 1970. *The Bureau of Outdoor Recreation.* New York: Praeger Publishers.

Foresta, Ronald A. 1984. *America's National Parks and Their Keepers.* Washington, DC: Resources for the Future.

Frome, Michael. 1984. *The Forest Service.* Boulder, CO: Westview Press.

Gates, Paul W. 1968. "History of Land Law Development." Public Land Law Review Commission study report. Washington, DC: Government Printing Office.

General Services Administration. 1986. *The United States Government Manual 1986/87.* Washington, DC: Government Printing Office.

Ise, John. [1961] 1967. *Our National Park Policy: A Critical History.* Baltimore: Johns Hopkins University Press.

Kieley, James F. 1981. "...Enter Mather and Albright." In U.S. Department of the Interior, National Park Service, *Sixty-fifth Anniversary, National Park Service,* 3-6. Washington, DC: U.S. Department of the Interior, National Park Service.

McKechnie, W. S. 1958. *Magna Carta: A Commentary on the Great Charter of King John.* New York: Burt Franklin & Company.

McMillon, Bill. 1983. *The Old Lodges and Hotels of Our National Parks.* South Bend, IN: Icarus Press.

Marsh, George P. 1874. *The Earth as Modified by Human Action.* New York: Scribner, Armstrong. [1970] St. Clair Shores, MI: Scholarly Press.

National Conference on Outdoor Recreation. 1928. "National Conference on Outdoor Recreation: A Report Epitomizing the Results of Major Fact-Finding Surveys and Projects Which Have Been Undertaken Under the Auspices of the National Conference on Outdoor Recreation." 70th Cong., 1st sess., May 1928. S. Doc. 158. Washington, DC: Government Printing Office.

The Nature Conservancy. 1977. *Preserving Our Natural Heritage.* Vol. I, *Federal Activities.* Washington, DC: Government Printing Office.

ORRRC. *See* Outdoor Recreation Resources Review Commission.

Outdoor Recreation Resources Review Commission. 1962a. "Outdoor Recreation for America." Washington, DC: Government Printing Office.

———. 1962b. "Public Outdoor Recreation Areas: Acreage, Use, Potential." ORRRC Study Report no. 1 (prepared by commission staff). Washington, DC: Government Printing Office.

———. 1962c. "List of Public Outdoor Recreation Areas: 1960." ORRRC Study Report no. 2 (prepared by commission staff). Washington, DC: Government Printing Office.

———. 1962d. "Wilderness and Recreation: A Report on Resources, Values, and Problems." ORRRC Study Report no. 3 (prepared by the Wildland Research Center, University of California, Berkeley). Washington, DC: Government Printing Office.

———. 1962e. "Shoreline Recreation Resources of the United States." ORRRC Study Report no. 4 (prepared by George Washington University). Washington, DC: Government Printing Office.

———. 1962f. "The Quality of Outdoor Recreation: As Evidenced by User Satisfaction." ORRRC Study Report no. 5 (prepared by the Department of Resource Development, Michigan State University). Washington, DC: Government Printing Office.

———. 1962g. "Hunting in the United States: Its Present and Future Role." ORRRC Study Report no. 6 (prepared by the Department of Conservation, School of Natural Resources, University of Michigan). Washington, DC: Government Printing Office.

———. 1962h. "Sport Fishing: Today and Tomorrow." ORRRC Study Report no. 7 (prepared by the Bureau of Sport Fisheries and Wildlife, U.S. Department of the Interior). Washington, DC: Government Printing Office.

———. 1962i. "Potential New Sites for Outdoor Recreation in the Northeast." ORRRC Study Report no. 8 (prepared by the Economic Research Service, U.S. Department of Agriculture). Washington, DC: Government Printing Office.

————. 1962j. "Alaska Outdoor Recreation Potential." ORRRC Study Report no. 9 (prepared by The Conservation Foundation). Washington, DC: Government Printing Office.

————. 1962k. "Water for Recreation: Values and Opportunities." ORRRC Study Report no. 10 (prepared by the Geological Survey, U.S. Department of the Interior). Washington, DC: Government Printing Office.

————. 1962l. "Private Outdoor Recreation Facilities." ORRRC Study Report no. 11 (prepared by the Economic Research Service, U.S. Department of Agriculture). Washington, DC: Government Printing Office.

————. 1962m. "Paying for Recreation Facilities." ORRRC Study Report no. 12 (prepared by the National Planning Association). Washington, DC: Government Printing Office.

————. 1962n. "Federal Agencies and Outdoor Recreation." ORRRC Study Report no. 13 (prepared by the Fredrick Burk Foundation for Education, San Francisco State College). Washington, DC: Government Printing Office.

————. 1962o. "Directory of State Outdoor Recreation Administration." ORRRC Study Report no. 14 (prepared by commission staff, based on an American Political Science Association study). Washington, DC: Government Printing Office.

————. 1962p. "Open Space Action." ORRRC Study Report no. 15 (prepared by William H. Whyte). Washington, DC: Government Printing Office.

————. 1962q. "Land Acquisition for Outdoor Recreation: Analysis of Selected Legal Problems." ORRRC Study Report no. 16 (prepared by Norman Williams, Jr.). Washington, DC: Government Printing Office.

————. 1962r. "Multiple Use of Land and Water Areas." ORRRC Study Report no. 17 (prepared by John Shanklin). Washington, DC: Government Printing Office.

————. 1962s. "A Look Abroad: The Effect of Foreign Travel on Domestic Outdoor Recreation and a Brief Survey of Outdoor Recreation in Six Countries." ORRRC Study Report no. 18 (prepared by Pauline Tait). Washington, DC: Government Printing Office.

————. 1962t. "National Recreation Survey." ORRRC Study Report no. 19 (prepared by commission staff, based on data collected by the Bureau of the Census). Washington, DC: Government Printing Office.

————. 1962u. "Participation in Outdoor Recreation: Factors Affecting Demand Among American Adults." ORRRC Study Report no. 20 (prepared by Eva Mueller and Gerald Gurin, with assistance from Margaret Wood). Washington, DC: Government Printing Office.

————. 1962v. "The Future of Outdoor Recreation in Metropolitan Regions of the United States." 3 vols. ORRRC Study Report no. 21 (prepared by commission staff and selected universities and planning agencies). Washington, DC: Government Printing Office.

———— 1962w. "Trends in American Living and Outdoor Recreation." ORRRC Study Report no. 22 (prepared by various authors). Washington, DC: Government Printing Office.

————. 1962x. "Projections for the Years 1976 and 2000: Economic Growth, Population, Labor Force and Leisure, and Transportation." ORRRC Study Report no. 23 (prepared by commission staff and others). Washington, DC: Government Printing Office.

————. 1962y. "Economic Studies of Outdoor Recreation." ORRRC Study Report no. 24 (prepared by commission staff and others). Washington, DC: Government Printing Office.

————. 1962z. "Public Expenditures for Outdoor Recreation." ORRRC Study Report no. 25 (prepared by commission staff). Washington, DC: Government Printing Office.

————. 1962aa. "Prospective Demand for Outdoor Recreation." ORRRC Study Report no. 26 (prepared by commission staff). Washington, DC: Government Printing Office.

————. 1962bb. "Outdoor Recreation in the U.S.: Its Literature and History." 2 vols. ORRRC Study Report no. 27 (prepared by the Library of Congress and Arthur Hawthorne Carhart). Washington, DC: Government Printing Office.

President's Commission on Americans Outdoors. 1987. *Americans Outdoors: The Legacy, the Challenge.* Washington, DC: Island Press.

Robinson, Glen O. 1975. *The Forest Service.* Baltimore: Johns Hopkins University Press.

Runte, Alfred. [1979] 1981. *National Parks: The American Experience.* Lincoln: University of Nebraska Press.

————. 1987. *National Parks: The American Experience.* 2d ed. Lincoln: University of Nebraska Press.

Sax, Joseph L. 1976. "America's National Parks: Their Principles, Purposes, and Prospects." *Natural History* (special supplement, October 1976). (Not paginated.)

Southern Appalachian National Park Commission. 1931. "Final Report of the Southern Appalachian National Park Commission to the Secretary of the Interior, June 30, 1931." Washington, DC: Government Printing Office.

U.S. Congress. Senate. Committee on Interior and Insular Affairs. 1974. "The Recreation Imperative." 93d Cong., 2d sess. Washington, DC: Government Printing Office.

————. 1975. "The Nationwide Outdoor Recreation Plans: Critiques by State Officials." Report prepared by the Environmental Policy Division, Congressional Research Service, Library of Congress. 94th Cong., 1st sess. Washington, DC: Government Printing Office.

U.S. Department of Agriculture. Forest Service. 1987. "The National Forests: America's Great Outdoors!" Staff papers prepared for presentation at the National Recreation Strategy Symposium, Lake Geneva, WI, November 15-17, 1987. Washington, DC: U.S. Department of Agriculture, Forest Service.

U.S. Department of the Interior. Bureau of Outdoor Recreation. 1973. "Outdoor Recreation: A Legacy for America." Washington, DC: Government Printing Office.

U.S. Department of the Interior. National Park Service. 1938. "Recreation Use of Lands in the United States." Washington, DC: Government Printing Office.

———. 1941. "A Study of the Park and Recreation Problem of the United States." Washington, DC: Government Printing Office.

———. 1972a. "Part One of the National Park Service System Plan: History." Washington, DC: Government Printing Office.

———. 1972b. "Part Two of the National Park Service System Plan: Natural History." Washington, DC: Government Printing Office.

———. 1989. "Land and Water Conservation Fund Grants-in-Aid Program, Annual Report: Fiscal Year 1988." Washington, DC: Government Printing Office.

Wellman, J. Douglas. 1987. *Wildland Recreation Policy*. New York: John Wiley & Sons.

Widner, Ralph R., ed. 1968. *Forests and Forestry in the American States*. Washington, DC: National Association of State Foresters.

Wirth, Conrad L. 1980. *Parks, Politics, and the People*. Norman: University of Oklahoma Press.

CHAPTER VII

The Nation's Wildlife and the National Wildlife Refuge System

The nation's wildlife resources are managed through a complicated system of federal, state, and private lands and federal and state laws. Federal government involvement affects primarily federal lands but may govern the activities of U.S. citizens wherever they occur.

A NATIONAL PERSPECTIVE

In his classic text *Game Management,* Aldo Leopold ([1933] 1948) recognized five classes of game management:

1. Restriction of hunting.
2. Predator control.
3. Reservation of game lands (such as parks, forests, refuges, etc.).
4. Artificial replenishment (restocking and game farming).
5. Environmental controls (control of food, cover, special factors, and disease). (Leopold [1933] 1948, 4, 5)

All levels of government, as well as private and corporate landowners, have practiced most or all of the above, frequently in a historical sequence from (1) to (5). In these efforts state governments have focused upon management of resident wildlife on private lands, primarily through regulation of the harvest. The federal government has concentrated more on migratory species, interstate commerce, and refuges—in recent years with a strong emphasis on rare and endangered species. All agencies—and particularly the nongovernmental landowners who control most of the nation's land—have a profound impact upon wildlife populations through the deliberate or incidental application of environmental controls. Among the federal agencies, those managing the most land, particularly the Bureau of Land Management and the Forest Service, also produce the most wildlife and related recreational opportunities.

From a national perspective, wildlife continues to be produced largely as a by-product of land managed for some other purpose—agriculture, timber, water, and so forth. The science of wildlife management through intentional habitat manipulation for the primary benefit of wildlife is a relative newcomer in the field of natural resources. Increasingly, however, wildlife management objectives are becoming injected into land management policies, and in many cases wildlife production may be the primary objective of land management.

Attainment of such objectives rests heavily upon appropriate policy, technology, and trained personnel, all of which were emphasized by the "father" of wildlife management in the United States, Aldo Leopold.

A WORD ABOUT LEOPOLD

Rand Aldo Leopold was born in Burlington, Iowa, on January 11, 1887, the eldest child of Clara Starker and Carl A. Leopold. Aldo's home was on a bluff above the Mississippi River, and he spent many boyhood days exploring the river marshes and the adjacent countryside. During this time he also was indoctrinated in "the ethics of outdoor behavior by his sportsman father" (McCabe 1987, x)—which he practiced throughout his later life.

After attending preparatory school at Lawrenceville Academy, New Jersey, and the Sheffield Scientific School at Yale University, Leopold enrolled in the forestry program at Yale and received a master's degree from that institution in 1909. Immediately upon leaving Yale, he reported to the Southwest District headquarters of the Forest Service in Albuquerque, New Mexico, from which he embarked on a career as a field forester. His first assignment was at a remote location in central Arizona, at the edge of Apache National Forest, and there he became a westerner—"horse, saddle, boots, spurs, chaps, ten-gallon hat and all the other accoutrements of the local cow-culture" (Flader 1973, 29, 30).

While at Apache National Forest, Leopold directed an inventory of wilderness areas (not a very great success), but as his skills improved he was promoted to supervisor of Carson National Forest in New Mexico. During his tour of duty in New Mexico, he contracted nephritis following a field trip during severe weather and nearly died. After a year and a half's convalescence, he was able to return to office work, but his weakened condition precluded his returning to an active field career (McCabe 1987, xi).

His experience in the Apache imbued Leopold with a sense of the value of wilderness, and in 1921 he proposed designation of wilderness areas within the National Forest System "premised wholly on highest recreational use" (Leopold 1921, 719). Following his guidance the first such area was established in Gila National Forest in 1922 (Allin 1982, 70) (see chapter 8).

In 1924 he left the Southwest to join the U.S. Forest Products Laboratory in Madison, Wisconsin, as associate director, with the anticipation that he would soon become director. That did not occur, however, and in 1928 he left the Forest Service to conduct a game survey of Wisconsin, Minnesota, Michigan, Ohio, Missouri, Illinois, and Iowa for the Sporting Arms and Ammunition Manufacturer's Institute. He completed the game survey report in 1931 (McCabe 1987, xi).

Soon after Leopold began the game survey, the chairman of the American Game Association appointed him chairman of a committee to draft an "American Game Policy" (McCabe 1987, xi). The results of this effort, adopted at the Seventeenth American Game Conference in 1930, stressed the continued production of game through the management of habitat rather than preservation of residual and declining populations through refuges and artificial breeding, as had been espoused previously (Flader 1974, 23).

The stock market crash of 1929 eliminated Leopold's source of financial support, and, although he did obtain a few small jobs following completion of the game survey, he found himself largely unemployed during the early depression years—with a wife and five children to support. Undismayed by this turn of events, he began writing a wildlife management textbook (Flader 1974, 23).

Publication of *Game Management* in 1933 marked the recognition of wildlife management as a natural resource profession. *Game Management* was the, and the only, text in the field for at least the next decade or two, and most of its principles are as valid today as they were then. But some of Leopold's early ideas proved erroneous.

Like most outdoorsmen of his time, Leopold initially had a bad impression of predators:

> Aldo saw a hawk pin a quail to an *Atriplex* bush. Shot the hawk. Saw a roadrunner with a quail chick in its beak. Shot the roadrunner. Predators kill our game, he told [his son] Starker. Wolves, too—they eat our deer. Eradicate them. (Gibbons 1981, 690)

But in later years, he came to understand and appreciate the role of predators in natural systems:

When our rifles were empty, the old wolf was down, and a pup was drag-
ging a leg into impassable slide-rocks.

We reached the old wolf in time to watch a fierce green fire dying in
her eyes. I realized then and have known ever since, that there was something new to me in those eyes—something known only to her and to the
mountain. I was young then, and full of trigger itch; I thought that
because fewer wolves meant more deer, that no wolves would mean
hunters' paradise. But after seeing the green fire die, I sensed that neither
the wolf nor the mountain agreed with such a view. (Leopold [1949]
1987, 130)

In the same year that his text was published, Leopold was "given a
five-year trial...to develop a training program in this new discipline at
the University of Wisconsin" (McCabe 1987, xii). While with the
Department of Wildlife Management at the University of Wisconsin
(1933-1948), Leopold directed the work of twenty-six graduate students,
eight of whom became university professors, educating a second generation of wildlife biologists (McCabe 1987, 165, 166). Two of these,
Robert A. McCabe and Joseph Hickey, continued the Leopold tradition
at Wisconsin: "For the next thirty-odd years we provided departmental
leadership, and attempted to maintain the bond that makes the educational experience in Aldo Leopold's department something special." The
thousands of professional fish and wildlife biologists educated in the
United States since then bear tribute to Leopold's academic success.

In early 1934 President Franklin Roosevelt appointed Leopold, cartoonist J. N. ("Ding") Darling, and publisher Thomas Beck to the
President's Committee on Wildlife Restoration and charged the group
with formulating a proposal to merge the federal program for acquisition
of submarginal farmland with a program for wildlife restoration. Leopold
stood alone on the committee in advocating a stronger federal role, but
he subsequently declined appointment as chief of the U.S. Biological
Survey. At the time Leopold was more interested in building a research
program, efforts that led to creation of the Cooperative Wildlife Research
Unit Program in 1935 (Flader 1974, 27, 28).

Three other events in 1935 changed the course of Leopold's life. In
January he, Robert Marshall (chapter 8), and others formed The
Wilderness Society, a national organization that has since educated and
lobbied effectively for the appreciation and preservation of wilderness
areas. Leopold adopted and spread the philosophy espoused by the leaders
of this movement and reoriented his own approach toward wilderness
"from a historical and recreational to a predominantly ecological and eth-

ical justification." In April he purchased a worn-out, abandoned farm on the sandy floodplain of the Wisconsin River, a natural laboratory, vacation spot, and hideaway for future years. On this sand county farm, he practiced the techniques of "observation, activity, and reflection" exemplified in his later writings. And in the autumn of 1935, he spent three months in Germany studying the highly artificialized forestry and wildlife management practiced there, an experience that required him to rethink many of his ideas concerning environmental control of wildlife populations (Flader 1974, 29, 30).

Of all his accomplishments, the book *A Sand County Almanac*, published after his death, has received the greatest public acclaim. Part one of the book is a year's calendar of events on the sand county farm. The second part contains accounts of his experiences "here and there" through which he acquired his concept of conservation. The third conveys the Leopold land ethic for which he is most famous:

> [It] sets forth, in more logical terms, some of the ideas whereby we dissenters rationalize our dissent. Only the very sympathetic reader will wish to wrestle with the philosophical questions in Part III. I suppose it may be said that these essays tell the company how it may get back into step. (Leopold [1949] 1987, viii)

But the Leopold ethic is woven throughout the book in a manner that evangelizes, educates, and entertains, with a smooth, graphic, and flowing style that has disappeared from much of modern literature:

> There are two spiritual dangers in not owning a farm. One is the danger of supposing that breakfast comes from the grocery, and the other that heat comes from the furnace.
>
> To avoid the first danger, one should plant a garden, preferably where there is no grocer to confuse the issue.
>
> To avoid the second, he should lay a split of good oak on the andirons, preferably where there is no furnace, and let it warm his shins while a February blizzard tosses the trees outside. (Leopold [1949] 1987, 6)

> The show begins on the first warm evening in April at exactly 6:50 p.m. The curtain goes up one minute later each day until 1 June, when the time is 7:50. This sliding scale is dictated by vanity, the dancer demanding a romantic light intensity of exactly 0.05 foot-candles. Do not be late, and sit quietly, lest he fly away in a huff.
>
> The stage must be an open amphitheater in woods or brush, and in its center there must be a mossy spot, a streak of sterile sand, a bare outcrop

of rock, or a bare roadway. Why the male woodcock should be such a stickler for a bare dance floor puzzled me at first, but I now think it is a matter of legs. The woodcock's legs are short, and his struttings cannot be executed to advantage in dense grass or weeds, nor could his lady see him there. I have more woodcock than most farmers because I have more mossy sand, too poor to support grass....

He flies in low from some neighboring thicket, alights on the bare moss, and at once begins the overture: a series of queer throaty *peents* spaced about two seconds apart....

Suddenly the peenting ceases and the bird flutters skyward in a series of wide spirals, emitting a musical twitter. Up and up he goes, the spirals steeper and smaller, the twittering louder and louder, until the performer is only a speck in the sky. Then, without warning, he tumbles like a crippled plane, giving voice in a soft liquid warble that a March bluebird might envy....

What I do not yet know about the sky dance is: where is the lady, and just what part, if any, does she play? I often see two woodcocks on the peenting ground, and the two sometimes fly together, but they never peent together. Is the second bird a hen, or a rival male? (Leopold [1949] 1987, 30-33)

A land ethic, then, reflects the existence of an ecological conscience, and this in turn reflects a conviction of individual responsibility for the health of the land. Health is the capacity of the land for self-renewal.

Conservation is our effort to understand and preserve this capacity....
It is inconceivable to me that an ethical relation to land can exist without love, respect, and admiration for land, and a high regard for its value. By value, I of course mean something far broader than mere economic value: I mean value in the philosophical sense.

Perhaps the most serious obstacle impeding the evolution of a land ethic is the fact that our educational and economic system is headed away from, rather than toward, an intense consciousness of land....In short, land is something [we have] "outgrown." (Leopold [1949] 1987, 221, 223, 224)

Sometime in 1946 Leopold's health began to fail. He contracted tic douloureux, an inflammation of the facial area around the trigeminal nerve, for which he underwent surgery at the Mayo Clinic. He never fully recovered, however, and thereafter was subject to temporary loss of memory, paralysis of the left side of his face, and a general lack of vigor. During this time he frequently spent weekends at "the shack," a converted chicken coop on the Leopold farm (McCabe 1987, 94, 141, 142).

On the morning of April 21, 1948, Leopold spotted a grass fire on a neighbor's property and, with his wife and daughter Estella, promptly attacked the blaze. It was too much for them, however, and Aldo sent Estella to summon assistance from the local fire department or the Wisconsin Department of Conservation while he continued to fight the fire. Leopold did not survive.

> He was lying on his back with his hands folded on his stomach and his head resting on a small hummock. I surmise that he was aware of the situation and lay down in the hope that the seizure would subside. It did not....Thus, in a matter of less than an hour, in a fire-fighting effort on a neighbor's farm on an April morning, a great man passed from us. A heart attack was the proximate cause of death, but tic douloureux was the ultimate factor that denied us that kind, wise and articulate gentleman and colleague. (McCabe 1987, 144)

To the natural science field Leopold left his research, his writings, his philosophy—-and his family. Of Leopold's five children, Starker is retired from a career as a wildlife and forestry professor at the University of California, Berkeley; Luna became a hydrologist at Berkeley; Estella became a palynologist and director of the Quarternary Research Center in Seattle; Carl became a plant physiologist at Cornell University; and Nina and her husband operated the Leopold Memorial Reserve, the family farm in Wisconsin (Gibbons 1981, 702).

Although Leopold was a prolific writer of a wide variety of material and was well known, at least by reputation, to everyone in the wildlife profession, little biographical information concerning the man emerged for almost forty years after his death (exceptions are Flader 1973, 1974). Then, around the centennial of his birth, at least four full-length books (McCabe 1987, 1988; Tanner 1987; Meine 1988) appeared, *A Sand County Almanac* was republished (Leopold [1949] 1987) and a companion volume issued (Callicott 1987), and numerous magazine and journal articles appeared (e.g., Allen 1987, Earley 1987, Meine and Watkins 1987, Taylor 1987). Today, at long last, the story of his life and works is readily available.

WILDLIFE ON FEDERAL LAND

During the late 1800s and early 1900s, wildlife in the United States generally was considered to be a common property resource, held in trust by state government and protected through a combination of property rights

and police powers (Tober 1981, 148). Absent treaty provisions or interstate commerce, the federal government had no authority to manage
wildlife, even on federal land. Since 1900, however, additional legislation
and evolving case law have injected the federal government into almost
every facet of wildlife management.

Despite the early premise that resident wildlife was exclusively a state
concern, federal efforts to manage (i.e., protect) wildlife in national parks
and national wildlife refuges went unchallenged for many years. But
when the secretary of agriculture directed the removal of excess deer from
Kaibab National Forest in 1924, state officials rebelled (Flader 1974,
84). Those carrying out the secretary's directive were arrested, and the
federal government brought suit to enjoin the state's action. The ensuing
Supreme Court decision declared "the power of the United States to thus
protect its lands and property does not admit of doubt...the game laws
or any other statute of the state...notwithstanding" (*Hunt v. United States,*
cited in Bean 1983, 22).

The *Hunt* precedent lasted for forty years: The federal government had
the right to control wildlife populations on federal land *in order to protect
that land.* Whether the federal property clause could be applied to the
wildlife itself was still in doubt. The next round began with a 1964
opinion of the Office of the Solicitor for the Department of the Interior
regarding hunting and fishing regulations on national wildlife refuges.
In the solicitor's opinion,

[u]nder the Constitution the United States may acquire land for many
purposes, including wildlife refuges; may make all needful rules and regulations respecting this land; and may delegate such powers to the Secretary
of the Interior. These rules and regulations are superior to those of the
State where there is a conflict....

The authority to regulate hunting and fishing on Federally owned land
within the national Wildlife Refuge System has been delegated to the
Secretary of the Interior by specific legislation....

When the Federal Government owns land which is under the administration of the Secretary of the Interior as part of the National Wildlife
Refuge System, the Secretary may make rules and regulations for the control and management of resident species of game on the land even though
these regulations may be more restrictive than the hunting and fishing
laws of the State within which the land is located. These rules and regulations take supremacy over State law where there is a conflict. (71 Interior
Dec. 469 (Dec. 1, 1964))

But a solicitor's opinion is just that: a statement of administration policy, a position to be taken should the opportunity arise—but not *law*. It riled the states, and final resolution rested with the Supreme Court. The case began with New Mexico authorities removing burros, protected by the newly passed Wild and Free-Roaming Horses and Burros Act of 1971, from lands under the jurisdiction of the Bureau of Land Management. Following demands that the burros be returned, New Mexico sued to have the act declared unconstitutional. While the lower court agreed with the state, the Supreme Court reversed the decision: "[The] furthest reaches of the power granted by the property clause have not yet been definitely resolved...[, but it] includes the power to regulate and protect the wildlife living there" (*Kleppe v. New Mexico*, cited in Bean 1983, 24). The issue is settled: The federal government has the legal right to manage all wildlife on its property, regardless of state and local laws. This is the law, but not the politics. In practice regulations governing the taking of fish and wildlife on most federal land, most of the time, are consistent with those of the state or states in which the land is located.

Constitutional authority notwithstanding federal agencies have always managed wildlife on their property. The act creating Yellowstone National Park directed the secretary of the interior to "provide against the wanton destruction of the fish and game found within said park, and against their capture or destruction for the purposes of merchandise or profit" (17 Stat. 23). In 1877 the secretary of the interior published rules prohibiting hunting, trapping, or fishing in the park, "except for recreation or to supply food for visitors or...residents" (Ise 1961, 19). Recreational hunting and fishing continued, however, and estimates of wildlife populations ranged from "hardly worth protecting" in 1877 to "vast herds" in 1878 and 1879. Kills totaled "some 2000 hides of elk, nearly as many each of bighorn sheep, deer, and antelope, and scores if not hundreds of moose and bison" in 1875, and catches were as high as "a man and wife catching more than five hundred fish in two days, as late as 1900" (Ise 1961, 23-25). Statutory assistance came in 1894 with passage of the Act to Protect the Birds and Animals in Yellowstone National Park, which prohibited all hunting (except to protect humans), restricted fishing, and prescribed severe penalties for violations (Ise 1961, 45, 46). The National Park Service carried out more active wildlife management in Yellowstone as well. In 1883 a hunter and pack of hounds were retained to hunt down mountain lions, and in 1896 a coyote eradication program was instituted. Wolves were eliminated from the park; mountain lions were almost exterminated; thousands of elk starved to death on the overstocked range during the winters of 1916-1917 and 1919-1920; and a 1923 act (42 Stat. 1214) authorized disposition of surplus elk, bison, bear, beaver, and predatory animals (Ise 1961, 205).

While wildlife management in Yellowstone was perhaps more dramatic than that in other units, similar activities were being conducted throughout the National Park System during the early 1900s. Not until 1939 did the Park Service adopt its present policy: "Every species shall be left to carry on its struggle for existence unaided, as being to its greatest ultimate good, unless there is real cause to believe that it will perish if unassisted" (Ise 1961, 586). Exotics are the exception: They "shall be either eliminated or held to a minimum provided complete eradication is not feasible" (Ise 1961, 601). This policy has been a source of some frustration to Park Service personnel, for the exotics often refuse to cooperate. Despite years of effort toward eradication, the feral hog population in Great Smoky Mountains National Park is increasing and expanding its range.

Fish are treated somewhat differently from birds and mammals. Most national parks permit fishing, and, at least until 1954, the Park Service stocked harvestable fish in park streams to supplement natural production (Ise 1961, 603).

Recognition of the importance of natural processes and a minimum of human interference was embodied in the report of the Leopold Committee, chaired by A. Starker Leopold. The report emphasizes that biotic communities are constantly changing in response to natural factors and that national park management must recognize the function of fire, predation, insect outbreaks, and other seemingly adverse environmental factors. If the National Park System is to perpetuate conditions characteristic of presettlement times, as Leopold advocates, it must permit these limiting factors to play out their respective roles (Runte 1987, 197-201).

The National Forest System plays a major role in managing the nation's wildlife populations. Theodore Roosevelt envisioned a system of "great forest preserves, which shall also be breeding grounds and nurseries for wild game" (Tober 1981, 129). The Multiple-Use Sustained Yield Act of 1960 directed that "the national forests are established and shall be administered for...wildlife and fish purposes," although it conditioned the directive by stating that "[n]othing herein shall be construed as affecting the jurisdiction or responsibilities of the several States with respect to wildlife and fish on the national forests" (16 U.S.C. 475). Today the National Forest System accounts for about 30 percent of the nation's big game harvest—more than 80 percent of the elk, bighorn sheep, and mountain goat; nearly 60 percent of the mule deer; and 35 percent of the bear and black-tailed deer. It contains 128,000 miles of fishing streams; more than 2.2 million acres of lakes; habitat for a number of endangered species; and millions of small game animals, upland game birds, and waterfowl (Frome 1984, 156, 157).

Forest Service fish and wildlife policy, enunciated on July 8, 1980, states:

> "Specific requirements of all management practices for National Forest System lands, to be met in accomplishing goals and objectives, will protect streams, streambanks, shorelines, lakes, wetland areas, and other bodies of water. Management practices also will provide for and maintain diversity of plant and animal communities to meet overall multiple-use objectives. Practices will be monitored and evaluated to assure that they protect fish, wildlife, watersheds, soils, recreation, aesthetic values, and vegetation productivity." (Cited in Frome 1984, 166)

In many cases, however, Forest Service practices have not supported the fish and wildlife policy. Short timber rotations on national forest lands, desirable from a production quantity standpoint, reduce mast production and may destroy squirrel, turkey, and deer habitat (Frome 1984, 162, 163). The service proposed roading and logging on an important bear reproduction area in Pisgah National Forest, North Carolina, over the objections of biologists from the North Carolina Wildlife Resources Commission (Frome 1984, 167). And above all is the continuing controversy over clear-cutting—necessary to regenerate early-succession plant and animal species but detrimental to old-growth species; increasing between-stand diversity but decreasing within-stand diversity.

Public controversy over wildlife management on Forest Service lands will never end. The service is second only to the Bureau of Land Management (BLM) in the size of its holdings and controls more land than the U.S. Fish and Wildlife Service and the National Park Service combined (table 3.5). Its lands are open to hunting and fishing, and it *manages* its lands. Management inevitably requires helping some interests while hurting others, and a heterogeneous public cannot, and will not, agree on what should be helped and what should be hurt.

While legislation governing lands managed by the BLM generally parallels that of the Forest Service, the BLM's effect on wildlife generally has not attracted as much public attention (Bean 1983, 150, 151). The Taylor Grazing Act of 1934, which provided the first legislative structure for the public domain, directed the secretary of the interior "pending its final disposal" to "provide for the orderly use, improvement, and development of the range" (48 Stat. 1269, 1270) and to cooperate with "official State agencies engaged in conservation or propagation of wild life interested in the use of the grazing districts" (48 Stat. 1273). More recently the Federal Land Policy and Management Act of 1976 (FLPMA), the BLM's organic act, declares that "the public lands [shall] be retained in Federal ownership, unless as a result of the land use planning procedure provided for in this Act, it is determined that disposal of a particular parcel will serve the national interest" (90 Stat. 2744). FLPMA directs the secretary of the interior to prepare land use plans for the public lands and to "protect and prevent irreparable damage to...fish and wildlife resources or other natural systems or processes" (90 Stat. 2744).

Agencies administering the largest federal landholdings inevitably have the greatest impact upon wildlife populations, but all federal agencies affect wildlife through their land management and other activities. Even military reservations have an important role. The Sikes Act "authorizes" the secretary of defense to develop and implement wildlife management programs on military reservations in cooperation with the secretary of the interior and appropriate state agencies and authorizes funding for such programs. Commanding officers of military establishments may issue special hunting and fishing permits, collect appropriate fees from hunters and fishermen, and use the receipts to further their management programs.

In sum, federal lands managed by agencies other than the U.S. Fish and Wildlife Service total some 650 million acres, almost all of which support some forms of wildlife and all of which are subsumed within the federal property clause of the Constitution—however broadly it may be interpreted.

ENFORCING FEDERAL LAW

Following the Norman Conquest, the Crown was viewed as the strict owner of the lands and the game thereon, bequesting both to subjects who enjoyed the king's favor (Tober 1981, 146). Taking of wildlife, then, was not a free right enjoyed by everyone but a social and political tool wielded by those in power. In England only those who were "qualified" (i.e., who had the requisite wealth and were loyal to the king) could partake (Bean 1983, 11, 12). Americans were quick to reject this premise, opting instead for "common rights to wildlife...manifested in doctrines that rejected landowner claims of special privilege and allowed free taking even on private lands" (Lund 1980, 24).

State intervention into wildlife management by regulation was based on a combination of police powers and public trust and was confirmed in state cases during the late nineteenth century. In an 1875 case, the New York Court of Appeals sustained the conviction of a game dealer, concluding:

"The legislature may pass laws the effect of which may be to impair or even destroy the right of property....The protection and preservation of game...may be justified on many grounds, one of which is for the purpose of food." (*Phelps v. Racey*, cited in Tober 1981, 148)

In 1894 the Minnesota Supreme Court proponed the common property/public trust doctrine. It questioned the right of the legislature "to declare all wild game the property of the state, in a proprietary sense," but found it

"to be correct doctrine in this country that the ownership of wild animals, so far as they are capable of ownership, is in the state, not as proprietor, but in its sovereign capacity, as the representative, and for the benefit, of all its people in common." (*State v. Rodman*, cited in Tober 1981, 148)

The first indication that state control over wildlife might not be exclusive came in the 1896 Supreme Court decision in *Geer v. Connecticut*. Geer had been convicted of legally taking game birds in Connecticut with the intention of shipping them out of state in violation of Connecticut law. The issues before the Court involved the relationship between state "ownership" of game and the constitutional power of Congress to regulate interstate commerce. After tracing the evolution of wildlife law since Greek and Roman times, the court concluded that states could "'control and regulate the common property in game...as a trust for the benefit of the people'" and brushed off the interstate commerce issue by asserting that states had the authority to utilize their police powers "'to preserve...a valuable food supply'" provided that interstate commerce was only "'remotely and indirectly affected'" (Bean 1983, 16, 17).

The Commerce Clase

In the *Geer* case, the Court raised the possibility (almost the certainty) that its decision would have gone against Connecticut had a more profound effect upon interstate commerce been demonstrated. At the time state efforts to control the harvest by proscribing sale of game were being thwarted by market hunters who shipped their quarry to states in which sale was permitted. The solution was to involve the federal government under the commerce clause (Lund 1980, 87). The instrument was the Lacey Act of 1900, enacted after "a drawn-out, four-year process, replete with the usual political machinations" and introduction of some highly questionable data concerning declining wildlife abundance (Tober 1981, 227, 247).

The act prohibits the interstate shipment of "any wild animals or birds" killed in violation of state law and the export or import of such animals in violation of the laws of either state. Its constitutionality has never been seriously questioned—no case has reached the Supreme Court, and the few lower court decisions have uniformly upheld it (Bean 1983, 106).

"Wildlife" in the context of the Lacey Act was limited to warm-blooded animals. Twenty-six years later, Congress extended the same provisions to fish through the Black Bass Act of 1926, and it later combined the features of both laws in the Lacey Act Amendments of 1981. Currently, then, it is generally a federal offense to cross state boundaries in the commission of any act involving any animal or plant when that act would be unlawful in either state.

The first federal incursion into wildlife law was a clear exercise of the commerce powers, but it affected only interstate movement of animals already "taken." The second effort addressed the taking issue and was less certain.

Treaty Powers

The last three decades of the nineteenth century saw game agencies established in most states (Trefethen 1975, 112) and seasonal protection afforded to many game species. But programs were not consistent across state lines (nor, in many cases, across county lines), and this lack of continuity was most troublesome in relation to migratory birds (Tober 1981, 151).

Around the turn of the century, market hunting of waterfowl was practiced wherever a sufficient number of birds was present (figure 7.1), and "sport" hunting over bait and live decoys killed a tremendous number of birds. An "opening day" report from the mouth of the Susquehanna River, at the head of Chesapeake Bay, gives some indication of the magnitude of the slaughter:

FIGURE 7.1. Shooting from a Sinkbox. (Photo from the Henry Walsh collection, courtesy Chesapeake Bay Maritime Museum)

"Havre de Grace, Md. Nov. 1.—Wild-duck shooting began on the Susquehanna Flats today and a rough estimate places the number of birds killed at 5,000. The number would have exceeded that figure by many thousands but for the calm weather, which stopped the flying. The largest number killed by any sinkbox was 235, and Jesse Poplar, of Havre de Grace, killed them all. The ducks were redheads, blackheads and baldpates. The greatest number of redheads killed was by Mr. William Linthicum's party from Baltimore. Of the 121 ducks killed by this party, 80 were redheads. The dealers paid $1.50 a pair for redheads, 50 cents for blackheads and 35 cents for coots....The average number of ducks killed from sinkboxes was about 90; from sneakboats about twenty-four." (Special Dispatch to the *Baltimore Sun*, 1893, cited in Walsh 1971, 131)

On December 5, 1904, Congressman George Shiras III of Pennsylvania introduced "A Bill to Protect Migratory Birds of the United States." No constitutional grounds were stated; no hearings were held; Shiras did not press for enactment; and the bill died. But Shiras's bill was widely circulated to sportsmen's clubs, naturalists, and state agencies and served as a basis for discussion, debate, and further action.

Even Congressman Lacey had misgivings regarding the constitutionality of federal intervention, though he offered the general welfare clause as a possible basis (Trefethen 1975, 148-150).

In 1908 Congressman John W. Weeks of Massachusetts reintroduced Shiras's bill (with minor amendments), but the first Weeks bill also failed. Early in 1912 Weeks and Senator George P. McLean of Connecticut tried again with identical bills, as did Congressman Daniel R. Anthony of Kansas with a similar bill. Then, in late 1912 and early 1913, the right combination emerged. First, an alliance in support of the measure was formed of arms and ammunition manufacturers, sportsmen, naturalists, and scientists, assisted by a full-time lobbyist employed by Henry Ford. Second, provisions of the Weeks-McLean bill were expanded to include "all species of insectivorous and songbirds that crossed national and state borders in migration," allying the agricultural interests with the cause. Third, the bill was hidden as a rider to the Agricultural Appropriations Bill, where it was overlooked by President William Taft in the waning days of his administration. So Taft, who had "regarded the entire proposal as fundamentally unconstitutional and had specifically warned Congress that he would veto any bill carrying a rider dealing with basic legislation," signed into law the Weeks-McLean Act (better known as the Migratory Bird Act of 1913) *without realizing what he was signing* (Trefethen 1975, 150-153).

Jubilance was short-lived, however. In *United States v. Shauver* and *United States v. McCullagh*, lower courts found the act of 1913 unsupportable on the basis of either the commerce clause or federal property powers. *McCullagh* was not appealed, and before *Shauver* could be decided in the Supreme Court, it was overtaken by events. On August 16, 1916, the United States signed the Convention for the Protection of Migratory Birds (also known as the Migratory Bird Treaty [Trefethen 1975, 154] and the Canadian Convention [Bean 1983, 68]), establishing a "treaty powers" basis for federal protection of migratory birds. (Note: The United States later signed conventions with Mexico [1936], Japan [1972], and the Soviet Union [1976]. While these treaties are similar to the 1916 convention in their general provisions, they differ in important details.)

The treaty with Great Britain affected three groups of birds: migratory game birds, migratory insectivorous birds, and other migratory nongame birds (art. I). It declared a "close season on all migratory game birds...between March 10 and September 1" and a "continuous close season" on most other species covered by the treaty but permitted Eskimos and Indians to take "auks, auklets, guillemots, murres, and puffins and their eggs" for food and clothing and allowed Indians to take scoters for food but not for sale (art. II). It also declared a "continuous close season" for ten years on most species of shorebirds, swans, and cranes (art. III) and prohibited the taking of nests and eggs of migratory birds except for scientific and propagation purposes, under permit (art. V). Destruction of migratory birds that had become "seriously injurious to agricultural or other interests" was authorized under permit (art. VII).

Two further actions were necessary before the Migratory Bird Treaty could be implemented in the United States. First, it must be ratified by a two-thirds vote of the Senate; and second, domestic legislation must be enacted to translate the obligations between nations into obligations between the central government and its subjects. The former was accomplished on August 29, 1916; the latter was effected two years later, through the Migratory Bird Treaty Act of 1918.

As frequently happens, the implementing statute

> amplified in a number of respects the narrow terms of the 1916 Convention. Thus, whereas the Convention prohibited the "hunting" of migratory birds during their close seasons, the Act made it unlawful, inter alia, "to hunt, take, capture, kill,...[or] possess" any bird protected by the Convention." (Bean 1983, 75)

The regulations that followed went even further, specifying permissible hunting methods, shooting hours, daily limits, tagging and identification requirements, hunting seasons, bag limits, and so on (50 C.F.R. 20). How far this process may extend the provisions of the underlying treaty becomes a matter for the courts to decide.

United States v. Shauver was lying unresolved in the Supreme Court, and enemies of federal involvement were eager to test the new federal authority. Their opportunity came when George L. Samples and W. C. De Lapp were charged in separate indictments with violating the Migratory Bird Treaty Act. They demurred on the ground that the act was unconstitutional, and the attorney general of Missouri filed a separate bill in equity seeking to restrain Ray P. Holland (a federal game warden) from enforcing the law in Missouri. The cases were consolidated for trial at the district court level, and the demurrers were overruled and the bill dismissed. *Missouri v. Holland* was subsequently appealed to the Supreme Court.

Missouri's case was a classic and lengthy summary of the states' position, documented with hundreds of references:

Under the ancient law, feudal law, and the common law of England, the absolute control of wild game was an attribute of government and a necessary incident of sovereignty. When, therefore, the United Colonies became free and independent states,...the power to control the taking of wild game passed to the states.

This power of the state over wild game within its borders...is derived from the peculiar nature of such property and its common ownership by all citizens of the state in their collective capacity. The state, in its sovereign capacity, is the representative of the people in their common ownership of the wild game within the borders of the state, and holds the same in trust for the benefit of all its people. (64 L. Ed. 642)

The power of the state over wild game within its borders is not dependent solely upon the authority which the state derives from common ownership and the trust for the benefit of the people; the power of the state to control wild game is a necessary incident of the power of police. The power of police is an attribute of state sovereignty.

The fact that the present act of Congress purports to give effect to a treaty...cannot validate such act...when its effect is not only to accomplish that which, under the Constitution, Congress has no power to do, but...that which is forbidden." (64 L. Ed. 643)

The government's case took less than a page:

The protection of migratory game is a proper subject of negotiations and treaties between the governments of the countries interested in such game.

The treaty-making power of the United States embraces all such power as would have belonged to the several states if the Constitution had not been adopted; in the exercise of that power the Federal government is the accredited agent of both the people of the United States and the states themselves.

The power of the Federal government to make treaties is not a limitation on the reserved powers of the states, but is the exercise of a power not reserved to the states under the 10th Amendment [reserved powers], being both expressly granted to the United States and prohibited to the states.

The power of the Congress to legislate to make treaties effective is not limited to subjects with respect to which it is empowered to legislate in purely domestic affairs.

The Constitution expressly grants to Congress the power to enact such laws as may be necessary to give effect to treaties. (64 L. Ed. 646)

The Supreme Court's decision (April 19, 1920) was written by Associate Justice Oliver Wendell Holmes:

> To answer this question it is not enough to refer to the 10th Amendment...because by article 2, [section] 2, the power to make treaties is delegated expressly, and by article 6, treaties made under the authority of the United States, along with the Constitution and laws of the United States, made in pursuance thereof, are declared the supreme law of the land. If the treaty is valid, there can be no dispute about the validity of the statute.... (64 L. Ed. 647)

> No doubt it is true that, as between a state and its inhabitants, the state may regulate the killing and sale of such birds, but it does not follow that its authority is exclusive of paramount powers. To put the claim of the State upon title is to lean upon a slender reed. Wild birds are not in the possession of anyone, and possession is the beginning of ownership. (64 L. Ed. 648)

> We see nothing in the Constitution that compels the government to sit by while a food supply is cut off and the protectors of our forests and of our crops destroyed. It is not sufficient to rely upon the states. The reliance is vain, and were it otherwise, the question is whether the United States is forbidden to act. We are of opinion that the treaty and statute must be upheld. (64 L. Ed. 648, 649)

"The Court's decision...decisively ended all doubt concerning the constitutionality of the Migratory Bird Treaty Act" (Trefethen 1975, 155) and of the regulations (then) enacted under it. The act has been subjected to a number of attacks based on more narrow grounds, however, the most far-reaching of which has been the allegation that "by prohibiting private landowners from hunting on their own lands, it deprives them of a valuable property right without just compensation" (Bean 1983, 76). In the first such case, involving private lands adjacent to Back Bay National Wildlife Refuge in Virginia, the United States Court of Appeals for the Fourth Circuit stated:

> "If the Government wishes to do more in the way of protecting migratory birds than prohibiting their slaughter, e.g., erect improvements to lessen the dangers resulting from the drainage of marshy areas, it must acquire some proprietary interest in the areas....[I]t does not follow that compensation must be made for all land closed to hunting." (*Bailey v. Holland*, cited in Bean 1983, 77)

A more recent test of the Migratory Bird Treaty Act and its implementing regulations concerned subsistence taking of waterfowl by native
Alaskans. Unlike the subsequent treaties with Japan and the Soviet
Union, the 1916 treaty with Great Britain (Canada) did not provide for
this culturally, and frequently nutritionally, important activity. The
Canadian treaty bans the taking of almost all migratory birds "between
March 10 and September 1," but the act states that "it shall be unlawful...to take...any migratory bird...included in the terms of the convention...unless and except as permitted by regulations made as hereinafter
provided" (40 Stat. 755). Until recently the U.S. Fish and Wildlife
Service "exercised its discretion to not strictly enforce the closed season
[against subsistence hunters]...provided that any birds taken are taken in
a non-wasteful manner and are used for food" (53 Fed. Reg. 16,880 (May
12, 1988)).

In January 1986 a U.S. district court ruled that "until subsistence
hunting regulations were established, Alaska Natives could take migratory birds for food at any time" (*Outdoor News Bulletin* 42 [11]: 2 (June 3,
1988)). On May 19, 1986, the service announced proposed rule making
to "permit and regulate subsistence hunting for migratory birds in
Alaska" (51 Fed. Reg. 18,349), and on October 9, 1987, the U.S. Court
of Appeals for the Ninth Circuit halted the rule-making procedure by
overturning the lower court's opinion, finding instead that "any rules for
subsistence hunting...must be in accordance with the 1916 Convention"
(53 Fed. Reg. 16,877); that is, they cannot permit hunting during the
closed season prescribed by treaty. The service was in an awkward position: For years it had condoned subsistence hunting, which was prohibited by treaty; the hunting had, at the least, contributed to a sharp decline
in the populations of the cackling Canada goose, emperor goose, Pacific
white-fronted goose, and black brant (and perhaps other species) but was
a well-established and politically popular component of native Alaskan
culture; and a circuit court had ruled that subsistence hunting could not
be permitted by regulation.

The service's solution was to issue a "policy statement" rather than a
"rule," stating:

> Service enforcement efforts during the closed season will be concentrated
> on violations that have the most serious impact on the resource. Special
> attention will be given to the protection of [the four species cited
> above]....
>
> As a second level of priority, the Service also will give attention to pro-
> tecting other species of waterfowl from taking during the nesting, brood-

rearing, and flightless periods, including the taking of their eggs....

Regardless of the prohibitions outlined above, the taking of migratory birds in...limited numbers to provide emergency food in...unforeseen emergency situations where food is unavailable and no means of transportation or other opportunities exist to obtain food...will not be referred to the United States Attorney for prosecution. (53 Fed. Reg. 16,881)

How long this expedient will prevail remains to be seen.

ANIMAL CONTROL

In America, control of wildlife thought to be injurious to man's interests goes back to earliest colonial times, when bounties were placed on wolves. Later, state and local governments placed bounties on a wide variety of animals—seals, wolves, cougars, black bears, foxes, coyotes, bobcats, hawks, owls, robins, blackbirds, bobolinks, gray and red squirrels, chipmunks, English sparrows, kingfishers, and even bald eagles (Trefethen 1975, 163).

The federal role in the eternal struggle against animal competitors fell to the same agency charged with protecting and preserving the nation's wildlife—the U.S. Fish and Wildlife Service. As early as 1887, its predecessor several times removed, the Division of Economic Ornithology and Mammalogy in the Department of Agriculture, was testing poisons to control English sparrows. In 1915 Congress appropriated $125,000 to the successor Bureau of Biological Survey (Department of Agriculture) to initiate predator control activities (Reed and Drabelle 1984, 75).

The bureau began work with a vengeance, as indicated in a report presented by bureau chief Dr. E. W. Nelson at the August 28, 1917, meeting of the International Association of Game, Fish and Conservation Commissioners:

"The western States are divided into districts, including one or two States, with an inspector in charge of each, who has a corps of expert hunters and trappers continuously hunting and poisoning predatory animals. We have from 175 to 300 of these hunters, the number varying with the season. As a result,...our men [have] taken the skins of 980 gray wolves, over 34,000 coyotes, about 110 bob-cats besides several stock-killing silver-tipped grizzly bears....There is little question that in five years we can destroy most of the gray wolves and greatly reduce the numbers of other predatory animals. In New Mexico we have destroyed more than fifty per cent of the gray wolves and expect to get the other fifty per cent in the next two or three years." (Trefethen 1975, 165)

Clear statutory authority for the program was granted in the Animal Damage Control Act of 1931, which authorized and directed the secretary of agriculture

> to determine, demonstrate, and promulgate the best methods of eradication, suppression, or bringing under control on national forests and other areas of the public domain as well as on State, Territory, or privately owned lands of mountain lions, wolves, coyotes, bobcats, prairie dogs, gophers, ground squirrels, jack rabbits, and other animals injurious to agriculture, horticulture, forestry, animal husbandry, wild game animals, fur-bearing animals, and birds...; and to conduct campaigns for the destruction or control of such animals: Provided, That in carrying out the provisions of this Act the Secretary of Agriculture may cooperate with States, individuals and public and private agencies, organizations, and institutions. (46 Stat. 1468)

Two aspects of the authorizing statute are noteworthy: It specifically sanctioned cooperative relationships between the federal agency and non-federal entities in executing field operations, and it authorized control activities on nonfederal lands (Bean 1983, 235). Combined, these provisions built a close working relationship between the program and recipient stock owners and landowners that continues to this day.

Activities of the Bureau of Biological Survey were subsequently transferred to the Branch of Predator and Rodent Control (PARC) in the Department of the Interior and later to the Division of Wildlife Services in the Bureau of Sport Fisheries and Wildlife (Cain 1978, 380).

Animal control has always been an emotional and controversial issue—"students of natural history want no predator control at all, while many hunters and farmers want as much as they can get up to complete eradication" (Leopold [1933] 1948, 230). In the classic 1930 enunciation of "the American game policy," a committee chaired by Aldo Leopold (Leopold 1930, 301, 302) recognized that "[j]ustifiable differences of opinion arise over the questions of where, when, what species, and how much control" and listed seven standards that "would make for greater harmony among conservationists, and sounder practice by public agencies and private owners." Among the most significant recommendations were the following:

> 2. No public agency should practice control in any region without establishing adequate fact-finding service in that region.
>
> 3. No predatory species should be exterminated over large areas.

4. Each public agency engaged in predator-control work should seek periodic review of its policy and operations by some independent scientific body without administrative or financial interest in control work....

6. Use of poisons...or other methods unlikely to discriminate between species...should be resorted to only in emergency or under careful safeguards. (Leopold 1930, 301, 302)

The Leopold Committee's recommendations appeared to have little impact, however, and animal control activities proceeded with little public opposition until the early 1960s. Then, with the development of the environmental movement, protests began to arise. Secretary of the Interior Stewart Udall appointed a committee chaired by A. Starker Leopold (Aldo Leopold's son) to investigate the matter, and the committee's report was highly critical of existing control programs. It recommended that "'[c]ontrol should be limited strictly to the troublesome species, preferably to the troublesome individuals, and in any event to the localities where substantial damage or danger exists'" and made a number of more specific recommendations, including appointing a permanent advisory board, expanding research, and regulating "'the distribution and use of 1080 or any other poisons capable of having severe secondary effects on nontarget wildlife species'" (Bean 1983, 236, 237). Few of the Leopold Committee's recommendations were implemented immediately, but most were gradually worked into federal predator control policies.

In 1972 the Advisory Committee on Predator Control, chaired by former assistant secretary of the interior Stanley Cain, recommended (among other things) the removal of "all existing toxic chemicals from registration and use for operational predator control...[and recommended] that these restrictions extend to those toxicants used in field rodent control whose action is characterized by secondary poisoning of scavengers" (Cain 1972, 5). As a consequence President Nixon banned the use of toxicants on federal land (Exec. Order No. 11,643, Feb. 8, 1972), and the EPA canceled the registration on all predacides (chemicals that kill predators) soon thereafter—but it registered sodium cyanide for use in M-44 ejectors against coyotes in 1975 (Reed and Drabelle 1984, 77).

Supporting the work of the advisory committee, a committee of the Wildlife Society in 1973 issued a list of "management concepts and policies concerned with predators":

"Indiscriminate predator control, applying to species or entire populations, is unwarranted. Bounty payments are wasteful, and seldom, if ever, accomplish anything useful.

"Predators have a desirable selective influence in the annual turnover of prey populations.

"Predator problems usually are local and temporary. Other forms of wildlife need no general protection from their natural enemies.

"Where plentiful predators are hunted, they should have game status for licensing and regulation.

"Scarce or declining predators should have legal protection effectively enforced. In cases of property damage, an alternative to eradication should be sought." (Allen 1973, cited in Cain 1978, 380)

With curtailment of the use of poisons, trapping and shooting became the primary means of coyote control, and they proved less efficient. Sheep owners claimed that losses to predation increased dramatically, and they kept political pressure on Interior to relax predacide restrictions (Reed and Drabelle 1984, 78).

Other wildlife problems were also accelerating during the 1970s. Bird concentrations in the vicinity of some airports became a hazard to aircraft. Winter blackbird roosts, sometimes containing millions of birds, constituted local nuisances and possible health hazards. Blackbirds, cowbirds, grackles, and robins were damaging agricultural crops (Cain 1978, 384, 385). "Urbanized" flocks of Canada geese became troublesome on golf courses, school grounds, and airports (Reed and Drabelle 1984, 82).

Nat Reed, assistant secretary of the interior for fish and wildlife and parks during this period, summed up the service's dilemma:

Even in the context of history, there remains something unpalatable about the FWS's animal damage control activities—something akin to the unpleasantness we experience when we recall that national park rangers often carry guns and issue tickets. Yet until Stanley Cain's call for devising other means of assisting the sheep industry is heeded, it seems likely that FWS will remain in the business of killing predators and pests. Although the animal damage control programs are not calculated to win FWS many friends apart from the programs' direct beneficiaries,...it is in the public interest for these programs to be conducted by an agency that is highly sensitive to the value and needs of wild animals. (Reed and Drabelle 1984, 83)

Federal funding for taking of red wolves ended in 1964 and for timber wolves in 1971 (both are now listed as endangered in the contiguous states). Beginning about 1970 PARC predator control activities showed a marked decline (Council on Environmental Quality 1984, 670) (table 7.1), and the service was not even winning friends among the program's "direct beneficiaries." "At least once in every session of Congress" over the past twenty years, efforts have been made to move the animal damage control program to a more sympathetic environment in the Department of Agriculture (131 CONG. REG. S13,192 (Oct. 15, 1985)). Three separate attempts were made during the Ninety-ninth Congress—the 1985 Farm Bill, the Department of Agriculture appropriations bill, and the continuing resolution providing interim funding for Interior and Agriculture. The first attempt failed, but a combination of the last two succeeded (U.S. Department of the Interior, U.S. Fish and Wildlife Service 1986a, 3). In October 1985 an Agriculture appropriations bill (H.R. 3037) was amended in Senate committee to transfer the program to Agriculture and to provide $20 million for its operations there (S. Rept. 99-137, 38). Although the House initially rejected the Senate amendment, the conference committee acceded to the transfer (H. Rept. 99-439, 13). Funds were included in the resultant continuing resolution (99 Stat. 1185), and animal damage control is now part of the Animal and Plant Health Inspection Service (APHIS) of the Department of Agriculture.

TABLE 7.1
Federal Animal Damage Control Activities, 1937-1983

	Animals Removed or Killed					
Years	*Bear*	*Bobcat*	*Coyote*	*Red Wolf*	*Timber Wolf*	*Mountain Lion*
1937-1940	1,794	34,260	362,254	4,757	79	922
1941-1945	2,993	47,056	536,571	5,662	45	885
1946-1950	3,764	39,323	444,292	6,137	142	755
1951-1955	3,910	84,532	273,956	8,568	645	1,037
1956-1960	5,040	116,033	354,235	14,459	5,401	465
1961-1965	4,012	95,397	482,135	10,700	50	1,427
1966-1970	2,290	50,593	369,793	—	73	773
1971-1975	824	22,834	376,697	—	14	221
1976-1980	682	6,653	338,497	—	—	282
1981-1983	520	1,700	171,993	—	—	238
Total	25,829	498,381	3,710,423	50,283	1,588	8,005

Source: Council on Environmental Quality, *Environmental Quality—1984* (Washington, DC: Government Printing Office, 1984), pp. 669, 670.

RESEARCH AND MANAGEMENT

The U.S. Fish and Wildlife Service carries out a wide spectrum of research and management activities (other than those on federal land) through a combination of cooperative wildlife research units at land grant colleges, cooperative research and management programs with state game and fish agencies, and its own laboratories. One year after taking office, President Franklin Roosevelt appointed J. N. ("Ding") Darling—a vigorous and enthusiastic phi beta kappa biology major, Pulitzer Prize-winning *Republican* political cartoonist, designer of the first "duck stamp," critic of New Deal wildlife programs, and inexperienced administrator—to head the Bureau of Biological Survey (Trefethen 1975, 219, 220). Darling had had some experience with wildlife policy, however. He was instrumental in removing political influence from the Iowa conservation department, was a member of the Iowa Game and Fish Commission, and had succeeded in implementing Aldo Leopold's recommendation "that a training school in fish and wildlife management be established in Iowa State College at Ames." When faced with a shortage of qualified personnel to staff the growing bureau, Darling turned to a national version of the Iowa approach, the Cooperative Wildlife Research Unit Program. U.S. Fish and Wildlife Service employees with faculty appointments staffed the units, and early graduates became faculty members for the wildlife management curricula being developed throughout the country and personnel for the federal aid programs of the following decades (Trefethen 1975, 219-226).

Apparently bureau contributions came from general administration funds, without specific statutory authorization until 1960. At that time Congress passed Public Law No. 86-686, authorizing the secretary of the interior to "continue to enter into cooperative agreements with colleges and universities, with game and fish departments..., and with non-profit organizations relating to cooperative research units."

The cooperative research program started with nine units, funded by the bureau, the host college or university, the American Wildlife Institute (now the Wildlife Management Institute), and the wildlife agency of the state in which the unit was located. In 1987 it contained thirty-six cooperative research units at universities throughout the country (Office of the Federal Register 1987, 345).

In 1937, four years after the cooperative wildlife research units were created, Senator Key Pittman of Nevada and Congressman A. Willis Robertson of Virginia introduced legislation that began "the most aggressive and constructive wildlife restoration program ever known" (Trefethen 1975, 228, 229). The Pittman-Robertson Act (officially the Federal Aid in Wildlife Restoration Act) provides a continuing source of federal cost sharing for state wildlife research and management programs. It created "The Federal aid to wildlife restoration fund," composed of revenues accruing from a 10 percent (later 11 percent) federal excise tax on "firearms, shells, and cartridges" (50 Stat. 917). Up to 8 percent of the annual revenue to the fund may be deducted to administer the act and the Migratory Bird Conservation Act, and the remainder is to be apportioned to the states based equally on each state's relative land area and its relative number of paid-hunting-license holders (50 Stat. 918). Almost any type of wildlife restoration project may be eligible for funding— research, land acquisition, construction, restoration and rehabilitation, maintenance, administration—but law enforcement and public relations activities are not eligible. Any state could participate, provided (1) it passed laws that "include a prohibition against the diversion of license fees paid by hunters for any purpose other than the administration of said State fish and game department" (50 Stat. 917) and (2) it provided at least 25 percent of the costs (50 Stat. 919). Puerto Rico, Guam, and the Virgin Islands became eligible under the amendments of 1970 but on slightly different terms (84 Stat. 110).

The Pittman-Robertson (P-R) program was immensely popular from the start. It provided a strong political-financial incentive to state game agencies wishing to gain control of their license receipts and a large, dependable source of funding. In return it required few concessions on the part of the states (though the secretary of the interior approved each state project funded [50 Stat. 918] and thereby could exercise considerable influence over the direction of state programs). Within its first year, forty-three of the (then) forty-eight states passed enabling acts, and the remainder did so soon thereafter; total federal excise tax receipts were almost $3 million that first year (Trefethen 1975, 228, 229). By 1983 annual P-R payments to the states and territories had grown to $107 million (Reed and Drabelle 1984, 127).

Two significant amendments were enacted in 1970. One directed that one-half of the federal excise tax paid on pistols and revolvers be apportioned among the states for hunting safety programs; the other permitted states to submit a "comprehensive fish and wildlife resource management plan" instead of individual project proposals.

In 1950 the Federal Aid in Fish Restoration Act (Dingell-Johnson Act) provided similar support for sportfishing programs, with the federal excise tax on "fishing rods, creels, reels, and artificial lures, baits, and flies" (64 Stat. 431) being apportioned to the states, based 40 percent on their area (including coastal and Great Lakes waters) and 60 percent on the relative "number of persons holding paid licenses to fish for sport or recreation" (64 Stat. 432). Although the act applies to "marine and/or fresh waters," it is designed specifically to apply to "species of fish which have material value in connection with sport or recreation" (64 Stat. 431). Thus the Dingell-Johnson (D-J) program is essentially a *freshwater sportfishing* program. Federal assistance for estuarine and marine fisheries came fourteen years later, with passage of the Commercial Fisheries Research and Development Act of 1964 (chapter 13).

The Fish and Wildlife Conservation Act of 1980 provided a further, but unsuccessful, expansion of the federal aid program. P-R and D-J programs were targeted on game and sport species; funds came from hunters and fishermen and were spent to benefit hunters and fishermen. No funds were available to provide the estimated $40 million per year needed to support a nongame species program, and environmentalists and supporters of nonconsumptive use of wildlife resources protested. The resulting "Non-game Act" (officially the Fish and Wildlife Conservation Act of 1980) was designed to fill that need but actually promoted comprehensive planning to benefit both game and nongame species (Bean 1983, 227). The act provided up to 90 percent federal reimbursement of the costs of developing a conservation plan through fiscal year 1984, 75 percent through fiscal year 1991, and none thereafter (94 Stat. 1326, 1327). Federal funds became available for up to 75 percent of the cost of implementing approved plans (94 Stat. 1327). Early versions of the nongame legislation provided that funds were to come from a special federal excise tax, but the act as passed required congressional appropriations from the general fund—a weakness that became apparent when Congress failed to appropriate the necessary funds (Bean 1983, 229).

Considerable overlap exists among the three programs (Bean 1983, 228), and the same project frequently could be financed through any of them. The confusion is probably more apparent than real, however; experienced bureaucrats are adept at operating under such situations. In sum the P-R, D-J, and nongame federal aid programs provide the foundation of state wildlife and freshwater fish research and management activities.

RARE, THREATENED, AND ENDANGERED SPECIES

Whether one argues species preservation from the utilitarian standpoint (we may need those commodities or genes someday), the ecological standpoint (what happens to the unfilled niche? the broken food chain? diversity?), or the moral-ethical viewpoint (a lost species is a broken trust), rare, threatened, and endangered species elicit strong and emotional reactions from almost everyone interested in natural resources (Reed and Drabelle 1984, 85, 86). Extinction itself is a natural phenomenon, but recent acceleration in the rate of extinction ensures that the subject will continue to attract attention. In the 200 years between 1600 and 1800, twenty-five bird species were lost; between 1800 and 1950, an additional seventy-eight disappeared, and mammals, reptiles, amphibians, and fish have also shown rising extinction rates (Nilsson 1983, 3).

Habitat alteration probably ranks first as the cause of extinction; trade is a close second (King 1978, 253). Efforts to preserve species and populations have addressed both factors. Concern over the bison led in part to reservation of Yellowstone National Park; destruction of pelicans led to creation of Pelican Island National Wildlife Refuge. The Lacey Act of 1900 was a tool to prevent interstate commerce in wildlife and could be employed to enforce state prohibitions. But it was not until 1966 that attempts were begun to integrate federal activities into an endangered species program.

Early Efforts

The first formal attempt to establish an endangered species program is contained in the Endangered Species Preservation Act of 1966. Prior to 1966 the Department of the Interior probably had the ability to conduct such a program under existing law, but Congress refused to appropriate funds for that purpose without clear statutory authorization. The 1966 act served that purpose; it authorized the secretary to use existing authorities, including the Land and Water Conservation Fund, "to carry out a program in the United States of conserving, protecting, restoring and propagating selected species of native fish and wildlife found to be threatened with extinction." It also directed the secretary to "publish in the Federal Register the names of the species of native fish and wildlife found to be threatened with extinction" (80 Stat. 926). But it failed to restrict the taking of or interstate commerce in endangered species; it had little real impact on habitat preservation efforts; and it provided protection only for native species (Bean 1983, 319-321). It was a beginning.

Progress toward correcting this last deficiency was afforded by the Endangered Species Conservation Act of 1969, which (1) directed the secretary to promulgate a list of fish and wildlife species or subspecies "threatened with worldwide extinction," (2) made it a crime to import any member of a listed species or subspecies (83 Stat. 275), and (3) directed the secretaries of state and the interior to "encourage bilateral and multilateral agreements...for the protection, conservation, and propagation of fish and wildlife" and toward that end to "seek the convening of an international ministerial meeting...[within which] shall be the signing of a binding international convention on the conservation of endangered species" (83 Stat. 278). The treaty emanating from this meeting, the Convention on International Trade in Endangered Species of Wild Fauna and Flora (CITES), provided the international forum and "treaty powers" justification for the United States's endangered species program.

CITES first defines "species" to include a "species, subspecies, or geographically separate population" (art. I), provides for a listing of affected species (art. II), and prescribes a system for control over trade in such species (art. III-V). The treaty recognizes three classes of species requiring protection: those "threatened with extinction which are or may be affected by trade" (app. I), those that are "not necessarily now threatened with extinction [but] may become so unless trade...is subject to strict regulation" (app. II), and those "which any party [has] identified as being subject to regulation within its jurisdiction" (app. III). Appendix I species "must be subject to particularly strict regulation...[and trade] must only be authorized under exceptional circumstances." Trade in listed species is authorized only under permit from the importing nation (Appendix I only) and the exporting nation, if the specimen has been lawfully taken, and (except for Appendix III species) upon a finding that "such export will not be detrimental to the survival of that species." CITES came into force in late 1975 (upon ratification by ten countries); by late 1976 it had thirty members (King 1978, 267), and by June 1982 seventy-seven had joined (Nilsson 1983, 209).

Prior to the implementation of CITES, two other domestic laws were enacted that (with CITES) complete the legal package upon which this country's endangered species program is based. The Marine Mammal Protection Act of 1972 contains several provisions relevant to the program. It was enacted through the combined efforts of a diverse group of supporters—commercial interests that anticipated a continuing utilizable resource under proper management, scientists concerned with the ecological role of marine mammals, and interested citizens who simply believed that the animals should be protected—all of whom were dissatisfied with the existing legal structure (Bean 1983, 281, 282). Among its provisions the act divides responsibilities between the secretary of commerce (National Marine Fisheries Service), with jurisdiction over cetaceans (whales and porpoises) and pinnipeds (seals) other than walruses, and the secretary of the interior (U.S. Fish and Wildlife Service), in respect to all other marine mammals covered by the act. It declared a moratorium on all takings and imports of marine mammals (with some exceptions) and extended protection beyond taxonomic species and subspecies to a "population stock," defined as "a group of marine mammals of the same species or smaller taxa in a common spatial arrangement, that interbreed when mature" (86 Stat. 1029)—a concept compatible with the "geographically separate population" of CITES.

The Endangered Species Act of 1973 put it all together. It sought to preserve not only all members of the plant and animal kingdoms but also "the ecosystems upon which [they] depend"; it directed "all Federal...agencies...to conserve endangered species and threatened species and...[to] utilize their authorities in furtherance of the purposes of this Act"; and it is "self-destructing," for it seeks "to bring any endangered species or threatened species to the point at which the measures provided pursuant to this Act are no longer necessary" (87 Stat. 885). The act provided for listing under a dual classification, "endangered" and "threatened" (87 Stat. 887), extended protection to local populations (as do CITES and the Marine Mammal Protection Act), and introduced a new concept, "critical habitat" (87 Stat. 892). Provisions of the Endangered Species Act have been tested repeatedly in the courts, and the law has been modified as a result. One of the earliest major confrontations involved a small fish and the Tennessee Valley Authority.

The Snail Darter and the Dam

Ten years before passage of the Endangered Species Act of 1973, the board of the Tennessee Valley Authority (TVA) launched the Tellico Dam Project on the Little Tennessee River. Like most TVA projects, it was justified on the basis of benefits from hydroelectric power generation, navigation, and flood control; and like most public works projects, it had its detractors (Wheeler and McDonald 1986, 24). In addition to displaced landowners, the Eastern Band of Cherokees opposed the project because it would inundate a number of old village sites. Some sportsmen and conservationists, including representatives of the Tennessee Game and Fish Commission and a small group of scientists at the University of Tennessee, also objected to impounding the free-flowing stream, but initial opposition was not particularly well organized or effective (Wheeler and McDonald 1986, 69, 185, 186). Construction began in 1967, and by mid-1973 the project was half complete (*TVA v. Hill,* 437 U.S. 197).

The opponents had filed a number of lawsuits, however, alleging violations of NEPA and the National Historic Preservation Act, and were successful in halting work through a temporary injunction from the U.S. Court of Appeals for the Sixth Circuit. But the court subsequently dissolved the temporary order, and construction resumed on November 12, 1973 (Wheeler and McDonald 1986, 188).

The opposition's strongest case had yet to be filed. It was based on a small fish, the snail darter, discovered at Coytee Springs on the Little Tennessee on August 12, 1973, by University of Tennessee zoologist David Etnier (Wheeler and McDonald 1986, 188). Just four months after Etnier's discovery, Congress passed the Endangered Species Act of 1973, and that act empowered citizens to file civil suits "to enjoin any person, including the United States and any other instrumentality or agency...who is alleged to be in violation of any provision of the Act or regulations issued under the authority thereof" (87 Stat. 900).

But before effective legal action could ensue, the snail darter had to be placed on the endangered species list, and the Tellico Project portion of the Little Tennessee River had to be declared critical habitat. Furthermore, section 7 of the act required "consultation" with the U.S. Fish and Wildlife Service in any situation in which a federal action could affect an endangered species or its critical habitat (87 Stat. 892). The first two details were effected on October 9, 1975, and May 3, 1976, respectively (40 Fed. Reg. 47,505, 41 Fed. Reg. 13,928). The last bogged down in interagency feuding and TVA's determination to complete the project as designed (Wheeler and McDonald 1986, 196).

The situation was again ripe for litigation and, following some initial setbacks at the district court level, opponents obtained a permanent injunction from the court of appeals on January 31, 1977. The appellate court held that the Endangered Species Act applied "regardless of when a project was started or how near completion it may be," found that TVA was in violation, and stated that the district court had "abused its discretion when it refused to enjoin a clear violation of law'" (U.S. Department of the Interior, U.S. Fish and Wildlife Service 1977, 1, 2). The injunction was to remain in effect "'until Congress, by appropriate legislation, exempts Tellico from compliance with the Act or the snail darter has been deleted from the list of endangered species or its critical habitat materially redefined'" (*TVA v. Hill,* 437 U.S. 154).

The arena now moved to the Congress, and a powerful additional player joined the opponent's team. The General Accounting Office (GAO) conducted a study of the Tellico Project and "took the agency to task for its parlous benefit-cost ratio, its double-counting, and its subsequent increasing of benefits with no apparent foundation." In the fall of 1977, the GAO recommended that Congress grant no further appropriations for the project until a more defensible cost analysis was produced (Wheeler and McDonald 1986, 200). So Congress now had to deal with money as well as endangered species and regional politics.

For well over a year, the Tellico Project languished. TVA had spent about $900,000 in public relations and lobbying, purchased 692 parcels of land and condemned 58 others, and expended over $116 million in total funds—yet construction was stopped until Congress acted (Wheeler and McDonald 1986, 202, 203). While Congress was embroiled in infighting and stratagems, the Supreme Court acted on TVA's appeal of the appelate court's decision. On June 15, 1978, by a six-to-three vote, the Court ruled as follows:

> Here we are urged to view the Endangered Species Act "reasonably," and hence shape a remedy "that accords some modicum of common sense and the public weal."...But is that our function? We have no expert knowledge on the subject of endangered species, much less do we have a mandate from the people to strike a balance of equities on the side of the Tellico Dam. Congress has spoken in the plainest of words, making it abundantly clear that the balance has been struck in favor of affording endangered species the highest of priorities....
>
> Our individual appraisal of the wisdom or unwisdom of a particular course consciously selected by the Congress is to be put aside in the process of interpreting a statute. Once the meaning of an enactment is discerned and its constitutionality determined, the judicial process comes to an end....
>
> We agree with the Court of Appeals that in our constitutional system the commitment to the separation of powers is too fundamental for us to pre-empt congressional action by judicially decreeing what accords with "common sense and the public weal". Our Constitution vests such responsibilities in the political branches. (*TVA v. Hill*, 437 U.S. 194, 195)

Shortly thereafter Congress acted, passing the 1978 amendments to the Endangered Species Act. Addressing the Tellico issue directly, the amendments established "the Endangered Species Committee...[which] shall review any application submitted to it...and determine...whether or not to grant an exception from the requirements" of the Endangered Species Act (92 Stat. 3753). The committee was to be composed of the secretaries of agriculture, army, and the interior; the chairman of the Council of Economic Advisors, the administrators of the Environmental Protection Agency (EPA) and the National Oceanic and Atmospheric Administration (NOAA), and one representative of each affected state (92 Stat. 3753). The amendments specifically directed the committee to review the Tellico Project within thirty days of passage and to grant exemption if

(1) there are no reasonable and prudent alternatives to the agency action; [and]

(2) the benefits of such action clearly outweigh the benefits of alternative courses of action consistent with conserving the species or its critical habitat, and such action is in the public interest. (sec. 7(h)(1)(A), 92 Stat. 3758)

On November 10 President Carter signed the Endangered Species Act Amendments of 1978, noting his misgivings over the exemption process and his desire that it be used judiciously:

> While I believe that this new exemption process is not necessary, I hope that as the Committee carries out its responsibilities, it will make the utmost efforts to protect the existence of the species inhabiting this planet. In the past, the act has worked well without this exemption process, because all agencies have made efforts to resolve conflicts and, where necessary, to pursue alternative courses of action....
>
> I am asking the Committee members to be exceedingly cautious in considering exemptions. (40 WEEKLY COMP. PRES. DOC. 2002 (Nov. 10, 1978))

On January 23, 1979, the Endangered Species Committee met to consider exemption of the Tellico Project. Led by comments from Charles Schultz of the Council of Economic Advisors, and after only a short discussion, the committee voted unanimously *not* to exempt (Wheeler and McDonald 1986, 211). The committee was to exempt Tellico (and the Grayrocks Dam and Reservoir Project sponsored by the Missouri Basin Electric Power Cooperative) only if it met the tests prescribed in the law. The Tellico case failed, but Grayrocks was exempted because it contained specific mitigation and enhancement measures that would maintain critical whooping crane habitat (U.S. Department of the Interior, U.S. Fish and Wildlife Service 1979a, 1, 2).

But the fight still was not over:

> Late in the afternoon of June 18, 1979, in a sleepy and near-empty House
> of Representatives, with a clerk laboring through the complete text of the
> 1980 public works appropriations bill, Congressman John Duncan
> [Tennessee] rose to offer an amendment. The clerk received the amend-
> ment and began droning his way through it, when Duncan moved that the
> reading be waived. Tom Bevill of Alabama rose to say that he had seen it
> and would approve it without its being read, and John Meyers echoed
> Bevill's sentiments. A voice vote was taken, and in forty-two seconds a
> drowsy fragment of the House membership had exempted Tellico from the
> Endangered Species Act. (Wheeler and McDonald 1986, 212)

The bill still had to pass the Senate. Senator Howard H. Baker, Jr., of
Tennessee had long been a staunch supporter of the project and was particularly riled by the committee's decision not to exempt. As one of the
most powerful senators, Baker was successful on his second try—but by
only four votes (Wheeler and McDonald 1986, 212). The final action was
in the White House:

> I accept, with regret, this action as expressing the will of the Congress in
> the Tellico matter. I am also convinced that even if I vetoed this bill,
> Tellico exemptions would be proposed repeatedly in the future.
>   Nevertheless, I believe firmly in the principles of the Endangered
> Species Act and will enforce it vigorously. I do not consider that the action
> by Congress on the Tellico matter implies congressional intent to overturn
> the general decision process for resolving conflicts under the act. I am con-
> vinced that this resolution of the Tellico matter will help assure the pas-
> sage of the Endangered Species Act reauthorization without weakening
> amendments or further exemptions. (15 WEEKLY COMP. PRES. DOC. 1760
> (Sept. 25, 1979))

One day later, on September 26, 1979, construction of Tellico Dam
resumed (U.S. Department of the Interior, Fish and Wildlife Service
1979b, 1). At last the battle was over. The dam was finished and the
reservoir filled. The snail darter still exists; some were successfully transplanted into the nearby Holston River, and others are held in a Tennessee
state fish hatchery and a TVA laboratory (U.S. Department of the
Interior, U.S. Fish and Wildlife Service 1979b, 11). The Indian villages
are forever inundated and the rural families displaced, but in time these
effects will fade from memory. Was the controversy justified? Was it
moral and ethical? Was it a proper use of private and public personal and

financial resources? Should endangered species be used as weapons in larger social, economic, and political controversies? There are no easy answers to these questions, but as long as threatened and endangered species receive special statutory protection, they will be centers of controversy employed by various interest groups with various motives. To date Tellico Dam probably has been the most complex example, but controversies surrounding the red-cockaded woodpecker in the Southeast and the northern spotted owl in the Pacific Northwest are close seconds.

The Program

The Endangered Species Program is an amalgam of the provisions of CITES, the Endangered Species Act and its amendments, and the Marine Mammal Protection Act. Its major components are (1) recognition of taxa that are threatened or endangered, (2) restraint on taking and trade of such species, and (3) programs to restore threatened and endangered populations. Except for species over which the National Oceanic and Atmospheric Administration (NMFS) was given authority by Reorganization Plan No. 4 of 1970, the secretary of the interior (FWS) has exclusive authority to list species as endangered or threatened and to change or eliminate such listings (16 U.S.C. 1533(a)(1) (1988)), and the FWS is "the keeper of the list" (16 U.S.C. 1533(c) (1988)). If the NMFS recommends listing or upgrading of a species over which it has jurisdiction, FWS must effectuate the change; but if FWS recommends downgrading or delisting, such change is not effective unless the NMFS concurs (16 U.S.C. 1533(a)(2)(C) (1988)). Proposals to list are accompanied by publication in the *Federal Register* and local newspapers, notice to scientific organizations and state and local governments, public hearings, receipt and consideration of comments, and other "due process" requirements (16 U.S.C. 1533(b)(5) (1988)). A decision to list is made "solely on the basis of the best scientific and commercial data available" (16 U.S.C. 1533(b)(1)(A) (1988)), regardless of economic implications.

An "endangered species" is one

> which is in danger of extinction throughout all or a significant portion of its range other than a species of the Class Insecta determined by the Secretary to constitute a pest whose protection...would present an overwhelming and overriding risk to man. (16 U.S.C. 1532(6) (1988))

A "threatened species" is one

which is likely to become an endangered species within the foreseeable future throughout all or a significant portion of its range. (16 U.S.C. 1532(20) (1988))

And "species" includes

any subspecies of fish or wildlife or plants, and any distinct population segment of any species of any vertebrate fish or wildlife which interbreeds when mature. (16 U.S.C. 1532(16) (1988))

Once a species is listed as endangered or threatened, no person subject to the jurisdiction of the United States may "take" it anywhere in the United States or its territorial sea or on the high seas (16 U.S.C. 1538(a)(1) (1988), 50 C.F.R. 17.21 (Oct. 1, 1989)), and "taking" is defined more broadly than in any other program:

The term "take" means to harass, harm, pursue, hunt, shoot, wound, kill, trap, capture, or collect, or to attempt to engage in any such conduct. (16 U.S.C. 1532(19) (1988))

"Harm" in the definition of "take" in the Act means an act which actually kills or injures wildlife. Such act may include significant habitat modification or degradation where it actually kills or injures wildlife by significantly impairing essential behavioral patterns, including breeding, feeding or sheltering. (50 C.F.R. 17.3(c) (Oct. 1, 1989))

The act recognizes the importance of "critical habitat":

(i) the specific areas within the geographical area occupied by the species...on which are found those physical or biological features (I) essential to the conservation of the species and (II) which may require special management considerations for protection; and

(ii) specific areas outside the geographic area occupied by the species at the time it is listed...upon a determination by the Secretary that such areas are essential for the conservation of the species. (16 U.S.C. 1532(5)(A) (1988))

While destruction of critical habitat by actions other than those of federal agencies is not specifically prohibited by the act, such an action could fall within the general definition of taking in that it "kills or injures wildlife by significantly impairing essential behavioral patterns, including breeding, feeding or sheltering." When federal actions are involved, however, a threat to critical habitat invokes the "consultation provisions."

Section 7 of the Endangered Species Act places special responsibilities on "any action authorized, funded, or carried out" by a federal agency (16 U.S.C. 1536(a)(2) (1988)). If "an endangered species or a threatened species may be present in the area affected...and...implementation of such action will likely affect such species," the agency must confer with the FWS to determine whether the proposed action is "likely to jeopardize the continued existence of any endangered species or threatened species or result in the destruction or adverse modification of critical habitat" (16 U.S.C. 1536 (a)(3), (a)(4) (1988)). "If jeopardy or adverse modification is found, the Secretary shall suggest...reasonable and prudent alternatives" (16 U.S.C. 1536 (b)(3)(A) (1988)). To assist this process, agencies are required "to conduct a biological assessment for the purpose of identifying any endangered species or threatened species which is likely to be affected" if "any species which is listed or proposed to be listed may be present in the area" (16 U.S.C. 1536(c) (1988)).

It is also unlawful to "remove or reduce to possession" endangered plants growing on "areas under Federal jurisdiction" (16 U.S.C. 1538(a)(2)(B) (1988)), but neither destruction in place nor lethal alteration of endangered plant habitat is prohibited (Bean 1983, 345).

One of the most important provisions of the endangered species legislation deals with "recovery plans," detailed provisions that, if successful, should lead to the delisting of species. The secretary of the interior is directed to "develop and implement...[such plans] for the conservation and survival of endangered species and threatened species" (16 U.S.C. 1533(f) (1988)). The plans are prepared with the assistance of "public and private agencies and institutions, and other qualified persons" organized as "recovery teams."

Much of the work under the Endangered Species Program may be carried out by the individual states under cooperative agreements. If the secretary of the interior finds that a state has an acceptable program for the "conservation of endangered species and threatened species" of animals and/or plants, he or she may provide up to 75 percent of the cost of implementation in the case of individual states or up to 90 percent if two or more states "enter jointly into an agreement with the Secretary" (16 U.S.C. 1535(d)(2) (1988)).

Penalties for violations may be very stiff. Those who "knowingly violate" may be assessed a civil penalty of $25,000 or assessed a criminal penalty of $50,000 and imprisoned for up to a year for each violation (16 U.S.C. 1540(a)(1), (b)(1) (1988)). In addition they may be required to forfeit all specimens and all guns, equipment, vessels, aircraft, and other equipment used in the unlawful act (16 U.S.C. 1540(e)(4) (1988)).

Success of the program cannot be measured by legal provisions, however. The test is whether it has conserved ecosystems upon which endangered and threatened species are dependent, slowed the extinction rate, and increased populations of endangered and threatened species to the point that they may be delisted. The record is mixed.

Since 1768 North America has lost eight unique forms of mammals and six kinds of birds—irretrievable and perhaps preventable, to be sure, but a very small part of our vertebrate biota, considering the magnitude of environmental change over the past three centuries. In 1975 the endangered species list contained thirty-one fishes, four amphibians, two reptiles, fifty-six birds, and sixteen mammals native to the United States and its territories. Nearly half (thirty-four) of the birds and mammals were insular species, found only on Puerto Rico and the Hawaiian Islands, and particularly susceptible to extinction. Of the twenty-three endangered birds and fifteen endangered mammals native to the continental United States, only seven birds and four mammals were true species in the taxonomic sense (Trefethen 1975, 298). If invertebrate animals, plants, and subspecific taxa are included, the list becomes much longer; some have estimated that more than 500 taxa have become extinct in the United States since colonial days (U.S. Department of the Interior, U.S. Fish and Wildlife Service 1980, 6).

As a result of increased statutory scope and attention, the United States's endangered species list had grown to 427 species by 1990—169 plants, 59 invertebrates, 51 fishes, 6 amphibians, 16 reptiles, 75 birds, and 51 mammals. An additional 138 species were listed as threatened, 256 recovery plans covering 307 species had been approved, and cooperative agreements had been executed with fifty-one states for fish and wildlife programs and with thirty-six states for plant programs (U.S. Department of the Interior, U.S. Fish and Wildlife Service 1990a, 8). By comparison, the United States in 1981 was estimated to contain 2,927 species and subspecies of vertebrates (Council on Environmental Quality 1981, 149). (Note, however, that "species" under the Endangered Species Act includes "distinct population segment[s]" of vertebrates [16 U.S.C. 1532(16) (1982)] and thus potentially many more taxa than true species and subspecies.)

Ecosystem preservation is approached through (1) the National Wildlife Refuge System, assisted by the Land and Water Conservation Fund, and (2) preservation of "critical habitat" and prohibition of "significant habitat modification or degradation." As of March 1980, more than 70,000 acres had been acquired at a cost of almost $40 million as a result of the Endangered Species Program. These new lands and other lands of the National Wildlife Refuge System provide essential habitat for fifty-eight endangered and threatened species on 248 refuges (U.S. Department of the Interior, U.S. Fish and Wildlife Service 1980, 6). Preservation of critical habitat is more difficult to ascertain, though federal agencies appear well aware of, and quite sensitive to, the requirement.

The Endangered Species Program has had some notable successes. The American alligator was downgraded from endangered to threatened in 1980 (Council on Environmental Quality 1980, 70). In 1987 it was removed from the list entirely but placed in a special category, "T/SA," "threatened due to similarity of appearance." Under this classification states may permit commercial hunting of the species but require tagging to ensure that protected crocodilian species are not passed off as alligators (U.S. Department of the Interior, U.S. Fish and Wildlife Service 1987a). The American bald eagle population in the coterminous United States more than doubled between 1974 and 1984, and in 1990 it was considered for reclassification from endangered to threatened (U.S. Department of the Interior, U.S. Fish and Wildlife Service 1990c, 3). The whooping crane population increased from 21 birds in 1941 to 143 in 1983. In 1984 the brown pelican became the first species to be delisted (Council on Environmental Quality 1984, 306, 671).

Perhaps the most dramatic recovery efforts are those directed at birds of prey—principally golden and bald eagles and peregrine falcons. Eggs are obtained from captive and wild birds and incubated under carefully controlled conditions, and the young are raised in captivity until almost ready to fly. At that time they are placed in "hacking towers" at protected locations containing suitable habitat. There they are slowly "weaned," are introduced to the wild, and learn the skills of flight and the hunt. As alternatives fertile peregrine eggs may be placed under wild peregrines with a history of unsuccessful egg production or under wild prairie falcons, or young captive-raised peregrines may be placed in the nests of wild peregrine falcons, where they are cared for by the foster parents.

This program has successfully reestablished the peregrine falcon over much of its range in the United States. In 1984 at least 27 pairs were nesting in the eastern United States (*The Peregrine Fund Newsletter* 1984, 1-4), and two years later no releases were made along the mid-Atlantic coast because it was felt that all available nesting sites were being utilized (*The Peregrine Fund Newsletter* 1986, 3). By 1988 at least 104 pairs were nesting in Oregon, Washington, California, and Idaho, where fewer than 10 pairs had nested in 1980 (U.S. Department of the Interior, U.S. Fish and Wildlife Service 1988b, 2).

Among other species the story is less heartening. As many as 2,500 plant species may be in jeopardy in the United States and have yet to be listed, and recovery plans are lagging far behind the listing process (Council on Environmental Quality 1980, 71). An intensive effort is under way to save the California condor. As a result of an egg-removal-and-incubation program, six young condors were produced in captivity in 1984, and another was hatched in the wild and subsequently taken into captivity. At that time the captive population contained ten females and six males. Unfortunately, several birds were lost from the wild population in 1985 (Council on Environmental Quality 1984, 306, 307). The U.S. Fish and Wildlife Service attempted to capture the remaining wild birds for safekeeping but during the process was restrained by a court order, leaving one female and four males in the wild and thirteen females and eight males in captivity (U.S. Department of the Interior, U.S. Fish and Wildlife Service 1986b). By 1987 the total California condor population consisted of twenty-seven birds, and the last wild bird was captured that year (U.S. Department of the Interior, U.S. Fish and Wildlife Service 1987b; U.S. Department of the Interior, U.S. Fish and Wildlife Service 1987d, 7). In the following spring, the first successful mating of captive California condors occurred (U.S. Department of the Interior, U.S. Fish and Wildlife Service 1988a, 2). By 1989 twenty-eight California condors existed, all in captivity, and plans for their eventual release into the wild were under way. Beginning early in that year, several Andean condors were released in the former range of the California condor in an attempt to determine whether suitable condor habitat still existed there. At the end of this experiment (fall 1990), these birds were to be recaptured and reintroduced into previously occupied areas in Colombia (Rees 1989, 8). By 1990 fifty California condors were in captive-breeding flocks at the Los Angeles Zoo and San Diego Wild Animal Park, and on February 14 of that year two of the birds were released to the wild in Ventura County (Haas 1991, 1, 15). Once again California condors soar over the California mountains.

Efforts are also under way to restore the endangered black-footed ferret. During the fall of 1986, the last individual in the last known black-footed ferret colony was captured; at that time the entire population consisted of 18 captive animals (U.S. Department of the Interior, U.S. Fish and Wildlife Service 1986c). Following several successful years of captive breeding, the ferret population reached 58 in 1988. The program's goal was to achieve 250 breeding pairs by 1991 and to make the first reintroductions into the wild that year (Rose 1988, 8). Disease and breeding problems severely hampered the program, but by 1989 the ferret population had reached 118 animals, and by the fall of 1990 it was 180. As of January 1991, reintroduction was planned for the fall of that year (U.S. Department of the Interior, U.S. Fish and Wildlife Service 1991, 1).

The situation is more bleak for another species. On June 16, 1987, the dusky race of the seaside sparrow became extinct. The last bird, a thirteen-year-old male, died at Walt Disney World's Discovery Island Zoological Park in Orlando, Florida. A breeding program to preserve some of the dusky gene pool through hybrids with another subspecies of seaside sparrow continues, but the pure duskies are gone (U.S. Department of the Interior, U.S. Fish and Wildlife Service, 1987c).

In December 1990 the U.S. Fish and Wildlife Service summarized accomplishments of the recovery program in a report to Congress. As of October that year,

• Five hundred eighty-one species were listed as endangered in the United States and/or trust territories.

• Three hundred fifty-two species (61 percent of those listed) have approved recovery plans, and an additional 22 percent have a recovery plan in some stage of development.

• Four hundred thirty-nine species (76 percent) have less than 25 percent of their recovery objectives achieved (U.S. Department of the Interior, U.S. Fish and Wildlife Service 1990b, vi, vii).

The Spotted Owl Controversy

One of the most intense, contentious, frustrating, and potentially most rewarding endangered species issues (if resolved) involves the northern spotted owl of the Pacific Northwest. The owl is characteristic of old-growth coniferous forests. Such forests have been largely eliminated from private lands. The remnants that are left are primarily on lands administered by the Bureau of Land Management (BLM) and the Forest Service (FS). The economy of much of the timber industry and of many towns in Oregon and Washington is dependent upon continued harvest of old-growth stands. The controversy contains elements of endangered species preservation, use of public lands, local and regional economics and politics, species versus ecosystem considerations, definitions of multiple use, numerous constituency groups, and all three branches of government—and more.

Executive Approaches

The executive branch precipitated the current controversy when the Forest Service released its final "Regional Guide for the Pacific Northwest Region" (U.S. Department of Agriculture, Forest Service 1984), but the controversy had been brewing for more than a decade. The owl was included as a possible candidate for federal listing as an endangered species in 1973; was a state-listed threatened species in Oregon in 1975; was the subject of a joint Oregon-BLM-FS management plan in 1977, which was modified in 1981 through efforts of the Spotted Owl Subcommittee of the Oregon-Washington Interagency Wildlife Committee; was reviewed by the U.S. Fish and Wildlife Service (FWS) for endangered species status in 1981 and 1987; and was the subject of numerous studies under the auspices of the Old Growth Wildlife Research and Development Program of the BLM and the FS beginning in 1982 (Thomas et al. 1990, 51-55).

Following an appeal from conservation groups that the 1984 "Regional Guide" was inadequate, the deputy assistant secretary of agriculture directed the Forest Service to prepare a supplemental EIS on spotted owl standards and guidelines (Thomas et al. 1990, 54). The final supplemental EIS and record of decision was released in late 1988, precipitating administrative appeals, litigation by both environmental groups and timber interests, and legislative proposals. In an effort to clarify the situation, the Forest Service recommended formation of the Interagency Spotted Owl Scientific Committee (ISC), chaired by Jack Ward Thomas, chief research wildlife biologist at the Forest Service's Pacific Northwest Research Station.

The ISC, formed in October 1989 from representatives of the BLM, FS, FWS, and NPS, was to "develop a scientifically credible conservation strategy for the northern spotted owl" (Thomas et al. 1990, 57). Its report, released in May 1990, contains an extensive and comprehensive review of the species' status and life requirements, and recommends a two-stage management strategy:

> The first stage, prescribes and implements the steps needed to protect habitat in amounts and distribution that will ensure the owl's long-term

survival. The second stage calls for research and monitoring to test the adequacy of the strategy and to seek ways to produce and sustain suitable owl habitat in managed forests. (Thomas et al. 1990, 2)

The ISC's management plan is based on large blocks of land termed habitat conservation areas (HCAs), each capable of supporting at least twenty pairs of owls, "spaced closely enough to facilitate dispersal between the blocks," and supplemented by smaller HCAs (Thomas et al. 1990, 3). The ISC's report was reasonably well received by professional wildlife managers, but it did not quell the controversy—it merely precipitated more study and confrontation.

While the Thomas Committee was working on management recommendations, the U.S. Fish and Wildlife Service was again considering the owl for listing under the Endangered Species Act (ESA). This time the agency found the owl in need of protection and listed it as threatened (55 Fed. Reg. 26,194 (June 26, 1990)), triggering the consultation requirements of section 7 of the act.

On the same day, the secretaries of agriculture and the interior announced creation of a "high level interagency task force, chaired by the secretary of agriculture, to begin work immediately on devising a forest management plan for the FS for fiscal year 1991...[to implement the president's charge of] finding a balance between protection of the owl and concern for jobs." The administration threatened to convene the Endangered Species Committee (affectionately called the "God Squad" [Wildlife Management Institute 1992, 1]) to seek exemption from section 7 of the ESA (16 U.S.C. 1536 (1988)) if the FWS were to determine that a proposed timber sale or harvest "jeopardize[d] the continued existence" of the owl in violation of that act (U.S. Department of Agriculture, Forest Service 1990, 20, 21).

In September 1991 the Forest Service released a "Draft Environmental Impact Statement on Management for the Northern Spotted Owl in the National Forests" to satisfy a court order "'to submit to the court and have in effect by March 5, 1991 revised standards and guidelines to ensure the northern spotted owl's viability, together with an environmental impact statement, as required by NFMA and its implementing regulations'" (U.S. Department of Agriculture, Forest Service 1991, 1-1). The report analyzes four management alternatives:

1. Spotted owl habitat areas (SOHAs)—the "no action" alternative utilizing "established networks of 1000 to 3000 acre Spotted Owl Habitat Areas (SOHAs)" prescribed in regional guides for the Pacific Northwest

and California national forests previously prepared under RPA (U.S. Department of Agriculture, Forest Service 1991, 2-7).

2. Habitat conservation areas (HCAs)—implementing recommendations of the conservation strategy developed by the ISC (Thomas et al. 1990). This preferred alternative is based on dispersed blocks of habitat suitable to support at least twenty pairs of owls, supplemented by HCAs of smaller size (U.S. Department of Agriculture, Forest Service 1991, 2-19, 2-26).

3. HCAs plus critical habitat—alternative (2) plus critical habitat outside the HCAs designated by the U.S. Fish and Wildlife Service (56 Fed. Reg. 20,816 (May 6, 1991)) (U.S. Department of Agriculture, Forest Service 1991, 2-39, 2-40).

4. HCAs plus all spotted owl habitat—alternative (3) plus all nesting, roosting, and foraging habitat (U.S. Department of Agriculture, Forest Service 1991, 2- 43).

While the environmental impact assessment process was under way in the Forest Service, a parallel activity was being undertaken in the Department of the Interior. On February 5, 1991, Secretary Manuel Lujan directed that the Northern Spotted Owl Recovery Team prepare a "scientifically credible plan that met the recovery standard set forth in the Endangered Species Act...[and that] 'to the extent feasible, addressed economic and social impacts.'" The draft recovery plan was submitted to the secretary in December 1991. However, in a letter dated February 14, 1992, outlining his review, the secretary stated that the plan met his directive but "requested the team to address certain concerns in the draft, most of which dealt either directly or indirectly with economic impacts....[S]ubject to compliance with my request and my subsequent final approval, publication of the draft for public comment could proceed." But before the recovery team could comply with the secretary's request, another complication arose. The president requested that all federal regulations and programs be evaluated and directed the secretary to "'identify and accelerate action on initiatives that will eliminate any unnecessary regulatory burden or otherwise promote economic growth.'" The secretary concluded, "Accordingly, it is not appropriate to publish the draft plan for public comment until such evaluation has been completed" (Lujan 1992c).

To undertake the evaluation, Secretary Lujan did not turn to the existing recovery team but instead created yet another body, the Work Group on Spotted Owl Management Options:

In an effort to comply with the goals of the program and regulatory review recently requested by the President, I believe we must expand the scope of planning efforts related to owl management and other land planning concerns, in order to develop and assess options which have lower economic impacts. I am fully aware that major structural changes in the timber industry are having significant effects on workers and communities and will continue to do so over the next several decades, notwithstanding Federal actions with respect to the northern spotted owl and forest management. However, I believe we have a responsibility to determine whether options are available which will not unduly exacerbate these effects, while at the same time providing for preservation of the owl. I am specifically interested in formulating and evaluating options whose implementation would result in significantly lower economic impacts and in a high probability of owl preservation and persistence, even though they might not achieve recovery of the species throughout its range or even in some physiographic provinces as required by the ESA....Because these options may require Congressional action to implement, your considerations vary from the requirements of ESA and other major land management statutes. (Lujan 1992b)

This proposal was immediately attacked by the environmental interests, who alleged:

The problem with such a plan is that its implementation would be in direct violation of the Endangered Species Act, which requires that any plan induce recovery, not mere existence. The Secretary's plan would also violate the National Forest Management Act, which says that the national forests must be managed to maintain viable populations of fish and wildlife. (Wildlife Management Institute 1992, 1)

On October 1, 1991, Secretary Lujan made good his threat to convene the Endangered Species Committee, following a finding by the FWS that forty-four BLM timber sales "were likely to jeopardize the continued existence of the northern spotted owl." More than seven months later, the committee released its decision:

As a result of applying the exemption criteria, the Committee finds for 13 sales that there are no reasonable and prudent alternatives, that the benefits clearly outweigh the benefits of alternative courses of action, that they are of regional significance, and that the Bureau of Land Management has not made any irreversible or irretrievable commitment of resources. (Lujan 1992a, 6)

Thus the committee exempted these sales from provisions of the ESA and permitted them to proceed (with the proviso that the BLM implement the final spotted owl recovery plan as soon as possible). For one or more of the reasons stated in the decision, exemptions for the remaining thirty-one proposed sales were denied.

At the time of the Endangered Species Committee's decision, there was no "final" recovery plan. The long-delayed draft plan, submitted to the secretary in December 1991, was released in May 1992 (Wildlife Management Institute 1992, 3). It is similar to the ISC plan, differing largely in having a stated objective of "removing the northern spotted owl from the list of threatened and endangered species," and includes analyses of economic and social effects and consideration of other species that would benefit from the plan. The habitat conservation areas (HCAs) of the ISC are renamed "designated conservation areas" (DCAs) but generally have the same attributes (Northern Spotted Owl Recovery Team 1992, vii, 588). The criterion of twenty or more pairs per area is retained, as are most of the other elements in the ISC report (Thomas et al. 1990). In comparison, the

DCAs contain approximately 275,000 more acres of NRF [nesting, roosting, and foraging] habitat than do the HCAs. Approximately 120 more owl pairs have been located in the DCAs than in the HCAs. Approximately 80,000 more acres suitable for timber production are contained in the DCAs than in the HCAs. (Northern Spotted Owl Recovery Team 1992, 590)

The 196 DCAs contain about 7.5 million acres, providing habitat for approximately 1,180 known pairs of spotted owls, about 48 percent of those currently on federal lands. When fully developed they will support about 2,320 pairs and will be the primary means of achieving recovery and delisting (Northern Spotted Owl Recovery Team 1992, ix). Implementation will carry a social and economic cost, however. The recovery team estimates that 18,900 jobs in the timber industry and 13,200 jobs in related sectors will be lost, the value of the timber harvest will be reduced by $470 million per year, receipts to the U.S. Treasury will be reduced by $328 million per year, and counties will lose $100 million per year in receipts (Northern Spotted Owl Recovery Team 1992, xiii).

Contemporaneous with release of the draft recovery plan, Secretary Lujan also released the draft preservation plan for the northern spotted owl (Lujan 1992d), prepared by the work group established by his

February 14, 1992, directive. Compared with the draft recovery plan, the draft preservation plan would increase timber harvest by almost a billion board feet (p. 9) and increase employment by about 17,000 jobs and receipts to counties by $68 million per year (p. 10). But it would remove protective measures from six of the eleven provinces within the owl's range, place only about half as much land in designated conservation areas, ultimately provide for 1,340 pairs of owls rather than 2,310, and be sufficient only "to provide a core of owl populations and habitat enabling reasonable assurance of the owl's survival" (pp. 2, 6). Implementation of the preservation plan requires congressional action because it conflicts with requirements of the Endangered Species Act and its implementing regulations and with Forest Service planning standards (p. 40).

The situation is convoluted and frustrating enough within the executive branch, but judicial and legislative considerations add further complicating dimensions.

Judicial Approaches

The controversy has spawned a plethora of litigation. On one side were various chapters of the Audubon Society and their allies, arguing for increased protection of the owl and the old-growth stands (ancient forests) that support it. On the other were the Northwest Forest Resource Council (NFRC) and its supporters, representing the timber industry. Over the intervening years, litigation has involved allegations that proposed timber sales on BLM and Oregon and California Railroad lands would violate the National Environmental Policy Act, the Migratory Bird Treaty Act, the Federal Land Policy and Management Act and other federal laws; constitutional tests of separation of powers; court-mandated development of a spotted owl management plan and designation of critical habitat; allegations that the BLM failed to enter into consultations with the FWS as required by the Endangered Species Act; and appeals to the U.S. Supreme Court (Rutzick 1991, 416-427). By June 1991 a spokesman for the NFRC declared:

> The spotted owl litigation in the Northwest has reached a crisis point. Despite the Congressionally-endorsed effort by the Forest Service and other agencies to develop the ISC conservation strategy, and despite the virtually universal acceptance of that strategy as one that will adequately protect spotted owls in the short term and the long term, the courts have now blocked the Forest Service from implementing the strategy, and have

indefinitely blocked most Forest Service timber sales in the 17 spotted owl forests while yet another plan is developed. Threats to BLM's ability to fulfill its statutory mandate to sell timber under the O&C Act is in serious doubt. (Rutzick 1991, 427, 428)

Legislative Approaches

Congress has responded by considering a number of legislative solutions. Section 318 of the Department of Interior and Related Agencies Appropriations Act, Fiscal Year 1989, specified conditions under which timber sales were to be conducted in the thirteen national forests and on Bureau of Land Management lands in Oregon that contained northern spotted owls and prohibited legal action to stop such sales for a period of one year (103 Stat. 745-750). These were stopgap measures, designed to delay irreversible commitments and to permit a cooling-off period during which a more permanent solution could be developed. The Hundred and First Congress considered four more comprehensive bills designed to permit timber sales in spotted owl areas (H.R. 1645), to protect ancient forests (H.R. 4492 and H.R. 5295), and to mandate preparation of plans that would "attempt to achieve timber sale levels greater than those available under a strict application of the ISC report" (H.R. 5116) (U.S. Congress, House 1990). None of these bills passed.

The Hundred and Second Congress also considered four bills (H.R. 842, H.R. 1309, H.R. 1590, and H.R. 2463) that contained provisions ranging from creating an ancient forest reserve system (H.R. 1590) to protecting the economy of communities dependent upon timber from the forests (H.R. 1309) (U.S. Congress, House 1991). As of June 1992 no definitive bill had passed, and there the matter rested.

Conclusion

The foregoing discussion is only a brief summary of an almost hopelessly complex situation. The northern spotted owl has become a symbol of endangered species, of old growth, of the conflict between consumptive and nonconsumptive uses of public (and private) lands, of "environment" versus "economy." The controversy has been used to muster support for only slightly similar issues throughout the country, and to put fear into the hearts of environmentalists and developers alike; it has intensified polarization among user groups; and it has stymied efforts by reasonable and competent professional resource managers to develop a solution that can withstand environmental, legal, economic, and political scrutiny. Perhaps there is no solution unless the owl becomes extinct, and even then the controversy would transfer to some other species and area. For the controversy is not about an owl. It is about the balance between consumptive and nonconsumptive uses of natural resources and about the allocation of those resources among users. It is an ecosystem argument, not a species argument. It is an argument about "how much" rather than "whether or not." Those who continue to work conscientiously toward rational resolution deserve our deepest gratitude.

THE NATIONAL WILDLIFE REFUGE SYSTEM

The National Wildlife Refuge System shares its heritage with the national forests and national parks. Beginning as an awakening to the disappearance of wildlife from developed areas and the public domain, it progressed through dedication of public lands, creation and evolution of a bureaucracy, acquisition of lands, and continued mission definition to a system of almost 570 national wildlife refuges and waterfowl production areas (General Services Administration 1984, 313).

Early Development

On December 24, 1892, President Benjamin Harrison used the authority provided by the Creative Act to "set apart and reserve...public lands...covered with timber or undergrowth...as public reservations" to reserve part of Afognak Island, Alaska (northeast of Kodiak Island), as the Afognak Forest and Fish Culture Reserve:

> And whereas, the public lands...known as Afognak Island, are in part covered with timber, and are required for public purposes, in order that the salmon fisheries in the waters of the Island, and the salmon and other fish and sea animals, and other animals and birds, and the timber, undergrowth, grass, moss and other growth...may be protected and preserved unimpaired....
>
> And whereas the United States Commissioner of Fish and Fisheries has selected Afognak Bay, River, and Lake, with their tributary streams...and the lands including the same on said Afognak Island, and within one mile of the shores thereof, as a reserve for the purpose of establishing fish culture stations....
>
> Now, therefore, I, BENJAMIN HARRISON, President of the United States...do hereby...set apart as a Public Reservation, including use for fish culture and stations, said Afognak Island, Alaska and its adjacent bays and rocks and territorial waters...Provided, That this proclamation shall

not be so construed as to deprive any bona fide inhabitant of said Island of any valid right he may possess under the Treaty for the cession of the Russian possessions. (27 Stat. 1052)

Six years later, on July 2, 1908, President Theodore Roosevelt consolidated the Afognak Forest and Fish Culture Reserve into the Chugach Forest Reserve by executive order, and in the next year, on February 23, 1909, he reinforced his order with a proclamation (35 Stat. 2231). Withdrawals were made subject to any preexisting rights, and the proclamation noted that withdrawal for a forest reserve was consistent with withdrawal for fish culture, "but the withdrawal for fish culture stations and for the use of the United States Commissioner of Fish and Fisheries shall be the dominant one" (35 Stat. 2232)—an early reference to *dominant use.*

During the 1970s the Forest Service recommended portions of Afognak Island (Tonki Cape and Devil Paw) for inclusion in the National Wilderness Preservation System (U.S. Department of Agriculture, Forest Service 1980, map). This was not to be, however, for the Alaska National Interest Lands Conservation Act of 1980 transferred the Devil Paw area to the U.S. Fish and Wildlife Service as part of Kodiak National Wildlife Refuge (94 Stat. 2391), released the Tonki Cape area to private ownership (Koniag, Inc.), and placed other portions of the original reservation within the Alaska Maritime Wildlife Refuge (94 Stat. 2389). None of the island is currently managed by the Forest Service (Ryan 1986). Confusing? Indeed! And perhaps for that reason Pelican Island (figure 7.2) is generally considered to be the first unit in the National Wildlife Refuge System.

Pelican Island lies about 2 miles east of Sebastian, Florida, in the Indian River estuary (Laycock 1973, 27). As early as 1882, it was recognized as an important brown pelican breeding colony (Lawrence 1891). Passing yachtsmen were also attracted by the concentrations of pelicans, however, and frequently used them for target practice (Riley and Riley 1981, 126). The American Ornithologists' Union attempted to acquire the island but was unsuccessful (nevertheless, it hired a local citizen, Paul Kroegel, as a "warden" for the area). Eventually appeals by conservationists reached President Roosevelt, who created the refuge by executive order on March 14, 1903:

It is hereby ordered that Pelican Island in Indian River in section nine, township thirty-one south, range thirty-nine east, State of Florida, be, and it is hereby, reserved and set apart for the use of the Department of Agriculture as a preserve and breeding ground for native birds.

FIGURE 7.2. The Pelicans of Pelican Island. (Photo courtesy USDI Fish and Wildlife Service)

Roosevelt probably had authority for his action under the Creative Act (the island supported mangrove vegetation [Laycock 1973, 27] and thus qualified as "public lands...in part covered with...undergrowth"), but it is doubtful that members of Congress had bird refuges in mind when they passed that forestry legislation. Three years later, on June 28, 1906, Congress confirmed the reservation and sanctioned the concept of bird refuges by prohibiting the hunting of birds "on all lands of the United States which have been set apart as breeding grounds for birds by any law, proclamation, or Executive order" except under regulations of the secretary of agriculture (34 Stat. 536, cited in Bean 1983, 22).

The pelicans were not yet safe, however. In late October 1910, Pelican Island was completely inundated by a hurricane for more than three weeks. The adult birds moved to a larger island 400 yards to the southeast, which Kroegel promptly posted and named "New Pelican Island." During World War I, fishermen blamed the pelicans for depleting Florida's fishery resources and advocated eradication of the colonies. Although this campaign led to the deaths of hundreds of birds, the pelicans survived—only to be threatened by land development. About this time (1963), the current warden, William Julian, found one of Kroegel's lantern slides, which showed a refuge sign on New Pelican Island, suggesting that the refuge was larger than the one 3-acre island commonly accepted. Further research led to the discovery of a second executive order, issued by Roosevelt on January 26, 1909, which enlarged the refuge to include "all small islands within sections 9 and 10," and on December 5, 1963, the Federal Land Register officially showed Pelican Island National Wildlife Refuge to contain 756 acres (Laycock 1973, 31-34). At last the pelicans' home was safe—but the birds were not. DDT had impaired their reproductive ability, their numbers were declining, and they were declared an endangered species in 1970 (35 Fed. Reg. 16,047, 35 Fed. Reg. 18,320). Today Pelican Island is administered as part of the 139,305-acre Merritt Island National Wildlife Refuge, which encompasses most of NASA's Kennedy Space Center (Riley and Riley 1981, 124-126).

Two years after the Pelican Island refuge was established, Congress and the president turned their attention to the future of the bison. By 1889 only about 541 bison remained in the United States—256 in captivity, 200 in Yellowstone National Park, and 85 "in the wild" (Tober 1981, 102). The "wild" animals were dispersed as small herds—four in "western Dakota" (Tober 1981, 117), ten in Montana, twenty-six in Wyoming, twenty in Colorado, and twenty-five generally near the intersection of Colorado, New Mexico, Oklahoma, and Kansas (Hornaday 1889, cited in Tober 1981, 98). By 1900 only about twenty animals remained outside captivity (Tober 1981, 102), in Yellowstone National Park, protected by the 1894 statute prohibiting all hunting and imposing strict penalties for poaching in the park (28 Stat. 73)—and by the U.S. Army. The Boone and Crockett Club, founded in 1887 at a dinner given by Theodore Roosevelt, had been active in fighting hounding of deer in New York's Adirondack Mountains, the destruction of game in Yellowstone National Park, and exploitation of the National Park System by private enterprise (Tober 1981, 189, 190). With "their man in the White House," the club turned its attention to saving the bison from extirpation (Udall 1963, 148). In January 1905 Congress empowered the president to set aside areas in the Wichita Mountains "for the protection of game animals and birds and [to] be recognized as a breeding place therefor." The New York Zoological Society donated a nucleus herd of fifteen bison on condition that Congress appropriate $15,000 for construction of a fence to enclose them—the beginnings of rehabilitation. But what Congress can create it can also destroy, and in 1956 the Department of Defense attempted a land grab. A bill was introduced that would have transferred 10,700 acres of refuge land to Fort Sill Military Reservation, which abuts the refuge. Testimony before the Subcommittee on Fisheries and Wildlife of the House Committee on Merchant Marine and Fisheries (May 23, 1956) was overwhelmingly opposed, and the bill failed (Laycock 1973, 15, 16). Today the 59,000-acre Wichita Mountains National Wildlife Refuge features elk, longhorn cattle, prairie dogs, Mississippi kites, bald and golden eagles, and many other species of wildlife in addition to the bison (Riley and Riley 1981, 429, 430).

Eighteen months after authorizing the Wichita Mountains National Wildlife Refuge, Congress passed an identical act affecting areas within the Grand Canyon National Forest (34 Stat. 607). This area later became part of Grand Canyon National Park (40 Stat. 1178). Creation of the National Bison Range (Montana) in 1908 and the National Elk Refuge (Wyoming) in 1912 largely completed the early refuge system. The National Bison Range was reserved from the public domain (35 Stat. 267; 35 Stat. 1051) in a manner similar to the preceding refuges, except that it involved lands within the Flathead Indian Reservation, and compensation to the Indians was required. The National Elk Refuge had a more complex beginning, involving private and public lands and powerful constituency groups.

Since long before the arrival of the white man, elk summering in what is now Yellowstone National Park and the Grand Tetons migrated through Jackson Hole, Wyoming, in the fall en route to their wintering range at lower elevations. With settlement, cattle, and fencing, the elk were no longer able to complete their journey. During the winter of 1908-1909, nearly half of the estimated 16,000 elk wintering around Jackson Hole died despite local, state, and federal efforts to provide food. A controversy also brewed among ranchers protecting their winter hay from elk depredation, commercial hunters who killed the animals for their canine teeth (sold to members of the Elk Lodge), and citizens concerned over possible extermination of the herd. Congress dispatched E. A. Preble of the Bureau of Biological Survey to investigate the situation and, based on his report, authorized a federal refuge for the indigent elk on August 12, 1912 (37 Stat. 293). Initially the refuge consisted of 1,760 acres purchased from local residents and 1,000 acres withdrawn from the public domain (37 Stat. 847). In 1925 the Izaak Walton League of America purchased and donated an additional 1,760 acres (44 Stat. 1246), and subsequent additions brought the refuge to its current size of 37 square miles. Elk on the refuge are managed by the Wyoming Game and Fish Commission, the National Park Service, and the U.S. Fish and Wildlife Service, and hunting regulations are adjusted to maintain the herd within the carrying capacity of its range (Laycock 1973, 91-101). Over the years, however, the elk management policy on the land adjacent to Yellowstone National Park has been neither consistent nor effective. The National Park Service's emphasis has vacillated from predator control to elk population control on and off parklands to reintroduction of predators to "leave things alone" (Chase 1986).

Migratory Bird Emphasis

National wildlife refuges have been established to protect big game, rare and endangered species, and other forms of wildlife, but historically the system's emphasis has been on protecting migratory waterfowl. The stimulus for a system of migratory bird refuges came from the Migratory Bird Treaty Act of 1918, but congressional authorization did not come until 1929 (Bean 1983, 120). The Migratory Bird Conservation Act created a Migratory Bird Conservation Commission, consisting of the secretaries of the interior (chairman), commerce, and agriculture and two members from the House of Representatives and two from the Senate, who "approved for purchase or rental...[or acquisition by] gift or devise, [areas] for use as inviolate sanctuaries for migratory birds." A state representative was included, ex officio, "for the purpose of considering and voting on all questions relating to the acquisition...of areas in his State." The act was subsequently amended to require the concurrence of the legislature of any state in which an acquisition was proposed (45 Stat. 1223) and to relax the prohibition against hunting on refuge lands. Hunting became permissible on up to 25 percent of a refuge in 1949 (63 Stat. 600), on up to 40 percent in 1958 (72 Stat. 486), on 40 percent if "compatible...with...major purposes for which...areas were established" in 1966 (80 Stat. 928), and on more than 40 percent if "beneficial to the species" in 1978 (92 Stat. 3114). The Migratory Bird Conservation Act was a good start. It had a treaty to back it up. It involved the executive and legislative branches of the federal government and a representative of state government in the decision making. It authorized gift, rental, or purchase. It remains the cornerstone of the National Wildlife Refuge System today; but it authorized only $200,000 per year for the entire system after 1939 (of which no more than 20 percent could be used for refuge administration and maintenance)—and that was dependent upon annual appropriations (45 Stat. 1224, 1225).

A solution to the fiscal problem came with passage of the Migratory Bird Hunting Stamp Act in 1934. Popularly known as the "duck stamp" law, this act (as amended in 1935) required all persons sixteen years of age and older to possess "an unexpired Federal migratory-bird hunting stamp validated by his signature written by himself in ink across the face of the stamp prior to [taking migratory waterfowl]" (48 Stat. 451). In 1934 a duck stamp cost $1.00. By 1987 the price had become $10.00; in 1989, $12.50; and in 1991 and thereafter, $15.00 (16 U.S.C. 718b(b)(1988)). Receipts are deposited in a special fund administered by the secretary of the interior to support the acquisition of migratory bird refuges and waterfowl production areas (72 Stat. 486).

While the Duck Stamp Act helped a great deal, it did not provide sufficient funding to keep pace with inflation, offset effects of wetland destruction (Bean 1983, p. 216), and maintain the growing refuge system. Subsequently Congress passed the Wetlands Loan Act of 1961 (75 Stat. 813), which authorized an advance interest-free appropriation to the fund of up to $105 million over seven years, with the ceiling raised to $200 million in 1976 (90 Stat. 189). Additional acquisition funds come from the Land and Water Conservation Fund, but support for maintenance and operation support still relies on the whims of Congress.

The Refuge System Today

In 1975 the National Wildlife Refuge System contained 284 migratory bird (waterfowl) areas, 70 migratory bird (general) areas, 16 big game areas, 4 national game ranges, 4 national wildlife ranges, and over 2,300 waterfowl production areas (The Nature Conservancy 1977, 61). The system had a decidedly waterfowl "flavor" then, and it still has today. But the Land and Water Conservation Fund Act, development of an endangered species program, and addition of the new Alaska refuges have modified the wetland-waterfowl dominance of the past.

The Land and Water Conservation Fund Act of 1965 was outdoor recreation legislation. Its purposes were "to assist in preserving, developing, and assuring accessibility to...such quality and quantity of outdoor recreation resources as may be available and are necessary and desirable for individual active participation in such recreation and to strengthen the health and vitality of the citizens of the United States" (78 Stat. 897). Yet, as frequently happens, subsequent amendments extended the act's provisions far beyond its original intent. Forty percent of appropriations from the fund were to be available to federal agencies for "acquisition of land, waters, and interests in land or waters" (among other purposes) provided "such acquisition is otherwise authorized by law," and allotments were to be made in the "same proportion as the number of visitor-days in areas...for which admission fees are charged." The act provided that funds could be used "[f]or any national area which may be authorized for the preservation of species of fish or wildlife that are threatened with extinction" and for "incidental recreation purposes" cited in section 2 of the Refuge Recreation Act of 1962 (76 Stat. 653).

The Refuge Recreation Act of 1962 (as amended) empowered the U.S. Fish and Wildlife Service to acquire land for "incidental fish and wildlife-oriented recreational development,...protection of natural resources,...[and] conservation of threatened and endangered species" and authorized appropriations from the LWCF for these purposes (16 U.S.C. 460k-1 (1988)). However, Congress insisted that any lands acquired with fund moneys must have recreational facilities constructed on them (Bean 1983, 232). Subsequent amendments, changes in policy, and additional legislation have combined to make the LWCF a major source of refuge funding.

With increasing demands on all public lands and continuing budgetary constraints, the National Wildlife Refuge System of the future will probably exhibit more multiple use management and commodity production than that of the past. The challenge will be to provide this increased array of benefits without diminishing the refuges' primary role of preserving and enhancing populations of waterfowl and other migratory birds, endangered species, and big game.

REFERENCES

Allen, Durwood L., ch. 1973. "Report of the Committee on North American Wildlife Policy." *Wildlife Society Bulletin* 1 (2): 73-92.

———. 1987. "Leopold the Founder." *American Forests* 93 (9-10): 26-29 (September-October).

Allin, Craig W. 1982. *The Politics of Wilderness Preservation.* Westport, CT: Greenwood Press.

Bean, Michael J. 1983. *The Evolution of National Wildlife Law.* New York: Praeger Publishers.

Cain, Stanley A., ch. 1972. "Predator Control—1971: Report to the Council on Environmental Quality and the Department of the Interior by the Advisory Committee on Predator Control." Washington, DC: Government Printing Office.

————. 1978. "Predator and Pest Control." In *Wildlife and America,* edited by Howard P. Brokaw, 379-395. Council on Environmental Quality. Washington, DC: Government Printing Office.

Callicott, J. Baird, ed. 1987. *Companion to A Sand County Almanac.* Madison: University of Wisconsin Press.

Chase, Alston. 1986. *Playing God in Yellowstone.* New York: Atlantic Monthly Press.

Council on Environmental Quality. 1980. *Environmental Quality—1980.* Washington, DC: Government Printing Office.

————. 1981. *Environmental Trends.* Washington, DC: Government Printing Office.

————. 1984. *Environmental Quality—1984.* Washington, DC: Government Printing Office.

Earley, Lawrence S. 1987. "The Father of Wildlife." *Wildlife in North Carolina* 51 (11): 20-23.

Flader, Susan. 1973. *The Sand Country of Aldo Leopold.* San Francisco: Sierra Club Books.

————. 1974. *Thinking Like a Mountain: Aldo Leopold and the Evolution of an Ecological Attitude Toward Deer, Wolves, and Forests.* Columbia: University of Missouri Press.

Frome, Michael. 1971. "Clearcutting the National Forests." *Field and Stream* 76 (3): 32, 34.

————. 1984. *The Forest Service.* Boulder, CO: Westview Press.

General Services Administration. 1984. *The United States Government Manual 1984/85.* Washington, DC: Government Printing Office.

Gibbons, Boyd. 1981. "Aldo Leopold: A Durable Scale of Values." *National Geographic* 160 (5): 682-708.

Haas, Ann. 1991. "History on the Wing: California Condors Restored to Home Skies." *Endangered Species Technical Bulletin* 16 (9-12): 1, 15.

Hornaday, William T. 1889. "The Extermination of the American Bison: With a Sketch of Its Discovery and Life History." In *The Annual Report of the U.S. National Museum for the Year Ending June 30, 1887,* 367-548. Washington, DC: Government Printing Office.

Ise, John. 1920. *The United States Forest Policy.* New Haven, CT: Yale University Press.

————. 1961. *Our National Park Policy.* Baltimore, MD: Johns Hopkins Press.

King, F. Wayne. 1978. "The Wildlife Trade." In *Wildlife and America,* edited by Howard P. Brokaw, 253-271. Council on Environmental Quality. Washington, DC: Government Printing Office.

Lawrence, Robert H. 1891. "A Breeding Place of *Pelecanus fuscus.*" *Auk* 8:231-232.

Laycock, George. 1973. *The Sign of the Flying Goose.* Garden City, NY: Anchor Natural History Books.

Leopold, Aldo. 1921. "The Wilderness and Its Place in Forest Recreational Policy." *Journal of Forestry* 29:718-721.

———. 1930. "Report to the American Game Conference on an American Game Policy." *American Game Conference* 17:284-309.

———. [1933] 1948. *Game Management*. New York: Charles Scribner's Sons.

———. [1949] 1987. *A Sand County Almanac*. New York: Oxford University Press.

Lujan, Manuel, Jr. 1992a. "Application for Exemption by the Bureau of Land Management to Conduct 44 Timber Sales in Western Oregon." Statement of decision of the Endangered Species Committee. Washington, DC: U.S. Department of the Interior, Endangered Species Committee.

———. 1992b. "Directive to the Work Group." Memorandum to members of the Work Group on Spotted Owl Management Options, February 14, 1992. Washington, DC: U.S. Department of the Interior, Office of the Secretary.

———. 1992c. "Northern Spotted Owl Recovery Planning Process." Memorandum to Donald R. Knowles, secretary's representative and recovery team coordinator and Marvin L. Plenert, recovery team leader, February 14, 1992. Washington, DC: U.S. Department of the Interior, Office of the Secretary.

———. 1992d. "Preservation Plan for the Spotted Owl: Draft." Washington, DC: U.S. Department of the Interior.

Lund, Thomas A. 1980. *American Wildlife Law*. Berkeley: University of California Press.

McCabe, Robert A. 1987. *Aldo Leopold: The Professor*. Amherst, WI: Palmer Publications.

———. 1988. *Aldo Leopold: Mentor*. Madison: University of Wisconsin, Russell Laboratories.

Meine, Curt. 1988. *Aldo Leopold: His Life and Work*. Madison: University of Wisconsin Press.

Meine, Curt, and T. H. Watkins. 1987. "How Leopold Learned to Think Like a Mountain." *Wilderness* 51 (179): 57-62 (Winter).

The Nature Conservancy. 1977. *Preserving Our Natural Heritage*. Vol. 1, *Federal Activities*. Washington, DC: Government Printing Office.

Nilsson, Greta. 1983. *The Endangered Species Handbook*. Washington, DC: The Animal Welfare Institute.

Northern Spotted Owl Recovery Team. 1992. "Recovery Plan for the Northern Spotted Owl." Washington, DC: Government Printing Office.

Office of the Federal Register. 1987. *The United States Government Manual 1987/88*. Washington, DC: Government Printing Office.

The Peregrine Fund Newsletter. 1984. No. 12 (Fall). (Published by The Peregrine Fund, Ithaca, New York.)

————. 1986. No. 14 (Fall). (Published by The Peregrine Fund, Ithaca, New York.)

Reed, Nathanial P., and Dennis Drabelle. 1984. *The United States Fish and Wildlife Service.* Boulder, CO: Westview Press.

Rees, Michael D. 1989. "Andean Condors Released in Experiment to Aid the California Condor." *Endangered Species Technical Bulletin* 14 (1-2): 8, 9.

Riley, William, and Laura Riley. 1981. *Guide to the National Wildlife Refuges.* New York: Anchor Press.

Robertson, F. Dale. 1990. "Concerning Old Growth Forests and the Northern Spotted Owl." In U.S. Congress, House, Committee on Interior and Insular Affairs, Subcommittee on National Parks and Public Lands, "Protection of Ancient Forests and Northern Spotted Owls," 89-90. 101st Cong., 2d sess. Serial 101-46. Washington, DC: Government Printing Office.

Rose, Sharon. 1988. "Black-footed Ferrets Moved to New Facilities." *Endangered Species Technical Bulletin* 13 (11-12): 8.

Runte, Alfred. 1987. *National Parks: The American Experience.* 2d rev. ed. Lincoln: University of Nebraska Press.

Rutzick, Mark C. 1991. "Testimony of Mark C. Rutzick." In U.S. Congress, House, Committee on Agriculture, Subcommittee on Forestry, Family Farms, and Energy, "Ancient Forest Protection Act of 1991; Community Stability Act of 1991; Ancient Forest Act of 1991; and the Forests and Families Protection Act of 1991," 416-429. 102d Cong., 1st sess. Serial 102-33. Washington, DC: Government Printing Office.

Ryan, Kevin. 1986. (Acting refuge manager, Kodiak National Wildlife Refuge, Alaska.) Personal communication, February 3.

Swanson, G. 1969. *Fish and Wildlife Resources on the Public Lands.* 2 vols. Springfield, VA: Clearing House for Scientific and Technical Information.

Tanner, Thomas, ed. 1987. *Aldo Leopold: The Man and His Legacy.* Ankeny, IA: Soil Conservation Society of America.

Taylor, J. Wolfred. 1987. "Aldo Leopold: A Celebration of the Land Ethic." *The Conservationist* 42 (3): 12-15 (November-December).

Thomas, J. W., ch., and E. D. Forsman, J. B. Lint, E. C. Meslow, B. R. Noon, and J. Verner. 1990. "A Conservation Strategy for the Northern Spotted Owl." Report by the Interagency Scientific Committee to Address the Conservation of the Northern Spotted Owl. Portland, OR: U.S. Department of Agriculture, Forest Service; U.S. Department of the Interior, Bureau of Land Management, Fish and Wildlife Service, National Park Service.

Tober, James A. 1981. *Who Owns the Wildlife? The Political Economy of Conservation in Nineteenth-Century America.* Westport, CT: Greenwood Press.

Trefethen, James B. 1975. *An American Crusade for Wildlife.* Piscataway, NJ: Winchester Press.

Stewart L. 1963. *The Quiet Crisis.* Orlando, FL: Holt, Rinehart and Winston.

U.S. Congress. House. Committee on Agriculture. Subcommittee on Forests, Family Farms, and Energy. 1991. "Ancient Forest Protection Act of 1991; Community Stability Act of 1991; Ancient Forest Act of 1991; and the Forests and Families Protection Act of 1991." 102d Cong., 1st sess. Serial 102-33. Washington, DC: Government Printing Office.

U.S. Congress. House. Committee on Interior and Insular Affairs. Subcommittee on National Parks and Public Lands. 1990. "Protection of Ancient Forests and Northern Spotted Owls." 101st Cong., 2d Sess. Serial 101-46. Washington, DC: Government Printing Office.

U.S. Department of Agriculture. Forest Service. 1980. "Draft Environmental Impact Statement, Withdrawal Request under FLPMA Section 204(c) for National Lands in Alaska." Alaska Region Report no. 113. Juneau, AK: U.S. Department of Agriculture, Forest Service.

———. 1984. "Regional Guide for the Pacific Northwest Region." Portland, OR: U.S. Department of Agriculture, Forest Service, Pacific Northwest Region.

———. 1990. "Yeutter and Lujan Announce Five-point Plan to Preserve Owl and Protect Jobs." News Release, June 26, 1990. In U.S. Department of Agriculture, Office of Public Affairs, "Selected Speeches and News Releases June 21-28, 1990," 19-21. Washington, DC: U.S. Department of Agriculture.

———. 1991. "Draft Environmental Impact Statement on Management for the Northern Spotted Owl in the National Forests." Washington, DC: U.S. Department of Agriculture, Forest Service.

U.S. Department of the Interior. U.S. Fish and Wildlife Service. 1977. "Appellate Court Prohibits Tellico Dam Closing; ES Legal Protections Defined." *Endangered Species Technical Bulletin* 2 (2): 1, 2.

———. 1979a. "Committee Exempts Grayrocks; Denies Exemption for Tellico Dam." *Endangered Species Technical Bulletin* 4 (1): 1, 6.

———. 1979b. "Tellico Dam Gets Go-ahead." *Endangered Species Technical Bulletin* 4 (10): 1, 3.

———. 1980. "Habitat Acquisition: Costly but Necessary to the Recovery of Many Endangered Species." *Endangered Species Technical Bulletin* 5 (6): 5-10.

———. 1986a. "ADC Returns to Agriculture." *Fish and Wildlife News* (January-February): 3.

———. 1986b. "Condor Update." *Endangered Species Technical Bulletin* 11 (4): 10.

——— 1986c. "Regional News: Region 6." *Endangered Species Technical Bulletin* 11 (10, 11): 11.

―――. 1987a. "Alligator Reclassified Rangewide." *Endangered Species Technical Bulletin* 12 (7): 1.

―――. 1987b. "Condors." *Endangered Species Technical Bulletin* 12 (5, 6): 3.

―――. 1987c. "Dusky Seaside Sparrow Becomes Extinct." *Endangered Species Technical Bulletin* 12 (5, 6): 1.

―――. 1987d. "Last Condor Captured." *Fish and Wildlife News* (April-May): 7.

―――. 1987e. "Regional News: Region 1." *Endangered Species Technical Bulletin* 12 (1): 2, 3.

―――. 1988a. "First Condor Egg." *Fish and Wildlife News* (March-April): 2.

―――. 1988b. "Regional News." *Endangered Species Technical Bulletin* 13 (9-10): 2.

―――. 1990a. "Box Score: Listings and Recovery Plans." *Endangered Species Technical Bulletin* 15 (2): 8.

―――. 1990b. "Endangered and Threatened Species Recovery Program." Washington, DC: Government Printing Office.

―――. 1990c. "Fish and Wildlife Service Undertakes Review of the Bald Eagle's Status." *Endangered Species Technical Bulletin* 15 (2): 3.

―――. 1991. "Black-footed Ferret Recovery Effort Progresses Toward Introduction." *Endangered Species Technical Bulletin* 16 (1): 1, 3-5.

Walsh, Harry M. 1971. *The Outlaw Gunner.* Centreville, MD: Tidewater Publishers.

Wheeler, William B., and M. J. McDonald. 1986. *TVA and the Tellico Dam.* Knoxville: The University of Tennessee Press.

Wildlife Management Institute. 1992. "Interior Ducks Owl Issue." *Outdoor News Bulletin* 46 (2): 1, 2.

CHAPTER VIII

Wilderness

Although the wilderness concept and philosophy infused many efforts to reserve and dedicate portions of the public domain and to acquire additional lands, legislative recognition of wilderness preservation per se as a legitimate public purpose was slow in coming. In fact, it emerged only after the more utilitarian functions had been institutionalized.

EARLY RUMBLINGS

George Catlin, a "lawyer turned painter who travelled in the upper Missouri River area during the summers of 1829-1832," is credited with some of the first wilderness proposals (Wellman 1987, 51). Contemplating the extinction of the Indian and the bison, he wrote as follows in 1832:

> "Such of nature's works are always worthy of preservation and protection; and the further we become separated...from that pristine wilderness and beauty, the more pleasure does the mind of enlightened man feel in recurring to those scenes, when he can have them preserved for his eyes and his mind to dwell upon....What a splendid contemplation...[that] they might in future be seen...preserved in their pristine beauty and wildness...." (Catlin 1913, 1:292-295, cited in Allin 1982, 14)

Later Henry David Thoreau became the best-known American advocate of wilderness preservation (Allin 1982, 13, 14); in 1892 the Sierra Club was formed (Fox 1981, 106, 107), and it championed the fight for preservation through the writings and life of John Muir; and still later, in 1935, Robert Marshall, Aldo Leopold, and others formed The Wilderness Society to continue the crusade (Fox 1981, 210). Vast areas were reserved as national forests and national parks through the efforts of these and other groups, yet none of these was dedicated to *wilderness*. National

forests came to be managed for timber, range, water, wildlife, and recreation. National parks were dedicated to preservation, true, but "because
visitor use...is a primary purpose for the establishment of Park system
units, and visitor uses are accommodated by physical facilities,...the
Park Service can not and does not practice strict preservation management of all natural resources within the boundaries of a unit of the Park
system" (The Nature Conservancy 1977, 33).

Although the Forest Service later acquired an antiwilderness reputation, Forest Service employees were the first to recognize wilderness values within land management plans. In 1919 Arthur H. Carhart, a landscape architect serving as a recreation engineer, was assigned to locate
homesites and the route for a proposed road through the Trapper's Lake
area of White River National Forest in Colorado. Carhart believed that
development in this area would be inappropriate and so informed his
superior, and the area remained roadless (Allin 1982, 69). Shortly thereafter Carhart met Aldo Leopold, then assistant district forester with the
Forest Service in Albuquerque, New Mexico, who had similar feelings
concerning wilderness. Leopold took wilderness dedication a step further.
In 1921 he published proposed principles for wilderness preservation:

> Some definitions are probably necessary at the outset. By "wilderness" I
> mean a continuous stretch of country preserved in its natural state, open
> to lawful hunting and fishing, big enough to absorb a two weeks' pack
> trip, and kept devoid of roads, artificial trails, cottages, or other works of
> man. Several assumptions can be made at once without argument. First,
> such wilderness areas should occupy only a small part of the total National
> Forest area—probably not to exceed one in each State. Second, only areas
> naturally difficult of ordinary industrial development should be chosen.
> Third, each area should be representative of some type of country of dis-
> tinctive recreational value, or afford some distinctive type of outdoor life,
> opportunity for which might disappear on other forest lands open to
> industrial development.
>
> The argument for such wilderness areas is premised wholly on highest
> recreational use. (Leopold 1921, 719)

These principles may appear somewhat odd in the light of present-day
wilderness policy—but one must remember that Leopold was a resource
manager and a follower of Pinchot:

> At this time Pinchot enunciated the doctrine of "highest use," and its cri-
> terion, "the greatest good to the greatest number," which is and must

remain the principle by which democracies handle their natural resources. (Leopold 1921, 718)

(Note: The statement "In the administration of the forest reserves it must be clearly borne in mind that all land is to be devoted to its most productive use for the permanent good of the whole people...and where conflicting interests must be reconciled the question will always be decided from the standpoint of the greatest good of the greatest number in the long run" appears in a letter from Secretary of Agriculture James Wilson to Gifford Pinchot [a letter that Pinchot wrote] dated February 1, 1905— the date of passage of the Transfer Act.)

In the same paper, Leopold proposed reservation of a wilderness area in Gila National Forest in New Mexico:

> Under the policy advocated in this paper, a good big sample of...[southwestern wilderness] should be preserved. This could easily be done by selecting such an area as the headwaters of the Gila River in the Gila National Forest. This is an area of nearly half a million acres, topographically isolated by mountain ranges and box canyons. It has not yet been penetrated by railroads and to only a very limited extent by roads. On account of the natural obstacles to transportation and the absence of any considerable areas of agricultural land, no net economic loss would result from the policy of withholding further industrial development, except that the timber would remain inaccessible and available only for limited local consumption. The entire area is grazed by cattle, but the cattle ranches would be an asset from the recreational standpoint because of the interest which attaches to cattle ranching under frontier conditions. The apparent disadvantage thus imposed on the cattlemen might be nearly offset by the obvious advantage of freedom from new settlers, and from the hordes of motorists who will invade this region the minute it is opened up. (Leopold 1921, 721)

In the following year (1922), district forester Frank Pooler set aside 574,000 acres in the Gila for wilderness recreation (Allin 1982, 70).

In 1930 Congress passed the Shipstead-Nolan Act, giving legislative recognition to Carhart's recreation plan for Superior National Forest, and at about the same time the Forest Service was developing the first regulations recognizing wilderness as a class of land use (Dana and Fairfax 1980, 133):

> Primitive or wilderness areas are something new in the policy of the U.S. Forest Service. A primitive area, in the language of the foresters, is a tract

of federally-owned land set aside to be kept in as near its natural and primitive condition as is physically and economically possible, in the interests of public education, research, and public recreation. Furthermore, no roads will ever be built into such areas, and only such trails as are necessary for their protection, nor shall any structures ever be built therein other than rude shelters of native or local materials needed for human protection from storms or the elements. (U.S. Department of Agriculture, Forest Service 1931, 31)

Regulation L-20 (1929) attempted to codify this policy, and during the next few years areas in many national forests were designated as "primitive." However, the effect of such a designation was greatly weakened by a directive in the *Forest Service Administrative Manual* that "'establishment of a primitive area ordinarily will not operate to withdraw timber, forage or water resources from industrial use'" (Allin 1982, 74). Regulation L-20 was unclear and inadequate, and many field foresters continued to fight the concept (Dana and Fairfax 1980, 134). But some Forest Service employees joined the other side and became leaders in the wilderness movement; Aldo Leopold was one, and Bob Marshall was another.

A WORD ABOUT MARSHALL

Bob Marshall grew up in New York, the son of a wealthy constitutional lawyer and civil libertarian (Fox 1981, 206)—and came to be the "most effective spokesperson the wilderness movement ever had" (Dana and Fairfax 1980, 155). His boyhood summers were spent in the Saranac Lake region of upstate New York, where "'the hundreds of things which make the woods so superior to the city'" directed him to an out-of-doors career (Fox 1981, 206). He spent fifteen months in the Koyukuk region of north-central Alaska in 1929-1931 and documented his experiences in a best-selling book, *Arctic Village* (Marshall 1933a). His second book, *The People's Forests* (Marshall 1933b), argues for public ownership and management of the nation's forests (Fox 1981, 206, 207). His socialist leanings got him into trouble with the House Un-American Activities Committee, but his older brother, James, maintained that "[h]e was accused of being a Communist, but he never was....[H]e had absorbed some Marxist doctrine, but I don't think he had much political background or judgment. He was emotional in these things, not practical" (Edwards 1985b, 682).

Marshall received forestry degrees from Harvard University and the

New York State College of Forestry and (while on leave from the Forest Service) a Ph.D. in plant physiology from Johns Hopkins University (Fox 1981, 206), yet he neither flaunted his degrees nor basked in his family's wealth (Edwards 1985b, 664, 669). Publication of "The Problem of the Wilderness" in *Scientific Monthly* (Marshall 1930) began his decade-long crusade for wilderness preservation (Allin 1982, 80, 81):

> I shall use the word *wilderness* to denote a region which contains no permanent inhabitants, possesses no possibility of conveyance by any mechanical means and is sufficiently spacious that a person in crossing it must have the experience of sleeping out. The dominant attributes of such an area are: first, that it requires any one who exists in it to depend exclusively on his own effort for survival; and second, that it preserves as nearly as possible the primitive environment.
>
> When Columbus effected his immortal debarkation, he touched upon a wilderness which embraced virtually a hemisphere. The philosophy that progress is proportional to the amount of alteration imposed upon nature never seemed to have occurred to the Indians. (Marshall 1930, 141)

> To-day there remain less than twenty wilderness areas of a million acres, and annually even these shrunken remnants of undefiled continent are being despoiled. (p. 142)

> A thorough study should forthwith be undertaken to determine the probable wilderness needs of the country....Once the estimate is formulated, immediate steps should be taken to establish enough tracts to ensure every one who hungers for it a generous opportunity of enjoying wilderness isolation.
>
> To carry out this program it is exigent that all friends of the wilderness ideal should unite. If they do not present the urgency of their view-point the other side will certainly capture popular support. (p. 148)

Marshall's liberal leanings involved him in numerous civil rights issues. He opposed religious and racial discrimination within the Forest Service and on Forest Service land, fought timber company influence within the service, and engaged in numerous skirmishes with leaders of the forestry profession and Congress:

> Bob Marshall...was one of the most liberal, eloquent, and controversial persons ever to practice forestry. He advocated the nationalization of 80 percent of the country's forests; he led the resistance against conservative tendencies in professional foresters' organizations, especially the Society of American Foresters; he may have been the first high-level official to seri

ously oppose racial and religious discrimination in Forest Service recreation policies; and he was among the first of many citizens to be wrongfully accused of disloyalty by congressional committees that in the end abused the very rights they were supposed to protect. (Glover and Glover 1986, 119)

In 1933 Marshall left the Forest Service to become director of forestry in the Bureau of Indian Affairs (then the Indian Service) in the Department of the Interior. During his five years at that job, he became "wilderness's most formidable advocate" (Edwards 1985b, 682). No longer a part of the Department of Agriculture, he was nevertheless successful in preventing road construction in de facto wilderness areas within the National Forest System—for New Deal road construction funds appropriated to the Public Works Administration were administered by the Department of the Interior, and Marshall was close to its secretary, Harold Ickes (Allin 1982, 81).

In 1934 Marshall delivered a speech before the American Forestry Association in Knoxville, Tennessee—and there began The Wilderness Society. On a field trip, he, Benton MacKaye (then a regional planner with the Tennessee Valley Authority [TVA]), Harvey Broome (lawyer, wilderness enthusiast, and activist in the Great Smoky Mountains Hiking Club), and Bernard Frank (associate forester for the TVA) outlined the principles for a new wilderness movement, and on October 19 they enrolled the four other founders of the society—Harold Anderson, Aldo Leopold, Ernest Oberholtzer, and Robert Sterling Yard (Frome 1974, 123). The Wilderness Society "was officially launched in January, 1935" (Fox 1981, 210). Goals of the new organization were "'to secure the preservation of wilderness, conduct educational programs concerning the value of wilderness, encourage scientific studies, and mobilize cooperation in resisting the invasion of wilderness'" (Frome 1974, 123). In the struggle for congressional recognition of wilderness areas that was to follow, The Wilderness Society and the Sierra Club would lead the way.

During his tenure with the Indian Service, Marshall established sixteen wilderness areas on Indian reservations (Fox 1981, 209), and he continued to bring pressure to bear on the Forest Service to protect more wilderness within that system. While these activities might well have aroused the ire of some Forest Service field personnel, Marshall retained the friendship and respect of Chief Forester F. A. Silcox, and in 1937 he was offered an opportunity to return to his old agency as chief of the Recreation and Lands Division (Allin 1982, 82). During his two years in this position, Marshall achieved passage of the "U-regulations" (Frome 1974, 125) and restricted road building and development on 14 million acres of national forest land (Fox 1981, 209).

Despite his knowledge of a congenital heart defect, Marshall led a strenuous life. He detested being shut in and delighted in long hikes through the wilderness. On more than two hundred occasions, he hiked more than 30 miles in one day, and he once walked 70 miles in a thirty-four-hour period (Fox 1981, 209).

On November 10, 1939, two months after enactment of the U-regulations, Marshall was found dead in a compartment aboard a train bound from Washington to New York. He was thirty-eight years old. From his $1.5 million estate (before taxes) one-fourth went to promote wilderness—mostly through The Wilderness Society—and the remainder was used to foster civil liberties and to further his philosophy of "production for use, not for profit" (Edwards 1985b, 689).

In the year after his death, the Forest Service named nearly a million acres of land within the Lewis and Clark and Flathead national forests in Montana the Bob Marshall Wilderness (Frome 1974, 126)—a fitting tribute to the short, tempestuous, and productive life of this wilderness crusader. Subsequently the contiguous Great Bear and Scapegoat wilderness areas were created under the provisions of the 1964 Wilderness Act, enlarging the Bob Marshall Wilderness to 1.5 million acres. Congress may add another one-half million acres, but the proposed additional lands, which may contain oil and gas reserves, are coveted by energy companies and speculators—so the fight goes on (Edwards 1985a, 690, 691).

TOWARD A NATIONAL WILDERNESS SYSTEM

The U-regulations were clearer and more restrictive than the L-regulations that they replaced. They (1) established three categories of roadless area—wilderness, wild, and recreation; (2) defined "wilderness" areas as tracts of not less than 100,000 acres in which roads, timber harvesting, motorized transportation, and occupancy would be prohibited (subject to existing rights); (3) designated similar areas of between 5,000 and 100,000 acres as "wild," to be treated in the same way as wilderness; and (4) prescribed that "recreation" areas be kept "substantially in their natural condition" (Dana and Fairfax 1980, 157).

Despite the new regulations and continued agitation by wilderness advocates, little progress occurred during the 1940s and early 1950s—other national concerns took priority. Then, in 1954, James P. Gilligan delivered a speech before the Society of American Foresters that got the ball rolling again. Gilligan's doctoral dissertation analyzed wilderness preservation during the early 1950s, and his findings were alarming:

The preservation of a system of large, unique wilderness regions in this country does not seem to fit into the shifting tides of emotion and economic change so characteristic of our changing democracy....Certainly the laws and administrative regulations governing the National Park Service and the Forest Service, which are necessary to prevent encroachment on wilderness conditions, give every sign of being inadequate.

Those interested in national forest wilderness preservation are easily lulled into complacency by the soothing and oft quoted figures of 13,000,000 acres of land reserved in 77 wilderness, wild, and primitive areas throughout the West. If we examine more closely the conditions in only 28 of the areas over 100,000 acres in size (comprising about 11,000,000 acres),...there are nearly 200 miles of road open to public travel in 9 of the so-called wilderness or primitive areas. There are about 145,000 acres of privately owned timber, agriculture, summer home, resort, and mineral lands inside 15 of the areas, in addition to 400-500 mining claims of unknown acreage within 20 areas....About 60 of the mining claims and patents are being worked [and]...some units are being explored for possible oil leasing....There are 24 air landing strips in 6 areas, 17 of which are under Forest Service jurisdiction....There are roughly...140,000 sheep and 25,000 cattle grazing seasonally within all but two of the larger units classified as wilderness or primitive areas. Grazing, without question, has drastically altered natural conditions in many areas....Timbered zones within wilderness areas that now can be logged are being removed from wilderness classification as rapidly as possible. Over 2,000,000 wilderness acres are now considered to be commercial timberland....Nearly 90 dams and water control structures have been built...[and] the Bureau of Reclamation has proposed large dams affecting 16 wilderness areas.

National Parks, too, often must justify their existence to the locality or state in which they are situated principally on economic grounds. As long as the drums throb for more tourist dollars, park administrators will find it hard to accommodate the increasing army of sightseers without extending development....[The National Park Service] is subject to the unrelenting pressures of mass use, and retreats gradually behind the cold logic that more areas must be developed to care properly for the public to whom the land belongs.

There is every indication that the wilderness areas of the future will consist of a series of small land units devoid of economic potentials. If attractive, these delicate natural zones will be swarming with outdoor enthusiasts trying to convince themselves that they are enjoying original conditions....Those who understand the problems of wilderness preservation on federal lands are convinced that Congressional action is necessary to retain wilderness areas for future generations. (Gilligan 1955, 119-122)

Gilligan's speech was published in *The Living Wilderness* (Spring-Summer 1955) and in the *Congressional Record* (102 CONG. REC. 12,314 (July 11, 1956)) (Allin 1982, 136). The interest it aroused, coupled with the increased use of and competition for national forest land that developed after World War II, brought wilderness before Congress.

The first proposal to include the wilderness concept in federal legislation was made in an amendment to the Multiple-Use Sustained Yield Act of 1960. Wilderness advocates, led primarily by Howard Zahniser, then executive secretary of the Sierra Club, attempted to get wilderness recognized as a "use" of national forest land, on par with timber, wildlife, outdoor recreation, water, and grazing. While they failed in this attempt, they were successful in inserting into the amendment the statement "The establishment and maintenance of areas of wilderness are consistent with the purposes and provisions of the Act" (Le Master 1984, 6).

The first national "wilderness bill" was written largely by Howard Zahniser (Frome 1974, 139), with assistance from the Citizens Committee on Natural Resources and the Council of Conservationists and with the cooperation of The Wilderness Society, the National Wildlife Federation, Trustees for Conservation, the National Parks Association, the Wildlife Management Institute, and others (Allin 1982, 105). It was based on Zahniser's speeches before the Second Biennial Wilderness Conference (San Francisco, 1951) (Frome 1974, 138) and the National Citizen's Planning Conference on Parks and Open Spaces for the American People. The latter speech caught the attention of Senator Hubert Humphrey of Minnesota, who had it reprinted in the *Congressional Record* (101 CONG. REC. A3809-A3812 (June 1, 1955)) (Allin 1982, 104, 105). A year later, on June 7, 1956, Humphrey introduced S. 4013—the first of four Humphrey wilderness bills.

As described by Craig Allin,

[the bill] was a strong preservationist document. It would create a national wilderness preservation system consisting of reasonably untouched areas of federal land in national forests, national parks, national monuments, wildlife refuges, and Indian reservations. Within these areas, all commercial enterprise would be banned including farming, logging, the grazing of domestic livestock, mining, and mineral prospecting. The building of roads or other structures would also be banned. The use of motorized vehicles would be forbidden except as necessary for the administration of the areas.

Some nonconforming uses were to be allowed to continue, however, where they were already well established. In this fashion, some toleration was granted to the use of motorboats and airplanes and to livestock grazing. An earlier draft had made some exceptions for mineral prospecting as well, but these had been deleted at the suggestion of the Izaak Walton League. (Allin 1982, 106)

Eighty areas in the national forests, forty-eight in national parks and national monuments, twenty in national wildlife refuges, and fifteen on Indian reservations were to constitute the initial system, and others could be added by executive order or by designation by the secretary of agriculture or the interior. Only Congress could remove areas from the system (Frome 1974, 138, 139).

S. 4013 began nine years of heated congressional debate. Understandably, the conservation groups mentioned earlier were staunch supporters, while the forest products industry and oil, grazing, and mining interests were opposed. So, too, were many career professionals in the National Park Service and the Forest Service (Frome 1974, 139). As stated by Richard E. McArdle, chief of the Forest Service, in testimony before the Senate Committee on Interior and Insular Affairs:

> [This bill] would give a degree of congressional protection to wilderness use of national forests not enjoyed by any other use. It would tend to hamper free and effective application of administrative judgment which now determines, and should continue to determine, the use, or combination of uses, to which a particular national-forest area is put. (U.S. Congress, Senate 1957, 93)

McArdle's letter succinctly stated the feelings of many trained natural resource managers who felt that natural resource decisions are best made by professionals (and should be made only by professionals) and that neither the public nor its elected officials should interfere.

Despite these objections, however, the time had come, and the wilderness bill passed the Senate by a vote of 73 to 12 on April 10, 1963, and the House (with one negative vote) on July 30, 1964. The two versions differed in one respect—a special dispensation to permit mining exploration in wilderness—which was compromised in conference committee in favor of the mining interests. On September 3, 1964, President Lyndon Johnson signed the Wilderness Act of 1964, creating our National Wilderness Preservation System. By then Leopold, Marshall, and Zahniser were all dead (Frome 1974, 140)—but their legacy lives on.

THE ACT AND THE SYSTEM

In order to assure that as increasing population, accompanied by expanding settlement and growing mechanization, does not occupy and modify, all areas within the United States and its possessions, leaving no lands designated for preservation and protection of their natural condition, it is hereby declared to be the policy of the Congress to secure for the American people of present and future generations the benefits of an enduring resource of wilderness. For this purpose there is hereby established a National Wilderness Preservation System to be composed of federally owned areas designated by Congress as "wilderness areas," and these shall be administered for the use and enjoyment of the American people in such manner as will leave them unimpaired for future use and enjoyment as wilderness, and so as to provide for the protection of these areas, the preservation of their wilderness character, and for the gathering and dissemination of information regarding their use and enjoyment as wilderness....A wilderness, in contrast with those areas where man and his own works dominate the landscape, is hereby recognized as an area where the earth and its community of life are untrammeled by man, where man himself is a visitor who does not remain...undeveloped Federal land retaining its primeval character and influence, without permanent improvements or human habitation, which is protected and managed so as to preserve its natural conditions and which (1) generally appears to have been affected primarily by the forces of nature, with the imprint of man's hand substantially unnoticeable; (2) has outstanding opportunities for solitude or a primitive and unconfined type of recreation; (3) has at least five thousand acres of land or is of sufficient size as to make practicable its preservation and use in an unimpaired condition; and (4) may also contain ecological, geological, or other features of scientific, educational, scenic, or historical value. (78 Stat. 890, 891)

All national forest areas previously classified as "wilderness" (eighteen, covering 6,898,014 acres), "wild" (thirty-five, covering 1,355,034 acres), and "canoe" (the 886,673-acre Boundary Waters Canoe Area in Minnesota) were included in the new system (about 9.1 million acres in all). The secretary of agriculture was directed to review all "primitive" areas (5,477,740 acres) within ten years to determine whether they should be included (Frome 1974, 145), and the secretary of the interior was to do likewise with roadless areas of 5,000 contiguous acres or more within his jurisdiction. Recommendations for wilderness designation were to return to Congress via the president, and areas could be added to the system only by act of Congress (78 Stat. 891, 892) (although it is unstated in the act, Congress also has the constitutional authority to remove units from the system, and even from federal ownership, if it so desires).

The act created no new bureaucracy to administer the system, leaving units within the agencies with which they were previously associated and appropriated no additional funds for their administration (78 Stat. 890).

In order to obtain passage of the act, wilderness advocates made several concessions. Prospecting and mineral leasing were permitted until December 31, 1983, and existing mining rights were recognized—including the right to remove and use mature timber "if the timber is not otherwise reasonably available." Within wilderness areas designated in national forests, water resource developments, power projects, transmission lines, and ancillary road construction and maintenance were allowed—a major intrusion into the wilderness concept—and preexisting grazing rights were recognized—remember Leopold's concept? In all cases development and use rights were to be exercised "subject to...restrictions" or "in accordance with such regulations as...may seem desirable," and the act clearly intended that these be sufficient to retain, as much as possible, the wilderness character of the land (78 Stat. 894, 895).

With nine years of congressional debate and hundreds of pages of rhetoric, one might think that the act would produce significant changes in federal land management. Yet it did not—at least in its early years. National park lands and national wildlife refuges were not managed for consumptive uses. Areas designated within national forests were already managed as wilderness (Dana and Fairfax 1980, 221), and relatively few of these contained recoverable mineral reserves or merchantable timber resources. Additional controversy erupted when new areas were proposed and when wilderness invaded the East.

TOWARD A BIGGER AND BETTER SYSTEM

As directed by the Wilderness Act, the Forest Service began reviewing its "primitive areas," holding hearings and conducting field studies. In general the work progressed on schedule and without major controversy *as long as it pertained to previously designated areas*. When new or enlarged primitive areas were proposed, controversy ensued (Frome 1974, 153; Frome 1984, 185). During the same period, the Forest Service was attempting to implement the fairly new Multiple-Use Sustained Yield Act of 1960 (placing recreation, range, wildlife, and water supplies on par with timber production), was engaged in congressional debate over a proindustry "Timber Supply Act" (which subsequently failed) (Dana and

Fairfax 1980, 324), was fighting to manage timber on de facto wilderness areas contiguous with primitive areas in Idaho and Colorado (and lost on both counts) (Allin 1982, 152-155), and began logging in the proposed Alpine Lakes Wilderness Area of the Pacific Northwest over the strong protestations of citizens' groups (Frome 1974, 153-156). It was indeed an exciting time for Forest Service personnel. They were beset on all sides by diverse interests demanding recognition and a share of the resource. Their technical competence as resource managers was being challenged by persons with no forestry training. Statutory requirements were increasing and becoming more complicated. The good old days were vanishing, and they did not like it.

On April 16, 1971, the Council on Environmental Quality (CEQ) in the Executive Office of the President attempted to intervene. The council was in its second year. The environmental movement was strong. President Nixon's power and awareness of environmental issues were at their height. Environmental groups were outraged by the Forest Service's apparent attempts to accelerate logging and road building in potential wilderness areas (thereby disqualifying them for wilderness designation), and officials in the Forest Service and their traditional allies in timber-using industries were lobbying for increased production from the forests. The CEQ drafted an executive order directing "the Forest Service to identify by December 3, 1972, all areas in the national forests 'that appear to have the character of wilderness as defined in Section 2(c) of the [Wilderness Act].'" The order required evaluation of "almost all of the 56 million acres of unroaded areas in the national forests, and...protect[ed] each...until the President and Congress could 'determine its suitability for designation as a wilderness area.'" Industry and agency opponents were too strong, however, and the executive order was never signed (Shepherd 1975, 249-251), but it contributed to the pressure that forced the Forest Service into RARE I—the first roadless area review and evaluation.

Whatever its motives in initiating RARE I, the Forest Service pursued it with extreme vigor, completing its evaluation of all roadless areas greater than 5,000 acres, holding hearings, and completing its report in ten months (from August 11, 1971, to June 30, 1972). It was a stupendous task—inventorying, evaluating, and making management recommendations on 56 million acres of remote, inaccessible, and often snow-covered land in less than a year. The task was poorly and precipitously executed; numerous duplications and omissions existed. Public reaction was intense—over 8,000 letters were generated. Timber and preservation interests became intensely and bitterly polarized, and court action followed, requiring maintenance of all de facto wilderness areas in wilderness condition (Shepherd 1975, 252-258).

To prevent logging and other activities in roadless areas, which would disqualify them for future wilderness designation, the Sierra Club filed suit against the Forest Service in the U.S. district court in San Francisco (*Sierra Club v. Butz*) but settled out of court when the Forest Service agreed to prepare environmental impact statements prior to permitting road building, logging, or other development in roadless areas (Stewart 1985, 5)—effectively removing all 56 million acres of RARE I lands from Forest Service management. And as if the service did not already have enough problems, it was hit by requirements of the National Environmental Policy Act (NEPA) in 1970, the Forest and Rangeland Renewable Resources Planning Act (RPA) in 1974, the Eastern Wilderness Act in 1975, and the National Forest Management Act (NFMA) in 1976. The Eastern Wilderness Act designated sixteen additional wilderness areas in the East (only three—Linville Gorge and Shining Rock in North Carolina and Great Gulf in New Hampshire—existed prior to the 1964 act [Frome 1984, 187]). It directed the secretary of agriculture to "review, as to its suitability or nonsuitability for preservation as wilderness[,]" seventeen additional areas and made it clear that "wilderness areas designated by...this Act shall be managed...in accordance with the provisions of the Wilderness Act [of 1964]." Wilderness study areas were to be managed "so as to maintain their presently existing wilderness character and potential for inclusion in the National Wilderness Preservation System" (88 Stat. 2100). No new definition of wilderness was provided, but inclusion of areas as small as 2,570 acres (Gee Creek Wilderness in Cherokee National Forest, Tennessee) and those that had been previously cut, farmed, abandoned, and reforested in second growth obviously weakened the more pristine concept of the 1964 act.

RARE II—AND BEYOND

Left with the shambles of RARE I, the Forest Service began anew in June 1977 and completed RARE II in May 1979. RARE II was designed to "somehow bring the whole National Forest System wilderness designation process to a timely resolution, using a planned and, insofar as it can be, controlled process" (address of M. Rupert Cutler, assistant secretary of agriculture for natural resources and environment, to the October 1977 national meeting of the Society of American Foresters, cited in Task Force on Rare II Legislation 1981, 5). Competing interests watched (and participated) in the RARE II process with a mixture of hope and concern. Commodity groups hoped that the process would find ways around the legal and political obstacles blocking use of de facto wilderness areas yet feared that the Carter administration would give in to pressure from the preservation lobby (Allin 1982, 162). Carter (Frome 1984, 188) had called the Wilderness Act a "landmark of American conservation policy" and had urged expansion of the system "before the most deserving of federal lands are opened to other uses and lost to wilderness forever." Preservationists, on the other hand, hoped that the commodity interests' worst fears would be realized but were concerned that lands not designated would permanently be lost to preservation. By all sides RARE II was considered the last chance to settle the question, How much wilderness on national forest lands? (Allin 1982, 162, 163). The Forest Service encouraged public participation, perhaps too much so: "To a great extent, RARE II owes its troubles to one fact glaringly obvious to many observers—it is largely a political exercise masquerading as a professional study" (Popovich 1978, 370). It involved 47,000 people in 227 workshops (Popovich 1978, 371) and generated tens of thousands of letters representing widely divergent points of view.

Of the 62 million acres considered in RARE II, 15.4 million (25 percent) were recommended for wilderness designation; 10.6 million (17 percent), for further planning; and 36 million (58 percent), for continued multiple-use management. The proposals would increase wilderness on national forest lands to 33.8 million acres (Task Force on RARE II Legislation 1981, 5). (Note: During deliberations on the 1964 act, Senator Frank Church and Congressman John P. Saylor had assured wilderness opponents that no more than 15 million acres of national forest land would be designated [Task Force on RARE II Legislation 1981, 4]. The 1975 RPA program stated a wilderness goal of 25-30 million acres [Day 1980b, 6].) Outside of Alaska the administration proposed adding fewer than 10 million acres to the wilderness system while releasing almost 29 million for multiple-use management—hardly a victory for the preservation community (Allin 1982, 163). (Note: The CEQ staff had sought to expand USDA wilderness recommendations by about 2 million acres, but the Carter administration's final position, stated earlier in this paragraph, was only about 200,000 acres more than the USDA had proposed [R. Smythe, personal communication].)

Litigation was not long in coming. In July of the same year (Allin

1982, 164), the state of California filed suit in the U.S. District Court for the District of Eastern California (*California v. Bergland*), challenging the adequacy of the Forest Service's programmatic environmental impact statement as it related to California areas not recommended for wilderness designation (Bean 1983, 168). On January 8, 1980, Judge Lawrence K. Karlton rendered his decision:

> [T]he environmental impact statement (EIS) supporting RARE II did not satisfy the requirements of the National Environmental Policy Act (NEPA)....[T]he Forest Service [was enjoined from] developing any of the 47 disputed nonwilderness areas in California, pending a proper consideration of wilderness values in compliance with NEPA....[P]rimary deficiencies...included:
>
> • Lack of site-specific data on RARE II areas;
> • Inadequate discussion of the wilderness values that would be foregone [should "nonwilderness" areas be developed];
> • Inadequate alternatives without an explanation of the range considered; and,
> • A flawed method of disclosure and public participation. (Day 1980a, 190)

Judge Karlton's decision presented the Forest Service with several alternatives, none of which was very pleasant. It could (1) appeal to the U.S. Court of Appeals for the Ninth Circuit, but the appeal probably would not be heard for two or three years, during which time the district court's decision would be binding, and prospects for reversal were not good; (2) seek a legislative remedy, but going to Congress is always dangerous, and the service might get much more than it bargained for; (3) comply with the court's order and face the tedious job of site-by-site analysis and several more years of work; or (4) abandon the national approach to wilderness studies and admit that RARE II was not working either (Day 1980a, 191).

The Forest Service chose the first alternative, and in 1982, in *California v. Block*, the U.S. Court of Appeals for the Ninth Circuit affirmed the findings of the district court:

> 1) the RARE II EIS failed to consider an adequate range of wilderness designation; 2) the EIS did not adequately examine the site-specific impacts of the allocations proposed; 3) the Forest Service did not provide sufficient opportunity for public comment on proposals for specific allocations,

when proposals had been changed substantially from those appearing in the draft EIS; and 4) the Forest Service did not adequately respond to public comments regarding individual areas. (*California v. Block*, cited in Council on Environmental Quality 1982, 242)

Although subsequent executive branch rule making and congressional action circumvented the precedential effect of the *California v. Block* decision, the foregoing enumerated items remain among the most important that should be accommodated in any environmental assessment process.

Even before the circuit court's decision, the arena had shifted to Congress. Neither side wanted a drawn-out legal battle, and the ultimate solution rested with the lawmakers. After considerable jockeying for position, compromise language was incorporated into the omnibus California wilderness bill, which served as a model for subsequent state-by-state and area-by-area consideration. The compromise provisions did not require that nondesignated lands be managed to preserve their wilderness attributes, nor did they require the Forest Service to manage them for nonwilderness uses (Allin 1982, 164, 165).

Based on RARE II recommendations, Congress passed laws adding national forest land to the National Wilderness Preservation System on a state-by-state basis. During 1980 wilderness on national forest land within the contiguous forty-eight states grew by 4.4 million acres. During the same year, the Alaska National Interest Lands Conservation Act added an additional 5.3 million acres, bringing the total to 25.4 million acres, and another 8 million could have been designated before the allocation process ended (Allin 1982, 267)—virtually the same amount as recommended in RARE II and more than twice the amount in the Church-Saylor assurances in 1964.

Yet despite all the furor, the rhetoric, the litigation, and the legislation, the impact upon the National Forest System would be minimal. If Allin's estimate is correct, between 17 and 18 percent of the system will be wilderness. Logging will be prohibited, but grazing and mineral exploration may be permitted in many of the areas. Outdoor recreational opportunities will be provided, wildlife habitat preserved, and watersheds protected. The only real "loss" from the array of multiple uses cited in the Multiple-Use Sustained Yield Act of 1960 is timber. Even this is not really a "loss," for these areas have remained "untrammeled by man" simply because it was uneconomic to do so. Sixty years ago Bob Marshall remarked:

Economic loss could be greatly reduced by reserving inaccessible and unproductive terrain. Inasmuch as most of the highly valuable lands have already been exploited, it should be easy to confine a great share of the wilderness tract to those lofty mountain regions where the possibility of material profit is unimportant. (Marshall 1930, 146)

So our wilderness areas in the national forests were and are the picturesque, the inaccessible, the unproductive, and the unwanted, and (given the current condition of the timber industry) many probably would have remained so for some time to come without a formal "wilderness" designation. The concept of wilderness has changed dramatically through time and will undoubtedly continue to do so. Even during a given period of time, different groups have far different perceptions of wilderness. And if at some future time the nation's need for timber increases—what Congress can do, Congress can undo.

WILDERNESS IN OTHER AGENCIES

Most of the controversy surrounding wilderness designation has been directed toward national forest land, for there existed the greatest apparent difference between past agency management (particularly logging) and the general public's concept of wilderness. But Congress can designate any "area of undeveloped Federal land retaining its primeval character and influence" as part of the National Wilderness Preservation System (78 Stat. 891), and national parks were specifically mentioned in the act (78 Stat. 892).

The Wilderness Act directed the secretary of the interior to "review every roadless area of five thousand contiguous acres or more in the...national park system and every such area of...the national wildlife refuges and game ranges...[and to] report to the President his recommendation as to the suitability or nonsuitability of each such area...for preservation as wilderness" by September 1984 (78 Stat. 892). Despite the apparent opportunity within the National Park System, only 3 million acres (about 4 percent of the system) were recommended and designated—and less than a million acres within the National Wildlife Refuge System (Task Force on RARE II Legislation 1981, 7). It remained for the Alaska National Interest Lands Conservation Act (ANILCA) to make the National Park Service the major custodian of wilderness. This act added 32.4 million acres of national park wilderness (all in Alaska), bringing the total to over 35 million acres (48 percent of the National

TABLE 8.1
The National Wilderness Preservation System, 1964-1990

Year	TOTAL SYSTEM, 1964-1990 Number of Areas	Acres (Millions)
1964	54	9.14
1980	257	79.83
1982	258	79.84
1983	276	80.5
1984	458	88.54
1988	463	88.9
1990	487	91.49

Agency	AREAS BY AGENCY, 1990 Number of Areas	Acres (Millions)
Department of Agriculture		
Forest Service	367	33.19
Department of the Interior		
National Park Service	43	38.50
U.S. Fish and Wildlife Service	66	19.33
Bureau of Land Management	25	0.47
Total	501[a]	91.49

Source: Council on Environmental Quality, *Environmental Quality—1984* (Washington, DC: Government Printing Office, 1984), p. 649; Gayle Backman Love, The Wilderness Society, telephone conversation with author, June 25, 1990.
[a]Fourteen areas are managed by more than one agency.

Park System). When the dedication process is complete, up to 70 percent of all national park lands (more than 50 million acres) may be in the system (Allin 1982, 270). After long and bitter debate over that unanswerable question How much wilderness?, ANILCA also created 19 million acres of Alaskan wilderness lands within the National Wildlife Refuge System (Allin 1982, 270).

Bureau of Land Management lands were not mentioned in the Wilderness Act, but Congress corrected that oversight in section 603 of the Federal Land Policy and Management Act of 1976 (FLPMA). This section requires the secretary of the interior to review "roadless areas of five thousand acres or more and roadless islands of the public lands...and from time to time report to the President his recommendation as to the suitability or nonsuitability of each such area or island for preservation as wilderness" (90 Stat. 2785). The secretary had fifteen years to complete this review (until October 1991); was required to report recommendations concerning areas previously identified as natural or primitive by July 1, 1980; and must manage "such lands...in a manner so as not to impair the suitability of such areas for reservation as wilderness." This last admonition is conditioned by the proviso "subject, however, to the continuation of existing mining and grazing leases and mineral leasing in the manner and degree in which the same [were] being conducted on the date of approval of this Act: Provided, That...the Secretary shall by regulation or otherwise take any action required to prevent unnecessary or undue degradation of the lands and their resources or to afford environmental protection" (90 Stat. 2785)—figure that one out! BLM has developed policy and guidelines for wilderness management and identified approximately 24 million acres in 758 wilderness study areas. How much of this area is to become designated remains to be seen—less than 100,000 acres had been designated by the summer of 1984 (Harmon 1984). Craig Allin (1982, 271) estimates that "from 10 to 20 million acres of present BLM wilderness study areas will eventually find their way into the National Wilderness Preservation System." If so the BLM will become an important—but definitely junior—partner in the system.

By 1990 the National Wilderness Preservation System had grown to over 90 million acres. The National Park System contained the most total acreage (almost 90 percent of which is in Alaska), but the national forests had nine times as many designated areas (table 8.1). The system probably is approaching its final size. Attention should now shift from designation to management, with primary emphasis on protecting designated areas from overuse by recreationists.

REFERENCES

Allin, Craig W. 1982. *The Politics of Wilderness Preservation.* Westport, CT: Greenwood Press.

Bean, Michael J. 1983. *The Evolution of National Wildlife Law.* New York: Praeger Publishers.

Catlin, George. 1913. *North American Indians.* 2 vols. Philadelphia: Leary, Stewart, and Company.

Council on Environmental Quality. 1982. *Environmental Quality—1982.* Washington, DC: Government Printing Office.

———. 1984. *Environmental Quality—1984.* Washington, DC: Government Printing Office.

Dana, Samuel T., and Sally K. Fairfax. 1980. *Forest and Range Policy: Its Development in the United States.* New York: McGraw-Hill Book Company.

Day, Robert D., Jr. 1980a. "California v. Bergland." *Journal of Forestry* 78:190-191.

————. 1980b. "The Wilderness System: Legacy of Uncertainty." *Journal of Forestry* 78:6.

Edwards, Mike. 1985a. "Battle for a Bigger Bob." *National Geographic* 167 (5): 690-692.

————. 1985b. "A Short Hike with Bob Marshall." *National Geographic* 167 (5): 664-689.

Fox, Stephen. 1981. *John Muir and His Legacy*. Boston: Little, Brown and Company.

Frome, Michael. 1974. *Battle for the Wilderness*. New York: Praeger Publishers.

————. 1984. *The Forest Service*. Boulder, CO: Westview Press.

Gilligan, James P. 1955. "The Contradiction of Wilderness Preservation in a Democracy." In *Proceedings, Society of American Foresters Meeting*. Bethesda, MD: Society of American Foresters, 119-122.

Glover, James M., and Regina B. Glover. 1986. "Robert Marshall: Portrait of a Liberal Forester." *Journal of Forest History* 30 (3): 112-119.

Harmon, David W. 1984. "Wilderness and the Bureau of Land Management: An Update." *Journal of Forestry* 82:684.

Le Master, Dennis C. 1984. *Decade of Change: The Remaking of Forest Service Statutory Authority During the 1970s*. Westport, CT: Greenwood Press.

Leopold, Aldo. 1921. "The Wilderness and Its Place in Forest Recreational Policy." *Journal of Forestry* 29:718-721.

Marshall, Robert. 1930. "The Problem of the Wilderness." *Scientific Monthly* 30:141-148.

————. 1933a. *Arctic Village*. New York: Literary Guild.

————. 1933b. *The People's Forests*. New York: H. Smith and R. Haas.

The Nature Conservancy. 1977. *Preserving Our Natural Heritage*. Vol. 1, *Federal Activities*. Washington, DC: Government Printing Office.

Pinchot, Gifford. 1947. *Breaking New Ground*. Seattle: University of Washington Press.

Popovich, Luke. 1978. "A Summer Rerun: The *Deja Vu* of RARE II." *Journal of Forestry* 76:370-373.

Shepherd, Jack. 1975. *The Forest Killers*. New York: Weybright and Talley.

Stewart, Alva W. 1985. *Wilderness Protection: A Bibliographic Review*. Monticello, IL: Vance Bibliographies.

Task Force on RARE II Legislation. 1981. "Wilderness Allocation in the Context of RARE II." *Journal of Forestry* 79: 8 pages following p. 298.

U.S. Congress. Senate. Committee on Interior and Insular Affairs. 1957. "National Wilderness Preservation Act." Hearings on S. 1176. 85th Cong., 1st sess., June 19-20, 1957. Washington, DC: Government Printing Office.

U.S. Department of Agriculture. Forest Service. 1931. Untitled statement. *Journal of Forestry* 29 (1): 31.

Wellman, J. Douglas. 1987. *Wildland Recreation Policy*. New York: John Wiley & Sons.

CHAPTER IX

Soil Conservation

Two rather unrelated events coincided during the mid-1930s: (1) drought and misguided agricultural practices created clouds of dust that enveloped the eastern half of the United States and extended far out into the Atlantic and (2) the nation's economy was hit by the highest level of unemployment in its history. The Dust Bowl and the Great Depression teamed up to catalyze government action, but it was the need to provide employment through a federal public works program that was the greatest incentive (Morgan 1965, 1, 2). These elements might not have been sufficient to launch an effective federal soil conservation effort had a third not been present, however. That third essential element—effective leadership—was supplied by Hugh Hammond Bennett.

BENNETT'S CRUSADE

The U.S. Department of Agriculture (USDA) began conducting soils research at agricultural experiment stations as early as 1894. Through the Cooperative Agricultural Extension Service, established by the Smith-Lever Act, the USDA had fostered the transfer of knowledge and technology to the agricultural community since 1914. No USDA program then provided soil conservation assistance directly to the farmers (Morgan 1965, 2), but within its Bureau of Chemistry and Soils was the man who was to become known as the "father of soil conservation" in America (Brink 1951).

Hugh Hammond Bennett's "Soil Erosion: A National Menace" (Bennett 1928) launched a personal crusade to publicize the extent and significance of "accelerated" erosion on cultivated land. Within the bureau he directed a research program to "(1) measure the rates of soil and water losses, (2)...determine the extent and location of damage by erosion, and (3) develop methods for controlling erosion" using research stations in nine states (Brink 1951, 78). Bennett's treatise, *Soil Conservation* (Bennett 1939), remains a classic documentation of the worldwide effects of soil erosion and an encyclopedia of remedial measures. He was a practical scientist, an evangelist, a shrewd politician, a dedicated public servant, and, perhaps more than anything else, a man with a mission and the drive to fulfill it.

The money and clout to promote Bennett's ideas were not within the Bureau of Chemistry and Soils, however. They were in the New Deal agencies that President Roosevelt had developed to combat the depression. One such agency, the Federal Emergency Administration of Public Works (PWA), was directed by Secretary of the Interior Harold Ickes, assisted by a Special Board for Public Works on which sat Bennett's superior, Assistant Secretary of Agriculture Rexford Tugwell. As frequently happens in matters of great significance, exact details, motives, and maneuvers are not clear, but on September 19, 1933, Hugh Bennett found himself in charge of the "first erosion control agency ever set up by an important nation in all history" (Brink 1951, 84). In this capacity he began directing a $5 million program *within the Department of the Interior.* Perhaps Bennett's appointment was an effort by Tugwell to "avoid the endless strife among bureaus of the Department of Agriculture" (Morgan 1965, 11), to circumvent the land-terracing fixation prevalent among engineers within Agriculture (with which Bennett did not agree), or to return a favor (Brink 1951, 83, 84). Perhaps it was the beginning of Ickes's plan to expand the Department of the Interior into a department of conservation (Morgan 1965, 10). Whatever the reasons, Bennett had the opportunity he wanted, and he made the most of it. In his two years as director of the U.S. Soil Erosion Service, he (1) recruited a large technical staff from colleges, universities, and experiment stations; the Cooperative Agricultural Extension Service; and agricultural industries (Brink 1951, 85, 86); (2) developed an approach for demonstrating erosion control measures; and (3) spent some $12 million (Hardin 1952, 55).

In November 1934 Bennett presented a report to the National Resources Board in which he outlined his proposal for a long-term national approach to the soil erosion problem:

(1) To coordinate action and to supply proper technical direction, the United States should maintain a single agency "charged with the responsibility for directing and coordinating erosion work generally, whether on Federal, state or private lands. Such an organization

would also coordinate and give general supervision to the erosion work of other federal agencies."

(2) A "fairly detailed survey" should be made to determine the needs for control.

(3) Legislation should be enacted authorizing the federal agency charged with erosion work to carry out necessary work on state and private lands "on a cost-sharing federal aid basis" with states providing adequate "contributions, cooperation, regulation and agreements controlling the use of the land." The federal government's share of the cost should be in proportion to the federal benefit contributed.

(4) Federal appropriations should be made for work on the Indian reservations.

(5) Federal, state, and local governments should acquire badly eroded lands unsuited to continuing safe agricultural use and convert them into forest or grazing preserves.

(6) Federal legislation should withhold federal loans and other types of credit from new agricultural developments on submarginal lands, including those subject to destructive erosion; farmers who cooperated with erosion control measures under the federal program should receive *"definite advantages and preferences."* . . .

(7) Through various procedures, especially "selective extension of Federal aid" for control of erosion, states should be encouraged to pass legislation authorizing: (a) cooperation with the federal government in erosion control; (b) the "organization of conservancy districts or similar legal sub-divisions with authority to carry out measures of erosion control; and (c) the establishment of state or local land-use zoning ordinances where lack of voluntary cooperation makes such ordinances necessary." (Morgan 1965, 14, 15)

This was Bennett's battle plan in 1934. Some have been won; some lost; and some are still being fought.

Bennett also became involved in a bureaucratic turf squabble between Interior, Agriculture, the Federal Emergency Relief Administration (FERA), the Association of Land-Grant Colleges and State Universities, and President Roosevelt over the proper role and administrative location for the soil erosion agency (Morgan 1965, 15-20)—a squabble that was settled for the time being by Congress. In April of the following year, Congress passed the Soil Conservation Act of 1935, the organic legislation for the Soil Conservation Service (SCS). The act accomplishes the following:

[R]ecognize[s] that the wastage of soil and moisture resources on farm, grazing, and forest lands of the Nation, resulting from soil erosion, is a menace to national welfare and that it is hereby declared to be the policy of Congress to provide permanently for the control of soil erosion....

[Provides that] the Secretary of Agriculture...shall coordinate and direct all activities with relation to soil erosion...[and authorizes the secretary]

(1) To conduct surveys, investigations, and research relating to the character of soil erosion and the preventive measures needed,...to disseminate the results..., [and] to carry on demonstrational projects...;

(2) To carry out preventive measures, including...engineering operations, methods of cultivation, the growing of vegetation, and changes in use of land;

(3) To cooperate or enter into agreements with, or to furnish financial or other aid to, any agency...or person...;

(4) To acquire lands, or rights or interests therein, by purchase, gift, condemnation or otherwise....

[Empowers the secretary to]...require—

(1) The enactment and reasonable safeguards for the enforcement of State and local laws imposing suitable permanent restrictions on the use of such lands and otherwise providing for the prevention of soil erosion;

(2) Agreements or covenants as to the permanent use of such land, and

(3) Contributions, money, or otherwise....

[Directs t]he Secretary of Agriculture...[to] establish an agency to be known as the "Soil Conservation Service," to exercise the powers conferred on him by this Act. (49 Stat. 163, 164)

It was a good organic act. It named the new agency and gave it legitimacy and the stamp of congressional approval. It gave the secretary of agriculture broad authority within a circumscribed (but large) area. Severe problems awaited the newborn SCS within the Department of Agriculture, however, problems that even good organic legislation and presidential and secretarial support could not solve.

INTERNECINE WARFARE

In 1935 Bennett and other personnel of the Soil Erosion Service were transferred to the Department of Agriculture by executive order (U.S. Department of the Interior 1935, VII) and became the nucleus of the SCS. Bennett was committed to "getting more actual soil conservation on the land—better and faster" (Brink 1951, 103), but he was forced to direct much of his attention to protecting his interests. Providing an aggressive, ambitious bureaucrat with a broad congressional charter and returning him to an old-line department was bound to cause trouble. Within a short time, "[d]eans of some of the agricultural colleges and chiefs of nine of the bureaus in the Department implored Secretary Wallace to curb Hugh Hammond Bennett and the new Soil Conservation Service" (Morgan 1965, 25). The Smith-Lever Act and a 1914 agreement between the secretary and the Executive Committee of the Association of American Agricultural Colleges and Experiment Stations (now the National Association of State Universities and Land-Grant Colleges) provided that all agricultural extension work was to be conducted by state colleges of agriculture through state extension services regardless of the source of funds (Morgan 1965, 26, 28)—but the Soil Conservation Act empowered the SCS to disseminate the results of research and studies. Neither the Extension Service, the Association of Land-Grant Colleges and State Universities, nor the Farm Bureau favored the SCS's being able to deal directly with the farmer.

SCS interagency problems involved agencies other than the Extension Service. A Department of Agriculture interbureau committee recommended in 1935 that all USDA agencies were to be involved in erosion control and that SCS operations should be subservient to extension activities and forbade SCS operations in the Tennessee Valley without the consent of the Tennessee Valley Authority (TVA). The committee report fueled controversies over Bennett's program for more than two decades (Morgan 1965, 31-34).

THE DISTRICTS: GOVERNMENTS
WITHIN GOVERNMENTS

Bennett's strategy required "conservancy districts or similar legal subdivisions with authority to carry out measures of erosion control"—soil conservation districts—with which the SCS could execute contracts for demonstration projects *and* that would constitute its advocacy group in time of need. The recommended district structure was set forth in *A Standard Soil Conservation Districts Law* (U.S. Department of Agriculture 1936)—a "Great Plan" prepared by Bennett with considerable advice and assistance from the solicitor's offices in both Agriculture and Interior, state officials, representatives of land grant colleges and universities, and others. "Nothing like it had ever been attempted in all history. It was a spectacular document, a masterly blueprint which was destined to become a powerful and inspiring and indispensable tool of rural democracy" (Brink 1951, 106, 107).

The districts were to have the power to conduct research, demonstration, and control operations; to enact and enforce land use regulations; to enter into agreements with land "occupiers" to carry out operations subject to conditions set by the governing board; to purchase or receive lands as gifts and to lease or sell such lands; and to receive and spend income and act as agents of the federal government. In essence the districts were to have all the powers normally attributed to local governments except the power of taxation. But they were to be separate and apart from existing government structure. They could be formed by groups of "interested parties" and cover "'naturally bounded area[s] like a watershed,'" whereas the Extension Service was organized along county units. They would be responsive to the secretary of agriculture, bypassing county and state officials. The program would not merely consist of demonstrations of techniques that farmers were free to adopt or reject but would also include conservation plans enforceable under state police power. The districts would utilize the technical expertise of the Extension Service and welcome the support of the Farm Bureau, but they would strengthen the power of the secretary relative to these institutions (Morgan 1965, 44-50).

Early in the next year, on March 22, 1937, the North Carolina General Assembly enacted the requisite enabling legislation (1937 N.C. Sess. Laws 393), and on August 4, 1937, the first soil conservation district was chartered. It was Brown Creek District, in Anson County, North Carolina; and it included Hugh Bennett's plantation birthplace (Sampson 1985, 32, 33).

On February 27, 1939, copies of the *Standard Law* were transmitted to state governors with a letter from President Roosevelt urging adoption (Brink 1951, 107-108). Five days after the letter was issued, Arkansas became the first state to enact soil conservation district legislation following distribution of the *Standard Law*, and by June 30 of that year eighteen states had joined the movement (Brink 1951, 108). By 1940 more than 300 districts had been organized, covering 190 million acres, and seven years later over a billion acres were under district programs (Sampson 1985, 33).

Districts were not "produced by spontaneous combustion" as many had anticipated, however. In many areas they were actively and openly opposed by the Extension Service and its constituency, and their creation and survival required diligent work (politicking) by SCS personnel. Nor did they represent natural geographic units, as Bennett had envisioned, but in almost all cases came to conform to county boundaries. Furthermore, the districts' role as advocates of comprehensive land use planning and regulation never was fully developed (Hardin 1952, 71-75), and expectations of state and local funding are unfulfilled—the districts remain largely an appendage of the SCS (Morgan 1965, 204, 230, 231).

Despite these shortcomings the soil conservation district (now the soil and water conservation district) concept lies at the foundation of SCS field operations. By 1964 districts encompassed more than 92 percent of the nation's farmland, covering most of the forty-eight coterminous states (Held and Clawson 1965, 204). They have been and are important vehicles for disseminating information and influencing public opinion (Held and Clawson 1965, 278). They provide opportunities for public-spirited farmers to exercise leadership (Hardin 1952, 79). They have been powerful advocates for additional congressional appropriations to the SCS and effective allies in institutional disagreements (Hardin 1952, 89-93). As long as the SCS exists, so shall the districts (and probably vice versa).

THE OTHER PART OF THE STORY

Bennett believed that demonstrations of efficient erosion control practices would be sufficient to entice farmers to apply them in their own self-interest. By conducting demonstrations only in states that had enacted district-enabling legislation, he sought to achieve both more erosion control and more districts. He believed that land use regulations would become necessary and that the government should enact enforceable soil erosion regulations (Hardin 1952, 70), but he recommended that regulatory measures be introduced gradually so as not to incur adverse reaction from the agricultural community (Morgan 1965, 84). While Bennett was implementing his program in the SCS, a parallel (and sometimes overlapping) approach was being developed within the same department.

The Agricultural Adjustment Act of 1933 authorized the secretary of agriculture, through the Agricultural Adjustment Administration, to impose a "processing tax" upon agricultural commodities and to use such moneys for direct payments to farmers upon their agreement to reduce the acreage or production of agricultural commodities. The act was part of the New Deal legislation, emergency measures brought on by farm surpluses and the depression, but it created a subsidy system offering economic incentives for instituting land management measures. In 1936, however, the Supreme Court, in *United States v. Butler*, invalidated most of the Agricultural Adjustment Act. The Court found that

> [d]espite a reference in its first section to a burden upon, and an obstruction of the normal currents of commerce, the act under review does not purport to regulate transactions in interstate or foreign commerce. Its stated purpose is the control of agricultural production, a purely local activity. Indeed, the Government does not attempt to uphold the validity of the act on the basis of the commerce clause, which, for the purpose of the present case, may be put aside. . . .
>
> The act invades the reserved rights of the states. It is a statutory plan to regulate and control agricultural production, a matter beyond the powers delegated to the federal government. The tax, the appropriation of the funds raised, and the direction for their disbursement, are but parts of the plan. They are but means to an unconstitutional end. (297 U.S. 63, 64, 68)

In place of the Agricultural Adjustment Act, Congress enacted the Soil Conservation and Domestic Allotment Act of 1936 and the Agricultural Conservation Program (ACP). (Note: Actually the Agricultural Adjustment Administration, created by the Agricultural Adjustment Act, became the Agricultural Adjustment Agency, part of the Agricultural Conservation and Adjustment Administration, in 1942 and was succeeded by the Production and Marketing Administration [PMA] in 1945. The PMA then administered the ACP [Morgan 1965, 115].) The ACP provided direct payments to farmers who carried out essentially annual soil conservation practices, whereas the SCS assisted in developing and implementing long-range farm plans without direct financial assistance. The SCS was composed largely of technical and scientific personnel; the ACP had very few such personnel (Hardin 1952, 112, 113). The SCS operated through a district structure; the ACP did not. Both, however, were in the same federal department, and both dealt with individual farmers and local agricultural committees. Both were concerned with the same people carrying out the same conservation practices on the same parcels of land. Annual practices subsidized by the ACP were part of long-term plans developed with assistance from the SCS. Conflict and competition were unavoidable, and aiding and abetting the controversy was a coalition of the Farm Bureau and the Extension Service. These agencies favored abolishing the SCS field organization to allow the Extension Service to assume all technical phases of soil conservation, with the ACP doling out the money (Morgan 1965, 132, 133).

ACCOMMODATION

The jurisdictional battle reached a climax in the late 1940s and early 1950s. "[S]candalous open warfare broke out between these two agencies [SCS and PMA] in several states...[portending] nothing but disaster for agricultural programs in general if such warfare continued" (Held and Clawson 1965, 51). Republican Thomas E. Dewey was projected to win the 1948 presidential election and was expected to staff the Department of Agriculture from among the leadership of the Farm Bureau and northern agricultural colleges—ensuring the demise of the SCS (Morgan 1965, 140). Harry Truman's unexpected victory dashed these hopes, leaving only the PMA-SCS relationship to be resolved. Skirmishing between the two agencies continued until 1951 and was finally settled in a memorandum from Secretary of Agriculture Charles F. Brannan:

> "The role of PMA under Memorandum 1278 was fixed simply. It retained general responsibility for formulating an annual national conservation program and it kept control of the money to pay farmers for applying practices authorized in state and county programs. The Memorandum also specifically directed each state PMA committee to initiate negotiations among the three agencies which were to have technical responsibility in the future—the Extension Service, SCS and the U.S. Forest Service. Each SCS state conservationist was to be 'responsible for all technical phases of the permanent type of soil-conservation work, except forestry,' undertaken by PMA and SCS (but not extension work) within a state under the direction of the Chief of the SCS. The Forest Service was directed to assume similar responsibility for forestry practices paid by PMA. Also, SCS and PMA officials were directed expressly to 'jointly encourage the creation and development of soil-conservation districts.'" (Morgan 1965, 153-154)

While all affected agencies could find something to gripe about in Brannan's memorandum, it provided a workable solution to the problem and generally described the division of labor that exists today. (Note: The Agricultural Stabilization and Conservation Service [ASCS] replaced the PMA in 1961; a 1953 reorganization divested SCS regional offices of their administrative role, and the SCS is now organized on a state-by-state basis [Morgan 1965, 170]. The ACP, administered by the ASCS, has evolved into an agricultural production subsidy program with little direct relationship to soil and water conservation.)

NATIONAL LAND USE PLANNING:
YOU CAN'T WIN 'EM ALL

Of all of Bennett's proposals, the concept of national land use planning and regulation remains the furthest from implementation. Soon after its creation, the SCS attempted to foster land use planning and zoning of rural lands (Wehrwein et al. 1938). On July 8, 1938, the Association of Land-Grant Colleges and State Universities and the Department of Agriculture agreed on a cooperative program for developing land use plans through local and state land use committees (Foster and Vogel 1940, 1140, 1141). One year later forty-five states had agreed to participate and forty-three had organized state committees; 1,120 counties and 70,000 farm men and women were involved; and 112 preliminary draft area maps and reports had been prepared (Foster and Vogel 1940, 1144). Despite this early promise, rural land use planning has not been popular in the United States, and comprehensive land use planning has rarely been employed at the district level (Held and Clawson 1965, 277).

At the national level, the history is even more bleak and the future less promising. In 1958 the secretary of agriculture appointed a USDA Land and Water Policy Committee and held the National Conference on Land and People to obtain assistance in developing USDA land and water policies. In the mid-1960s, the secretaries of agriculture and housing and urban development addressed problems of urbanization of agricultural land. Few concrete results emerged, however, and surely nothing resembling any federal regulatory control. The USDA policy was to encourage local involvement in land use decisions, with a limited federal role—primarily influencing development patterns through federal development investments (highways, airports, waste treatment plants, etc.) (Schnepf 1979, 150-153).

In his February 8, 1971, message on the environment, President Nixon indicated a change in course:

> "I propose legislation to establish a National Land Use Policy which will encourage the States, in cooperation with local government, to plan for and regulate major developments affecting growth and the use of critical land areas. This should be done by establishing methods for protecting lands of critical environmental concerns, methods for controlling large-scale development, and improving use of land around key facilities and new communities." (Council on Environmental Quality 1971, 295, 296)

Nixon's proposals were incorporated into administration bills (S. 992 and

H.R. 8816, Ninety-second Congress, first session) that would have provided $100 million over five years to assist states in assuming regulatory control over sensitive areas (Council on Environmental Quality 1971, 20). Nixon reiterated his support for a national policy in his environmental message of February 8, 1972, proposing amendments in the pending National Land Use Policy Act, which would have required states to control the siting of major transportation facilities and imposed sanctions on states that did not establish land use programs (Council on Environmental Quality 1972, 373). The act passed the Senate during the Ninety-second Congress but failed to pass the House. An administration bill was resubmitted during the first session of the Ninety-third Congress (Council on Environmental Quality 1973, 214), and Nixon endorsed it as a "high priority in [his] administration" in his State of the Union address on January 30, 1974 (Council on Environmental Quality 1974, 543). Consideration of land use legislation continued in Congress for several years, but by early 1975 the Ford administration had changed position and opposed passage of the legislation—ostensibly for budgetary reasons (U.S. Congress, Senate 1975, 44, 88). However, Secretary of the Interior Rogers C. B. Morton cautioned that "some turf battles…are going to have to be resolved," that Agriculture wanted "a piece of this action," and that city planners and the Department of Housing and Urban Development wanted to be involved (U.S. Congress, Senate 1975, 49), indicating that more than budgetary matters were involved.

Soil conservation interests themselves did not support the proposed national policy. In 1972 the Soil Conservation Society of America sponsored a special conference to discuss "(1) the need for a national land use policy, (2) components of land use planning, (3) implementation of land use policy and plans, and (4) future needs." After extensive discussion of these issues, the conference concluded, "In the final analysis, whether we develop *effective* and *acceptable* land use controls is a political question" (Soil Conservation Society of America 1973, vi, 192). In 1974 and 1975, the president of the National Association of Conservation Districts testified *against* national land use policy legislation (U.S. Congress, Senate 1975, 175).

By 1975 a national land use policy per se had disappeared from the federal agenda. The window, if there had ever been one, had closed. Defense of individual, state, and local prerogatives and opposition to federal sanctions were too great. The time had (has) not yet come. Although the SCS role in land use policy and planning has not reached the levels envisioned by some of its proponents, the agency has been and continues to be a major link between agricultural researchers and those who till the land. Over the almost six decades of its existence, SCS activities have profoundly influenced our attitudes toward and use of land and water resources.

ACHIEVEMENTS

Although the SCS's role in land us policy and planning has not reached the levels envisioned by some of its proponents, the agency has been and continues to be a major link between agricultural researchers and those who till the land. Over the almost six decades of its existence, the SCS's activities have profoundly influenced our attitudes toward and use of land and water resources.

Soil Classification and Survey

Since its inception the SCS has been involved in developing a taxonomy of soil classification and applying it in mapping the distribution of the nation's soils. The current system recognizes about 10,500 soil "series"— the lowest category in the system (U.S. Department of Agriculture, Soil Conservation Service 1975, 80). In addition to the classification system based on soil series, the SCS has developed a system based on "land-capability classes" that "place[s] soils in broad groups with similar hazards and limitations for use, in light of their tendencies for erosion or in view of their other limitations" (Held and Clawson 1965, 123). Bennett originally recognized five classes of agricultural soils, representing increasing limitations and constraints:

> Class I. Lands that can be cultivated safely on a sustained-production basis for at least moderate to good yields of adaptable crops, without the need for special practices or treatments....

> Class II. Lands that cannot be cultivated safely on a sustained-production basis for at least moderate to good yields of adaptable crops without the application of some special practice or treatment of simple character....

> Class III. Lands that cannot be cultivated safely on a sustained-production basis for at least moderate to good yields of adaptable crops without the application of extensive practices or measures, such as contour cultivation, strip cropping in narrow bands, terracing, tile drainage, fertilization, or systematic rotations.

Class IV. Lands that cannot be cultivated safely under any plan of continuous use but that can be used safely for pasture grasses and tame hay with such cultivation as may be necessary to maintain a good cover.

Class V. Lands that cannot be cultivated safely at any time and that are suitable only for permanent cover. (Bennett 1939, 957, 958)

Bennett limited his system to soils that had at least some potential for agricultural production. Subsequently three other classes were added, reflecting the SCS's concern with a comprehensive land-capability classification:

CLASS VI. Soils...[with] extreme limitations that restrict their use largely to pasture or range, woodland, or wildlife....

CLASS VII. Soils...[with] very severe limitations which restrict their use to grazing, woodland, or wildlife....

"CLASS VIII....[S]oils that should not be used for any kind of commercial plant production. Their use is restricted to "recreation, wildlife, water supply, or aesthetic purposes." (Brady 1974, 350)

The land-capability classification system is much more subjective than that based on soil series, but it is more effective in interpreting land use opportunities and constraints. Together the two systems provide a comprehensive and systematic basis for characterizing the nation's soils.

Land Banking

Bennett's original proposals for a national soil conservation program included the recommendation that "[f]ederal, state, and local governments should acquire badly eroded lands unsuited to continued safe agricultural use and convert them into forest or grazing preserves" (Morgan 1965, 14).

The Resettlement Administration, created by Executive Order No. 7072 on April 30, 1935, was directed to do the following:

(a) To administer approved projects involving resettlement of destitute or low-income families from rural and urban areas....

(b) To initiate and administer a program of approved projects with respect to soil erosion, stream pollution, seacoast erosion, reforestation, forestation, and flood control

(c) To make loans...to finance...the purchase of farm lands...."
(Resettlement Administration 1936, 1)

The Resettlement Administration's objective was to purchase some 10 million acres of submarginal or substandard land, remove it from crop production, resettle the original owners and/or tenants, and convert the land to its "proper uses"—primarily grassland and forest (Resettlement Administration 1936, 2, 3).

By June 30, 1937, the agency had developed 206 resettlement projects and obtained title to 4.9 million acres of the 9.1 million then earmarked for acquisition. Subsequently almost all land acquired was conveyed to state conservation commissions or other state agencies, the National Park Service, the Forest Service, and the Office [Bureau] of Indian Affairs (U.S. Department of Agriculture, Resettlement Administration 1937, 9, 10). Today it resides in state and national parks, forests, and recreational areas.

A second effort at land banking was initiated by the Soil Bank Act of 1956. The act established an Acreage Reserve Program and a Conservation Reserve Program to "assist farmers to divert a portion of their cropland from the production of excessive supplies of agricultural commodities, and to carry out a program of soil, water, forest and wildlife conservation" (70 Stat. 188). By participating in the Acreage Reserve Program, farmers received payments in cash or kind, at least equal to the net income lost, in return for short-term reductions in acreage planted to wheat, cotton, corn, rice, tobacco, or peanuts. Participants in the Conservation Reserve Program entered into contracts (for up to fifteen years) under which they agreed to withdraw land from cultivation and to establish permanent conservation practices on it. In return they received reimbursement for up to 80 percent of the cost of the conservation practices plus annual payments (averaging $10 per acre) as compensation for income forgone (U.S. Department of Agriculture, Office of Information 1956). Between 1956 and 1963, 21 million acres were withdrawn from production and planted in permanent vegetative cover (U.S. Department of Agriculture, Agricultural Stabilization and Conservation Service 1964, 1). The program peaked in 1960, with more than 300,000 farms and almost 29 million acres under contract (table 9.1).

The Soil Bank Act was repealed by title VI of the Food and Agriculture Act of 1965, which instituted a Cropland Adjustment Program similar to the Acreage Reserve Program during the years 1965 through 1969 (amended to 1970). Although the primary purpose of this program was to hold land out of production, it was based on five- to ten-

TABLE 9.1
Participation in the Conservation Reserve Program, 1956-1972

Year	Number of Farms	Area (Thousands of Acres)
1956	16,327	1,429
1957	79,791	6,427
1958	125,502	9,887
1959	245,937	22,464
1960	306,186	28,661
1961	303,413	28,512
1962	271,240	25,805
1963	251,572	24,256
1964	167,064	17,456
1965	126,435	14,142
1966	124,284	13,577
1967	108,154	11,330
1968	90,485	9,658
1969	35,962	3,582
1970	1,877	71
1971	192	8
1972	4	—

Source: U.S. Department of Agriculture, Agricultural Stabilization and Conservation Service, *Conservation Reserve Program and Land Use Adjustment Program. Statistical Summary: 1963* (Washington, DC: Government Printing Office, 1964), pp. 4-7.

year contracts and required participants to "maintain...practices which will conserve soil, water, or forest resources, or establish or protect or conserve open spaces, natural beauty, wildlife or recreation resources, or prevent air or water pollution" (79 Stat. 1297).

A recent effort to dissuade farmers from cultivating erodible land was contained in the Food Security Act of 1985 (the 1985 Farm Act). Title XII of the act describes programs intended to discourage farming of highly erodible lands and wetlands (see chapter 12 for a discussion of the "swampbuster" program). In general (but with many exceptions), the "sodbuster" program denies agricultural subsidies (price supports, loans, crop insurance, and disaster payments) to any farmer who "in any crop year produces an agricultural commodity on a field on which highly erodible land is predominate" (99 Stat. 1506). Currently 117.9 million acres of cropland and 227.3 million acres of noncropland are "highly erodible"—24.5 percent of all agricultural lands, accounting for 58 percent of all cropland erosion (51 Fed. Reg. 23,497 (June 27, 1986)). As an additional incentive for farmers to remove such lands from production, the act establishes the Conservation Reserve Program (CRP) for the crop years 1986 through 1990, under which farmers may be compensated 50 percent of the cost of establishing conservation practices, plus annual rental payments, for "converting highly erodible cropland normally devoted to the production of an agricultural commodity...to a less intensive use...such as pasture, permanent grass, legumes, forbs, shrubs, or trees, substantially in accordance with a schedule outlined in the [approved] plan" (99 Stat. 1509, 1510).

By July 1988 more than 25.5 million acres had been placed in the CRP, reducing crop surpluses, promoting soil and water conservation, and improving wildlife habitat (Wildlife Management Institute 1988a). By January 1990 almost 34 million acres were enrolled, providing nearly 2.2 million acres planted to trees and almost 9,000 acres of filter strips (narrow vegetated strips that trap sediment, nutrients, and pesticides) along more than 500 miles of streams, rivers, and lakes. At that time the program was credited with reducing annual soil erosion by more than 660 million tons (Wildlife Management Institute 1990). Some CRP lands are not producing all the public benefits anticipated, however. As a result of the 1988 drought, the USDA opened to haying CRP lands in more than 200 counties in thirteen states—even though the act states that CRP lands should be closed to grazing and haying, and the farmers had received payment from the USDA and, in many cases, from state wildlife agencies as well (Wildlife Management Institute 1988b).

Soil Conservation Practices

Since 1936 the Agricultural Conservation Program has assisted an average of 1.8 million farms per year to install soil conservation measures at a total cost of more than $8 billion. Despite these commendable accomplishments, soil erosion continues to be a serious problem in the United States. A General Accounting Office (GAO) report to Congress estimated that the ACP had spent nearly $15 billion for soil conservation between 1935 and 1977, yet agricultural soil erosion losses were higher in 1977 than in 1934 (U.S. Congress, General Accounting Office 1977, 3, 6).

The GAO estimate is somewhat misleading, however. Seventy percent of soil erosion greater than 5 tons per acre came from only 8.6 percent of the nation's tilled land (Batie 1985, 17), and much of this land was placed into production during the 1970s in order to take advantage of increases in grain exports (primarily to the Soviet Union). From 1973 to 1974, harvested acreage increased by 24 million acres. In the process much of the previous commitment to soil conservation became lost in the desire for short-term income (Batie 1985, 15). In an effort to evaluate the effects of these developments, Congress passed the Soil and Water Resources Conservation Act of 1977, directing the USDA to review its accomplishments, revise its programs based on the reviews, and make the results of the process known to Congress and the public. Although the act has greatly improved the USDA's information base, so far it has had little impact upon field operations (Batie 1985, 17). The Food Security Act of 1985, with its "sodbuster" and "swampbuster" provisions, may be more successful.

REFERENCES

Batie, Sandra. 1985. "Soil Conservation in the 1980s: A Historical Perspective." In *The History of Soil and Water Conservation,* edited by Douglas Helms and Susan L. Flader, 5-21. Washington, DC: Agricultural History Society.

Bennett, Hugh H. 1928. "Soil Erosion: A National Menace." U.S. Department of Agriculture Circular no. 33. Washington, DC: Government Printing Office.

———. 1939. *Soil Conservation.* New York: McGraw-Hill Book Company.

Brady, Nyle C. 1974. *The Nature and Properties of Soils.* 8th ed. New York: Macmillan Publishing Company.

Brink, Wellington. 1951. *Big Hugh, the Father of Soil Conservation.* New York: Macmillan Publishing Company.

Council on Environmental Quality. 1971. *Environmental Quality—1971.* Washington, DC: Government Printing Office.

———. 1972. *Environmental Quality—1972.* Washington, DC: Government Printing Office.

———. 1973. *Environmental Quality—1973.* Washington, DC: Government Printing Office.

———. 1974. *Environmental Quality—1974.* Washington, DC: Government Printing Office.

Foster, Ellery A., and Harold A. Vogel. 1940. "Cooperative Land Use Planning: A New Development in Democracy." In *Farmers in a Changing World: 1940 Yearbook of Agriculture,* 1138-1156. Washington, DC: Government Printing Office.

Hardin, Charles M. 1952. *The Politics of Agriculture.* New York: Free Press.

Held, R. Burnell, and Marion Clawson. 1965. *Soil Conservation in Perspective.* Baltimore: Johns Hopkins University Press.

Morgan, Robert J. 1965. *Governing Soil Conservation: Thirty Years of the New Decentralization.* Baltimore: Johns Hopkins University Press.

Resettlement Administration. 1936. "First Annual Report." Washington, DC: Government Printing Office.

Sampson, R. Neil. 1985. *For Love of the Land: A History of the National Association of Conservation Districts.* League City, TX: National Association of Conservation Districts.

Schnepf, Max. 1979. *Farmland, Food, and the Future.* Ankeny, IA: Soil Conservation Society of America.

Soil Conservation Society of America. 1973. *National Land Use Policy.* Proceedings of a conference in Des Moines, IA, November 27-29, 1972. Ankeny, IA: Soil Conservation Society of America.

U.S. Congress. General Accounting Office. 1977. *Report to the Congress: To Protect Tomorrow's Food Supply, Soil Conservation Needs Priority Attention.* Washington, DC: Government Printing Office.

U.S. Congress. Senate. Committee on Interior and Insular Affairs. Subcommittee on Energy and the Environment. 1975. "Land Use and Resource Conservation." 94th Cong., 1st sess. Serial 9-7. Washington, DC: Government Printing Office.

U.S. Department of Agriculture. 1936. *A Standard Soil Conservation Districts Law.* Washington, DC: Government Printing Office.

————. Agricultural Stabilization and Conservation Service. 1964. *Conservation Reserve Program and Land Use Adjustment Program. Statistical Summary: 1963.* Washington, DC: Government Printing Office.

————. 1981. *Agricultural Conservation Program, 45-year Statistical Summary, 1936 Through 1980.* Washington, DC: Government Printing Office.

U.S. Department of Agriculture. Office of Information. 1956. *The Soil Bank Program.* Washington, DC: Government Printing Office.

U.S. Department of Agriculture. Resettlement Administration. 1937. "Report of the Administrator of the Resettlement Administration, 1937." Washington, DC: Government Printing Office.

U.S. Department of Agriculture. Soil Conservation Service. 1975. *Soil Taxonomy.* Agricultural Handbook no. 436. Washington, DC: Government Printing Office.

U.S. Department of the Interior. 1935. "Annual Report of the Secretary of the Interior." Washington, DC: Government Printing Office.

Wehrwein, George S., Clarence I. Hendrickson, M. H. Saunderson, P. M. Glick, C. C. Taylor, F. R. Kenney, and M. Harris. 1938. "The Remedies: Policies for Private Lands." In *Soils and Man: 1938 Yearbook of Agriculture,* 241-265. Washington, DC: Government Printing Office.

Wildlife Management Institute. 1988a. "CRP Climbs 3.3 Million Acres." *Outdoor News Bulletin* 42 (12): 1 (June 17).

————. 1988b. "USDA Reneges on CRP." *Outdoor News Bulletin* 42 (13): 1 (July 1).

————. 1990. "CRP Nearly 34 Million Acres." *Outdoor News Bulletin* 44 (1): 3 (January 1).

CHAPTER X

Water Law

The legal framework governing use of water resources is among the most complex and intriguing in renewable natural resources. It derives from a mixture of common-law heritage, constitutional and statutory law (federal, state, and local), local custom, judicial decisions, and international convention. It is a mosaic of laws affecting ownership and use of the land adjacent to and beneath water bodies, the waters themselves, transportation over and through such waters, and access to the living resources contained therein.

TIDELANDS, STREAMBEDS, AND SHORES

About the time of the Norman Conquest (A.D. 1066), the Crown claimed ownership over all English lands and waters and the living resources therein. In time two distinct types of ownership became recognized. The highlands and other nontidal lands and their resources were held by the Crown *jus privatum,* as a private proprietary right, and were freely alienable. Tidelands, however, were held by the Crown *jus publicum* and, as a general rule, could not be conveyed:

> In 1601, *Sir Henry Constable's Case* held that a Crown grant of land upon the seacoast was, under the general rule, a conveyance of only those lands above the high water mark. This rule applied to lands situated on the seacoast and royal rivers which, according to the 1604 decision in *The Royal Fishery of the Banne,* included "[e]very navigable river, so high as the sea flows and ebbs in it...." The high water mark itself was determined by "the line of the medium high tide between the springs and the neaps" on the theory that the land below that line was "not capable of ordinary cultivation or occupation" while the land above that line was "for the most part dry and maniorable."
>
> Royal waters, both coastal and inland, were waters in which the public, due to the *jus publicum* character of these waters, had a common right of

both navigation and fishery. The unbridgeable common right of navigation extended further to encompass other waters in which the tide did not ebb and flow, *i.e.*, non-tidal navigable waters, although the law did allow private persons to receive grants conveying lands beneath these non-tidal waters. It was also possible to receive from the Crown an exclusive or several fishery in non-tidal navigable waters, but such rights were subject to the paramount common right to use the stream for navigation. (Rice 1968, 6, 7)

The transition from Crown rule to laws of the United States is described in great detail in the 1894 case *Shively v. Bowlby,* involving ownership of land beneath the Columbia River in the state of Oregon:

I. By the common law, both the title and the dominion of the sea, and of rivers and arms of the sea, where the tide ebbs and flows, and of all the lands below high water mark, within the jurisdiction of the Crown of England, are in the King. Such waters, and the lands which they cover, either at all times, or at least when the tide is in, are incapable of ordinary and private occupation, cultivation, and improvement; and their natural and primary uses are public in their nature, for highways of navigation and commerce, domestic and foreign, and for the purpose of fishing by all the King's subjects. Therefore the title, *jus privatum,* in such lands, as of waste and unoccupied lands, belongs to the King as the sovereign; and the dominion thereof *jus publicum,* is vested in him as the representative of the nation and for the public benefit. (152 U.S. 11)

It is equally well settled that a grant from the sovereign of land bounded by the sea, or by any navigable tide water, does not pass any title below high water mark, unless either the language of the grant, or long usage under it, clearly indicates that such was the intention. (152 U.S. 12)

II. The common law of England upon this subject, at the time of emigration of our ancestors, is the law of this country, except so far as it has been modified by the charters, constitutions, statutes or usages of the several colonies and states, or by the Constitution and laws of the United States. (152 U.S. 14)

III. The governments of the several colonies, with a view to induce persons to erect wharves for the benefit of commerce and navigation, early allowed to the owners of lands bounding on tide waters greater rights and privileges in the shore below high water mark than they had in England. But the nature and degree of such rights and privileges differed in the different colonies, and in some were created by statute, while in others they rested upon usage only. (152 U.S. 18)

IV. The new states admitted into the Union since the adoption of the Constitution have the same rights as the original states in the tide waters, and in the lands below the high water mark, within their respective boundaries. (152 U.S. 26)

VI. The decisions of this court...regarding the shores of waters where the ebb and flow of the tide from the sea is not felt, but which are really navigable, should be considered with reference to the facts upon which they were made, and keeping in mind the local laws of the different states, as well as the provisions of the acts of Congress relating to such waters.... "[S]ome of the cases assert that by navigable rivers are meant rivers in which there is no flow or reflow of the tide. This [tidal flux] definition may be very proper in England, where there is no river of considerable importance as to navigation, which has not a flow of the tide; but it would be highly unreasonable when applied to our larger rivers." (152 U.S. 31)

VII. The later judgments of this court clearly establish that the title and rights of riparian proprietors in the soil below high water mark of navigable waters are governed by the local laws of the several states, subject, of course, to the rights granted to the United States by the Constitution. (152 U.S. 40)

VIII. Notwithstanding the *dicta* contained in some of the opinions of this court...to the effect that Congress has no power to grant any land below high water mark of navigable waters in a territory of the United States, it is evident that this is not strictly true. (152 U.S. 47)

IX. But Congress has never undertaken by general laws to dispose of such lands....The Congress...has constantly acted upon the theory that those lands...above high water mark, may be taken up by actual occupants, in order to encourage the settlement of the country; but that the navigable waters and the soils under them, whether within or above the ebb and flow of tide, shall be and remain public highways; and...shall not be granted away during the period of territorial government; but...shall be held by the United States in trust for the future states, and shall vest in the several states, when organized and admitted to the Union, with all the powers and prerogatives appertaining to the older states. (152 U.S. 48, 49)

Despite its admonition that "there is no universal and uniform law upon the subject [of tideland ownership]" (152 U.S. 26 (1894)), the

Court in *Shively v. Bowlby* recognized as a general rule that unencumbered private ownership ended at the high water line or landward limit of navigability. If private ownership were recognized below that line, it was subject to the navigational servitude and other common property constraints. Ownership of unoccupied and unclaimed lands passed from the Crown to the original states and from United States territories to new states as they were formed; thus tidelands are state, not federal, property. But precise determination of the line of demarcation between tidelands and uplands awaited later resolution.

In *Borax Consolidated Ltd. v. City of Los Angeles* (1935), the Court was faced with the issue of locating the seaward limit of private ownership in land bordering Los Angeles Harbor—land that had passed through Mexican and U.S. territorial rule to the state of California and thence either to the city of Los Angeles (which claimed title under a grant from the state) or to Borax Consolidated Ltd. (which claimed title under a preemption patent issued by the United States prior to statehood):

> Upon the acquisition of the territory from Mexico, the United States acquired the title to tidelands equally with the title to upland, but held the former only in trust for the future states which might be erected out of that territory. (296 U.S. 15)

> There is no question that the United States was free to convey the upland, and the patent [to Borax Consolidated Ltd.] affords no ground for holding that it did not convey all title that the United States had in the premises. The question as to the extent of this federal grant, that is, as to the limit of the land conveyed, or the boundary between the upland and the tideland, is necessarily a federal question...which concerns the validity and effect of an act done by the United States. (296 U.S. 22)

> The tideland extends to the high water mark....This does not mean...a physical mark made upon the ground by the waters; it means the line of high water as determined by the course of the tides. By the civil law [of Justinian], the shore extends as far as the highest waves in winter...[, but] by the common law, the shore "is confined to the flux and reflux of the sea at ordinary tides."...It is the land "between ordinary high and low water mark, the land over which the daily tides ebb and flow. When, therefore, the sea, or a bay, is named as a boundary, the line of ordinary high-water mark is always intended where the common law prevails." (296 U.S. 22, 23)

> In order to include the land that is thus covered, it is necessary to take the mean high tide line, which...is neither the spring tide nor the neap tide,

but a mean of all the high tides....[I]n order to ascertain the mean high
tide line with requisite certainty in fixing the boundary of valuable tidelands,..."an average of 18.6 years should be determined as near as possible." (296 U.S. 26, 27)

Borax Consolidated settled the legal definition of the upper tideland
boundary. Local mean high tide data are determined by the National
Ocean Survey and adjusted for successive nineteen-year epochs—the
complete tidal cycle (Shalowitz 1964, 59). Establishing the tideland
boundary on level terrain remains a problem, however, for it is the intersection of a horizontal plane (mean high tide) with one that is almost
horizontal (the earth's surface).

The foregoing cases fairly well establish the limit of private ownership
adjacent to and beneath tidal watercourses, and in general they are
applicable to nontidal navigable streams as well (Clark 1967, 207, 257).
(Note: In lands beneath nonnavigable streams, private ownership usually
is considered to extend to midstream.) These principles have nothing to
do with rights in the water itself, however. This is a separate body of law.

THE WATERS WITHIN

Since the days of Justinian, waters in running streams have not been subject to private ownership, but owners of lands abutting streams were
entitled to certain rights of use. Such a right is termed *"usufructuary"* and
"'consists not so much of the fluid itself as the advantage of its use. A
right may be acquired to its use that will be regarded and protected as
property, but this right carried with it no specific property in the water
itself'" (Wiel 1911, sec. 18, cited in Martz 1979, 28). Water within the
stream remained *res nullius* and was owned by no one, while the right of
transportation over such waters was a public right, *res publicae*, protected
by law (chapter 1).

Eastern Water Law

The "common-law riparian doctrine" of water law, characteristic of all
states east of the Dakota, Nebraska, and Kansas tier, evolved from this
usufructuary right of riparian owners. It appears to have emerged in the
mid-nineteenth century, prior to which "English law granted the right to
use waters flowing through one's land to the first appropriator" (Martz
1979, 69). As described in *Lux v. Haggin* (1886):

"'As *a general proposition,* every riparian proprietor has a natural and equal right to the use of water in a stream adjacent to his land, *without diminution or alteration.* 'Washb.Easem. 319. 'Riparian proprietors are entitled, in the absence of a grant, license, or prescription limiting their rights, to have the stream which washes their lands flow as is wont by nature, without *material* diminution or alteration. Gould, Waters, §204. Each riparian proprietor has a right to the natural flow of the watercourse undiminished, except by its reasonable consumption by upstream proprietors. Ang. c. 4, *passim.* The right to the flow of the water *is inseparably annexed to the soil,* and passes with it, not as an easement or appurtenant, *but as a parcel. Use* does not create, and *disuse* cannot destroy or suspend it. Each person through whose land a water-course flows has (in common with those in like situation) an equal right to the benefit of it as it passes through his land, for all useful purposes to which it may be applied; and no proprietor of land on the same water-course has a right *unreasonably* to divert it from flowing through his premises, or to obstruct it in passing from them, or to corrupt or destroy it. Chief Justice Shaw in Johnson v. Johnson, 2 Metc. 239....Priority of occupancy of the flowing waters of a river *creates no right,* unless the appropriations be for a period which the law deems a presumption of right. Mr. Justice Story in *Tyler v. Wilkinson,* 4 Mason 397." (cited in Martz 1979, 70, 71)

In the early days of our country, the riparian doctrine worked reasonably well in the well-watered East, where conflicts and competition were minimal and the prior English principle of "first come, first served" was evoked to protect prescriptive rights. Such rights became more important as water demands increased with the coming of the industrial revolution (Clark 1967, 288, 289). In time the "natural flow" theory of riparian rights was modified to accommodate the concept of "reasonable use," wherein

each riparian may put water to any beneficial and consumptive use recognized by the customs of his community and the needs of his society, so long as he does no material damage to his neighbors below him. *Lux v. Haggin,* 69 Cal. 255, 4 P. 919, 10 P. 674 (1886), at p. 756.

Among the uses which have been held to be reasonable, under this theory, are fishing, bathing, boating, floatage, power and commercial irrigation, though the effect of the use is to substantially reduce the flow of the stream through riparian lands below. (Martz 1979, 119)

While "reasonableness" may vary widely depending on local conditions, it may not include such uses as diversion and use by nonriparian owners or diversion by a riparian owner for sale or for the benefit of a nonriparian owner (Martz 1979, 125).

As population density and competition for water in the East increase, irrigation of agricultural crops becomes more common, and droughts inject their limiting effect, riparian doctrine states find it necessary to depart from strict interpretation and to develop more flexibility on the one hand and more control over use on the other. Municipalities are given statutory authority to divert water to nonriparian owners and to discharge effluent into watersheds other than the one of origin. Additional water users are preempted by prior users. Withdrawals of surface water and/or groundwater are controlled by permit systems (Goldfarb 1984, 8-11). In combination these constraints move the eastern states closer to the prior appropriation doctrine practiced by their western neighbors.

Western Water Law

Conditions in the arid West presented pioneers with a different situation. Water supplies were often inadequate for the needs of potential users, and competition among users required a system of "allocation." Some areas were subject to water management long before the coming of the white man. Prior water rights had been established in others, and Washington was a long way off and its territorial laws thinly spread over the land.

By about A.D. 1000, native Americans were irrigating crops in the Southwest. In what is now southwestern Colorado, they built check dams and irrigation ditches more than 4 miles in length. In northwestern New Mexico, a similar system supported a Chaco population of more than 10,000 persons. The Hohokim people of central and southern Arizona built more than 125 miles of irrigation canals, constituting a well-engineered and efficient irrigation system—comparable structures were maintained by the Anasazi, Zuni, and Hopi (Meyer 1984, 12-15).

With Spanish settlement during the sixteenth and seventeenth centuries, the Indians increasingly found themselves on the short side of the water issue, and eventually Spanish land grants, in their initial form or by subsequent addition, came to include water rights (Meyer 1984, 58, 133). When portions of these lands later became territories of the United States through the Treaty of Guadalupe Hidalgo (1848) and the Gadsden Purchase (1853), the law of prior appropriation already pertained to them (Clark 1967, 74, 75).

Four characteristics distinguish the prior appropriation doctrine from the common-law riparian system:

First, since appropriation rights are based on priority of beneficial use, not on ownership of riparian land, anyone can acquire an appropriative right for use at any location. Realistically, appropriative rights are limited only by the economics of applying water from a particular source for use in a particular place.

Second, an appropriative right exists for a definite amount of water, and is not correlative with other diversion rights. If an appropriator can make beneficial use of all the unappropriated water in a watercourse, he can lawfully appropriate the entire quantity unless the state imposes a "minimum flow" restriction. When a water shortage occurs, the burden falls on the "junior appropriators" (later diverters): they are closed down completely in inverse order of priority, i.e., the latest allocation granted is the first to be closed. There is no sharing of the burden of shortage as in riparianism....

Third, an appropriative diversion right, being separate from the land ownership, is in almost all western states transferrable to a different holder, a different place, and to a new or different use. Moreover, the present holder is legally entitled to change the nature of use, point of diversion, or method of diversion....

Finally, an appropriative water right is of indefinite duration as long as it is used in accordance with the law. However, unlike a riparian right, an appropriative right can be lost through nonuse....Should a rightholder not use his right, or part of it, for a statutory period of time, and intend not to use it, his water right may be lost by abandonment in a proceeding brought by the state or a junior appropriator. (Goldfarb 1984, 16, 17)

The states of Arizona, Colorado, Idaho, Montana, Nevada, New Mexico, Utah, Wyoming, and Alaska adhere to the doctrine of prior appropriation (also called the "Colorado doctrine") (Martz 1979, 69). An appropriation is obtained by (1) giving notice of an intent to create a water diversion, (2) creating such a diversion, and (3) applying the diverted water to a useful industry. Once validly constituted an appropriation exists as long as the appropriator continues to use the volume specified in the appropriation permit or decree, under whatever other conditions may be stipulated (Martz 1979, 69, 164, 219).

The generally less arid states east and west of the Colorado doctrine states exercise a mixture of riparian and prior appropriation doctrines. These states (Washington, Oregon, California, North Dakota, South Dakota, Nebraska, Kansas, Oklahoma, and Texas) attempted to retain some portion of riparian doctrine while recognizing appropriations made from the public domain and the state. As competition for water becomes more acute, their policies fuse with those of the Colorado doctrine states (Martz 1979, 236-238).

LITTORAL AND MARITIME CONSIDERATIONS

As one proceeds seaward from the uplands, he or she crosses consecutive zones of ownership—private, state, federal, and international. Much of the law concerning the littoral and maritime portions of this continuum is of relatively recent vintage. Many areas are not completely resolved and, particularly in the international arena, are still evolving.

Domestic Issues

The earlier discussion established the mean high water line as the general boundary between private and public (state) ownership of tidelands; the boundary between state and federal ownership is another matter. The tidelands and lands beneath navigable waters are in the individual states, out to some offshore limit. The location of this boundary was of little importance as long as the bottom had little or no economic value. Its location was therefore ignored—until California began leasing oil and gas rights in the Santa Barbara Channel during the 1920s. Even then the federal government took twenty years to initiate action to resolve the issue. The litigation, *United States v. California*, began in 1945 when the government invoked the original jurisdiction of the Supreme Court by filing suit against the state of California. The United States claimed ownership over all lands and resources "'lying seaward of the ordinary low-water mark on the coast of California and outside the inland waters of the State, extending seaward three nautical miles.'" California claimed the same area as part of the tidelands acquired by the original colonies upon independence, to which it was entitled upon admission to the union "on an equal footing" (Shalowitz 1962, 3-5).

The Court declared that the concept of a marginal maritime belt over which a nation could exercise exclusive jurisdiction dated only to the end of the eighteenth century, after formation of the United States. The original colonies did not have this jurisdiction, nor did states admitted later (Shalowitz 1962, 6, 7). Thus the Court found "that the federal government rather than the state has paramount rights in and power over that belt, an incident to which is full dominion over the resources of the soil under that water area, including oil" (332 U.S. 38). Subsequently, in *United States v. Louisiana* and *United States v. Texas*, the Court reaffirmed its *California* ruling as it applied to a state claiming more than 3 miles seaward of the baseline (Louisiana) and one that was an independent republic prior to joining the Union (Texas).

It took Congress three years from the *Louisiana* and *Texas* decisions to enact a statute reversing the Supreme Court decisions. The Submerged Lands Act of May 22, 1953, defined by statute littoral and maritime concepts previously existing in case law and common law (changing some in the process):

Sec. 2. When used in this Act—

(a) The term "lands beneath navigable waters" means—

   (1) all lands within the boundaries of each of the respective States which are covered by nontidal waters that were navigable under the laws of the United States at the time such State became a member of the Union, or acquired sovereignty over such lands and waters thereafter, up to the ordinary high water mark as heretofore or hereafter modified by accretion, erosion, and reliction;

   (2) all lands permanently or periodically covered by tidal waters up to but not above the line of mean high tide and seaward to a line three geographical miles distant from the coast line of each such State and to the boundary line of each such State where in any case such boundary as it existed at the time such State became a member of the Union, or as heretofore approved by Congress, extends seaward (or into the Gulf of Mexico) beyond three geographical miles, and

   (3) all filled in, made, or reclaimed lands which formerly were lands beneath navigable waters, as hereinabove defined;

(b) [I]n no event shall the term "boundaries" or the term "lands beneath navigable waters" be interpreted as extending from the coast line more than three geographical miles into the Atlantic Ocean or the Pacific Ocean, or more than three marine leagues [nine geographical miles] into the Gulf of Mexico;

(c) The term "coast line" means the line of ordinary low water along that portion of the coast which is in direct contact with the open sea and the line marking the seaward limit of inland waters; . . .

(e) The term "natural resources" includes, without limiting the generality thereof, oil, gas, and all other minerals, and fish, shrimp, oysters, clams, crabs, lobsters, sponges, kelp, and other marine animal and plant life but does not include water power, or the use of water for the production of power....

Sec. 4. Seaward Boundaries.—The seaward boundary of each original coastal State is hereby approved and confirmed as a line three geographical miles distant from its coast line or, in the case of the Great Lakes, to the international boundary. Any State admitted subsequent to the formation of the Union which has not already done so may extend its seaward boundaries to a line three geographical miles distant from its coast line, or to the international boundaries of the United States in the Great Lakes or any other body of water traversed by such boundaries....Nothing in this section is to be construed as questioning or in any manner prejudicing the existence of any State's seaward boundary beyond three geographical miles if it was so provided by its constitution or laws prior to or at the time such State became a member of the Union, or if it has been heretofore approved by Congress....

Sec. 6. Powers Retained by the United States.—(a) The United States retains all its navigational servitude and rights in and powers of regulation and control of said lands and navigable waters for the constitutional purposes of commerce, navigation, national defense, and international affairs, all of which shall be paramount to, but shall not be deemed to include, proprietary rights of ownership, or the rights of management, administration, leasing, use, and development of the lands and natural resources which are specifically recognized, confirmed, established, and vested in and assigned to the respective States. (67 Stat. 29-32)

The Submerged Lands Act settled a number of important issues in littoral and maritime law. The seaward boundaries of the states were to be 3 geographical miles offshore of the baseline or as they were when individual states joined the Union, but control over use of the overlying waters for commerce, navigation, and other national and international purposes remained in the United States. The coastline, and thus the baseline from which all offshore boundaries are measured, was to be (generally) the seaward limit of internal waters or the mean low water line along the ocean shore, whichever was relevant. The problem of physically determining the location of the coastline remained, however, and was as difficult as the task of locating the mean high water line. The "historical" boundary of each coastal state was left to future determination, and the legal regime for lands and waters seaward of the "3-mile limit" was not addressed.

President Harry Truman had previously acted on the last issue, however. On September 28, 1945, by executive proclamation, he had unilaterally extended United States jurisdiction over some vague "contiguous zone" by declaring

the natural resources of the subsoil and sea bed of the continental shelf beneath the high seas but contiguous to the coasts of the United States as appertaining to the United States, subject to its jurisdiction and control....The character as high seas of the waters above the continental shelf and the right to their free and unimpeded navigation are in no way thus affected. (Proclamation No. 2667, 59 Stat. 884, 885)

The proclamation did not define the offshore boundary of the contiguous zone, but an accompanying press release interpreted it to extend to the 100-fathom depth (Wenk 1972, 254). In extending the contiguous zone so far offshore, Truman was meddling in international affairs with no sanction from the international community, but he did not let minor details like that bother him. He staked out his turf; it was up to others to approve, condone, or object. Thirteen years later they did.

As to the precise offshore limits of individual states, lawsuits began flying almost immediately. Alabama sued Texas, Louisiana, Florida, and California; the secretaries of the treasury, navy, and the interior; and the treasurer of the United States. Rhode Island filed a similar suit against the same defendants. The United States sued Louisiana, Texas, Mississippi, Alabama, and Florida (Shalowitz 1962, 126, 129). In each case the basic issue was whether, and to what degree, Gulf Coast states were to receive more than the 3-geographical-mile zone accorded other coastal states—and the oil lease revenues from the extended area.

Only *United States v. Louisiana* was subsequently heard by the Supreme Court. The complicated case encompassed almost five years (filed December 19, 1955; decided May 31, 1960) and culminated in six written opinions. The Court's decision was based "on the two-fold test incorporated in the act—boundaries which existed at the time of admission and boundaries heretofore approved by Congress" (Shalowitz 1962, 134). Of the Gulf Coast states, only two met the test—Texas and Florida. The offshore boundary of the Republic of Texas, as described in its declaration of independence from Mexico, ran "'west along the Gulf of Mexico three leagues from land,'" and the same boundary was confirmed by Congress in the 1838 Convention Between the United States of America and the Republic of Texas (8 Stat. 511) and in the joint resolution approving the annexation of Texas (Shalowitz 1962, 136).

In finding for the state of Florida, the court relied on the second part of the test. In 1868 Congress had approved the Florida Constitution, which declared the state boundary to run "'southwestwardly along the edge of the Gulf Stream and Florida Reefs to and including the Tortugas Islands; thence northeastwardly to a point three leagues from the mainland; thence northwestwardly three leagues from land, to a point west of the mouth of the Perdido River" (Shalowitz 1962, 147).

In summary, then, the seaward boundary of all coastal states except Florida and Texas is 3 geographical miles seaward from the baseline—the mean low water line on the ocean or Gulf shore or the seaward limit of internal waters. In the case of Texas and the Gulf Coast of Florida, the boundary is 3 leagues (9 geographical miles) seaward of the baseline. Within this zone the federal government retains jurisdiction over interstate and foreign commerce and defense; beyond it the states have no jurisdiction.

International Matters

Although other nations had laid claim to offshore areas prior to Truman's outer continental shelf proclamation, his action provided the impetus for serious international discussion of maritime boundaries. By one stroke of his pen, he added to the United States an area estimated to encompass 760,000 square miles—almost three times the size of France (Shalowitz 1962, 188, 189), more than the Gadsden Purchase, more than the Florida Purchase, almost one-sixth the area of the original colonies—and at no cost to the United States!

Such claims, "including the United States claim, were all unilateral in nature and had no binding force on the international community other than the voluntary respect that nations chose to accord them, or as the nations involved were able to enforce." It fell on the International Law Commission (ILC), an agency of the United Nations, to express the feelings of the international community (Shalowitz 1962, 189). Before they could act, however, the United States backed up the Truman proclamation with a statute.

The Outer Continental Shelf Lands Act, passed only three months after the Submerged Lands Act, stated the following:

Sec. 3. Jurisdiction Over Outer Continental Shelf.—

(a) It is hereby declared to be the policy of the United States that the subsoil and seabed of the outer Continental Shelf appertain to the United States and are subject to its jurisdiction, control, and power of disposition as provided in this Act.

(b) This Act shall be construed in such manner that the character as high seas of the waters above the outer Continental Shelf and the right of navigation and fishing shall not be affected.

Sec. 4. Laws Applicable to Outer Continental Shelf.—(a)(1) The Constitution and laws and civil and political jurisdiction of the United

States are hereby extended to the subsoil and seabed of the outer Continental Shelf...to the same extent as if the outer Continental Shelf were an area of exclusive Federal jurisdiction located within a State: *Provided, however,* That mineral leases on the outer Continental Shelf shall be maintained or issued only under the provisions of this Act. (67 Stat. 462)

While the act was painfully clear in its intent, it was quite nebulous as to the offshore boundary of the area concerned. The outer continental shelf was defined rather circularly as

all submerged lands lying seaward and outside of the area of lands beneath navigable waters as defined in...the Submerged Lands Act..., and of which the seabed and subsoil appertain to the United States....(67 Stat. 462)

International efforts to codify maritime legal jurisdiction coalesced in 1958 at the First Geneva Conference on the Law of the Sea. The two-month-long conference, attended by representatives of eighty-six states (countries), considered draft rules prepared by the ILC and produced four international conventions: (1) the Convention on the Territorial Sea and Contiguous Zone, (2) the Convention on the Continental Shelf, (3) the Convention on the High Seas, and (4) the Convention on Fishing and Conservation of the Living Resources of the High Seas. The conventions created little new law, but they did codify "'existing international law and practice'" (Shalowitz 1962, 210, 211).

The Territorial Sea and Contiguous Zone

The Convention on the Territorial Sea and Contiguous Zone confirms that "the normal baseline for measuring the breadth of the territorial sea is the low water line along the coast" and gives procedures for establishing the baseline on irregular coasts, on bays, around artificial structures, and between opposite or adjacent states. Waters landward of the baseline are internal waters of the state, and the "outer limit of the territorial sea is the line every point of which is at a distance from the nearest point of the baseline equal to the breadth of the territorial sea" (sec. II).

Ships of all states "enjoy the right of innocent passage through the territorial sea," and "[p]assage is innocent so long as it is not prejudicial to the peace, good order, or security of the coastal State" and includes a limited right of stopping and anchoring. Even foreign warships may traverse the territorial seas of other states, provided they "comply with the regulations of the coastal State concerning passage through the territorial sea"— but submerged submarines are not "innocent." Nor are fishing vessels operating in violation of "such laws and regulations as the coastal State may make and publish to prevent these vessels from fishing in the territorial sea." While a state "may take the necessary steps in its territorial sea to prevent passage which is not innocent," it "must not hamper innocent passage" (sec. III).

In addressing the contiguous zone, the treaty went far beyond the limited and nebulous words of the Truman proclamation, specifying the maximum width of the zone and the nature of coastal state jurisdiction within it:

1. In a zone of the high seas contiguous to its territorial sea, the coastal State may exercise the control necessary to:
   (a) Prevent infringement of its customs, fiscal, immigration or sanitary regulations within its territory or territorial sea;
   (b) Punish infringement of the above regulations committed within its territory or territorial sea.
2. The contiguous zone may not extend beyond twelve [geographical] miles from the baseline from which the territorial sea is measured. (Art. 24)

While the foregoing provisions clarified many aspects of the nature and use of the territorial sea and contiguous zone, they failed to resolve two major issues—the width of the territorial sea and the nature of fishing rights within the contiguous zone (Shalowitz 1962, 209).

The Continental Shelf

Prior to the Geneva Conference, the concept of a territorial sea was reasonably well understood and accepted, and recognition of a limited contiguous zone within which a coastal state could exercise "customs, fiscal, immigration or sanitary regulations" did not evoke much emotion at the conference. The continental shelf was another matter. Here was oil. Oil was money. States unilaterally had claimed and were claiming extensive rights over shelf areas, and no uniformity or international consensus existed (Shalowitz 1962, 245). Thus the Convention on the Continental Shelf represented a major accomplishment in precedent and substance:

Article 1
For the purpose of these articles, the term "continental shelf" is used as referring (a) to the seabed and subsoil of the submarine areas adjacent to the coast but outside the area of the territorial sea, to a depth of 200 meters or, beyond that limit, to where the depth of the superjacent waters

admits of the exploitation of the natural resources of the said areas; (b) to the seabed and subsoil of similar submarine areas adjacent to the coasts of islands.

Article 2

1. The coastal State exercises over the continental shelf sovereign rights for the purpose of exploring it and exploiting its natural resources.

2. The rights referred to in paragraph 1 of this article are exclusive in the sense that if the coastal State does not explore the continental shelf or exploit its natural resources, no one may undertake these activities, or make a claim to the continental shelf, without express consent of the coastal State.

3. The rights of the coastal State over the continental shelf do not depend on occupation, effective or notional, or on any express proclamation.

4. The natural resources referred to in these articles consist of the mineral and other non-living resources of the seabed and subsoil together with the living organisms belonging to sedentary species, that is to say, organisms which, at harvestable stage, either are immobile on or under the seabed or are unable to move except in constant physical contact with the seabed or the subsoil.

Article 3

The rights of the coastal State over the continental shelf do not affect the legal status of the superjacent waters as high seas, or that of the airspace above those waters.

The remaining sections of the treaty addressed measures to minimize conflicts between exploration and exploitation of shelf resources and laying and maintenance of submarine pipelines and cables, legitimate activities on the high seas, and between adjacent states sharing a common continental shelf. Among the more controversial sections were those limiting the freedom to conduct scientific investigations:

8. The consent of the coastal State shall normally be obtained in respect of any research undertaken there. Nevertheless, the coastal State shall not normally withhold its consent if the request is submitted by a qualified institution with a view to purely scientific research into the physical or biological characteristics of the continental shelf, subject to the proviso that the coastal State shall have the right, if it so desires, to participate or to be represented in the research, and that in any event the results shall be published. (Art. 5)

It does not take a great deal of imagination to envision a host of potential problems with this provision. Progressive developed nations were fearful of being impeded by conservative protective states. Those carrying out covert activities were fearful of discovery. Mandatory disclosure of results bothered scientists, industrialists, and the defense establishment. Scientists made a great deal of fuss; intelligence agencies said very little. In practice it is not "a serious obstacle to world-wide scientific inquiry, but it has the potential of becoming such an obstacle" ("Report of the International Panel" 1969, VIII-70). The *threat* was there; that is what counted, and the controversy remains today.

The High Seas

The Convention on the High Seas simply codified recognized rules of international law pertaining to the high seas—"all parts of the sea that are not part of the territorial waters of a State" (art. 1). It declared the right of all states, both coastal and noncoastal, to the four freedoms of the high seas: freedom of navigation, freedom of fishing, freedom to lay submarine cables, and freedom to fly over the high seas. The convention dealt primarily with rules of conduct on the high seas and had little relevance to natural resource matters. Those were covered in the following convention.

Living Resources of the High Seas

Since at least 1839, when England and France entered into an agreement concerning fishing in the English Channel, the dual issues of the threat of overfishing and expansion of high seas fisheries produced a plethora of international agreements and unilateral claims. On the same day that President Truman issued his statement on the continental shelf, he issued a second proclamation setting forth the "policy of the United States with respect to coastal fisheries in certain areas of the high seas":

> In view of the pressing need for conservation and protection of fishery resources, the Government of the United States regards it as proper to establish conservation zones in those areas of the high seas contiguous to the coasts of the United States wherein fishing activities have been or in the future may be developed and maintained on a substantial scale. Where such activities have been or shall hereafter be developed and maintained by its nationals alone, the United States regards it as proper to establish explicitly bounded conservation zones in which fishing activities shall be subject to the regulation and control of the United States. Where such

activities have been or hereafter shall be legitimately developed and maintained jointly by nationals of the United States and nationals of other States, explicitly bounded conservation zones may be established under agreements between the United States and such other States; and all fishing activities in such zones shall be subject to regulation and control as provided in such agreements....(Proclamation No. 2668, September 28, 1945, 59 Stat. 885)

Although the proclamation recognized "[t]he right of any State to establish conservation zones off its shores in accordance with the above principles...provided that corresponding recognition is given to the interests of nationals of the United States which may exist in such areas" (59 Stat. 886), it was a flagrant unilateral move without any semblance of international sanction. Other nations soon followed suit but without "corresponding recognition" of U.S. fishing interests. Chile, Ecuador, and Peru asserted that "'each of them possesses sole sovereignty and jurisdiction over the areas of the sea adjacent to the coast of its own country and extending not less than two hundred nautical miles from the said coast'" ("Declaración Sobre Zona Marítima" 1957, 714, cited in "Report of the International Panel" 1969, VIII-56). Soon thereafter the "CEP" countries (Chili, Ecuador, and Peru) began seizing U.S. tuna vessels and their catches within the claimed waters, precipitating congressional action to reimburse the vessel owners (Fishermen's Protective Act of 1954). During the late 1940s and early 1950s, with rapid and extensive expansion of distant-water fisheries following the end of World War II, the high seas fisheries situation was chaotic and becoming more so. The Convention on Fishing and Conservation of the Living Resources of the High Seas attempted to provide an orderly framework for these fisheries, giving particular attention to fisheries adjacent to territorial seas. In so doing it sanctioned many of the provisions of the Truman proclamation.

Recognizing (and restating) the situation just described, the treaty went on to declare the basic freedom of fishing on the high seas, with some constraints:

1. All States have the right for their nationals to engage in fishing on the high seas, subject (a) to their treaty obligations, (b) to the interests and rights of coastal States as provided for in this Convention, and (c) to the provisions contained in the following articles concerning conservation of living resources of the high seas. (Art. 1)

The treaty then prescribed an obligation to develop "measures...for the purpose of the conservation of the living resources affected" and a protocol for doing so (art. 3). Such measures may be unilateral (when only one nation is fishing the stocks) or multilateral (when "the nationals of two or more States are engaged in fishing the same stock or stocks" [art. 4]). They are obligatory among all participating states (art. 5) and are enforceable under dispute proceedings described later in the treaty (art. 9).

The most far-reaching provisions of the Convention on Fishing and Conservation of the Living Resources of the High Seas were enacted in an effort to recognize the interests of coastal states in fisheries adjacent to but beyond their territorial seas without sanctioning excessive unilateral claims to the world's high seas fisheries:

1. A coastal State has a special interest in the maintenance of the productivity of the living resources in any part of the high seas adjacent to its territorial sea.

2. A coastal State is entitled to take part on an equal footing in any system of research and regulation for the purposes of conservation of the living resources of the high seas in that area, even though its nationals do not carry on fishing there.

3. A State whose nationals are engaged in fishing in any area of the high seas adjacent to the territorial sea of a coastal State shall, at the request of that coastal State, enter into negotiations with a view to prescribing by agreement the measures necessary for the conservation of the living resources of the high seas in that area.

4. A State whose nationals are engaged in fishing in any area of the high seas adjacent to the territorial sea of a coastal State shall not enforce conservation measures in that area which are opposed to those which have been adopted by the coastal State. (Art. 6)

In addition to the cooperative ventures described in articles 4 and 6, a coastal state may "adopt unilateral measures" to conserve stocks in the high seas adjacent to its territorial sea, and those measures, under prescribed circumstances, "shall be valid as to other States" (art. 7). Furthermore, any state that "has a special interest in the conservation of the living resources" in such areas "may request the State or States whose nationals are engaged in fishing there" to adopt conservation measures "even if its nationals are not engaged in fishing in" the area (art. 8).

Of the four treaties emanating from the Geneva Conference, only the treaty on living resources contained measures for dispute resolution. It provided for hearings before a special five-member commission (art. 9) and stipulated criteria to be followed in conflict resolution (art 10.). Decisions of the commission are "binding on the States concerned" (art. 11). According to the Optional Protocol of Signature Concerning the Compulsory Settlement of Disputes (1958), disputes under this treaty and all other treaties "arising out of the interpretation or application of any Convention on the Law of the Sea shall lie within the compulsory jurisdiction of the International Court of Justice [World Court], and may accordingly be brought before the Court by an application made by any party to the dispute being a party to this Protocol" (art. I).

Progress Since the Geneva Conference

Progress in international maritime law during the years following the Geneva Conference has been frustratingly slow and tedious.

Between January 1967 and January 1969 the President's Commission on Marine Science, Engineering, and Resources (primarily through its Panel on Marine Resources and its International Panel) assessed the international situation as part of its charge to "make a comprehensive investigation and study of all aspects of marine science in order to recommend an overall plan for an adequate national oceanographic program" (80 Stat. 206). The commission focused on three unresolved jurisdictional areas: breadth of the territorial sea and exclusive fisheries zones, seabed resources of the continental shelf and deep oceans, and freedom of scientific inquiry.

After discussing problems resulting from varying (but expanding) widths of territorial seas and exclusive fisheries zones ("Report of the International Panel" 1969, VIII-55), the commission failed to recommend any concrete solution, recommending merely "that an attempt be made to reach international agreement on the maximum breadth of the territorial sea," that international fishery organizations be strengthened to ensure "that the geographical area subject to international fisheries management be large enough to permit regulation on the basis of ecological units rather than species and, when necessary, include the territorial seas," and that "renewed diplomatic efforts be made to persuade all important fishing nations of the world to adhere to the Convention on Fishing and Conservation of the Living Resources of the High Seas" (Commission on Marine Science, Engineering, and Resources 1969, 111, 113).

The commission felt that the accepted definition of the continental shelf was both overly restrictive and vague. As an alternative, it recommended that the continental shelf extend to the 200-meter isobath or 50 nautical miles from the baseline, whichever gave the coastal state the greater shelf. Beyond the redefined continental shelf would be an "intermediate zone," extending to the 2,500-meter isobath or 100 nautical miles from the baseline, whichever gave the coastal state the greater area. Within this zone only the coastal state would be authorized to exploit mineral resources; the area beyond it would be governed by the legal regime of the deep seabed. Mineral claims in the deep seabed would be registered with an "International Registry Authority" that would have regulatory authority, and registration fees would deposited in an "International Fund" and be used "to compensate the common owners of the mineral resources of the deep seas...for purposes that the international community agrees will promote the common welfare" (Commission on Marine Science, Engineering, and Resources 1969, 147-151).

None of the Marine Science Commission's international recommendations has been enacted in exactly the form expressed by the commission. Most have appeared, from time to time, in executive branch policy statements, and much of their substance is embodied in the Convention on the Law of the Sea.

In December 1982, after fourteen years of negotiations by more than 150 countries, the Third United Nations Conference on the Law of the Sea convened at Montego Bay, Jamaica, for the purpose of signing a Convention on the Law of the Sea (*The Law of the Sea* 1983, xxix). By December 1984, when the period for signing expired, 159 signatures and fourteen ratifications had been received (the treaty comes into force one year after it receives sixty ratifications) (Burke 1985, 2). The new treaty recodified and amplified many of the customs and procedures cited in the treaties of 1958 but sailed far beyond precedent into uncharted and stormy waters.

The treaty contained 320 articles and nine annexes, covering in great detail all aspects of maritime activities. Although negotiations were long, tedious, and sometimes heated, 130 countries voted to adopt the convention, 4 voted against, and 17 abstained (*The Law of the Sea* 1983, 192). On the first day it was open to signature, 119 countries signed the convention—acceptance unprecedented "in the annals of international law" (*The Law of the Sea* 1983, xxxiii).

In an attempt to resolve the disparate territorial seas claimed by coastal states, the treaty authorized each state to extend its territorial sea to a maximum of 12 nautical miles from its coastline (art. 3). Within this area it may exercise broad authority, including designation of sea

lanes and traffic separation schemes and limited criminal and civil jurisdiction over foreign vessels, but all ships may exercise the right of innocent passage through territorial seas (arts. 17-26). Because the extended
territorial seas of opposite states could subsume all waters in what were
formerly high seas in recognized international straits, a new concept,
"transit passage," was offered to permit "freedom of navigation and overflight during continuous and expeditious passage or for the purposes of
entering or leaving a state bordering on the strait." Ships in transit passage enjoy almost all of the rights and obligations of those in innocent
passage except the right to stop and anchor temporarily—passage must
be "continuous and expeditious" (Jarman 1985a, 9).

The treaty also addressed the width of the contiguous zone—that area
contiguous with the territorial sea in which a coastal state may enforce
"customs, fiscal, immigration or sanitary laws." Coastal states are permitted a contiguous zone not to exceed a width of 24 nautical miles from the
baseline (art.. 33).

Article 57 of the Convention on the Law of the Sea established a 200-
mile exclusive economic zone (EEZ), within which a coastal state has the
sovereign but not exclusive right to exploit the natural resources (art. 56).
Coastal states also have an obligation to abstain from overfishing (art. 61)
but are to permit other states to harvest stocks in their EEZ that otherwise would be underexploited (art. 62).

The treaty attempted to resolve the nebulous and narrow boundary of
the continental shelf by prescribing that it may be coextensive with the
area of the EEZ or may be larger under certain conditions (art. 76). In
practice the formula for extension beyond the EEZ is so complicated and
costly to invoke that it may rarely be used; for practical purposes, the area
of the EEZ and the continental shelf are the same (Jarman 1985b, 21,
22).

In the area of deep-sea mining, conducted on the "'sea-bed and ocean
floor and the subsoil thereof, beyond the limits of national jurisdiction,'"
the Law of the Sea Treaty addressed the most controversial matters. It created an international registry for mineral claims in the deep sea and an
International Sea-Bed Authority to regulate mining activities and stated
that "no claims to recovered minerals are to be recognized internationally
except those made in conformity with the treaty" (Jarman 1985c, 17, 18).

For fourteen years the nations of the world labored over the wording of
the Law of the Sea Treaty, and the United States was in the forefront of
the negotiations. Yet when it came time to sign, the United States
refused to do so! The kindest thing that might be said is that we reneged.

[T]he United States rejects the treaty as a whole because it objects to one small part of it, that dealing with deep seabed mining. The Reagan Administration believes that this part of the Treaty is fatally flawed because it is allegedly antithetical to the free enterprise system that the Administration thinks should prevail in the mining of deep seabed resources....

[When] in July, 1982, the United States announced its rejection of the treaty because it objected to the deep seabed mining regime, it struck many participants that the United States was going back on an understanding that had been the essential underpinning of the entire negotiation [that the treaty was a package deal]. Nations were particularly aggrieved at the United States because the latter had been a leader in the negotiations and during the past four years had succeeded in securing literally dozens of favorable changes in the proposed treaty. (Burke 1985, 2, 3)

The president of the Third United Nations Conference on the Law of the Sea, Tommy Koh of Singapore, was a bit pointed in his reaction:

All speakers have addressed an earnest appeal to the United States to reconsider its position. The United States is a country which has, throughout its history, supported the progressive development of international law and has fought for the rule of law in relations between States. The present position of the United States Government towards this Convention is, therefore, inexplicable in the light of its history, in the light of its specific law of the sea interests and in the light of the leading role which it has played in negotiating the many compromises that have made this treaty possible. (*The Law of the Sea* 1983, xxxv)

The long-range effects of the Reagan administration's action remain to be seen (and the U.S. position can certainly change under future administrations), but it did not make us any friends.

Summary: Critical Maritime Zones and Boundaries

Maritime zones and boundaries recognized by the United States and in international conventions are illustrated in figure 10.1 and defined in the list that follows. Definitions come from Shalowitz (1962, 1964) and relevant international conventions.

• *The high water line*—in lunar tidal areas, the line formed by the intersection of the plane formed by the earth's surface and that formed by the

OFFSHORE JURISDICTION

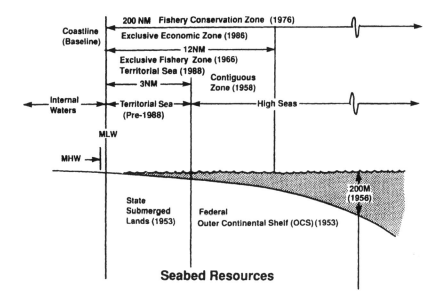

FIGURE 10.1. Critical Maritime Zones and Boundaries

average of all high waters (high tides) over a period of 18.6 years (in practice, 19 years). In the United States, private ownership of land below this line is generally prohibited by state law. If permitted, private ownership is encumbered by navigational servitude and other expressions of common property resources and public trust. Synonymous with "high tide line" and "shoreline."

• *The low water line*—in lunar tidal areas, the line formed by the intersection of the plane formed by the earth's surface and that formed by the average of all the low waters (low tides) over a period of 18.6 years (in practice, 19 years). Synonymous with "low tide line" and "coastline."

• *Tidelands*—the land surface between the mean high and mean low water lines, generally under state jurisdiction. Synonymous with "shore" and "shorelands."

• *The baseline*—the line from which all offshore jurisdictional boundaries are measured. Along the open ocean coast, it is the mean low water line. Across bays, river mouths, and inlets, it is a "closure line" connecting points on the mean low water line of both sides and defining the boundary between internal waters and the marginal sea.

• *Internal waters*—waters of a country lying landward of the territorial sea and those within its land territory (such as rivers and lakes), over which the nation has complete sovereignty.

• *Territorial sea*—a zone extending seaward from the baseline 12 geographical (nautical) miles (Convention on the Law of the Sea). Within this zone the coastal state (nation) has exclusive jurisdiction, subject to foreign vessels' right of innocent passage. Synonymous with "marginal sea." Historically the United States territorial sea was 3 geographical miles wide, and seabed resources within the territorial sea (the "inner continental shelf") appertained to the contiguous (domestic) state. Off the coast of Texas and the western coast of Florida, state ownership of seabed resources extended beyond the territorial sea to a distance of 9 geographical miles (3 leagues) from the baseline. The Reagan Declaration of December 27, 1988 (54 Fed. Reg. 777) extended the United States territorial sea to a line 12 geographical miles seaward of the baseline but did not affect state boundaries or ownership of seabed resources (Saurenman 1990, 42, 43). In an effort to clear up ambiguities and settle questions concerning the legality of Reagan's declaration, Congressman Walter Jones, a Democrat from North Carolina, introduced H.R. 3842 (137 CONG. REC. H10,841 (Nov. 21, 1991)), a bill that would (1) confirm extension of the U.S. territorial sea from 3 to 12 miles, (2) extend the U.S. contiguous zone from 12 to 24 miles, and (3) direct a study of the adequacy of existing authorities to manage natural resources within the extended territorial sea. The House Merchant Marine and Fisheries Committee held hearings on H.R. 3842 (138 CONG. REC. D65 (Feb. 4, 1992)) and reported the bill to the House of Representatives on August 12 (138 CONG. REC. H8144 (Aug. 12, 1992)), but it failed to become law during the Hundred and Second Congress (138 CONG. REC. D1337 (Oct. 29, 1992)).

• *High seas*—all waters seaward of the territorial sea, within which all nations exercise broad but not unlimited freedoms of navigation, fishing, overflight, and laying of submarine cables and pipelines (Convention on the High Seas) as well as construction of artificial islands and scientific research (Convention on the Law of the Sea).

• *Contiguous zone*—a portion of the high seas, contiguous with the territorial sea, within which a coastal state may enforce its laws regarding customs, fiscal matters, immigration, and sanitation. The contiguous zone may extend up to 24 geographical miles seaward of the baseline (Convention on the Law of the Sea). Prior to the Reagan declaration, the U.S. contiguous zone was recognized as a band 9 miles wide contiguous with the outer boundary of the territorial sea (territorial sea plus contiguous zone extended 12 miles seaward from the baseline). Apparently the contiguous zone is now coterminous with and subsumed within the U.S. territorial sea.

• *Continental shelf*—the submerged portion of a continent extending seaward from the outer limit of the territorial sea to a depth of 200 meters (100 fathoms) or beyond that depth to "where the depth of the superjacent waters admits of the exploitation of the natural resources of said areas" (Convention on the Continental Shelf), but it may extend seaward as far as 200 miles from the baseline (Convention on the Law of the Sea). In the United States, synonymous with "outer continental shelf."

• *Exclusive economic zone (EEZ)*—a 200-mile-wide zone extending seaward from the baseline, within which the coastal state (nation) may exercise sovereign but not exclusive rights to exploit the natural resources with a concomitant obligation to protect the environment (Convention on the Law of the Sea). Although the United States has not signed the Law of the Sea Treaty, the 1986 amendments to the Fishery Conservation and Management Act of 1976 establish an exclusive fishery conservation zone extending seaward 200 miles from the baseline, within which the United States exercises exclusive authority over marine species.

REFERENCES

Burke, William T. 1985. "The Law of the Sea Treaty, Customary Law, and the United States." *Water Log* (newsletter of the Mississippi-Alabama Sea Grant Consortium) 5 (2): 2-6.

Clark, Robert E., ed. 1967. *Waters and Water Rights*. Vol. 1. Indianapolis: Allen Smith Company. (With 1978 supplement.)

Commission on Marine Science, Engineering, and Resources. 1969. *Our Nation and the Sea*. Washington, DC: Government Printing Office.

"Declaración Sobre Zona Marítima." 1957. In *U.N. Legislative Series, Laws and Regulations on the Regime of the Territorial Sea*, Art. II, XIV. U.N. Doc. no. St/Leg./Ser/.B16, Treaty no. 20.

Goldfarb, William. 1984. *Water Law*. Stoneham, MA: Butterworth Publishers.

Jarman, M. Casey. 1985a. "The 1982 Law of the Sea Treaty as Applicable to Marine Transportation and Commerce." *Water Log* (newsletter of the Mississippi-Alabama Sea Grant Consortium) 5 (2): 7-12.

———. 1985b. "Continental Shelf Resources and the Law of the Sea Treaty." *Water Log* (newsletter of the Mississippi-Alabama Sea Grant Consortium) 5 (2): 21, 22.

———. 1985c. "Deep Seabed Mining." *Water Log* (newsletter of the Mississippi- Alabama Sea Grant Consortium) 5 (2): 17-20.

The Law of the Sea. 1983. New York: United Nations.

Martz, Clyde O. 1979. Reprint edition. *Cases and Materials on the Law of Natural Resources.* New York: Arno Press.

Meyer, Michael C. 1984. *Water in the Hispanic Southwest.* Tucson: University of Arizona Press.

"Report of the International Panel." 1969. In *Panel Reports of the Commission on Marine Science, Engineering and Resources.* Vol. 3, *Marine Resources and Legal-Political Arrangements for Their Development,* VIII-1 to VIII-153. Washington, DC: Government Printing Office.

Rice, David A. 1968. *Estuarine Lands of North Carolina: Legal Aspects of Ownership, Use and Control.* Chapel Hill: University of North Carolina, Institute of Government.

Saurenman, John A. 1990. "The Effects of a Twelve-Mile Territorial Sea on Coastal State Jurisdiction: Where Do Matters Stand?" *Territorial Sea Journal* 1 (1): 39-79.

Shalowitz, Aaron L. 1962. *Shore and Sea Boundaries.* Vol. 1, *Boundary Problems Associated with the Submerged Lands Cases and the Submerged Land Acts.* Washington, DC: Government Printing Office.

———. 1964. *Shore and Sea Boundaries.* Vol. 2, *Interpretation and Use of Coast and Geodetic Survey Data.* Washington, DC: Government Printing Office.

Wenk, Edward, Jr. 1972. *The Politics of the Ocean.* Seattle: University of Washington Press.

Wiel, Samuel C. 1911. *Water Rights in the Western States.* 3d ed. 2 vols. San Francisco: Bancroft-Whitney Company.

CHAPTER XI

Federal Water Resource Development

Water is the lifeblood of the land, but often there is too little (or too much), it is too deep (or too shallow), or it simply is in the wrong place. In efforts to "correct" these perceived discrepancies, the federal government has evolved a complex multiagency approach with primary objectives of enhancing navigation, flood control, and water supplies. Because of the pervasive nature of water, however, the effects of water resource development projects go far beyond their primary intention—to local, regional, and national economic development; wildlife and fisheries habitats; outdoor recreation; urban, suburban, and recreational real estate development; the location and distribution of agricultural land; in essence, everywhere.

Of all the federal programs, those of the U.S. Army Corps of Engineers are the oldest and most far-reaching. Almost every federal land-managing agency carries out some water resource development practices; those of the Soil Conservation Service, the Tennessee Valley Authority, and the Bureau of Reclamation are also discussed.

THE U.S. ARMY CORPS OF ENGINEERS

Authorization to construct public water resource projects was initiated in 1824 by a $75,000 appropriation to the U.S. Army Corps of Engineers to be used for improving navigation and removing sandbars in the Ohio River and for removing snags in the Ohio and Mississippi rivers (4 Stat. 32). In the ensuing century and a half, Corps water resource development activities have had more impact upon land use and wildlife habitat than those of any other federal agency. They have created water bodies where there were none and removed water where there was some. They have made shallow waters deep and deep waters shallow. They have destroyed natural shellfish beds and provided new ones on dredged material. They have built islands essential for the nesting of some birds and eliminated others. Over the years Corps activities tied to the commerce clause have grown and diversified with broadening interpretations of that clause. And with growth and diversification have come increasing conflicts with environmental and natural resource interests.

Navigation

While improvements to navigation were first authorized in 1824, it was not until after the Civil War that great expenditures were made. In an effort "to divert the tremendous energy then at work, from the paths of war to conquests of peace," bills were passed in 1866 authorizing work on at least forty-eight projects at a cost of almost $4 million (Ruffner 1886, 7, 8).

Federal navigation projects are generally limited to public waterways. They include inland waterways, deep-draft harbors and channels, and small-boat harbors and channels and may include such features as anchorages, turning basins, locks and dams, harbor areas, and protective jetties and breakwaters (U.S. Army Corps of Engineers, Office of the Chief of Engineers 1983, 11-1, 11-2). Prior to construction of any navigation project, nonfederal interests must agree to

(1) provide to the Federal Government lands, easements, and rights-of-way, and to provide dredged material disposal areas and perform the necessary relocations required for construction, operation, and maintenance of such project;

(2) hold and save the United States free from any damages due to the construction or operation and maintenance of the project, except for damages due to the fault or negligence of the United States or its contractors;

(3) provide to the Federal Government the non-Federal share of all other costs of construction of such project; and

(4) in the case of a deep draft harbor [greater than 45 feet deep], be responsible for the non-Federal share of operation and maintenance [generally 50 percent of the excess cost of a harbor of greater than 45-foot depth]. (100 Stat. 4083, 4084)

Reservoirs

As early as 1852, the Corps was considering dams at the headwaters of the Mississippi, and in 1868 the St. Paul district engineer recommended a study to determine the possibility of retaining floodwaters to be released during low-flow conditions as an aid to navigation. Study funds were appropriated in 1874 (Merritt 1984, 3), and construction moneys were included in the Rivers and Harbors Acts of 1880 (21 Stat. 193) and 1881 (21 Stat. 481). The Corps' dam building was under way, clearly related to navigation and clearly supported by the commerce clause of the Constitution.

But while a clear relationship existed between navigation and interstate commerce, a similar federal role in reservoir construction for other purposes initially was not obvious to Congress. The issue was debated extensively before the Senate in 1899. One section of the Rivers and Harbors Bill of 1899 would have authorized funds for construction of three reservoirs in Wyoming at the headwaters of the Missouri River, and another called for a general survey of potential reservoir sites throughout the arid region—both were introduced as Senate amendments (32 CONG. REC. 2268 (Feb. 24, 1899)). Objections were raised by Senator Joseph L. Rawlins of Utah, who feared conflicts with western water law:

> [I]t would be almost impossible to survey, construct, and maintain a reservoir without interfering with vested rights to the use of water which have already accrued, and leading to complications, the nature of which can not now be fully anticipated....
>
> I want the Senate to understand that this is the dedication of this money to the creation of these reservoirs for the benefit of private individuals, who already in many cases are in possession of the title to the use of the water. (32 CONG. REC. 2269 (Feb. 24, 1899))

A second line of attack came from Senator John C. Spooner of Wisconsin, who endorsed reservoirs for flood control and to enhance navigation (32 CONG. REC. 2271 (Feb. 24, 1899)) but questioned the motivation and precedent of the new provisions:

> [T]he real object of this proposed legislation is to secure the construction of reservoirs in the States for irrigation purposes; and it is a work, if that be the purpose, upon which the Congress...ought not to engage, I think, at this time, if ever....
>
> [T]his is the beginning of an elaborate system which, in my judgment, before it is ended will cost this Government hundreds of millions of dollars for the reclamation of what is known as the arid-land region. (32 CONG. REC. 2269 (Feb. 24, 1899))
>
> This ought not simply to be considered a barrel of pork out of which each State and each community is to have, without regard to the merits of the proposition itself, its share....I do not know what right Congress has

to go into a State to construct reservoirs for irrigation....[W]hen you boil it down it is little more and little less than a proposition to turn the United States, so far as the arid-land region is concerned, into a great water company. (32 CONG. REC. 2271 (Feb. 24, 1899))

The bill passed the Senate with only three dissenting votes (32 CONG. REC. 2302 (Feb. 24, 1899)) but ran into trouble with the House members of the conference committee, who prevailed in deleting the reservoir provisions. When the conference report was presented to the Senate on March 3, a lengthy and passionate debate ensued, led by Senator Francis E. Warren of Wyoming, who implored the Senate to reject the report (32 CONG. REC. 2815-2843 (Mar. 3, 1899)). Warren's speech appeared to have lasted well over an hour on the last business day of the Fifty-fifth Congress and resulted in two votes to recommit the bill to conference (32 CONG. REC. 2824, 2843 (Mar. 3, 1899)). The second vote was successful, and a second conference meeting was held with only hours remaining in the session—a highly unusual procedure. The House members held firm, however. The second conference committee report was unchanged and was accepted by both houses with little additional comment (32 CONG. REC. 2843, 2925 (Mar. 3, 1899)).

While the Corps failed in its initial attempts to construct reservoirs for irrigation, Congress subsequently expanded Corps activities to include hydroelectric power generation (1912, 1917), flood control (1917, 1927, 1936, 1974), recreation (1944, 1962, 1965), water supply (1944, 1958, 1965), and water quality (1961, 1972, 1974) (U.S. Army Corps of Engineers, Office of the Chief of Engineers 1983, 2-3). Project planning generally begins by addressing one or a few limited problems and expands to a "multipurpose" reservoir project with a favorable bene-fit-cost ratio.

A need to include diverse interests in the planning process has accompanied the increased complexity of water resource development projects. In order to assist the Corps in meeting the environmental demands of the 1970s, Lieutenant General Frederick J. Clarke, then chief of engineers, appointed a six-member Environmental Advisory Board on April 2, 1970. Charter members of the board were particularly exemplary conservationists: Roland Clement, vice-president, National Audubon Society; Lynton K. Caldwell, professor of political science, University of Indiana; Charles H. W. Foster, executive director, New England Natural Resources Center; Harold Gilliam, environmental reporter, San Francisco *Chronicle;* Richard H. Pough, chairman of the board, Open Space Action Institute and America the Beautiful Fund; and Charles H. Stoddard, environmental consultant and former director of the Bureau of Land Management (Reuss 1983, 1). The board represented a personal and professional risk to its members and a bureaucratic risk to the Corps, and its early days were marked by frequent controversy and confrontation (Reuss 1983, 67). During its first ten years of existence, however, the board was instrumental in easing the Corps into the environmental decade with a minimum of trauma, illustrating the value of this kind of administrative mechanism.

To Get a Project

Corps projects begin as local problems recognized by local leaders, who bring them to the attention of cognizant district engineers. The Corps makes a point of this distinction, stating, "The Corps of Engineers never initiates a project" (U.S. Army Corps of Engineers, South Atlantic Division 1981, 9), but as a project develops from an initial idea to an operational feature, Corps personnel become increasingly associated with its success or failure. The Corps' district office becomes increasingly dependent upon the project for operational funding, and there comes a time during the planning process when the Corps begins to assume a proprietary and paternalistic attitude. Nevertheless, the distinction is important: The Corps reacts to local pressures and follows the mandates of Congress; it does not follow its own whims wherever they may lead.

The path to a successful Corps project is long and tortuous. With some variations, the process is generally as follows (U.S. Army Corps of Engineers 1986):

1. *Action by local people if they perceive water resource problems.* When local interests identify a problem that could be solved by a Corps project—flood control, reservoir, navigation, shore protection, clearing and snagging, and the like—they contact the district engineer of the local U.S. Army Engineer District. In discussions with the district engineer, they learn the type of project most applicable to their problem, and the district engineer learns the magnitude of the problem and the nature and amount of local support for a possible project. Local interests also inform local and state political leaders and their senators and/or representatives in Congress.

2. *Action by congressional delegation and Congress.* If convinced of the need and appropriateness of Corps involvement, a senator or representative requests study authorization through the appropriate public works com-

mittee. If a previous Corps study has been made on the area, a resolution may suffice; if no previous authorization exists, legislation is normally required.

3. *Initial funding of study.* If the resolution or bill passes and a study is authorized, funds are included in annual energy and water development appropriations acts.

4. *Accomplishing the study.* The chief of engineers assigns the study to the appropriate division engineer, who refers it to the cognizant district engineer (back where the process began). The district engineer becomes responsible for conducting the study, including cooperation and coordination with local authorities and state and other federal agencies, holding public meetings, performing environmental assessments, and complying with the Fish and Wildlife Coordination Act, in addition to the necessary engineering and economic analyses. Studies are usually conducted in two phases—reconnaissance and feasibility. Reconnaissance studies are entirely federally funded; feasibility studies require local cost sharing. The studies produce a "definite project report" and an environmental impact statement (EIS), which are forwarded to the Corps' division office.

5. *Division (regional) review.* The division engineer reviews the report and EIS and transmits them to the Board of Engineers for Rivers and Harbors or the Mississippi River Commission for review. In addition to being provided opportunities for public input at the district level, all interested persons are notified of the findings of the district and division engineers and are entitled to present their views to the board.

6. *Board review.* The appropriate board or commission then prepares its report and recommendations, which are transmitted to the chief of engineers.

7. *Preparation of the chief of engineer's report.* The proposed chief of engineer's report and final EIS (FEIS) are sent to the governors of the states affected and to other federal agencies. The FEIS is filed with the Environmental Protection Agency and distributed to the public. The chief of engineers considers all comments received and prepares his report to the secretary of the army.

8. *Administration review.* The assistant secretary of the army (civil works) reviews the chief of engineer's report, obtains comments from the Office of Management and Budget (OMB), and transmits the report to Congress.

9. *Continuation of planning and engineering (CP&E) or advance engineering and design (AE&D).* In some cases planning may continue pending con-

gressional authorization (CP&E); in others planning and design are terminated pending congressional authorization and appropriations based on the definite project report (AE&D).

10. *Congressional authorization.* The House Committee on Public Works and Transportation and the Senate Committee on Environment and Public Works receive the chief of engineer's reports and hold hearings prior to formulating a bill (usually a water resources development bill [omnibus bill]) containing authorization of the project. If the bill passes, the project becomes "authorized," but construction is not yet funded.

11. *Plans and specifications for project implementation.* The district engineer completes plans and specifications for initial project implementation.

12. *Funding for project implementation.* Budget recommendations are made based on state support and the willingness and ability of local sponsors to provide their share of the project cost. Federal construction funds are normally included in annual energy and water resources development appropriations acts.

13. *Contract between the federal government and nonfederal sponsors.* The secretary of the army and the nonfederal sponsors sign a formal agreement obligating the sponsors to participate in implementing, operating, and maintaining the project in accordance with congressional and administration requirements.

14. *Project implementation.* Federal funds are included in the president's annual budget. Construction is managed by the Corps but performed by private contractors.

15. *Operation and maintenance.* Most projects are operated and maintained by nonfederal sponsors. Where federal funds are required, they are requested in the president's annual budget.

Depending on the act or resolution authorizing a particular project, the process just described may be repeated several times and may be interrupted for long periods, until construction and operation are finally authorized and funded (or deauthorized)—often two to four decades after initiation. One may marvel that any project ever succeeds in transiting the maze over so long a time, yet two factors weigh heavily toward success.

The first is the process of "getting hooked"; the second is the politics of the pork barrel. The first step in the project initiation process usually involves local political leaders, and state leaders soon become participants. At these early stages, project costs and adverse impacts are poorly known (if known at all), and the matter is presented as a reasonable solution to a pressing problem. Politicians have little choice but to give their endorsements. As project development proceeds, more and more unfavorable attributes may be discovered, but the politicians have already become aligned with the project—they are "hooked." Even if planning proceeds through several local and state administrations and serious adverse effects become apparent, the tendency is not to break precedent.

"Pork barrel politics" also weighs heavily on the outcome. Because of the preponderance of federal funds in Corps projects, almost every project is economically viable *at the local level.* Politicians are elected and remain in office because of votes from their *local* areas. If they support a project that is locally popular but is not in the best interests of the larger area, they may lose a few friends there, but they will win votes from the local area benefited. If, on the other hand, they fail to support a local project that is adverse to the state or national interest, they may win a few friends outside their district but lose the next election. When elected officials consider proposals for projects in others' districts, it is a matter of "you scratch my back and I'll scratch yours"—a difficult system to beat.

Many have tried. In 1949 the first Hoover Commission on Organization of the Executive Branch of the Government criticized both the Bureau of Reclamation and the Corps and recommended that they be combined to form a Water Development and Use Service in the Department of the Interior. It did not happen. Even "Franklin D. Roosevelt, generally regarded as a strong President, lost every round he fought with the Corps. Although the Champ swung angrily and often, he never laid a glove on the Army Engineers" (de Roos and Maass 1949, 21, 22). Only in the most recent administrations have efforts to reform the Corps begun to have some effect, and these resulted from economic and environmental constraints rather than political considerations.

Not all Corps projects must go through the process described earlier. "Smaller" projects may be executed without specific congressional approval if their cost does not exceed the following limits (U.S. Army Corps of Engineers 1986):

- $4 million for flood damage reduction.
- $2 million for navigation projects.
- $1 million for beach erosion projects.
- $250,000 for clearing and snagging.
- $250,000 for emergency bank protection.

Among the more controversial of the "small project" programs have been those authorized under section 205 of the Flood Control Act of 1948. Under this program the Corps channelized and straightened thousands of miles of natural stream channels, with severe impacts on wetland communities. In recent years activities under section 205 have been limited largely to "clearing and snagging," greatly reducing the associated environmental impacts.

THE BUREAU OF RECLAMATION (BUREC)

While the Corps failed to receive congressional authorization to construct reservoirs for irrigation in 1899, efforts were under way in the Department of the Interior that succeeded three years later. Under the direction of John Wesley Powell, the Geological Survey had embarked on a course leading to the Reclamation Act of 1902 (chapter 4). The act authorized the secretary of the interior

> to make examinations and surveys for, and to locate and construct... irrigation works for the storage, diversion, and development of waters....
>
> [T]he Secretary of the Interior shall...withdraw from public entry the lands required for any irrigation works contemplated under the provisions of this Act. (32 Stat. 388)

To implement the act, the secretary established the Reclamation Service in the Geological Survey, and the service became the Bureau of Reclamation (BuRec) in 1923 (Office of the Federal Register 1987, 331, 332). BuRec serves the seventeen western states, an area of 1.8 million square miles, with (in 1984) a system of 335 storage reservoirs, 360 diversion dams, and more than 17,000 miles of canals, tunnels, and pipelines. As of September 30, 1984, it was providing 25.7 million acre-feet of irrigation water on 9.8 million acres of land annually and producing 62.7 billion kilowatts per year of electric power from fifty-two power plants, furnishing 3.9 million acre-feet of water annually to municipalities and other nonagricultural users, and providing 50.4 million annual visitor days of recreation in 291 recreation areas (U.S. Department of the Interior, Bureau of Reclamation 1984, 1, 2).

THE TENNESSEE VALLEY AUTHORITY (TVA)

The Tennessee Valley Authority (TVA) is generally considered a child of the Great Depression, a product of the "first 100 days" of the Franklin

Roosevelt administration. Its roots predate the Roosevelt era, however. They had begun to grow more than a decade earlier with the efforts of Senator George Norris, a Republican from Nebraska, to fight the increasing power of private utilities and to salvage a government nitrate plant at Muscle Shoals on the Tennessee River near Florence, Alabama. Under the authority of the National Defense Act of 1916, President Woodrow Wilson had designated Muscle Shoals as the location for a plant to produce nitrate (an essential component of explosives) and a dam to provide power for the plant.

The Muscle Shoals project was largely unsuccessful, and after the war the government was faced with disposition of a $13 million nitrate plant, a $69 million power-generating facility, and a $47 million dam. Then commenced a series of attempts to dispose of the plants to private industry for fertilizer production, culminating in a $5 million offer from Henry Ford. Ford's offer stimulated renewed interest within government as well as considerable opposition from power companies in the area (which saw his proposal as a move to obtain a competing power plant at an extremely low cost) and resulted in Norris's introducing a bill in 1921 to provide for government operation of the properties there. This bill failed to pass, as did a similar effort in 1924 (Pritchett 1943, 5-11).

Norris was unsuccessful again in 1928 and once more in 1930, when President Herbert Hoover vetoed the TVA bill. With the depression, the New Deal, and President Roosevelt, Norris found a benevolent environment, and the Tennessee Valley Authority Act was passed on May 18, 1933 (Chandler 1984, 2).

The TVA represented the first effort to institutionalize water resource planning and development across state boundaries on the basis of a river basin (Teclaff 1967, 119-121), but it went far beyond any narrow concept of water resource development. The TVA, an independent federal agency, was

> [t]o improve the navigability and to provide for the flood control of the Tennessee River; to provide for reforestation and the proper use of marginal lands in the Tennessee Valley; to provide for the agricultural and industrial development of said valley; to provide for the national defense by the creation of a national corporation for the operation of government properties at and near Muscle Shoals in the State of Alabama, and for other purposes. (48 Stat. 58)

The new agency was faced with a number of challenges. The Tennessee River was shallow and presented numerous obstacles to navigation. Only

25 percent of the valley's population lived in cities; 51 percent were on farms, and the remainder lived in rural areas. Eighty-five percent of the region had been damaged by soil erosion; 2 million acres were so badly damaged that recovery was questionable, and another 9 million acres were gullied and visibly eroded. Only 4.2 percent of the farms had electricity; net farm income was about one-third of the national average, and the illiteracy rate among adults was almost twice the national average (Tennessee Valley Authority 1983, 7, 10, 13, 14).

The TVA inherited a 1930 study of the Tennessee Valley, conducted over a period of eight years by the U.S. Army Corps of Engineers, which envisioned a series of dams to control floods and improve navigation (Kyle 1958, 9). One proposal in the Corps' study was selected as the initial TVA project, and soon Norris Dam was rising near the newly created town of Norris, Tennessee (Kyle 1958, 15). The TVA recognized the recreational potential of Norris Lake and solicited the cooperation of the National Park Service and the CCC to develop three demonstration recreational facilities on the shores of the lake (Kyle 1958, 27).

From its start at Norris, the TVA system grew swiftly. By 1941 eight dams were operating; by 1943 there were twenty-eight (Pritchett 1943, 142, 314). The flow of the Tennessee was controlled and coordinated with that of the lower Mississippi, and the TVA had affected the lives of practically everyone in the valley.

Twenty-five years after its creation, the TVA's claims were most impressive. Average incomes in the valley had risen by 350 percent since 1929, compared with the national average of 250 percent. Manufacturing incomes had increased by 502 percent, compared with 321 percent on a national basis. Ninety-five percent of rural housing had the TVA's low-cost electricity. Shipping on the Tennessee River had increased sixty-five-fold. And perhaps most significantly, the TVA's unique institutional form had been accepted by state and local governments, and by the people, in the region (Kyle 1958, 11, 12).

The second twenty-five years brought great changes. Cheap electricity and economic growth generated demands for more electricity, and by the late 1940s projections were exceeding the TVA's hydropower capacity. In the 1950s the TVA began constructing coal-fired plants, and by 1970 the coal plants were generating six times as much power as was produced from the dams. Then came nuclear power. The TVA began its nuclear power program in 1966, and the first plant, Browns Ferry, came on line in 1974—and in 1967 came the first of many rate increases. Between 1965 and 1985, the TVA's generating capacity doubled, but the cost to the residential consumer more than tripled between 1973 and 1985 (Tennessee Valley Authority 1983, 42-49).

Environmental problems also are besetting the agency. Water pollution from mining, pesticides, and silt threatens the streams, while atmospheric deposition threatens the land. Efforts to remove pollutants from liquid and gaseous waste create sludge, which must be disposed of. The nuclear plants upon which the TVA so heavily invested create their own distinctive waste problem (Tennessee Valley Authority 1983, 202-204).

And to add to its woes, some analysts (e.g., Chandler 1984) are questioning the validity of many of the TVA's economic claims and the structure of the agency itself. On June 30, 1988, the TVA announced the layoff of 7,500 employees, 15.3 percent of its total staff, in order to achieve its "goal of converting the bloated, top-heavy bureaucracy to a businesslike structure capable of competing with privately owned companies" (Associated Press 1988, 1A). Forty percent of contract personnel and 17 percent of the TVA employees in the nuclear power branch were to be released, and construction of two planned nuclear units was to be delayed (Associated Press 1988, 13A).

THE SOIL CONSERVATION SERVICE (SCS)

In the Flood Control Act of 1936, Congress recognized the importance of upstream land management and flood control measures in any comprehensive flood control program and authorized the USDA to begin instituting such measures. Implementation of the act began a long dispute between the Corps, which had been engaged in large flood control reservoir and other publicly operated downstream flood control works, and the Soil Conservation Service (SCS), with its traditional emphasis on smaller-scale, upstream activities conducted under the aegis of local conservation districts. After a hiatus during the war years, the controversy resumed in Congress during the late 1940s and early 1950s, with the House Public Works Committee (which handles Corps legislation) arguing the Corps' point of view and the House Agriculture Committee supporting the SCS's position (Sampson 1985, 130, 133).

Congress authorized the Corps to construct small watershed projects under section 205 of the Flood Control Act of 1948 and authorized the SCS to engage in similar activities under the Watershed Protection and Flood Protection Act of 1954 (commonly referred to as "P.L. 566"). While the statutes do grant overlapping jurisdiction and controversies between supporters of each agency continue, the agencies generally have worked out their differences. In most cases Corps "205 projects" are located on the more downstream portions of watersheds, while SCS "566 projects" tend to be in the more upstream portions.

The SCS program permits local agencies (districts) to receive federal assistance for projects on watersheds no larger than 250,000 acres. The watershed work plan is developed largely by the SCS, and it may contain land treatment measures, reservoirs, levees and dikes, floodwater diversions, and "clearing, straightening, and enlarging of stream channels" (Simms 1970, 44). When implemented the project may include contributions from many more federal agencies—cost sharing from the Agricultural Stabilization and Conservation Service, loans from the Farmers Home Administration, forestry aid from the Forest Service, and wildlife management assistance from the U.S. Fish and Wildlife Service—as well as numerous state and local agencies (Simms 1970, 44, 46).

During the 1970s the environmental impacts of the "566 program" (and the Corps' similar "205 program") attracted national attention. Support from the National Association of Conservation Districts and others sympathetic toward the SCS was countered by objections from the Department of the Interior and from Friends of the Earth and other environmental groups. Nathaniel Reed, assistant secretary of the interior for fish, wildlife and parks, testifying before the Conservation and Natural Resources Subcommittee of the House Committee on Government Operations, stated that "there is 'shocking and irrefutable evidence of the severe damage to fish habitat and populations in the immediate area of channel alterations'" (Sampson 1985, 215). The controversy became heated, extending over the public, the agencies, and Congress and into the courts.

Among the more publicized cases was *Natural Resources Defense Council v. Grant* (Coffey 1982). The case concerned the 35,000-acre Chicod Creek watershed project, in eastern North Carolina. The watershed contained 10,000 acres of cropland, at least half of which was being damaged by floods on the average of once every four years. The SCS proposed to channelize 66 miles of the stream, create a 12-acre warm-water fish pond, and preserve 61 acres of wetland as mitigation for the loss of fish and wildlife habitat. Twenty days after invitations to bid had been issued, the Natural Resources Defense Council filed suit, alleging that completion of the project would violate the National Environmental Policy Act and a number of other federal statutes, regulations, and policies. Litigation lasted six years, during which time the sponsors revised the project's environmental impact statement, agreed to obtain the necessary Corps of

Engineers' section 404 permit, and made numerous project modifications. Some of the most important modifications, which became precedent for other 566 projects, were the following (Coffee 1982, 81, 82):

1. Channelization was not performed in the wooded swamp habitat type—fallen trees and other debris were removed from the channel (clearing and snagging), but no excavation was done.

2. Construction was not conducted from February 1 to June 30 to avoid damage to herring runs.

3. Sediment traps were constructed and will be maintained at critical points in the channel.

4. A 15-foot-wide grass buffer strip was established on both banks where the channel runs through nonforest land.

5. Channels were excavated from one side only.

6. All spoil was seeded to protective vegetation to reduce erosion and sedimentation.

7. In wooded areas, clumps of trees along the channel were preserved at intervals of 200 to 300 feet.

The court also directed that extensive pre- and postconstruction studies be made to document the project's environmental impact. Contrary to the fears of many environmentalists, the postconstruction study, conducted ten years after project completion, failed to find any profound environmental changes attributable to the project (Lunk and Adams 1988).

THE RIVER BASIN CONCEPT

Following the successful creation of the TVA, President Roosevelt attempted to organize much of the country into seven regional agencies, based partially on drainage boundaries, but failed to obtain congressional approval (Teclaff 1967, 130, 131). Less ambitious approaches subsequently emerged following recommendations of a report by the Water Resources Council (1967), which identified eight basin-oriented patterns of water resource administration:

1. *Interstate compacts.* Agreements between two or more states, consented to by Congress, in which the federal government may assist but is not a member. Twenty-nine such compacts are in effect (Witmer 1968, VII).

2. *Federal-interstate compacts.* Agreements between two or more states and the federal government, with the consent of Congress. Two such compacts exist: the Delaware River Basin Compact and the Susquehanna River Basin Compact (U.S. Army Corps of Engineers, Office of the Chief of Engineers 1979, 4-8).

3. *River basin commissions (title II).* Established by the president pursuant to title II of the Water Resources Planning Act of 1965, river basin commissions include representatives of the member states and federal agencies. Unlike the compacts, river basin commissions are limited to planning and coordinating activities and do not have authority to construct and operate projects (U.S. Army Corps of Engineers, Office of the Chief of Engineers 1979, 4-9).

4. *Basin interagency committees.* Composed of the member states and interested federal agencies, the committees may manage water resource framework studies and river basin plans but are not created by statute and have no statutory powers of their own (U.S. Army Corps of Engineers, Office of the Chief of Engineers 1979, 4-9).

5. *Regional federal-state commissions.* Created to foster the economic growth of specific regions of the country, these multistate-federal commissions consider water resource planning in the larger context of economic development. Two regional commissions were established: the Appalachian Regional Commission and the Coastal Plains Regional Commission.

6. *Intrastate special districts.* Special resource-oriented districts that may conform to drainage basins but more frequently follow political boundaries. Drainage districts and soil and water conservation districts are examples.

7. *Federal regional agencies.* The Tennessee Valley Authority, discussed earlier, is the only example.

8. *A single federal administrator.* An example is the administration of the Colorado River by the secretary of the interior (Water Resources Council 1967, 4).

While basin-oriented administrative units are theoretically desirable, they have been only marginally successful. Only a relatively small portion of the nation is included in interstate basin compacts and commissions, and creation of additional ones is doubtful. The public appears willing to consider hydrologic units as superior to counties but inferior to states (i.e., they are acceptable for intrastate efforts but not for interstate ones).

BENEFITS AND COSTS

Because most statutes authorize construction of federal water resource development projects only "if the benefits are in excess of the costs," the process of benefit-cost analysis becomes critically important. Economic analyses of water resource development agencies are frequently criticized by project opponents, and often with just cause, but the *analysis process* utilized is prescribed by detailed guidelines that have evolved over at least four decades.

The basic principles of formulation and evaluation were first outlined in a report titled "Proposed Practices for Economic Analysis of River Basin Projects," prepared by the Inter-Agency Committee on Water Resources in 1950 and revised in 1958 (U.S. Army Corps of Engineers, Office of the Chief of Engineers 1979, 3-3). On May 15, 1962, President John Kennedy approved for application a report developed by the secretaries of the army; agriculture; health, education, and welfare; and the interior titled "Policies, Standards, and Procedures in the Formulation, Evaluation, and Review of Plans for Use and Development of Water and Related Land Resources." That report was printed as Senate Document 97 of the Eighty-seventh Congress, second session (U.S. Congress, Senate 1962). In his statement introducing the report to the Senate, Senator Clinton P. Anderson of New Mexico said:

> This action will place Federal water resource [project] proposals in a realistic and forward-looking context that will enable both the executive and the legislative branches to make informed judgments of the merits and desirability of the projects. Thus a significant advance has been made in the resources field. As a consequence, it will be possible soundly to devise, authorize, and execute the large programs that are urgently needed to match water supplies to the water requirements of our rapidly growing population and expanding economy. (U.S. Congress, Senate 1962, III)

Senate Document 97 became the water resource project evaluation bible for the next ten years.

Section 103 of the Water Resources Planning Act of 1965 directed the Water Resources Council to develop new guidelines for this process, and the resultant "Principles and Standards for Planning Water and Related Land Resources" (P&S) (38 Fed. Reg. 24,778-24,862 (Sept. 10, 1973)) replaced Senate Document 97 in 1973. The P&S set forth two objectives—national economic development (NED) and environmental quality (EQ)—which were to receive equal consideration. Member agencies were to develop alternative NED and EQ plans and to display the potential impacts of plans in a system of accounts (U.S. Army Corps of Engineers, Office of the Chief of Engineers 1981, 2-6).

Soon after taking office, President Jimmy Carter directed the Water Resources Council, the Office of Management and Budget (OMB), and the Council on Environmental Quality to review water resource policy and to provide recommendations for policy coordination and reform by early 1978 (Council on Environmental Quality 1977, 97). In his Water Resource Reform message of June 6, 1978, Carter reaffirmed his support for the P&S but urged that water conservation be included as a component of the EQ and NED objectives and that nonstructural alternatives be considered in water resource project planning (U.S. Army Corps of Engineers, Office of the Chief of Engineers 1979, 3-3). The P&S were revised by the Water Resources Council and subsequently became codified at 18 C.F.R. 711, 713, and 714 (U.S. Army Corps of Engineers, Office of the Chief of Engineers 1981, 2-6).

Three years later, President Ronald Reagan took office and soon indicated his desire to abolish the Water Resources Council and to rescind the P&S (Caulfield 1984, 224). James G. Watt, then secretary of the interior and chairman of the Water Resources Council, was given the job.

On September 9, 1982, the Water Resources Council voted to repeal the existing P&S and to establish a set of new "principles and guidelines" that more accurately reflected the new president's policies (Water Resources Council 1983, iii). Under the resultant Economic and Environmental Principles and Guidelines for Water and Related Land Resources Implementation Studies (Water Resources Council 1983), water resource development agencies are required to formulate a number of alternative plans and to evaluate the effect of each on several "accounts."

Alternative plans include the following:

(a) A plan that reasonably maximizes net national economic development [NED] benefits, consistent with the Federal objective....

(b) Other plans which reduce net NED benefits in order to further address other Federal, State, local, and international concerns not fully addressed by the NED plan. (Water Resources Council 1983, iv)

Each alternative is to be evaluated in terms of one or more of the following:

(a) The national economic development (NED) account[, which] displays changes in the economic value of the national output of goods and services.

(b) The environmental quality (EQ) account[, which] displays nonmonetary effects on significant natural and cultural resources.

(c) The regional economic development (RED) account[, which] registers changes in the distribution of regional economic activity that result....

(d) The other social effects (OSE) account[, which] registers plan effects from perspectives that are relevant to the planning process, but are not reflected in the other three accounts. (Water Resources Council 1983, v)

Evaluation by the NED account is required (the others are optional), and the NED plan is to be recommended "unless the Secretary of a department or head of an independent agency grants an exception" (Water Resources Council 1983, v). The Reagan-Watt guidelines abolish multiobjective planning oriented toward both environmental quality and national economy and substitute a single "'federal objective' of 'national economic development consistent with protecting the nation's environment'" (Caulfield 1984, 224).

The fifteen-year life of the Water Resources Council ended during the Reagan administration. Its coordinative function was assumed by the Cabinet Council on Natural Resources and Environment and the Assistant Secretaries Working Group on Water. The river basin commissions also were essentially disbanded, and most water resource planning funds to the states were curtailed. The council was a political entity within the executive branch; it drew its power from the support of the chief executive. During the days of the "Great Society," that support existed; now it does not (Grigg 1985, 161).

WHAT OF TOMORROW?

The era of federal water resource development and large-scale projects probably ended in the mid-1960s—overcome by a combination of resource exhaustion, ineffectiveness, environmentalism, budget constraints, and the new federalism (Holmes 1979, 111, 113, 118, 131).

After more than a century of water resource development, dams have been built on most good sites and navigation projects have been authorized on most navigable streams. Opportunities for additional large federal projects are limited simply because most available sites are already occupied.

Since the mid-1960s, a number of persons have contended that large reservoirs are poor solutions to flood problems. The issues of "big dams versus small dams" and "dams versus no dams" are far from settled; many believe that nonstructural solutions such as floodplain zoning, flood-proofing, and warning systems are much more effective and are more appropriate for state or local implementation (Caulfield 1984, 221). Where structural alternatives are desirable (usually in concert with land treatment provisions), they are more often of small size, located high up in the watershed, and amenable to action by state and local governments (Peterson 1954).

Irrigated agriculture is of little interest to the urban voting majority (Caulfield 1984, 220) and is a poor economic investment at the national level. Where desirable it is more appropriately developed and administered through small projects, administered at the state or regional level.

In the days of Gifford Pinchot, Theodore Roosevelt, and John Wesley Powell, the environmental-conservation interests were solidly behind large-scale water resource planning and development with a strong federal flavor (Caulfield 1984, 218). As time progressed, however, these projects came into increasing conflict with environmentalists, whose positions received support from such legislation as the Wild and Scenic Rivers Act of 1968, the Wilderness Act of 1964 and the Eastern Wilderness Act of 1974, and the National Environmental Policy Act of 1969. As a consequence proposals for many water resource projects have failed in recent years (Caulfield 1984, 220, 221).

Decline in public support for water resource development is evinced by actions in the legislative and executive branches of the federal government. Since 1968 the Bureau of Reclamation has received no significant new authorizations, and the lowest average five-year appropriations to the Corps of Engineers during the period 1945-1975 (in constant dollars) occurred in the last four years of that period (Caulfield 1984, 220). During the next five years, appropriations remained relatively constant. The low discount rate used to advantage in computing project benefits and costs has been under attack by the Bureau of the Budget and its successor, the OMB, since Senate Document 97, and in recent years it has been rising toward a more realistic value (Holmes 1979, 118).

Soon after taking office, President Carter initiated a review of 325 active water resource projects and subsequently recommended that funding for eighteen be deleted. After much debate and negotiation with Congress, funds for nine projects were deleted for fiscal year 1978. Among the projects not funded were the Corps' Merrimac Park Lake

Project in Missouri, which would have inundated 75 miles of Ozark streams and over 12,000 acres of farmland and forest at a cost of more than $88 million, and the Bureau of Reclamation's Fruitland Mesa Project, which would have provided irrigation water to fewer than seventy landowners at a federal cost of over $82 million (Council on Environmental Quality 1977, 96, 97).

Continuing his fight against unsound water resource development, Carter vetoed the fiscal 1979 public works appropriations bill because it contained funds "for more than two dozen water projects that did not meet minimum Administration economic or environmental standards and would ultimately have cost $1.8 billion to construct"—and the House sustained the president's veto (Council on Environmental Quality 1979, 388). Economists within the Carter administration also tightened the P&S to the degree that economic justification of most projects—and particularly irrigation projects—became almost impossible, and Reagan economists followed with an even more restrictive approach in their *Economic and Environmental Principles and Guidelines for Water and Related Land Resource Implementation Studies* (Caulfield 1984, 223, 224).

The Reagan administration also brought a change in resource philosophy:

> The Administration believes that the participation of individuals in problem solving is encouraged by using the level of government closest to the problem. Clearly, this philosophy and the local nature of most water problems suggest that the states should take the lead in water resource management and development....
>
> The federal government continues to have a role in water development, but its activities will not be independent of the states. Rather, the federal government is concentrating its efforts on affirming the authority of the states, and allowing them to be accountable for their actions. This is being done through a strong partnership in water development, full cost pricing of water, nonfederal participation in financing, management reforms to give greater deference to state leadership and the reduction of uncertainty over water availability. (Council on Environmental Quality 1982, 164, 165)

The Water Resources Development Act of 1986 brought things to a head. It codified conditions for local cooperation (see the earlier discussion in this chapter); instituted nonfederal cost sharing in navigation projects; increased cost sharing on flood control projects; assessed fees for use of harbor facilities; and unauthorized almost 300 flood control, navigation, and hydroelectric projects with a total authorized cost of $11.1 billion (100 Stat. 4202-4223).

Title I of the act describes the new cost-sharing arrangements. Instead of improvements to commercial navigation being federal responsibilities, at federal cost (U.S. Army Corps of Engineers, Office of the Chief of Engineers 1983, 5-21, 10-4), costs are now shared with nonfederal interests. During the period of construction, nonfederal interests must pay

(A) 10 percent of the cost of construction of the portion of the project which has a depth not in excess of 20 feet; plus

(B) 25 percent of the cost of construction of the portion of the project which has a depth in excess of 20 feet but not in excess of 45 feet; plus

(C) 50 percent of the cost of construction of the portion of the project which has a depth in excess of 45 feet. (100 Stat. 4082)

Nonfederal interests must pay an additional 10 percent of the costs of general navigation features over a period of thirty years, but the value of lands, easements, rights-of-way, relocations, and dredged material disposal areas provided under terms of local cooperation are credited toward this payment. Operation and maintenance of navigation projects continue to be a federal expense, except that in activities related to deep draft harbors, nonfederal interests bear 50 percent of the cost attributable to a depth greater than 45 feet (100 Stat. 4082, 4083).

For flood control projects other than nonstructural measures, nonfederal interests must now

(A) pay 5 percent of the cost of the project assigned to flood control during construction of the project;

(B) provide all lands, easements, rights-of-way, and dredged material disposal areas required only for flood control and perform all necessary relocations, and

(C) provide that portion of the joint costs of lands, easements, rights-of-way, dredged material disposal areas, and relocations which are assigned to flood control. (100 Stat. 4084)

In the event that the nonfederal costs just described are less than 25 percent of the project costs, nonfederal interests must pay 25 percent of the project costs assigned to flood control; but nonfederal costs cannot exceed 50 percent of total project costs (100 Stat. 4094). The nonfederal share of nonstructural flood control measures will be 25 percent of such costs (100 Stat. 4095). The nonfederal share of other project purposes will be as follows:

(1) hydroelectric power: 100 percent;

(2) municipal and industrial water supply: 100 percent;

(3) agricultural water supply: 35 percent;

(4) recreation, including recreational navigation: 50 percent of the separable costs and, in the case of any harbor or inland harbor or channel project, 50 percent of joint and separable costs allocated to recreational navigation;

(5) hurricane and storm damage reduction: 35 percent; and

(6) aquatic weed control: 50 percent of control operations. (100 Stat. 4085)

In order to provide a portion of the federal costs of navigation projects, the act creates two new trust funds and sources of revenue. Receipts from a harbor maintenance tax, assessed at the rate of 0.04 percent of the value of commercial cargos imported or exported through U.S. ports (100 Stat. 4266), will be deposited in the Harbor Maintenance Trust Fund (100 Stat. 4269), which may furnish up to 40 percent of harbor maintenance and operations costs (100 Stat. 4106). The federal tax on fuels used in commercial transportation on inland waterways will be $.10 per gallon until 1990, then it will increase gradually to $.20 per gallon after 1994. Receipts from this inland waterways tax will be deposited in the Inland Waterways Trust Fund (100 Stat. 4271) and will be used to pay 50 percent of the federal cost of constructing the Inland Waterways Transportation System (100 Stat. 4084).

REFERENCES

Associated Press. 1988. "TVA to Lay Off 7,500 Employees, Citing Need for 'Survival.'" *Atlanta Constitution* (June 30): 1A, 13A.

Caulfield, Henry P., Jr. 1984. "U.S. Water Resources Development Policy and Intergovernment Relations." In *Western Public Lands: The Management of Natural Resources in a Time of Declining Federalism,* edited by John G. Francis and Richard Ganzel, 213-231. Totowa, NJ: Rowman and Allanheld.

Chandler, William U. 1984. *The Myth of TVA.* Cambridge, MA: Ballinger Publishing Company.

Coffey, Albert. 1982. "Stream Improvement: The Chicod Creek Episode." *Journal of Soil and Water Conservation* 37 (2): 80-82 (March-April).

Council on Environmental Quality. 1977. *Environmental Quality—1977.* Washington, DC: Government Printing Office.

————. 1979. *Environmental Quality—1979.* Washington, DC: Government Printing Office.

————. 1982. *Environmental Quality—1982.* Washington, DC: Government Printing Office.

de Roos, Robert, and Arthur A. Maass. 1949. "The Lobby That Can't Be Licked: Congress and the Army Engineers." *Harpers* 199 (August): 21-30.

Grigg, Neil S. 1985. *Water Resources Planning.* New York: McGraw-Hill Book Company.

Holmes, Beatrice Hort. 1979. *History of Federal Water Resources Programs and Policies, 1961-70.* U.S. Department of Agriculture Miscellaneous Publication no. 1379. Washington, DC: Government Printing Office.

Kyle, John H. 1958. *The Building of TVA.* Baton Rouge: Louisiana State University Press.

Lunk, Edward M., and David A. Adams. 1988. "A Pre- and Post-Construction Evaluation of the Chicod Creek Watershed, N.C." Vegetation Analysis Subreport, Habitat Inventory Subreport, and Wildlife Resource Utilization Subreport. Raleigh, NC: Soil Conservation Service.

Merritt, Raymond H. 1984. *The Corps, the Environment, and the Upper Mississippi River Basin.* Written for the Historical Division, Office of Administrative Services, Office of the Chief of Engineers, Department of the Army. Washington, DC: Government Printing Office.

Office of the Federal Register. 1987. *The United States Government Manual 1986/87.* Washington, DC: Government Printing Office.

Peterson, Elmer T. 1954. *Big Dam Foolishness.* New York: Devin-Adair Company.

Pritchett, C. Herman. 1943. *The Tennessee Valley Authority.* Chapel Hill: University of North Carolina Press.

Reuss, Martin. 1983. *Shaping Environmental Awareness: The United States Army Corps of Engineers Environmental Advisory Board 1970-1980.* EP 870-1-10. U.S. Department of Defense, Department of the Army, U.S. Army Corps of Engineers, Office of the Chief of Engineers. Washington, DC: Government Printing Office.

Ruffner, Capt. E. H. 1886. *The Practice of the Improvement of the Non-Tidal Rivers of the United States, with an Examination of the Results Thereof.* New York: John Wiley & Sons.

Sampson, R. Neil. 1985. *For Love of the Land.* League City, TX: National Association of Conservation Districts.

Simms, D. Harper. 1970. *The Soil Conservation Service.* New York: Praeger Publishers.

Teclaff, Ludwik A. 1967. *The River Basin in History and Law.* The Hague, Netherlands: Martinus Nijhoff.

Tennessee Valley Authority. 1983. *The First Fifty Years: Changed Land, Changed Lives.* Knoxville: Tennessee Valley Authority.

U.S. Army Corps of Engineers. 1983. "Annual Report FY 83 of the Chief of
    Engineers on Civil Works Activities." Washington, DC: Government
    Printing Office.
————. 1986. "Fifteen Steps to a Civil Works Project." EP 1105-2-10.
    Washington, DC: U.S. Department of Defense, Department of the Army,
    U.S. Army Corps of Engineers. (Fold-out pamphlet.)
————. Office of the Chief of Engineers. 1979. *Digest of Water Resources Policies
    and Authorities.* Washington, DC: U.S. Department of Defense,
    Department of the Army, U.S. Army Corps of Engineers, Office of the
    Chief of Engineers.
————. 1981. *Digest of Water Resources Policies and Authorities.* Washington, DC:
    U.S. Department of Defense, Department of the Army, U.S. Army Corps
    of Engineers, Office of the Chief of Engineers.
————. 1983. *Digest of Water Resources Policies and Authorities.* Washington, DC:
    U.S. Department of Defense, Department of the Army, U.S. Army Corps
    of Engineers, Office of the Chief of Engineers.
U.S. Army Corps of Engineers. South Atlantic Division. 1981. *Water Resources
    Development in North Carolina 1981.* Atlanta, GA: U.S. Department of
    Defense, Department of the Army, U.S. Army Corps of Engineers, South
    Atlantic Division.
U.S. Congress. Senate. 1962. "Policies, Standards, and Procedures in the
    Formulation, Evaluation, and Review of Plans for Use and Development
    of Water and Related Land Resources." 87th Cong., 2d sess. S. Doc. 97.
    Washington, DC: Government Printing Office.
U.S. Department of the Interior. Bureau of Reclamation. 1984. *Summary
    Statistics.* Vol. 1, *Water, Land, and Related Data.* Washington, DC:
    Government Printing Office.
Water Resources Council. 1967. "Alternative Institutional Arrangements and
    Guidelines for Managing River Basin Operations." Report of the Task
    Force on Institutional Arrangements for River Basin Planning.
    Washington, DC: Government Printing Office.
————. 1983. *Economic and Environmental Principles for Water and Related Land
    Resources Implementation Studies.* Washington, DC: Government Printing
    Office.
Witmer, T. Richard, ed. 1968. *Documents on the Use and Control of the Waters of
    Interstate and International Streams.* 90th Cong., 2d sess. H. Doc. 319.
    Washington, DC: Government Printing Office.

CHAPTER XII

Water Resource Protection

The distribution and maintenance of renewable natural resources are so closely tied to water resources that professional resource managers must have an understanding of the legal and administrative structures governing water resource protection. As in many other natural resource areas, federal involvement began in the later years of the nineteenth century. Initially based on commerce considerations and narrowly oriented, the federal role has since grown in breadth and depth.

NAVIGATION

The first federal efforts toward water resource protection produced some of the most long-lived legislation in the field of natural resources—legislation directed not toward environmental impacts but toward protection of waterborne commerce; not toward natural resource agencies but toward the U.S. Army Corps of Engineers. In one quick vote, Congress gave the Corps authority and responsibility for maintaining the integrity of the nation's waterways, and the Corps has executed that authority since 1899.

The Foundation

On the evening of Friday, February 24, 1899, barely a week before adjournment, the United States Senate resumed debate on the Rivers and Harbors Bill (H.R. 11795), "making appropriations for the construction, repair, and preservation of certain public works on rivers and harbors, and for other purposes" (32 CONG. REC. 2268 (Feb. 24, 1899)). After lengthy and heated debate on a proposal to construct a system of reservoirs for irrigation and flood control (chapter 11) and on a proposed canal across the Isthmus of Panama (32 CONG. REC. 2268-2282 (Feb. 24, 1899)), Senator William P. Frye of Maine, chair of the Committee on Commerce, introduced a letter from the Corps of Engineers requesting that ten additional sections be added to the bill. As the letter explained, "these new sections contain no new matter, but simply revise and make clearer and more definite laws that have already been enacted," so Frye moved for their adoption (32 CONG. REC. 2297 (Feb. 24, 1899)).

Senator Richard F. Pettigrew of South Dakota was the sole objector:

> [I]t seems to me a bad precedent that we should codify the laws upon this subject, bring it in here at the last minute, at the end of the day, and without reading it, without having it printed and laid on our desks, without any chance to consider or think about it, practically knowing nothing about it, put it through as an amendment to an appropriation bill. (32 CONG. REC. 2297 (Feb. 24, 1899))

And so, without further ado, the Senate passed and sent to conference the regulatory provisions of the Rivers and Harbors Act of 1899—the most far-reaching and longest-lived federal land use regulations this nation has ever known.

The conference committee, appointed on March 1 (32 CONG. REC. 2622, 2662 (Mar. 1, 1899)), returned its report to the Senate on March 3 (32 CONG. REC. 2814 (Mar. 3, 1899)). The conference report debate in both houses occupies more than thirty pages in the *Congressional Record*—queries concerning local project funding and long harangues over reservoir authorization and the feasibility and desirability of a Panama Canal—but not one word about the regulatory provisions. On March 3, 1899, the day before adjournment, the Rivers and Harbors Act of 1899 became law (30 Stat. 1121).

Sections 9, 10, and 13 contain the act's most important regulatory provisions:

> Sec. 9. It shall not be lawful to construct or commence the construction of any bridge, dam, dike, or causeway over or in any port, roadstead, haven, harbor, canal, navigable river, or other navigable water of the United States until the consent of Congress to the building of such structures shall have been obtained and until the plans for the same shall have been submitted to and approved by the Chief of Engineers and by the Secretary of War: *Provided,* That such structures may be built under authority of the legislature of a State across rivers and other waterways the navigable portions of which lie wholly within the limits of a single State. (Presently codified, with amendments, as 33 U.S.C. 401 (1988))

> Sec. 10. The creation of any obstruction not affirmatively authorized by

Congress to the navigable capacity of any of the waters of the United States is hereby prohibited, and it shall not be lawful to build or commence the building of any wharf, pier, dolphin, boom, weir, breakwater, bulkhead, jetty, or other structures in any port, roadstead, haven, harbor, canal, navigable river, or other water of the United States outside established harbor lines, or where no harbor lines have been established, except on plans recommended by the Chief of Engineers and authorized by the Secretary of War; and it shall not be lawful to excavate or fill, or in any manner to alter or modify the course, location, condition, or capacity of any port, roadstead, haven, harbor, canal, lake, harbor of refuge, or inclosure within the limits of any breakwater, or of the channel of any navigable water of the United States, unless the work has been recommended by the Chief of Engineers and authorized by the Secretary of War prior to beginning the same. (Presently codified as 33 U.S.C. 403 (1988).)

Sec. 13. It shall not be lawful to throw, discharge, or deposit, or cause, suffer, or procure to be thrown, discharged, or deposited either from or out of any ship, barge, or other floating craft of any kind, or from the shore, wharf, manufacturing establishment, or mill of any kind, any refuse matter of any kind or description whatever other than that flowing from streets and sewers and passing therefrom in a liquid state, into any navigable water of the United States, or into any tributary of any navigable water from which the same shall float or be washed into such navigable water; and it shall not be lawful to deposit, or cause, suffer, or procure to be deposited material of any kind in any place on the bank of any navigable water, or on the bank of the tributary of any navigable water, where the same shall be liable to be washed into such navigable water either by ordinary or high tides, or by storms, or floods, or otherwise, whereby navigation shall or may be impeded or obstructed: *Provided,* That nothing herein contained shall extend to, apply to, or prohibit the operations in connection with the improvement of navigable waters or construction of public works, considered necessary and proper by the United States officers supervising such improvement or public work: *And provided further,* That the Secretary of War, whenever in the judgment of the Chief of Engineers anchorage and navigation will not be injured thereby, may permit the deposit of any material above mentioned in navigable waters, within limits to be defined and under conditions to be prescribed by him, provided application is made to him prior to depositing such material. (Presently codified as 33 U.S.C. 407 (1988).)

All of this may be summarized as follows:

1. Do not build any dams or bridges across navigable waters of the

United States without the approval of Congress (section 9).

2. Do not build any structure, do any dredging, or deposit any fill in navigable waters without a permit from the Corps of Engineers (section 10).

3. Do not let any trash get into navigable waters of the United States (section 13).

Congressional Embellishment

Without doubt the initial intent of Congress was to protect navigation in the interests of interstate commerce, an authority clearly provided by the commerce clause of the U.S. Constitution (art. I, sec. 8). Yet, as frequently happens, application grew in scope, geographic extent, and complexity far beyond the narrow consideration of effects upon interstate navigation.

The first complication arose with passage of the Fish and Wildlife Coordination Act Amendments of 1958. In order to "provide that wildlife conservation shall receive equal consideration and be coordinated with other features of water-resource development programs," the Coordination Act provides that

> whenever the waters of any stream or other body of water are proposed or authorized to be impounded, diverted,...or...otherwise controlled or modified for any purpose whatever, including navigation and drainage, by...any public or private agency under Federal permit or license, such...agency shall first consult with the United States Fish and Wildlife Service, Department of the Interior, and with the head of the agency exercising administration over the wildlife resources of the particular State wherein the...facility is to be constructed, with a view to the conservation of wildlife resources by preventing loss of and damage to such resources as well as providing for the development and improvement thereof in connection with such water-resource development. (72 Stat. 564)

Despite these provisions of the Coordination Act, Corps district engineers implementing permit provisions were slow to accommodate environmental considerations. In hearings on a national estuarine protection program authorized by H.R. 25 of the Ninetieth Congress (progenitor of the coastal zone management program), dredging and filling was cited as one of the most important causes, if not the most important cause, of estuarine destruction (U.S. Congress, House, Committee on Merchant Marine and Fisheries 1967, 30, 31, passim). As late as 1963, the Corps' public notices issued in response to permit applications carried the following statement:

> "The Federal courts have ruled that the decision of the Department of the Army must be based on the effect the proposed work would have upon navigation, and not on its effect on property values and other considerations having nothing to do with navigation." (U.S. Congress, House, Committee on Merchant Marine and Fisheries 1967, 33)

The caveat was somewhat softened by 1966:

> "While a Department of the Army permit merely expresses assent so far as the public rights of navigation are concerned, information from interested persons on aspects of the proposed work other than navigation will be accepted and made a part of the record." (U.S. Congress, House, Committee on Merchant Marine and Fisheries 1967, 33)

Yet the Corps continued to place little weight on comments received under the Coordination Act, and in a number of cases it issued permits over the objection of the U.S. Fish and Wildlife Service (U.S. Congress, House, Committee on Merchant Marine and Fisheries 1967, 189-206). Relations between the Corps and state and federal fish and wildlife agencies were strained at best.

Judicial Amplification: Zabel v. Tabb

The most dramatic change in the Corps' permit policy and in national policy toward regulation of work in navigable waters was already developing at the time of the hearings on H.R. 25, but it was not fully developed until 1971. Alfred G. Zabel and David H. Russell owned land riparian to and beneath Boca Ciega Bay, an arm of Tampa Bay, Florida, navigable waters of the United States. Zabel and Russell desired to dredge and fill in their land for a trailer park, a common practice in Florida at that time, and secured the state and local permits required for their development. They then applied for a Corps permit under the provisions of 33 U.S.C. 403—section 10 of the Rivers and Harbors Act of 1899 (1 Env't. Rep. 1449).

Following public hearings in November and December 1966, the Corps' district engineer, Colonel R. H. Tabb, found that "'the proposed work would have no material adverse effect on navigation'" but recommended to the division engineer that the permit be denied:

"Careful consideration has been given to the general public interest in this case. The virtually unanimous opposition to the proposed work as expressed in the protests which were received and as exhaustively presented at the public hearing have convinced me that approval of the application would not be in the public interest. The continued opposition of the U.S. Fish & Wildlife Service despite efforts on the part of the applicants to reduce the extent of damage leads me to the conclusion that approval of the work would not be consistent with the intent of Congress as expressed in the Fish & Wildlife Coordination Act, as amended, 12 August 1958. Further, the opposition of the State of Florida and of county authorities...gives additional support to my conclusion that the work should not be authorized." (1 Env't. Rep. 1450)

The division engineer and chief of engineers concurred, and the secretary of the army denied the permit application on February 28, 1967, because it

1. would result in a distinctly harmful effect on the fish and wildlife resources of Boca Ciega Bay.
2. would be inconsistent with the purposes of the Fish and Wildlife Coordination Act of 1958, as amended (16 U.S.C. 662).
3. is opposed by the Florida Board of Conservation on behalf of the State of Florida, and by the County Health Board of Pinellas County and the Board of County Commissioners of Pinellas County, and
4. would be contrary to the public interest. (1 Env't. Rep. 1450)

The landowners then instituted a suit to compel the secretary of the army to issue the permit, alleging that the proposed work would not hinder navigation and that the secretary had no authority to refuse the permit on other grounds but acknowledging that ecological damage would result. The government supported denial of the permit based on the discretionary authority of the River and Harbor Act of 1899 and the consultation requirements of the Fish and Wildlife Coordination Act. The district court found for the landowners and directed issuance of the permit:

"The taking, control or limitation in the use of private property interests by an exercise of the police power of the government or the public interest or general welfare should be authorized by legislation which clearly outlines procedure which comports to all constitutional standards. This is not the case here.
"As this opinion is being prepared the Congress is in session. Advocates of conservation are both able and effective. The way is open to

obtain a remedy for future situations like this one if one is needed and can be legally granted by the Congress." (1 Env't. Rep. 1451)

The government appealed to the United States Court of Appeals for the Fifth Circuit, which began its deliberations by considering two fundamental issues:

(1) Does Congress for ecological reasons have the power to prohibit a project on private riparian submerged land in navigable waters? (2) If it does, has Congress committed the power to prohibit to the Secretary of the Army? (1 Env't Rep. 1451)

As to the first issue,

[t]he test for determining whether Congress has the power to protect wildlife in navigable waters and thereby to regulate the use of private property for this reason is whether there is a basis for the Congressional judgment that the activity regulated has a substantial effect on interstate commerce....That this activity meets this test is hardly questioned. In this time of awakening to the reality that we cannot continue to despoil our environment and yet exist, the nation knows, if the courts do not, that the destruction of fish and wildlife in our estuarine waters does have a substantial, and in some cases a devastating, effect on interstate commerce. ...Because of these potential effects, Congress has the power to regulate such projects. (1 Env't. Rep. 1451, 1452)

As to the second, the court first found that the federal government did not relinquish the right to control interstate commerce when it conveyed the tidelands to the states under the Submerged Lands Act. It then confirmed the provisions of the Rivers and Harbors Act that any obstruction to the navigable capacity of any waters of the United States was prohibited unless authorized by the Corps of Engineers (1 Env't. Rep. 1452-1454). Finally, it addressed the most important issue—can the Corps deny a section 10 permit on ecological grounds alone?

Common sense and reason dictate that it would be incongruous for Congress in the light of the fact that it intends conservation to be considered in private dredge and fill operations...not to direct the only federal agency concerned with licensing such projects both to consult and to take such factors into account....The Secretary must weigh the effect a dredge and fill project will have on conservation before he issues a permit lifting the Congressional ban.

> [The National Environmental Policy Act] essentially states that every
> federal agency shall consider ecological factors when dealing with activi-
> ties which may have an impact on man's environment....Although this
> Congressional command was not in existence at the time the permit in
> question was denied, the correctness of that decision must be determined
> by the applicable standards of today....In rejecting a permit on non-navi-
> gational grounds, the Secretary of the Army does not abdicate his sole
> ultimate responsibility and authority. Rather in weighing the application,
> the Secretary of the Army is acting under a Congressional mandate to col-
> laborate and consider all these factors. (1 Env't. Rep. 1457-1459)

Finally, the court dealt with the landowners' contention that denial of
the permit constituted taking of private property without compensation
in violation of the Fifth Amendment of the U.S. Constitution. As later
applied in the then embryonic national coastal zone management program, this part of the decision completely changed coastal protection
strategy—from emphasis upon ownership to use of the commerce clause
and police powers:

> Our discussion of this contention begins and ends with the idea that there
> is no taking. The waters and underlying land are subject to the paramount
> servitude in the Federal government which the Submerged Lands Act
> expressly reserved as an incident of power incident to the Commerce
> Clause. (1 Env't. Rep. 1460)

Subsequent to this adverse ruling by the circuit court, the landowners
petitioned the U.S. Supreme Court for *certiorari* (review). Their petition
was denied in 1971, however, essentially confirming the lower court's
decision. In the years since *Zabel v. Tabb,* application of the commerce
clause to environmental issues has continued to grow; in the late 1960s
and early 1970s, the *Zabel v. Tabb* decision was precedent setting.

At the same time that *Zabel v. Tabb* was progressing through the courts,
Congress was looking into Corps activities. Concerned over the narrow tra-
ditional Corps approach to permit activities, the House Committee on
Government Operations issued the following recommendations:

> The Corps of Engineers should instruct its district engineers and other
> personnel involved in considering applications for fills, dredging, or other
> work in estuaries, rivers, and other bodies of navigable waters to increase
> their emphasis on how the work will affect all aspects of the public inter-
> est, including not only navigation but also conservation of natural

resources, fish and wildlife, air and water quality, esthetics, scenic views, historic sites, ecology, and other public interest aspects.

[The Corps]...should permit no further landfills or other work in the nation's estuaries, rivers, and other waterways except in those cases where the applicant affirmatively proves that the proposed work is in accord with the public interest, including the need to avoid piecemeal deterioration of these water areas.

[The Corps]...should vigorously enforce the Refuse Act of 1899 which prohibits discharge of refuse into navigable waters and deposit of polluting material on their banks. (U.S. Congress, House, Committee on Government Operations 1970, 6, 17)

From this guidance the Corps developed new policies for evaluating permit applications:

The decision whether to issue a permit will be based on an evaluation of the probable impacts, including cumulative impacts, of the proposed activity and its intended use on the public interest....The benefits which reasonably may be expected to accrue from the proposal must be balanced against its reasonably foreseeable detriments. The decision...[is] determined by this balancing process....

The following criteria will be considered in the evaluation of every application:

(i) The relative extent of the public and private need for the proposed work;

(ii) Where there are unresolved conflicts as to resource use, the practicability of using reasonable alternative locations and methods to accomplish the objective of the proposed structure or work; and

(iii) The extent and permanence of the beneficial and/or detrimental effects which the proposed structure is likely to have on the public and private uses to which the area is suited....

(b) *Effect on wetlands*....No permit will be granted which involves the alteration of wetlands identified as important...unless the district engineer concludes...that the benefits of the proposed alteration outweigh the damage to the wetlands source.

(c) *Fish and wildlife*....The Army will give full consideration to the views of [state and federal fish and wildlife agencies] in deciding on the issuance, denial, or conditioning of individual or general permits.

(d) *Water quality*. Applications...will be evaluated for compliance with

applicable effluent limitations and water quality standards, during
construction and subsequent operation of the proposed activity.

(e) *Historic, cultural, scenic, and recreational values....*Due consideration
[will] be given to the effect [on such values]. (51 Fed. Reg. 41,223,
41,224 (Nov. 13, 1986))

Through the public interest review, the Corps attempts to act as an
"honest broker," according all interests equal representation; integrating
all applicable laws and policies; weighing the environmental, social, and
economic costs; and judging the permit application accordingly. Theirs is
a goal that is impossible to achieve but imperative to attempt.

WATER AND WETLANDS

Prior to 1948 the federal government played no role in water pollution
control per se, though the Refuse Act (section 13) and the other regulatory provisions of the Rivers and Harbors Act of 1899 gave it some lever-
age in cases affecting navigable water. The federal program began as an
effort to protect public health through abatement of pollution in interstate waters and has grown to affect the use of almost every water body,
wetland, and watershed—in essence, the entire country.

Water Pollution Control

Since its inception in 1948, the national water pollution control program
has expanded to include the following major elements: (1) a water classification system by which the "best use" of each water resource is determined and standards are set for each class of water; (2) permits and
licenses, by which desirable acts that otherwise would be unlawful may
be permitted; (3) penalties for violations of standards or permit provisions; (4) a system of incentives to facilitate compliance; and (5) a
research, surveillance, demonstration, and monitoring program to under-
gird the pollution control activities.

The Federal Water Pollution Control Act of 1948 (FWPCA) contained most of these elements. It began with a broad policy statement,
carefully tied to interstate commerce and public health and dutifully recognizing state primacy:

[I]n connection with the exercise of jurisdiction over the waterways of the
Nation and in consequence of the benefits resulting to the public health

and welfare by the abatement of stream pollution, it is hereby declared to be the policy of Congress to recognize, preserve, and protect the primary responsibilities and rights of the States in controlling water pollution...and to provide Federal technical services to State and interstate agencies and to industries, and financial aid to State and interstate agencies and to municipalities, in the formulation and execution of their stream pollution abatement programs. (62 Stat. 1155)

The 1948 act provided the foundation for our present program, but it was sadly lacking in enforcement mechanisms. Before the government could bring suit in a federal court, the surgeon general had to give formal notice of the offense to the alleged polluter. If no remedial action occurred, the surgeon general was required to give a second notice and to notify the cognizant state or regional water pollution agency. If there was still no action, the administrator of the Federal Security Agency would hold a public hearing on the matter, and, if the hearing board was convinced that a pollution problem existed, it could recommend abatement procedures. Finally, if the polluter still took no action "after a reasonable time," the federal security administrator could request the attorney general to bring suit—after notifying and obtaining consent from the state in which the offense occurred (62 Stat. 1156, 1157). Not many cases were prosecuted.

The Water Quality Act of 1965 attempted to remedy some of the weaknesses in the 1948 act. It created the Federal Water Pollution Control Administration in the Department of Health, Education, and Welfare (79 Stat. 903) and provided that the secretary could promulgate water quality standards for interstate waters if the states failed to act. But even the 1965 act left most initiative in state hands. While the federal government could impose standards and plans if the states failed to do so, the legislative language indicated that Congress did not relish that possibility (Peskin 1986). The Federal Water Pollution Control Act Amendments of 1972 clearly established federal leadership. (Note: The Federal Water Pollution Control Administration was transferred to the Department of the Interior in 1966 [Reorganization Plan No. 2], and on December 2, 1970, the independent Environmental Protection Agency (EPA) was created and assumed most federal pollution control responsibilities [Reorganization Plan No. 3].)

The 1972 act begins with an eloquent statement of goals and policy, realistic perhaps in the environmental glow of the early 1970s but far too optimistic in hindsight:

(1) [I]t is the national goal that the discharge of pollutants into the navigable waters be eliminated by 1985;

(2) it is the national goal that wherever attainable, an interim goal of water quality which provides for the protection and propagation of fish, shellfish, and wildlife and provides for recreation in and on the water be achieved by July 1, 1983 [the "fishable and swimmable" provisions];

(3) it is the national policy that the discharge of toxic pollutants in toxic amounts be prohibited;

(4) it is the national policy that Federal financial assistance be provided to construct publicly owned waste treatment works;

(5) it is the national policy that areawide waste treatment planning processes be developed and implemented to assure adequate control of pollutants in each State; and

(6) it is the national policy that a major research and demonstration effort be made to develop technology necessary to eliminate the discharge of pollutants into the navigable waters, waters of the contiguous zone, and the oceans. (86 Stat. 816)

Since 1972 almost every Congress has added to or amended prior water pollution control legislation, but the statements of goals and policy remain intact (and largely unfulfilled). Most of the subsequent acts have been titled "the Federal Water Pollution Control Act Amendments of (Year)," though several (e.g., the Water Quality Act of 1965 and the Clean Water Act of 1977) have had their own distinctive names. This continual tinkering has produced an almost impossible maze from a historical perspective and a complicated mess from a technical viewpoint. This text does not attempt to unravel the situation; unless otherwise indicated, the discussion that follows is based primarily on title 33 of the *United States Code* as published in 1988, much of which originated in the Federal Water Pollution Control Act Amendments of 1972. Nor does this text attempt to cover in detail all provisions of the national program—that task is best left to courses in environmental law. The most important pollution control elements are touched upon, and provisions with important land use and renewable resource policy implications are discussed.

Resource Classification and Standards

Prior to the 1972 legislation, most states had classified their water resources and developed water quality standards sufficient (in their view) to maintain the uses specified by the classification system. The Clean Water Act requires states to review and revise their water quality classifications and standards at least every three years,

> taking into consideration their use and value for public water supplies, propagation of fish and wildlife, recreational purposes, and agricultural, industrial, and other purposes, and...their use and value for navigation. (33 U.S.C. 1313(c)(2)(A) (1988))

State standards are to be reviewed by the administrator of the EPA, who may issue federal standards if the state standards do not meet requirements of the act or the EPA's implementing guidelines (33 U.S.C. 1313(b) (1988)).

All point sources discharging pollutants "require application of the best available technology economically achievable for such category or class" (33 U.S.C. 1311(b)(2)(A) (1988)). If such technology is not sufficient to maintain the standards assigned to the receiving water in any particular situation, more stringent effluent limitations must be established that "can reasonably be expected to contribute to the attainment or maintenance of such water quality" (33 U.S.C. 1312(a) (1988)).

Permits and Licenses

A central, key provision of the federal water pollution control legislation is the permit required for the discharge of pollutants, termed, oddly enough, a "National Pollutant Discharge Elimination System," or NPDES, permit. With such a permit, a person may discharge pollutants, subject to terms and conditions sufficient to protect the water quality classification and relevant standards. NPDES permits may be issued by the administrator of the EPA but are more frequently issued by state administrators of approved programs (33 U.S.C. 1342 (1988)).

Enforcement and Penalties

Penalties for violation of the federal water pollution laws can be quite severe. Any person who negligently violates provisions of the Clean Water Act may be assessed a criminal penalty of $2,500 to $25,000 and/or up to one year in prison per day of violation for the first offense. For subsequent offenses the act authorizes a fine of up to $50,000 and/or imprisonment of up to two years per day of violation. If a person knowingly violates the act, the corresponding penalties are $5,000 and three years for the first offense and up to $100,000 and six years for subsequent offenses. If a person knowingly endangers others by his or her polluting activities, the criminal penalty may reach $1 million per day of violation (33 U.S.C. 1319(c) (1988)).

Unless the offense is willful or negligent (i.e., a criminal offense), a civil penalty "not to exceed $25,000 per day of violation" may be assessed (33 U.S.C. 1319(d) (1988)). The provision that each day of violation constitutes a separate violation becomes important in situations in which discharges or permit violations occur over extended periods. Forty days of wetland filling, unauthorized discharge of a pollutant, or violation of permit conditions could warrant a $1 million civil penalty. In practice, of course, penalties tend to be much closer to the minimum than to the maximum.

The act also grants standing to any citizen to bring a civil action

(1) against any person (including (i) the United States, and (ii) any other governmental instrumentality or agency...) who is alleged to be in violation of (A) an effluent standard or limitation...or (B) an order issued by the Administrator or a State with respect to such standard or limitation, or

(2) against the Administrator where there is alleged a failure...to perform any act or duty under this Act which is not discretionary with the Administrator. (33 U.S.C. 1365(a) (1988))

No citizen's suit may be initiated prior to sixty days after giving notice to the alleged violator, the administrator of the EPA, and cognizant state officials; nor may any citizen bring suit if a civil or criminal action is under way (33 U.S.C. 1365(b) (1988)).

Incentives

Incentives are scattered throughout the legislation—funds for pilot programs for training operators of waste treatment plants (33 U.S.C. 1254(g)(1) (1988)); cooperative studies of the effects of pollution in estuaries (33 U.S.C. 1254(n)(1) (1988)); demonstration projects on numerous subjects (33 U.S.C. 1255, 1257, 1258 (1988)); and many others—but the greatest incentive is offered through federal grants for construction of waste treatment works.

The subsidized waste treatment management plans and practices are to "provide for the application of the best practicable waste treatment technology before any discharge into receiving waters, including reclaiming and recycling of water, and confined disposal of pollutants so that they will not migrate to cause water or other environmental pollution and shall provide for consideration of advanced waste treatment techniques" (33 U.S.C. 1281(b) (1988)). The federal share is generally 55 percent of the construction costs, with a 20 percent bonus (a total of 75 percent) if the "treatment works or any significant portion thereof...[utilizes] innovative or alternative wastewater treatment processes and techniques" (33 U.S.C. 1282(a)(1), (a)(2) (1988)).

While these provisions have provided the incentive for thousands of municipalities to construct and operate waste treatment programs, their effectiveness has been greatly hampered by the complicated bureaucratic process leading to funding (Council on Environmental Quality 1977, 27-35). Under the 1972 act, three separate, serial submissions generally were required—for facility planning, for construction plans and specifications, and for the building and erection of the treatment works. Each submission was approved at the local, state, and federal levels, and if funds were limited each had to pass through the priority list extant at the time of submission. Many applications required revision and amplification prior to approval, and the complete process often took several years. The resultant inefficiencies contributed to impoundment of funds by the OMB, inability to spend appropriated funds in the time allotted, and subsequent budget reductions.

Areawide Waste Treatment Management: A Start Toward Land Use Management

At the same time that a national land use policy was being debated and eventually defeated (chapter 9), a national land use policy was being approved as part of the 1972 act. Under the provisions of section 208 of that act (86 Stat. 839), plans were to be prepared that would identify the treatment facilities needed over the succeeding twenty years, address all point and nonpoint sources of pollution, and identify the agencies required for plan implementation. The "208 plans" were to include the impacts of agriculture, silviculture, mining, and construction and were to prescribe methods for controlling pollution emanating from these activities.

Such plans were to be developed for "each area...which, as a result of urban-industrial concentrations or other factors, has substantial water quality problems" as identified by a state's governor, and each governor was to designate the boundaries of the area and "a single representative organization, including elected officials from local governments or their designees, capable of developing effective areawide waste treatment management plans" (86 Stat. 839). For portions of a state not so designated, the state was to act as the planning agency (86 Stat. 840). Thus the 208 planning process was statewide and nationwide, ostensibly only in those areas suffering from water quality problems resulting from "urban-industrial concentrations or other factors" but in reality covering much of the nation.

The planning approach was comprehensive and innovative. Initial plans were to be certified by state governors and submitted to the EPA within three years of funding (86 Stat. 840), and the governors were required to "designate one or more waste treatment management agencies...for each area" that were to *carry out the plan.* Once an areawide plan was approved, no construction grants or NPDES permits could be issued except in conformance with the plan (86 Stat. 842).

As with much of the 1972 act, section 208 was overly optimistic and overly ambitious. The Council on Environmental Quality (1976, 24) commented that "no additional Section 208 planning agencies have been funded since July 1, 1975. It is not clear whether the agencies given this planning responsibility have either the necessary authority or access to adequate financial and technical resources to cope with the nonpoint source problem." The CEQ concluded that "there has been little constructive progress in...regulation [of nonpoint source pollution]" (Council on Environmental Quality 1976, 23).

Yet section 208 accomplished much. It provided technical planning assistance through the EPA, the Corps of Engineers, the U.S. Fish and Wildlife Service, and the Department of Agriculture (33 U.S.C. 1288(g), (h), (i), (j) (1988)), and it forced those agencies to communicate and cooperate. It introduced the concept of "best management practices"—commonsense, nonenforceable approaches to land management that reduce nonpoint source pollution—and made "BMPs" part of our natural resource vocabulary. It instituted a program of cost sharing for implementing best management practices on agricultural land (33 U.S.C. 1288(j)(1) (1988)). And probably most important, it got people talking about nonpoint source problems and fostered a realization of their importance and complexity.

The Water Quality Act of 1987

In 1982 Congress began work on the next significant amendments to the FWPCA (Davis 1987b). After four years of deliberation and debate, the House passed the Federal Water Pollution Control Act Amendments of

1986 by a vote of 408 to 0, and the Senate followed, 96 to 0 (132 CONG. REC. 10,942, 10,943 (Oct. 15, 1986); 132 CONG. REC. 16,610, 16,611 (Oct. 16, 1986)). Then Congress adjourned. Despite the overwhelming endorsement of Congress and the constituencies it served, President Reagan pocket vetoed the bill on November 6 because it "cost too much" (Congressional Quarterly, Inc. 1987, 136).

The One Hundredth Congress lost no time in resurrecting the legislation. The House passed H.R. 1 (406 to 8) on January 8, and the Senate followed (93 to 6) on January 21 (Davis 1987a). Reagan vetoed the bill again.

> I am returning without my approval HR 1, the "Water Quality Act of 1987."...The cleanup of our nation's rivers, lakes, and estuaries is, and has been for the past 15 years, a national priority of the highest order. This Administration remains committed to the objectives of the Clean Water Act and to continuing the outstanding progress we have made in reducing water pollution. But the issue facing me today does not concern the ensuring of clean water for future generations. The real issue is the Federal deficit—and the pork-barrel and spending boondoggles that increase it.
>
> The Clean Water Act construction grant program, which this legislation funds, is a classic example of how well-intentioned, short-term programs balloon into open-ended, long-term commitments costing billions of dollars more than anticipated....
>
> HR 1 gave the Congress the opportunity to demonstrate whether or not it is serious about getting Federal spending under control. The Congress should fulfill its responsibility to the American people and support me on these important fiscal issues. Together we can cut the deficit and reduce spending. But by passing such measures as HR 1, the Congress divides our interests and threatens our future. (Reagan 1987)

We shall have an opportunity to see whether Reagan's dire predictions were correct, for this time Congress was in session and promptly overrode his veto by votes of 401 to 26 in the House and 86 to 14 in the Senate. The Water Quality Act of 1987 became law on February 4, 1987 (Davis 1987a).

Among other provisions, the new amendments (1) attempt to simplify the procedures for funding wastewater treatment plants, (2) change the facilities grants program to one based on loans, (3) make a second attempt at solving nonpoint source problems, and (4) provide for a national estuary program.

Much of the criticism of facilities grants was levied against the lengthy and expensive system for evaluating and processing grant applications, particularly in relation to funding support for smaller systems operated by smaller units of government. The 1987 act provides for a simplified procedure—a single submission for projects of $8 million or less (101 Stat. 17). After 1990, however, federal grants for wastewater treatment plants were to end, replaced by a loan program administered by the states. The act authorizes $1.2 billion in fiscal years 1989 and 1990 and $2.4 billion in 1991 to assist the states in establishing revolving loan funds. From such funds they may make loans for up to twenty years to any "municipality, intermunicipality, interstate, or State agency" for the cost of publicly owned wastewater treatment facilities or the development and implementation of water conservation and management programs (101 Stat. 22-24). After 1991 authorizations decline by $600 million per year, phasing out in 1994 (101 Stat. 27)—future Congresses must decide what happens then.

The 1987 act expands federal assistance (and direction) in areas of nonpoint source pollution. Following up on the rather ineffectual performance of section 208 of the earlier legislation, the new amendments require the governor of each state to identify navigable waters in which standards are being contravened by nonpoint source pollution, to identify the sources, and to describe best management practices for dealing with them (101 Stat. 52, 53).

The act then directs each governor to develop and submit to the administrator of the EPA a nonpoint source management program to be implemented during the "first four fiscal years beginning after the date of submission." The plan must identify best management practices for each type of nonpoint source and the programs to implement them. It must also contain an implementation schedule and a certification that the state has obtained or will obtain sufficient authority to implement the programs (101 Stat. 53, 54).

Each state had eighteen months (until August 1988) in which to submit its report and management program (101 Stat. 54). If it did not do so, the administrator had an additional twelve months to prepare the report, and a local public agency or organization could prepare and implement the management program (101 Stat. 55). Federal funds, up to 60 percent of the cost, are authorized for implementation of the management program (101 Stat. 57).

Section 404: A National Wetland Policy?

On December 23, 1970, in the absence of effective water pollution control legislation, President Nixon issued an executive order directing the U.S. Army Corps of Engineers to "implement a permit program under the aforesaid section 13 of the Act of May 3, 1899 [the Refuse Act]," the existing Federal Water Pollution Control Act, the Fish and Wildlife Coordination Act, and the National Environmental Policy Act (Exec. Order No. 11,574). This was a stopgap measure, a "field expedient" in military terms, something to tide the nation over until the Federal Water Pollution Control Act Amendments of 1972 could be passed. Nixon's ploy was effective; it bought time, but it was not a permanent solution. We are in a similar situation in regard to wetland legislation. Many people recognize the value of wetlands and are concerned over the mounting loss of these areas. We have no statutory national wetland policy, so we improvise with section 404.

The 1972 Provisions

This short, highly controversial, three-paragraph restriction on the "discharge of dredged or fill material into the navigable waters" divided jurisdiction between the U.S. Army Corps of Engineers (already issuing similar permits under the Rivers and Harbors Act of 1899) and the EPA (custodian of the nation's water quality). It authorized the secretary of the army to issue permits for such discharges into specified disposal areas, defined through guidelines developed by the administrator of the EPA. It also gave the administrator a "veto power" by empowering him to prohibit discharges that would have unacceptable adverse environmental effects (86 Stat. 884).

Defining the Waters

Much of the controversy over section 404 revolved around definition of the phrase "navigable waters"—"waters of the United States, including the territorial seas" (86 Stat. 886)—and the more familiar term "navigable waters of the United States." At the center of the controversy was inclusion, by regulation, of wetland areas within the definition of "waters of the United States" even though the term "wetlands" did not appear in the statute.

The Corps' initial position was that "the section 404 program was to be applicable only as to those water areas which are under the classical definition of navigable waters" (U.S. Congress, House, Committee on

Public Works and Transportation 1975, 3)—a position that soon landed the Corps in court. In *Natural Resources Defense Council v. Callaway*, the district court found for the plaintiff and directed the Corps, in cooperation with the EPA, to draft new regulations expanding Corps jurisdiction to all "waters of the United States." The Corps did so, publishing proposed regulations in May 1975 (40 Fed. Reg. 19,766 (May 6, 1975)) and interim final regulations in July (40 Fed. Reg. 31,320 (July 25, 1975)). The Corps offered four alternatives, ranging from the traditional concept of control over navigable waters of the United States to what then seemed a radical extension to include private waters and wetlands (about what we have today), and included commentary that was somewhat inflammatory. (Note: Over 4,500 comments were received in response to the proposed regulations, many of which attacked the statutory 404 program as a whole rather than addressing the Corps' regulatory proposals.) "Considerable controversy ensued over whether the construction and maintenance of farm ponds and irrigation ditches and even the plowing of fields would be subject to Corps permit authority. Over a dozen bills were introduced seeking to clarify or restrict this section of the law" (Council on Environmental Quality 1975, 206).

Under the 1975 proposals, the Corps implemented section 404 in three phases. Phase I began immediately, on July 25, 1975, and included "coastal waters and coastal wetlands contiguous or adjacent thereto...[and] inland navigable waters of the United States and freshwater wetlands contiguous or adjacent thereto." Phase II began on July 1, 1976, and included "primary tributaries, freshwater wetlands contiguous or adjacent to primary tributaries, and lakes greater than five acres in surface area." Phase III became effective on July 1, 1977, encompassing the remaining "navigable waters subject to this regulation" (40 Fed. Reg. 31,326 (July 25, 1975)).

Phase I caused little concern; these were areas already regulated under section 10 and in most cases were regulated under state coastal zone management programs. Phase II caused a bit of a stir, but still nothing too serious. But when phase III became fully implemented, and particularly after 1984, when headwater areas were included as a result of a consent decree in *National Wildlife Federation v. Hanson* (623 F. Supp. 1539 (E.D.N.C. 1985)) and the Corps' regulatory activities were extended far beyond its traditional jurisdiction, discussions became heated. The major issues concerned the definition and delineation of wetlands and the concepts of "adjacent" and "isolated" wetlands.

The 1977 Amendments

The Clean Water Act of 1977 expanded section 404 from three paragraphs to seven pages but did little to clarify the wetlands definition problem. Instead it concentrated on administrative efficiency and the kinds of activities regulated.

In order to reduce the number of individual permit applications processed and to eliminate situations that "cause only minimal adverse environmental effects," the amendments provide for issuance of "general permits," each of which applies to a category of activities on a nationwide, regional, or state basis. Under this concept minor actions such as filling of less than 1 acre of wetlands in headwater areas may be permitted without individual permit, application, or even notice, and filling of between 1 and 10 acres of wetlands in headwater areas may be permitted upon notice to the district engineer (51 Fed. Reg. 41,255, 41,256 (Nov. 13, 1986)).

In an effort to reduce opposition from agricultural and forestry interests, the 1977 amendments provided that except for "any activity having as its purpose bringing an area of the navigable waters into a use to which it was not previously subject" or "where navigability might be impaired," the discharge of dredged or fill material from "normal farming, silviculture, and ranching activities" was not subject to section 404 or other regulatory provisions of the act (except for effluent standards). Construction of farm ponds and ditches and construction and maintenance of farm and forest roads were also exempted, as were activities covered by an approved 208 plan (91 Stat. 1600, 1601).

In deference to those states that requested assumption of the 404 program, the act now permits states to do so under a rather detailed and laborious process (91 Stat. 1601, 1604). Not all of section 404 is assumable, however. Even under state assumption, the U.S. Army Corps of Engineers would continue to issue permits for activities in impoundments of Corps-regulated waters and all "phase I" waters other than those "historically used for navigation but no longer used or susceptible for use for navigation" (Gale, Propst, and Sappie 1985, 2). A number of states— for example, Alaska, Nebraska, North Carolina, Michigan, Rhode Island, and South Carolina—have conducted feasibility studies to ascertain their interest in assuming 404 responsibilities, but as of 1985 only Michigan had done so (Gale, Prospt, and Sappie 1985, 1). Michigan was regulating dredging and filling in waterways and wetlands prior to enactment of section 404 (Michigan Department of Natural Resources, Division of Land Resource Programs, 1983). Assumption did not impose a great additional burden for Michigan, but other states have not found this to be the case.

The OTA Assessment

In March 1984 the Office of Technology Assessment (OTA), an arm of Congress, released the results of a wetlands study (U.S. Congress, Office of Technology Assessment 1984) that had been undertaken at the request of the Subcommittee on Environmental Pollution of the Senate Committee on Environment and Public Works. The comprehensive report "describes the ecological values of wetlands, trends in wetlands use, and the effect of Federal and State wetland programs on wetlands." Although it covered many aspects of wetlands and their uses, much of the study related directly to the 404 program (U.S. Congress, Office of Technology Assessment 1984, iii).

The OTA is a policy development and analysis agency; it provides guidance to Congress but does not necessarily recommend specific courses of action. Thus its report, *Wetlands: Their Use and Regulation,* defined major policy issues facing the nation, suggested alternative courses of action, and analyzed their implications, but it did not recommend elements of a national wetland program or even recommend that there should be a national program. The OTA identified three major policy issues:

1. Should Federal involvement in protecting wetlands be increased or decreased?
2. Should the Federal Government improve its policymaking capability through a systematic collection and analysis of additional information about wetlands?
3. Should the Federal Government develop a more integrated approach for managing the use of wetlands? (U.S. Congress, Office of Technology Assessment 1984, 14)

A number of the OTA's options have since been implemented in whole or in part—removing the incentive for agricultural conversions (pp. 15, 77-81); increasing appropriations for wetland acquisition (pp. 16, 72-74); expanding the use of general permits (pp. 16, 72); and accelerating the U.S. Fish and Wildlife Service's National Wetland Inventory (p. 19). However, the most basic issue, the proper federal statutory role in wetland management, remains unsettled.

Regulatory Definitions

While the 1977 amendments did much to allay the fears of agricultural and forestry interests, they did little to reduce the controversy concerning the geographic extent of the program and the policies under which permit applications were evaluated. Much of the controversy and resultant adjudication revolves around definitions contained in the federal regulations, the most pertinent of which are as follows (33 C.F.R. 328.3, 51 Fed. Reg. 41,250-41,251 (Nov. 13, 1986)):

(a) The term "waters of the United States" means

    (1) All waters which are currently used, or were used in the past, or may be susceptible to use in interstate or foreign commerce, including all waters which are subject to the ebb and flow of the tide;

    (2) All interstate waters including interstate wetlands;

    (3) All other waters [isolated waters and wetlands]...the use, degradation or destruction of which could affect interstate or foreign commerce...;

    (4) All impoundments of waters otherwise defined as waters of the United States under the definition;

    (5) Tributaries of waters identified in paragraphs (a) (1)-(4) of this section;

    (6) The territorial seas;

    (7) Wetlands adjacent to waters...identified [above]....

(b) The term "wetlands" means those areas that are inundated or saturated by surface or ground water at a frequency and duration sufficient to support, and that under normal circumstances do support, a prevalence of vegetation typically adapted for life in saturated soil conditions. Wetlands generally include swamps, marshes, bogs, and similar areas.

(c) The term "adjacent" means bordering, contiguous, or neighboring. Wetlands separated from other waters of the United States by manmade dikes or barriers, natural river berms, beach dunes and the like are "adjacent wetlands."

Adjudication

One of the first tests of the extent of Corps jurisdiction was *United States v. Riverside Bayview Homes.* In 1952 George Short began assembling property (Riverside) near the Clinton River in Harrison Township, Macomb County, Michigan, and by the mid-1970s he had accumulated approximately 80 acres of land. In 1973 high water levels on Lake Saint Clair, some three-quarters of a mile east of the Riverside property, caused the Corps and Harrison Township to construct a dike, which disrupted the normal drainage from the property. Thus Riverside could not develop its property without filling. When a source of fill became available in 1976, Riverside attempted to ascertain whether a Corps permit was required, but "uncertainty and confusion existed as to what area the Corps claimed was subject to its permit requirements." (Note: At the time, the Corps was operating under the 1975 regulations, which defined jurisdiction under section 404 to include "freshwater wetlands...contiguous or adjacent to other navigable waters" and which defined "freshwater wetlands" as "[t]hose areas that are periodically inundated and that are normally characterized by the prevalence of [wetland] vegetation" (40 Fed. Reg. 31,324-31,325 (July 25, 1975).) Despite these uncertainties, Riverside applied for a Corps permit on November 15, 1976.

Riverside also obtained a fill permit from Harrison Township. When it had not commenced filling by December 1976, Riverside was notified by the township that its lands constituted a nuisance under the applicable local zoning ordinance and that it stood to sustain substantial fines unless the land were filled. Work began immediately, and on December 22, 1976, the Corps issued a cease and desist order prohibiting further filling. Caught between a rock and a hard place, Riverside continued filling, and the Corps brought an enforcement action on January 7, 1977 (Brief for Respondent at 3-6, *Riverside* (No. 84-701)).

The Corps alleged that the filled area was an "adjacent wetland" under the 1975 regulations and that Riverside had violated section 301(a) of the Federal Water Pollution Control Act by depositing fill on the area without a permit as required by section 404. The district court agreed and issued a preliminary injunction on February 24, 1977. During the two and one-half years of litigation that ensued, the Corps refused to process an application for an after-the-fact permit covering the area, maintaining that it "was precluded by regulation 33 C.F.R. 326.4(e) (1981), from accepting an after-the-fact permit application from Riverside until final disposition of the judicial proceedings" (Brief for Appellee at 2, 3, 13, 14, *United States v Riverside Bayview Homes*. 729 F.2d 391 (6th Cir. 1984) (Nos. 81-1405, 81-1498). Riverside then filed a counterclaim, asking "that the district court declare this regulation unconstitutional and a de facto taking of Riverside's property" (Brief for Appellee at 14, *United States v Riverside Bayview Homes*. 729 F.2d 391).

In its final opinion, on June 20, 1979,

the district court found that Riverside had violated the temporary restraining order and was in contempt of court. The court also declared the Corps' delay in processing an after-the-fact permit to be an unconstitutional taking without statutory authority. (Civ. Action No. 77-70041 (Feb. 24, 1977); Civ. Action No. 77-70041 (June 21, 1979))

Both parties appealed. The issues presented in the appeals were (1) whether portions of Riverside's property were wetlands under the jurisdiction of section 404 and (2) whether the Corps' regulation concerning after-the-fact permits was constitutional and a valid exercise of statutory authority (Brief for Appellee at 2). But in the more than four years that had transpired since Riverside began filling, Corps regulations had changed.

The court of appeals remanded the case to the district court for consideration of the 1977 regulations. Riverside lost again and appealed again. In the second appeal, the United States Court of Appeals for the Sixth Circuit reversed the lower court's decision:

The [circuit] court construed the Corps' regulations to exclude from the category of adjacent wetlands—and hence from that of "waters of the United States"—wetlands that were not subject to flooding by adjacent navigable waters at a frequency to support the growth of aquatic vegetation. The court adopted this construction of the regulations because, in its view, a broader definition of wetlands might result in the taking of private property without just compensation. The court also expressed its doubt that Congress, in granting the Corps jurisdiction to regulate the filling of "navigable waters," intended to allow regulation of wetlands that were not the result of flooding by navigable waters. Under the court's reading of the Corps' regulation, respondent's property was not within the Corps' jurisdiction, because its semiaquatic characteristics were not the result of frequent flooding by the nearby navigable waters. Respondent was therefore free to fill the property without obtaining a permit. (*Riverside*, 474 U.S. at 125)

As to the constitutionality of the Corps regulation, the appellate court "vacate[d] as moot the declaratory judgment issued by the District Court in the first proceeding" (Petition for a Writ of Certiorari to the United States Court of Appeals for the Sixth Circuit at app. A, 1a, *Riverside* (No. 84-701) 729 F2d at 392).

We construed the Corps wetlands definition narrowly and concluded the Riverside's property is not a wetland and that, therefore, the Corps has no

jurisdiction over it. Riverside is now free to develop its land as it wishes.
Moreover, the challenged regulation has since been amended to suggest a
strong presumption in favor of processing applications for after-the-fact
permits....We should not pass unnecessarily on the constitutionality of
the Corps regulation. The declaratory judgment of the District Court is
therefore vacated and the claim dismissed. (Petition for a Writ of
Certiorari to the United States Court of Appeals for the Sixth Circuit at
app. A, 17a, 18a, 729 F2d at 399)

The government appealed to the Supreme Court. As phrased by the
government, the question was "[w]hether, under the Clean Water Act of
1977,...federal jurisdiction to regulate discharges into 'wetlands' is limited to areas that support aquatic vegetation only by virtue of 'frequent
flooding' from adjacent streams, lakes, or seas" (Petition for a Writ of
Certiorari to the United States Court of Appeals for the Sixth Circuit at
(I)). As phrased by the Supreme Court, the issue was somewhat broader:

> We granted certiorari to consider the proper interpretation of the Corps'
> regulation defining "waters of the United States" and the scope of the
> Corps' jurisdiction under the Clean Water Act, both of which were called
> into question by the Sixth Circuit's ruling. (*Riverside,* 474 U.S at 126)

Interest groups on both sides of the issue recognized the importance of
Riverside and were quick to enter the case as *amici curiae.* At least twenty-
two states and conservation organizations entered in support of the
United States, and at least seven development-oriented groups entered in
support of Riverside. (Note: States and conservation organizations
included the National Wildlife Federation, the American Fisheries
Society, the Environmental Defense Fund, and the Sierra Club; the states
of Florida and Michigan; and local and regional organizations such as the
Chesapeake Bay Foundation, Scenic Hudson, and the Louisiana Wildlife
Federation (Motion for Leave to File Brief and Proposed Brief as *Amici
Curiae* in Support of Petitioner at 1, *Riverside* (No. 84-701)).
Development interests allied with Riverside, including the United States
Chamber of Commerce, the Pacific Legal Foundation, the National
Cattlemen's Association, the Resource Development Council for Alaska,
the American Petroleum Institute, the Mid-Atlantic Developers
Association, and the Citizens of Chincoteague for a Reasonable Wetlands
Policy, filed *amici* briefs on behalf of Riverside Bayview Homes (Briefs of
Amici Curiae [of the various parties] in Support of the Respondents).)
The Supreme Court first considered whether a narrow interpretation

of the Corps' regulation was necessary to avoid a taking without just compensation in violation of the Fifth Amendment:

> We have frequently suggested that government land-use regulation may under extreme circumstances amount to a "taking" of the affected property...[but w]e have never precisely defined those circumstances....Only when a permit is denied and the effect of the denial is to prevent "economically viable" use of the land in question can it be said that a taking has occurred.
>
> [S]o long as compensation is available for those whose property is in fact taken, the governmental action is not unconstitutional....[This is b]ecause the Tucker Act,...which presumptively supplies a means of obtaining compensation for any taking that may occur through operation of a federal statute,...is available to provide compensation for takings that may result from the Corps' exercise of jurisdiction over wetlands. (*Riverside*, 474 U.S. at 126-128)

Having dispensed with the constitutional issue, the Court considered whether Riverside was a wetland under the Corps' definition:

> The District Court found that respondent's property was "characterized by the presence of vegetation that requires saturated soil conditions for growth and reproduction,"...and that the source of the saturated soil conditions...was ground water. There is no plausible suggestion that these findings are clearly erroneous, and they plainly bring the property within the category of wetlands as defined by the current regulations. In addition, the court found that the wetland...was adjacent to a body of navigable water, since the area characterized by wetland vegetation extended beyond the boundary of the respondent's property to Black Creek, a navigable waterway....Together, these findings establish that the...property is a wetland adjacent to a navigable waterway...part of the "waters of the United States." (*Riverside*, 474 U.S. at 130-131)

The last question was by far the most significant: Just what did Congress intend to include within the concept of "waters of the United States," and did the Corps' regulations conform to that congressional intent? The Court's opinion here would be precedent for defining the area subject to wetland regulations across the nation. This was a matter of great concern to conservationists and developers throughout the United States.

The Court researched congressional documents in an effort to determine "the legislative history and underlying policies of its statutory grants of authority," conceded that "[n]either of these sources provided unambiguous guidance for the Corps in this case" (*Riverside*, 474 U.S. at 132), and then concluded:

> [T]he evident breadth of congressional concern for the protection of water quality and aquatic ecosystems suggests that it is reasonable for the Corps to interpret "waters" to encompass wetlands adjacent to waters as more conventionally defined....In view of the breadth of federal regulatory authority contemplated by the Act itself and the inherent difficulties of defining precise bounds to regulable waters, the Corps' ecological judgment about the relationship between waters and their adjacent wetlands provides an adequate basis for a legal judgment that adjacent wetlands may be defined as waters under the act.
>
> This holds true even for wetlands that are not the result of flooding or permeation by water having a source in adjacent bodies of water...and we therefore conclude that a definition of "waters of the United States" encompassing all wetlands adjacent to other bodies of water over which the Corps has jurisdiction is a permissible interpretation of the Act.
>
> [And so in conclusion, w]e are thus persuaded that the language, policies, and history of the Clean Water Act compel a finding that the Corps has acted reasonably in interpreting the Act to require permits for discharge of fill material into wetlands adjacent to "waters of the United States." Accordingly, the judgment of the Court of Appeals is *Reversed.* (*Riverside*, 474 U.S. at 133-139)

The Court in *Riverside* mentioned the Tucker Act as a means of obtaining compensation for a taking resulting from operation of a federal statute. This act authorizes the United States Claims Court to "render judgment upon any claim against the United States founded either upon the Constitution, or any Act of Congress or any regulation of an executive department" (28 U.S.C. 1491). In land use cases, the claim arises from the government's taking of property through exercise of regulatory powers, for which it must pay compensation. The Tucker Act was invoked in *Florida Rock Indus. v. United States*, in which a section 404 "permit denial made it impossible to profitably mine rock on the company's property" (52 U.S.L.W. 2577). In the words of the claims court,

> [t]he fact that plaintiff's proposed mining operation would involve wetlands does not by some peculiar alchemy protect the government from the fifth amendment's takings clause any more than the other incantations it has involved....[W]hen the government treats private land as if it were its

own, ignoring the interest of the property owner and rendering the property economically useless, it has worked a taking and, under our constitution, compensation is due. (8 Cl. Ct. 179 (1985))

The court determined that mining was impossible because of regulatory constraints on 98 of the 1,560 acres purchased by Florida Rock Industries, awarded $1,029,000 ($10,500 per acre) as compensation for the land, and ruled that the plaintiff was entitled to recover $311,174 in attorneys' fees and $189,373 in expenses (9 Cl. Ct. 288, 292 (1985)).

While *Riverside*, originating in the Midwest, was proceeding through the United States Court of Appeals for the Sixth Circuit, a similar case was under way in the Deep South (*Avoyelles Sportmen's League v. Marsh*). In Avoyelles Parish, Louisiana, a number of private landowners were engaged in converting 80,000 acres of bottomland hardwood forest into agricultural land, primarily for soybean production. The particular area in question, the Lake Long Tract, contained approximately 20,000 acres. Before clearing commenced the land was logged of all commercially valuable timber. Then the residual vegetation was removed by shearing at or just above ground level, the trees and other debris were piled and burned, and the stumps and ashes were disked into the ground by machinery. The Avoyelles Sportsmen's League filed a citizens' suit under section 505 of the Clean Water Act (33 U.S.C. 1365) against the U.S. Army Corps of Engineers, the Environmental Protection Agency, and the landowners, alleging that pollution was being discharged into waters of the United States without a section 404 permit, in violation of the act (715 F.2d 901). During the course of the litigation, Louisiana state agencies and the Louisiana Landowners Association intervened, expert witnesses were extensively utilized by both sides, and the trial court provided its own interpretation of the area of wetland affected (later reversed).

In a long, complicated, and detailed decision, the United States Court of Appeals for the Fifth Circuit found the following:

(1) That the bulldozers and backhoes were "point sources" within the meaning of the Clean Water Act;

(2) That in filling in the sloughs and leveling the land, the landowners were redepositing fill material into waters of the United States, and that therefore, these activities constituted a "discharge of a pollutant";

(3) That the landclearing activities were not exempt from the Corps' permit requirements [as normal farming]...because those activities constituted a change in use of wetlands. (715 F.2d 929, 930)

Other events were transpiring on the eastern seaboard. On Chincoteague Island, Virginia, Edward Tull was filling irregularly flooded tidal marsh and converting it into trailer lots and other developable property at Ocean Breeze Mobile Homes Site, Mire Pond Properties, Eel Creek, Fowling Gut Extended, and Ocean Breeze. The government sought injunctive relief under section 1319(a) of the Clean Water Act and the maximum civil penalty authorized by section 1319(d)—$22,890,000. The district court found Tull guilty, imposing civil fines of $80,000 and assessing an additional $250,000, which was suspended "'on the specific condition that he restore the extension of Fowling Gut to its former navigable condition'"—$330,000 in all (*Tull v. United States*, 481 U.S. 412, 415 (1987)). The court of appeals affirmed the lower court's opinion over a dissent, and Tull appealed to the Supreme Court. The Supreme Court reversed the decision and remanded the case "for further proceedings consistent with this opinion" (Tull, 481 U.S. at 427).

Tull's appeal and the Supreme Court's decision had nothing to do with wetland laws per se, but instead involved a constitutional issue. Prior to trial by the district court, Tull had demanded, and been denied, a trial by jury as guaranteed by the Seventh Amendment of the U.S. Constitution ("In Suits at common law, where the value in controversy shall exceed twenty dollars, the right to trial by jury shall be preserved"). The Supreme Court's decision sent the case back to the district court for a trial before a jury. Tull and the government reached an agreement before the trial date, however, and the retrial was never held. By such means are cases won.

Soil Conservation Service Involvement

The "swampbuster" provisions of the Food Security Act of 1985 brought the Soil Conservation Service (SCS) into wetland identification and delineation activities under generally the same statutory definition as in the Clean Water Act. Persons who produce an agricultural commodity on wetland converted to agricultural production after December 23, 1985, are ineligible for price supports, loans, crop insurance, and other subsidies, and those farming highly erodible soils may be similarly affected (chapter 9). The Department of Agriculture implements the Food Security Act (often called the 1985 Farm Act) through the Agricultural Stabilization and Conservation Service (ASCS), the Farmers Home Administration, the Federal Crop Insurance Corporation, and the SCS (see appendix A for a discussion of agency responsibilities). The SCS "determines whether the land is highly erodible, wetland or converted wetland, whether the producer is actively applying a conservation plan, and whether crop production on converted wetlands is permissible because the effect on wetland values will be minimal" (U.S. Department of Agriculture, Soil Conservation Service 1986, 3).

The Art as It Is Practiced

Since 1972 the Corps has been implementing section 404, yet until 1989 there was no uniform, agreed-upon methodology for identifying jurisdictional wetlands (those that came under the provisions of section 404). Even more important, there was no process for delineating the boundary between such wetlands and nonwetlands (Adams, Buford, and DuMond, 1987).

Three somewhat independent processes evolved. The U.S. Fish and Wildlife Service, engaged in the National Wetlands Inventory, developed its definition and methodology for that purpose. Wetlands identified in the inventory are those areas that

> must have one or more of the following three attributes: (1) at least periodically, the land supports predominantly hydrophytes, (2) the substrate is predominantly undrained hydric soil, and (3) the substrate is nonsoil and is saturated with water or covered by shallow water at some time during the growing season of each year. (Cowardin et al. 1979, 3)

The foregoing definition uses three parameters—vegetation, soil, and hydrology—in an "either-or" context (i.e., "one or more of the following"). It is a U.S. Fish and Wildlife Service definition for use in the National Wetland Inventory and is *not relevant to the definition and delineation of jurisdictional wetlands under the provisions of section 404.* The relevant definition is that developed by the Corps and the EPA, the cognizant section 404 agencies. The Corps-EPA definition uses the same parameters but in a "both-and" context (i.e., all must be present). It was developed and published independently by the Corps and the EPA in 1987 (U.S. Army Corps of Engineers Environmental Laboratory Station 1987; Sipple 1987), was field-tested, and subsequently emerged as an "interagency cooperative publication" in 1989 (Federal Interagency Committee for Wetland Delineation 1989 [hereinafter cited as *Delineation Manual* 1989]). The *Delineation Manual* was a cooperative effort of the Corps and the EPA as well as the U.S. Fish and Wildlife Service and the Soil Conservation Service. It is used by those agencies for purposes of section 404 and the Food Security Act of 1985 but not for the National Wetlands Inventory.

To be a jurisdictional wetland, an area must possess vegetation, soils, and hydrologic conditions characteristic of wetlands (*Delineation Manual* 1989, 9). For section 404 purposes, Corps or EPA personnel identify the plant species within an area and classify them as "obligate [wetland]," "facultative wetland," "facultative," "facultative upland," and "nonwetland," using the list in *National List of Plant Species That Occur on Wetland* (U.S. Department of the Interior, U.S. Fish and Wildlife Service 1986). An area meets the vegetative requirements of a wetland if "more than 50 percent of the dominant species from all strata" are facultative, facultative wetland, or obligate species (*Delineation Manual* 1989, 10). The Soil Conservation Service uses a similar approach, relying on the same vegetation and soils reference documents just cited. However, rather than use an indication of vegetative "prevalence" based on the sum of facultative, facultative wetland, and obligate plant species, the SCS employs a weighted mean of frequency of occurrence. Obligate species are assigned an "ecological index" value of 1; facultative wetland species, 2; facultative species, 3; facultative upland species, 4; and nonwetland species, 5. A prevalence index for an area is calculated based on weighted relative frequency of occurrences: if the index is less than 3.0, the area is a wetland for the purposes of the Food Security Act of 1985 (*Delineation Manual* 1989, app. C).

Hydric soil characteristics are indicated if detailed soils maps of the area show it to possess hydric soil series as listed in *Hydric Soils of the United States* (U.S. Department of Agriculture, Soil Conservation Service 1985). In areas where soil mapping is inadequate or filling has occurred, hydric conditions may be inferred from the presence of organic matter in the upper profile, from soil color, and from other field characteristics (*Delineation Manual* 1989, 43).

Hydrologically an area is a wetland if it is permanently or periodically inundated or the soil is saturated to the surface sometime during the growing season. While these characteristics may be more difficult to ascertain than soil and vegetation indicators, they can often be inferred from floodplain management maps, stream gage data, National Wetland Inventory maps, and other available information (*Delineation Manual* 1989, 27-30).

Having determined that jurisdictional wetland occurs within an area to be filled, the Corps must decide whether or not the proposed action is in the public interest and thus is permittable. A part of this balancing of expected benefits against probable impacts includes the concept of mitigation within an overall nationwide goal of "no net loss of the nation's remaining wetland base." Only the "least environmentally damaging practicable alternative" may be permitted. In arriving at this alternative, the Corps must ensure that first, wetland impacts are avoided wherever possible; second, residual impacts are minimized; and third, "compensatory mitigation is…[performed] for unavoidable adverse impacts which remain." Compensatory mitigation may include restoration of degraded wetlands, creation of new wetlands, or withdrawal of wetland "credits" previously earned through restoration, preservation, or creation and placed in a recognized "mitigation bank" (Page and Wilcher 1990, 2-4).

The *Delineation Manual* and the Page-Wilcher memorandum of agreement have greatly improved the 404 program, but many problems remain. Wetland identification is routine, but delineation of the precise boundary between that land which may be filled with impunity (upland) and that which probably cannot be lawfully filled (jurisdictional wetland) is still more art than science. The classification of activities included within the silvicultural and agricultural exemptions incorporated into the 1977 amendments is controversial at best. The list of filling activities resulting in *de minimus* impacts, which could be authorized through general permits rather than individual evaluations, is open to question. And we continue to use a water quality statute as an expedient for a wetland policy law.

Many persons considered the 1989 delineation manual to be an imperfect but usable handbook that could be perfected through subsequent use and amendment (Sipple 1992, 5). Others considered it to expand the concept of wetlands into areas that Congress did not intend and that most persons did not consider "wet." The latter group prevailed upon the Bush administration to revise the manual to "increase the burden of proof required to identify and delineate a wetland" (U.S. Environmental Protection Agency 1991, "Backgrounder," 5). Although the revisions contained a number of provisions that would have restricted the wetlands definition, the most significant would "[r]equire inundation for 15 or more consecutive days, or saturation to the surface for 21 or more consecutive days during the growing season" in order to meet the hydrology criterion (U.S. Environmental Protection Agency 1991, "Questions and Answers," 8). The 1989 manual required saturation to the surface "at some point in time during an average rainfall year," which could be inferred if the water table were between 0.5 and 1.5 feet below the surface "usually one week or more during the growing season," depending on soil permeability (*Delineation Manual* 1989, 7). As soon as the revisions were released (56 Fed. Reg. 40,446-40,480 (Aug. 14, 1991)), opposition arose:

The administration's proposed revisions to the 1989 [manual]...will result in tremendous losses of wetland functions nationwide, and will cost both society as a whole as well as developers far more than previous manuals....This is because the manual is technically unsound, requires excessive field testing, does not provide field personnel with the ability to achieve repeatable results, and the delineations that result eliminate areas clearly possessing functions attributable to wetlands....An early review...by many federal, state, and private sector scientists and regulators has provided reports that from 20 to 60 percent of wetlands in various states will lose their status as jurisdictional wetlands. (Huffman 1992, 10)

First, significant wetland areas in quantity and function will be lost from all wetland types in New England....The second obvious casualty of the proposed manual will be good wetlands science. The approach identified for wetlands delineation in the proposal is driven predominantly by policy considerations, not scientific ones....The third casualties...are simplicity and consistency—an ironic result because workability in the field and streamlined field testing procedures were among the principal intentions of the Bush administration....The final, and perhaps most unfortunate, casualty of the proposed approach is public credibility. (Shelley 1992, 13, 14)

On January 21, 1992, after five months and two extensions, the comment period on the proposed revisions finally ended. By that time the EPA had received more than 50,000 comments (*National Wetlands Newsletter* 1992b), and by June the EPA had reported receiving 80,000 comments (telephone conversation with EPA Wetlands Hotline, June 11, 1992). State governors and politicians of various persuasions (including the Democratic presidential candidate) (*National Wetlands Newsletter* 1992a) also joined the original cadre of environmentalists, scientists, and regulators in opposition to the revised manual, and when the Bush administration ended in January 1993, it still had not been officially adopted.

In the meantime much of the immediate significance of the controversy had been removed by Congress. The Energy and Water Development Appropriations Act of 1992, passed on August 17, 1991, prohibited the Corps from identifying or delineating jurisdictional wetlands using the 1989 manual "or any subsequent manual not adopted in accordance with the requirements for notice and public comment of the rule-making process of the Administrative Procedure Act." In view of the intensity and complexity of the situation, that requirement may not be met for some time. In the interim, the Corps must revert to its 1987 manual, the only document meeting Congress' requirements.

Toward a National Policy?

In October 1986, after four years of debate, Congress passed the Emergency Wetland Resources Act. The act (1) extends the Wetlands Loan Act of 1961 until September 30, 1988, permitting the U.S. Fish and Wildlife Service to continue to borrow from the Treasury to buy wetlands (100 Stat. 3584); (2) doubles the price of migratory bird hunting and conservation stamps ("duck stamps") to $15 over a period of five years (100 Stat. 3586); (3) transfers duties collected on imported sporting arms and ammunition into the Migratory Bird Conservation Fund, from which it may be used for wetland acquisition (100 Stat. 3586); and (4) sets a deadline of September 30, 1998, for completion of the much-delayed National Wetland Inventory in the contiguous United States (100 Stat. 3588). But it is not a national wetland policy act.

In March 1987 Senator John Breaux of Louisiana introduced S. 655, a bill that would have directed the U.S. Army Corps of Engineers, in cooperation with the states and other federal agencies, to identify coastal wetland systems that have particular value for fish and wildlife and, within two and one-half years after passage, to develop action plans to protect the ten most threatened wetland systems. But Breaux's bill was not a national wetland policy bill.

Subsequently Congress has considered many bills, conducted many hearings, and amassed volumes of testimony. But as of mid-1992, the nation still had no national wetland policy. Perhaps the individual states will preempt the federal government by enacting their own wetland policies, within or without section 404. Perhaps, after the 1992 election, Congress and the new administration will be able to formulate a rational and politically acceptable solution. Or perhaps wetlands, like northern spotted owls, will constitute an insoluble problem for some time to come.

REFERENCES

Adams, David A., Marilyn A. Buford, and David M. DuMond. 1987. "In Search of the Wetland Boundary." *Wetlands* 7:59-70.
Congressional Quarterly, Inc. 1987. *Congressional Quarterly Almanac: 1986.* Vol. 47. Washington, DC: Congressional Quarterly.
Council on Environmental Quality. 1975. *Environmental Quality—1975.* Washington, DC: Government Printing Office.
———. 1976. *Environmental Quality—1976.* Washington, DC: Government Printing Office.
———. 1977. *Environmental Quality—1977.* Washington, DC: Government Printing Office.

Cowardin, Lewis M., Virginia Carter, Francis C. Golet, and Edward T. LaRoe. 1979. *Classification of Wetlands and Deepwater Habitats of the United States.* Washington, DC: Government Printing Office.

Davis, Joseph A. 1987a. "Congress Easily Overrides Veto of $20 Billion Clean Water Bill." *Congressional Quarterly Weekly Report* 45 (6): 240, 241.

———. 1987b. "Senate Clears Clean Water Bill, Urges President Not to Veto." *Congressional Quarterly Weekly Report* 45 (4): 164.

Delineation Manual. See Federal Interagency Committee for Wetland Delineation.

Federal Interagency Committee for Wetland Delineation. 1989. *Federal Manual for Identifying and Delineating Jurisdictional Wetlands.* Cooperative technical publication. Washington, DC: U.S. Army Corps of Engineers; U.S. Environmental Protection Agency; U.S. Fish and Wildlife Service; U.S. Department of Agriculture, Soil Conservation Service.

Gale, Judith A., C. Luther Propst, and Ruth E. Sappie. 1985. "404 Feasibility Study Final Project Report." Raleigh: North Carolina State University, Center for Environmental Studies.

Huffman, Terry. 1992. "A Return to Ecological Concepts." *National Wetlands Newsletter* 13 (6): 10-12.

National Wetlands Newsletter. 1992a. "Manual Opposition." News Briefs. *National Wetlands Newsletter* 14 (2): 16.

———. 1992b. "Wetlands Docket." News Briefs. *National Wetlands Newsletter* 14 (2): 17.

Michigan Department of Natural Resources. Division of Land Resource Programs. 1983. "Michigan 404 Program." Lansing, MI: Department of Natural Resources.

Page, Robert W., and LaJuana S. Wilcher. 1990. "Army/EPA MOA Concerning Determination of Mitigation under the Section 404(b)(1) Guidelines." Washington, DC: Department of the Army; Environmental Protection Agency.

Peskin, Henry M. 1986. "Nonpoint Pollution and National Responsibility." *Resources* 83 (Spring): 10, 11.

Reagan, Ronald. 1987. "President Reagan's Message on Veto of Clean Water Act." *Congressional Quarterly Weekly Report* 45 (6): 253.

Shelley, Peter. 1992. "Losing Our Wetlands, Science, and Credibility." *National Wetlands Newsletter* 13 (6): 13-14.

Sipple, William S. 1987. *Wetlands Delineation Manual* (interim final). 2 vols. Office of Wetlands Protection, Office of Water. Washington, DC: U.S. Environmental Protection Agency.

U.S. Army Corps of Engineers. Environmental Laboratory. 1987. *Corps of Engineers Wetlands Delineation Manual.* Technical Report Y-87-1. Vicksburg, MS: U.S. Army Engineer Waterways Experiment Station.

———. 1992. "Time to Move On." *National Wetlands Newsletter* 14 (2): 4-6.

U.S. Congress. House. Committee on Government Operations. 1970. "Our Water and Wetlands: How the Corps of Engineers Can Help Prevent Their Destruction and Pollution." 91st Cong., 2d sess. H. Rept. 91-917. Washington, DC: Government Printing Office.

U.S. Congress. House. Committee on Merchant Marine and Fisheries. Subcommittee on Fisheries and Wildlife Conservation. 1967. *Estuarine Areas.* Hearings on H.R. 25, H.R. 1397, H.R. 4505, and similar bills, March 6, 8, 9, 1967. 90th Cong., 1st sess. Serial 90-3. Washington, DC: Government Printing Office.

U.S. Congress. House. Committee on Public Works and Transportation. Subcommittee on Water Resources. 1975. *Development of New Regulations by the Corps of Engineers, Implementing Section 404 of the Federal Water Pollution Control Act Concerning Permits for Disposal of Dredge or Fill Material.* 94th Cong., 1st sess., July 15, 16, 17, 1975. Serial 94-18. Washington, DC: Government Printing Office.

U.S. Congress. Office of Technology Assessment. 1984. *Wetlands: Their Use and Regulation.* OTA-O-206. Washington, DC: Government Printing Office.

U.S. Department of Agriculture. Soil Conservation Service. 1985. *Hydric Soils of the United States 1985.* Washington, DC: Government Printing Office.

———. 1986. "LTP: SCS Highly Erodible Land-Wetland Conservation Draft Procedures." National Bulletin no. 300-6-18, July 7, 1986. Washington, DC: U.S. Department of Agriculture, Soil Conservation Service.

U.S. Department of the Interior. Fish and Wildlife Service. 1986. *National List of Plant Species That Occur on Wetland.* St. Petersburg, FL: U.S. Department of the Interior, U.S. Fish and Wildlife Service.

U.S. Environmental Protection Agency. 1991. "Proposed Revisions to the Federal Manual for Delineating Wetlands." Washington, DC: U.S. Environmental Protection Agency, Office of Wetlands, Oceans, and Watersheds. (Various pagination.)

CHAPTER XIII

Fisheries

National fisheries policy has evolved through a combination of federal jurisdiction under the commerce clause and treaty provisions and state control over inland waters and bottoms within the territorial sea (chapter 10). Although similar to wildlife policy in many ways, it differs in that with the exception of high seas fisheries, the states control almost all of the "land" upon which fisheries are based. Thus the states control the habitat and, subject to exercise of the federal property powers on federal land, regulate the taking of fish and seafood in internal waters. National fisheries policy places relatively more emphasis on commercial and international aspects than does wildlife policy, however, and fisheries management is more often effected through control of harvest than through manipulation of habitat. Thus the federal government has placed more emphasis on the regulatory aspects in fisheries management than it has in matters affecting wildlife.

INSTITUTIONAL MATTERS

One of the earliest cases regarding ownership of bottoms and the fisheries they support (*Martin v. Waddell*, 1842) involved oyster beds in the Raritan River of New Jersey. Waddell's lessee claimed ownership of riparian and submerged lands under a grant traceable to the Crown, which conveyed "all lands, islands, soil, rivers,...marshes, waters, lakes, fishings, hawkings, huntings, and fowlings." Martin claimed shellfish on the same area under a lease from the state. The court ruled that prior to independence, "dominion and property in navigable waters and in the lands under them [were] held by the king as a public trust"—they were held as a public right, *jus publicum*, rather than a private right, *jus privatum*. Under this concept the king had no authority to convey them, for they belonged to the people as a whole.

At the time of independence, powers of "the [C]rown or of Parliament...became immediately and rightfully vested in the state...subject to the rights since surrendered by the Constitution to the general government." As successors to the Crown, states can have no greater right than the Crown had and thus cannot convey their waters or submerged lands. However, they can and do grant rights to a several (i.e., exclusive) fishery through grants and leases of shellfish bottoms, and they can convey the privilege to participate in a common fishery by license.

The degree of state control is not complete and exclusive. States may regulate the taking of fish (*Manchester v. Massachusetts*) and the planting of shellfish (*McCready v. Virginia*) within their bays and internal waters, but they can neither exclude nonresidents from fishing privileges afforded residents (*Douglas v. Seacoast Products, Tangier Sound Waterman's Ass'n v. Douglas*) nor exclusionarily discriminate against nonresidents in terms of license fees or other requirements (*Toomer v. Whitsell*).

In an effort to reduce the pressure upon fish populations without necessarily decreasing fishing efficiency, some states are moving toward a system of "limited entry," in which the total number of entrants or units of gear is controlled. Alaska attempted limited entry into salmon fisheries in 1962 and again in 1969, but both attempts denied entry to nonresidents and were struck down by the courts on constitutional grounds (Rogers 1979, 785). Alaska tried again through a 1972 constitutional amendment that authorized limited entry "'for purposes of resource conservation, to prevent economic distress among fishermen..., and to promote the efficient development of aquaculture'" (Rogers 1979, 186). Residency requirements were not mentioned. Under the 1973 act that implements this provision, Alaska has successfully limited entry into specific elements of its salmon and herring fisheries. Under a complicated system that considers social considerations in addition to biological and economic ones, permits are issued to individuals for use of a specific type of gear in a specific area of Alaskan waters (Adasiak 1979). While the system appears to be working satisfactorily in these situations, Adasiak (1979, 781) cautions:

> Based on Alaska's experience, the general political formula for establishing a limited entry system seems to be that it is not possible to get action before a crisis or a disaster....Absent a spur that sharp, it is not likely that there will be successful movement toward the establishment and implementaton of limited entry systems.

Although federal authority to regulate the United States fishing industry beyond the territorial sea is obvious, and the power to regulate domestic fisheries wherever they occur is afforded through the commerce clause, the federal government has been slow in intervening.

The origin of the federal fisheries agency had much in common with the creation of the federal parks, forestry, and soil conservation agencies. In all four cases, much of the success was due to a public crisis, and the leader of the effort became the head of the new agency. In the case of fisheries, the issue was alleged depletion of marine fisheries resulting from operation of fish traps (Allard 1978, 76), and the leader was Spencer Fullerton Baird. During the summer of 1870, Baird (assistant secretary of the Smithsonian Institution, member of the National Academy of Sciences, and author of a major paper on the distribution and migration of North American birds [Allard 1978, 53-54]) became aware of the fish trap controversy and recognized it as an opportunity to obtain increased research funds. He approached Congressman Henry Dawes of Massachusetts, chairman of the House Appropriations Committee, with a request for $5,000 and an authorization to spend it and, after one initial setback, obtained the resolution he sought (Allard 1978, 77-83).

The position of commissioner of fish and fisheries was created in the Department of Commerce on March 3, 1871, with the duty to

> prosecute investigations and inquiries on the subject [of fisheries], with the view of ascertaining whether any and what diminution in the number of the food fishes of the coast and lakes of the United States has taken place; and, if so, to what causes the same is due; and also whether any and what protective, prohibitory, or precautionary measures should be adopted in the premises; and to report upon the same to Congress. (16 Stat. 593)

(Note: Persons with experience in fisheries matters will recognize the directive—it has been repeated innumerable times since, and the "diminution in the number of food fishes" is still with us.)

Baird was appointed commissioner on March 8, 1871 (the act required appointment "from among the civil officers or employees of the government, one person of proved scientific and practical acquaintance with the fishes of the coast, to be commissioner" (16 Stat. 593)). While serving as commissioner of fish and fisheries, Baird also was instrumental in founding the National Museum and served as secretary of the Smithsonian Institution and director of the National Museum. He held all three posts until his death at the age of sixty-four on August 19, 1887. In accordance with the authorizing legislation, he served as commissioner "without additional salary," but he continued to draw his salary, from the Smithsonian. His efforts toward fisheries regulation and fish culture met with limited success, but the foundation of scientific research that he established within the U.S. Fish Commission and its research facility at Woods Hole, Massachusetts, continue today (Allard 1978, 347-355).

The Fish Commission subsequently became the Bureau of Fisheries and was removed from the Department of Commerce in 1939 as part of Reorganization Plan No. II, in an effort to consolidate federal fish and wildlife functions in the Department of the Interior. In the following year, the Bureau of Fisheries and the Bureau of Biological Survey (from the Department of Agriculture) became the Fish and Wildlife Service (Reorganization Plan No. III, sec. 3).

The Fish and Wildlife Act of 1956 created a Bureau of Commercial Fisheries and a Bureau of Sport Fisheries and Wildlife within the renamed United States Fish and Wildlife Service, illustrating at least one of the problems of fisheries management. Whereas federal concerns over forests, wildlife, and parks are located within a single agency, jurisdiction over fisheries was then split between two services and is now divided between two departments. The resource is shared not only among state, federal, and international interests but also between "sport" and "commercial" interests. Neither interest has been sufficiently large to attract much congressional funding, and each manages to feud with the other whenever possible.

Following recommendations of the Commission on Marine Science, Engineering and Resources (1969, 232), the Bureau of Commercial Fisheries and the migratory marine game fish functions of the Bureau of Sport Fisheries and Wildlife were moved from the Department of the Interior into the new National Oceanic and Atmospheric Administration in 1970 and became the National Marine Fisheries Service (Reorganization Plan No. 4 of 1970). The locus and organization of the federal fisheries function are still being questioned, however. In 1986 the American Fisheries Society appointed a committee to, among other things, "review the current distribution of major fishery research and management authority among federal agencies [and]...'to formulate a proposal for the reorganization of the U.S. federal government role in this nation's fisheries resources affairs'" (Harville 1986, 2). The committee found that the federal effort continued to be so fragmented that it was ineffective in developing and implementing national fisheries policy. It recommended that a "single Federal Fishery Agency" be created, consoli-

dating the fisheries functions of the National Marine Fisheries Service
and the U.S. Fish and Wildlife Service, to become the lead federal agency
in all matters affecting fisheries (Harville 1986, 4, 5).

FEDERAL AID TO THE STATES

As in the case of wildlife programs (chapter 7), federal fisheries aid to the
states has been instrumental in increasing knowledge, developing management expertise, and creating jobs for fisheries biologists and scientists. Because jurisdiction over fisheries is divided between the National
Marine Fisheries Service and the U.S. Fish and Wildlife Service at the
federal level and is often similarly divided at the state level between an
agency oriented toward coastal, commercial fisheries and one oriented
toward inland, sport fisheries, administration of the programs becomes
somewhat complicated.

The Dingell-Johnson Act

Thirteen years after providing federal aid to wildlife restoration through
the Pittman-Robertson Act (P-R), Congress passed the Dingell-Johnson
Act of 1950 (D-J), providing similar assistance to fisheries management.
The act authorized appropriations of "an amount equal to the revenue
accruing from tax imposed...on fishing rods, reels, and artificial lures,
baits, and flies" (64 Stat. 431) to be used for "fish restoration and management projects" to be agreed upon by the secretary of the interior and
the state fish and game department. Addressing a controversial issue of
the times, the act denies eligibility to any state which has not "passed
laws for the conservation of fish, which shall include a prohibition
against the diversion of license fees paid by fishermen for any other purpose than the administration of said fish and game department" (64 Stat.
430). Projects could include

(a) such research into the problems of fish management and culture as
    may be necessary to efficient administration affecting fish resources;
(b) the acquisition of such facts as are necessary to guide and direct the
    regulation of fishing by law....
(c) the formulation and adoption of plans of restocking waters with food
    and game fishes....
(d) the selection, restoration, and improvement of areas of water or land

adaptable as hatching, feeding, resting, or breeding areas for fish. (64 Stat. 431)

Funds were apportioned to the states based "40 per centum [o]n the ratio which the area of each State including coastal and Great Lakes waters...bears to the total area of all States and 60 per centum [o]n the ratio which the number of persons holding paid licenses to fish for sport or recreation in the State...bears to the number of such persons in all the States," with the proviso that no state may receive less than 1 percent nor more than 5 percent of the available funds (64 Stat. 432). In general, federal funds could be used for 75 percent of project costs (64 Stat. 432).

Annual apportionments to the states during the period 1981-1985 averaged $33.8 million (U.S. Department of the Interior, U.S. Fish and Wildlife Service n.d., table III), to be used for the following:

1. Development projects—restoration of fishing waters, habitat improvements, lake and stream rehabilitation, and installation of public use facilities.

2. Land control for public use—easements, land acquisition, and fishing access entry points.

3. Fishery research—information on fish populations and characteristics, resource inventories, management techniques, nutritional requirements, disease and parasite problems, and so forth (U.S. Department of the Interior, U.S. Fish and Wildlife Service 1984, vi, 3).

The Dingell-Johnson Act undoubtedly marked the beginning of a sustainable national program in fisheries research, development, and management, but it created some problems in states with divided fisheries jurisdictions (i.e., those having a primarily freshwater sportfishing agency and a primarily saltwater commercial fishing agency). Only one agency in each state could be designated the recipient of D-J funds, and that agency was invariably (and logically) the agency having jurisdiction over sportfishing or sport fisheries. Yet in coastal and Great Lakes states, the "commercial" fisheries agency frequently governed a larger water area and more sport (as well as commercial) fishermen. Furthermore, the area of these "coastal" waters was included in the formula by which the other, often competing, fisheries agency received federal funds.

Fourteen years later the Congress addressed this issue. The Wallop-Breaux Act (section 1014 of the Tax Reform Act of 1984) provided that

[e]ach coastal State, to the extent practicable, shall equitably allocate the
following sums between marine fish projects and freshwater fish projects
in the same proportion as the estimated number of marine anglers and the
estimated number of freshwater anglers, respectively, bear to the estimated number of all resident anglers in that State. (98 Stat. 1015)

The "following sums" refer generally to a 10 percent tax on sportfishing
equipment, a 3 percent federal tax on the sale of electric outboard motors
and sonar devices, import duties on fishing tackle and boats, and federal
motorboat fuel taxes (98 Stat. 1017-1020). Estimating the numbers of
anglers involved, the basis for allocation, is a difficult and imprecise task
in the absence of saltwater sportfishing licenses.

During fiscal year 1986, the first year that Wallop-Breaux funds
became available, almost $95 million was apportioned to the states—
almost triple the average of the preceding five years (U.S. Department of
the Interior, U.S. Fish and Wildlife Service n.d., table III).

The Commercial Fisheries Research and Development Act of 1964

Reacting to the continued decline in the relative position of United
States commercial fisheries and their omission from provisions of the
Dingell-Johnson Act, Congress passed Public Law No. 88-309 "for the
research and development of the commercial fisheries of the nation" (78
Stat. 197). Appropriations for this act were to come from general federal
revenues and (as in the previous federal aid programs) were to be available to the states on a three-to-one federal-state matching basis. Funds
were allocated based on the "average of the value of raw fish harvested by
domestic fishermen and received within the State...[and] the average of
the value to the manufacturer of manufactured and processed fishery
merchandise manufactured within each State," relative to the nation as a
whole (78 Stat. 198). Unlike the P-R and D-J programs, Public Law No.
88-309 contained two additional programs administered largely at the
secretary of commerce's discretion. The first provided for federal funds to
"be made available to the States in such amounts as the Secretary may
determine appropriate" or to be used "directly by the Secretary" in the
event of "a commercial fishery failure due to a resource disaster arising
from natural or undetermined causes" (78 Stat. 197). The second provided for funds "to be made available to the States in such amounts as the
Secretary may determine for developing a new commercial fishery" (78
Stat. 198). Through fiscal year 1984, almost $90 million in 88-309

funds had been distributed to the states (U.S. Department of Commerce, National Marine Fisheries Service 1984, 2). The 1986 amendments to the Fishery Conservation and Management Act repealed Public Law No. 88-309, replacing it with a new interjurisdictional fisheries research program under the Interjurisdictional Fisheries Act of 1986.

The Anadromous and Great Lakes Fisheries Act of 1965

One might think that any possible need for federal fisheries assistance to the states could be met with the D-J and 88-309 programs, and perhaps it could, but Congress was not through yet. The anadromous fisheries program, often termed "89-304" after its public law number, authorized fifty-fifty federal-nonfederal cost sharing for work directed toward the development and enhancement of anadromous fisheries—fisheries based on species that spend their adulthood in marine or estuarine waters but ascend streams to spawn. Whereas D-J is administered by the U.S. Fish and Wildlife Service and 88-309 is administered by the National Marine Fisheries Service, 89-304 is jointly administered by the two federal fisheries agencies. Similar arrangements exist in counterpart state agencies.

REGULATORY FUNCTIONS

Federal fisheries regulatory activities are carried out through a system of unilateral actions affecting fisheries products taken under the commerce clause and a series of complex bilateral and multilateral arrangements involving the states, regional entities, and foreign nations.

The Black Bass Act of 1926

Following the precedent of the Lacey Act of 1900, the Black Bass Act of 1926 prohibited the interstate shipment of fish contrary to the laws of any affected state. Initially it pertained only to two black bass species—largemouth (*Micropterus salmoides*) and smallmouth (*M. dolomieu*)—but it was amended in 1947 to apply to other game fish, in 1952 to apply to all fish, and by the Endangered Species Conservation Act of 1969 to include products imported or exported in violation of the laws of any foreign country. In 1981 the Black Bass Act was repealed, and its provisions were combined with those of the Lacey Act of 1900 and expanded in the Lacey Act Amendments of 1981 (chapter 7).

Multistate Marine Fisheries Commissions

A move toward something broader than State control over domestic fisheries resources came with creation of the three marine fisheries commissions during the 1940s. The Atlantic States Marine Fisheries Compact,
created in 1942, included all Atlantic Coast states from Maine through
Florida. The commission was composed of three representatives from
each member state—the head of the state fisheries agency, a member of
the legislature, and an interested citizen—and was to

> promote the better utilization of the fisheries, marine, shell, and anadro-
> mous[,] of the Atlantic seaboard by the development of a joint program
> for the promotion and protection of such fisheries, and by the prevention
> of the physical waste of the fisheries from any cause. (56 Stat. 267)

The Fish and Wildlife Service was to serve as the research agency of
the commission, with cooperation from research agencies of the member
states. In 1950 the compact was amended to provide that "any two or
more consenting States could designate the Commission as a joint regulatory agency...for the regulation of the fishing operations of the citizens
and vessels of the designating States" (64 Stat. 467). In 1949 the Gulf
States Marine Fisheries Compact created a similar body comprised of
Florida, Alabama, Mississippi, Louisiana, and Texas.

The West Coast commission, the Pacific States Marine Fisheries
Commission, was created by the Pacific Marine Fisheries Compact of
1947. It differed from the others in designating state fisheries agencies as
its research arm and in not providing that the commission may act as a
regulatory agency.

To date no marine fisheries commission has been given regulatory
authority, but the commissions have been valuable in obtaining congressional fishery appropriations, in promoting fishery research, and in providing advice and counsel to the member states and the federal government (Tinsley and Nielsen 1987, 304).

The Fishery Conservation and Management Act
and the Regional Councils

The federal government entered the domestic fisheries resource management arena through a combination of policy declarations and statutes. In
1945 the Truman Declaration claimed for the United States special
rights in fisheries lying seaward of and contiguous with the territorial sea

(chapter 10). Then, in 1953, Congress affirmed the rights of the states to "title...and ownership of the lands beneath navigable waters within the boundaries of the respective States, and the natural resources within such lands and waters" (67 Stat. 30). Natural resources were defined to include "fish, shrimp, oysters, clams, crabs, lobsters, sponges, kelp, and other marine animal and plant life," and lands beneath navigable waters included all those "nontidal waters that were navigable under the laws of the United States" and lands beneath tidal waters seaward to the offshore limits of State jurisdiction (67 Stat. 29; see the discussion in chapter 10). These two actions produced a system in which the states exercised jurisdiction over fisheries in internal waters and the territorial sea, and the federal government claimed the fisheries resources of the contiguous zone (to 12 geographical miles offshore) but did not exercise that jurisdiction against United States fishermen. The Fishery Conservation and Management Act of 1976 (the FCMA, or the Magnuson Act) finally created a framework for federal involvement in domestic marine fisheries management. The act first states congressional findings:

(1) The fish off the coasts of the United States, the highly migratory species of the high seas, the species which dwell on or in the Continental Shelf appertaining to the United States, and the anadromous species which spawn in United States rivers or estuaries, constitute valuable and renewable natural resources. These fisheries contribute to the food supply, economy, and the health of the Nation and provide recreational opportunities.

(2) As a consequence of increased fishing pressure and because of the inadequacy of fishery conservation and management practices and controls (A) certain stocks of such fish have been overfished to the point where their survival is threatened, and (B) other stocks have been so substantially reduced in number that they could become similarly threatened.

(3) Commercial and recreational fishing constitutes a major source of employment and contributes significantly to the economy of the Nation....

(4) International fishery agreements have not been effective in preventing or terminating the overfishing of these valuable fishery resources....

(5) Fishery resources are finite but renewable....

(6) A national program for the conservation and management of the fishery resources of the United States is necessary to prevent overfishing, to rebuild overfished stocks, to insure conservation, and to realize the full potential of the Nation's fishery resources.

(7) A national program for the development of fisheries which are under-

utilized or not utilized by the United States fishing industry, including bottom fish off Alaska, is necessary to assure that our citizens benefit from the employment, food supply, and revenue which could be generated thereby. (90 Stat. 331-332)

Having laid the factual groundwork, the act then proceeded to state parallel purposes and policy and to design a program implementing the policy. The program consisted of a claim of authority by which the United States could exercise jurisdiction over fish stocks and a mechanism by which that authority might be expressed. It established a "fishery conservation zone" beginning at the offshore limit of state jurisdiction and extending 200 miles seaward from the baseline. It then claimed "exclusive fishery management authority" for the United States for all fish within the conservation zone, for all anadromous species that spawned in U.S. waters throughout their migratory range (except when they are in areas subject to the jurisdiction of other countries), and for all fishery resources of the continental shelf (90 Stat. 336). Declaration of an exclusive fisheries zone on the high seas was a unilateral action on the part of the United States, but it was in consort with actions being taken by numerous coastal countries.

With a fishery resource to manage, the act then prescribed the standards for fishery management plans:

(1) Conservation and management measures shall prevent overfishing while achieving, on a continuing basis, the optimum yield from each fishery.

(2) Conservation and management measures shall be based upon the best scientific information available.

(3) To the extent practicable, an individual stock of fish shall be managed as a unit throughout its range, and interrelated stocks of fish shall be managed as a unit or in close coordination.

(4) Conservation and management measures shall not discriminate between residents of different States....

(5) Conservation and management measures shall, where practicable, promote efficiency in the utilization of fishery resources; except that no such measure shall have economic allocation as its sole purpose.

(6) Conservation and management measures shall take into account and allow for variations among, and contingencies in, fisheries, fishery resources, and catches.

(7) Conservation and management measures shall, where practicable, minimize costs and avoid unnecessary duplication. (90 Stat. 346, 347)

The standards enunciate important and valid management concepts but are almost impossible to implement precisely. The concept of achieving "optimum yield," the overall management objective, is itself extremely evasive. Traditionally, renewable natural resources have been managed with an objective of achieving maximum sustainable yield (MSY), the greatest volume or mass that can be harvested over the long run. Economists would argue that maximum economic yield (MEY), maintaining the harvest level that maximizes long-term economic return, is a more rational goal. In recent years the concept of optimum sustainable yield (OSY), or simply optimum yield (OY), has emerged. OSY is that level of sustained harvest which will maximize public benefits, taking into account (at least) all economic, sociological, and biological factors. Conceptual definition of OSY is difficult enough; quantitative definition "based on the best scientific information available" is virtually impossible (Roedel 1975).

The FCMA established eight regional fishery councils to implement the framework prescribed—New England, Mid-Atlantic, South Atlantic, Caribbean, Gulf, Pacific, North Pacific, and Western Pacific. Each council consisted of the "principal State official with marine fishery management responsibility and expertise in each constituent State," the "regional director of the National Marine Fisheries Service for the geographic area concerned," and four to twelve additional members appointed by the secretary of commerce (90 Stat. 347, 348). Councils were to prepare fishery management plans for each fishery in their region in accordance with the standards set forth in the act, and could require permits or prescribe fees for fishing rights, limit gear and otherwise limit the catch, establish a system of limited access to a fishery, and otherwise take all actions consistent with sound fishery management (90 Stat. 351, 352).

The FCMA also affected treaties and other international agreements. While it recognized treaties then in effect, it also directed that those in conflict with the new act be renegotiated (90 Stat. 337) and required vessels of foreign nations fishing in the fisheries conservation zone to abide by a number of operating conditions. As a matter of policy, "[t]he total allowable level of fishing [by foreign vessels]...shall be that portion of the optimum yield...which will not be harvested by vessels of the United States" (90 Stat. 338). Furthermore, all foreign vessels fishing on stocks governed by the FCMA must possess a permit issued by the secretary of commerce with the advice and counsel of the secretary of state, the secretary of the department in which the Coast Guard is operating, and the appropriate regional council (90 Stat. 342, 343).

Designation of the 200-mile zone was changed from "fisheries conservation zone" to "exclusive economic zone" (EEZ) by the 1986 amendments to the FCMA to conform with the proclamation establishing the EEZ (Proclamation No. 5030, 19 WEEKLY COMP. PRES. DOC. 384 (Mar. 10, 1983)).

International Arrangements

The right of all nations to fish the high seas has been recognized since the beginning of the seventeenth century, but the boundary between the high seas and the territorial sea (wherein a coastal nation has exclusive jurisdiction) has been a cause of continual disputes. Complicating the issue is the degree to which a coastal nation can exercise control over fishing in the high seas adjacent to its coast (Bean 1983, 384-385).

In 1948 President Harry Truman declared that the United States would regard it proper to establish conservation zones in such waters, within which fishing activities of all nations would be subject to U.S. regulation (59 Stat. 884). While Truman apparently sought only to negotiate agreements with nations fishing the high seas off the United States coast, some interpreted his remarks to indicate that the United States would unilaterally regulate fishing in such waters. Chile responded by declaring a 200-mile conservation zone, and other nations followed suit (Bean 1983, 384, 385).

The current overall framework for international arrangements governing fisheries is described in the Convention on Fishing and Conservation of the Living Resources of the High Seas, one of the treaties resulting from the First Geneva Conference on the Law of the Sea in 1958 (chapter 10). Provisions of individual treaties made under the general umbrella of the convention vary, but most provide for an administrative organization and describe its powers and duties (usually a commission composed of representatives of the member state parties), stipulate conservation objectives, detail budget provisions, authorize research activities, and provide some sort of enforcement mechanism. The last provision is perhaps the weakest—no fishery convention provides for an international enforcement system; the conventions generally entrust each member state with the job of policing its citizens ("Report of the International Panel" 1969, VIII-54).

However, some domestic legislation includes sanctions that can be invoked against nations that violate fishing agreements. The Pelly Amendment to the Fisherman's Protective Act of 1954 authorizes the president to prohibit importation of fish products from such countries; the Packwood Amendment to the FCMA mandates a 50 percent reduction in any catch allocations to which a nation might be due, if that nation violates the provisions of the International Convention for the Regulation of Whaling (IWC). In 1974 an attempt was made to invoke the Pelly Amendment against the Soviet Union and Japan for violations of minke whale quotas set by the International Whaling Commission (IWC). President Gerald Ford refused to invoke the sanctions, however, stating that such actions would disrupt the domestic economy by halting imports of fish products and that the two countries would abide by IWC quotas in the future (Bean 1983, 266).

Multilateral fisheries treaties to which the United States was a party as of January 1, 1987, are as follows (U.S. Department of State 1986, 251, 252, 305, 306, 323, 324):

• International Convention for the Regulation of Whaling (1935)—fifty-seven countries; all whale fisheries.

• International Convention for the Regulation of Whaling with Schedule of Whaling Regulations (1948)—forty-one countries.

• International Convention on the High Seas Fisheries of the North Pacific Ocean (1953)—Canada, Japan, United States; primarily halibut, herring, and salmon.

• Interim Convention on Conservation of North Pacific Fur Seals (1957)—Canada, Japan, Soviet Union, United States; limited to fur seals.

• Convention for the Establishment of an Inter-American Tropical Tuna Commission (1950)—France, Japan, Nicaragua, Panama, United States; yellowfin and skipjack tuna and other fish taken by tuna vessels in the eastern Pacific Ocean.

• Amended Agreement for Establishment of the Indo-Pacific Fisheries Commission (1961)—twenty countries.

• International Convention for the Conservation of Atlantic Tunas (1966)—twenty-two countries; all tuna and tunalike fisheries.

• Convention on Fishing and Conservation of the Living Resources of the High Seas (1966)—thirty-five countries.

• Convention for the Conservation of Antarctic Seals (1978)—eleven countries.

• Convention on the Conservation of Salmon in the North Atlantic (1983)—Canada, Denmark, European Communities, Iceland, Norway, Sweden, Soviet Union, United States.

In addition to the foregoing multilateral agreements, the United States has bilateral conventions with Canada concerning the halibut fishery of the northern Pacific Ocean and the Bering Sea (1953), the Pacific salmon fisheries (1985), and the Great Lakes fisheries (1954). It has also entered into agreements with the Soviet Union (1976) and Japan (1982) concerning fisheries off the United States coasts.

REFERENCES

Adasiak, A. 1979. "Alaska's Experience with Limited Entry." *Journal of the Fisheries Research Board of Canada* 36:770-782.

Allard, Dean Conrad, Jr. 1978. *Spencer Fullerton Baird and the U.S. Fish Commission.* New York: Arno Press.

Bean, Michael J. 1983. *The Evolution of National Wildlife Law.* New York: Praeger Publishers.

Commission on Marine Science, Engineering and Resources. 1969. *Our Nation and the Sea.* Washington, DC: Government Printing Office.

Harville, John P. 1986. "Summary Report and Recommendations of the AFS Committee on Federal Fisheries Responsibilities." *Fisheries* 11 (4): 2-6 (July-August).

"Report of the International Panel." 1969. In *Panel Reports of the Commission on Marine Science, Engineering and Resources*, Vol. 3, *Marine Resources and Legal-Political Arrangements for Their Development*, VIII-1 through VIII-153. Washington, DC: Government Printing Office.

"Report of the Panel on Marine Resources." 1969. In *Panel Reports of the Commission on Marine Science, Engineering and Resources*, Vol. 3, *Marine Resources and Legal-Political Arrangements for Their Development*, VII-1 through VII-253. Washington, DC: Government Printing Office.

Roedel, Philip M., ed. 1975. *Optimum Sustainable Yield as a Concept in Fisheries Management.* Special Publication no. 9. Washington, DC: American Fisheries Society.

Rogers, George W. 1979. "Alaska's Limited Entry Program: Another View." *Journal of the Fisheries Research Board of Canada* 36:783-788.

Tinsley, V. Randall, and L. A. Nielsen. 1987. "Interstate Fisheries Arrangements: Application of a Pragmatic Classification Scheme for Interstate Arrangements." *Virginia Journal of Natural Resource Law* 6 (2): 263-321.

U.S. Department of Commerce. National Marine Fisheries Service. 1984. *Grant-in-Aid for Fisheries: Program Activities 1984.* Washington, DC: Government Printing Office.

U.S. Department of the Interior. U.S. Fish and Wildlife Service. 1984. *Federal Aid in Fish and Wildlife Restoration 1984.* Washington, DC: Government Printing Office.

————. n.d. "Statistical Summary for Fish and Wildlife Restoration." Washington, DC: U.S. Department of the Interior, U.S. Fish and Wildlife Service, Division of Federal Aid.

U.S. Department of State. 1986. *Treaties in Force: A List of Treaties and Other International Agreements in Force on January 1, 1987.* Washington, DC: Government Printing Office.

CHAPTER XIV

The Coastal Zone

The coastal zone is a diffuse band within the continuum from the deep ocean to the high land. It begins and ends where one wants it to, for whatever purposes one defines it; and all of us have some mental concept of the "coast" or "coastal zone." For years it sustained the many demands placed upon it with little federal involvement, except for marine transportation and waterfowl management. Marine-oriented agencies looked seaward; land-oriented agencies looked landward. Then, in the mid-1960s, the coastal zone was discovered as an entity—valuable, beautiful, fragile, and dangerous. During the next decade, government intervention in management of the coastal zone became one of the hottest natural resource and environmental issues in the country.

About 75 percent of the nation's population then lived in coastal and Great Lakes states, and the coastal population was growing at a faster rate than was the total U.S. population ("Report of the Panel on Management and Development of the Coastal Zone" 1969, III-10). Two-thirds of the commercial fisheries (in value and number of species) and almost all of the coastal sport fish species are dependent upon estuaries (U.S. Department of the Interior, U.S. Fish and Wildlife Service 1970, IV-97, IV-167), and the coastal margin has always been popular with fishermen and sunseekers.

The coastal zone paid a price for our intense use. Of the nation's 8 million acres of estuaries, over 7 percent had been destroyed by dredging and filling by 1967 (U.S. Congress, House, Committee on Merchant Marine and Fisheries 1967, 31), and many important coastal areas—more than 50 percent of the original marsh—and other tidal habitat had been destroyed (Clark 1967, 11). Many coastal industries and municipalities considered the estuaries as convenient depositories for pollution and, while engineering works were essential to support marine transportation, their adverse environmental impacts were often profound (National Council on Marine Resources and Engineering Development 1968, 71).

At that time the full value of the coastal zone was not known, and its functions were imperfectly understood. The first national estuarine conference, held at Jekyll Island, Georgia, in 1964 (Lauff 1967) brought together estuarine scientists from throughout the United States and from many foreign countries and served as a catalyst for the accelerated and expanded scientific investigations that bore fruit during the following decade.

While society was exacting a price from the coastal zone, the coastal zone was reciprocating. Between 1954 and 1967, nineteen major storms swept the Atlantic and Gulf coasts, causing more than 1,000 deaths and almost $6 billion in damages ("Report of the Panel on Management and Development of the Coastal Zone" 1969, III-33). Erosion caused by these and other storms precipitated congressional action in the River and Harbor Act of 1968, which directed the U.S. Army Corps of Engineers to identify areas where serious erosion problems existed and to recommend remedial action. Of the nation's 84,000 miles of shoreline, the resultant report identified more than 20,000 experiencing significant erosion (U.S. Army Corps of Engineers 1973, 20).

The national coastal zone management program began as an effort to control physical destruction of the nation's estuaries and coastal waters, largely as a result of inadequately regulated dredge and fill activities. (Note: Arguably, the origin may also be traced through water pollution control legislation to the Rivers and Harbors Act of 1899 [Wenk 1972, 541], but these earlier efforts were much narrower than the comprehensive areawide approach that began in the mid-1960s.) The concept grew into a wide-ranging and complex experiment in intergovernmental relations with an accent on land use planning and management in the broadest context.

LEGISLATIVE PRECURSORS

Several states instituted coastal land use programs during the 1960s. Massachusetts and Maine required local and state permits for dredging or filling in wetlands bordering coastal waters. North Carolina required permits for dredging or filling in estuaries or state-owned lakes and began preparing a long-range plan for estuarine conservation and management. New Jersey's program was based on estuarine land acquisition. Florida and New York combined acquisition with regulation, and California concentrated on problems surrounding San Francisco Bay (Heath 1971, 154-162).

The federal (national?) program developed slowly, evolving as it came. Its roots were in sections 9, 10, and 13 of the 1899 Rivers and Harbors Act (chapter 12), and these provisions (plus section 404 of the subsequent Clean Water Act of 1977) continue to provide the substance of *federal regulatory authority* in the coastal zone. The Rivers and Harbors Act was supplemented by the consultation and coordination requirements of the Fish and Wildlife Coordination Act of 1934 (as amended in 1958), incorporating the views of state and federal fish and wildlife agencies into permit decisions. But the process did not work very well, and by 1966 Congress and the federal executive branch had begun six years of deliberations that would culminate in the Coastal Zone Management Act of 1972.

H.R. 25

The first attempts toward a national program were contained in Congressman John D. Dingell's H.R. 13,447 of the Eighty-ninth Congress (1966). His bill was poorly publicized, stimulated little interest at the state level, and failed to pass the House under suspension of the rules by three votes (Adams 1971, 20). Dingell vowed to introduce a similar bill early in the Ninetieth Congress, and he did—with H.R. 25. Soon thereafter identical or similar bills were introduced by Congressmen Herbert Tenzer, William F. Ryan, Richard L. Ottinger, and Congresswoman Edna F. Kelly (New York); Frank Thompson, Jr. (New Jersey); Rogers C. B. Morton (Maryland); and Hastings Keith (Massachusetts).

As described by Dingell in his introductory remarks at the March 6, 1967, hearing on H.R. 25 and related bills,

> the bills to be heard would authorize the Secretary of the Interior, in consultation with the States and other Federal agencies, to conduct a nationwide study of estuarine areas....The first phase would be to identify areas that are relatively [unspoiled] or partially spoiled, but which should be protected from further adverse effects. The second phase would be to conduct a more detailed study of the identified areas to determine the estuarine areas that should be preserved or protected, or, where possible, restored, which are valuable for sport and commercial fishing, wildlife conservation, recreation and scenic beauty....
>
> The Secretary would be authorized to acquire and develop lands and waters within a designated area, but only after the designation has been approved by a subsequent act of Congress.
>
> With respect to [publicly] owned areas of national significance, the Secretary would be authorized to enter into agreements with States and

local subdivisions for the management and development of those areas. (U.S. Congress, House, Committee on Merchant Marine and Fisheries 1967, 1-2)

In his introductory comments, Dingell failed to mention some of the bill's more controversial provisions—authority for the secretary of the interior to "issue regulations...specifying standards for zoning bylaws" (sec. 6 (a)) and the requirement for a permit from the secretary of the interior "in addition to any other permit that may be required...[for] dredging, filling, or excavation work within any estuary of the United States or in the Great Lakes and connecting waterways" (sec. 12 (a)). In the hearings that followed (U.S. Congress, House, Committee on Merchant Marine and Fisheries 1967), the Sport Fishing Institute, the League of Women Voters, The Izaak Walton League of America, The Conservation Foundation, and other conservation groups universally supported the legislation. Many states opposed it, however (because of its apparent infringement upon traditional state and local jurisdiction), as did the U.S. Army Corps of Engineers (dual Interior and Corps permits) and affected development interests.

H.R. 25 focused on the physical alteration of estuarine systems, primarily through dredging and filling subject to Corps permits. Its recommended solution was a study and a federally dominated management system. It had already been preempted on the former, and the nation was unwilling to accept the latter.

The preceding Congress had passed the Clean Water Restoration Act of 1966, section 201(b) of which directed the secretary of the interior to conduct a study of pollution in the nation's estuaries and to prepare "recommendations for a comprehensive national program for the preservation, study, use, and development of estuaries of the Nation, and the respective responsibilities that should be assumed by Federal, State and local governments and by public and private interests" (80 Stat. 1248)— in essence, a national coastal zone management program. The report was to be completed by November 3, 1969. It was focused on *pollution* rather than on physical alteration of the estuaries; the study was conducted by the Federal Water Pollution Control Administration; and the bill came through the House Committee on Public Works and Transportation rather than Dingell's Subcommittee on Fisheries and Wildlife Conservation of the House Committee on Merchant Marine and Fisheries. But the National Estuarine Pollution Study was already under way as H.R. 25 was being debated, and its existence detracted from the prominence of Dingell's efforts.

Marine Affairs

A second avenue for congressional interest came through concern over the nation's activities in the marine arena and was oriented (at least initially) more toward marine science and federal and international institutional arrangements than toward coastal matters and land use. Following a long sequence of bickering among constituency groups, executive department agencies, and congressional committees and a presidential veto over support for the nation's oceanographic effort, Congress developed two approaches. The Senate emphasized a council structure, drawn from within the executive branch and chaired by the vice-president, assisted by an advisory commission. The House was skeptical of a council structure and placed its emphasis on a commisson. Neither side retreated, and the resultant act contained both, operating under a unique working relationship (Wenk 1972, 82-92).

The Marine Resources and Engineering Development Act of 1966 stated a national policy "to develop, encourage, and maintain a coordinated, comprehensive, and long-range national program in marine science for the benefit of mankind" (80 Stat. 203). It created two bodies to carry out the policy, a council within the Executive Office of the President and a fifteen-member commission drawn from "government, industry, universities, laboratories and other institutions engaged in marine scientific or technological pursuits," with representation from Congress (80 Stat. 206). (Note: The official name of the council was the National Council on Marine Resources and Engineering Development, but it became known as the Marine Sciences Council. Similarly, the commission was the Commission on Marine Science, Engineering, and Resources, but it became known as the Stratton Commission, after its chairman, Julius A. Stratton.) Activities of the two bodies were in many ways parallel—both were to review marine science activities, conduct studies, and the like—but they differed in several important aspects.

The Marine Sciences Council was an "in-house" organization, chaired by the vice-president and composed of cabinet-level officers and the heads of two independent agencies. (Note: Council members were the vice-president; the secretaries of state, navy, interior, commerce, treasury, and health, education, and welfare; the chairman of the Atomic Energy Commission, and the director of the National Science Foundation.) While the legislation charged the council with developing "a comprehensive program of marine science activities" and "the planning and conduct of a coordinated Federal program" (80 Stat. 205), it was to do so through existing agencies within the existing executive branch structure. The council was part of the Executive Office of the President. It reported to the president, and it became deeply involved in the day-to-day workings of the executive branch.

Members of the commission were appointed by the president, largely from outside the federal government, but the commission contained three members of the administration and two each from the House and Senate (Note: Administration members represented the Departments of the Navy, the Interior, and Commerce. Norris Cotton, a Republican from Ohio, and Warren G. Magnuson, a Democrat from Washington, represented the Senate; Alton A. Lennon, a Democrat from North Carolina, and Charles A. Mosher, a Republican from New Hampshire, represented the House.) The commission was to "recommend an overall plan for an adequate national oceanographic program that will meet present and future needs" and to "[r]ecommend a Governmental organizational plan with estimated cost" (80 Stat. 206). Except for its reviews of existing marine programs as bases for its recommendations, it did not become heavily involved in current agency activities.

The commission was to make one final report "to the President, via the Council, and to the Congress not later than eighteen months after [its] establishment" (80 Stat. 207). The president was to make annual reports to Congress on the status of the nation's marine science activities, including recommendations for legislation. (Note: This report was prepared by the council, transmitted by the vice-president to the president, and thence to Congress.) Neither the commission nor the council was to be a permanent agency; the commission was to expire 30 days, and the council 120 days, after submission of the commission report (80 Stat. 205, 207).

In neither case was there any statutory directive to become involved in coastal or estuarine affairs or land use management. Both groups were decidedly marine and primarily federal to international in their orientation, and (at least initially) both were concerned mainly with marine science activities. Yet both were to play major roles in developing a national coastal zone program.

WITHIN THE EXECUTIVE BRANCH

As Congress debated the desirability and characteristics of a national coastal zone management program, the council and the commission were engaged in similar activities within the executive branch. Both branches contributed to the program which ultimately emerged.

The Marine Sciences Council

The Marine Sciences Council held its first meeting on August 17, 1966, two months after the Marine Resources and Engineering Development Act was passed (National Council on Marine Resources and Engineering Development 1967, 23). During the remainder of its first year, the council identified nine "new initiatives," one of which, "estuary study," recognized the problem of estuarine pollution and initiated a study of the situation, focusing initially on Chesapeake Bay (National Council on Marine Resources and Engineering Development 1967, 33, 73). This first annual report of the council did not mention coastal zone management per se, but the next one did, and so did every one thereafter (National Council on Marine Resources and Engineering Development 1967, 1968, 1969, 1970). In 1967 the council established a Committee on Multiple Uses of the Coastal Zone (CMUCZ), composed of members representing fifteen different federal agencies (Wenk 1972, 190). The CMUCZ became the forum for administration debates on coastal zone matters. Through it, and its successor, a special White House task group under the leadership of undersecretary of the interior Russell E. Train, the council attempted to develop coastal zone management legislation. However, its efforts were stymied by differences among the agencies and the transition between the Johnson-Humphrey and Nixon-Agnew administrations, and initiative fell to the commission and to Congress (Wenk 1972, 199-201).

The Stratton Commission

While the Marine Sciences Council was engaged with affairs within the administration, the president's Commission on Marine Science, Engineering, and Resources (the Stratton Commission) was conducting its deliberations. The commission was to "undertake a review of existing and planned marine science activities of the United States in order to assess their adequacy" (80 Stat. 206).

The Stratton Commission was oriented toward *marine science and engineering,* not estuaries or land use problems. In its initial organization, none of its panels was assigned investigation of coastal zone problems—indeed, there was some question of whether the commission's charter included this arena. But on a bus trip while attending a Naval Academy football game, several members of the Panel on Environmental Monitoring engaged in an enthusiastic discussion of coastal zone issues. Soon thereafter a new panel was created—the Panel on Management and Development of the Coastal Zone—with membership identical to that of the Panel on Environmental Monitoring. Interestingly, the chairman's foreword to the "Panel Reports" speaks of "seven working panels," and the list of "Panels of the Commission" that follows contains one "Panel on Environmental Monitoring and on Management of the Coastal Zone"—but the document contains an eighth panel report, the "Report of the Panel on Management and Development of the Coastal Zone" (*Panel Reports of the Commission on Marine Science, Engineering and Resources* 1969).

The commission's deliberations on coastal matters and the recommendations that followed were among its most significant accomplishments. The Stratton Commission recommended that

> a Coastal Zone Management Act be enacted which will provide policy objectives for the coastal zone and authorize Federal grants-in-aid to facilitate the establishment of State Coastal Zone Authorities empowered to manage coastal waters and adjacent land." (*Our Nation and the Sea* 1969, 57)

> [t]he National Oceanic and Atmospheric Agency administer the grants in support of planning and enforcement activities of the State Coastal Zone Authorities. It should be empowered to revoke or withhold the grants if Authorities are not acting in compliance with plans NOAA has approved.
>
> All Federal agencies providing grants-in-aid to States or engaging in coastal activities review their projects for consistency with plans of the State Coastal Zone Authorities.
>
> NOAA assist the States in an effort to resolve problems resulting from the divergent objectives of other Federal agencies.
>
> NOAA develop and continually update its plans for the development and use of coastal areas not within State jurisdiction and coordinate the activities of other Federal agencies in these areas. (*Our Nation and the Sea* 1969, 62)

THE COASTAL ZONE MANAGEMENT ACT OF 1972 (CZMA)

The National Estuarine Pollution Study was completed by the Federal Water Pollution Control Administration in November 1969. The U.S. Fish and Wildlife Service's National Estuary Study (U.S. Department of the Interior, U.S. Fish and Wildlife Service 1970), authorized by a watered-down H.R. 25, was under way and would be completed in January 1970 (the Estuary Protection Act of 1968). The Marine Sciences Council in the Executive Office of the President was "taking steps to encourage the States to strengthen and expand the necessary institutional framework for carrying out planned use of the Coastal Zone in the national interest" (National Council on Marine Resources and Engineering Development 1969, 79). Through its Committee on Multiple Uses of the Coastal Zone, the council also was slowly bringing agencies of the executive branch toward support of a national coastal zone management program (Wenk 1972, 190-197). The Stratton Commission's report was released in January 1969. The environmental movement was gathering momentum. The stage was set for legislative action.

The Ninety-first Congress

Senator Warren G. Magnuson's bill (S. 2802), introduced on August 8, 1969, was the first to emerge. Magnuson was a member of the Stratton Commission, a staunch supporter of NOAA, a powerful ally of commercial fishing interests, chairman of the Senate Committee on Commerce, and a Democrat. Staff members of the Marine Sciences Council had cooperated with the senator in preparing his bill. They had also been working with members of the Department of the Interior and the Bureau of the Budget (BOB), attempting to obtain support for coastal zone management legislation from a somewhat recalcitrant Nixon administration (Wenk 1972, 201). Shortly after S. 2802 was introduced, the Marine Sciences Council's staff received a telephone call from the cognizant staff person in the BOB. "Have you seen Magnuson's bill?" he asked. "Yes," was the response. "What do you think of it?" "We've fiddled around with this issue for at least four years. It's a good bill. We should go with it." There was an awkward moment of silence on the BOB end of the line, then "That's too bad. He's in the wrong party." Such is partisan politics.

The administration's bills (H.R. 14845 and S. 3183) were introduced three months later, in late November of 1969. By the end of the Ninety-first Congress, six similar bills were pending before Congress. S. 2802 and S. 3460 were in the Senate Commerce Committee; H.R. 15099 and H.R. 16155 were in the House Merchant Marine and Fisheries Committee—these generally followed the Stratton Commission's recommendations and placed jurisdiction in the Marine Sciences Council (NOAA was not created until 1970). S. 3183 and H.R. 14845, administration bills that would give the new program to the Department of the Interior, were in the public works committees of both houses. All committees except the House Public Works Committee held hearings during

1969 and 1970, with the Senate Commerce Committee being most active—fourteen days of hearings, fifty-two witnesses, and eighty-two items of information received (U.S. Congress, Senate, Committee on Commerce 1976, 5). However, the Ninety-first Congress failed to act.

The Ninety-second Congress

Deliberations began anew in the early days of the Ninety-second Congress. In the House, Congressman Alton Lennon (also a member of the Stratton Commission) introduced H.R. 2492 and H.R. 2493 on January 29, and H.R. 9229 on June 17, 1971. All of these were referred to the House Committee on Merchant Marine and Fisheries, of which Lennon was a member. H.R. 4332, an administration bill introduced in February, would have given jurisdiction to the Department of the Interior. Senate bills were introduced in early February of 1971: S. 582 and S. 638 would have placed jurisdiction in the newly formed NOAA and were referred to Magnuson's Commerce Committee; S. 632 and S. 992 (February 25), a companion bill to H.R. 4332, were referred to the Senate Committee on Interior and Insular Affairs (U.S. Congress, Senate, Committee on Commerce 1976, 5-8).

All bills contained the same basic concept—federal cost sharing to states for a largely state-operated land and water use planning and management program. The basic concept received almost universal support, yet intense efforts over almost twenty-one months were required to obtain enactment.

Administration Support

The administration's position changed dramatically between the Ninety-first Congress and the Ninety-second Congress. In the former it had been a reluctant supporter of the coastal zone management concept, provided the program was in Interior. In the latter it was an enthusiastic supporter of the idea as *part of the larger concept of a national land use policy*. This position greatly weakened the testimony of administration witnesses before the Senate Commerce Committee and the House Merchant Marine and Fisheries Committee and frequently put administration witnesses at odds with committee members:

> MR. LENNON....We would like your views, Mr. Secretary, as to whether you think we ought to wait at this point in time and do nothing about the creating of a coastal zone management program until such time

as we could get a land-use bill through Congress. I think you gentlemen
know that some of us have lived with this problem for years and have felt
the need for an independent oceanic and atmospheric agency; and we recognize with the administration taking another view that it would be years
before that could be brought into being....

SECRETARY LOESCH [assistant secretary of the interior for public land
management]. Mr. Chairman, let me observe that I do not share your view
in the first place.

MR. LENNON. No, sir; I do not expect you to. You would not be here in
the first place if you did.

SECRETARY LOESCH. No sir; I do not share your view that there is
likely to be a great delay in passage of a land-use planning bill. I do not
say that [it] will necessarily be the administration's bill, but I think this
Congress will devote itself, it has, in part, already, to a general land-use
planning bill....I just do not think we ought to settle for half a loaf if we
can get it all, and I believe we can get it all. (U.S. Congress, Senate,
Committee on Commerce 1976, 158)

S. 3507, the first bill to receive action in the Ninety-second Congress,
placed jurisdiction in the Department of Commerce (ostensibly in
NOAA, as recommended by the Stratton Commission). The House
Committee on Merchant Marine and Fisheries reported a new bill (H.R.
14146) containing the results of its deliberations and placing the new
program in Interior, and this bill passed the full House. The House then
amended S. 3507 to conform to H.R. 14146, changing jurisdiction from
NOAA to Interior, and passed the amended Senate version in lieu of H.R.
14146 (U.S. Congress, Senate, Committee on Commerce 1976, 7). The
Senate refused to accept House amendments, and the bill went to conference. Subsequently, conferees agreed on a NOAA locus, reversing the
House action:

Therefore, what the conferees agreed upon was basically a water-related
coastal zone program administered by the Secretary of Commerce...
requir[ing] full coordination with and concurrence of the Secretary of
Interior. This compromise recognizes the need for making coastal zone
management fully compatible with national land use policy, while making
use of the special technical competence of the National Oceanic and
Atmospheric Administration in the Department of Commerce in managing the nation's coastal areas. (U.S. Congress, Senate, Committee on
Commerce 1976, 456)

During all the legislative maneuvering, the Nixon administration played a passive role, avoiding taking sides between two powerful senators—Magnuson (NOAA-based coastal zone management) and Henry Jackson (Interior-based national land use policy). The administration opted instead to bide its time, waiting for passage of a land use policy that would place the entire package in Interior (Wenk 1972, 205). But this was not to be.

President Nixon begrudgingly signed the Coastal Zone Management Act on October 27, 1972 (the same day that it would have become law without his signature), commenting as he did so:

> S. 3507 locates administrative responsibility for this program in the Department of Commerce rather than in the Department of the Interior which I would have preferred—and as I called for in my proposed Land Use Policy Act. This action is not sufficient reason in my judgment for vetoing the bill, but it does underscore once again the importance of creating a new Department of Natural Resources, as I have recommended, so that we can reverse the trend toward fragmentation and fractionalization of Federal programs and begin to coordinate our environmental efforts more effectively. (U.S. Congress, Senate, Committee on Commerce 1976, 459)

The chronology of legislative action culminating in the Coastal Zone Management Act of 1972 is summarized in figure 14.1.

Congressional Policy

In the five years between introduction of H.R. 25 and passage of the Coastal Zone Management Act, Congress broadened and modified its policy toward coastal resources. The objectives of the former act were simply "to preserve, protect, develop, and, where possible, restore and make accessible for the benefit of all the people selected parts of the Nation's diminishing estuarine areas which are valuable for sport and commercial fishing, wildlife conservation, outdoor recreation, and scenic beauty" (sec. 1). The national policy enunciated in the Coastal Zone Management Act was

> (a) to preserve, protect, develop, and where possible, to restore or enhance, the resources of the Nation's coastal zone for this and succeeding generations, (b) to encourage and assist the states to exercise effectively their responsibilities in the coastal zone through the development and implementation of management programs..., (c) for all Federal agencies engaged in programs affecting the coastal zone to cooperate and partici-

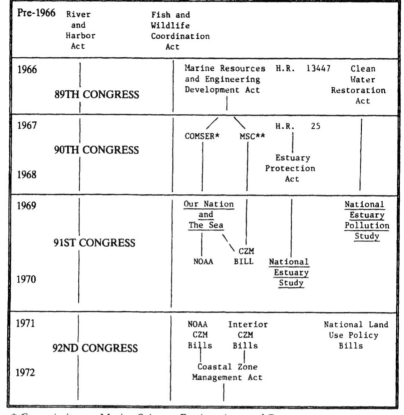

Pre-1966	River and Harbor Act	Fish and Wildlife Coordination Act			
1966	89TH CONGRESS	Marine Resources and Engineering Development Act	H.R. 13447		Clean Water Restoration Act
1967 1968	90TH CONGRESS	COMSER* MSC**	H.R. 25 Estuary Protection Act		
1969 1970	91ST CONGRESS	Our Nation and The Sea CZM NOAA BILL	National Estuary Study		National Estuary Pollution Study
1971 1972	92ND CONGRESS	NOAA Interior CZM CZM Bills Bills Coastal Zone Management Act			National Land Use Policy Bills

* Commission on Marine Science, Engineering, and Resources
** National Council on Marine Resources and Engineering Development

FIGURE 14.1. Chronology of the Coastal Zone Management Act of 1972. The chronology of legislative action culminating in the Coastal Zone Management Act of 1972.

pate with state and local governments and regional agencies in effectuating the purposes of this chapter, and (d) to encourage the participation of the public, of federal, state, and local governments and of regional agencies in the development of coastal zone management programs. (Sec. 303)

The objective of H.R. 25 was retained as the first policy element of the new act. State management programs—initially in a narrow sense, later in a broad perspective—were the crux of the legislation. The program that evolved was indeed a great experiment in interagency and intergovernmental coordination and cooperation, but participation of "regional agencies" and later encouragement of "interstate and regional agreements" have not yet borne fruit.

Defining the Coastal Zone

In addition to the agency jurisdictional battle, definition of the geographic area affected by the legislation became a controversial issue. The seaward limit was generally agreed upon—the offshore limit of the territorial sea. The landward boundary was general and vague, however, "to allow for adequate coordination with the proposed national land use legislation" (U.S. Congress, Senate, Committee on Commerce 1976, 201), leaving precise definition and delineation up to the individual states:

> "Coastal Zone" means the coastal waters...and the adjacent shorelands...strongly influenced by each other and in proximity to the shorelines of the several coastal states, and includes transitional and intertidal areas, salt marshes, wetlands, and beaches. The zone extends, in Great Lakes waters, to the international boundary between the United States and Canada and, in other areas, seaward to the outer limit of the United States territorial sea. The zone extends inland from the shorelines only to the extent necessary to control shorelands, the uses of which have a direct and significant impact upon the coastal waters. (86 Stat. 1281)
>
> [A state] management program shall include:
> (1) an identification of the boundaries of the coastal zone subject to the management program. (86 Stat. 1282)

Federal Consistency

Among the more novel attributes of the CZMA were the "consistency provisions." Lands "the use of which is by law subject solely to the discretion of or which is held in trust by the Federal Government, its officers or agents" are specifically excluded from the definition of "coastal zone" (86 Stat. 1281) and from state management plans. "Laws of the United States which shall be made in Pursuance [of the Constitution]...shall be the supreme Law of the Land;...any Thing in the Constitution or Laws of any State to the Contrary notwithstanding" (U.S. Constitution, art. VI). As federal laws tend to prescribe the duties and powers of federal agencies, they also tend to preempt state authority in such areas. But in the CZMA,

> [e]ach Federal agency conducting or supporting activities directly affecting the coastal zone shall conduct or support those activities in a manner which is, to the maximum extent practicable, consistent with approved state management programs....

> Any Federal agency which shall undertake any development project in the coastal zone of a state shall insure that the project is, to the maximum extent practicable, consistent with approved state management programs. (86 Stat. 1285)

> State and local governments submitting applications for Federal assistance under other Federal programs affecting the coastal zone shall indicate the views of the appropriate state or local agency as to the relationship of such activities to the approved management program for the coastal zone....Federal agencies shall not approve proposed projects that are inconsistent with a coastal state's management program, except...[when] consistent with the purposes of this chapter or necessary in the interest of national security. (86 Stat. 1286)

The origin of the consistency concept may be found in the Stratton Commission's recommendation that "[a]ll Federal agencies providing grants-in-aid to States or engaging in coastal activities review their projects for consistency with plans of the State Coastal Zone Authorities" (*Our Nation and the Sea* 1969, 62), but the rationale for this recommendation is missing. In fact, discussions in the commission and panel reports and the draft legislation that follows fail to mention federal consistency with state programs (*Our Nation and the Sea* 1969, 56-62; "Report of the Panel on Management and Development of the Coastal Zone" 1969, III-148 to III-157, III-183 to III-187). On the contrary, the commission's reports emphasize *federal review* of *state* programs to ensure "that the National interests be protected and if for any reason a Coastal Zone Authority cannot act in the public interest, the Federal Government should participate in the actions of the Coastal Zone Authority" ("Report of the Panel on Management and Development of the Coastal Zone" 1969, III-155). "The Federal Government should not make decisions for the State Authority, but it should oversee the Authority and withdraw funding support and delegation of specific Federal functions if the Authority performs inadequately" (*Our Nation and the Sea* 1969, 61).

The concept of federal consistency with approved state programs appeared in Magnuson's S. 2802 of the Ninety-first Congress, the first coastal zone management bill introduced, and was a part of almost all subsequent bills (including administration bills). Very little administration testimony addressed the consistency provisions. In testimony before the Ninety-second Congress, Russell Train, then chairman of the Council on Environmental Quality, recognized their significance—"A Federal agency such as the Corps would not be permitted...to undertake any act, including the granting of a license or permit, which is inconsistent with an approved State plan....And I think that could prove in practice a very substantial incentive to the States" (U.S. Congress, Senate, Committee on Commerce 1976, 100, 103). In general, administration witnesses did not view consistency as a serious threat to the federal bureaucracy and concentrated their efforts (at least during the Ninety-second Congress) toward defending the Nixon administration's proposal for national land use legislation in preference to a coastal program.

Major Provisions of the CZMA

The Coastal Zone Management Act of 1972 contained four action-oriented elements—management program development grants, administrative grants, interagency coordination and cooperation, and estuarine sanctuaries. Other sections contained statements of congressional findings (sec. 302), recognizing the importance of the coastal zone and the need for protection and more effective utilization; congressional policy (sec. 303), stating the intention to "preserve, protect, develop, and where possible to restore, the resources of the Nation's coastal zone" with emphasis on state implementation, federal cooperation, and federal, state, local, and regional participation; creation of a fifteen-person Coastal Zone Management Advisory Committee (sec. 311); and various administrative and fiscal provisions (secs. 304, 307-310, 313-315).

Management Program Development Grants (Section 305)

The first step in the national program was to develop state management programs, for which not more than two-thirds of the costs were offset by federal grants for no more than three years per state. State programs must include

(1) an identification of the boundaries of the coastal zone subject to the management program;

(2) a definition of what shall constitute permissible land and water uses within the coastal zone which have a direct and significant impact on the coastal waters.

(3) an inventory and designation of areas of particular concern within the coastal zone;

(4) an identification of the means by which the state proposes to exert control over the land and water uses referred to in paragraph (2) of this subsection, including a listing of relevant constitutional provisions, legislative enactments, regulations, and judicial decisions;

(5) broad guidelines on priority of uses in particular areas, including specifically those uses of lowest priority;

(6) a description of the organizational structure proposed to implement the management program, including the responsibilities and interrelationships of local, areawide, state, regional, and interstate agencies in the management process. (86 Stat. 1282)

Administrative Grants (Section 306)

Upon approval of its program, a state became eligible for two-thirds federal cost sharing for program implementation. In addition to meeting the requirements of section 305, states must show that all interested parties shared in development of the programs, that development plans of other jurisdictions were considered, and that an "effective mechanism for continued consultation and coordination" among all interests existed (86 Stat. 1284). Eligible state agencies must have the power

(1) to administer land and water use regulations, [to] control development in order to ensure compliance with the management program, and to resolve conflicts among competing uses; and

(2) to acquire fee simple and less than fee simple interests in lands, waters, and other property through condemnation or other means when necessary to achieve conformance with the management program. (86 Stat. 1284)

Considerable latitude and opportunity for imagination and creativity were left to the states in developing management arrangements. State programs could provide

(1) for any one or a combination of the following general techniques for control of land and water uses within the coastal zone;

(A State establishment of criteria and standards for local implementation, subject to administrative review and enforcement of compliance;

(B) Direct state land and water use planning and regulation; or

(C) State administrative review for consistency with the management program of all development plans, projects, or land and water use regulations, including exceptions and variances thereto, proposed by any state or local authority or private developer, with power to approve or disapprove after public notice and an opportunity for hearings.

(2) for a method of assuring that local land and water use regulations within the coastal zone do not unreasonably restrict or exclude land and water uses of regional benefit. (86 Stat. 1284)

States could allocate a portion of the federal funds received to local governments or other agencies, modify their programs from time to time, and adopt segments of their programs sequentially (86 Stat. 1285). Ultimately, however—"as soon as...reasonably practicable"—each participating state had to convince NOAA that it was willing, able, and fully intended to carry out a program meeting the objectives of the act.

Interagency Coordination and Cooperation (Section 307)

While the "guts" of this section remained the federal consistency provisions discussed earlier, their impacts were somewhat softened by requirements for cooperation, consultation, and consideration among all levels of government before actions were taken. The section also contained the usual provisions that "[n]othing in this title shall be construed—(1) to diminish either Federal or state jurisdiction, responsibility, or rights in the field of planning, development, or control of water resources, submerged lands, or navigable waters...[or] (2) as superceding, modifying, or repealing existing laws applicable to the various Federal agencies" (86 Stat. 1286). While these provisions were undoubtedly intended to mollify federal agencies that might have felt threatened by the CZMA and are typical "boilerplate" in statutes of this type, their validity here seems dubious in view of the far-reaching impacts of the act.

Estuarine Sanctuaries (Section 312)

In an effort to provide a better factual basis for coastal zone management decisions, the act encouraged establishment of estuarine sanctuaries "as natural areas set aside primarily to provide scientists the opportunity to make baseline ecological measurements" (U.S. Congress, Senate, Committee on Commerce 1976, 208). It authorized up to $2 million in federal funds, on a fifty-fifty matching basis, for the "acquisition, development, and operation of estuarine sanctuaries" (U.S. Congress, Senate, Committee on Commerce 1976, 190). The estuarine sanctuary provisions emerged as part of the "second wave" of legislation during the second session of the Ninety-first Congress. Initially they were strongly supported by the academic and research constituencies, but they were felt by many administrators to be somewhat peripheral to the main purpose of the act—to manage use of the lands and waters of the coastal zone. Their inclusion in the act constituted the first attempts to broaden the national coastal zone management program beyond these narrow regulatory objectives.

AMENDMENTS TO THE ACT

Almost every subsequent Congress has considered amending the CZMA. In toto, the amendments reflect expansion and proliferation of activities during the first decade as the program gained public acceptance, with subsequent retrenchmnent and reduction of federal support during recent years. Only the most important amendments are discussed here.

The Ninety-fourth Congress

Despite numerous funding problems at all levels of government, all eligible states and three of the four eligible territories were participating in the program by 1976. Encouraged by initial successes and burdened by complicating developments on national and international scales, the Congress undertook to broaden the program further through the Coastal Zone Management Act Amendments of 1976. The Arab oil embargo was changing attitudes toward energy and increasing efforts toward domestic production and conservation. Interest in the petroleum resources of the outer continental shelf (OCS) intensified, and sole federal jurisdiction over resources of the OCS was reconfirmed by the Supreme Court (Council on Environmental Quality 1976, 102-111; *United States v. Maine*). As a result, efforts were made to clarify and strengthen the consistency provisions and to provide funds to lessen the impacts upon "communities adversely affected by energy development" (Council on Environmental Quality 1977, 100). Additional provisions sought to expand the program, to attract a broader constituency, to soften the program's reputation as a purely regulatory measure, and to make it more financially attractive to the states. Toward these ends federal support also was provided for research and training, public access to beaches, and preservation of islands—and federal cost sharing was increased from two-thirds to 80 percent (U.S. Congress, Senate, Committee on Commerce 1976, 579, 628).

off-shore coast oil interests

Consistency and Mediation (Section 6)

In an effort to strengthen the state role in OCS activities, Congress added a new subsection to the provisions for interagency coordination and cooperation:

> (B) After the management program of any coastal state has been approved..., any person who submits to the Secretary of the Interior any plan for the exploration or development of, or production from, any area which has been leased under the Outer Continental Shelf Lands Act...shall...attach to such plan a certification that each activity...complies with such state's approved management program and will be carried out in a manner consistent with such program. No federal official or agency shall grant such person any license or permit for any activity...in such plan until such state or its designated agency receives a copy of such certificate and plan. (90 Stat. 1018)

While subsequent subsections afforded the secretary of commerce an override, Congress's intent appears clear—OCS programs were to be subject to state coastal zone management plans. Yet subsequent litigation illustrates the complexities of full consistency implementation.

Coastal Energy Impact Program (Section 7)

Affectionately termed "the Louisiana Repurchase" because of the funds provided to that state, this complex section "consist(s) of the provision of financial assistance to meet the needs of coastal states and local governments...resulting from specified activities involving energy development" (90 Stat. 1019).

Coastal Energy Impact Program (CEIP) funds could be used for almost anything related to coastal energy development:

> public facilities and public services which are required as a direct result of...Outer Continental Shelf energy activity...[and other coastal energy activities, including] highways and secondary roads, docks, navigation aids, fire and police protection, water supply, waste collection and treatment (including drainage), schools and education, and hospitals and health care.
> ...prevention, reduction, or amelioration of any unavoidable loss...of any valuable environmental or recreational resource if such loss results from coastal energy activity. (90 Stat. 1022)

Federal grants, loans, bonds, or other indebtedness guarantees could be provided to states or local units of government, depending on the circumstances. CEIP funds were apportioned among the states by a complex formula involving (1) the amount of newly leased OCS acreage adjacent to the state, (2) the volume of oil and natural gas produced during the preceding fiscal year from OCS leases adjacent to the state, (3) the amount of OCS oil and gas that was first landed in the state, and (4) the number of residents who obtained new employment as a result of OCS energy activities (90 Stat. 1020).

During its first year, an appropriation of $50 million was authorized for the CEIP—an amount equivalent to that authorized for administrative (sec. 306) grants (90 Stat. 1031). For a few years, the CEIP was a powerful enticement for coastal states to withdraw their opposition to OCS development (see the discussion later in this chapter).

Research and Training Assistance (Section 9)

To broaden the program further, the secretary of commerce (NOAA) was empowered to provide grants to states to assist them "in carrying out research, studies, and training required with respect to coastal zone management" (90 Stat. 1029). Other agencies in the federal executive branch could participate through interagency agreements and cost reimbursement. While the authorized funding was limited ($10 million per year, half of which was earmarked for federal agencies (90 Stat. 1031)), the intent was clear—NOAA's Office of Coastal Zone Management was to be much more than a regulatory agency.

Acquisition of Access to Public Beaches and Other Public Coastal Areas (Section 12)

The land acquisition and management provisions of the CZMA were also expanded to include "acquiring lands to provide access to public beaches and other public coastal areas of environmental, recreational, aesthetic, ecological, or cultural value, and for the preservation of islands" (90 Stat. 1030). These provisions were added to the estuarine sanctuary program, providing up to $2 million to pay not more than 50 percent of state costs incurred in acquiring such areas (90 Stat. 1031).

With passage of the 1976 amendments, the national coastal zone management program reached maturity. It had grown from a narrow regulatory concept, centered upon protecting the nation's estuaries from physical destruction, into a broadly based effort involving land use planning at all levels of government, research, land acquisition and management, and intricate intergovernmental relations. However, the authorization of appropriations for many sections expired on September 30, 1980 (90 Stat. 1031), necessitating congressional reauthorization the following fiscal year.

The Ninety-sixth Congress

The Coastal Zone Management Improvement Act of 1980 reaffirmed Congress's interest in the national program. The act rewrote and expanded the congressional statement of policy and added sections dealing with improvement of resource management and congressional review and disapproval of regulations.

Under the 1980 act, earlier requirements that state government plans give "full consideration to ecological, cultural, historic, and esthetic values as well as to needs for economic development" (86 Stat. 1281) were amplified to require that they provide for

(A) the protection of natural resources, including wetlands, floodplains, estuaries, beaches, dunes, barrier islands, coral reefs, and fish and wildlife and their habitat, within the coastal zone,

(B) the management of coastal development to minimize the loss of life and property caused by improper development in flood-prone, storm surge, geological hazard, and erosion-prone areas and in areas of subsidence and saltwater intrusion, and by the destruction of natural protective features such as beaches, dunes, wetlands, and barrier islands.

(C) priority consideration...to coastal-dependent uses and orderly processes for siting major facilities related to national defense, energy, fisheries development, recreation, ports and transportation, and the location, to the maximum extent practicable, of new and commercial and industrial developments. (94 Stat. 2060, 2160)

A new program of resource management improvement grants authorized federal grants to assist states in preserving or restoring areas having "recreational, ecological or esthetic values," in redeveloping "underutilized urban waterfronts and ports," and in providing access to "public beaches and other public coastal areas and to coastal waters" (94 Stat. 2063). Exemplary as this section may have been, it was not funded (Zinn 1985, 1). Many states are conducting activities cited in the section (e.g., preserving ecologically valuable areas) but have been employing other provisions of the CZMA to do so (e.g., the estuarine sanctuary provisions (16 U.S.C. 1461)).

The congressional disapproval procedure of the 1980 act introduced a complicated and highly questionable procedure into coastal zone management—congressional approval of executive rule making. The secretary of commerce (NOAA) was required to forward all final rules to Congress, where they would be reviewed by relevant committees in both houses. If either house objected to the rule, it could, through a concurrent resolution, disapprove the rule, whereupon the rule-making procedure must start again. Aware that it might have been infringing upon the powers of the executive branch (and perhaps being a bit sensitive), Congress granted standing to any person to test the constitutionality of the section and provided for an expedited Supreme Court review.

In 1981, early in the Reagan administration, the disapproval provisions were employed against proposed regulations that could have removed OCS leasing decisions from consistency review (46 Fed. Reg. 26,660). As such would have been contrary to the implied requirements of section 307(c)(1) of the CZMA and the explicit requirements of the new section 307(b)—section 6 of the 1976 amendments—the House Committee on Merchant Marine and Fisheries voted overwhelmingly to veto the regulations (H.R. REP. NO. 97-269, 97th Cong., 1st sess., 7-8 (1982)). The proposed regulations were subsequently withdrawn, averting a head-on confrontation (47 Fed. Reg. 4231).

Fortunately for all, the congressional disapproval procedure expired by statute on September 30, 1985.

The Ninety-ninth Congress

Since inception of the CZMA, the proper balance of federal-state funding and the intent of that funding have been debated. On the one side, the administration (particularly the Reagan administration) has favored reducing or eliminating federal funding, contending that the program was intended only to provide seed money and has fulfilled that purpose. On the other side, the Coastal States Organization and the individual states have argued for continued and increased federal support, contending that the states cannot continue the program without substantial federal assistance (Zinn 1985, 4).

The Coastal Zone Management Reauthorization Act of 1985 reflected the former view and the realities of the federal budget. The federal-state funding ratio for administrative and resource management improvement grants (sections 306, 306A) decreased from the previous 4 to 1 to 2.3 to 1 in fiscal year 1987, 1.5 to 1 in 1988, and 1 to 1 thereafter (100 Stat. 124).

The 1985 reauthorization also changed the national estuarine sanctuaries program (lowercase) to the National Estuarine Reserve Research System, institutionalizing Congress's original intent that these are areas to be used for research, requiring that NOAA "give priority consideration to research that used the System" (100 Stat. 126), and authorizing withdrawal of federal support if, among other conditions, "research being conducted...is not consistent with the research guidelines developed" (by the secretary of commerce). As further reductions in federal support for coastal zone management, the act repealed provisions for federal grants for research and technical assistance and eliminated the Coastal Zone Management Advisory Committee (100 Stat. 128).

The Hundred and First Congress

The 1990 amendments added provisions that may (1) strengthen the national coastal zone management program by increasing its breadth or (2) embroil management agencies in turf battles that may weaken the program.

Section 309 provides 100 percent federal funding (withheld from funds otherwise available for program implementation) for "development and implementation of [the following] coastal zone enhancement objectives":

(1) Protection, restoration, or enhancement of the existing coastal wetlands base, or creation of new coastal wetlands.

(2) Preventing or significantly reducing threats to life and destruction of property by eliminating development and redevelopment in high-hazard areas....

(3) Attaining increased opportunities for public access....

(4) Reducing marine debris entering the Nation's coastal and ocean environment by managing uses and activities that contribute to the entry of such debris.

(5) Development and adoption of procedures to assess, consider, and control cumulative and secondary impacts of coastal growth and development....

(6) Preparing and implementing special area management plans for important coastal areas.

(7) Planning for the use of ocean resources.

(8) Adoption of procedures and enforceable policies to help facilitate the siting of energy facilities and Government facilities and energy-related

activities and Government activities which may be of greater than
local significance. (104 Stat. 1388-309, 1388-310)

Although all enhancement objectives may be justifiable components of
a state coastal zone management plan, almost all involve the jurisdiction
of other agencies. Objective (1) interacts with section 404 of the Federal
Water Pollution Control Act (33 U.S.C.S. 1344 (1990)) and with mitigation requirements of the Council on Environmental Quality (40 C.F.R.
1508.20 (1992)). Objective (2) is related to activities of the Federal
Emergency Management Agency and the National Flood Insurance
Program, under review in the Hundred and Second Congress (S. 1659).
Objective (5) is part of the environmental assessment process prescribed
in regulations of the Council on Environmental Quality (40 C.F.R.
1508.27 (1991)) and may approach or exceed the state of the art.
Objective (8) confronts federal consistency requirements (16 U.S.C.S.
1456 (1990)), provisions that were also strengthened in the 1990 amendments (104 Stat. 1388-307). States are now implementing section 309.
It remains to be seen how the jurisdiction and coordination issues will be
resolved.

A new element of the national program, section 6217, requires states
to "prepare and submit to the Secretary [of the Department of
Commerce] and the Administrator [of the EPA] a Coastal Nonpoint
Pollution Control Program" that is subject to approval of both federal
officials (104 Stat. 1388-314). These requirements overlap those of sections 208 and 319 of the Federal Water Pollution Control Act (33 U.S.C.
1288, 33 U.S.C. 1329 (1988)), which in most states are not implemented
through the coastal zone management agency. The new section further
directs the secretary and the administrator to review the "inland coastal
zone boundary of each coastal State program which has been approved or
is proposed for approval...to determine whether the State's coastal zone
boundary extends inland to the extent necessary to control the land and
water uses that have a significant impact on coastal waters of the State"
and to "recommend appropriate modifications...[if] necessary to more
effectively manage land and water uses to protect coastal waters" (104
Stat. 1388-317). The intent is clearly to expand geographic jurisdiction
of state coastal zone management agencies, jurisdiction that was resolved
for most states many years ago. "Guidance" (rule-making authority) for
nonpoint source pollution in coastal waters is given to the administrator
of the EPA, in consultation with other agencies (104 Stat. 1388-317,
1388-318). Efforts to control nonpoint sources of pollution in coastal

areas and to bolster statewide efforts being made under the Federal Water Pollution Control Act are commendable and may well be justified. But giving the EPA direct oversight authority in state coastal programs; expanding those programs into areas traditionally the realm of statewide water pollution agencies; and reopening potential constitutional questions concerning the definition and delineation of the coastal zone at a time of retrenchment in environmental regulation may prove dangerous.

THE NATIONAL PROGRAM

The long delay in obtaining federal legislation, the political climate of the early 1970s, and the novel intergovernmental relationship contained in the CZMA created a climate for rapid implementation. Even before the act was passed, states were developing coastal zone management programs that were to become part of the national system.

Early Implementation

State reception and implementation were enthusiastic and immediate. Prior to 1969 only Massachusetts, Florida, and New Hampshire controlled filling and drainage of wetlands; between 1969 and 1971, while the congressional debates were taking place, Connecticut, North Carolina, New Jersey, Maryland, Georgia, Delaware, and Rhode Island enacted wetlands legislation. In 1970 the National Governor's Conference created the Coastal States Organization to provide a focal point for state activities (Wenk 1972, 182, 184).

Although the CZMA became effective in October 1972, no funding was provided until more than a year later—in December 1973. Within its first effective year, thirty-one of the thirty-four eligible states and territories applied for and received planning grants, the entire fiscal year 1974 appropriation of $7.2 million was utilized, and a backlog of $890,000 in requests existed (U.S. Congress, Senate, Committee on Commerce 1976, 533).

In 1973 the Coastal Zone Management Advisory Committee was appointed and the first of a series of annual national coastal zone conferences was held at Annapolis, Maryland (U.S. Department of Commerce, National Oceanic and Atmospheric Administration 1974, 4, 5). In the following year, the first estuary sanctuary grant was obligated, guidelines for management approval were drafted, and the Second National Coastal

Zone Conference was held, with 450 persons attending (U.S. Department of Commerce, National Oceanic and Atmospheric Administration 1975, 1, 12).

By 1976 the program was maturing. The first state (Washington) had achieved approval of its management program and became eligible for section 306 funds, and four other state programs had been completed and were under NOAA review. Three estuarine sanctuaries had been established; initial funding under the Coastal Energy Impact Program became available; draft regulations on federal consistency were being circulated—and the program was audited by the General Accounting Office (GAO) (U.S. Department of Commerce, National Oceanic and Atmospheric Administration 1977, 1-3).

An Uncertain Future?

The 1976 GAO report, "The Coastal Zone Management Program: An Uncertain Future," found that the states generally believed that they were making progress in developing management programs, but cited a number of actual and potential problems. Of the thirty states responding to the GAO's questionnaire, sixteen had a coastal management authority of some sort prior to the CZMA and thus were able to progress faster than the others (Comptroller General of the United States 1976, 11). While many of the problems cited in the GAO report have been resolved, perpetuation of the national coastal zone management program as a federal-state partnership remains in doubt.

Local Opposition

Almost all states encountered strong local opposition to the program and were forced to refight the state-federal battle at the state-local level. In the opinion of the GAO,

> resistance exists because (1) local governments may regard coastal zone management as an example of Federal-State interference in planning decisions traditionally made by localities and (2) the public, especially coastal landowners, contend that State management programs infringe on their private property rights and affect property values by restricting the uses to which their land can be put. (Comptroller General of the United States 1976, 27)

In addition, states were encountering the backlash engendered by the proliferation of environmental regulations and government intervention that occurred during the 1960s. In combination, local government opposition and the change in political climate caused considerable delay and frustration among some of the state leaders (Louisiana, North Carolina, Michigan, and Maine), and probably among others as well, and resulted in Maine's temporary withdrawal of its application for program approval (Comptroller General of the United States 1976, iii, 29, 33).

The constitutionality of the new program was soon tested. In *Adams v. N.C. Dep't of Natural and Economic Resources*, the plaintiffs owned land in Carteret County, North Carolina, one of the counties included in that state's coastal zone program. Residents of Carteret County were overwhelmingly opposed to a coastal zone management program, as were many of North Carolina's coastal residents, and the plaintiffs sought a declaratory judgment ruling the state's Coastal Area Management Act (CAMA) unconstitutional. The case was not particularly well prepared, but it illustrates the kinds of issues raised and the mistakes made in contesting these kinds of laws.

The plaintiffs alleged the following:

1. That the Act is a prohibited local act under Article II, section 24 of the North Carolina Constitution.

2. That the Act delegates authority to the Coastal Resources Commission (hereinafter referred to as CRC) to develop and adopt "State Guidelines" for the coastal area without providing adequate standards to govern the exercise of the power delegated in violation of Article I, section 6 and Article II, section 1 of the North Carolina Constitution.

3. That the provisions of the Act, and the State guidelines adopted by the CRC, deprive them of their property without due process of law in violation of the Fifth and Fourteenth Amendments [of the United States Constitution] and in violation of Article I, section 19 of the North Carolina Constitution.

4. That Section 113A-126 of the Act authorizes warrantless searches by the CRC which are repugnant to the Fourth Amendment of the United States Constitution and Article I, section 20 of the North Carolina Constitution. (295 N.C. at 685-686)

Section 24 of the North Carolina Constitution prohibits "any local, private, or special act or resolution" relating to "health, sanitation, and the abatement of nuisances;...non-navigable streams;...[or r]egulating labor, trade, mining, or manufacturing" but authorizes general laws regulating these matters. "General laws may be enacted for classes defined by population or other criteria...[and must be made applicable] without classification or exception in every unit of local government of like kind, such as every county, or every city or town, but need not be made applicable in every unit of local government in the state" (art. XIV, sec. 3). CAMA begins with legislative findings that (1) the "coastal area, and in particular the estuaries, are among the most biologically productive regions of this State and of the nation"; (2) the area "has an extremely high recreational and esthetic value which should be preserved and enhanced"; (3) it "has been subjected to increasing pressures which are the result of an [expanding society]"; and (4) "an immediate and pressing need exists to establish a comprehensive plan for the protection, preservation, orderly development, and management of the coastal area of North Carolina" (N.C. GEN. STAT. § 113A-102(a) (1974)). The coastal area is further defined as those counties "that (in whole or in part) are adjacent to, adjoining, intersected by or bound by the Atlantic Ocean...or any coastal sound" (N.C. GEN. STAT. § 113A-103(2) (1974)) upstream to "the limit of saltwater encroachment" (N.C. GEN. STAT. § 113A-103(3) (1974)). After commenting on the inexactness of legislative classifications, the North Carolina Supreme Court declared:

> We conclude that the western boundary of the coastal zone as determined by use of the seawater encroachment criterion is reasonably related to the purpose of the Act. The record shows, and a look at any map of eastern North Carolina will confirm, that the twenty counties included within the purview of the Act under the statutory definition of coastal area are the counties which are substantially bounded by the large bodies of water which may be logically, scientifically, or otherwise, considered to be coastal sounds. The coastal area as defined includes all those counties which intimately affect the quality of North Carolina's valuable estuarine waters. We thus hold that the Act is a general law which the General Assembly had power to enact. Since we hold that the Act is a general law we need not determine whether it relates to or regulates one of the subjects as to which the Constitution prohibits local legislation. (295 N.C. at 696)

Concerning delegation of legislative power, the North Carolina Constitution declares that "legislative, executive, and judicial powers of the State government shall be forever separate and distinct from each other" (art. I, sec. 6) and that the "legislative power of the State shall be vested in the General Assembly" (art. II, sec. 1). Admitting that the state constitution (as well as the United States Constitution) did not provide for delegation of even a part of this legislative authority, the court also recognized that a "modern legislature must be able to delegate—in proper instances—'a *limited* portion of its legislative powers' to administrative bodies...provided that such transfers are accompanied by adequate guiding standards to govern the exercise of the delegated powers." The issue became, then, whether the General Assembly of North Carolina had provided *adequate guiding standards* in delegating rule-making authority to the CRC. The court considered two aspects: (1) declarations of legislative goals and policies that the CRC was to apply when exercising its delegated powers and (2) whether the delegation was supported by guiding standards in the form of procedural safeguards. It found that the act's statements of legislative findings and the criteria for designating AECs (areas of environmental concern, within which development was to be regulated) were "'as specific as the circumstances permit'" and sufficient to "provide the members of the CRC with an adequate notion of the legislative parameters within which they" were to operate. Furthermore, procedural safeguards provided in the act, those contained in the North Carolina Administrative Procedure Act, an Administrative Rules Review Committee established by the General Assembly, and "sunset" legislation previously adopted were decreed adequate procedural safeguards.

The last two allegations—deprivation of property without due process and warrantless searches—were dismissed perfunctorily. "'The inherent function of judicial tribunals is to adjudicate genuine controversies between antagonistic litigants with respect to their rights, status, or other legal relations,'" not "to give a purely advisory opinion which the parties might, so to speak, put on ice to be used if and when occasion might arise." As no final AECs had been determined, no permits applied for (much less denied), no rights taken, and no searches initiated, no controversy existed.

All of the landowners' allegations failed. The constitutionality of CAMA was upheld and was not tested again.

Federal Participation

Although the CZMA declared a national policy for "all Federal agencies involved with programs affecting the coastal zone to cooperate and participate with State and substate agencies developing coastal zone management programs," many did not choose to do so. As of December 1975, three years after enactment, only the Departments of Defense and the Interior, the Federal Energy Administration, and the U.S. Army Corps of Engineers had formulated overall policy. Not surprisingly, these are the agencies most concerned with coastal activities, generally with precedent state-federal coordinating mechanisms, and the ones whose activities would be most threatened by strong state programs. Coastal zone management was a novel concept and an unfunded add-on to normal federal agency activities; thus, in many cases (at least early in the program), responses to state requests for information, technical assistance, and involvement were nonexistent or inadequate. As a result many state programs were later found deficient during NOAA's formal consideration of federal agency comments during program approval (Comptroller General of the United States 1976, 47-63).

Federal Consistency

The agencies may have underestimated the impact of the consistency provisions during congressional debate, but all players soon felt its effects. In commenting on the GAO report, the secretary of commerce "felt that Federal consistency remains the principal incentive of the program for many States and thus it will be a key factor in continued State participation." Conflicts have always existed between federal and state priorities and programs, and they always will, and federal agencies did not take kindly to an apparently superior state position. OCS resource development was the issue; California was the arena; and the consistency requirements were up for the test (Comptroller General of the United States 1976, 71).

The Department of the Interior intended to lease 10 million acres of OCS lands during 1975, of which up to 1.6 million lay off the coast of southern California. California's opposition was based on several motives:

—A desire to avoid adverse impacts, especially environmental damage of the kind that followed the 1969 Santa Barbara oil spill.

—The belief that Interior had rushed into the leasing program before demonstrating the need for rapid OCS development and before California had a chance to deal with the impacts....

—A desire to obtain, before any southern California leasing, a share of OCS lease revenues and Federal funds to compensate for adverse impacts sustained by California entities [as later would be provided by the coastal energy impact provisions of the CZMA]. (Comptroller General of the United States 1976, 66)

After repeated unsuccessful attempts to negotiate a delay through legislative and executive channels, California brought two lawsuits, alleging that the OCS lease program violated NEPA and the CZMA. Both suits failed, and the lands were leased on December 11, 1975. In the interim California also attempted to block Interior's move by prohibiting construction of a pipeline across state-controlled waters until such time as the state coastal plan were implemented (Comptroller General of the United States 1976, 67).

The importance of the consistency provisions and the controversy over their interpretation contributed greatly to the delay in issuing implementing regulations for this part of the program. Promulgation of proposed regulations was delayed until 1976 and precipitated intense interagency debate, numerous comments, and an OMB review (U.S. Department of Commerce, National Oceanic and Atmospheric Administration 1979, 47). Not until 1978, six years after passage of the CZMA, were final regulations promulgated (Council on Environmental Quality 1979, 509).

Through the years the consistency provisions continued to be among the most controversial elements of the national program. In arguing for reduced federal funding, administration officials opined that consistency was sufficient motivation for states to remain in the program, even without federal funding. Others were equally convinced that states would not be able to implement the consistency provisions effectively without strong federal financial support. Even under funding arrangements of the 1970s, many states were disappointed in their attempts to invoke consistency (Zinn 1985, 6). States frequently employed federal consistency as a means of constraining federal construction projects and federally permitted activities, particularly those related to OCS development:

Section 307(c)(1). Each Federal agency conducting or supporting activities directly affecting the coastal zone shall conduct or support those activities in a manner which is, to the maximum extent practicable, consistent with approved state management programs. (16 U.S.C. 1456(c)(1) (1988))

Section 307(c)(2). Any Federal agency which shall undertake any development project in the coastal zone of a state shall insure that the project is, to the maximum extent practicable, consistent with approved state management programs. (16 U.S.C. 1456(c)(2) (1988))

Section 307(c)(B). After the management program of any coastal state has been approved by the Secretary…, any person who submits…any plan for the exploration or development of, or production from, any area which has been leased under the Outer Continental Shelf Lands Act…shall…attach to such plan a certificate that each activity which is described in detail in the plan complies with such state's approved management program and will be carried out in a manner consistent with such program. No federal official or agency shall grant such person any license or permit...until...such state or its designated agency...concurs with such person's certification...or...the Secretary finds...that each activity...is consistent with the objectives of this title or is otherwise necessary in the interest of national security. (16 U.S.C. 1456(c)(3)(B) (1988))

During the first twelve years of the program, at least twenty-three lawsuits based upon these provisions were brought against federal agencies, nine of which involved OCS leases (U.S. Congress, Senate, Committee on Commerce, Science, and Transportation 1984, 4). One of the most significant, thorough, and complicated decisions, *Secretary of the Interior v. California*, was issued by the Supreme Court on January 11, 1984:

> In 1977, the Department of Commerce approved the California Coastal Management Plan. The same year, Interior began preparing Lease Sale No. 53—a sale of OCS leases off the California coast near Santa Barbara....In October 1978, Interior announced the tentative selection of 243 tracts....
>
> On July 8, 1980 the California Coastal Commission informed Interior that it had determined Lease Sale No. 53 to be an activity "directly affecting" the California coastal zone. The state commission therefore demanded a consistency determination—a showing by Interior that the lease sale would be "consistent" to the "maximum extent practicable" with the state coastal zone management program. Interior responded that the Lease Sale would not "directly affect" the California coastal zone...[but] decided to remove 128 tracts,...[leaving] 115 tracts in the Santa Maria Basin.
>
> On December 16, 1980, the state commission reiterated its view that the sale of the remaining tracts in the Santa Maria Basin "directly affected" the California coastal zone. The commission expressed its concern that oil spills on the OCS could threaten the southern sea otter, whose range was within 12 miles of the 31 challenged tracts...[and] concluded that 31 more tracts should be removed from the sale because "leasing within 12 miles of the Sea Otter Range in Santa Maria Basin would not be consistent" with the California Coastal Management Program.
>
> Interior rejected the State's demands. In the Secretary's view, no consistency review was required because the lease sale did not engage CZMA §307(c)(1)....On April 10, 1981, Interior announced that the lease sale of the 115 tracts would go forward, and on April 27 issued a final notice of sale....
>
> Respondents [the state of California, the Natural Resources Defense Council, the Sierra Club, Friends of the Earth, Friends of the Sea Otter, and the Environmental Coalition on Lease Sale 53] filed two substantially

similar suits in federal court to enjoin the sale of 29 tracts situated within 12 miles of the Sea Otter Range. Both complaints alleged, inter alia, Interior's violation of §307(c)(1) of CZMA. They argued that leasing sets in motion a chain of events that culminates in oil and gas development, and that leasing therefore "directly affects" the coastal zone within the meaning of §307(c)(1).

The district court entered a summary judgment for respondents [*California et al.*]. The Court of Appeals for the Ninth Circuit affirmed that portion of the district court judgment that required a consistency determination before the sale. We granted certiorari, and we now reverse. (52 U.S.L.W. 4064-4065)

The Supreme Court found that "sale of OCS oil and gas leases is not an activity 'directly affecting' the coastal zone within the meaning of §307(c)(1), and thus a consistency review is not required under that section before such sales are made" (52 U.S.L.W. 4063). It based its decision on the legislative history of the definition of "directly affecting" and a specific and narrow meaning of "lease sales" and indicated a more appropriate course for future OCS consistency litigation.

Both sides conceded that lease sales per se had no significant effect on the coastal zone but were one "in a series of decisions that may culminate in activities directly affecting that zone" (52 U.S.L.W. 4065). The Court therefore ascertained the source and intended definition of "directly affecting." The original bill passed by the Senate defined the coastal zone to exclude "lands the use of which is by law subject solely to the discretion of or which is held in trust by the Federal Government." The corresponding House version included federal lands within the definition of "coastal zone," making federal activities on such lands subject to consistency. Neither bill included submerged lands on the OCS within the coastal zone, and all federal activities on the OCS were thus to be exempt from the consistency provisions. The Conference Committee subsequently adopted the narrower Senate definition of the coastal zone "but then expanded §307(c)(1) to cover activities on federal lands not 'in' but 'directly affecting' the zone." On at least four occasions, the Ninety-second Congress debated and rejected proposals to extend the CZMA of 1972 to OCS activities (52 U.S.L.W. 4066).

To recapitulate, the "directly affecting" language in §307(c)(1) was, by all appearances, only a modest compromise, designed to offset in part the narrower definition of the coastal zone favored by the Senate and adopted by the Conference Committee. Section 307(c)(1)'s "directly affecting" language was aimed at activities conducted or supported by federal agencies on federal lands physically situated in the coastal zone but excluded from the zone as formally defined by the Act. Consistent with this view, the same Conference Committee that wrote the "directly affecting" language rejected two provisions in the House bill that would have required precisely what respondents seek here—coordination of federally sponsored OCS activities with state coastal management and conservation programs. In light of the Conference Committee's further, systematic rejection of every other attempt to extend the reach of the CZMA to the OCS, we are impelled to conclude that the 1972 Congress did not intend §307(c)(1) to reach OCS lease sales. (52 U.S.L.W. 4068)

The Court then discussed the distinction between "lease" and "permit" and went on to suggest that section 307(c)(3)(B) was more applicable than section 307(c)(1) to OCS matters—but not to lease sales. Section 307(c)(3)(B) was added by the Ninety-fourth Congress in the CZMA amendments of 1976. House and Senate committees of that Congress both reported bills that would have included leases within section 307(c)(1). Congress ultimately rejected these provisions, opting instead to add a new section, 307(c)(3)(B), that specifically provided "that applicants for federal licenses to explore, produce, or develop oil or gas on the OCS must first certify consistency with affected state plans...[but omitting any] suggestion that a lease sale by Interior requires any review of consistency with state management plans" (52 U.S.L.W. 4069). Much of the confusion here stems from the use of such terms as "OCS leases" and "OCS leasing program" in a general sense rather than in strict accord with statutory definitions. The Outer Continental Shelf Lands Act of 1953 (OCSLA) defined "mineral lease" broadly to be "any form of authorization for the exploration for, or development or removal of deposits of, oil, gas, or other minerals" (67 Stat. 462). Under such a definition, "lease" could have included extractive activities affecting the coastal zone and subject to the consistency provisions. In 1978, however, the OCSLA was amended to define

> four distinct statutory stages to developing an offshore oil well: (1) formulation of a five year leasing plan by the Department of the Interior; (2) lease sales; (3) exploration by the lessees; (4) development and production. Each stage involves separate regulatory review and may, but need not, include the transfer to lease purchasers of rights to conduct additional activities on the OCS. And each stage includes specific requirements for consultation with Congress, between federal agencies, or with the States. *Formal review of consistency with state coastal management plans is expressly reserved for the last two stages* [emphasis added]. (52 U.S.L.W. 4070)

A lease conveys only limited rights to conduct activities preliminary to full-scale OCS exploration—only "geophysical and other surveys that do not involve seabed penetrations greater than 300 feet and that do not result in any significant environmental impacts" (30 C.F.R. 250.34-1 (1982)). The purchaser of such leases receives "no right to proceed with full exploration, development, or production that might trigger CZMA §307(c)(3)(B); the lessee acquires only a priority in submitting plans to conduct those activities" (52 U.S.L.W. 4070). The Court thus concluded that there was nothing in the lease sales program that could directly affect the coastal zone of a state and require a consistency determination.

Exploration, development, and production are another matter, not relevant to the case at issue. When these later stages of the OCS administrative procedures are invoked, the consistency requirements of section 307(c)(3)(B) operate without question (52 U.S.L.W. 4070).

Five members of the nine-member Court found for Interior, but in handing the state a defeat the Supreme Court also pointed the way to a solution, simply delaying the final battle until later stages in OCS lease development. The remaining four judges filed a lengthy and passionate dissenting opinion, arguing that

[t]he Court's first theory is refuted by the plain language of the 1972 Act, its legislative history, the basic purpose of the Act and the findings of the District Court. The Court's second theory, which looks at post-1972 legislative developments, is simply overwhelmed by a series of unambiguous legislative pronouncements that consistently belie the Court's interpretation of the intent of Congress. (52 U.S.L.W. 4072)

The five-to-four decision and the strength of the dissenting opinion indicate that all is not peaceful within the consistency provisions. The boundaries within which consistency operates, particularly including such considerations as "the maximum extent practicable," are a long way from being resolved.

The Coastal Energy Impact Program

The bill I am introducing today [February 5, 1975]...provid[es] a means for assisting coastal States in the amelioration of the socioeconomic and environmental problems resulting from the location of support facilities onshore needed to service the expiration [exploration?] and development activities on the OCS and to ensure consistency of these activities with State coastal zone managemement programs....[The bill establishes a]

coastal impact fund to provide up to $200 million in annual grants to States
for alleviating coastal impacts of offshore drilling and the siting of all types
of energy facilities and for providing the necessary public services and facilities. (U.S. Congress, Senate, Committee on Commerce 1976, 615)

With these words, Senator Ernest Hollings of South Carolina introduced S. 586 to the Ninety-fourth Congress. It came soon after the Arab
oil embargo of 1973, when energy independence was a high priority and
a national objective, when accelerated OCS development was being
strongly advocated, and when the Supreme Court in *United States v. Maine*
had decreed that coastal states were not to share in OCS revenues. In five
days of joint hearings held by the Senate Committees on Interior and
Insular Affairs and Commerce, fifty-four witnesses testified and 114 communications were received, most of which addressed OCS issues (U.S.
Congress, Senate, Committee on Commerce 1976, 577-579).

The feeble objections of a few inland and non-oil-producing coastal
states produced many pages of debate (see, for example, U.S. Congress,
Senate, Committee on Commerce 1976, 635-687) and an intricate allocation formula (90 Stat. 1020, 1021), but the nation was rich, domestic
energy production was in vogue, and there were simply too many potential winners—the Coastal Energy Impact Program (CEIP) had to pass.

From the states' standpoint, the CEIP has been among the most lucra-
tive aspects of the national coastal zone management program. During
the CEIP's approximately eight years of life, coastal states received
$238.7 million in grants and loans, compared with $69.7 million in program development grants and $180.5 in administrative grants (Zinn
1985, 2). States that bordered producing areas of the OCS received the
lion's share of CEIP funds, but all qualifying coastal states benefited substantially. However, neither the magnitude of coastal energy development
nor its "adverse economic effects" materialized to the degree envisioned
by the CEIP's original sponsors. No funds have been appropriated since
1981, and the program is now moribund, if not dead.

Yet $148 million of the CEIP payments were loans, and

[i]f the Secretary finds that any coastal state or unit of general purpose
local government is unable to meet its obligations pursuant to a loan or
guarantee...because the actual increases in employment and related population resulting from coastal energy activities and the facilities associated
with such activity do not provide adequate revenues...the Secretary shall,
after review of the information submitted by such state or unit...take any
of the following actions:

(A) Modify appropriately the terms and conditions of such loan guarantee.

(B) Refinance such loan.

(C) Make a supplemental loan...which shall be applied to the payment of the interest and principal due....

(D) Make a grant to such state or unit the proceeds of which shall be applied to the payment of interest and principal due under such loan or guarantee. (90 Stat. 1023)

Times have changed. Oil-producing areas whose future looked so bright in the oil shortage days of the mid-seventies, during which the CEIP was born, are sunk in recession in the oil glut of the eighties and nineties. Indebtedness under CEIP loans and loan guarantees can extend for up to thirty years (16 U.S.C. 1456a(e)(3)C) (1988)). We may not have heard the last of the CEIP.

The Reagan Territorial Sea Proclamation

When President Reagan extended the United States territorial sea "to 12 nautical miles from the baselines of the United States," he did nothing that "extends or otherwise alters existing Federal or State law or any jurisdiction, rights, legal interests, or obligations derived therefrom" (54 Fed. Reg. 777 (Dec. 27, 1988)). Perhaps. Implications relative to other maritime boundaries and international law were discussed briefly in chapter 10; those relative to domestic law, despite the disclaimer, may be far more important.

Since 1793 the territorial sea of the United States has been recognized as a 3-nautical-mile band seaward of the baseline within which the United States is sovereign (i.e., it has sole power to govern within the zone, subject only to a vessel's right of innocent passage) (Kmiec 1990, 4, 9). The CZMA defines the coastal zone as extending "seaward to the outer limit of the United States territorial sea" (86 Stat. 1281)—a distance undefined. It requires state programs to include "an identification of the boundaries of the coastal zone subject to the [state] management program" (86 Stat. 1282)—inferring that this "coastal zone" might not be coterminous with the "coastal zone" defined above. It excludes from the definition lands "the use of which is by law subject to the discretion of or which is held in trust by the Federal Government" (86 Stat. 1281) but requires that "[e]ach Federal agency conducting or supporting activities directly affecting the coastal zone shall...[do so] in a manner which is, to the maximum extent practicable, consistent with approved state management programs" (86 Stat. 1285)—the consistency provisions.

Prior to Reagan's proclamation, the State Department asked the Department of Justice to determine

> (1) whether the President has the authority to unilaterally extend the territorial sea; (2) what effect such an extension would have on domestic law and in particular the Coastal Zone Management Act (CZMA); and (3) whether the President can limit the effect of the Proclamation on domestic law. (Rieser and Eichenberg 1990, iv)

...to which Justice responded:

> [T]he President's constitutional role as the representative of the United States in foreign relations empowers him to extend the territorial sea and assert sovereignty over it, although most such claims in our nation's history have been executed by treaty....The domestic effect of the extension of the territorial sea on federal statutes that refer to the territorial sea must be determined by examining Congress' intent in passing each relevant statute. We have concluded that the better view is that extension of the territorial sea will not extend coverage of the Coastal Zone Management Act....However, we recognize that the effect of the proclamation on the CZMA and numerous other federal statutes will continue to be uncertain until final judicial resolution. Therefore, we recommend that the President seek legislation providing that no federal statute is affected by the President's proclamation. (Kmiec 1990, 37)

The California attorney general's office had a somewhat different viewpoint:

> California...accepts that the President possessed the authority to alter the breadth of the territorial sea by proclamation. Thus, the California opinion assumes that the twelve mile territorial sea was immediately effective without any further action by the President or by the Congress. (Saurenman 1990, 41, 42)

> [T]he limitations on the state coastal zone, as defined in the [California] Coastal Act, have no impact on the federal definition of the coastal zone. These definitions have always been different. (P. 61)

> [E]xtension of the seaward boundary of the coastal zone does impact on the implementation of the consistency provisions of the CZMA. The extension does not alter the basic relationship between the state and the federal government, but it does expand the area which will be subject to the consis-

tency provisions. Thus, more federally supported or conducted activities will affect land or water uses in the coastal zone.

In sum, the effect on the Coastal Commission of the President's proclamation extending the territorial sea is limited to the consistency provisions of the CZMA. The proclamation neither alters the grant made to the state in the Submerged Lands Act nor extends the state's permit jurisdiction. However, the proclamation does have the effect of extending to twelve miles the seaward boundary of the coastal zone, and this change in the seaward boundary...has an impact on the implementation of the CZMA by enlarging the area subject to the consistency provisions. (P. 65)

Resolution of these differences awaits congressional or judicial action or both, but resolution may be slow in coming. States have little to gain by attempting to extend their jurisdiction seaward. Ownership of bottom resources is defined by the Submerged Lands Act, the Outer Continental Shelf Lands Act, and relevant treaties and cannot be affected by a presidential proclamation. Similarly, fisheries management is afforded through the Fishery Conservation and Management Act. Controversies over consistency provisions can be resolved through negotiation, coordination, and cooperation without ever mentioning "consistency." Thus the states may continue to manage their previously defined coastal zones in accordance with the CZMA as if the proclamation had never happened. Time will tell.

Who Pays the Bill?

The final element in assessing the future of the nation's coastal zone management program is the inevitable bottom line. The program began as a novel experiment in intergovernmental relations, justified by congressional recognition that

[t]he coastal zone is rich in a variety of natural, commercial, recreational, industrial, and esthetic resources of immediate and potential value to the present and future well-being of the Nation;...[and] increasing and competing demands upon lands and waters of our coastal zone occasioned by population growth and economic development, including the requirements for industry, commerce, residential development, recreation, extraction of mineral resources and fossil fuels, transportation and navigation, waste disposal, and harvesting of fish, shellfish, and other living marine resources, have resulted in the loss of living marine resources, wildlife, nutrient-rich areas, permanent and adverse changes in ecological systems, decreasing open space for public use, and shoreline erosion. (86 Stat. 1280)

Federal funding began at two-thirds of state planning and administrative costs and soon increased to 80 percent. With increasing federal budget constraints, recent administrations have requested fewer and fewer federal funds, elimination of some program elements, and constriction of the overall program. In the early stages of this process, strong state and congressional support succeeded in restoring (or prolonging) many authorized activities. But Congress is feeling the fiscal squeeze, and the states may not be as enthusiastic as they become saddled with more and more of the costs. The 1985 amendments clearly signal Congress's intent to phase out federal funding. How much additional burden the states, with their own severe financial problems, are willing to accept remains to be seen.

What Have We Accomplished?

Despite the difficulties incurred and an uncertain future, the national coastal zone program has been a successful experiment in natural resource management. More than anything else, the program has been an experience in intergovernmental and interpersonal relations. The complex management systems that have developed require all levels of government to work together, and for the most part the systems have worked. Provisions for citizen participation and for public education exist where none did before. Public awareness of coastal problems and approaches to their solutions have increased manyfold.

Of the thirty-five states and territories eligible to participate in the national program in 1985, twenty-eight had approved state programs by the mid-1980s (Georgia's program was not approved; Illinois, Indiana, Minnesota, Ohio, and Texas had withdrawn; and Virginia's program was pending and was later approved [Coastal States Organization 1985, app. B]). The following are a few specific accomplishments:

> The Massachusetts legislature appropriated $27 million to purchase the Commonwealth's few remaining underdeveloped coastal areas after evaluating a $30,000 CZM-funded study recommended their acquisition. (Coastal States Organization 1985, 6)

> Rhode Island converted a large surplus Navy base...into a major onshore support base used for offshore oil and gas exploration in the mid- and North Atlantic. (P. 6)

> The Corps of Engineers was able to dredge a severely silted Wicomico River for the first time in 10 years after a $35,000 Maryland CZM project identified suitable upland areas for dredge disposal. (P. 7)

Oregon developed a sophisticated "mitigation bank" system to assess habitat types and to prevent a loss of estuarine acreage and habitats from various development projects. (P. 9)

American Samoa and Guam developed a comprehensive mapping system that affords better protection for the territories' extensive coral reefs. (P. 10)

In Mississippi, 70,000 acres of prime marshland have been acquired by the state to prevent their development. (P. 10)

Rhode Island, Connecticut, South Carolina and Michigan have all used CZM funds to identify suitable locations for the construction of access-ways that make reaching a beach, launching a boat or strolling along the shore much easier. (P. 11)

To reduce permit processing delays, states such as North and South Carolina, Connecticut, New York, Louisiana and Maine issue public notices for proposed projects jointly with the Corps of Engineers. (P. 14)

The list could go on and on, but the conclusion should be clear—the national coastal zone management program has touched virtually every activity and every person along the nation's coasts. It has not stopped damage to the coastal environment, nor has it stopped coastal development, but without it our coastal ecosystems would have been seriously degraded and our coastal economy diminished.

REFERENCES

Adams, David A. 1971. "Management Systems Under Consideration at the Federal-State Level." In *Coastal Zone Resource Management*, edited by James C. Hite and James M. Stepp, 20-32. New York: Praeger Publishers.

Clark, John. 1967. "Fish and Man: Conflict in the Atlantic Estuaries." Special Report no. 5. Highlands, NJ: American Littoral Society.

Coastal States Organization. 1985. *America's Coasts: Progress and Promise*. Washington, DC: Coastal States Organization.

Comptroller General of the United States. 1976. *The Coastal Zone Management Program: An Uncertain Future*. Washington, DC: Government Printing Office.

Council on Environmental Quality. 1976. *Environmental Quality—1976*. Washington, DC: Government Printing Office.

———. 1977. *Environmental Quality—1977*. Washington, DC: Government Printing Office.

————. 1979. *Environmental Quality—1979*. Washington, DC: Government Printing Office.

Heath, Milton S. 1971. "Descriptions of Illustrative State Programs of Estuarine Conservation." In *Coastal Zone Resource Management*, edited by James C. Hite and James M. Stepp, 154-165. New York: Praeger Publishers.

Kmiec, Douglas W. 1990. "Legal Issues Raised by the Proposed Presidential Proclamation to Extend the Territorial Sea." *Territorial Sea Journal* 1 (1): 1-38.

Lauff, George F., ed. 1967. *Estuaries*. American Association for the Advancement of Science Publication no. 83. Washington, DC: American Association for the Advancement of Science.

National Council on Marine Resources and Engineering Development. 1967. *Marine Science Affairs: A Year of Transition*. Washington, DC: Government Printing Office.

————. 1968. *Marine Science Affairs: A Year of Plans and Progress*. Washington, DC: Government Printing Office.

————. 1969. *Marine Science Affairs: A Year of Broadened Participation*. Washington, DC: Government Printing Office.

————. 1970. *Marine Science Affairs: Selecting Priority Programs*. Washington, DC: Government Printing Office.

Our Nation and the Sea. 1969. Report of the Commission on Marine Science, Engineering, and Resources. Washington, DC: Government Printing Office.

Panel Reports of the Commission on Marine Science, Engineering, and Resources. 1969. Vol. 1, *Science and the Environment*, I-1 through I-65, II-1 through III-74, II-1 through III-187, IV-1 through IV-14. Washington, DC: Government Printing Office.

"Report of the Panel on Management and Development of the Coastal Zone." 1969. In *Panel Reports of the Commission on Marine Science, Engineering, and Resources*. Vol. 1, *Science and Environment*, III-1 through III-187. Washington, DC: Government Printing Office.

Rieser, Alison, and Timothy Eichenberg. 1990. "Introduction from the Editors." *Territorial Sea Journal* 1 (1): i-viii.

Saurenman, John A. 1990. "The Effects of a Twelve-Mile Territorial Sea on Coastal State Jurisdiction: Where Do Matters Stand?" *Territorial Sea Journal* 1 (1): 39-79.

U.S. Army Corps of Engineers. 1973. *Report of the Chief of Engineers on the National Shoreline Study*. Vol 1. Washington, DC: Government Printing Office.

U.S. Congress. House. Committee on Merchant Marine and Fisheries. Subcommittee on Fisheries and Wildlife Conservation. 1967. *Estuarine Areas*. Hearings on H.R. 25, H.R. 1397, H.R. 4505, and similar bills, March 6, 8, 9, 1967. 90th Cong., 1st sess. Serial 90-3. Washington, DC: Government Printing Office.

U.S. Congress. Senate. Committee on Commerce. 1976. *Legislative History of the Coastal Zone Management Act of 1972, as Amended in 1974 and 1976 with a Section-by-Section Index.* Washington, DC: Government Printing Office.

U.S. Congress. Senate. Committee on Commerce, Science, and Transportation. 1984. *Hearing before the National Ocean Policy Study of the Committee on Commerce, Science, and Transportation on S. 2324.* 98th Cong., 2d sess., March 28, 1984. Serial 98-81. Washington, DC: Government Printing Office.

U.S. Department of Commerce. National Oceanic and Atmospheric Administration. 1974. "Coastal Zone Management: Annual Report for Fiscal Year 1973." Washington, DC: Government Printing Office.

————. 1975. "Report to the Congress on Coastal Zone Management, July, 1973 through June, 1974." Washington, DC: Government Printing Office.

————. 1977. "Report to the Congress on Coastal Zone Management. Public Law 92-583. Fiscal Year 1976." Washington, DC: Government Printing Office.

————. 1979. *The First Five Years of Coastal Zone Management: An Initial Assessment.* Washington, DC: U.S. Department of Commerce, National Oceanic and Atmospheric Administration, Office of Coastal Zone Management.

———— 1984. *Biennial Report.* Washington, DC: U.S. Department of Commerce, National Oceanic and Atmospheric Administration, Office of Coastal Zone Management.

U.S. Department of the Interior, U.S. Fish and Wildlife Service. 1970. *National Estuary Study.* 7 vols. Washington, DC: Government Printing Office.

Wenk, Edward, Jr. 1972. *The Politics of the Ocean.* Seattle: University of Washington Press.

Zinn, Jeffrey. 1985. "Coastal Zone Management: Reauthorization and Other Issues in the 99th Congress." Issue brief, updated April 18, 1985 (order code IB85070). Washington, DC: U.S. Congress, Congressional Research Service, Environmental and Natural Resources Policy Division.

CHAPTER XV

A National Environmental Policy

The nation's environmental policy is an umbrella over individual (and frequently artificially defined) natural resource concerns. It attempts to meld these disparate and often competing and conflicting interests into some cohesive whole, and in so doing it both offers a hope for the future and runs counter to traditional organization and operation of government.

As in the case of the nation's coastal zone management program, our environmental policy is a product of the environmental fervor of the late 1960s, which bore fruit during the early 1970s. It is a new concept to society, still relatively unproven. The magnitude and distribution of benefits and costs associated with environmental quality are still uncertain. However, the American people have repeatedly expressed their support for improvement of the nation's environmental quality (Council on Environmental Quality 1980).

THE ENVIRONMENTAL SETTING

By the middle of the twentieth century, jurisdiction over the nation's natural resources was relatively well allocated among federal and state agencies. Organic legislation (with some exceptions) had defined their powers and duties. Prior to the hiatus caused by World War II, considerable progress had been made in forest fire protection, soil erosion control, migratory bird conservation, water resource development, and many other natural resource areas (Whitaker 1976, 21).

The dominant policy (ethic?) in these activities was that of conservation—the "wise use" of natural resources, an inheritance from Pinchot, Leopold, the Roosevelts, and other earlier leaders. Even with the economic boom and concomitant resource consumption following the war, few people saw a need to protect natural resources beyond the tenets of conservation (Whitaker 1976, 23).

By the 1950s and 1960s, however, disquieting signs were beginning to appear. Rachel Carson (1962) awakened the world to the dangers of persistent pesticides. During the 1960s, urban noise increased significantly, and noise from traffic and aircraft were affecting an estimated 16 million Americans (Council on Environmental Quality 1970, 124). By 1969 Americans were discarding more than 4.3 billion tons of solid waste per year (Council on Environmental Quality 1970, 107). Hunters, hikers, and fishermen found overcrowding to be an increasing problem (Udall 1963, 177). Some people reread the earlier warnings of William Vogt (1948), Fairfield Osborn (1948, 1953), and Paul Sears (1958) and began to believe them. Others read articles in such periodicals as *Atlantic, Harper's, Saturday Review,* and *Life* and became convinced that we did not have to pay such an environmental price for economic growth (Caldwell 1975, 24). Still others reviewed the doctrines of Marsh (1864), Leopold (1949), Marshall (1930), White (1967), and others and adopted an environmental ethic.

The Mood of the 1960s

The decade of the 1960s was one of the most momentous periods of change in American history. It was marked by the rise to prominence and political power of black Americans, a revolution in attitudes toward sex, violence and rebellion in colleges and universities, and massive rejection of traditional patriotic values in protest against the war in Southeast Asia, which corroded the nation's civic life from 1965 to the withdrawal of American participation in 1973. The decade also saw the rise of consumer advocacy, personified by Ralph Nader and frankly aimed at using political methods, especially public interest lawsuits, to establish and maintain new standards of accountability in business and government for public health and safety. It was a period of rapid population increase and migration to California, the southwestern States, and the larger metropolitan areas. There was also a massive out-migration from the central cities to suburbs, facilitated by the private automobile and the interstate highway system. Concomitant with these changes were escalating land values, destruction of the suburban countryside, general collapse of intercity and commuter transportation by rail, and rapid deterioration of the quality of air, water, and landscape over large areas of the nation. (Caldwell 1973, 23)

America today stands poised on a pinnacle of wealth and power, yet we live in a land of vanishing beauty, of increasing ugliness, of shrinking open space, and of an overall environment that is diminished by pollution and noise and blight. (Udall 1963, viii)

The velocity and complexity of social evolution in the decade of the 1960s were difficult to comprehend, even for a culture accustomed to rapid change. And from this caldron emerged the thing called "the environmental movement," a force often misinformed, misdirected, and misunderstood—but a force to be reckoned with.

What produced the environmental movement? Certainly it was a combination of a number of interrelated factors. One thesis begins with the growth of the U.S. economy following World War II, which increased water and air pollution and also raised the nation's standard of living. Increased leisure provided time to consider and become concerned about the environment; increased affluence provided the capacity to do something about it. An increasing population at the same time placed additional strain on the sociopolitical-environmental system (Davies 1970, 21, 22).

Caldwell (1975, 25-30) explains the changing attitudes of Americans toward environmental quality that were evident during the 1960s in terms of affluence, health, and ecology. Growing affluence consumed resources and spewed pollution while at the same time providing the means to protect environmental quality. Public concern over the health consequences of pollution became a major national issue. The public became more aware of environmental interrelationships and believed that science and technology were capable of meeting the environmental challenge. So came the environmental movement.

John Whitaker, deputy assistant to President Richard Nixon on energy and environment and undersecretary of the interior (1973-1975), acknowledges the effect of affluence and scientific and technological development but believes that "advocacy journalism," particularly through television, was a contributing cause. Finally, Whitaker speculates that we simply may have needed a challenge with which to occupy ourselves, and nothing better arose (Whitaker 1976, 24, 25). Regardless of the precise cause of the environmental movement of the 1960s and 1970s, in less than a decade it drastically changed the nation's relationship with its surroundings.

Two events that brought environmental concerns into the public arena early in the decade were the report of the Outdoor Recreation Resources Review Commission (ORRRC) and the White House Conference on Conservation, both of which occurred in 1962.

Increasing concern over diminishing and degraded outdoor recreational opportunities in the face of increasing population, leisure time, and financial resources led Congress to pass the Outdoor Recreation Resources Review Act of 1958. The act established the ORRRC, fifteen persons "informed about and concerned with the preservation and development of outdoor recreation resources and opportunities, and experienced in resource conservation planning for multiple resources uses." Laurance S. Rockefeller, a man of considerable ability and influence, chaired the commission. A Recreation Advisory Council, composed of fifteen federal agency representatives and twenty-five persons representing state and private interests throughout the country, assisted the ORRRC. The commission was to conduct "a nationwide inventory and evaluation of outdoor recreation resources and opportunities,...[gather] information available concerning trends in population, leisure, transportation, and other factors...and recommend what policies should best be adopted and what programs be initiated, at each level of government and by private organizations" (72 Stat. 240). The ORRRC report, *Outdoor Recreation for America*, (1) proposed a comprehensive national outdoor recreation policy, specifying the roles of the federal government, state and local governments, and the private sector; (2) urged adoption of a system of recreational land classification based on attributes of the land and needs of the people; (3) recommended expanded programs of public recreational land acquisition and management at all levels of government; (4) outlined a federal grants-in-aid program to assist states in planning, acquiring, and developing recreational lands; and (5) proposed establishment of a Bureau of Outdoor Recreation in the Department of the Interior to coordinate federal programs and administer the grants-in-aid program and other technical assistance to the states (Outdoor Recreation Resources Review Commission 1962, 6-10).

The White House Conference on Conservation was held in May 1962, attended by 280 delegates and 300 observers and addressed by President John Kennedy. The president's speech, "while concerned primarily with the material aspects of resources conservation, concluded with an emphasis on the role of government in maintaining environmental quality and natural beauty." The dominant theme of the conference was the "traditional sense of provident use of natural resources," but discussions frequently centered on issues of environmental quality. Many participants used the conference to voice their growing concern "about the deteriorating quality of their surroundings and the irreversible foreclosure of opportunities for choice and variety in the environment of the future" (Caldwell 1975, 32).

Following these two precedents, President Lyndon Johnson called the national Conference on Natural Beauty in March 1965. Laurance Rockefeller was again appointed chairman, and the Recreation Advisory Council was active in organizing and implementing the program (Caldwell 1975, 36, 37). While the conference achieved few concrete results, it did serve to maintain momentum and visibility and to increase public environmental awareness (Caldwell 1975, 36-40). And it led to another conference.

In September 1965 Russell E. Train, then president of The Conservation Foundation, presented the keynote address to a joint meeting of the National Council of State Garden Clubs and the American Forestry Association in Grand Teton National Park, Wyoming.

> I propose that the President establish a Council of Ecological Advisors, or alternatively, an interdisciplinary group of environmental advisors having a strong ecological orientation. And let me make it clear that I am not just talking about an interdepartmental committee. With one such bold stroke, concern for the quality of the environment would be given an important new status in planning and policy-making at the highest level of government. It would give ecology a new posture in public affairs, and a new sense of responsibility for making its knowledge applicable and relevant to the needs of our day. (Train 1965, 46)

Here was the germ of the Council on Environmental Quality from the man who, five years later, would become its first chairman.

Partly as a result of the class of persons associated with the environmental movement of the 1960s, partly as a result of incidents in its early history, and partly as a result of the sharp social divisiveness of that decade, the movement became identified largely with white upper-middle-class society, and it focused on outdoor recreation, beauty, aesthetics, air and water pollution, historical heritage, and other issues considered by many less fortunate individuals and societies as "cosmetics" (Caldwell 1975, 41) and luxuries. This emphasis and association may have been unfortunate in the longer run, diverting attention from the more basic linkages among environment, economy, and survival. At the time, however, it suited the mood of the times and provided the zest and appeal required to effect action.

The 1964 presidential campaign provided a platform for each major party to record its attitudes toward natural resource and environmental issues. Lyndon Johnson recognized the political value of the environmental movement but probably did not comprehend its potential depth and breadth. "Environment" was not yet a household word, and Johnson incorporated the context in his concepts of the "new conservation," "natural beauty," and the Great Society. He appealed to the middle-class American, frustrated by pollution, urban sprawl, water shortages, inadequate recreation areas, and vanishing public transportation. And he was successful. The Republican leaders seemed unable to comprehend these issues (Caldwell 1975, 33).

The enthusiasm of the environmental movement seems to have been wasted on the presidential candidates of 1968. Richard Nixon prepared eighteen radio addresses near the end of his campaign, and only one covered natural resources (Nixon 1968b, cited in Whitaker 1976, 1). In one Nixon campaign publication, 64 pages were devoted to foreign policy, 110 were devoted to domestic policy, and only 5 pages of the latter dealt with the environment, natural resources, and energy (Nixon 1968a, cited in Whitaker 1976, 1).

LEGISLATIVE HISTORY

The legislative branch also was active during the early to mid-1960s. The Wilderness Act of 1964, the Federal Water Pollution Control Act Amendments of 1965, the Land and Water Conservation Fund Act of 1965, and the Endangered Species Preservation Act of 1966 all reflected a favorable political climate for environmental legislation.

The policy enunciated in the National Environmental Policy Act of 1969 (NEPA) contains three basic elements: (1) a statement of policy, goals, aspirations, and standards; (2) a mechanism for organizing and directing government activities; and (3) an administrative locus in the Executive Office of the President. All three have statutory precedents.

Section 4(f) of the Department of Transportation Act of 1966, as amended by section 18 of the Federal-Aid Highway Act of 1968, provides an early statement of national environmental policy and standards:

> It is hereby declared to be the national policy that special effort should be made to preserve the natural beauty of the countryside and public park and recreation lands, wildlife and waterfowl refuges, and historic sites. The Secretary of Transportation shall cooperate and consult with the Secretaries of the Interior, Housing and Urban Development, and Agriculture, and with the States in developing transportation plans and programs that include measures to maintain or enhance the natural beauty of the lands traversed....[T]he Secretary shall not approve any program or project which requires the use of any publicly owned land from a public

park, recreation area, or wildlife or waterfowl refuge of national, State, or local significance as determined by the Federal, State, or local officials having jurisdiction thereof, or any land from an historic site of national, State, or local significance as determined by such officials unless (1) there is no feasible and prudent alternative to the use of such land, and (2) such program includes all possible planning to minimize harm to such park, recreational area, wildlife and waterfowl refuge, or historic site resulting from such use. (82 Stat. 824)

The provisions of section 4(f), now found at 49 U.S.C. 303 (1986), still apply to activities carried out by units of the Department of Transportation, and implementing regulations have been merged with those of NEPA (23 C.F.R. 135 (1986)).

The second precedent addressed the process of intergovernmental coordination. Under the 1958 amendments to the Fish and Wildlife Coordination Act,

whenever the waters of any stream or other body of water are proposed or authorized to be impounded, diverted, the channel deepened,...[or] otherwise controlled or modified for any purpose whatever,...by any department or agency of the United States, or by any public or private agency under Federal permit or license, such department or agency first shall consult with the United States Fish and Wildlife Service, Department of the Interior...and with the head of the agency exercising administration over the wildlife resources of the particular State...with a view to the conservation of wildlife resources by preventing loss and damage to such resources as well as providing for the development and improvement thereof in connection with such water-resource development. [R]eports and recommendations of the Secretary of the Interior on the wildlife aspects of such projects, and any report of the head of the State agency...shall be made an integral part of any report prepared or submitted by any agency of the Federal Government for...such projects when such reports are presented to Congress....Recommendations of the Secretary...shall be as specific as practicable with respect to features recommended for wildlife conservation and development, lands to be utilized or acquired for such purposes, [and] the results expected, and shall describe the damage to wildlife attributable to the project and the measures proposed for mitigation or compensating for these damages. (72 Stat. 564)

As discussed in chapter 12, the Fish and Wildlife Coordination Act provided a mechanism to consider habitat-related impacts of water resource developments. As a result of its provisions, the U.S. Army Corps of Engineers and wildlife agencies had long before developed working relationships and were in a better position to implement the new NEPA than many other agencies.

The third precedent stems from an unlikely source, the Employment Act of 1946, and relates to the form and locus of oversight. Following the end of World War II, the nation faced the task of converting a wartime, defense-oriented economy to a peacetime, consumer-oriented one. To ease the severe economic relocation that this process caused, Congress provided for assistance from the highest levels of government:

> There is hereby created in the Executive Office of the President a Council of Economic Advisors (hereinafter called the "Council"). The Council shall be composed of three members who shall be appointed by the President, by and with the advice and consent of the Senate, and each of whom shall be a person who, as a result of his training, experience, and attainments, is exceptionally qualified to analyze and interpret economic developments, to appraise programs and activities of the Government...and to formulate and recommend national economic policy to promote employment, production, and purchasing power under free competitive enterprise. (60 Stat. 24)

While the power of the Council of Economic Advisors has waxed and waned with presidential styles and national priorities, its structure provided the pattern for the Council on Environmental Quality.

Congressional Action

Congressional proposals relating to a national environmental policy were considered as early as 1959, and several bills were introduced during the mid-1960s (Andrews 1976, 7). John Dingell introduced H.R. 7796, a bill to create a Council on Environmental Quality, on March 23, 1967 (113 CONG. REG. 7870). The bill was referred to the House Committee on Interior and Insular Affairs, then, by request, rereferred to the Subcommittee on Science, Research and Development of the Committee on Science and Astronautics (113 CONG. REG. 9708 (Apr. 17, 1967)). There it was joined by H.R. 13211 and H.R. 14605, bills introduced in September 1967 and January 1968, respectively, that would create a Council of Ecological Advisors in the Executive Office of the President (U.S. Congress, House, Committee on Science and Astronautics 1968a). H.R. 7796 was never reported out of committee, the subcommittee feeling that "Congress should establish a permanent presidential council...only if interagency environmental coordination efforts were unsuccessful" (Liroff 1976, 21). As in the case of Dingell's initial estuary protection bill, H.R. 13447 of the Eighty-ninth Congress, the effort was premature.

Congressional reports issued during the summer of 1968 provided the impetus for legislative action. A report by Congressman Emilio Daddario's Subcommittee on Science, Research and Development, *Managing the Environment* (U.S. Congress, House, Committee on Science and Astronautics 1968b), examined the relationships between environmental quality and the structure of the federal government. A *National Policy for the Environment,* published by Senator Henry Jackson's Committee on Interior and Insular Affairs (1968b), defined a national environmental policy in terms of the total human environment, the "'life support systems—natural and manmade—upon which the health, happiness, economic welfare, and physical survival of human beings depend,'" and discussed the wide range of issues that must be included in the development of such a policy (Andrews 1976, 8, 9).

The two committee reports were followed in July 1968 by a "'Joint Senate-House Colloquium to discuss a national policy on the environment'" sponsored by the House Committee on Science and Astronautics. The resulting "Congressional White Paper" (U.S. Congress, Senate, Committee on Interior and Insular Affairs 1968a) contained the elements for a national environmental policy (Andrews 1976, 8).

Two years after his initial effort, on February 17, 1969, Dingell tried again, introducing H.R. 6750, a bill "[t]o amend the Fish and Wildlife Coordination Act to provide for the establishment of a Council on Environmental Quality, and for other Purposes." At least one motive in Dingell's approach was to ensure that the bill would be referred to a friendly committee (the Committee on Merchant Marine and Fisheries, and thence to the Subcommittee on Fisheries and Wildlife, which Dingell chaired). He rationalized as follows:

> Before starting with our first witness, I might point out that the subcommittee's basic jurisdiction is over matters relating to fisheries and wildlife, and we would like to ask the witnesses for their particular comments on this aspect of the legislation.
>
> However, we can no longer hide from the fact that fish and wildlife are affected adversely by many other factors, including air pollution, water pollution, and the increasing misuse of pesticides. If we are to accomplish the intended purpose, we must consider the interrelationships of these problems in formulating legislative policy. Therefore, the subcommittee will in the course of its hearings hear testimony covering a broad range of

environmental questions. (U.S. Congress, House, Committee on Merchant Marine and Fisheries 1969, 2)

At least nine identical bills followed in rapid succession. These early versions of NEPA contained a short statement of congressional findings and policy, required an annual report on the condition of the nation's environment, and established the Council on Environmental Quality in the Executive Office of the President. However, they lacked the longer discussion of national policy and the "action-forcing" environmental impact statement of the final bill.

On June 16, 1969, Congressman Lucien N. Nedzi introduced H.R. 12143, which provided the missing elements. Seven days of hearings were held on the House bills in May and June 1969—H.R. 12143 was included on June 20, 23, 26, and 27. Nedzi's bill was hardly acknowledged by witnesses, and its provisions were omitted from the bill reported by the committee. Neither committee members nor administration witnesses recognized the significance of section 1(d) of H.R. 12143, which was to become incorporated into section 102 of NEPA (U.S. Congress, House, Committee on Merchant Marine and Fisheries 1969).

The House bills were supported by the conservation-environmental constituency (e.g., the National Audubon Society, the Wildlife Management Institute, the Sierra Club, the Izaak Walton League of America, and the American Forestry Association). They also had the support of some elements of the chemical industry and labor (e.g., E. I. du Pont de Nemours & Company; the Oil, Chemical, and Atomic Workers International Union; and the AFL-CIO). Testimony before the House (such as it was) was almost unanimously favorable—except for that offered by representatives of the administration (U.S. Congress, House, Committee on Merchant Marine and Fisheries 1969). On the whole, NEPA was not highly controversial in its initial passage through the House, nor did it elicit much attention from the interest groups that later were to be affected by its provisions (Liroff 1976, 10, 11).

One day after introduction of Dingell's bill, on February 18, 1969, the Senate began its own deliberations. Senator Jackson's S. 1075 authorized the Department of the Interior to conduct ecological research and established the Council on Environmental Quality to advise the president and to prepare an annual environmental report. As in the early House bills, S. 1075 did not contain provisions for an environmental impact statement.

In testimony before the Senate Committee on Interior and Insular Affairs, Lynton K. Caldwell, a political scientist at Indiana University, first raised the issue. (Note: At the time, Caldwell was engaged as a consultant to the same committee to assist in drafting NEPA [Le Master 1984, 10].)

> "Congress indeed has a responsibility to develop and could enunciate such a policy. But beyond this, I would urge that in the shaping of such policy, it have an action-forcing, operational aspect. When we speak of policy we ought to think of a statement which is so written that it is capable of implementation; that it is not merely a statement of things hoped for; not merely a statement of desirable goals or objectives; but that it is a statement which will compel or reinforce or assist all of these things, the executive agencies in particular, but going beyond this, the Nation as a whole, to take the kind of action which will protect and reinforce what I have called the life support system of the country.
>
> "Let me give you just a few illustrations of what I mean, by policy-forcing or operational aspect of a policy statement. For example, it seems to me that a statement of policy by the Congress should at least consider measures to require the Federal agencies, in submitting proposals, to contain within the proposals an evaluation of the effect of these proposals upon the state of the environment." (U.S. Congress, Senate, Committee on Interior and Insular Affairs 1969b, 116)

Following the hearings Senator Jackson amended his bill to expand its policy statement and added section 102—requirements for development of environmental impact findings by executive agencies (U.S. Congress, Senate, Committee on Interior and Insular Affairs 1969a; 3, 9, 21, 22). S. 1075 was then reported out of committee on July 9, 1969 (115 CONG. REG. 18865).

But things were not to go smoothly for the Jackson bill. On June 12, 1969, Senator Edmund Muskie, with forty cosponsors, introduced S. 2391, an amendment to the omnibus water pollution bill that was being considered by his committee. Muskie's bill sparked a controversy in philosophy and committee jurisdiction:

> At the heart of the disagreement between Senators Muskie and Jackson, two of the Senate's strongest advocates of environmental protection, was a fundamental difference over the conduct of environmental policy. Senator Jackson's view was that with the enactment of NEPA, mission-oriented public works agencies would internalize environmental values as they began to develop evaluations of projects' environmental impacts. But Senator Muskie and the Public Works Committee staff harbored grave misgivings about the self-enforcement qualities of NEPA's action-forcing

provisions. They believed that some form of external policing mechanism was needed; the mission-oriented agencies could not be trusted to consider seriously the environmental consequences of their actions and the requirement for environmental findings provided but the narrowest basis for outside review. In Senator Muskie's view, external policing could be provided by federal water and air pollution control agencies. (Liroff 1976, 18-19)

History shows that Senator Muskie's suspicions were well founded—but the remedy lay with the judiciary rather than the legislative branch.

A compromise was eventually worked out between the senators, and a reamended S. 1075 was presented to the Senate on October 8 (Liroff 1976, 19; 115 CONG. REG. 29,050 (Oct. 8, 1969)).

In the meantime Dingell was having trouble in the House. H.R. 6750 was slightly revised and reported as H.R. 12549 on July 11, 1969—without any provisions for an environmental impact statement. It promptly ran afoul of Congressman Wayne N. Aspinall, whose Interior Committee had considered but failed to report an environmental quality bill during the preceding session of Congress (Liroff 1976, 24). The Dingell-Aspinall feud was similar in many ways to the Jackson-Muskie controversy—a mixture of substance and turfdom:

Congressman Aspinall was greatly concerned about the bill's potentially sweeping impact upon executive agencies. He was not quite sure what its effects would be, but he felt uneasy nevertheless. In his view, two changes were needed. First, it should stand on its own rather than be a part of the fish and wildlife law over which Congressman Dingell's subcommittee had jurisdiction. Second, it needed a specific provision indicating that the authority of existing agencies would not be changed. Such a provision would assure a continued preeminent role for those congressional committees supporting agencies' traditional missions. Agencies would examine their policies, propose changes consonant with the new environmental policy, and then offer legislative recommendations that would be reviewed by each oversight committee. (Liroff 1976, 25)

With accommodation of Aspinall's desires, a revised H.R. 12549 reached the House floor on September 23, 1969, and was passed (115 CONG. REG. 26,590).

During all the congressional maneuvering, the administration was attempting to prevent statutory establishment of another agency in the Executive Office of the President. On May 29, President Nixon created a cabinet-level Environmental Quality Council and Citizens' Advisory Committee on Environmental Quality (Exec. Order No. 11,472). The council was to be composed of the secretaries of agriculture; commerce; health, education, and welfare; housing and urban development; the interior; and transportation. It would be chaired by the vice-president and staffed by the Office of Science and Technology, whose chairman would serve as executive secretary. The Citizens' Advisory Committee was to replace the Citizens' Advisory Committee on Recreation and Natural Beauty, chaired by Laurance Rockefeller, who would continue as chairman of the new committee.

Thus administration witnesses could not endorse the proposed legislation without conflicting with the president's action, and of course they could not do that. The Department of Agriculture did "'not believe that establishment of the Environmental Quality Council proposed by H.R. 12143...[was] necessary at...[that] time'" (U.S. Congress, House, Committee on Merchant Marine and Fisheries 1969, 12). The National Council on Marine Resources and Engineering Development, a statutory body in the Executive Office of the President similar to the proposed Environmental Quality Council, felt it "'desirable to obtain the guidance of Congress in developing a national policy for use of the total environment,'" but, "'[i]n view of...[the president's] action,'" suggested that Congress "'may want to [re]consider the need for establishment of a statutory council of advisors'" (U.S. Congress, House, Committee on Merchant Marine and Fisheries 1969, 14). Even Russell Train, who had espoused the concept five years previously and was at that time undersecretary of the interior, expressed reservations:

> We recognize that the type of Council proposed in H.R. 6750, would differ in some details from the new Environmental Quality Council established by the President, and, accordingly, that it might offer certain advantages not presented by the new Council.
>
> It should be recognized, however, that the functions...would to a substantial degree overlap the functions of the President's Council. In the quest for strong leadership, it is possible that such duplication could create confusion and weaken the overall structure.
>
> On balance, it is our judgment that creation of a second Council under the present circumstances would be of marginal value.
>
> If, however, it is the judgment of the Congress that the establishment of an additional Council would be beneficial, the Department of the Interior would be willing to accept that judgment. We, therefore, do not oppose enactment of H.R. 6750. (U.S. Congress, House, Committee on Merchant Marine and Fisheries 1969, 213, 214)

Of course, Congress did not intend to continue the council created by executive order. Section 2 of H.R. 12143 would redesignate that body as the "Interagency Committee on Environmental Quality"—a powerless entity without a statutory mission. These provisions were not carried into NEPA, but the cabinet-level Environmental Quality Council was soon "abolished by Reorganization Plan No. 2 of 1970, which established a Domestic Council in the Executive Office of the President" (Council on Environmental Quality 1970, 20). (Note: While Reorganization Plan No. 2 does establish a Domestic Council, which is virtually identical in membership to the Environmental Quality Council, it does not mention the latter agency.)

Beyond this petty power struggle, Congress had more substantive objections to the president's approach:

1. Cabinet-level officers would not be able to devote sufficient effort to environmental affairs or, if they did, discussions would bog down in turf disputes (U.S. Congress, House, Committee on Merchant Marine and Fisheries 1969, 219, 363, 392; U.S. Congress, Senate, Committee on Interior and Insular Affairs 1969a, 15, 16).

2. Leadership, staffing, and funding provided by the Office of Science and Technology—never a particularly strong group— would be inadequate (U.S. Congress, House, Committee on Merchant Marine and Fisheries 1969, 225, 369-374, 395; U.S. Congress, Senate, Committee on Interior and Insular Affairs 1969a, 16).

3. The Department of Defense, and in particular the U.S. Army Corps of Engineers, was not a member of the president's council (U.S. Congress, House, Committee on Merchant Marine and Fisheries 1969, 226).

With passage of H.R. 12549 by the House and S. 1075 by the Senate, the stage was set for conference deliberations. Senate Conference Committee members were Jackson, Frank F. Church, Gaylord A. Nelson, Gordon L. Allott, and Leonard B. Jordan—all members of the Senate Interior Committee; those representing the House were Dingell and Edward A. Garmatz, of Merchant Marine and Fisheries, and Wayne N. Aspinall and John P. Saylor, representing the House Interior Committee. Of the issues to be resolved, by far the most important was the fate of section 102—part of S. 1075, included in H.R. 12143 but subsequently abandoned in passage of H.R. 12549.

This section of the conference substitute is based on section 102 of the Senate bill. There was no comparable provision in the House amendment. Under the conference substitute, the Congress authorizes and directs that, *to the fullest extent possible:* (1) the Federal laws, regulations, and policies be administered in accordance with the policies set forth in the bill;...

...the phrase "to the fullest extent possible" applies with respect to those actions which Congress authorizes and directs to be done under both clauses (1) and (2) of section 102....

The purpose of the new language is to make it clear that each agency of the Federal Government shall comply with the directives set out in subparagraphs (A) through (H) of clause (2) of section 102...unless the existing law applicable to such agency's operations expressly prohibits or makes full compliance with one of the directives impossible....Thus, it is the intent of the conferees that the provision "to the fullest extent possible" shall not be used by any Federal agency as a means of avoiding compliance with the directives set out in section 102....[N]o agency shall utilize an excessively narrow construction of its statutory authorizations to avoid compliance. (U.S. Congress, House 1969, 8-9)

Shortly before the Christmas break, the conference committee's report was accepted by both houses with little debate. The most serious dissent (and prophesy) came from Congressman William Harsha, a member of the Public Works Committee:

I must warn the Members that they should be on guard against the ramifications of a measure that is so loose and ambiguous as this....

[T]his is a major revision of the administrative functions of the U.S. Government and is indeed far beyond the concept of that which the House in its wisdom thought it was passing....

The impact of S. 1075, if it becomes law, I am convinced, would be so wide sweeping as to involve every branch of the Government, every committee of Congress, every agency, and every program of the Nation. (115 CONG. REG. 40,927-40,928 (Dec. 22, 1969))

The Act

The National Environmental Policy Act (NEPA) begins with an eloquent and far-reaching statement of policy, establishing NEPA's limits in time, space, and breadth. In the environmental aura of the late 1960s, Congress left little doubt that it believed the nation's economy and environment were closely linked, we could have the best of both, and environmental decisions were to be made in the broadest context possible. Even if no other sections had followed, section 101 could have provided the basis for a national environmental program:

> Sec. 101(a). The Congress, recognizing the profound impact of man's activity on the interrelations of all components of the natural environment...and recognizing further the critical importance of restoring and maintaining environmental quality to the overall development of man, declares that it is the continuing policy of the Federal Government, in cooperation with State and local governments, and other concerned public and private organizations,...to create and maintain conditions under which man and nature can exist in productive harmony, and fulfill the social, economic, and other requirements of present and future generations of Americans. (83 Stat. 852)

The next section of NEPA provides specific instructions to the executive branch, first by making clear Congress's intention that the policy of section 101 be implemented throughout government and then by prescribing in section 102(2)(C) specific requirements for "major Federal actions significantly affecting the quality of the human environment." These last provisions, relating to preparation of environmental impact statements (EISs), are the most far reaching, controversial, and poorly drafted provisions of the act. Their redundancy and ambiguity have complicated implementation and caused continuing problems for those associated with federal environmental issues.

> Sec. 102. The Congress authorizes and directs that, to the fullest extent possible: (1) the policies, regulations, and public laws of the United States shall be interpreted and administered in accordance with the policies set forth in this Act, and (2) all agencies of the Federal Government shall—
>
> (A) utilize a systematic, interdisciplinary approach...in planning and in decisionmaking which may have an impact on man's environment;
> (B) identify and develop methods and procedures...which will insure that presently unquantified environmental amenities and values may be given appropriate consideration in decisionmaking along with economic and technical considerations;
> (C) include in every recommendation or report on proposals for legislation and other major Federal actions significantly affecting the quality of the human environment, a detailed statement by the responsible official on—

  (i) the environmental impact of the proposed action,

 (ii) any adverse environmental effects which cannot be avoided should the proposal be implemented,

(iii) alternatives to the proposed action,

(iv) the relationship between local short-term uses of man's environment and the maintenance and enhancement of long-term productivity, and

 (v) any irreversible and irretrievable commitments of resources which would be involved in the proposed action should it be implemented....

(D) study, develop, and describe alternatives to recommended courses of action in any proposal which involves unresolved conflicts...;

(E) recognize the worldwide and long-range character of environmental problems. (83 Stat. 853)

In order to ensure that no existing statutory, regulatory, or policy provisions interfered with full implementation of NEPA, Congress mandated a review and corrective action:

Sec. 103. All agencies of the Federal Government shall review their present statutory authority, administrative regulations, and current policies and procedures...and shall propose to the President not later than July 1, 1971, such measures as may be necessary to bring...[them] into conformity with...this Act. (83 Stat. 854)

Provisions for an annual presidential report on the nation's environment and for an executive office Council on Environmental Quality (CEQ) to provide assistance and oversight were contained in a second title of NEPA. As is the case with all executive office agencies, the CEQ is as strong as the president wants it to be. It is primarily a staff agency, with few personnel of its own; its power is that of the president, effected through influence upon other agencies of the executive branch. Yet whatever the president's persuasions, his oath to "faithfully execute the Office of the President of the United States" requires that he fulfill the mandates of title II:

Sec. 201. The President shall transmit to the Congress annually, beginning July 1, 1970, an Environmental Quality Report...which shall set forth (1) the status and condition of the major natural, manmade, or altered environmental classes of the Nation...; (2) current and foreseeable trends in...such environments and the effects of those trends on the social, economic, and other requirements of the Nation; (3) the adequacy of avail-

able natural resources for fulfilling human and economic requirements...;
(4) a review of the program and activities...of the Federal Government,
the State and local governments, and nongovernmental entities and individuals, with particular reference to their effect on the environment...; (5)
a program for remedying the deficiencies....

Sec. 202. There is hereby created in the Executive Office of the President a
Council on Environmental Quality....The Council shall be composed of
three members...appointed by the President...by and with the advice and
consent of the Senate....

Sec. 204. It shall be the duty and function of the Council—

(1) to assist and advise the President in the preparation of the
    Environmental Quality Report required by section 201;
(2) to gather timely and authoritative information concerning conditions
    and trends in the quality of the environment...;
(3) to review and appraise the various programs and activities of the
    Federal Government in the light of the policy set forth in title I [sec-
    tions 101 and 102] of this Act...;
(4) to develop and recommend to the President national policies to foster
    and promote the improvement of environmental quality...;
(5) to conduct investigations...[etc.] relating to ecological systems and
    environmental quality;
(6) to document and define changes in the natural environment. (83 Stat. 854)

NEPA did not provide adequate staff and fiscal support for the CEQ,
an oversight that was remedied by the Environmental Quality
Improvement Act of 1970. This statute, passed as title II of the Water
Quality Improvement Act of 1970, established an Office of
Environmental Quality in the Executive Office of the President to pro-
vide "the professional and administrative staff and support for the
Council on Environmental Quality," and it more than doubled CEQ's
authorized budget (84 Stat. 115).

At the time of its passage, no one understood the implications of
NEPA. It was neither extensively lobbied nor thoroughly debated. While
most national conservation groups supported the legislation, they did so
with little enthusiasm. Development-minded interest groups gave it little attention, and not one timber industry trade association testified during the hearings. Even among the federal agencies, only the Atomic
Energy Commission showed much interest (Le Master 1984, 13).

NEPA is not particularly well written. Its goals and objectives, in hindsight, are naively optimistic. Many agencies did not take it seriously. But it changed for all time the way federal agencies do business.

ORGANIZING THE BUREAUCRACY

On January 29, 1970, President Nixon nominated Russell E. Train as chairman and Robert Cahn and Gordon J. F. MacDonald as members of the Council on Environmental Quality, and all were confirmed by the Senate on February 6. Train had previously served as undersecretary of the interior and had been president of The Conservation Foundation from 1965 to 1969. Cahn had been a correspondent with the Washington bureau of the *Christian Science Monitor* since 1965 and had received a Pulitzer Prize in 1969 for his series of articles on the national parks. MacDonald had been vice-chancellor for research and graduate affairs at the University of California, Santa Barbara; had been a member of the President's Science Advisory Committee (1965-1969); and was a member of the National Academy of Sciences and the National Research Council (Council on Environmental Quality 1972, 349, 350). All were extremely competent and well qualified individuals. They had the president's support, and the time was right.

But the task was not easy. The new CEQ was faced with implementing a national policy that crossed agency lines, required agencies to work together, expanded agency considerations beyond traditional organic legislation, and contained a mandatory reporting procedure (the EIS) that exposed the whole process to the public. On March 5, 1970, the president issued Executive Order No. 11,514, which generally restated the provisions of NEPA but added the requirement that the CEQ shall

[i]ssue guidelines to Federal agencies for the preparation of detailed statements on proposals for legislation and other Federal actions affecting the environment, as required by section 102(2)(C) of the act. (35 Fed. Reg. 4247 (Mar. 7, 1970))

By this action President Nixon established the CEQ's preeminence in matters relating to EIS preparation and provided the other federal agencies with an excuse for not acting until CEQ guidelines were promulgated—more than a year later ("interim" guidelines were published on April 30, 1970) (35 Fed. Reg. 7390 (May 12, 1970)). The revised guidelines (36 Fed. Reg. 7724-7729 (Apr. 23, 1971)) expanded fifteen lines of the statute into six pages in the *Federal Register*, beginning a proliferation process that ultimately would reach into the hundreds of pages. They also perpetuated the redundancy of sections 102(2)(C)(i)-(v) by repeating them as "points...to be covered," thereby establishing the organization of EISs for the next seven and a half years—until changed by the regulations of 1978 (43 Fed. Reg. 55,990 (Nov. 28, 1978)).

One of the most difficult tasks was interpreting the language of section 102(2)(C) and amplifying it into federal regulations. Almost every element in this critical and ambiguous section required definition before the agencies could begin implementation. What did the Congress mean by *"major* Federal actions," *"significantly* affecting," *"human* environment," *"adverse* environmental effects," *"local short-term* uses," *"long-term* productivity," *"irreversible* and *irretrievable* commitments," and even *"resources"* (italics added)? In one sense it was a regulation writer's nightmare; in another it was an invitation for excessive innovation. The 1971 CEQ guidelines attempted to clarify some of the terms (Council on Environmental Quality 1972, 231), but in most cases resolution was left to trial, error, and the courts.

The language of NEPA was not the only problem faced by the agencies. The "NEPA process" required active cooperation among engineers, planners, ecologists, economists, lawyers, and representatives of other disciplines, many of whom had never tried to work together. Even simple communications were a problem, for the technical jargon of one discipline was foreign to another. Implementation was complex, but it proceeded expeditiously, abetted by the zeal of the environmental movement and the public visibility ensured by the Freedom of Information Act and by NEPA itself.

Public emotion over environmental matters reached its peak on Earth Day, April 22, 1970. An estimated 20 million citizens participated, involving 2,000 college campuses, 10,000 high schools, and 2,000 communities nationwide (Council on Environmental Quality 1970, 217). Many functions were politically oriented, at the same time showing support for government environmental action and putting the agencies on notice that their activities were being watched.

Faced with a task for which they were unprepared, many agencies chose to contract preparation of EISs to the private sector, but architectural and engineering firms (and even the new environmental consultants who appeared on the scene) were as ill prepared as the federal government. On top of these difficulties rested the fact that EISs cost money, and none had been provided.

Despite these adversities, almost 2,000 draft statements were prepared during the first full year of implementation. Many of these represented projects that were ongoing at the time NEPA was enacted; annual production soon diminished to about 1,100 statements.

President Nixon gave strong personal support to NEPA and the CEQ during their early years, even though many of his advisors did not share his enthusiasm. The act was a potential threat, for it represented a legislative, rather than an executive, initiative; and Nixon had initially opposed its passage. At the same time, he recognized the political opportunities presented by aggressive implementation (Andrews 1976, 22). In his 1970 Message on the Environment, Nixon outlined "a 37-point program, embracing 23 major legislative proposals and 14 new measures to be taken by administrative action or Executive Order," organized into five major categories—water pollution control, air pollution control, solid waste management, parklands and public recreation, and organizing for action (Council on Environmental Quality 1970, 255).

Nixon's 1971 environmental message to Congress outlined a wide-ranging program including recommendations for a federal procurement program to encourage recycling of paper, a national land use policy, substantial expansion of designated wilderness areas, an Environmental Institute, and a World Heritage Trust to preserve parks and cultural areas throughout the world (Council on Environmental Quality 1971, 284-308). His 1972 message repeated many of the earlier initiatives, adding proposals for a Toxic Wastes Disposal Control Act, creation of a 547,000-acre Big Cypress National Fresh Water Reserve, development of national recreation areas around New York City and the Golden Gate, and establishment of a United Nations Fund for the Environment (Council on Environmental Quality 1972, 365-383). By early 1972, however, the president's ardor was beginning to cool, and by mid-1973 all charter members of the CEQ had resigned. The time had passed. Initiative fell to the individual agencies, to the public, and to the courts (Caldwell 1975, 87-89).

THE OTHER BRANCH: ASSISTANCE FROM THE JUDICIARY

Within the first year and a half of NEPA's existence, more than twenty federal district court decisions based on citizens' challenges to federal actions under the act were reported (NEPA does not explicitly grant standing to interested citizens, but the courts have consistently found that such standing exists). Many of the early cases tested NEPA's applicability to various federal agencies and their activities, defining the act's scope in space, time, and subject matter (Council on Environmental Quality 1971, 156, 157). By the end of the third year, at least 149 separate litigations had ensued, most of which concerned agency compliance with section 102 (Caldwell 1975, 90).

How Broad Is NEPA?

Among the more important early judicial interpretations of NEPA was *Calvert Cliffs' Coordinating Comm. v. Atomic Energy Comm'n*, initially decided on July 23, 1971. Calvert Cliffs is a nuclear power plant on Chesapeake Bay in Maryland. At the time of the litigation, it was under construction but had not yet been issued an operating license. For fifteen years, the Atomic Energy Commission (AEC) had been operating under its organic legislation, the Atomic Energy Act of 1954, and it apparently intended to continue to do so with a minimum of inconvenience from NEPA (the AEC was not alone in this attitude; most federal development agencies, licensees, and permittees held similar positions in the early days of NEPA).

The petitioners in the case, the Calvert Cliffs' Coordinating Committee, chose not to attack the plant directly but to concentrate on implementing regulations enacted by the AEC. Having unsuccessfully petitioned the AEC to revise its proposed guidelines for implementing NEPA, the committee brought suit (Liroff 1976, 64). Specifically, they argued that the following regulatory provisions violated the provisions of section 102:

(1) Although environmental factors must be considered by the agency's regulatory staff under the rules, such factors need not be considered by the hearing board...unless affirmatively raised by outside parties or staff members.

(2) ...[N]on-radiological environmental issues [may not be raised] at any hearing if the notice of that hearing appeared in the Federal Register before March 4, 1971.

(3) ...[T]he hearing board is prohibited from conducting an independent evaluation and balancing of certain environmental factors if other responsible agencies have already certified that their own environmental standards are satisfied by the proposed federal action.

(4) ...[W]hen a construction permit for a facility has been issued before NEPA compliance was required and when an operating license has yet

to be issued, the agency will not formally consider environmental factors or require modifications in the proposed facility until the time of issuance of the operating license. (2 E.R.C. 1784)

All of the foregoing provisions tended to limit the scope of section 102 and to shift responsibility as much as possible from the lead federal agency. The court found to the contrary.

As to the first issue:

We believe that the Commission's crabbed interpretation of NEPA makes a mockery of the Act....NEPA establishes environmental protection as an integral part of the Atomic Energy Commission's basic mandate. The primary responsibility for fulfilling that mandate lies with the Commission. Its responsibility is not simply to sit back, like an umpire, and resolve adversary contentions at the hearing stage. Rather, it must itself take the initiative of considering environmental values at every distinctive and comprehensive stage of the process beyond the staff's evaluation and recommendation. (2 E.R.C. 1785)

As to the second:

Congress passed the final version of NEPA in late 1969, and the Act went into full effect on January 1, 1970. Yet the Atomic Energy Commission's rules prohibit any consideration of environmental issues by its hearing boards at proceedings officially noticed before March 4, 1971. This is 14 months after the effective date of NEPA....In view of the importance of environmental consideration during the agency review process...such time lag is shocking....[A] blanket banning of such issues until March 4, 1971 is impermissible under NEPA. (2 E.R.C. 1786-1787)

On the third point, the court ruled:

We believe the Commission's rule is in fundamental conflict with the basic purpose of the Act. NEPA mandates a case-by-case balancing judgment on the part of federal agencies....Certification by another agency that its own environmental standards are satisfied involves an entirely different kind of judgment....Certifying agencies do not attempt to weigh that damage against the opposing benefits. Thus the balancing analysis remains to be done. (2 E.R.C. 1788-1789)

And finally:

By refusing to consider requirement of alterations until construction is completed, the Commission may effectively foreclose the environmental protection desired by Congress. It may also foreclose rigorous considera- tion of environmental factors at the eventual operating license proceed- ings. If "irreversible and irretrievable commitment[s] of resources" have already been made, the license hearing (and any public intervention there- in) may become a hollow exercise. This hardly amounts to consideration of environmental values "to the fullest extent possible."

A full NEPA consideration of alterations in the original plans of a facility, then, is both important and appropriate well before the operating license proceedings. (2 Env't. Rep. Cas. 1792-1793)

In summary, the court in *Calvert Cliffs* found (1) that federal agencies must strictly adhere to NEPA, and particularly to the provisions of sec- tion 102(2)(C); (2) that all environmental impacts must be considered, not just those under the jurisdiction of the lead agency; and (3) that NEPA applies to all actions taking place after its enactment (January 1, 1970).

After *Calvert Cliffs*, the agencies took NEPA more seriously.

Who Prepares the EIS?

Although NEPA places the responsibility for EIS preparation directly upon "all of the Federal Government," various agencies sought to side- step this obligation by delegating the work to permittees or contractors. The Federal Power Commission (FPC) attempted to use an EIS prepared by the Power Authority of the State of New York, which had applied for an FPC power line right-of-way license. In *Greene County Planning Bd. v. Federal Power Comm'n*, the court held that the FPC violated the spirit of NEPA—each federal agency must prepare its own statements. In many cases, however, agencies continue to contract preparation of the environ- mental impact statement but retain sufficient control and participate to a sufficient degree to claim authorship.

What Alternatives Need to Be Considered?

The act and the 1971 CEQ guidelines that followed were silent on this issue. As it related to offshore oil leases, the court held that the Department of the Interior must fulfill the obligations set by the policy enunciated in section 101; *reasonable* alternatives included those outside the lead agency's jurisdiction, such as modifying oil import quotas, but did not include producing power by solar radiation (*Natural Resources Defense Council v. Morton*).

Furthering the *Morton* decision, the court extended its interpretation of "alternatives" to include alternative analytical techniques, questioning the U.S. Army Corps of Engineers' benefit-cost procedures as it did so. In *Environmental Defense Fund v. Corps of Engineers,* the court found that non-structural alternatives (which were not in the Corps' institutional interests) should have been considered, and a critical analysis of the Corps' economic claims should have been included (Liroff 1976, 171).

NEPA AND THE EIS: GUTS OR FACADE?

More than two decades after its passage, the true value of NEPA and its proper future role remain a bit clouded. In its early days, the law and the assessment process it required stopped construction of the Cross-Florida Barge Canal and development of a major jetport in Florida's Big Cypress Swamp. They produced a nine-volume, 18-pound analysis of the trans-Alaska pipeline and caused numerous modifications in that project. They forced the Federal Highway Administration to pay more attention to Indian sites that lay in the path of highway construction, caused modification of a Bureau of Reclamation dam in Idaho, and reduced the acreage sprayed for gypsy moths. They provided employment for 200 employees in the AEC alone, at a cost of $6 million in 1973 (less than 1 percent of the agency budget). They cost the Forest Service $2 million per year and cost the Department of the Interior $8 million and the diversion of 400 to 600 man-years to NEPA-related activities (Gillette 1972). But they did not stop the Tennessee-Tombigbee Waterway or the Tellico Dam.

One issue that still remains to be resolved is the degree to which the EIS, the "statement," is the basis for environmental decisions rather than merely being a form of public disclosure. Since its inception, the CEQ has consistently argued the former. Others argue to the contrary, pointing out that the environmental assessment process, the "NEPA process," is the decision-making element. They note that the EIS is issued long after all significant decisions are made. If major decisions are based on the EIS, the process has failed. (Note: An exception to this situation would occur when an EIS is submitted in support of proposed legislation, in which case Congress would be the decision maker.) The current CEQ regulations differentiate between the "NEPA process" (pt. 1501) and the environmental impact statement (pt. 1502) but insist that

[t]he primary purpose of an environmental impact statement is to serve as an action-forcing device to insure that the policies and goals defined in the Act are infused into the ongoing programs and actions of the Federal Government. It shall provide full and fair discussion of significant environmental impacts and shall inform decisionmakers and the public of the reasonable alternatives which would avoid or minimize adverse impacts or enhance the quality of the human environment....An environmental impact statement is more than a disclosure document. It shall be used by Federal officials in conjunction with other relevant material to plan actions and make decisions. (40 C.F.R. 1502.1 (1986))

In the first few years of NEPA, many mid-level federal bureaucrats considered the act to be a form of impedence and harassment:

So far, the highest government official to say so publicly is John A. Carver, Jr., a Democratic appointee to the Federal Power Commission (FPC). In a recent speech to a petroleum industry group, Carver said that "NEPA has a minimal impact in any substantive way," and that, while it may be a laudable expression of policy, "its sole observable function has been that of furnishing a weapon to those who would use it for that purpose." (Gillette 1972, 147)

Carver's comments were undoubtedly accurate representations of the way he and many other development-oriented individuals felt toward NEPA. They also reflected the quality of the EISs prepared by those groups and their general disregard for environmental considerations. In most cases "the alleged burden of the 102 statement is the attempt of agencies to manipulate the requirement so as to justify procedurally such projects as were substantively inconsistent with the purpose of the Act" (Caldwell 1975, 81).

By 1973 Nixon's priorities had shifted from the environment to energy and the economy (moving shortly thereafter to political survival) (Andrews 1976, 22-24), but by then most of the foundation for NEPA implementation had been laid, and the act was gaining acceptance by the federal agencies. As stated by John Whitaker, President Nixon's assistant principally concerned with environmental affairs and CEQ's primary conduit to the White House during its early days (Liroff 1976, 56):

By 1976 CEQ probably passed the zenith of its influence on the Executive Office of the President, primarily because so much had been accomplished that the institution had tended to work itself out of a job. Nearly all of the major legislation, much of it created by CEQ and sent to Congress, had either become law or was under congressional consideration at the time Nixon left office. The advice CEQ gave to President Ford did, as Nixon had expected, become so routinely predictable as to be discounted or taken for granted. In the author's opinion a time will come, probably by 1980, when CEQ should cease to exist. By then if the job has been well done, protection of the environment will be built into federal decison making and the executive branch will not need an environmental watchdog. But almost anyone from the Washington-based iron triangle environmental constituency would disagree with this statement and that is why, Washington being what it is, the CEQ will probably exist long after its useful life is over. (Whitaker 1976, 52)

ENVIRONMENTALISM AND REAGANISM

The coming of the Reagan administration in 1981 brought a profound change in administration attitudes toward the environment, most of which were motivated by ideological preferences rather than sound economic and scientific analysis (Vig and Kraft 1984a, 23). In transmitting his first annual environmental report to Congress, President Reagan stated:

> To operate more efficiently, I believe we must take two major initiatives. First, we must create a more innovative and flexible regulatory and economic framework in which our environmental programs operate. Regulations should complement, not stifle[,] market forces in determining the most cost-effective methods of proper environmental management.
>
> Second, I believe that environmental decisions should be brought closer to the people most affected by them. Particularly in the past decade, the various state and local governments have substantially improved their capability for dealing with environmental issues. Therefore, we should increase our reliance upon that expertise. (Council on Environmental Quality 1981, iii)

The Reagan CEQ amplified:

> [W]hile this Administration recognizes and reaffirms the nation's traditional commitment to environmental protection and natural resource management, it has reevaluated federal government policy in those areas in light of four basic principles: 1) balancing costs and benefits; 2) allowing the marketplace to work; 3) decentralizing government responsibilities; and 4) continuing global cooperation. The application of these four principles in light of lessons learned during the 1970s will foster further improvement in environmental quality during the 1980s, while at the same time reducing the costs that are imposed on taxpayers. (Council on Environmental Quality 1982, 3, 4)

Reagan's policies were carried out primarily through actions relating to personnel and budgetary and fiscal matters.

Personnel

In July 1980 the CEQ contained fifty-four professionals and nineteen interns (Council on Environmental Quality 1980, 485). Shortly after taking office, Reagan cut the agency's professional staff to six (Vig and Kraft 1984a, 20). By the end of 1984, the professional and support staff consisted of seven full-time employees and one part-time employee, and by June 30, 1985, it had increased to nine, plus one part-time assistant and three detailees from other agencies (Council on Environmental Quality 1984, 563).

Reagan's attitude toward environmental matters was reflected in the quality of his appointments as well. His choice for EPA administrator, Anne McGill Burford (Gorsuch), resigned in the midst of a political scandal in March 1983, and more than twenty top EPA officials were subsequently fired. James G. Watt, his secretary of the interior, left on October 9, 1983, following a Senate resolution asking for his removal (Vig and Kraft 1984a, 3).

Reagan replaced Burford with William D. Ruckelshaus, the first administrator of the EPA and a person of proven competence and credibility. He replaced the colorful and controversial Watt with judge William Clark, "a God-fearing Westerner, fourth-generation rancher, a person I trust" (Kraft and Vig 1984, 367). Both have done less harm to the nation's environment than their predecessors did, but even Bill Ruckelshaus found it difficult to make much progress in the face of Reagan's overall environmental and fiscal policies.

Budgetary and Fiscal Policies

Reagan's commitment to the environment was also illustrated in his fiscal policies. During the 1970s, with the environmental movement in full swing, federal expenditures for environmental protection and natural resources increased from 1.5 percent to 2.4 percent of the federal budget. By 1984 they had fallen to 1.2 percent. Seeking to restore some semblance of public confidence (after the removal of Burford and Watt), the administration requested an 8.5 percent increase in the EPA's budget for fiscal year 1985—which would restore its purchasing power to that of 1975 (Vig and Kraft 1984b, ix).

A comparison of federal expenditures on environmental programs during the Ford and Carter administrations with those of the first two years of the Reagan administration graphically illustrates the change in budgetary policy (tables 15.1 and 15.2). Between 1973 and 1976, federal expenditures increased at a rate of almost 30 percent per year, more than doubling during the Ford administration. Obviously, this rate of growth was impossible to sustain; during the next four years (the Carter adminis-

TABLE 15.1

Federal Expenditures on Environmental Programs 1973-1982, by Administration (in Millions of Dollars)

Activity	Ford				Carter			Reagan		
	1973	1974	1975	1976	1977	1978	1979	1980	1981	1982
Pollution abatement and control										
a. EPA	1,113	1,417	2,528	4,228	5,115	4,139	4,799	5,602	5,256	4,770
(Percent annual change)	(—)	(27.3)	(78.5)	(67.2)	(20.1)	(-19.1)	(15.9)	(16.7)	(-6.2)	(-9.2)
b. Other	812	657	1,042	308	1,714	1,805	2,146	2,030	1,964	2,184
(Percent annual change)	(—)	(-19.1)	(58.6)	(-70.4)	(455.7)	(10.5)	(13.3)	(-5.4)	(-3.3)	(11.2)
Subtotal	1,925	2,074	3,571	4,536	6,829	6,034	6,945	7,632	7,220	5,954
(Percent annual change)	(—)	(7.7)	(72.2)	(27.0)	(50.6)	(-11.6)	(15.1)	(9.9)	(-5.4)	(-3.7)
Protection and enhancement										
a. Aid to state and local governments	248	333	403	392	426	847	856	891	1,063	851
(Percent annual change)	(—)	(34.3)	(21.0)	(-2.7)	(8.7)	(98.8)	(1.1)	(4.1)	(19.3)	(-19.9)
b. Other	572	537	725	902	1,072	1,841	1,758	1,858	1,520	1,415
(Percent annual change)	(—)	(-6.1)	(35.0)	(24.4)	(18.9)	(71.7)	(-4.5)	(5.7)	(-18.2)	(-6.9)
Subtotal	820	870	1,128	1,294	1,498	2,688	2,614	2,749	2,583	2,266
(Percent annual change)	(—)	(6.1)	(29.7)	(4.7)	(15.8)	(79.4)	(-2.8)	(5.2)	(-6.0)	(-12.3)
Understanding, prescribing, predicting	956	1,065	1,296	1,651	1.885	2,155	2,423	2,376	2,698	2,603
(Percent annual change)	(—)	(11.4)	(21.7)	(27.4)	(14.2)	(14.3)	(12.4)	(-1.9)	(3.6)	(-3.5)
Total[a]	3,701	4,009	5,995	7,481	10,212	10,887	11,982	12,757	12,501	11,823
(Percent annual change)	(—)	(8.3)	(49.5)	(24.8)	(36.5)	(6.5)	(10.2)	(6.5)	(-2.0)	(-5.4)

Source: Council on Environmental Quality, *Environmental Quality—1983* (Washington, DC: Government Printing Office), 1983, p. 326.

[a]Computed as sum of subtotals; totals differ from those in the original document.

TABLE 15.2

Comparison of Environmental Expenditures: Ford, Carter, and Reagan Administrations (in Millions of Dollars)

	Average Annual Budget			Average of Annual Changes		
	Ford	Carter	Reagan	Ford	Carter	Reagan
Pollution abatement and control						
a. EPA	2,321	4,914	5,013	57.7	8.7	-7.7
(Percent change)	(—)	111.7	2.0	(—)	-84.9	(-188.5)
b. Other	705	1,946	2,074	-10.3	118.5	4.0
(Percent change)	(—)	176.0	6.6	(—)	125.0	(-96.7)
Subtotal	3.027	6,860	7,087	35.6	16.0	-4.54
(Percent change)	(—)	(126.7)	3.3	(—)	(-55.1)	(-128.4)
Protection and enhancement						
a. Aid to state and local governments	344	755	957	17.5	28.2	-0.3
(Percent change)	(—)	(119.5)	(26.8)	(—)	(61.1)	(-101.1)
b. Other	684	1,632	1,468	17.8	22.9	-12.6
(Percent change)	(—)	(138.6)	(-10.1)	(—)	(28.7)	(-155.0)
Subtotal	1,028	2,387	2,425	16.8	24.4	-9.2
(Percent change)	(—)	(132.2)	(26.8)	(—)	(45.2)	(-137.7)
Understanding, prescribing, predicting	1,242	2,210	2,651	20.2	9.8	5.0
(Percent change)	(—)	(77.9)	(20.0)	(—)	(-51.0)	(50.0)
Total[a]	5,297	11,457	12,162	27.6	14.9	-3.7
(Percent change)	(—)	(116.3)	(6.2)	(—)	(-46.0)	(-124.8)

[a]Computed as sum of subtotals; totals differ from those in the original document.

tration) the rate of growth declined by almost one-half—but the environmental budget was still increasing by about 15 percent per year. Abruptly with the first Reagan budget, expenditures for environmental programs actually decreased by 2 percent, and they decreased by an additional 5 percent during the second year. While rapid growth in the environmental budget during the preceding two administrations had undoubtedly produced some inefficiencies, the message sent by Reagan's budget cuts left no doubt of his intentions.

Although funds for the EPA and other agencies were reduced significantly, no agency suffered as much as the CEQ. In addition to losing virtually all of its staff, the CEQ's budget was cut by almost 75 percent, and whereas Congress frequently increased funding above that requested by the administration, in the case of the CEQ (in 1984) it appropriated $0.2 million less than the administration requested—so dissatisfied was Congress with the CEQ's performance under Reagan (Bartlett 1984, 132).

Reagan's fiscal constraints went beyond the budgetary process. Even before assuming office, his transition team was working toward reducing the "regulatory burden," and by mid-January 1981 it had produced a "'hit list' of some 242 regulations for possible reconsideration and a shorter list of 110 for early attention" (Andrews 1984, 162, 163). Within a month of his inauguration, Reagan issued an executive order (Exec. Order No. 12,291, 3 C.F.R. 127 (Feb. 17, 1981)) requiring all federal agencies to consider the economic effects of their rules and regulations and to promulgate future regulations only "if the potential benefits to society outweigh the potential costs of the proposed action." Agencies were to perform a regulatory impact analysis (RIA) on all proposed "major" regulations—those that were likely to cause the following:

An annual effect on the economy of $100 million or more;

A major increase in the costs or prices for consumers, individual industries, federal, state or local government agencies, or geographic regions; or

Significant adverse effects on competition, employment, investment, productivity, innovation, or the ability of U.S.-based enterprises to compete with foreign-based enterprises in domestic or export markets. (Council on Environmental Quality 1982, 176)

Vice-president George Bush directed the regulatory relief efforts. The process was not the cure that the Reagan administration had perceived, however. The executive order assumed that benefit-cost analyses of complicated environmental regulations were possible, that the methodology existed and the results would be accepted. In most cases these assumptions were not met. A great deal of judgment was required, and there was ample room for disagreement (Smith 1984, 6).

One of the first applications of the regulatory reform policy concerned effluent guidelines for the iron and steel industry. The EPA estimated the proposed regulations' economic effect on the iron and steel industry under two scenarios ("fairly profitable" and "less profitable") and concluded that it would be "moderate when compared to in-place controls." The agency then assessed effects on price, production, domestic market share, and employment under the same scenarios and determined that these effects were also small. Next, the cost-effectiveness of the new regulations was compared with that of similar guidelines for other industries, and again they passed the test. And finally, the benefits to recreational uses, aesthetic values, human health, diversionary use, and commercial fisheries were estimated. Despite admitted weaknesses in the process, the EPA concluded that the benefits exceeded the costs and that the proposed regulations were justified (Council on Environmental Quality 1982, 178-180).

In this illustration (cited by Reagan's CEQ), RIA did not appear to hinder the regulatory process. But overall, results were not so exemplary:

> At the request of representatives of the gasoline blending industry,...the Bush [T]ask [F]orce [on Regulatory Relief] and OMB persuaded EPA to relax its regulations limiting lead additives in gasoline, despite the well-documented evidence of automotive lead's serious effects on urban children....
>
> A package of 18 regulatory relief measures was adopted to benefit the auto industry, including proposals to relax heavy-truck emission standards and average diesel particulate emissions....
>
> In the regulation of hazardous waste disposal, EPA abruptly lifted its ban on disposing liquids into chemical landfills—apparently to benefit, at least in part, a particular firm in Gorsuch's home state of Colorado, which reportedly had large volumes of these materials lined up and ready to dump in anticipation of the change....
>
> Perhaps equally important as its actions were areas in which EPA did *not* act under Gorsuch. New regulations came slowly, if at all. By July 1982 EPA had adopted only three of twelve new source performance standards for air quality that had been proposed at the time Gorsuch took office, and it had proposed only one of eleven others that were technically ready for issuance. (Andrews 1984, 170)

A Price to Pay?

Reagan's misinterpretation of the voter "mandate" cost him what little rapport he might have retained with conservation and environmental interests, and his failure to change direction in support of Ruckelshaus as EPA administrator eliminated any hope of progress on an environmental agenda during his tenure (Mitchell 1984, 71). Opinion polls during 1982 and 1983 indicated that the administration's environmental policies were opposed by a large majority of the American public, and two-thirds of the candidates endorsed by the League of Conservation Voters were elected in the 1982 elections (Kraft 1984, 46). Nevertheless, Reagan chose to maintain his course:

While the administration did pay a steep political price eventually, it may have succeeded in using the opportunity to restructure the political agenda for the next decade. The long-term impact of the Reagan administration's efforts to do so will depend on public reaction, the way the national media cover environmental and resource issues, the activities of the nation's environmental groups, and how other policy makers evaluate the new climate for environmental issues. (Kraft 1984, 47)

Reagan's environmental philosophy continued throughout the Bush administration. Although advocating "no net loss" of wetlands and alleging to be an environmentalist, President Bush in many ways perpetuated the policies of the prior administration (of which he had been a part). His adoption of an "environment versus economy" posture; his go-slow attitude regarding reduction of acid emissions and greenhouse gases; his reliance upon environmental counsel from within the White House staff (primarily from John Sununu, his chief of staff) rather than from the director of the EPA or other, more environmentally inclined, persons; his emphasis on "the costs of cleaning up pollution" rather than on the costs of enduring it; and the federal budget deficit and the national debt all meant little administration support for a revitalized environmental program. Yet there are signs that the American people may be willing (or may be forced) to commit more resources to environmental matters. The grounding of the *Exxon Valdez* demonstrated the potential magnitude of oil spills and our inability to cope with them. Earth Day 1990, while not evoking the furor of the original celebration, reminded us that the activists are still active. Droughts and water shortages are changing the economics, politics, and technology of providing dependable supplies. Data supporting climatic change are beginning to accumulate, and the results may be profound and inevitable, at least in the near term. Other nations—particularly those of western Europe—are exposing our environmental transgressions in the international arena and are demanding remedial efforts. Most recent surveys have supported the thesis that Americans want a clean and productive environment and are willing to pay for it. Who, how much, when, and how remain to be seen.

REFERENCES

Andrews, Richard N. L. 1976. *Environmental Policy and Administrative Change.* Lexington, MA: Lexington Books.

———. 1984. "Deregulation: The Failure at EPA." In *Environmental Policy in the 1980s: Reagan's New Agenda,* edited by Norman J. Vig and Michael E.

Kraft, 161-180. Washington, DC: Congressional Quarterly, CQ Press.

Bartlett, Robert V. 1984. "The Budgetary Process." In *Environmental Policy in the 1980s: Reagan's New Agenda*, edited by Norman J. Vig and Michael E. Kraft, 121-143. Washington, DC: Congressional Quarterly, CQ Press.

Caldwell, Lynton K. 1975. *Man and His Environment: Policy and Administration.* New York: Harper & Row, Publishers.

Carson, Rachel. 1962. *Silent Spring.* Boston: Houghton Mifflin Company.

Council on Environmental Quality. 1970. *Environmental Quality.* Washington, DC: Government Printing Office.

———. 1971. *Environmental Quality—1971.* Washington, DC: Government Printing Office.

———. 1972. *Environmental Quality—1972.* Washington, DC: Government Printing Office.

———. 1980. *Public Opinion on Environmental Issues: Results of a National Opinion Survey.* Washington, DC: Council on Environmental Quality.

———. 1981. *Environmental Quality—1981.* Washington, DC: Government Printing Office.

———. 1982. *Environmental Quality—1982.* Washington, DC: Government Printing Office.

———. 1984. *Environmental Quality—1984.* Washington, DC: Government Printing Office.

Davies, J. Clarence. 1970. *The Politics of Pollution.* New York: Pegasus.

Gillette, Robert. 1972. "National Environmental Policy Act: How Well Is It Working?" *Science* 176:146-148.

Kraft, Michael E. 1984. "A New Environmental Policy Agenda: The 1980 Presidential Campaign and Its Aftermath." In *Environmental Policy in the 1980s: Reagan's New Agenda*, edited by Norman J. Vig and Michael E. Kraft, 29-50. Washington, DC: Congressional Quarterly, CQ Press.

Kraft, Michael E., and Norman J. Vig. 1984. "Epilogue." In *Environmental Policy in the 1980s: Reagan's New Agenda*, edited by Norman J. Vig and Michael E. Kraft, 359-374. Washington, DC: Congressional Quarterly, CQ Press.

Le Master, Dennis C. 1984. *Decade of Change: The Remaking of Forest Service Statutory Authority during the 1970s.* Westport, CT: Greenwood Press.

Leopold, Aldo. 1949. *A Sand County Almanac.* New York: Oxford University Press.

Liroff, Richard A. 1976. *A National Policy for the Environment.* Bloomington: University of Indiana Press.

Marsh, George P. 1864. *Man and Nature.* New York: Charles Scribner.

Marshall, Robert. 1930. "The Problem of the Wilderness." *Scientific Monthly* 30:141-148.

Mitchell, Robert Cameron. 1984. "Public Opinion and Environmental Politics." In *Environmental Policy in the 1980s: Reagan's New Agenda*, edited by Norman J. Vig and Michael E. Kraft, 51-74. Washington, DC: Congressional Quarterly, CQ Press.

Nixon, Richard M. 1968a. *Nixon on the Issues.* New York: Nixon-Agnew Committee. (Not reviewed.)

———. 1968b. *Nixon Speaks Out: Major Speeches and Statements in the Presidential Campaign of 1968.* New York: Nixon-Agnew Committee. (Not reviewed.)

Osborn, Fairfield. 1948. *Our Plundered Planet.* Boston: Little, Brown & Company.

———. 1953. *The Limits of the Earth.* Boston: Little, Brown & Company.

Outdoor Recreation Resources Review Commission. 1962. *Outdoor Recreation for America.* Washington, DC: Government Printing Office.

Sears, Paul. 1958. "The Inexorable Problem of Space." *Science* 127 (3288): 9-16. (January 3).

Smith, V. Kerry. 1984. *Environmental Policy under Reagan's Executive Order.* Chapel Hill: University of North Carolina Press.

Train, Russell E. 1965. "The Keynote Address: America the Beautiful." *American Forests* 71 (10): 16-19, 46-50.

Udall, Stewart L. 1963. *The Quiet Crisis.* Orlando, FL: Holt, Rinehart and Winston.

U.S. Congress. House. 1969. *National Environmental Policy Act of 1969: Conference Report.* 91st Cong., 1st sess. H. Rept. 91-765. Washington, DC: Government Printing Office.

———. Committee on Merchant Marine and Fisheries. Subcommittee on Fisheries and Wildlife Conservation. 1969. *Environmental Quality.* 91st Cong., 1st sess. Serial 91-6. Washington, DC: Government Printing Office.

U.S. Congress. House. Committee on Science and Astronautics. Subcommittee on Science, Research, and Development. 1968a. *Environmental Quality.* H.R. 7796, H.R. 13211, H.R. 14605, H.R. 14629. 90th Cong., 2d sess. Washington, DC: Government Printing Office.

———. 1968b. *Managing the Environment.* 90th Cong., 2d sess. Washington, DC: Government Printing Office.

U.S. Congress. Senate. Committee on Interior and Insular Affairs. 1968a. *Congressional White Paper on a National Policy for the Environment.* 90th Cong., 2d sess. Serial T. Washington, DC: Government Printing Office.

———. 1968b. *A National Policy for the Environment.* Report by William J. Van Ness, special counsel to the committee, with a statement by Henry M. Jackson. 90th Cong., 2d sess. Washington, DC: Government Printing Office.

———. 1969a. *National Environment Policy Act of 1969.* 91st Cong., 1st sess. S. Rept. 91- 296. Washington, DC: Government Printing Office.

———. 1969b. *National Environmental Policy: Hearing on S. 1075, S. 237, and S. 1752.* 91st Cong., 1st sess. Washington, DC: Government Printing Office.

Vig, Norman J., and Michael E. Kraft. 1984a. "Environmental Policy from the Seventies to the Eighties." In *Environmental Policy in the 1980s: Reagan's New Agenda,* edited by Norman J. Vig and Michael E. Kraft, 3-26. Washington, DC: Congressional Quarterly, CQ Press.

—————. 1984b. *Environmental Policy in the 1980s: Reagan's New Agenda.* Washington, DC: Congressional Quarterly, CQ Press.

Vogt, William. 1948. *Road to Survival.* New York: William Sloane Associates.

Whitaker, John C. 1976. *Striking a Balance.* Washington, DC: American Enterprise Institute for Public Policy Research; Stanford, CA: Hoover Institution on War, Revolution, and Peace.

White, Lynn, Jr. 1967. "The Historical Roots of Our Environmental Crisis." *Science* 155:1203-1207.

Federal Government Organization

Almost every federal agency has some involvement with natural resource issues. Some of the more important and influential agencies are listed here with the aim of providing readers with an understanding of (1) where to go for information and services in specific natural resource areas and (2) the distribution of jurisdiction among the agencies. Unless otherwise noted, information was obtained from the *United States Government Manual 1989/90* (National Archives and Records Administration 1989). This document, the official handbook of the federal government, is published annually by the Office of the Federal Register in the National Archives and Records Administration. A companion public document, the *Congressional Directory* (U.S. Congress, Joint Committee on Printing 1989), and two similar documents published by a private source, the *Federal Staff Directory* (Brownson 1989b) and the *Congressional Staff Directory* (Brownson 1989a), provide lists of current key federal employees.

THE LEGISLATIVE BRANCH

In addition to Congress, the legislative branch contains several agencies that relate to natural resource matters.

United States Botanic Garden

The Botanic Garden was founded in 1820 under the auspices of the Columbia Institute for the Promotion of Arts and Sciences. It later became the repository for botanical collections of the United States Exploring Expedition to the South Seas (1838-1842) and subsequent collections from all over the world. Today the Botanic Garden contains more than 10,000 living specimens and is open to the public. It also provides limited research facilities, assists in the identification of rare plants, and furnishes information on the plants' culture. The Botanic Garden is located on the Mall at the west end of the Capitol Grounds in Washington, DC (National Archives and Records Administration 1989, 45).

General Accounting Office

The General Accounting Office (GAO) assists the Congress in carrying out its legislative and oversight responsibilities, particularly in the areas of legal and fiscal affairs and government operations. It conducts special audits, surveys, and reviews at the request of Congress and its committees and members; provides information and services to the Congressional Budget Office; and monitors and evaluates the operation of government programs.

Under the direction of the comptroller general, the GAO cooperates with the secretary of the treasury, the director of the Office of Management and Budget, and the heads of other agencies of the executive branch in developing standardized information, data processing, and fiscal and budgetary systems. As an independent, professional, nonpartisan agency, it is particularly valuable in obtaining accurate and objective audits of government contracts and agency expenditures (pp. 47-49).

Government Printing Office

The Government Printing Office (GPO) provides many of the printing and publication distribution services for all branches of the federal government. It provides catalogs of available material and sells approximately 20,000 different government publications through mail order and government bookstores (p. 52). Two of its more widely distributed publications are the daily *Federal Register,* which provides information about agency rule making and other activities of the executive branch, and the *Congressional Record,* which provides similar information about the legislative branch.

Library of Congress

Originally a repository for "such books as may be necessary for the use of Congress," the Library of Congress has grown to become the national library of the United States. In addition to maintaining an exhaustive collection of books, musical works, photographs, maps, and motion pictures, it provides limited reference service through correspondence, interlibrary loans, and photoduplication services. It also administers the copyright law, which protects authors, songwriters, choreographers, photographers, and other artists from duplication of their works for sale. Research facilities of the library are open to the public without charge. The Congressional Research Service is a special arm of the library that conducts analyses and studies for Congress (pp. 54-59).

THE JUDICIAL BRANCH

Our system of federal courts contains three levels, district, circuit, and Supreme, which hear cases involving violations of federal laws (treaties, statutes, and regulations), interstate controversies, violations of maritime law, and controversies in which the United States is a party. In understanding government operations, it is important not to confuse the *judiciary* (the judicial branch and its system of courts, which hears cases and renders decisions) and the *Justice Department* (a unit of the executive branch that prepares and prosecutes cases on behalf of the government and defends the government in cases against it).

The Supreme Court

The chief justice and eight associate justices constitute the United States Supreme Court. Supreme Court justices are appointed by the president (by and with the advice and consent of the Senate), and all federal justices hold office for life ("during good Behaviour"). Justices may, however, retire at age seventy after ten years of service or at age sixty-five after fifteen years of service. In cases involving "Ambassadors, other public Ministers and Consuls," and those "in which a State shall be party," the Supreme Court has original jurisdiction (U.S. Constitution, art. III, sec. 2); in all other situations, the Supreme Court hears cases appealed from lower courts (p. 67).

Courts of Appeals

The intermediate judicial level consists of twelve courts of appeals, one for each of the twelve judicial circuits plus one that has nationwide jurisdiction. Each state and territory is assigned to a circuit court, as is the District of Columbia. Each court consists of a circuit justice assigned from the Supreme Court and 6 to 28 judges (168 in all), depending on the work load, and normally hears cases in panels of three judges (p. 69).

District Courts

The district court is the trial court of the federal system. Each state, the District of Columbia, and Puerto Rico has at least one district court (for a total of ninety-one) consisting of 2 to 27 judges (for a total of 541). Normally a single judge hears and decides a case in district court, but in special instances (e.g., injunction orders) three judges may be required (p. 73).

THE EXECUTIVE BRANCH

The organization of the executive branch results from a combination of legislative initiatives (organic acts and enabling legislation) and presidential actions issued periodically as reorganization plans. Details may vary from time to time, but the general format remains, and functions (as dictated by statute) endure.

The basic structure of the executive branch consists of a chief executive officer and a number of functional agencies, replicated through government from the highest level (president and cabinet officers) down through the ranks to the most insignificant office. The chief executive may have an alter ego (a deputy) who acts in his stead. Higher-level, policy-making personnel tend to be appointees of the current administration and change as presidents come and go; lower-level people tend to be career public servants, protected by civil service legislation, who serve the nation whomever the president might be.

The programs of most executive branch agencies include research and development (in-house and through outside grants or contracts), law enforcement (treaties and federal laws and regulations), grants-in-aid to state and local government, land management, and education and extension services.

The President

The president is the administrative head of the executive branch, which contains fourteen departments and many independent agencies. The president's cabinet consists of the secretaries of agriculture, commerce, defense, education, energy, health and human services, housing and urban development, the interior, labor, state, transportation, the treasury, and veterans affairs and the attorney general (p. 85).

The original executive departments—Treasury, War, Navy, Post Office, and Attorney General—reflected a young nation's concern with finances, defense, and essential services. This organization remained much the same until the mid-1800s (of major natural resource agencies, only the U.S. Army Corps of Engineers is older). The Department of the Interior was established in 1849; the Department of Agriculture was created in 1862; and most natural resource bureaus, offices, and services are creatures of the twentieth century.

Executive Office of the President

The Executive Office of the President is the staff agency to the president. It contains the president's personal staff and a number of specialized technical, scientific, fiscal, and management groups that provide information and counsel. Although the executive office has no line authority—it has no jurisdiction over executive branch departments or other agencies— personnel within the office exert their influence through the president, who may then effect action through the respective secretaries or other line agency heads. The interplay between members of the executive office and the cabinet, as each attempts to sway the president, is complicated, profound, and ever changing as individuals come and go or win and lose in the eternal power struggle. Although most of the executive office changes with each administration, many technical and scientific professionals may persist.

The White House Office

The White House Office comprises the president's personal staff (p. 90). Others *may* have access to the president; the president's chief of staff and other executives in the White House Office *have* access to the president. Depending on each president's particular style of management, cabinet officers may have more or less influence (usually less) than these officials, but (1) the secretaries and other agency heads will be required to carry out the policies developed here and enunciated by the president, and (2) line officers and White House staff members will be continually testing each other's strength.

Office of Management and Budget

Next to the president and the president's personal staff, the director of the Office of Management and Budget (OMB) is probably the most powerful person in the executive branch. In addition to preparing the annual budget and fiscal program for the president, the director of the OMB has general oversight responsibilities throughout the executive branch. He or she supervises and controls administration of the budget, occasionally impounding or otherwise prohibiting expenditure of funds appropriated by Congress. He or she clears all executive department statements presented to Congress supporting or opposing pending legislation, thereby ensuring that the administration's position is expressed (a position that the director has been instrumental in preparing). He or she assists in developing regulatory reform and paperwork reduction proposals—efforts that have affected environmental regulatory programs. He or she may prepare executive orders and other proclamations that enunciate administration policy. In essence, the OMB is the watchdog for the president, ensuring that "the Laws...[are] faithfully executed" in accordance with the goals and objectives of the current administration (pp. 91, 92).

Council of Economic Advisors

Established by the Employment Act of 1946, the Council of Economic Advisors (CEA) analyzes the national economy, appraises government economic programs and policies, and assists in developing the president's economic policy (p. 93). In this last capacity, it interacts with the OMB and the secretary of the treasury; in recent years it has lost the three-way power struggle that results.

Council on Environmental Quality

Established by the National Environmental Policy Act of 1969 (NEPA), the Council on Environmental Quality (CEQ) consists of three persons, assisted by a staff, who develop and recommend environmental policy to the president. In addition to evaluating trends in the national environment and efforts of the administration, the CEQ prepares the president's annual environmental quality report to Congress (p. 96). During the early to mid-1970s, the CEQ exerted considerable national influence, and its annual reports, titled *Environmental Quality*, were valuable descriptions of government activities and environmental conditions. However, with the waning of the environmental movement and the advent of Reaganism, the CEQ's staff, budget, and power diminished drastically.

Office of Science and Technology Policy

Established by the National Science and Technology Policy Organizations and Priorities Act of 1976 as successor to the Office of

Science and Technology, the Office of Science and Technology Policy (OSTP) serves as a source of scientific and technological information for the president, assists the OMB in preparing the budget, and provides leadership in coordinating research and development programs within the federal government (p. 97).

Statutory agencies within the Executive Office of the President (CEA, CEQ, and OSTP) cannot be abolished by presidential proclamation, executive order, or reorganization plan. Their importance ebbs and flows, however, with national politics and administration policy and budget. In recent administrations the power within the administration appears to have been concentrated within the White House office, with other executive office and cabinet agencies assuming much less importance.

Department of Agriculture

Created by an act of Congress on May 15, 1862, the Department of Agriculture works to improve the condition of the agricultural sector of our economy. It provides technical assistance and funds to individuals, sponsors and conducts research programs, and manages the National Forest System. Its activities have a profound effect upon the nation's soil, water, forests, and other natural resources (p. 105).

Line agencies (usually called "administrations" and "services") answer to undersecretaries and assistant secretaries responsible for program areas—for example, small communities and rural development (Farmers Home Administration), natural resources and environment (Forest Service and Soil Conservation Service), and science and education (Agricultural Research Service, Cooperative State Research Service, and Extension Service) (p. 104).

Animal and Plant Health Inspection Service

Established to protect and improve animal and plant health, the Animal and Plant Health Inspection Service enforces plant and animal quarantines, regulates veterinary biological products, and regulates genetically engineered organisms. Its animal damage control program conducts research on predator-prey relationships and control methods, advises farmers and ranchers on animal control measures, and suppresses nuisances and health threats caused by wildlife (pp. 116, 117).

Farmers Home Administration

Through a network of 2,200 county and district offices, the Farmers Home Administration (FmHA) provides loans to rural residents who are unable to obtain adequate arrangements elsewhere. In addition to granting operating loans of up to $200,000 to operators of family farms to cover costs of equipment, seed, feed, and fertilizer and other operational costs, the FmHA provides funds for a number of activities related to natural resources. Soil and water conservation loans enable farmers (including corporations) to develop their land and water resources. Watershed protection and flood prevention loans enable local organizations to finance their share of flood control projects. Resource conservation and development loans and community program loans provide assistance to sponsors of projects and to public bodies for conservation and resource-related facilities such as water and waste disposal systems. Loans are granted by the FmHA or by cooperating lending institutions (with FmHA guarantee) for periods of of thirty to fifty years and may provide up to $10 million per project (watershed protection and flood prevention loans), with interest rates generally following the cost of government borrowing. In sum, FmHA projects permit farmers to stay in business when other lines of credit are foreclosed and to develop otherwise unobtainable natural resources (pp. 106-109). While instrumental in developing rural America, FmHA projects have been criticized in the past as facilitating overexploitation of resources and extending farmers' credit beyond their repayment abilities.

Agricultural Stabilization and Conservation Service

Through more than 3,000 county committees, the Agricultural Stabilization and Conservation Service (ASCS) administers commodity and related land use programs. Its loans, purchases, and subsidy payments tend to stabilize the markets for wheat, corn, cotton, soybeans, peanuts, rice, tobacco, and other agricultural products by adjusting production. The Conservation Reserve Program (CRP), established by the Food Security Act of 1985, conserves soil and water resources on highly erodible land through agreements with participants, who maintain cover crops and carry out other conservation programs on the land. The Agriculture Conservation Program (ACP) provides up to 80 percent of farmers' costs incurred while implementing other soil and water conservation and management measures. In cooperation with ACP and State forestry programs, the Forestry Incentives Program (FIP) may reimburse a landowner for up to 65 percent of the cost of reforestation and stand improvement (maximum annual cost share per participant is $10,000). The Water Bank Program enables landowners to enter into ten-year agreements and receive payments in return for preserving important waterfowl nesting areas. The experimental Rural Clean Water Program

(RCWP) is authorized to provide up to 75 percent federal cost sharing and technical assistance in efforts to control nonpoint source pollution from agricultural lands (pp. 122-125). In support of its programs, the ASCS periodically obtains aerial photographs of agricultural regions, which are available for inspection in county and state offices and may be purchased by the public. File photographs extend back to the 1930s and provide natural resource specialists with excellent chronologies of land use changes.

Forest Service

In exercising its responsibility for national leadership in forestry, the Forest Service manages the National Forest System to provide a continuous flow of renewable and nonrenewable resources, executes cooperative programs with other federal and state agencies and local governments, and conducts research on renewable resource management. The National Forest System contains 156 national forests, nineteen national grasslands, and fifteen land utilization projects encompassing 191 million acres in forty-four states, the Virgin Islands, and Puerto Rico. Dedicated to the principles of multiple use and sustained yield, the Forest Service balances the need to provide wood and paper products with equally important obligations to maintain recreational opportunities and natural beauty, wildlife habitat, livestock forage, and water supplies. Within the National Forest System are about 32 million acres designated as wilderness and an additional 175,000 acres set aside as primitive areas. No timber is harvested from wilderness and primitive areas.

Through its cooperative state and private forestry programs, the Forest Service provides technical assistance and financial support for rural forestry assistance, insect and disease control, fire prevention and control, and other programs to improve the quality of natural resources on nonfederal land and to encourage their use. The Forest Service also conducts research in cooperation with state agricultural colleges under the provisions of the McSweeney-McNary Act. Much of the labor in national forests is provided through the Youth Conservation Corps, the Volunteers in the National Forests, the Job Corps, and the Senior Community Service Employment programs—providing worthwhile employment and meaningful outdoor experiences at minimum public cost (pp. 132, 133).

Soil Conservation Service

Through a system of about 3,000 soil and water conservation districts (usually counties), the Soil Conservation Service (SCS) implements a national program of soil and water conservation. It provides soil mapping, farm planning, and other technical assistance to landowners and cooperates with other federal, state, and local agencies in conducting river basin surveys, planning and executing small watershed projects, and reducing damage due to flooding (pp. 134, 135). In many Department of Agriculture programs, the Extension Service (see the discussion that follows) provides general information to the agricultural community, the SCS supplies technical assistance, the ASCS furnishes cost-sharing funds, and the FmHA provides loans for the nonfederal costs for soil and water conservation projects. Extension Service, SCS, and ASCS personnel frequently share office space at the district (county) level, and the average citizen often fails to differentiate among them.

Agricultural Research Service

The Agricultural Research Service (ARS) administers a broad program of basic, applied, and developmental research at 138 locations within the United States, in the Virgin Islands and Puerto Rico, and in eight foreign countries (p. 128).

Cooperative State Research Service

Agricultural research stations in the fifty states, the territories, and the District of Columbia are financed through the Cooperative State Research Service (CSRS). Individual research projects at state agricultural research stations are funded through the Hatch Act (p. 129).

Extension Service

Land grant universities, county governments, and the Extension Service participate in the Cooperative Extension Service. Extension programs are available in all states, the District of Columbia, Puerto Rico, the Virgin Islands, Guam, American Samoa, and Micronesia. Specialists in local offices are in day-to-day contact with the agricultural community, providing an effective information transfer mechanism from academe and the bureaucracy to the farmer and rancher (p. 130).

Department of Commerce

Created from the Department of Commerce and Labor on March 4, 1913, the Department of Commerce contains a wide variety of programs designed to promote international trade, economic growth, and technological advancement. Activities range from providing assistance to promote domestic economic development to working to improve knowledge of the earth's physical and oceanic resources (p. 147).

National Oceanic and Atmospheric Administration

Formed in 1970 by combining the functions of the National Weather Service (NWS), the National Ocean Survey (NOS), and the National Marine Fisheries Service (NMFS), the National Oceanic and Atmospheric Administration (NOAA) is the department's major environmental monitoring and natural resource management agency. Since its creation it has assumed responsibility for the federal role in coastal zone management, protection of marine mammals, creation and management of marine sanctuaries, protection of rare and endangered marine species, and management of marine fisheries. NOAA is the public source of weather forecasts and long-term environmental information and of nautical and aeronautical charts. It also administers the National Sea Grant college program, which provides grants to institutions for marine research, education, and advisory services (pp. 157, 158).

National Technical Information Service

A collector, organizer, publisher, and distributor of scientific literature, the National Technical Information Service (NTIS) has files that contain more than 1.8 million titles, all of which are available for sale to the public. In addition to providing an outlet for government-sponsored research reports, the NTIS regularly reviews and publishes foreign technology and marketing information. It distributes more than 3 million documents annually, is financially self-sustaining from the sale of publications and other services, and maintains an on-line Bibliographic Data Base available to the public through contracting agencies (pp. 163, 164).

Department of Defense

U.S. Army Corps of Engineers

The first federal natural resource management agency, the Corps has held civil works responsibility since passage of the Act of May 24, 1824. The Corps is the nation's major water resource development agency. Its civil works program involves construction and operation of facilities related to rivers, harbors, and waterways. In addition to the Corps' role as water resource developer, it administers laws designed to protect and preserve navigable waterways and wetlands (p. 216).

Department of Housing and Urban Development

Operating under the assistant secretary for housing, the Department of Housing and Urban Development (HUD) implements the Interstate Land Sale and Full Disclosure Act. This act requires developers of subdivisions containing fifty or more lots, who sell through interstate commerce, to maintain a current registration statement with the Office of Interstate Land Sales Registration and to furnish prospective buyers a "property report" prior to purchase (p. 339). By requiring full disclosure of projects' environmental, economic, and legal conditions, the program protects buyers from unscrupulous and incompetent developers.

Department of the Interior

Originally a group of caretaker agencies (the General Land Office, the Office of Indian Affairs, the Pension Office, the Patent Office, the Commissioner of Public Buildings, the Warden of the Penitentiary of the District of Columbia, etc.), the Department of the Interior (DOI) has evolved into the nation's principal conservation agency. Its activities include administration of more than 550 million acres of federal and trust lands; conservation and development of water, mineral, fish and wildlife, and recreational resources; preservation of scenic, natural, and historic areas; reclamation of arid western lands; management of hydroelectric systems; coordination and operation of manpower and youth training programs; and social and economic programs in the trust territories and among the Indian tribes (pp. 346, 348).

Line natural resource agencies operate under the assistant secretary for fish and wildlife and parks (the National Park Service and the United States Fish and Wildlife Service), the assistant secretary for water and science (the Geological Survey, the Bureau of Reclamation, and the Bureau of Mines), and the assistant secretary for land and minerals management (the Bureau of Land Management; the Office of Surface Mining, Reclamation, and Enforcement; and the Minerals Management Service) (p. 347).

National Park Service

Established in 1916, the National Park Service (NPS) administers more than 337 parks, parkways, monuments, historic sites, and recreation areas. The service manages these areas for public enjoyment and education while protecting their natural environment. It interprets the areas' natural and historical significance to the visiting public through talks, tours, exhibits, and other media and operates campgrounds and other visitor facilities. The NPS also administers the state portion of the Land and Water Conservation Fund, formulates the Nationwide Outdoor Recreation Plan and oversees development of state comprehensive outdoor recreation plans (SCORPs), conducts the planning functions of the National Wild and Scenic Rivers System, administers the National Trails System, and maintains the National Register of Historic Places (p. 356).

United States Fish and Wildlife Service

Formed in 1940 through consolidation of the Bureau of Fisheries (from Commerce) and the Bureau of Biological Survey (from Agriculture), the United States Fish and Wildlife Service (FWS) discharges the nation's responsibilities to conserve, protect, and enhance its fish and wildlife resources. The FWS has undergone numerous reorganizations since its inception, the most significant of which transferred the Bureau of Commercial Fisheries (now the National Marine Fisheries Service) to the Department of Commerce in 1970. Major activities now include maintaining 450 national wildlife refuges and 150 waterfowl production areas, which comprise more than 91 million acres; cooperating in planning and assessing the environmental impacts of water resource development; operating cooperative fish and wildlife research units at universities and providing research and management funds to state fish and game agencies; preserving and restoring populations of endangered fish and wildlife (other than marine mammals); and enforcing federal fish and wildlife laws and regulations (pp. 354, 355).

Geological Survey

The Geological Survey (GS) is primarily a scientific and technical agency engaged in investigating and understanding the nation's water and mineral resources. The GS prepares topographic and geologic maps; inventories and assesses mineral resources on public lands prior to lease; and investigates earthquakes, volcanoes, landslides, floods, and other hazardous geologic phenomena (pp. 357, 358).

Bureau of Reclamation

Created by the Reclamation Act of 1902, the Bureau of Reclamation (BuRec) develops water resources in the seventeen contiguous western states. While its projects primarily provide dependable sources of water for irrigation, hydropower, and municipalities, they also furnish outdoor recreation, fish and wildlife habitat, and flood control and navigation benefits. Among other facilities, BuRec operates 355 water storage reservoirs, 15,855 miles of canals, and 54 hydroelectric power plants. About 81 percent of direct project costs are repaid by beneficiaries (pp. 362, 363). The U.S. Army Corps of Engineers is the primary federal water resource development agency over most of the United States, but in much of the West, BuRec is *the* water resource development agency.

Bureau of Land Management

Formed by the consolidation of the General Land Office and the Grazing Service in 1946, the Bureau of Land Management (BLM) is the nation's primary land manager. It is responsible for 272 million acres of public lands and an additional 300 million acres on which mineral rights have been reserved by the federal government. As guardian of the public domain, the BLM manages the total resources of these lands as authorized by the Federal Land Policy and Management Act of 1976, including timber, solid minerals, oil and gas, geothermal energy, wildlife habitat, endangered species, recreation, and cultural values—the works—under the principles of multiple use and sustained yield. The BLM also oversees leasing of energy and mineral resources on public lands and administers a system of payments in lieu of taxes to counties and other units of local government (pp. 361, 362).

Office of Surface Mining Reclamation and Enforcement

Established by the Surface Mining Control and Reclamation Act of 1977, the Office of Surface Mining Reclamation and Enforcement assists the states in developing programs to ensure that surface mining for coal can be done without damage to water and land resources. Currently most coal-mining states have assumed responsibility for the program under the office's oversight (p. 358).

Minerals Management Service

Created in 1982 by Secretarial Order No. 3071, the Minerals Management Service (MMS) assumed responsibility for all outer continental shelf (OCS) leasing and for the collection and distribution of royalties, rents, and other revenues received from mineral leasing throughout the public domain. Such revenues are among the largest nontax sources of federal income and are distributed to the states, to the general fund of the Treasury, and to Indian tribes and others in accordance with several statutes (pp. 360, 361). OCS revenues provide the majority of receipts to the Land and Water Conservation Fund, from which state and local park and recreation agencies derive much of their financial support.

Department of Justice

The Department of Justice is the federal government's law office, furnishing counsel and representing it in litigation, just as a private law firm does for individuals. In addition Justice conducts investigations, obtains evidence, enforces federal laws in the field, and houses and rehabilitates federal prisoners. It is a combination of law enforcement officers, prosecutors, and counselors serving the federal establishment, but it does not include the federal courts—they are in the judicial *branch* of government, separate and equal.

The Department of Justice was established on June 22, 1870, with the attorney general as its head. The department operates through its central Washington office and a system of U.S. attorney district offices (under the supervision of the associate attorney general) corresponding to the federal court districts (p. 371).

Office of Legal Counsel

The Office of Legal Counsel provides legal opinions to executive department agencies, particularly regarding agency disputes and constitutional matters. Such opinions are not law, as are opinions of the judiciary, but they are given great weight by government agencies and are the closest thing to case law short of litigation. In addition to this function, the Office of Legal Counsel reviews all executive orders and proclamations for form and legality (p. 373).

Civil Division

Attorneys of the Civil Division defend the government in suits resulting from alleged negligence of government employees, represent the government in maritime litigation, and prosecute other federal civil suits. They also are responsible for securing injunctions (to stop an unlawful activity) and for representing the federal government in litigation testing the constitutionality of federal laws, regulations, and other decisions and actions (pp. 381, 383).

Criminal Division

The Criminal Division handles all criminal prosecutions except those specifically assigned to other divisions. It contains sections concerned with organized crime and racketeering, narcotics and dangerous drugs, and national security (pp. 384-386).

Land and Natural Resources Division

The Land and Natural Resources Division is the environmental arm of the Justice Department. It is responsible for both criminal and civil actions involving public lands and natural resources, environmental quality, Indian lands and claims, and wildlife resources. Over much of its seventy-five-year history, the division's litigation focused on management of federal lands; in more recent years, pollution abatement activities of the Environmental Protection Agency have occupied the majority of its time (pp. 386, 387).

Department of State

All formal government business with foreign countries is conducted through the State Department. It negotiates treaties, speaks for the United States in the United Nations and in more than fifty major international organizations, and represents the United States in more than 800 international conferences annually (pp. 431, 433).

Bureau of Oceans and International Environmental and Scientific Affairs

The Bureau of Oceans and International Environmental and Scientific Affairs formulates and implements international scientific and technical policies and is concerned with international issues relating to the oceans, fisheries, the environment, population, and nuclear and energy technology (p. 436).

Department of Transportation

In establishing and executing the nation's transportation policy, the Department of Transportation exerts a profound influence upon land, energy conservation, and technological change (p. 453).

United States Coast Guard

A branch of the armed forces, the Coast Guard serves under the Department of Transportation in peacetime and is a part of the United States Navy in wartime. It enforces federal laws and international agreements on the high seas and in waters under United States jurisdiction. In addition to its duties in maritime law enforcement, search and rescue operations, and boating safety, the Coast Guard has major responsibilities for protecting the marine environment. It oversees all marine activities that might result in discharge of pollutants into waterways and maintains a National Strike Force, which can respond swiftly in the event of a major pollution incident (pp. 458, 459). In addition the Coast Guard issues permits for the construction of bridges over navigable waters of the United States as authorized by the Rivers and Harbors Act of 1899.

Federal Aviation Administration

As the agency with overall responsibility for the nation's air transportation system, the Federal Aviation Administration (FAA) has been involved in major environmental issues concerned with air and noise pollution, airport location and construction, and safety (pp. 462, 463).

Federal Highway Administration

In funding the 42,500-mile National System of Interstate and Defense Highways, 800,000 miles of other federal-aid roads and streets, and more than 80,000 miles of federally owned roads on federal land, the Federal Highway Administration (FHWA) is constantly confronted with environmental problems. The agency has been instrumental in funding research related to the environmental impacts of highway construction and in conducting exhaustive environmental assessments of highway construction projects (pp. 464-467).

Independent Agencies

A number of federal agencies are directed not by a cabinet-level officer but by a lower-level executive (usually an "administrator") and report to the president through a representative in the Executive Office of the President.

Agency for International Development

Closely associated with the State Department, the Agency for International Development (AID) implements foreign policy through economic assistance programs. Major program areas include agriculture, rural development, and nutrition; health; population planning; child survival; AIDS; education and human resource development; and private sector, environment, and energy activities. AID conducts humanitarian activities overseas in response to earthquakes, drought, floods, and other natural calamities and is instrumental in distributing U.S. agricultural commodities to the poor in foreign nations (pp. 734-737).

Environmental Protection Agency

The Environmental Protection Agency (EPA) was established by Reorganization Plan No. 3 of 1970, effective December 2, 1970, from several preexisting agencies (primarily from the Departments of Health and the Interior). The EPA's mission is to control pollution—air, water, solid waste, pesticides, radiation, and toxic substances—in cooperation with state and local governments. Agency activities are organized around program areas (air, water, etc.) and are carried out through a system of regional offices, which interact closely with state counterparts. Each program area is generally authorized by its own specific legislation and consists of pollution standard development, regulations, and enforcement; technology development and transfer; and financial assistance (pp. 553-556).

REFERENCES

Brownson, Ann L., ed. 1989a. *1989 Congressional Staff Directory/2.* Mount Vernon, VA: Staff Directories.

———. 1989b. *1989 Federal Staff Directory.* Mount Vernon, VA: Staff Directories.

National Archives and Records Administration. 1989. *United States Government Manual 1989/90.* Washington, DC: Government Printing Office.

U.S. Congress. Joint Committee on Printing. 1989. *1989-90 Congressional Directory.* Washington, DC: Government Printing Office.

APPENDIX B

Treaties and Federal Statutes Cited

Act of April 20, 1832, ch. 71, 4 Stat. 505—to reserve Hot Springs, Arkansas

Act of April 27, 1935, ch. 85, 49 Stat. 163 (codified as amended at 16 U.S.C. §§ 590a-590f (1982))—to establish the Soil Conservation Service

Act of August 12, 1912, ch. 284, 37 Stat. 269, 293 (current version at 16 U.S.C. § 673 (1982))—to establish a winter game (elk) reserve in Wyoming

Act of February 9, 1871, res. 22, 16 Stat. 593—appointment of a commissioner of fish and fisheries

Act of February 12, 1938, ch. 27, §§ 5-6, 52 Stat. 29 (current version at 16 U.S.C. §§ 403i-403j (1982))—to purchase lands to complete the Great Smoky Mountains National Park

Act of February 21, 1925, ch. 281, 43 Stat. 958—to determine boundaries of Shenandoah, Smoky Mountains, and Mammoth Cave national parks

Act of February 25, 1927, ch. 205, 44 Stat. 1246 (current version at 16 U.S.C. § 673a (1982))—to accept title to lands adjacent to the winter elk refuge in Wyoming

Act of February 26, 1919, ch. 44, § 5, 40 Stat. 1178 (codified as amended at 16 U.S.C. §§ 225-228, 687 (1982))—to include parts of Grand Canyon National Game Preserve in Grand Canyon National Park

Act of January 24, 1905, ch. 137, 33 Stat. 614 (current version at 16 U.S.C. §§ 684-686 (1982))—to protect birds and animals in Wichita Forest Reserve

Act of January 24, 1923, ch. 42, 42 Stat. 1174, 1214—disposal of surplus animals in Yellowstone National Park

Act of June 6, 1900, ch. 791, 31 Stat. 588, 618 (codified as amended at 16 U.S.C. § 78 (1982))—to authorize use of troops in Sequoia, Yosemite, and General Grant national parks

Act of June 14, 1926, ch. 578, 44 Stat. 741—acquisition or use of public lands by states, counties, or municipalities for recreational purposes

Act of June 15, 1934, ch. 538, 48 Stat. 964 (current version at 16 U.S.C. §§ 403b, 403g, 403h (1982))—to establish a minimum area for the Great Smoky Mountains National Park

Act of June 22, 1870, ch. 150, 16 Stat. 162 (current version at 28 U.S.C. §§ 501, 503 (1982))—to create the Department of Justice

Act of June 28, 1906, ch. 3565, 34 Stat. 536—to protect birds and their eggs in preserves

Act of June 28, 1916, ch. 179, 39 Stat. 238 (current version at 16 U.S.C. § 26 (1982))—to punish crimes in Yellowstone National Park

Act of June 29, 1906, ch. 3593, 34 Stat. 607 (current version at 16 U.S.C. §§ 684-686 (1982))—to protect wild animals in Grand Canyon Forest Reserve

Act of June 30, 1864, ch. 184, 13 Stat. 325—grant of Yo-Semite Valley and Mariposa Big Tree Grove

Act of March 1, 1872, ch. 24, 17 Stat. 32—to establish Yellowstone Park

Act of March 2, 1831, ch. 66, 4 Stat. 472—to protect timber on naval timber reserves

Act of March 2, 1887, ch. 314, 24 Stat. 440 (1887) (codified as amended at 7 U.S.C. §§ 361a-361i (1982))

Act of March 3, 1875, ch. 191, 18 Stat. (Pt. III) 517—to establish Mackinac Island National Park

Act of March 3, 1883, ch. 143, 22 Stat. 603, 627 (current version at 16 U.S.C. § 23 (1982))—to authorize use of troops in Yellowstone National Park

Act of March 3, 1891, ch. 561, 26 Stat. 1095 (current version at 16 U.S.C. § 471 (1982))—to repeal the Timber Culture Act and the Creative Act

Act of March 4, 1909, ch. 301, 35 Stat. 1039, 1051 (current version at 16 U.S.C. § 671 (1982))—to enlarge the Montana National Bison Range

Act of March 4, 1913, ch. 141, 37 Stat. 736 (current version at 15 U.S.C. § 1501 (1982))—to create the Department of Commerce from the Department of Commerce and Labor

Act of March 4, 1913, ch. 145, 37 Stat. 828, 847 (current version at 16 U.S.C. § 673 (1982))—to enclose the winter elk refuge in Montana

Act of March 4, 1925, ch. 556, 43 Stat. 1313, 1331—to pay expenses of the Temple Commission

Act of March 19, 1828, ch. 17, § 3, 4 Stat. 256—appropriations for a naval timber reserve

Act of March 31, 1933, ch. 17, 48 Stat. 22—for the relief of unemployment (establishes Civilian Conservation Corps)

Act of May 7, 1894, ch. 72, 28 Stat. 73—to protect birds and animals in Yellowstone National Park

Act of May 8, 1914, ch. 79, 38 Stat. 372 (current version at 7 U.S.C. §§ 341-349 (1982))—to create the Agricultural Extension Service

Act of May 15, 1862, ch. 72, 12 Stat. 387—to create the Department of Agriculture

Act of May 18, 1933, ch. 32, 48 Stat. 58—to establish the Tennessee Valley Authority

Act of May 22, 1926, ch. 363, 44 Stat. 616 (current version at 16 U.S.C. §§ 403a-403c (1982))—to provide for establishment of Shenandoah and Great Smoky Mountains national parks

Act of May 23, 1908, ch. 192, 35 Stat. 251, 267 (current version at 16 U.S.C. § 671 (1982))—to reserve the National Bison Range

Act of May 24, 1824, ch. 134, 4 Stat. 32—first appropriations to the U.S. Army Corps of Engineers for work in navigable waters

Act of May 29, 1830, ch. 208, 4 Stat. 420—the Preemption Act of 1830

Act of October 2, 1888, 24 Stat. 255—to reserve funds for Irrigation Survey

Act of September 4, 1841, ch. 16, § 11, 5 Stat. 453, 456—preemption rights and sale of public lands—the Log Cabin Bill

Afognak Island, Alaska, Proclamation No. 39, 27 Stat. 1052 (1892)—to withdraw and reserve lands

Agreement Between the United States and Japan Concerning Fisheries off the Coasts of the United States, September 10, 1982, United States-Japan, 34 U.S.T. 2060, T.I.A.S. No. 10480

Agreement Between the United States and the Soviet Union Concerning Fisheries off the Coasts of the United States, November 26, 1976, United States-Soviet Union, 28 U.S.T. 1847, T.I.A.S. No. 8528

Agricultural Act of 1956, ch. 327, 70 Stat. 188 (repealed in part)—the Soil Bank Act

Agricultural Adjustment Act of 1933, ch. 25, tit. I, §§ 1-21, 48 Stat. 31 (codified as amended at 7 U.S.C. §§ 601-605, 607-623 (1982))

Agricultural Appropriations Act of 1905, ch. 1405, 33 Stat. 861, 873 (codified as amended at 16 U.S.C. § 559 (1982))—to authorize Forest Service employees to make arrests

Agricultural Appropriations Act of 1907, ch. 2907, 34 Stat. 1256

Agricultural Appropriations Act of 1908, ch. 192, 35 Stat. 251, 260 (codified as amended at 16 U.S.C. § 500 (1982))

Agriculture and Consumer Protection Act of 1973, Pub. L. No. 93-86, § 1(28), 87 Stat. 221 (codified as amended at 16 U.S.C. §§ 1501-1510 (1982))

Agriculture and Food Act of 1981, Pub. L. No. 97-98, 95 Stat. 1213 (codified as amended in scattered sections of 7 and 16 U.S.C.)

Alaska National Interest Lands Conservation Act, Pub. L. No. 96-487, 94 Stat. 2371 (1980) (codified as amended at 16 U.S.C. §§ 3101-3233 (1982))

Alaska Native Claims Settlement Act, Pub. L. No. 92-203, 85 Stat. 688 (1971) (current version at 43 U.S.C. §§ 1601-1624 (1982))

Amended Agreement for Establishment of the Indo-Pacific Fisheries Commission, November 23, 1961, 13 U.S.T. 2511, T.I.A.S. No. 5218, 418 U.N.T.S. 348

Anadromous and Great Lakes Fisheries Act of 1965, Pub. L. No. 89-304, 79 Stat. 1125 (codified as amended at 16 U.S.C. §§ 757a-757f (1982))

Animal Damage Control Act of 1931, ch. 370, 46 Stat. 1468 (1931) (current version at 7 U.S.C. § 426 (1982))

Antiquities Act of 1906, ch. 3060, § 2, 34 Stat. 225 (1906) (current version at 16 U.S.C. § 431 (1982))

Atlantic States Marine Fisheries Compact, Pub. L. No. 539, 56 Stat. 267 (1942)

Atlantic States Marine Fisheries Compact Amendments of 1950, Pub. L. No. 721, 64 Stat. 467 (1950)

Atomic Energy Act of 1954, Pub. L. No. 703, 68 Stat. 919 (codified as amended in scattered sections of 42 U.S.C.)

Black Bass Act, ch. 346, 44 Stat. 576 (1926) (repealed in 1981)

Black Bass Act Amendments of 1947, ch. 348, 61 Stat. 517 (repealed in 1981)

Black Bass Act Amendments of 1952, ch. 911, 66 Stat. 736 (repealed in 1981)

Canada Forest Fire Protection Compact, Pub. L. No. 340, 66 Stat. 71 (1952)

Carey Act of 1894, ch. 301, § 4, 28 Stat. 372, 422 (1894) (codified as amended at 43 U.S.C. § 641 (1982))

Chugach National Forest Additions, Proclamation of February 23, 1909, 35 Stat. 2231

Civilian Conservation Service Act of 1933, 48 Stat. 22

Clarke-McNary Act of 1924, ch. 348, 43 Stat. 653 (1924) (codified as amended at 16 U.S.C. §§ 471, 499, 505, 515, 564-568, 569, 570 (1982))

Classification and Multiple Use Act of 1964, Pub. L. No. 88-607, 78 Stat. 987 (current version at 43 U.S.C. §§ 1411-1418 (1982) (omitted))

Clean Water Act of 1977, Pub. L. No. 95-217, 91 Stat. 1566 (codified as amended at 33 U.S.C. §§ 1251-1265, 1281-1292, 1311-1328, 1341-1345, 1361-1376 (1982))

Clean Water Restoration Act of 1966, Pub. L. No. 89-753, 80 Stat. 1246 (repealed)

Coastal Zone Management Act Amendments of 1976, Pub. L. No. 94-370, §§ 2-14, 90 Stat. 1013 (current version at 16 U.S.C. §§ 1451, 1453-1464 (1982))

Coastal Zone Management Act Amendments of 1990, Pub. L. No. 101-508, 104 Stat. 1388-299 (codified at 16 U.S.C.S. § 1451 et seq. (Supp. III 1991))

Coastal Zone Management Act of 1972, Pub. L. No. 92-583, 86 Stat. 1280 (codified as amended at 16 U.S.C. §§ 1451-1464 (1982))

Coastal Zone Management Improvement Act of 1980, Pub. L. No. 96-464, 94 Stat. 2060 (current version at 16 U.S.C. §§ 1451-1464 (1982))

Coastal Zone Management Reauthorization Act of 1985, Pub. L. No. 99-272, 100 Stat. 124 (current version at 16 U.S.C. §§ 1451-1463 (Supp. IV 1986))

Commercial Fisheries Research and Development Act of 1964, Pub. L. No. 88-309, 78 Stat. 197 (codified as amended at 16 U.S.C. §§ 742c, 779 (1982))

Convention Between the United States and Canada for the Preservation of the Halibut Fishery of the Northern Pacific Ocean and Bering Sea, March 2, 1953, 5 U.S.T. 5, T.I.A.S. No. 2900, 222 U.N.T.S. 77

Convention Between the United States and the Republic of Texas, April 25, 1838, 8 Stat. 511

Convention Concerning the Conservation of Migratory Birds and Their Environment, United States-U.S.S.R., 29 U.S.T. 4647, T.I.A.S. No. 9073

Convention for the Conservation of Salmon in the North Atlantic, March 2, 1982, 1 U.S.T. 230, T.I.A.S. No. 2044, 80 U.N.T.S. 3

Convention for the Establishment of an Inter-American Tropical Tuna Commission, May 31, 1949, United States-Costa Rica, 1 U.S.T. 230, T.I.A.S. No. 2044, 80 U.N.T.S. 3

Convention for the Protection of Migratory Birds, August 16, 1916, United States-Great Britain, 39 Stat. 1702, T.S. No. 628

Convention for the Protection of Migratory Birds and Birds in Danger of Extinction, and their Environment, March 4, 1972, United States-Japan, 25 U.S.T. 3329, T.I.A.S. No. 7990

Convention for the Protection of Migratory Birds and Game Mammals, February 7, 1936, United States-Mexico, 50 Stat. 1311, T.S. No. 912

Convention on Fishing and Conservation of the Living Resources of the High Seas, April 29, 1958, 17 U.S.T. 138, T.I.A.S. No. 5969, 559 U.N.T.S. 285

Convention on International Trade in Endangered Species of Wild Fauna and Flora (CITES), March 3, 1973, 27 U.S.T. 1087, T.I.A.S. No. 8249, 993 U.N.T.S. 243

Convention on Nature Protection and Wildlife Preservation in the Western Hemisphere, October 12, 1940, 56 Stat. 1354, T.S. No. 981, 161 U.N.T.S. 193

Convention on the Continental Shelf, April 29, 1958, 15 U.S.T. 471, T.I.A.S. No. 5578, 499 U.N.T.S. 311

Convention on the Great Lakes Fishery, September 10, 1954, United States-Canada, 6 U.S.T. 2836, T.I.A.S. No. 3326, 238 U.N.T.S. 97

Convention on the High Seas, April 29, 1958, 13 U.S.T. 2312, T.I.A.S. No. 5200, 450 U.N.T.S. 11

Convention on the Territorial Sea and Contiguous Zone, April 29, 1958, 15 U.S.T. 1606, T.I.A.S. No. 5639, 516 U.N.T.S. 205

Cooperative Forestry Assistance Act of 1978, Pub. L. No. 95-313, 92 Stat. 365 (current version at 16 U.S.C. §§ 2101-2111, 1606 (1982))

Cooperative Research Unit Act of 1960, Pub. L. No. 86-686, 74 Stat. 733 (codified as amended at 16 U.S.C. §§ 753a-753b (1982))

Creative Act, ch. 561, § 24, 26 Stat. 1095 (1891) (repealed by the Federal Land Policy and Management Act of 1976, § 704(a), Pub. L. No. 94-579, 90 Stat. 2743, 2792)

Deep Seabed Hard Mineral Resources Act, Pub. L. No. 96-283, 94 Stat. 553 (1980) (codified as amended at 30 U.S.C. §§ 1401-1470 (1982))

Deep Water Port Act of 1974, Pub. L. No. 93-627, 88 Stat. 2126 (codified as amended at 33 U.S.C. § 1340 (1982))

Department of Interior and Related Agencies Appropriations Act, Fiscal Year 1988, Pub. L. No. 100-446, 102 Stat. 1774 (codified in scattered sections of 2, 16, 25, 30, 43, and 48 U.S.C.)

Department of Interior and Related Agencies Appropriations Act, Fiscal Year 1989, Pub. L. No. 101-121, 103 Stat. 701, 745 (codified in scattered sections of 16, 25, 30, 42, and 48 U.S.C.)

Department of Transportation Act of 1966, Pub. L. No. 89-670, 80 Stat. 930 (codified as amended in scattered sections of 23 U.S.C.)

Desert Land Act of 1877, ch. 107, 19 Stat. 377 (codified as amended at 43 U.S.C. §§ 321-323 (1982))

Dingell-Johnson Act, ch. 658, 63 Stat. 430 (1950) (codified as amended at 16 U.S.C. §§ 777-777k (1982))

Eastern Wilderness Act of 1974, Pub. L. No. 93-622, 88 Stat. 2096 (1975)

Emergency Wetland Resources Act of 1986, Pub. L. No. 99-645, 100 Stat. 3582 (current version at 16 U.S.C. §§ 3901-3911, 3921-3922, 3931 (Supp. IV 1986))

Employment Act of 1946, ch. 33, 60 Stat. 23 (codified as amended at 15 U.S.C. §§ 1021-1024 (1982))

Endangered Species Act Amendments of 1978, Pub. L. No. 95-632, 92 Stat. 3751 (codified as amended at 16 U.S.C. §§ 1531-1536, 1538-1540, 1542 (1982))

Endangered Species Act Amendments of 1982, Pub. L. No. 97-304, 96 Stat. 1411 (codified as amended at 16 U.S.C. §§ 1531-1533, 1535-1537a, 1538-1540, 1542 (1982 and Supp. IV 1986))

Endangered Species Act of 1973, Pub. L. No. 93-205, 87 Stat. 884 (codified as amended at 7 U.S.C. § 136 and 16 U.S.C. §§ 460k-1, 460l-8, 668dd, 715i, 715s, 1362, 1371, 1372, 1402, 1531-1543 (1982))

Endangered Species Conservation Act of 1969, Pub. L. No. 91-135, 83 Stat. 275 (codified as amended at 16 U.S.C. §§ 668, 705, 851, 852 and 18 U.S.C. 43, 44, 3054, 3112 (1982))

Endangered Species Preservation Act of 1966, Pub. L. No. 89-669, 80 Stat. 926 (repealed in 1973)

Energy and Water Development Appropriations Act of 1992, Pub. L. No. 102-104, 105 Stat. 510

Environmental Quality Improvement Act of 1970, Pub. L. No. 91-224, tit. I, §§ 202-205, 84 Stat. 114 (codified as amended at 42 U.S.C. §§ 4371-4374 (1982))

Estuary Protection Act of 1968, Pub. L. No. 90-454, 82 Stat. 625 (current version at 16 U.S.C. §§ 1221-1226 (1982))

Federal-Aid Highway Act of 1966, Pub. L. No. 89-574, 80 Stat. 766 (codified as amended in scattered sections of 23 U.S.C.)

Federal-Aid Highway Act of 1968, Pub. L. No. 90-495, 82 Stat. 815 (codified as amended in scattered sections of 49 U.S.C.)

Federal Aid in Fish Restoration Act, Pub. L. No. 681, 64 Stat. 430 (1950) (codified as amended at 16 U.S.C. § 777 (1982))—Dingell-Johnson Act

Federal Aid in Wildlife Restoration Act, ch. 899, 50 Stat. 917 (1937) (codified as amended at 16 U.S.C. § 669 (1982))

Federal Aid in Wildlife Restoration Act Amendments of 1970, Pub. L. No. 91-503, 84 Stat. 1097 (current version at 16 U.S.C. §§ 669b, 669c, 669g (1982))

Federal Land Policy and Management Act of 1976, Pub. L. No. 94-579, 90 Stat. 2744 (codified as amended in scattered sections of 7, 10, 16, 25, 30, 42, 43, and 49 U.S.C.)

Federal Water Pollution Control Act Amendments of 1965, Pub. L. No. 89-234, 79 Stat. 903

Federal Water Pollution Control Act Amendments of 1972, Pub. L. No. 92-500, 86 Stat. 816 (codified as amended in scattered sections of 12, 15, 31, and 33 U.S.C.)

Federal Water Pollution Control Act of 1948, ch. 758, 62 Stat. 1155

Fish and Wildlife Act of 1956, ch. 1036, 70 Stat. 1119 (codified as amended at 16 U.S.C. §§ 742a-742j-2 (1982))

Fish and Wildlife Conservation Act of 1980, Pub. L. No. 96-366, 94 Stat. 1322 (codified as amended at 16 U.S.C. §§ 2901-2911 (1982))

Fish and Wildlife Coordination Act Amendments of 1958 (Pub. L. No. 85-624, 72 Stat. 563 (current version at 16 U.S.C. §§ 661-664, 1008 (1982))

Fish and Wildlife Coordination Act of 1934, ch. 55, 48 Stat. 401 (codified as amended at 16 U.S.C. §§ 661-666 (1982))

Fish and Wildlife Improvement Act of 1978, Pub. L. No. 95-616, 92 Stat. 3114 (current version at 16 U.S.C. §§ 460k-3, 666g, 668a, 668dd(d)(1)(A), 668dd(f), 690e, 695i, 695j-1, 706, 712, 718f, 742 (1982))

Fisheries Agreement Concerning Fisheries of the Coasts of the United States, with Agreed Minutes, November 26, 1976, U.S.S.R.-United States, 28 U.S.T. 1847, T.I.A.S. No. 8528

Fishermen's Protective Act of 1967, Pub. L. No. 680, 68 Stat. 883 (codified as amended at 22 U.S.C. §§ 1971-1976 (1982))

Fishery Conservation and Management Act Amendments of 1986, Pub. L. No. 99-659, 100 Stat. 3706 (current version at 16 U.S.C. §§ 1801-1802, 1811-1813, 1821-1822, 1824, 1826-1827, 1852-1861, 1881-1882 (Supp. IV 1986)

Fishery Conservation and Management Act of 1976, Pub. L. No. 94-265, 90 Stat. 331 (codified as amended at 16 U.S.C. §§ 1801-1882 (1982))

Flood Control Act of 1936, 49 Stat. 1570 (current version at 33 U.S.C. § 701 (1982))

Flood Control Act of 1944, 58 Stat. 887 (current version at 33 U.S.C. § 701 (1982))

Flood Control Act of 1948, 62 Stat. 1182 (current version at 33 U.S.C. § 701s (1982))

Food and Agriculture Act of 1965, Pub. L. No. 89-321, 79 Stat. 1187 (codified as amended in scattered sections of 7 U.S.C.—Cropland Adjustment Program is at 7 U.S.C. § 1838 (1982))

Food Security Act of 1985, Pub. L. No. 99-198, 99 Stat. 1355 (current version in scattered sections of 7, 12, 15, 16, 21, 29, and 42 U.S.C.)

Forest and Rangeland Renewable Resources Planning Act of 1974, Pub. L. No. 93-378, 88 Stat. 476 (codified as amended at 16 U.S.C. §§ 581h, 1600-1614 (1982))

Forest and Rangeland Renewable Resources Research Act of 1978, Pub. L. No. 95-307, 92 Stat. 353 (codified as amended at 16 U.S.C. §§ 1641-1647 (1982))

Forest Homestead Act, ch. 3074, 34 Stat. 233 (1906) (repealed in 1962)

Forest Lieu Lands Act, ch. 2, § 1, 30 Stat. 36 (1897) (current version at 16 U.S.C. §§ 473, 478-482 (1982))

Forest Lieu Lands Act Repeal, ch. 1495, 33 Stat. 1264 (1905)

Forest Management Act of 1897, ch. 2, 30 Stat. 34 (codified as amended at 16 U.S.C. §§ 473-482 (1982))—also called the Organic Administration Act, or Organic Act, of 1897

Forest Reserve Act, ch. 561, 26 Stat. 1095, 1103 (1891) (codified as amended at 16 U.S.C. §§ 471, 607-610; 25 U.S.C. §§ 426, 495 (1982); and scattered sections of 43 U.S.C.)

Freedom of Information Act, Pub. L. No. 89-487, 80 Stat. 250 (1966) (codified as amended at 5 U.S.C. § 522 (1982))

Free Timber Act, ch. 150, 20 Stat. 88 (1878) (current version at 16 U.S.C. § 604 (1982))

Grand Canyon National Forest Act, ch. 3593, 34 Stat. 607 (1906) (current version at 16 U.S.C. §§ 684-686 (1982))

Gulf States Marine Fisheries Compact, ch. 128, 63 Stat. 70 (1949)

Hatch Act, ch. 314, 24 Stat. 440 (1887) (codified as amended at 7 U.S.C. §§ 361a-361i (1982))

Historic Sites Act of 1935, 49 Stat. 666

Homestead Act of 1862, ch. 75, 12 Stat. 392

Interim Convention on Conservation of North Pacific Fur Seals, February 9, 1957, 8 U.S.T. 2283, T.I.A.S. No. 3948, 314 U.N.T.S. 105

Interjurisdictional Fisheries Act of 1986, Pub. L. No. 99-659, 100 Stat. 3706, 3731 (current version at 16 U.S.C. §§ 4101-4107 (Supp. IV 1986))

International Convention for the Conservation of Atlantic Tunas, May 14, 1966, 20 U.S.T. 2887, T.I.A.S. No. 6767, 673 U.N.T.S. 63

International Convention for the Regulation of Whaling, September 24, 1931, 49 Stat. 3079, T.S. 880, 155 L.N.T.S. 349

International Convention for the Regulation of Whaling with Schedule of Whaling Regulations, December 2, 1946, 62 Stat. 1716, T.I.A.S. No. 1849, 161 U.N.T.S. 72

International Convention on the High Seas Fisheries of the North Pacific Ocean, May 9, 1952, Canada-Japan-United States, 4 U.S.T. 380, T.I.A.S. No. 2786, 205 U.N.T.S. 65

Interstate Land Sales Full Disclosure Act, Pub. L. No. 90-448, 82 Stat. 590 (1968) (codified as amended at 15 U.S.C. § 1701 note (1982))

Japanese-United States Fisheries Agreement, September 10, 1982, 34 U.S.T. 2060, T.I.A.S. No. 10480

Knutson-Vandenberg Act of 1930, ch. 416, 46 Stat. 527 (codified as amended at 16 U.S.C. §§ 576-576b (1982))

Lacey Act Amendments of 1981, Pub. L. No. 97-79, 95 Stat. 1073 (current version at 16 U.S.C. §§ 667e, 851-856, 3401-3408 and 18 U.S.C. §§ 42c, 43, 44, 3054, 3112 (1982))

Lacey Act for the Protection of the Yellowstone Park, ch. 72, 28 Stat. 73 (1894) (codified as amended at 16 U.S.C. §§ 24-30 (1982))

Lacey Act of 1900, ch. 553, 31 Stat. 187 (codified as amended at 16 U.S.C. §§ 667e, 701 and 18 U.S.C. §§ 42-44 (1982))

Land and Water Conservation Fund Act Amendments of 1968, Pub. L. No. 90-401, 82 Stat. 354 (codified as amended at 16 U.S.C. 4601-5, 4601-7, 4601-9, 4601-10, 4601-22 (1982))

Land and Water Conservation Fund Act Amendments of 1970, Pub. L. No. 91-485, 84 Stat. 1084 (codified as amended at 16 U.S.C. § 4601-5 and 40 U.S.C. § 484 (1982))

Land and Water Conservation Fund Act Amendments of 1974, Pub. L. No. 93-303, 88 Stat. 192 (current version at 16 U.S.C. §§ 4601-6a, 4601-8, 4601-10a (1982))

Land and Water Conservation Fund Act Amendments of 1976, Pub. No. 94-422, 90 Stat. 1313 (current version at 16 U.S.C. §§ 4601-5, 4601-7 through 4601-10, 4601-10d (1982))

Land and Water Conservation Fund Act Amendments of 1977, Pub. L. No. 95-42, 91 Stat. 210 (codified as amended at 16 U.S.C. §§ 4601-7, 4601-9(a)(3), 4601-9(b), 4601-9(c) (1982))

Land and Water Conservation Fund Act of 1965, Pub. L. No. 88-578, 78 Stat. 897 (codified as amended at 16 U.S.C. §§ 460d, 4601-4 through 4601-11 (1982))

Log Cabin Bill, ch. 16, § 11, 5 Stat. 453, 456 (1841)

McIntire-Stennis Act of 1962, Pub. L. No. 87-788, 76 Stat. 806 (codified as amended at 16 U.S.C. §§ 582a-582a-7 (1982))

McNary-Woodruff Act of 1928, ch. 461, 45 Stat. 468

McSweeney-McNary Act of 1928, ch. 678, § 1, 45 Stat. 700 (repealed in 1978)

Magnuson Fishery Conservation and Management Act, Pub. L. No. 94-265, 90 Stat. 331 (1976) (codified as amended at 16 U.S.C. §§ 1801-1882 (1982))

Magnuson Fishery Conservation and Management Act Amendments of 1986. *See* Fishery Conservation and Management Act Amendments of 1986

Marine Mammal Protection Act of 1972, Pub. L. No. 92-522, 86 Stat. 1027 (codified as amended at 16 U.S.C. §§ 659, 1361, 1362, 1371-1384, 1401-1407 (1982))

Marine Resources and Engineering Development Act Amendments of 1968, Pub. L. No. 90-242, 81 Stat. 780 (current version at 33 U.S.C. §§ 1102, 1104 (1982))

Marine Resources and Engineering Development Act of 1966, Pub. L. No. 89-454, 80 Stat. 203 (codified as amended at 33 U.S.C. §§ 1101-1108 (1982))

Middle Atlantic Interstate Forest Fire Protection Compact, ch. 719, 70 Stat. 636 (1956)

Migratory Bird Conservation Act of 1929, ch. 257, 45 Stat. 1222 (codified as amended at 16 U.S.C. §§ 715-715r (1982))

Migratory Bird Hunting Stamp Act Amendments of 1935, ch. 261, 49 Stat. 378 (current version at 16 U.S.C. §§ 141b, 715k-3, 718a-718e and 18 U.S.C. §§ 382-394 (1982))

Migratory Bird Hunting Stamp Act Amendments of 1949, ch. 421, 63 Stat. 599 (codified as amended at 16 U.S.C. §§ 718b, 718d (1982))

Migratory Bird Hunting Stamp Act Amendments of 1958, Pub. L. No. 85-585, 72 Stat. 486 (current version at 16 U.S.C. §§ 718b, 718d (1982))

Migratory Bird Hunting Stamp Act Amendments of 1978, Pub. L. No. 95-552, 92 Stat. 2071 (current version at 16 U.S.C. § 718b (1982))

Migratory Bird Hunting Stamp Act of 1934, ch. 71, 48 Stat. 451 (codified as amended at 16 U.S.C. §§ 718-718h (1982))

Migratory Bird Treaty Act of 1918, ch. 128, 40 Stat. 755 (codified as amended at 16 U.S.C. §§ 703-711 (1982))

Multiple-Use Sustained Yield Act of 1960, Pub. L. No. 86-517, 74 Stat. 215 (current version at 16 U.S.C. §§ 528-531 (1982))

National Bison Range Act, ch. 192, 35 Stat. 267 (1908) (current version at 16 U.S.C. § 671 (1982))

National Defense Act of 1916, ch. 134, 39 Stat. 166

National Environmental Policy Act of 1969, Pub. L. No. 91-190, 83 Stat. 852 (codified as amended at 42 U.S.C. §§ 4321-4347 (1982))

National Flood Insurance Program Act Amendments of 1971, Pub. L. No. 92-213, 85 Stat. 775 (current version at 42 U.S.C. §§ 4012, 4013, 4021, 4156 (1982))

National Forest Management Act of 1976, Pub. L. No. 94-588, 90 Stat. 2949 (codified as amended at 16 U.S.C. §§ 472a, 476, 500, 513-516, 518, 521b, 576b, 581h, 1600-1614 (1982))

National Historic Preservation Act of 1966, Pub. L. No. 89-665, 80 Stat. 915 (current version at 16 U.S.C. § 470 (1982))

National Park Service Organic Act, ch. 408, 39 Stat. 535 (1916) (current version at 16 U.S.C. §§ 1-4, 22, 43, 1457 (1982))

National Science and Technology Policy Organization and Priorities Act of 1976, Pub. L. No. 94-282, 90 Stat. 459, 463 (codified as amended in scattered sections of 42 U.S.C.)

National Trails System Act of 1968, Pub. L. No. 90-543, 82 Stat. 919 (codified as amended at 16 U.S.C. §§ 1241-1249 (1982))

National Wildlife Refuge System Administration Act of 1966, Pub. L. No. 89-669, §§ 4-5, 80 Stat. 926 (codified as amended at 16 U.S.C. §§ 668dd, 668ee (1982))

Newlands Act of 1902, ch. 1093, 32 Stat. 388 (current version at 43 U.S.C. §§ 372, 373, 391, 392, 411, 416, 419, 421, 431, 432, 434, 439, 461, 491, 498 (1982))

Northeastern Interstate Forest Fire Protection Compact, ch. 246, 63 Stat. 271 (1949)

Occupational Safety and Health Act of 1970 (OSHA), Pub. L. No. 91-596, 84 Stat. 1590 (codified as amended in scattered sections of 5, 15, 18, 29, 42, and 49 U.S.C.)

Optional Protocol of Signature Concerning the Compulsory Settlement of Disputes, U.N. Doc. A /Conf./ 13 L.57 (1958)

Organic Act of 1897. *See* Forest Management Act of 1897

Outdoor Recreation Programs Act of 1963, Pub. L. No. 88-29, 77 Stat. 49 (codified as amended at 16 U.S.C. § 1601 (1988))

Outdoor Recreation Resources Review Act of 1958, Pub. L. No. 85-470, 72 Stat. 238 (codified as amended at 16 U.S.C. § 17 note (1982))

Outer Continental Shelf Lands Act, ch. 345, 67 Stat. 462 (1953) (codified as amended at 10 U.S.C. §§ 7421-7426, 7428-7438 and 43 U.S.C. §§ 1331-1343 (1982))

Outer Continental Shelf Lands Act Amendments of 1978, Pub. L. No. 95-372, 92 Stat. 629 (codified as amended in scattered sections of 16, 30, and 43 U.S.C.)

Pacific Marine Fisheries Compact, 61 Stat. 419 (1947)

Park, Parkway, and Recreational Area Study Act of 1936, ch. 735, 49 Stat. 1894 (codified as amended at 16 U.S.C. §§ 17k-17n (1982))

Pittman-Robertson Act, ch. 899, § 1, 50 Stat. 917 (1937) (codified as amended at 16 U.S.C. §§ 669-669j (1982))

Pittman-Robertson Act Amendments of 1970, Pub. L. No. 91-503, 84 Stat. 1097 (current version at 16 U.S.C. §§ 669b, 669c, 669g (1982))

Preemption Act, ch. 16, 5 Stat. 453 (1841)

Proclamation No. 39, 27 Stat. 1052 (1892)—to withdraw and reserve lands on Afognak Island, Alaska

Proclamation of February 23, 1909, 35 Stat. 2231—additions to Chugach National Forest

Public Land Law Review Act of 1964, Pub. L. No. 88-606, 78 Stat. 982

Public Rangelands Improvement Act of 1978, Pub. L. No. 95-514, 92 Stat. 1803 (codified as amended at 43 U.S.C. §§ 1901-1908 (1982))

Reclamation Act of 1902, ch. 1093, 32 Stat. 388 (codified as amended in 43 U.S.C.)

Recreational Boating Safety and Facilities Improvement Act of 1980, Pub. L. No. 96-451, 94 Stat. 1983, 1991 (codified as amended at 16 U.S.C. § 1606a and in scattered sections of 23, 26, and 46 U.S.C.)

Refuge Recreation Act of 1962, Pub. L. No. 87-714, 76 Stat. 653 (codified as amended at 16 U.S.C. §§ 460k-460k-4 (1982))

Renewable Resources Extension Act of 1978, Pub. L. No. 95-306, 92 Stat. 349 (current version at 16 U.S.C. §§ 1671-1676 (1982))

Reorganization Plan No. II of 1939, §§ 4(e), 4(f), 53 Stat. 1423, 1433

Reorganization Plan No. III of 1940, § 3, 54 Stat. 1231, 1232

Reorganization Plan No. 2 of 1970, 84 Stat. 2085

Reorganization Plan No. 3 of 1946, § 403, 60 Stat. 1097, 1100

Reorganization Plan No. 3 of 1950, 64 Stat. 1262

Reorganization Plan No. 3 of 1970, 84 Stat. 2086

Reorganization Plan No. 4 of 1970, 84 Stat. 2090

Resource Conservation and Recovery Act of 1976 (RCRA), Pub. L. No. 94-580, 90 Stat. 2795 (current version at 42 U.S.C. §§ 3251-3254, 3256-3259, 6901-6907, 6911-6916, 6921-6931, 6941-6949, 6951-6954, 6961-6964, 6971-6979, 6981-6987 (1982))

Rivers and Harbors Act of 1880, ch. 211, 21 Stat. 180

Rivers and Harbors Act of 1881, ch. 136, 21 Stat. 468

Rivers and Harbors Act of 1899, ch. 425, 30 Stat. 1151 (codified as amended at 33 U.S.C. §§ 401, 403, 404, 406-409, 411-415, 418, 502, 549, 686, 687 (1982))

Rivers and Harbors Act of 1968, Pub. L. No. 90-483, 82 Stat. 731 (current version at 33 U.S.C. §§ 59c-1, 59g-59i, 426i, 562a (1982))

Shipstead-Nolan Act, ch. 881, 46 Stat. 1020 (1930) (current version at 16 U.S.C. §§ 577-577b (1982))

Sikes Act, Pub. L. No. 86-797, 74 Stat. 1052 (1960) (codified as amended at 16 U.S.C. §§ 670a-670o (1982))

Sikes Act Extension of 1974, Pub. L. No. 93-452, 88 Stat. 1369, 16 U.S.C. §§ 670g-670o (1982)

Smith-Lever Act of 1914, ch. 79, 38 Stat. 372 (codified as amended at 7 U.S.C. §§ 341-348e (1982))

Soil and Water Resources Conservation Act of 1977, Pub. L. No. 95-192, 91 Stat. 1407 (current version at 16 U.S.C. §§ 2001-2009 (1982))

Soil Bank Act, ch. 327, 70 Stat. 188 (1956) (codified as amended at 7 U.S.C. §§ 1801-1814, 1821-1824, 1831-1832 (1982))

Soil Conservation Act of 1935, ch. 85, 49 Stat. 163 (codified as amended at 16 U.S.C. §§ 590a-590q (1982))

Soil Conservation and Domestic Allotment Act of 1936, ch. 104, 49 Stat. 1148 (codified as amended at 16 U.S.C. §§ 590g-590q, 612c, 624 (1982))

South Central Interstate Forest Fire Protection Compact, 68 Stat. 783 (1954)

Southeastern Interstate Forest Fire Protection Compact, 68 Stat. 536 (1954)

Submerged Lands Act, ch. 65, 67 Stat. 29 (1953) (current version at 10 U.S.C. §§ 7421-7426, 7428-7438 and 43 U.S.C. §§ 1301-1303, 1311-1315 (1982))

Sundry Civil Expenses Appropriations Act of 1888, ch. 902, 24 Stat. 222, 255

Sundry Civil Expenses Appropriations Act of 1890, ch. 873, 25 Stat. 371

Surface Mining Control and Reclamation Act of 1977, Pub. L. No. 95-87, 91 Stat. 445 (codified as amended at 18 U.S.C. § 1114 and scattered sections of 30 U.S.C.)

Tax Reform Act of 1984, Pub. L. No. 98-369, 98 Stat. 494 (current version in scattered sections of 26 U.S.C.)

Taylor Grazing Act Amendments of 1936, ch. 842, 49 Stat. 1976

Taylor Grazing Act Amendments of 1939, ch. 270, 53 Stat. 1002

Taylor Grazing Act Amendments of 1947, ch. 507, 61 Stat. 790

Taylor Grazing Act of 1934, ch. 865, 48 Stat. 1269 (codified as amended at 43 U.S.C. §§ 315-315n, 315o-1, 485, 1171 (1982))

Tennessee Valley Authority Act of 1933, ch. 32, 48 Stat. 58 (codified as amended at 16 U.S.C. §§ 831-831dd (1982))

Timber and Stone Act of 1878, ch. 76, 20 Stat. 46 (current version at 16 U.S.C. §§ 601, 602 (1982))

Timber Culture Act of 1873, ch. 277, 17 Stat. 605

Transfer Act, ch. 288, 33 Stat. 628 (1905) (codified as amended at 16 U.S.C. §§ 472, 476, 495, 524, 551, 554, 614b (1982))

Treaty Concerning Pacific Salmon, January 28, 1985, U.S.T., T.I.A.S. No.

Tucker Act, ch. 359, 24 Stat. 505 (1887) (current version at 28 U.S.C. § 1491 (1982))

Wallop-Breaux Act of 1984, Pub. L. No. 98-369, 98 Stat. 494, 1015 (current version at 16 U.S.C. § 777 (Supp. III 1985)

Water Quality Act of 1965, Pub. L. No. 89-234, 79 Stat. 903 (superseded in 1972)

Water Quality Act of 1987, Pub. L. No. 100-4, 101 Stat. 7 (codified in scattered sections of 33 U.S.C.)

Water Resources Development Act of 1974, Pub. L. No. 93-251, 88 Stat. 12 (codified as amended in scattered sections of 16 U.S.C.)

Water Resources Development Act of 1986, Pub. L. No. 99-662, 100 Stat. 4082

Water Resources Planning Act of 1965, Pub. L. No. 89-80, 79 Stat. 244 (codified as amended in scattered sections of 42 U.S.C.)

Watershed Protection and Flood Prevention Act of 1954, ch. 656, 68 Stat. 666 (codified as amended at 16 U.S.C. §§ 1001-1008 (1982))—"Public Law No. 566"

Weeks Act, ch. 186, 36 Stat. 961 (1911) (codified as amended at 16 U.S.C. §§ 480, 500, 513-519, 521, 552, 563 (1982))

Wetlands Loan Act of 1961, Pub. L. No. 87-383, 75 Stat. 813, 16 U.S.C. §§ 715k-3 through 715k-5 (1988))

Wetlands Loan Extension Act of 1976, Pub. L. No. 94-215, 94 Stat. 189 (current version at 16 U.S.C. §§ 668dd(b)(3), 715a, 715k-3, 715k-5, 718a, 718b, 718 (1982))

Wichita National Forest Game Preserve Act, ch. 137, 33 Stat. 614 (1905) (codified as amended at 16 U.S.C. §§ 684-686 (1982))

Wild and Scenic Rivers Act of 1968, Pub. L. No. 90-542, 82 Stat. 906 (codified as amended at 16 U.S.C. §§ 1271-1287 (1982))

Wilderness Act of 1964, Pub. L. No. 88-577, 78 Stat. 890 (codified as amended at 16 U.S.C. §§ 1131-1136 (1982))

Yellowstone Park Act, ch. 24, 17 Stat. 32 (1872)

APPENDIX C

Cases Cited

Adams v. N.C. Dep't of Natural and Economic Resources, 295 N.C. 683, 249 S.E.2d 402 (1978)

Avoyelles Sportsmen's League v. Marsh, 715 F.2d 897 (5th Cir. 1983)

Bailey v. Holland, 126 F.2d 317 (4th Cir. 1942)

Baldwin v. Montana Fish and Game Comm'n, 436 U.S. 371 (1978)

Borax Consol. v. City of Los Angeles, 296 U.S. 10 (1935)

California v. Bergland, 483 F. Supp. 465 (E.D. Cal. 1980), *modified sub nom.*, *California v. Block*, 690 F.2d 753 (9th Cir. 1982)

California v. Block, 690 F.2d 753 (9th Cir. 1982)

Calvert Cliffs' Coordinating Comm. v. Atomic Energy Comm'n, 449 F.2d 1109 (D.C. Cir. 1971), *cert. denied*, 404 U.S. 942 (1972)

Chicago v. Commonwealth Edison, 24 Ill. App. 2d 624, 321 N.E.2d 412 (1974)

Const. Indus. Ass'n v. City of Petaluma, 522 F.2d 897 (9th Cir. 1975), *cert. denied*, 424 U.S. 934 (1976)

Coyle v. Smith, 221 U.S. 559 (1911)

Dapson v. Daly, 257 Mass. 195, 153 N.E. 454 (1926)

Douglas v. Seacoast Products, 431 U.S. 265 (1977)

Environmental Defense Fund v. Corps of Engineers, 325 F. Supp. 728 (E.D. Ark. 1971)

Florida Rock Indus. v. United States, 8 Cl. Ct. 160 (1985); *Florida Rock Indus. v. United States*, 9 Cl. Ct. 285 (1985)

Foster-Fountain Packing Co. v. Haydel, 278 U.S. 1 (1929)

Geer v. Connecticut, 161 U.S. 519 (1896), *overruled*, *Hughes v. Oklahoma*, 441 U.S. 322 (1978)

Greene County Planning Bd. v. Federal Power Comm'n, 455 F.2d 412 (2d Cir. 1972), *cert. denied*, 409 U.S. 849 (1972)

Grimaud v. United States, 220 U.S. 506 (1911)

Hunt v. United States, 278 U.S. 96 (1928)

Kleppe v. New Mexico, 426 U.S. 529, *reh'g denied* (1976)

Lux v. Haggin, 69 Cal. 255, 4 P. 919, 10 P. 674 (1886)

McCarty v. Natural Carbonic Gas Co., 189 N.Y. 40, 82 N.E. 549 (1907)

McCready v. Virginia, 94 U.S. 391 (1876)

Manchester v. Massachusetts, 139 U.S. 240 (1890)

Marshall v. Barlow's, 436 U.S. 307 (1978)

Martin v. Waddell, 41 U.S. (16 Pet.) 234 (1842)

Missouri v. Holland, 258 F. 479 (W.D. Miss. 1919), *aff'd*, 252 U.S. 416 (1920)

National Wildlife Federation v. Hanson, 623 F. Supp. 1539 (E.D. N.C. 1985)

Natural Resources Defense Council v. Callaway, 524 F.2d 79 (2d Cir. 1975)

Natural Resources Defense Council v. Grant, 355 F. Supp. 280 (E.D. N.C. 1973)

Natural Resources Defense Council v. Morton, 388 F. Supp. 829 (D.D.C. 1974)

People v. Livingston, 8 Barb. 253 (1850)

Phelps v. Racey, 60 N.Y. 10 (1875)

Scenic Hudson Preservation Conference v. FPC, 354 F.2d 608 (2d Cir. 1965), *cert. denied*, 384 U.S. 941 (1966)*Secretary of the Interior v. California*, 464 U.S. 312 (1984)

Shively v. Bowlby, 152 U.S. 1 (1894)

Sierra Club v. Butz, 349 F. Supp. 934 (N.D. Cal. 1972)

Sierra Club v. Morton, 405 U.S. 727 (1972)

State v. Pinckney, 22 S.C. 484 (1885)

State v. Rodman, 58 Minn. 393, 59 N.W. 1098 (1894)

Tangier Sound Waterman's Ass'n v. Douglas, 541 F. Supp. 1287 (E.D. Va. 1982)

Territory v. Burgess, 8 Mont. 57, 19 P. 558 (1888)

Toomer v. Whitsell, 334 U.S. 385 (1948)

Tull v. United States, 481 U.S. 412 (1986), 107 S. Ct. 1831 (1987)

TVA v. Hill, 437 U.S. 153 (1978)

United States v. Butler, 297 U.S. 1 (1936)

United States v. California, 332 U.S. 19 (1947), *aff'd sub nom.*, 252 U.S. 416 (1919)

United States v. De Lapp, 258 F. 479 (W.D. Miss. 1919)

United States v. Light, 220 U.S. 523 (1911)

United States v. Louisiana, 339 U.S. 699 (1950)

United States v. Louisiana, 363 U.S. 1 (1960)

United States v. McCullagh, 221 F. 288 (D. Kan. 1915)

United States v. Maine, 420 U.S. 515 (1975)

United States v. Riverside Bayview Homes, 474 U.S. 121 (1985)

United States v. Samples, 258 F. 479 (E.D. Mo. 1919), *aff'd sub nom.*, 252 U.S. 416 (1919)

United States v. Shauver, 214 F. 154 (E.D. Ark. 1914), *diss'd*, 248 U.S. 594 (1919)

United States v. Students Challenging Regulatory Agency Procedures, 412 U.S. 669 (1973)

United States v. Texas, 339 U.S. 707 (1949), *modified*, 340 U.S. 848 (1950)

West Virginia Div. of the Izaak Walton League of America v. Butz, 522 F.2d 945 (4th Cir. 1975), *aff'g* 367 F. Supp. 422 (N.D. W. Va. 1973)

Woodward v. Price, 282 S.C. 366, 318 S.E.2d 584 (S.C. Ct. App. 1984)

Zabel v. Tabb, 430 F.2d 199 (5th Cir. 1970), *cert. denied*, 401 U.S. 910 (1971)

Zieske v. Butz, 406 F. Supp. 258 (D. Alaska 1975)

Index

Acadia National Park, 192
Acquisition era of federal land ownership,
    59–61
Acreage Reserve Program, 319
*Adams v. North Carolina Department of
    Natural and Economic Resources*, 455
Adasiak, A., 413–14
Ad Council, 162
Afognak Forest and Fish Culture Reserve,
    272–73
Agencies, federal:
    executive orders affecting, 40
    internal regulations, 40
    rules and regulations issued by, 39–40
    see also specific agencies
Agency for International Development,
    524–25
Agricultural Adjustment Act, 312, 313
Agricultural Adjustment Administration,
    312, 313
Agricultural Adjustment Agency, 313
Agricultural Appropriations Acts (1905
    and 1907), 126
Agricultural Conservation and Adjustment
    Administration, 313
Agricultural Conservation Program (ACP),
    313, 314, 321
Agricultural Research Service, 517
Agricultural Stabilization and
    Conservation Service (ASCS), 314,
    363, 404, 515–16
Agriculture and Consumer Protection Act,
    168
Alabama water law, 335
Alaska, limited entry to fisheries, 413
Alaska National Interest Lands
    Conservation Act, 273, 302–303
Alaska Native Claims Settlement Act, 202
Alaska natives, subsistence taking of
    waterfowl by, 242–43

Alaskan national parks, 202
Albright, Horace M., 185, 187–91, 194–
    95
Alligators, 262
Allin, Craig, 293–94, 301, 303
Allott, Gordon L., 485
American Fisheries Society, 400, 415
American Forestry Association, 117, 146,
    160
American Game Association, 225
American Petroleum Institute, 400
*Americans Outdoors: The Legacy, the
    Challenge*, 213
Anadromous fisheries program, 419
Anderson, Clinton P., 366
Anderson, Harold, 290
Animal Damage Control Act, 244
Anthony, Daniel R., 238
Antiquities Act (Legacy Act), 70–71,
    184–85, 191, 192, 251
    Amendments of 1981, 236
Appalachian forests, 127–34
Appalachian Regional Commission, 365
Army Corps of Engineers, U.S., 84, 85,
    132, 216, 363–64, 390, 478–79,
    485, 518
    coastal zone management and, 429,
        431, 457
    navigation and, 352, 375, 378–84
    water resource development and, *see*
        Water resource development,
        federal, Army Corps of Engineers
    wetlands and, 393–94, 395, 397–403,
        405–407, 408, 409
Aspinall, Wayne N., 483, 485
Assistant Secretaries Working Group on
    Water, 368
Association of American Agricultural
    Colleges and Experiments Station,
    310

Association of Land-Grant Colleges and State Universities, 308, 310, 315
Atlantic States Marine Fisheries Compact, 420
Atomic Energy Commission, 489, 493–95
Audubon Society, 143, 270
Avoyelles Sportsmen's League v. Marsh, 403

Baird, Spencer Fullerton, 414–15
Baker, Howard H., Jr., 257
Bald eagle, 262
Ballinger, Richard A., 135, 160
Bennett, Hugh Hammond, 306–12, 318
Bible, 3–5
Bill of Rights, 43–48, 49
   bear arms, right to, 43–44
   cruel and unusual punishment, 28, 46–47
   due process, 27, 28, 44–45, 46
   eminent domain, 44, 45
   search and seizure, 44
   state powers, 47–48
Biltmore Forest School, 123
Bison, 275–76
Black Bass Act, 236, 419
Black-footed ferret, 263–64
Board of Engineers for Rivers and Harbors, 356
Bob Marshall Wilderness, 291
Bobwhite Quail: Its Habits, Preservation, and Increase, The (Stoddard), 162
Borax Consolidated Ltd. v. City of Los Angeles, 327–28
Botanic Garden, U.S., 508–509
Brannan, Charles F., 314
Bridger, Jim, 181
Broome, Harvey, 290
Brown pelican, 262
Budgetary process, federal, 40–41
Bureau of Fisheries, 415
Bureau of Indian Affairs, 165, 319
Bureau of Land Management (BLM), 74–79, 82, 84, 85, 165, 233–34, 268, 521
   grazing lands, 74, 78, 79, 84, 90, 108, 110–11
   wilderness protection and, 303
   wildlife and, 224, 231, 264, 270
      northern spotted owl, 265, 270

Bureau of Oceans and International Environmental and Scientific Affairs, 523
Bureau of Outdoor Recreation, 208, 209–14, 475
Bureau of Reclamation, 72, 73, 85, 216, 520–21
   water reserve development, 351, 359, 369, 370
Burford (Gorsuch), Anne McGill, 499, 503
Bush, George, 502, 503
Bush administration, 109, 407–408, 504

Cabinet Council on National Resources and the Environment, 368
Cahn, Robert, 490
Cain, Stanley, 245
Caldwell, Lynton K., 354, 474, 481–82
Calendar of the U.S. House of Representatives and History of Legislation, 33, 34
California:
   outer continental shelf lands, 458–59
   water rights, 332
California condor, 263
California v. Block, 300–301
Calvert Cliffs' Coordinating Committee v. Atomic Energy Commission, 493–95
Canadian Convention, 238, 239
Canute, King, 13–14
Cape Cod National Seashore, 203
Carhart, Arthur H., 286, 287
Carson, Rachel, 473
Carta de Foresta, 19, 20, 23–24
Carter, Jimmy, 213, 256, 257, 299, 500–501
   water resource development and, 367, 369
Carver, John A., Jr., 497
Case law, 41–42, 43
Catlin, George, 285, 286
Cattle grazing, *see* Grazing and grazing lands
Chamber of Commerce, U.S., 400
Chesapeake Bay Foundation, 400
Chugach Forest Reserve, 273
Church, Frank, 299, 485
Citizens Committee on National Resources, 293

Citizens of Chincoteague for a Reasonable
  Wetlands Policy, 400
Citizen suits:
  under Clean Water Act, 388, 403
  under Endangered Species Act, 254
  against Forest Service, 138–43
  under NEPA, 492–93
Civilian Conservation Corps, 135, 194–
  97, 361
Civilian Conservation Service Act, 194
Civil War battlefields, 203
Clapp, Earle H., 156
Clark, William, 499
Clarke, Frederick J., 354
Clarke-McNary Act, 134, 155, 161, 168
Classification and Multiple Use Act, 76–
  77, 78
Clean Air Act, 51
Clean Water Act, 387–88
  wetlands and, 395–96, 403, 404
Clean Water Restoration Act, 431
Clement, Roland, 354
Cleveland, Grover, 119–20, 121
Clinton administration, 109
Coastal Energy Impact Program, 447–48,
  463–65
Coastal Plains Regional Commission, 365
Coastal States Organization, 450
Coastal zone, 428–69
  Coastal Zone Management Act, *see*
    Coastal Zone Management Act
  erosion of, 429
  intense use of, 428
  legislation prior to Coastal Zone
    Management Act, 429–33
  Marine Sciences Council, 432–33, 434
  national program for managing the,
    453–69
    accomplishments of, 468–69
    Coastal Energy Impact Program,
      447–48, 463–65
    constitutionality of, 455–57
    early implementation of Coastal Zone
      Management Act, 453–54
    federal agencies, participation of,
      457–58
    federal consistency, 458–63
    funding of, 467–68
    local opposition to, 454–57

  Reagan territorial sea proclamation
    and, 465–67
  Stratton Commission, 432, 433, 434–35
Coastal Zone Management Act, 81, 430,
  439–53
  administrative grants, 444–45
  amendments to, 446–53
  Coastal Energy Impact Program, 447–
    48, 463–65
  defining the coastal zone, 441
  efforts leading to, 429–39, 440
  estuarine sanctuaries, 445–46, 451
  federal consistency with state
    management programs, 441–43,
    446, 447, 459
  implementation of, *see* Coastal zone,
    national program for managing the
  interagency coordination and
    cooperation, 445
  management program development
    grants, 443–44
  policy enunciated in, 439–40
  public beaches and other public control
    areas, acquisition and access to,
    448–49
  research and training assistance, 448
Coast and Geodetic Survey, 102
Coast Guard, U.S., 523–24
Code of Federal Regulations, 40
Commerce clause of the Constitution, 35–
  36, 86, 235–36, 378, 382
Commercial Fisheries Research and
  Development Act, 250, 418–19
Committee on Multiple Uses of the
  Coastal Zone (CMUCZ), 434, 436
Committee on Natural Resources, 144
Committees of Congress, 32–33
  conference committee, 33
  functions of, 33
  hearings, 33
  major committee considering natural
    resources issues, 32
Common law, 48
Common property resources, 52–53
Congaree Swamp National Monument, 202
Congress:
  legislative process, *See* Legislative
    process
  powers of, 35–37, 38–39, 87

Congressional Record, 33, 34, 293, 376
Conness, John, 179
Conservation Foundation, 431
Conservation Reserve Program (CRP),
    168–69, 319, 320, 321
Constitution, U.S., 27–49
    Bill of Rights, *see* Bill of Rights
    budgetary process and, 40–41
    commerce clause, 35–36, 86, 235–36,
        378, 382
    Congressional powers, 35–37, 38–39,
        87
    defense, power to provide for, 37, 86
    executive branch, *see* Executive branch of
        the federal government
    executive orders, 40
    federal property clause, 36, 87
    general welfare provision, 37, 86
    judicial branch, *see* Judicial branch
    legislative branch, 29–37, 87
    legislative process, *see* Legislative
        process
    personnel matters, 38–39
    rules and regulations of executive
        branch, 39–40
    states, powers reserved to, 29
    as supreme law, 29
    treaty powers, 38, 86, 236–43
Consultation and confrontation era of
        federal land ownership, 75–83
Continental shelf, international law of,
    338–40, 343–44, 345, 349
Convention for Protection of Migratory
    Birds, 238, 239
Convention on International Trade in
    Endangered Species of Wild Fauna
    and Flora (CITES), 252, 253
Convention on the Law of the Sea,
    344–46
Cook, Charles W., 181
Coolidge, Calvin, 204
Cooperative Agricultural Extension
    Service, 306, 310, 311, 313, 517
Cooperative Forestry Assistance Act, 155,
    163, 168
Cooperative State Research Service, 517
Cotton, Norris, 433
Council of Conservationists, 293
Council of Economic Advisors, 479, 513

Council on Environmental Quality (CEQ),
    297, 299, 367, 390, 452, 492,
    497–98
    creation of, 476, 481
    NEPA provisions, 488–89
    Reagan administration, 498–99, 501
    regulations interpreting NEPA, 490–
        91, 496
Court system, federal, 41, 42–43
Coville, Fredrick V., 92, 93
Crafts, Edward C., 209, 212
Creative Act, 91, 272, 274
Cropland Adjustment Program,
    319–20
Cruel and unusual punishment, 28, 46
Culhane, Paul J., 59, 76, 82, 83
Custodial management era of federal land
    ownership, 72–75

Daddario, Emilio, 480
Damages for violation of environmental
    law, 46
Dams, *see* Water resource development,
    federal; Water resource protection
Darling, J.N., 226, 248
Dawes, Henry, 414
Delaware River Basin Compact, 365
Delineation Manual, 405–408
Department of Agriculture, U.S., 36, 72,
    84, 308, 484, 514–17
    Division of Forestry, 117, 124, 125,
        128, 155, 156
    wilderness protection and, 299
    *see also specific agencies of the Department of
        Agriculture, e.g.* Forest Service; Soil
        Conservation Service
Department of Commerce, 517–18
Department of Defense, U.S., 72, 85, 276,
    457, 485, 518
Department of Housing and Urban
    Development, 519
Department of the Interior, U.S., 72, 78,
    84, 94–95, 132, 135, 162, 308,
    519–21
    coastal zone management program and,
        457
    Division of Grazing, 106–108
    northern spotted owl controversy and,
        267–70

Department of the Interior (*continued*)
outer continental shelf lands, leasing of, 458–63
Soil Conservation Service and, 363
wildlife policy, 230–31
see also specific agencies of the Department of the Interior
Department of Justice, U.S., 42, 466, 522–23
Department of State, 523
Department of Transportation, 523–24
Department of Transportation Act, 477–78
Dewey, Thomas E., 314
Dingell, John D., 430–31, 479, 480–81, 483, 485
Dingell-Johnson Act, 249–50, 416–18
Disposal era of federal land ownership, 61–68
Doane, Gustavus C., 181
Due process, 21, 27, 44–45, 46, 48–49
Dusky seaside sparrow, 264

Earth Day 1970, 491
Eastern Wilderness Act, 81, 124, 137, 298, 369
Economic and Environmental Principles and Guidelines for Water and Related Land Resource Implementation Studies, 370
Eisenhower, Dwight D., 200
Elk refuge, 276–77
Emergency Wetland Resources Act, 490
Emerson, Ralph Waldo, 178
Eminent domain, 44, 45
Employment Act, 479
Endangered species, *see* Rare, threatened, and endangered species
Endangered Species Act, 47, 81, 253, 260
Amendments of 1978, 255–56
Endangered Species Committee, 255–56, 266, 268–69
Endangered Species Conservation Act, 419
Endangered Species Preservation Act:
of 1966, 477
of 1969, 251–52
Energy and Water Development Appropriations Act, 408

Environmental Advisory Board, 354–55
Environmental Defense Fund, 400
Environmental Defense Fund v. Corps of Engineers, 496
Environmental impact statements (EISs), 82, 137, 356, 363, 490, 491–92, 495
Council on Environmental Quality guidelines for, 490–91, 496
NEPA provision, 481, 487–88
purpose of, 496–97
RARE II, 300–301
on spotted owl standards, 265
Environmental policy, national, 472–504
Bush administration, 504
legislative history, 477–486
Reagan administration, 498–504
setting for, 472–77
mood of the 1960s, 473–477
see also National Environmental Policy Act
Environmental Protection Agency (EPA), 38, 245, 356, 388, 502–503, 525
administration of, 51, 499–501, 503
funding of, 500–501
pollution control responsibilities, 387, 390, 403
wetlands and, 393, 394, 403, 405–408
Environmental Quality Improvement Act, 489
Equal protection, 28, 49–50
Etnier, David, 254
Everglades National Park, 190
Exclusive economic zones (EEZ), 345, 349, 424
Executive branch of the federal government, 37–41, 511–25
budgetary process, 40–41
personnel matters, 38–39
rules and regulations, 39–40
treaty powers, *see* Treaties
Executive Office of the President, 512
Executive orders, 40
Extinction of species, 251
prevention of, *see* Rare, threatened, and endangered species

Farm Act of 1985, *see* Food Security Act
Farm Bureau, 310, 311, 313, 314

Farmers Home Administration, 363, 404, 514–15
Fechner, Robert, 194
Federal-Aid Highway Act, 477–78
Federal Aid in Fish Restoration Act, 249–50
Federal Aviation Administration, 524
Federal Crop Insurance Corporation, 404
Federal Emergency Administration of Public Works (PWA), 307
Federal Emergency Management Act, 452
Federal Emergency Relief Administration (FERA), 308
Federal Energy Administration, 457
Federal government, organization of, 508–25
Federal Highway Administration, 524
Federal Land Policy and Management Act (FLPMA), 78–79, 84, 234, 303
Federal Power Commission, 495
Federal Register, 39, 40, 258, 491
Federal Water Pollution Control Act, 142, 384–85, 452, 453
  Amendments of 1965, 477
  Amendments of 1972, 47, 385–86, 389, 390
    standing to sue under, 41
    wetlands and section 404, 393–94, 398, 405–407
Federal Water Pollution Control Administration, 385, 431, 435
Federal Water Project Recreation Act, 211
Fee simple ownership, 61
Fernow, Bernhard Eduard, 117, 122–23, 124
Fire protection for forests, 158–67
Fish and Wildlife Act, 415
Fish and Wildlife Conservation Act, 250, 356
Fish and Wildlife Coordination Act, 378, 430, 478–79
Fish and Wildlife Service, U.S., 363, 390, 415, 416, 419, 420, 520
  Army Corps of Engineers and, relations with, 378–79
  creation of, 72, 415
  Endangered Species Act and, 254, 258, 260, 263, 264, 265, 266
  holdings of, 84, 85
  legislation affecting, 76, 80, 415

National Estuary Study, 435
National Wetland Inventory, 396, 405, 406, 409
  wetlands purchases by, 409
  wilderness preservation and, 304
  wildlife management, 233, 242, 273, 277, 279
    animal control, 243, 246
    research, 248–50
Fish Commission, U.S., 415
Fisheries, 412–26
  federal aid to the states, 416–19
  federal fisheries agencies, history of, 414–16
  Fish and Wildlife Service, *see* Fish and Wildlife Service, U.S.
  historical background, 412–16
  limited entry, approach to, 413
  multilateral international treaties, 425–26
  National Marine Fisheries Service, 415, 416
  regulatory functions, 419–26
    domestic, 419–24
    international, 424–26
  state control, degree of, 413
Fisherman's Protective Act, Pelly Amendment to, 424–25
Fishery Conservation and Management Act, 419, 421–24, 467
  Packwood Amendment to, 425
Fishing, *see* Fisheries; Wildlife
Fishing rights on the high seas, 340–43
Flood Control Act, 216, 359, 362
Floodplains, 81
Florida, 400
  water law, 335, 336
Florida Rock Industries v. United States, 402–403
Folsom, David E., 181
Food Security Act, 168, 320, 321, 404, 405, 406
Ford, Henry, 360
Ford administration, 151, 316, 425, 498, 500–501
Forest and Rangeland Renewable Resources Planning Act (RPA), 144–48, 149–52, 157, 298, 299
Forest Commission, 116, 117

Forest Lieu Lands Act, 126–27
Forest Management Act (Organic Act),
  119, 120–22, 140–43
  amendment of, 148
Forest Reserve Act, 70, 117–18
Forestry Incentives Program, 155, 168
Forests, 72, 114–73
  Carta de Foresta, 19, 20, 23–24
  clear-cutting, 137–43, 149, 171, 233
  Congressional authority, 36, 127, 131
  desires of forest owners, 170–71
  Division of Forestry of Department of
    Agriculture, 117, 124, 125
  Forest Laws, 15–18, 24
  Forest Service, *see* Forest Service
  Magna Carta, 22–23
  management of outside national forests,
    155–69
    cooperative research, 156–58
    fire protection, 158–67
    public education, 162–63
    reforestation, 167–69
  multiple use and sustained-yield issue,
    136–37, 169–70
  National Forest System, *see* National
    Forest System
  outdoor recreation and, 214–16
  persistent problems, 169–73
  reserves, 114–55
    Agricultural Appropriations Acts,
      126
    the beginnings of, 116–17
    debate over use of, 118, 122
    development of policy for
      administration and management
      of, 119
    in the East, 127–35
    Forest Management Act (Organic
      Act), 120–22, 129, 140–43, 148
    funds for managing, 126, 127
    Multiple-Use Sustained Yield Act,
      136–37
    for naval purposes, 114–16
    1970s legislation and its effects,
      144–55
    Transfer Act, 125–26
  Royal Forests, 14–15, 18, 25
  secretary of interior's powers, 121
  "the system," 171–73

Forest Service, 72, 78, 82, 84, 85, 126,
  127, 135, 172–73, 319, 363,
  516
  eastern forest reserves and, 131
  Forest and Rangeland Renewable
    Resources Planning Act and, 144–
    48, 149–52
  grazing lands, 79, 84, 90, 93–94, 95,
    104, 106–108, 109–10
  legislation defining role of, 76, 126,
    136–37
  management of forests outside national
    forests, 155–69
  National Forest Management Act and,
    148–49, 152–54
  opposition to forestry practices of, 137–
    43
  outdoor recreation and, 214–16
  planning process, 149–55
  wilderness and, 286–87, 291,
    296–302
    RARE I, 297–98
    RARE II, 298–301
  wildlife and, 233, 242, 264, 273
    endangered species, 265, 266–67
Foster, Charles H. W., 354
Frank, Bernard, 290
Freedom of Information Act, 491
Friends of the Earth, 144, 146, 363
Frome, Michael, 158
Frye, William P., 375–76

Game management, *see* National Wildlife
  Refuge System; Wildlife
Game Management (Leopold), 223, 225
Garmatz, Edward A., 485
Geer v. Connecticut, 235–36
General Accounting Office (GAO), 166,
  255, 321, 454, 458, 509
General Land Office (GLO), 74, 93, 102,
  125
Geneva Conference on the Law of the Sea,
  First, 337, 424
  continental shelf, 338–40
  high seas, 340
  living resources on the high seas, 340–
    43, 424
  territorial sea and contiguous zone,
    337–38

Geological Survey, U.S., 102–104, 128, 132, 181, 185, 359, 520
  Irrigation Survey, 103, 104
Gila National Forest, 225, 287
Gilliam, Harold, 354
Gilligan, James P., 291–93
Giltmier, James W., 146
Golden eagle, 262
Government Printing Office, 509
Grand Canyon National Park, 276
Grant, Ulysses S., 181, 183
Grazing and grazing lands, 74, 78, 84, 90–111
  Bureau of Land Management and, *see* Bureau of Land Management, grazing lands
  cattle drives of the 1800s, 90–91
  competition between cattle and sheep, 90–91
  Forest Service and, *see* Forest Service, grazing lands
  grazing fees, 79–80, 107–109
  history of, 90–190
  legislation, 91–92, 104–106
  permits, 79–80, 92–95, 104–107
  Taylor Grazing Act, 104–106
Great Smoky Mountains National Park, 193, 194
Greeley, William, 160, 167
Greene County Planning Board v. Federal Power Commission, 495
Guadelupe Mountains National Park, 202
Gulf States Marine Fisheries Compact, 420
Harbor Maintenance Trust Fund, 372
Harrison, Benjamin, 118, 272–73
Harsha, William, 486
Hartzog, George, 202
Hawley, Ralph C., 170–71
Hayden, Ferdinand Vandeveer, 181
Heritage Conservation and Recreation Service, 213
Hickel, Walter J., 212
Hickey, Joseph, 226
High seas, international law of, 340, 348
  living resources on the, 340–43, 424
Hill, Louis W., 190
Historical background of protection of renewable resources:
  Bible, 3–5

Constitution, U.S., *see* Constitution, U.S.
Constitutions of original thirteen states, 27–28
  England before the Magna Carta, 13–19
  Magna Carta and Carta de Foresta, 19, 20, 23–24, 27, 28
  Roman law, 5–13
Historic preservation, 70–71
Historic Sites Act, 203
Hofe, G. Douglas, Jr., 212
Hollings, Ernest, 464
Holmes, Joseph A., 123–24
Holmes, Oliver Wendell, 241
Homesteading, 66–67, 73, 74, 104–105, 106
Hoover, Herbert, 360
Hoover Commission on Organization of the Executive Branch, 358
House of Representative, U.S., *see* Legislative process
Humphrey, Hubert, 146, 149, 151, 293
Hunting, *see* National Wildlife Refuge System; Wildlife
Hydric Soils of the United States, 406

Ickes, Harold, 307
Inland Waterways Transportation System, 372
Intensive management era of federal land ownership, 75
Inter-Agency Committee on Water Resources, 366
Interagency Spotted Owl Scientific Committee (ISC), 265–66, 269
Interest groups, *see* Public participation
Interjurisdictional Fisheries Act, 419
International Convention for the Regulation of Whaling (IWC), 425
International Law Commission (ILC), 336
International Sea-Bed Authority, 345
International water law, *see* Water law, international
Interstate commerce, *see* Commerce clause of the Constitution
Interstate Commerce Commission, 51
Irrigation Survey, 103, 104

Izaak Walton League of America, 138,
143, 276–77, 431

Jackson, William Henry, 181, 182, 213,
439, 480, 481, 482
Jefferson, Thomas, 58
Johnson administration, 213, 294, 475–
77
Jones, Walter, 348
Jordan, Leonard B., 485
Judeo-Christian tradition, 3–5
Judicial branch, 41–43, 510–11
activist environmental role of, 83
case law, 41–42, 43
Constitutional powers, 41
court system, 41, 42–43
prosecution of natural resource cases,
42–43
Julian, William, 275
Justinian's Codification, 5–6

Karlton, Lawrence K., 300
Kelly, Edna F., 430
Kennedy, John F., 209, 366, 475
King, Clarence, 102–103
Kodiak National Wildlife Refuge, 273
Koh, Tommy, 346

Lacey, John F., 184, 185, 238
Lacey Act (Antiquities Act), 70–71, 184–
85, 191, 192, 236, 251
Amendments of 1981, 236
Land and Water Conservation Fund, 202,
209–10, 214, 251, 261, 278, 279
Land and Water Conservation Fund Act,
81, 84, 209, 278–79, 477
Land use planning, national, 315–17
Lane, Franklin K., 187–88, 189–90
Langford, Nathanial Pitt, 181, 183
Laws, process of creating and passing, *see*
Legislative process
League of Conservation Voters, 503
League of Women Voters, 431
Legislative process:
Article 1 on the Constitution, 29–30
committees of congress, *see* Committees
of Congress
origination of the legislation, 31
Presidential actions, 34

publication and numbering of laws,
34–35
Lennon, Alton A., 433, 437–38
Leopold, A. Starker, 232, 245
Leopold, Aldo, 223, 224–29, 248, 285,
294, 473
committee on animal control headed by,
244–45
wilderness preservation and, 286, 287,
288, 290
Library of Congress, 509–10
Living Wilderness, The (Gilligan), 293
Locke, John, 58
"Log Cabin Bill" of 1841, 65–66
Louisiana Landowners Association, 403
Louisiana water law, 333, 335
Louisiana Wildlife Federation, 400
Lujan, Manuel, 267–68, 269–70
Lux v. Haggin, 328–29

MacKaye, Benton, 290
McArdle, Richard E., 294
McCabe, Robert A., 226
McDonald, Gordon J. F., 490
McGuire, John R., 146, 151
McIntire-Stennis Act, 155, 156–57
McKinley, William, 120
McLean, George P., 238
McSweeney-McNary Act, 155, 156
Magna Carta, 13, 19–25, 27, 28, 46, 49
events preceding the, 13–19
Magnuson, Warren G., 433, 436, 439,
442
Mammoth Cave National Park, 193
Managing the Environment, 480
Marine Mammal Protection Act, 81, 252–
53
Marine Resources and Engineering
Development Act, 432, 434
Marine Sciences Council, 432–33, 434,
435–36
Marsh, George Perkins, 69, 178, 473
Marshall, Robert B., 185, 226, 285, 288–
91, 294, 301–302, 473
Mather, Stephen T., 185, 186, 187–91,
204
Michigan, 395–96, 400
Mid-Atlantic Developers Association, 400
Migratory Bird Act, 238

Migratory Bird Conservation Act, 249, 277
Migratory Bird Conservation Fund, 409
Migratory Bird Hunting Stamp Act, 81, 278
Migratory Bird Treaty, 238
Migratory Bird Treaty Act, 241–42, 270, 277
Miller, Adolph C., 188
Minerals Management Service, 521
Mississippi River Commission, 356
Mississippi water law, 335
Missouri v. Holland, 239–41
Monongahela National Forest, 131, 137–43
Moran, Thomas, 181
Morton, Rogers C. B., 316, 430
Mosher, Charles A., 433
Muir, John, 124, 178, 183, 188, 285
Multiple-Use Sustained Yield Act, 136–37, 142, 215, 232, 296
  amendments to, 293
Muscle Shoals project, 360
Muskie, Edmund, 482–83

National Association of Conservation Districts, 316, 363
National Association of State Foresters, 162, 165
National Bison Range, 276
National Cattlemen's Association, 400
National Council on Marine Resources and Engineering Development, 80, 484
National Defense Act, 360
National Elk Refuge, 276
National environmental policy, *see* Environmental policy, national
National Environmental Policy Act (NEPA), 45, 81–82, 83, 270, 298, 363, 369, 382, 486–90
  basic elements of, 477
  conference committee deliberations, 485–86
  Council on Environmental Quality, *see* Council on Environmental Quality
  efforts leading to, 477–86
  environmental impact statements, *see* Environmental impact statements
  evaluation of effectiveness of, 496–98
  federal regulations implementing, 490–91
  forests and, 142, 151, 157
  litigation testing, 492–96
  provisions of, 486–89
  statement of purpose of, 487
National Flood Insurance Program, 452
National Forest Commission, 119
National Forest Management Act (NFMA), 144, 148–49, 152–54, 298
National Forest Reservation Commission, 132, 133, 134
National Forest System, 36, 126, 135
  outdoor recreation and, 214–16
  wildlife and, 232–33
  see also Forests
National Historic Preservation Act, 203
National land use planning, 315–17
National List of Plant Species That Occur on Wetland, 406
National Marine Fisheries Service, 415, 416, 419
National Oceanic and Atmospheric Administration (NOAA), 76, 258, 415, 435, 437, 518
  coastal zone management and, 435, 437, 438, 445, 448, 454, 458
National Ocean Survey, 328
National Parks Association, 293
National Park Service, 72, 73, 82, 84, 85, 124, 135, 319, 361, 519–20
  forest fire management and, 164, 165, 166
  funding of, 198–201
  outdoor recreation and, 206–207, 212, 213
  wilderness protection and, 286, 302–303
  wildlife management and, 231–32, 277
  see also National park system; Outdoor recreation
National Park Service Organic Act, 185–86, 188, 189, 204
National park system, 36, 178–204
  Civilian Conservation Corps and, 194–97
  eastern national parks, 191–94
  the first national park, 178–84

National park system (*continued*)
Mission 66, 197–201
modern national park system, 202–204
movement toward, 184–88
organization of, 188
purpose of national parks, 186
railroads and, 186–87
regulations, 189–90
see also individual parks
National Rifle Association, 143–44
National Technical Information Service,
518
National Trails System Act, 211
National Wilderness Preservation System,
301, 302, 303, 304
National Wildlife Federation, 143, 293,
400
National Wildlife Federation v. Hanson, 394
National Wildlife Refuge System, 216,
261, 262, 272–79, 302, 303
currently, 278–79
early development of, 272–77
migratory bird emphasis, 277–78
Natural Resources Defense Council v.
Callaway, 394
Natural Resources Defense Council v. Grant,
363–64
Natural Resources Defense Council v. Morton,
496
Navigation, 372
Army Corps of Engineers projects, 352,
375, 378–84
Magna Carta, 20, 21–22
nonfederal interests, cost sharing by, 371
Roman law, 12–13
water resource protection, *see* Water
resource protection
Nedzi, Lucien N., 481
Nelson, Dr. E. W., 243
Nelson, Gaylord A., 485
Nelson, Thomas C., 139
New York Act of 1885, 117
New York Zoological Society, 275
Niagara Falls, 180
Nixon administration, 146–47, 204,
212, 213, 245, 297, 315–16, 393,
477
coastal zone management and, 436,
437, 439

Council on Environmental Quality and,
490, 492
NEPA and, 483–85, 492, 497–98
Norris, George, 360
North Carolina, 455–57
Northern spotted owl controversy,
264–72
Northwest Forest Resource Council, 270
Nuisance, 51–52

Oberholtzer, Ernest, 290
Occupational Safety and Health Act
(OSHA), 44
Office of Management and Budget (OMB),
151, 356, 367, 369, 389, 459,
503, 512–13
Office of Science and Technology Policy,
485, 513–14
Office of Surface Mining Reclamation and
Enforcement, 521
Office of Technology Assessment, 154–55,
396
Olmsted, Frederick Law, 179–80
Oregon and California Railroad, 270
Osborn, Fairfield, 473
Ottinger, Richard L., 430
Outdoor recreation, 204–18, 474–75
attempts at creating a national policy
for, 204–208
Bureau of Outdoor Recreation and, 208,
209–14
Forest Service and, 214–16
funding of, 217–18
management of, 217–18
National Park Service and, 206–207,
212, 213
on other federal lands, 216
Outdoor Recreation Resources Review
Commission and, 208
"Outdoor Recreation: A Legacy for
America," 213
Outdoor Recreation for America, 475
Outdoor Recreation Programs Act,
209
Outdoor Recreation Resources Review
Commission (ORRRC), 208, 474,
475
Outer continental shelf (OCS) lands,
leasing of, 458–63

Outer Continental Shelf Lands Act, 336–37, 467
Ozark National Scenic Riverways, 203

Pacific Legal Foundation, 400
Pacific States Marine Fisheries Commission, 420
Park, Parkway, and Recreation Area Study Act, 206–207
Pelican Island National Wildlife Refuge, 251, 273–75
Penalties for violation of environmental law, 46–47
    water pollution statutes, 387–88
Peregrine falcon, 262–63
Peterson, William, 181
Pettigrew, Richard F., 376
Pinchot, Gifford, 74, 93, 94, 95, 119, 121, 122–27, 128, 129, 132, 135, 157–58, 160, 167, 180, 187, 214
    as author, 156
    philosophy of, 124, 286–87
Pisgah National Forest, 124, 134, 233
Pittman, Key, 248–49
Pittman-Robertson Act, 249
Police power of states, 45, 47–48, 51, 235, 382
Policy for the Environment, 480
Pollution:
    air, 51
    water, *see* Water pollution control
Pooler, Frank, 287
Potter, Albert F., 94, 95
Pough, Richard H., 354
Powell, John Wesley, 95–104, 105, 106, 359
Practice of Silviculture, The (Hawley), 170–71
Preble, E. A., 276
Predatory animals, control of, 243–50
Preemption, principle of, 65–66
Presidency, 511–12
President's Commission on Americans Outdoors, 213–14, 217
President's Commission on Marine Science Engineering and Resources, 343–44
President's Committee on Wildlife Restoration, 226

"Problem of the Wilderness, The," 289
Production and Marketing Administration, 313, 314
Property clause of the Constitution, 36, 87
Public domain, 55–87
    after the Continental Congress of 1777, 57
    boundaries of original states, 57
    colonial period, 56–57
    Constitutional authority to hold and manage land, 86–87
    early land tenure systems, 55–57
    federal land managers, 84–87
    federal landownership, eras of, 58–83
        acquisition, 59–61
        consultation and confrontation, 75–83
        custodial management, 72–75
        disposal, 61–68
        reservation, 68–72
    ideology of land ownership, 58
    intensive management, 75
Public Land Law Review Commission, 72, 76, 77–78
Public land sales, 64–65
Public land surveys, 63–64
Public participation in agency policy, 82–83
Public Rangelands Improvement Act (PRIA), 108–109
Public trust doctrine, 53

Railroads, 186–87
Randolph, Jennings, 149
Rare, threatened, and endangered species, 250–72
    early efforts to protect, 251–53
    Endangered Species Program, 258–64
    spotted owl controversy, 264–72
    Tellico Dam and the snail darter, 253–58
Rawlins, Joseph L., 353
Reagan administration, 38, 41, 72, 84, 213, 346, 348, 391, 450
    environmental policy, 498–504
    territorial sea proclamation, 348, 465–67
    water resources development policy, 367–68, 370

Reclamation Act, 359
Recreation, *see* Outdoor recreation
Recreation Advisory Council, 209
"Recreation Imperative, The," 212–13
Reed, Nathaniel, 246, 363
Refuge Recreation Act, 216, 279
Refuse Act, 142, 383, 384, 393
Regulations and rules, federal, 39–40
Report on the Lands of the Arid Region of the United States (Powell), 95, 100–102
Research:
  forestry, 156–58
  wildlife, 248–50
Reservation era of federal land ownership, 68–72
Reservoirs, Army Corps of Engineers and, 352–55
Resettlement Administration, 318–19
Resource Conservation and Recovery Act (RCRA), 44
Resource Development Council for Alaska, 400
Rhode Island water law, 335
River basins and water resource administration, 364–65
Rivers and Harbors Act of 1968, 429
Rivers and Harbors Acts of 1880 and 1881, 353
Rivers and Harbors Act of 1899, 375–78, 379, 380, 381, 384, 393, 429, 430
Robertson, A. Willis, 248–49
Robertson, F. Dale, 216
Rockefeller, John D., 192
Rockefeller, John D., Jr., 193
Rockefeller, Laurance S., 208, 475, 476, 484
Roman law, 5–13
  Justinian's Code, 5–6
  land, 8–12, 52
  Law of Things (Property), 6–8
  navigation, 12–13
Roosevelt, Franklin D., 194, 206, 226, 248, 307, 308, 311
  water resource development and, 358, 359–60, 364
Roosevelt, Theodore, 122, 125, 126, 127, 129, 131, 232, 273–75
Ruckelshaus, William, 38, 499, 503

Rules and regulations, federal, 39–40
Ryan, William F., 430

Sagebrush Rebellion, 72, 84
Sales of public lands, 64–65
Sand County Almanac, A (Leopold), 227–28, 229
Sargent, Charles Sprague, 124, 180
Saylor, John P., 299, 485
Scenic Hudson, 400
Schenck, Carl A., 123
Schultz, Charles, 256
Scientific Monthly, 289
Sears, Paul, 473
Secretary of the Interior v. California, 460–63
Senate, U.S., *see* Legislative process
Sequoia National Park, 190
Sheep grazing, *see* Grazing and grazing lands
Shenandoah National Park, 193
Shipstead-Nolan Act, 287
Shiras, George, III, 237, 238
Shively v. Bowlby, 325–27
Sierra Club, 51, 124, 138, 143, 146, 285, 290, 293, 298, 400
Sikes Act, 234
Smith, Adam, 58
Smith, Hoke, 92, 119
Smith-Lever Act, 306, 310
Snail darter and Tellico Dam Project, 253–58
Soil and Water Resources Conservation Act, 322
Soil Bank Act, 319
Soil conservation, 306–22
  Bennett's 1934 proposal for, 307–309, 318
  conflict among government agencies over, 308–14
  national land use planning, proposals for, 315–17
  Soil Conservation Act, 308–309, 310
  soil conservation districts, 310–12
  Soil Conservation Service, *see* Soil Conservation Service
Soil Conservation (Bennett), 307
Soil Conservation Act, 308–309
Soil Conservation and Domestic Allotment Act, 3

Soil Conservation Service (SCS), 110, 308–22, 516–17
  achievements of, 317–22
    land banking, 318–22
    soil classification and survey, 317–18
    soil conservation practices, 321–22
    water resource development and, 351, 362–64
    wetlands and, 404–405, 406
Soil Conservation Society of America, 316
"Soil Erosion: A National Menace," 309
Soil Erosion Service, 307–10
Southern Appalachian National Parks Commission, 192–93
Sport Fishing Institute, 431
Squatter's rights, 65–66
Standard Soil Conservation Districts Law, A, 310–11
Standing to sue, 48, 50–51
  under NEPA, 492–93
States, powers of the, 27, 29, 45, 47–48
  interstate commerce and, 36, 235–36
  police power, 45, 47–48, 51, 235, 382
Statutes at Large, 34
Stoddard, Charles H., 76, 354–55
Stoddard, Herbert L., 162
Stratton Commission, 423, 433, 434–35, 436, 437, 442
Submerged Lands Act, 333–34, 381, 382, 467
Supreme Court, U.S., 41, 42–43, 51, 70, 93–94, 313, 510
  leasing of outer continental shelf lands and Coastal Zone Management Act, 460–63
  water rights decisions, 332, 335
  wetlands regulation and, 400–402, 404
  wildlife decisions, 230, 231, 235–36, 239–41
Surveys of public land, 63–64
Susquehanna River Basin Compact, 365

Tabb, R. H., 379–80
Taft, William Howard, 127, 160, 238
Taking of property, 45
Taylor Grazing Act, 104–106, 233–34
Technical Committee on Recreation, 207
Tellico Dam Project, 253–58

Tennessee Valley Authority (TVA), 216, 253–58, 310
  creation of, 360
  water resource development and, 351, 359–62, 365
Tennessee Valley Authority Act, 360
Tenzer, Herbert, 430
Territorial sea and contiguous zone, international law of, 337–38, 343, 348–49, 465–67
Texas water law, 332, 335, 336
Theodore Roosevelt National Park, 202
Thomas, Jack Ward, 265
Thompson, Frank, Jr., 430
Thoreau, Henry David, 178, 285
Threatened species, *see* Rare, threatened, and endangered species
Tidelands, 324–28, 347
Tongass National Forest, 143, 173
Torts, 50
Towell, William E., 146
Train, Russell E., 434, 442–43, 476, 484, 490
Transfer Act of 1905, 125–26
Treaties:
  Constitutional power to make, 38, 86, 236–43
    multilateral fisheries treaties, 425–26
  see also individual treaties
Trespass, 52
Trials, local, 28
  see also Due process
Trout Unlimited, 144
Truman, Harry S., 314, 334–35, 336, 421, 424
Trustees for Conservation, 293
Tucker Act, 401, 402
Tugwell, Rexford, 307
Tull, Edward, 404

Udall, Stewart, 245
U.S. Department of . . ., *see* Department of . . ., U.S.
United States Code, 34, 35
United States Code Service, 35
United States v. Butler, 313
United States v. California, 332
United States v. Louisiana, 332, 333, 335

United States v. Riverside Bayview Homes,
   397–403
United States v. Shauver, 238, 239
United States v. Texas, 332

Vogt, William, 473
Vucanovich, Barbara, 213–14

Wallop, Malcolm, 214
Wallop-Breaux Act, 417–18
Warren, Francis E., 354
Washburn, Henry Dana, 181
Waste treatment management, 388–90,
   391, 392
Water law, 324–49
   common law riparian system, 328–30,
     331
   domestic littoral and maritime law,
     332–36
   Eastern water law, 328–30
   international, 336–49
     continental shelf, 338–40, 343–44,
       345, 349
     critical maritime zones and
       boundaries, 346–49
     high seas, 340, 348
     living resources on the high seas,
       340–43, 424
     Outer Continental Shelf Lands Act,
       336–37
     progress since First Geneva
       Conference, 343–46
     territorial sea and contiguous zone,
       337–38, 343, 348–49, 465–67
   prior appropriation, law of, 330–31
   tidelands, 324–28, 347
   transportation over waters, 328
   usufractory rights, 328
   waters running in streams, 328
   Western water law, 330–31
   see also Water resource development,
     federal; Water resource protection
Water pollution control, 384–92
   Clean Water Act, 387–88
   enforcement of statutes, 387–88
   EPA and, 385, 387, 390
   Federal Water Pollution Control Act
     and Amendments, 384–86, 389,
     390

   incentives, 388–89
   nonpoint source management, 389–90,
     391, 392
   NPDES permits, 387
   penalties for violation of statutes, 387–
     88
   resource classification and standards,
     386–87
   waste treatment management, 388–90,
     391, 392
   Water Quality Act, 385, 390–92
Water Quality Act, 385, 390–92
Water resource development, federal, 351–
   72
   Army Corps of Engineers, 351–59, 361,
     362–63, 369
   navigation, 352
   paths to successful Corps project,
     355–59
   politics and, 357–59
   reservoirs, 352–55
   benefit-cost analysis, 366–68, 370
   Bureau of Reclamation, 359, 369, 370
   the future for, 368–72
   river basin concept, 364–65
   Soil Conservation Service, 351, 362–64
   Tennessee Valley Authority, 351, 359–
     62, 365
   see also Water law; Water resource
     protection
Water resource protection, 375–409
   navigation, 375–84
     Army Corps of Engineers and, 375,
       378–84
     Rivers and Harbors Act, 375–78,
       379, 380, 381
     Zabel v. Tabb, 379–82
   water pollution control, *see* Water
     pollution control
   wetlands, *see* Wetlands
   see also Water law; Water resource
     development
Water Resources Council (WRC), 80,
   364–65, 366, 367–68
Water Resources Development Act, 370–
   72
Water Resources Planning Act, 265, 366
Watershed Protection and Flood
   Protection Act, 362

Waterways Trust Fund, 372
Watt, James, 38, 367, 499
Webster, Daniel, 62
Weekly Compilation of Presidential Documents, 34, 40
Weeks, John W., 238
Weeks Act, 132, 155, 160
Wetlands, 81
  Clean Water Act, 395–96
  definition of, 404
  Emergency Wetland Resources Act, 409
  jurisdictional wetlands, delineation of, 405–406, 407–408
  litigation, 397–404
  OTA assessment, 396
  regulatory definitions, 397
  Section 404 of Federal Water Pollution Control Act Amendments of 1972, 393–94, 398, 405–407
  Soil Conservation Service involvement, 404–405, 406
Wetlands Loan Act, 278, 409
Wetlands: Their Use and Regulation, 396
Whitaker, John, 474, 497–98
White House Conference on Conservation of 1962, 474, 475
White House Office, 512
White Mountains, 131, 134
Whooping crane, 262
Wild and Scenic Rivers Act, 203, 211, 369
Wilderness, 285–304
  Bureau of Land Management and, 303, 304
  creation of National Wilderness Preservation System, 294
  designation of wilderness area, 295–302
  Fish and Wildlife Service and, 304
  Forest Service and, 286–87, 291, 296–302, 304
    RARE I, 297–98
    RARE II, 298–301

Humphrey wilderness bills, 293–94
National Park Service and, 286, 302–303, 304
Regulation L-20, 288
U-regulations, 291
Wilderness Act, 81, 124, 137, 294, 295–96, 299, 302, 369, 477
Wilderness Society, 143, 291, 293
  creation of, 226, 285, 290
Wildlife, 223–79
  animal control, 243–50
  enforcement of federal law, 234–43
    commerce clause, 235–63
    treaty powers, 236–43
  federal land, wildlife on, 229–34
  rare, threatened, and endangered species, *see* Rare, threatened, and endangered species
  research and management, 248–50
  see also National Wildlife Refuge System
Wildlife Management Institute, 144, 293
Wildlife Society, 245–46
Wilson, James, 129, 130, 287
Wilson, Woodrow, 185, 188, 189, 192, 360
Wirth, Conrad L., 191, 198–201
Witchita Mountains National Wildlife Refuge, 276

Yard, Robert Sterling, 290
Yellowstone National Park, 70, 251, 275
  establishment of, 181–84, 231
  fires in, 164–67
  forest preserves, 118
  regulation of hunting, trapping, and fishing in, 183–84
Yellowstone Park Act, 181–82, 186, 231
Yosemite National Park, 179

Zabel v. Tabb, 42, 379–82
Zahniser, Howard, 293, 294
Zoning, 47